STATE ARCHIVES OF ASSYRIA STUDIES

VOLUME XVI

STATE ARCHIVES OF ASSYRIA STUDIES

Published by the Neo-Assyrian Text Corpus Project
of the University of Helsinki
in co-operation with
the Finnish Oriental Society

Project Director
Simo Parpola

Managing Editor
Robert M. Whiting

VOLUME XVI

Mikko Luukko

GRAMMATICAL VARIATION IN NEO-ASSYRIAN

THE NEO-ASSYRIAN TEXT CORPUS PROJECT

State Archives of Assyria Studies is a series of monographic studies relating to and supplementing the text editions published in the SAA series. Manuscripts are accepted in English, French and German. The responsibility for the contents of the volumes rests entirely with the authors.

Set in Times
The Assyrian Royal Seal emblem drawn by Dominique Collon from original
Seventh Century B.C. impressions (BM 84672 and 84677) in the British Museum
Custom fonts by Robert M. Whiting
Typesetting and layout by Greta Van Buylaere

Printed in Finland
by Vammalan Kirjapaino Oy

ISBN 951-45-9059-7 (Volume 16)
ISSN 1235-1032 (Series)

GRAMMATICAL VARIATION IN NEO-ASSYRIAN

By

Mikko Luukko

THE NEO-ASSYRIAN TEXT CORPUS PROJECT
2004

To the memory of

Karlheinz Deller

ACKNOWLEDGEMENTS

This study was submitted as a doctoral thesis at the University of Helsinki in April, 2004.

It is my great pleasure to thank those who have constantly helped, encouraged and supported me in this project.

First of all, I want to thank my teacher and supervisor, Professor Simo Parpola. Without him, I would not have studied Assyriology at all. Over the years I was able to discuss numerous grammatical details of the Neo-Assyrian dialect with him. Moreover, he always gave me plenty of valuable advice and allowed access to the project's database and to grammatical material he himself had collected. In other words, he kept me on the straight and narrow intellectual path when I attempted to tackle the extant Neo-Assyrian letters in an unwise manner. I would also like to thank him for accepting this study for publication in the series *State Archives of Assyria Studies*.

My warmest thanks are due to the reviewers of my thesis, Professors Frederick Mario Fales (Udine) and Martti Nissinen (Helsinki). I also owe many thanks to Professor Jaakko Hämeen-Anttila (Helsinki) for his suggestions and corrections to the manuscript.

I am very grateful to Kate Moore for editing my English and to Robert Whiting and Simo Parpola for additional corrections.

I also want to thank all the people of the State Archives of Assyria Project, in particular, Simo Parpola, Robert Whiting, Raija Mattila and Laura Kataja. They all have taught me Akkadian in the past. They have also contributed to the building-up and maintenance of the database. My research has benefited enormously from access to the Neo-Assyrian Text Corpus Project's database.

I would like to express my sincere thanks to the people who gave me a chance to see the "real things," i.e., tiny Neo-Assyrian letters full of odd cuneiform characters: Dr. Christopher Walker of the British Museum, Dr. Evelyn Klengel-Brandt and Dr. Joachim Marzahn of the Vorderasiatisches Museum and Prof. Dr. Johannes Renger of the Freie Universität, Berlin. I am also indebted to Prof. Dr. E. Cancik-Kirschbaum who together with J. Renger supervised an inspiring seminar in 1997-1998 on the problems of Akkadian grammar while I studied at the Freie Universität, Berlin.

In the late 1990's, I had the honour to attend some of the classes of Prof. Emeritus Karlheinz Deller as a guest in Heidelberg. At that time he was teaching Neo-Assyrian, Middle Assyrian and Old Assyrian. His enthusiasm and dedication to the systematic study of Assyrian made an indelible impression on me. Even though I know that he would not agree with some of my interpretations, I want to dedicate this study to him because of his remarkable contribution toward the understanding of the Assyrian dialect.

I want to express my gratitude to the Finnish Cultural Foundation and the Graduate School of the Institute of Asian and African Studies of the University of Helsinki, which made this study possible financially.

Last but certainly not least, I owe many thanks to my wife Greta Van Buylaere who not only encouraged me when I was down, but offered me extensive technical assistance and gave invaluable suggestions to improve the manuscript of this volume. I also want to thank my parents for their unrelenting support over a very long time. Thank you!

Any errors in this study remain entirely my own responsibility.

Ostend, January 2004 Mikko Luukko

CONTENTS

ABBREVIATIONS AND SYMBOLS

Bibliographical abbreviations

A	Tablets in the collections of the Istanbul Museum
ABL	R.F. Harper, *Assyrian and Babylonian Letters* (London and Chicago 1892-1914)
AfO	Archiv für Orientforschung
AnOr	Analecta Orientalia
AnSt	Anatolian Studies
AOAT	Alter Orient und Altes Testament
AoF	Altorientalische Forschungen
ArOr	Archiv Orientální
AS	Assyriological Studies
BaM	Baghdader Mitteilungen
BiOr	Bibliotheca Orientalis
BM	Tablets in the collections of the British Museum
BT	B. Parker, "Economic Tablets from the Temple of Mamu at Balawat," *Iraq* 25 (1963) 86-103
CRRAI	Rencontre assyriologique internationale, comptes rendus
CTN	Cuneiform Texts from Nimrud
GAG	W. von Soden, *Grundriss der akkadischen Grammatik*, AnOr 35 (Roma 1952/1969/1995)
GPA	J.N. Postgate, *The Governor's Palace Archive*. CTN 2 (London 1973)
IM	Tablets in the collections of the Iraq Museum, Baghdad
JNES	Journal of Near Eastern Studies
KAV	O. Schroeder, *Keilschrifttexte aus Assur verschiedenen Inhalts* (Leipzig 1920)
LAS	S. Parpola, *Letters from Assyrian Scholars to the Kings Esarhaddon and Assurbanipal I, II*. AOAT 5/1-2 (Neukirchen-Vluyn 1970, 1983)
LAS II A	S. Parpola, *Letters from Assyrian Scholars to the Kings Esarhaddon and Assurbanipal. Part II A: Introduction and Appendices* (Kevelaer and Neukirchen-Vluyn 1971)
MSL	Materials for the Sumerian Lexicon
NAIT	K. Deller and I.L. Finkel, "A Neo-Assyrian Inventory Tablet of Unknown Provenance," *ZA* 74 (1984) 76-91
ND	Field numbers of tablets excavated at Nimrud

NL	H.W.F. Saggs, "The Nimrud Letters." Parts I-VIII. Published originally in *Iraq* 17-18, 20-21, 25, 27-28 and 36 (1955-1974). All these letters are now republished in CTN V
NWL	J.V. Kinnier Wilson, *The Nimrud Wine Lists*. CTN 1 (London 1972)
OLA	Orientalia Lovaniensa Analecta
OLZ	Orientalistische Literaturzeitung
Or.	Orientalia, Nova Series
PIHANS	Publications de l'Institut historique-archéologique néerlandais de Stamboul = Uitgaven van het Nederlands Historisch-Archaeologisch Instituut te Istanbul
PKTA	E. Ebeling, *Parfümrezepte und kultische Texte aus Assur* (Rome 1952)
PNA	*The Prosopography of the Neo-Assyrian Empire* (Helsinki 1998-)
RA	Revue d'assyriologie
Rfdn	Al-Rāfidān
RIMA	The Royal Inscriptions of Mesopotamia. Assyrian Periods
SAA	State Archives of Assyria
SAAB	State Archives of Assyria Bulletin
SAAS	State Archives of Assyria Studies
StAT	Studien zu den Assur-Texten
StOr	Studia Orientalia (Helsinki)
TCS	Texts from Cuneiform Sources
TH	J. Friedrich et al., *Die Inschriften von Tell Halaf. Keilschrifttexte und aramäische Urkunden aus einer assyrischen Provinzhauptstadts*, AfO-Beiheft 6 (1940)
UF	Ugarit-Forschungen
VAT	Tablets in the collections of the Vorderasiatisches Museum
VS	Vorderasiatische Schriftdenkmäler der Staatlichen Museen zu Berlin
ZA	Zeitschrift für Assyriologie

Non-bibliographical abbreviations and symbols

acc.	accusative
adj.	adjective
assimil.	assimilation
Babyl.	Babylonianism
C	consonant
cohort.	cohortative
cont.	context
coord.	coordination (between clauses/sentences)
dat.	dative
dissimil.	dissimilation
DN	divine name
e.	edge
ellipt.	elliptical
env.	envelope
f.	feminine
frg	fragment
gen.	genitive
GN	geographical name
imperat.	imperative
infinit.	infinitive
int.	intonation
liter.	literally
m.	masculine
MA	Middle Assyrian
mg.	morphographemic gemination
metat.	metathesis
NA	Neo-Assyrian

NB	Neo-Babylonian
nom.	nominative
O, obj.	object
OA	Old Assyrian
obv.	obverse
P	predicate
pf	perfect
pl.	plural; plate
PN	personal name
prep.	preposition
prc	precative
procl.	proclitic
progr.	progressive
pros.	prosodic
prs	present
prt	preterite
r.	reverse
RN	royal name
S	subject
s.	side (i.e. left edge)
sg.	singular
stat	stative
st. cstr.	status constructus
subj.	subjunctive
suff.	suffix
unkn.	unknown (sender of a letter)
V	vowel
var.	variant
vent.	ventive
verb.adj.	verbal adjective
!	collation
!!	emendation
?	uncertain reading
: :.	cuneiform division marks
|	vertical word-divider
/	line break
//	end of obverse
*	graphic variants (see LAS I p. xx)
0	uninscribed space or non-existent sign
x	broken or undeciphered sign
( )	supplied word or sign
[[ ]]	erasure
[...]	minor break
[......]	major break

1 INTRODUCTION

1.1 Aims

In this work, I study the grammatical variation attested in Neo-Assyrian letters. To this end, I concentrate on the internal Neo-Assyrian variation, not on the variation existing, for instance, between Neo-Assyrian and Neo-Babylonian, or between Neo-Assyrian and Middle Assyrian. Furthermore, I do not attempt to clarify how Neo-Assyrian relates to other languages spoken in the Near East at that time, i.e. Aramaic[1] and Hebrew in particular. I have thus reduced the provable variation concerning loanwords and proper names to a minimum. Nevertheless, I could not disregard completely the relation of Neo-Assyrian to other languages, or to the earlier forms of Assyrian, as these all influenced the grammatical variation in Neo-Assyrian.

First, I will review the evidence. Ample examples prove the existence of variation in the Neo-Assyrian dialect. I will cite as many examples as possible to illustrate, describe and clarify the linguistic mechanisms working within Neo-Assyrian. These examples serve above all to collect the various grammatical manifestations – variants – in Neo-Assyrian. The interpretation and analysis of these variation examples are only secondary goals in this study, but they have received considerable attention even if not to the same depth as the primary goals. Unfortunately, since the topic is so wide, many important grammatical phenomena in which variation exist are only quickly mentioned or even completely passed over. So, in a way, this study represents a selective grammatical cross section.

The classification of different variation types is closely linked with the clarification of the whole variation. I introduce all the different variation types in the introductory chapter (see 1.5.1-1.5.13). Here I pay attention to the possible factors underlying the different types of variation, and observe the potential causes behind variation in order to avoid some of the most straightforward, but not necessarily most likely, explanations.

[1] However, see the references for the entry "Aramaic influence/Aramaisms" of the Indices. For the language contact with Aramaic, see Kaufman (1974) 15-19, 22-27.

I have tried to compress the most essential features of the constituent parts of the traditional grammar (morphology [Chapter 5], syntax [Chapter 6], and also phonology[2] [Chapter 4]) into my work. I have reserved one chapter for all the main parts of the grammar, but partial overlaps cannot be avoided, since many different elements of the grammar are often combined in one phenomenon (e.g. orthography provides immediate information about phonology). Furthermore, I have added a chapter on semantic variation (see Chapter 7), which in fact, belongs more to the scope of a lexical than to a grammatical study.

Owing to the special nature of cuneiform writing (being essentially syllabic, but as well logographic, which is markedly different from alphabetic writing) I have also treated some orthographic features (see Chapter 3), since their interpretation is closely connected with all the grammatical conclusions.[3] Thus, the grammatical variation of cuneiform writing is a somewhat wider phenomenon than the variation attested in our modern, alphabetic writing system.

1.2 Definition of the key terms

Neo-Assyrian. By Neo-Assyrian – as a dialect, historical period, culture, etc. – I refer to the era between about 1000 BCE and 612 BCE, the year when Nineveh was destroyed. Neo-Assyrian is the youngest of the three chronologically consecutive forms of the Assyrian dialect (Old Assyrian, Middle Assyrian, Neo-Assyrian). However, the differences between, for instance, Neo-Assyrian and Middle Assyrian writings are in many cases very slight.

The end of Middle Assyrian and the beginning of Neo-Assyrian are easier to define in the light of historical events than by linguistic features: the Middle Assyrian era ended at the time Assyrian power declined, when the Assyrian kings were no longer able to control the Aramaic tribes who made more and more raids into the Assyrian heartland as well as into other areas formerly held and controlled by Assyrian kings and their officials.

Correspondingly, the Neo-Assyrian era begins with the recovery of the Assyrian (military) power: the restoration of public order first had to be realized in Assyria and thereafter, Assyria had to gain enough strength and ability to repel the assaults of the Aramaic tribes. A new strategy was then developed for dealing with the former enemy: many Aramaic tribal chiefs were rewarded by the king of

---

[2] A traditional grammar includes morphological and syntactic knowledge and their study, but excludes phonetics, phonology and semantics as specialized areas of linguistics, see Bussmann (1996) 194 sub grammar.

[3] The grammar of a certain language is a description of the structure of the language. In the case of Neo-Assyrian, the orthography plays a greater role than usual in describing the structure of the language. Nonetheless, I am well aware of the fact that nowadays there are many divergent notions, opinions, orientations and tendencies concerning the composition of a grammar: what should be included in it and what, in proportion, should be completely left outside. For one example of an evaluation of the composition of an Akkadian grammar, see Gelb (1955) 94-95.

Assyria with high offices. While the Assyrian empire extended, it also turned into a genuinely bilingual empire: Assyrian-Babylonian and Aramaic were the prevalent languages. At the time of the formation of the empire, both the Assyrian-Babylonian and Aramaic languages influenced each other's further development.

Assyrian is usually considered to be a dialect of Akkadian, along with Babylonian, and not an independent language. However, the distinction between a dialect and a language is not a linguistic one, but rather a socio-political one.[4]

Variation. Complete uniformity creates neither any alternation nor variation. But when it comes to alternation or variation, the cuneiform writing offers it amply. The combination of two different ways of writing, syllabic and logographic, typical of Akkadian language, definitely favours the existence of variation at least on the surface level. Logographic writing functions in Neo-Assyrian letters as a type of shorthand to abbreviate (common) nouns in particular. Many common nouns, such as *ekallu* "palace," *ekurru* "temple," *eqlu* "field," *ilu* "god," *mar'u* "son," *mê* "water," *sissû* "horse," *šarru* "king," *urdu* "servant" and so on, were regularly written by their logographic equivalents in Neo-Assyrian letters: É.GAL, É.KUR, A.ŠÀ, DINGIR, DUMU/A, A.MEŠ, ANŠE.KUR.RA, LUGAL/MAN, ARAD, and so on. Logographic writing is also used in Neo-Assyrian letters for verbs (cf. e.g. DU = *alāku*, KIN = *šapāru*) and other parts of speech as well, but then often with phonetic complements, and much less frequently and regularly than in many other types of documents.

In any case, syllabically written Assyrian (and Babylonian) serves the purpose of this study much better because it expresses phonological information directly. For this reason, I have not devoted much space to logographic writing, which historically originated and played a much greater role in ancient Sumerian writing, and which had an important but secondary role in the essentially syllabic script of Neo-Assyrian letters.

Even so, the syllabic writing alone presents ample evidence for variation. To those of us who always write words in the same manner (not taking into account personal handwritings), the abundant, visual variation of the cuneiform script may not occur to us in the first place.

(Syllabic) examples:  =  (*u* = *ù*) "and"

 =  (*ar-hi-iš* = *ár-hiš*) "quickly."

Logograms: 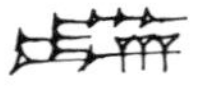 =  (LUGAL = MAN "king")

 =  (ŠEŠ = PAB "brother" and ŠEŠ = PAB "to guard").

[4] For the features which separate Assyrian from Babylonian, see e.g. Deller (1965A) 38.

1.3 Method

The starting point of this work was a careful acquaintance with the entire extant Neo-Assyrian letter corpus at hand, both the translations and transliterations of published texts and the non-published texts. From the latter group, I used predominantly transliterations extracted from the database of the State Archives of Assyria Project. Besides reading these letters, at this stage I collected a rather large Neo-Assyrian glossary, which includes a wide range of finite verb forms. Subsequently, I tried to analyze all the forms I had assembled.

In the next phase of the work, I searched, evaluated and sorted out the collected material. Then, I began to combine and parse the material from the letters to their relevant places and connections. Of course I had also become acquainted with the grammatical theories concerning Neo-Assyrian, which are published in various articles and books (see the Bibliography). I also took note of the linguistic theories of variation in order to provide a theoretical framework and to apply them in practice.

I personally have read or collated only about 100 original Neo-Assyrian letters – which is approximately 5% of the presently available letter corpus – at the British Museum in London and at the Vorderasiatisches Museum in Berlin. This is why the study is mainly based on published and unpublished cuneiform hand copies, as well as on transliterations, translations, commentaries, and grammatical theories.

When dealing with a phenomenon like linguistic variation, one can most plausibly choose a comparative research method by which one arranges the cuneiform sign values, single words, whole clauses and sentences, and even larger entities side by side.[5] Mostly in the main chapters of this book, the occurring variants are organized side by side. The "marked" (rare) forms are always represented first, after which the "unmarked" (common) forms follow. In presenting the various forms and interpretations of Neo-Assyrian linguistic variation, this book observes descriptive principles but pays attention to the proper use of Neo-Assyrian, too. Therefore, the following chapters include some normative remarks on the grammatical correctness of the dialect. However, regulative rules are only given when it is possible to point out grammatical errors and otherwise clear-cut examples of bad or awkward Neo-Assyrian.

It would have been easy to collect a long list of peculiarities in the Neo-Assyrian letter corpus and file them under the title "incomprehensible variants" or alike, but these "oddities" are principally attested in very broken contexts, in passages which are open to various very divergent interpretations. For this reason, I have seen no reason to include a chapter or section for a collection of oddities.[6]

---

[5] Some good examples of this type of research in the field of Assyriology are e.g. Deller (1959), (1969) 45-64 and LAS II 437-46.

[6] Cf. e.g. Reiner's ([1966] 18) words on the oddities within the framework of grammatical research.

The analysis of the Neo-Assyrian dialect and different theories about it are (primarily) based on the interpretation of the Neo-Assyrian writing system. Accordingly, we have to suppose that the writing system tried to serve the language to the best of its limited abilities.[7] Naturally we should be a bit sceptical and doubt if our comprehension of this difficult writing system is really good enough. Be that as it may, it is particularly noteworthy that all the linguistic features are to be read in the cuneiform script itself.[8] Though admittedly some features can only be interpreted indirectly, for instance, a written logogram can in some cases only theoretically be converted into a syllabic form. Of course, parallel examples with syllabic variants do often exist, but the reliability of the interpretation of these cases may vary significantly.

Since every natural language is a complicated and constantly changing system, there is not one single theory or hypothesis that can explain all linguistic phenomena. Instead, I have painstakingly tried to interpret some features in the development of the Neo-Assyrian dialect. Those features go in very diverse directions, depending on the cultural background and other complicated factors.

1.4 Principles for marking

The transliteration of quotations is given sign-by-sign according to the principles of the SAA series: syllable signs are written in lower case and the originally Sumerian (plus some later formations) logograms correspondingly are written in small capitals. Italics are used to transcribe Neo-Assyrian morphemes, words and clauses, but not for root radicals or proper names. The graphemes of the script are marked with < >. Square brackets [ ] are reserved for phonetic spelling, mainly for allophones, e.g. [*a*], whereas / / signals the more approximate, phonemic transcriptions. Moreover, I have often put examples of the lexemes and root radicals in parentheses ( ). With this practice, my purpose is to point out the expected or basic form of a word and thus refer to the dictionaries.

Most Neo-Assyrian transliterations and transcriptions longer than one or two words are now provided with translations. The purpose of this is to make the study more user-friendly and to reduce time-consuming cross-checking. I have taken the translations of Neo-Assyrian letters from the SAA series. However, when it seemed more appropriate to emphasize a specific grammatical feature, I deviated from the SAA translations and offered a more literal interpretation which – hopefully – also grammatically appears a bit more illustrative. The translations of unpublished texts are either my own, or if not so, the source of quotation is

[7] On the cuneiform writing and its interpretative limitations, see among others, Reiner (1973), and von Soden and Röllig (1967) xvii-xxvi.

[8] Cf. Parpola (1984) 201.

given.[9] In some examples, I have used boldface or underlining for the sake of emphasis, or to try to make the separation of the distinctive features clearer.

With regard to the line numbering, I follow the principle of the SAA series. In practice, the difference between many other text editions, such as CTN V, is that the reverse column and the left edge (= side = s.) of a tablet are numbered separately in the SAA series. Thus, numbers are not consecutive after the bottom and top edges, but begin anew on the new face of the tablet. Hence:

NOT: obv. 1, ... 11, 12, e. 13, 14, r.15 ... r. 27e ... s.29

BUT: obv. 1, ... 11, 12, e. 13, 14, r.1, 2 ... r.13e, s.1

This practice may cause some trouble when consulting text editions other than SAA but should not really make finding passages difficult.

The accent markers are ´ (as e.g. in *ū́*, however, note that a long vowel is not always stressed) and circumflex ^ (always stressed).

The length of a vowel is marked either as short (simple) or long: *a*, *ā*, *â*. In transcription, a macron is used for marking the stressed as well as the unstressed long vowel. The circumflex (^) is used when there is a realized vowel contraction (e.g. *i* + *u* > *û*, as *iqabbi* + subjunctive *-ūni* > *iqabbûni*), as well as in a small group of mono- and disyllabic words in which the (last) syllable is almost without exception written with a CV_1-V_1 sequence:[10] e.g.

> *adê* "treaty, covenant," *akê* "how," *alê* "where," *kî* "as, like," *šî* "she," *šû* "he," *ulâ* "or, alternatively," *ūmâ* "now."

For the usage of the circumflex, I have however deviated to some extent from the way it has been established in GAG,[11] and used it for interrogative intonation too.[12] This is orthographically based, since the interrogative intonation is always written as a plene.[13] For example,

> *abutu* > *a-bu-tu-u* (question)

1.5 Types of variation

Whereas conditional (1.5.4), phonological (1.5.6), and morphological (1.5.7) variations belong to the field of grammatical variation, the other discussed types of variation are external. They mainly concern the background factors of

---

[9] Simo Parpola kindly provided me with his own provisional translations for part of the yet unpublished Neo-Assyrian correspondence of Assurbanipal. The translations of letters that are not published in the SAA series may deviate significantly from editions, for example, the CTN V references are not the same as those found in the volume.

[10] In this respect, I follow the established forms given in the glossaries of the SAA series, although, for instance, the word for "where" in those glossaries is given as the lexeme *ali*; however, cf. 5.2.

[11] See GAG § 16, § 38g.

[12] Cf. ibid. § 39c and § 153d-g.

[13] On plene writing in Akkadian, see Aro (1953).

grammatical variation. These different types of variation are not presented side by side with the evidence in the main analytical chapters of the book (3-7), but are inserted in places where the weight of their evidence appears meaningful. The purpose of presenting these different types of variation is to explore the descriptional possibilities of grammatical variation in Neo-Assyrian by trying to explain some of the causes behind variations by means of factors that lie outside the categories of traditional grammar.

1.5.1 Geographical variation[14]

At its largest, the Neo-Assyrian empire reached from the Caspian sea to the Nile Valley and from Anatolia as far to the Persian Gulf. In spite of the empire's immense size, it is assumed here that within the Neo-Assyrian empire, there was only one literary form of Assyrian.[15] At least in official, administrative correspondence, a standard form of the dialect was in use.[16]

The Assyrian dialect used in all (formal) Neo-Assyrian letters is uniform enough in its essential characteristics to confirm a sole literary form of Assyrian. However, this fact does not exclude dialectal[17] and other kinds of differences in letters by different scribes, even though both the educational and social background of the scribes were in all probability quite the same.[18] In any case, when studying Neo-Assyrian letters, the existence of certain deviating features in writing cannot escape one's notice. For instance, the private and rather informal letters from Assur in the 7th century BCE are very distinctive when compared to the other letters of the corpus.[19] Presumably the "scribes" in Assur who wrote those private letters were neither very experienced nor very educated. Be that as it may, these letters are probably closer to the actual colloquial language than to the standard language used in official and other, more formal, letters. Thus far only a few private letters have been found elsewhere than in Assur. The evidence from these private letters is scanty.

---

[14] For examples on the Neo-Assyrian geographical variation outside the letter corpus, see Lambert (1959) 124-26, 128-29. For the local "languages" of the scholars, see LAS II A p. 27 nn. 3-4.

[15] It is not the purpose of this presentation to treat the other languages which were spoken or written inside the boundaries of the Neo-Assyrian empire.

[16] From the domain of a modern language, for example the (potential) classification of the English language into its standard form and to various differing subgroups, see e.g. Quirk (1995) 21-31, particularly the chart on page 23.

[17] A good example of the modern dialectal language research, dialectology, is Trudgill and Chambers (1991); see the Bibliography.

[18] Important was the hereditary nature of the office of many scribes in Assyria. For instance, a high scholarly office was often inherited by the son of an office-bearer, see Wiseman (1955) 9, LAS II xvii-xix and SAA IX 7:4 with its footnote.

[19] These can be roughly counted as about 40 letters, not much when considering that the whole corpus has approximately 2,250.

Geographical variation as such is attested, for example, in the parallel words for *šumma* "if" and *kīma* "when, if," viz. *aššummu* and *akkīma*, which can pretty often be found in letters from Der and Babylonia.[20] Wavering between the usage of <*s*> and <*š*> can often be seen as a sign that the letter did not come from Assyria proper.[21] On the other hand, for instance, the letters of the Balih and Khabur river areas are lacking the *lū* of the blessing formula, probably on purpose.[22]

Research on the Neo-Assyrian geographical variation is often complicated considerably by the fact that the exact sending place of a letter does not give reliable evidence as to the local language or dialect. Most, or almost all, of the scribes and officials in the remotest regions of the empire were not of local origin, but had been appointed to their new duties by the king himself and sent to execute their offices all over the empire. All of these officers and officials had had a similar type of education, were loyal servants and supporters of the Neo-Assyrian empire and its ideology and were often serving far away from the Assyrian heartland.

In fact, it is also important to emphasize that the so-called Babylonianisms[23] may often be more connected with a specific scribal education, particularly in the case of Assyrian scholars and their special fields and literature, than with the actual geographical background. In general, it is good to bear in mind that the tradition of copying earlier tablets was extremely strong in Assyria and Babylonia. The direct result of copying earlier tablets was that the nature and language of most of the Mesopotamian written records changed very slowly.

In the following main chapters of this book, the geographical variation is sometimes (when considered to be meaningful) observed by attaching the geographical origin (if known) of a letter with the "marked" forms.

The locations of the senders of the Neo-Assyrian letters are recorded in Appendix B.

1.5.2 Orthographic variation[24]

In orthography,[25] there are several alternating features, which can be decisive when distinguishing different scribes, such as the number of vowels and

---

[20] See Parpola (1997A) 318 n. 9 with examples.

[21] Ibid. 318 n. 10 with examples. See also 4.1.4.

[22] Parpola (1997A) 322 Appendix: 3.

[23] A Babylonianism is something characteristic of the Babylonian dialect or its writing system as distinct from the corresponding Neo-Assyrian characteristics. I have also treated the influences from the literary tradition as Babylonianisms. On the literary texts, their tradition and their background, see SAA III pp. xv-xxxi.

[24] Generally speaking, the orthography of cuneiform writing makes an arbitrary use of both the phonemic and morphophonemic method, Reiner (1973) 57. On the basically phonemic character of cuneiform writing, see Gelb (1970B) 526.

[25] Reiner (1973) 25 n. 31 gives illustrative examples – as a model of noun + possessive suffix – of diverging orthographies with an eye to transcription: morpheme-analytic (*qaqqas-sa*

consonants used in each scribe's personal sign inventory, abnormal vs. normal syllabification,[26] defectively vs. more completely written forms, the writing of foreign (non-Assyrian) loan words, the potential use of a "colon" (see 3.2), the total number of used cuneiform signs[27] and the qualitative selection of them, the differences in the realization of assimilation (partial, complete and non-assimilation), syllabic writing as well as the parallel use of logographic writing. On the whole, orthographic variation is closely connected to some other variation types (e.g. 1.5.5, 1.5.9). For examples of the orthographic variation, see especially 3.7. Note that Parpola has published an illustrative table on the characteristic orthographic features of the scholars.[28]

1.5.3 Free variation

Free variation,[29] which also appears in Neo-Assyrian writings, often hints at a change in language. [30] For example, a new and an old variant may coexist at a certain given time in any language, but in the so-called transitional period, the usage of one of the variants first decreases until its usage later, perhaps, ceases altogether.[31]

[sic], *qāt-su*), morphophonemic (*qaqqad-ša, qāt-šu*) and assimilative (*qaqqassa, qāssu*) orthography (the syllable works as a marker of morpheme boundary in the examples above).

[26] E.g. the word "Akkad" written syllabically (seldom) or the use of an exceptional reading value KI = *qí* can be seen as hints to identify a writer in question, see LAS II no. 124 discussion part.

[27] For an example of the orthography of one writer, Urdu-Nanaia, with his use of the sign *šú*, see LAS II ad no. 255 r.2 and p. 253 n. 450.

[28] LAS II pp. 443-46. See further Parpola (1987B) 269 and LAS II A p. 27 n. 2: scholars who practiced the same profession often used similar orthographic conventions in their letters, and this was surely the influence of their technical literature. For more on the characteristic orthographic features of the scholars, see the passage D) Characteristic features (under each scholar), ibid. pp. 28-45.

[29] See e.g. Reiner (1966) 115-16.

[30] See Paunonen (1973) 285. In the first place, Paunonen is not defining free variation as a concept in his article, but instead emphasizes that free variation is not totally free in reality, ibid. 285 n. 2. Besides, he clarifies the history of variation research and its study methods in an interesting way, ibid. pp. 285-90.

[31] As an example of dialectological research in which it is observed that the older dialectal forms may give way to the (potential) spread of (grammatically more correct) standard forms, see Ihalainen (1991) 104-19. See also Itkonen (1970), in particular pp. 427-30, 434, 437-38, who emphasizes that sound changes are often gradual in reality. Even with rapid sound changes, it takes some time before an increase in frequency shows that the innovation gains ground at the expense of the original item.

Free variation means that there is no grammatical difference in meaning or interpretation between two or more forms which exist side by side.[32]

E.g. nasals (*m*, *n*) are in free variation before a plosive: *ša-li-in-te* (gen.) SAA I 54:7 ~ *ša-lim-tu* (nom./acc.) SAA I 132:10

1.5.4 Conditional variation

All the different conditional clauses follow their own strict rules. Sometimes those rules slightly deviate from the ones applied in the normal, main and subordinate clauses with indicative predicates. Especially the use of tenses[33] is conspicuous in this respect. As examples of conditional clauses or other specialized clause types there are, for instance, (a) oaths (note the use of the subjunctive as a marker),[34] (b) *šumma/kīma* clauses (note the specialized use of the perfect and preterite: referring to the future), (c) variously formulated *maṣi* clauses and their specialized meanings,[35] (d) *udīni/a* clauses (*lā* + present) and (e) *lū* + preterite in irreal wishes of the past.[36]

1.5.5 Graphemic variation

Graphemic variation occurs on a fairly large scale in Neo-Assyrian, since the writers of letters could use different graphemes to express the same words. Two simple examples on graphemic variation may illustrate this point. In these examples, the difference is extreme, since every written grapheme of the first form of the word is different from that in the second form of the same word:

bat-te SAA I 93:7 ~ *ba-at-ti* SAA X 89 r.8 and
nak-kan-tu SAA X 369 r.8 ~ *na-kam-tú* NL 41 r.30e (CTN V 208ff)

These forms are not grammatically different from each other, but graphemically they look like the following:  ~  (*bat-te* ~ *ba-at-ti*);  ~  (*nak-kan-tu* ~ *na-kam-tú*).

In any case, the use of graphemes was for the most part rather strictly established and regular in Neo-Assyrian. This often meant in practice that scribes did not allow themselves great liberties in propagating graphemic variation, although graphemic variation is generally attested quite abundantly. There are at least two obvious reasons for this: (1) Practicality: With fewer signs, it is far easier to write Neo-Assyrian than by trying to learn and use all the possible signs and their reading values; (2) Limitations (of scribes): This point is naturally connected with the previous one. The education of (different types of) scribes is

[32] For the definition of free variation, cf. e.g. Carr (1993) 28.

[33] Also, the normal use of tenses has accurately regulated rules and functions, cf. 6.3.

[34] See SAA II, p. xxxviii ff.

[35] See Parker (1997B) 37-54.

[36] On these irreal *lū* clauses, see GAG § 152f.

the key question here, and it is difficult to determine how much the education of one scribe differed from that of another scribe. However, it seems evident that most of the Neo-Assyrian scribes were not specialized in several, different genres. Scholars were exceptional in this way because they clearly had opportunities to become well versed in all or most of the Mesopotamian sciences. At least on the basis of their written records, it seems that these scholars had relatively easy access to different type of writings and thus they could also be more innovative from time to time than other scribes in combining creatively the writings from their sources. I do not think that there was any prohibition on writing Assyrian in a more complicated manner. Actually, there is no reason to underestimate the significance of purposeful graphemic variation, but the great number of established, fixed grapheme inventories in writing is no less important.

There were striking differences in the number of graphemes used by the individual scribes (see 3.4).

Graphemic variation is, for instance, closely linked to orthographic variation (1.5.2) and, on the other hand, also to idiosyncratic and stylistic factors (1.5.8-9), as well as to free variation (1.5.3).

I am well aware of the fact that I have not treated the graphemic variation sufficiently in the following chapters, but cf. Chapter 3, particularly 3.14, where I have listed at least some rarely attested graphemes.

1.5.6 Phonological variation

The phonology of Neo-Assyrian is transmitted to us in Neo-Assyrian writings.[37] Consequently, the phonology of Neo-Assyrian, even at its best, is no more than an elaborate assumption based on the writing system. However, the careful and detailed analysis of the Neo-Assyrian writing combined with our present knowledge about other Semitic languages – both living and dead – must undeniably lead to the right kind of conclusions concerning the phonology of Neo-Assyrian.

Part of phonological variation[38] is, for instance, the alternation between a geminated consonant and a long vowel in writing. We assume that this type of alternation was realized in the actual speech itself. For example,

> *la mu-qa-an-ni* "We will not be able ..." SAA XIII 161 r.6 ~ *la e-mu-qa-a-ni* SAA XVI 140 r.9 and *di-i-bi* ("marked form") *an-nu-u-te* StAT 1 51 r.10 ~ *di-ib-bi an-nu-te* "these matters" SAA V 46 r.3 and passim

Chapter 4 is dedicated to analyzing this phonological variation.

---

[37] Information on Neo-Assyrian phonology can also be obtained by studying contemporary (dialects and) languages, such as Babylonian and Aramaic.

[38] For example, the majority of native English-speaking people differ linguistically relatively little from one another, whereas the biggest differences in language between these people are found in phonetics and phonology, see Trudgill and Chambers (1991) 2.

1.5.7 Morphological variation

Chapter 5 treats morphological variation which is, for example, perceivable in verbal conjugation, prepositions, adverbs and pronouns. In Neo-Assyrian, exemplary cases of morphological variation are, among other things, words which have two different plural forms. These plural forms that deviate from one another are identical in their sense; however, some nuances of meaning are of course possible. E.g.

> (*etinnu* "master builder") *etinnāni* ~ *etinnāti*: LÚ.TIN.MEŠ-*ni-ia* "my master builders" SAA V 56:7; LÚ.TIN.MEŠ-*ni* "master builders" SAA V 56 r.9 ~ LÚ.*e-tin-na-ti* SAA I 138:13 (for more examples of two different plural forms, see 5.3)

1.5.8 Idiolects and idiosyncrasies

Each person has an individual way to use language,[39] be it either spoken or written. Also, in Neo-Assyrian, a dialect which is known entirely from its written form, many scribes are identifiable by their personal characteristic features which appear in their writing.[40] These characteristics include handwriting, a selection of graphemes, the use of certain words[41] and phrases which may be repeated in the same type of context, as well as style (see 1.5.9), etc.

Moreover, sociological variation would undoubtedly deserve its own subheading, yet this is a difficult topic to cover with our present knowledge. The above-mentioned assumption of the similarity of the scribes' educational and social background is merely a simplification; certainly in reality there must have been a marked difference both in wealth and social appreciation between the so-called scholars (often persons who might have been close to the king) and the more ordinary scribes.[42] It is admittedly very difficult to evaluate these kinds of matters in general, especially within the limits of grammatical or some other type of linguistic research. Furthermore, the sociological variation easily overlaps with many other variation types, which may be more manageable. This overlap is particularly conspicuous under this subheading, as well as under the sections 1.5.1, 1.5.6 and 1.5.9.

In this respect, it is only natural to ask a difficult question: What is the relation between the idiolect of one individual (and his/her variation) and the language used in the whole society (and to its variation), especially if our purpose is to speculate on the strategy of a language change in practice.

---

[39] See e.g. Paunonen (1973) 287.

[40] On personal, characteristic features, see e.g. Deller (1969) 47-52 (about Adad-šumu-uṣur) and Parpola (1987B) 268-69 (about Urdu-Gula, son of Adad-šumu-uṣur). For details on the Neo-Assyrian scholars, see LAS II 437-46 and LAS II A pp. 27-45, especially passage D. Characteristic features (of each scholar are treated there).

[41] As an example of a rather exceptional choice of a word (*sūqu* "street" NB) in Neo-Assyrian, see LAS II ad no. 292 r.14′.

[42] For an example of a miserable falling of a highly esteemed scholar from the top of the hierarchy of government officials to the "bottom" of society, see Parpola (1987B).

Together with the "idiolectically marked" forms, I have in some cases also indicated the name of the sender of a letter. In this context, it is important to note that even though many of the so-called scholarly letters (in particular, those in SAA X) can be attributed with certainty to given scholars,[43] it is often not possible to establish the identity of the authors of other letters.[44] Furthermore, while I basically refer to the senders of the letters as "writers," in reality, many letters from high officials, for example, must have been written down by professional scribes.[45]

1.5.9 Stylistic variation

Usually when speaking about style it is desirable to distinguish between the high, "correct" (mostly literary[46]) and everyday, even "corrupt," (spoken) language. This distinction certainly holds for Neo-Assyrian too, but pointing out the more correct forms is not so obvious. Nevertheless, the stylistically more correct and esteemed forms were in all probability the longer and fuller forms in comparison with the shorter ones.[47] On the other hand, Babylonianisms[48] are frequently found in scholarly letters and were often used as stylistic devices or technical terms.[49]

Stylistic variation may occur, among other things, in the introductory formulae[50] of letters and in the form of address used in the letter itself; for example, the writer may suddenly change his previous usage of the "you" form into the "he" form when addressing the recipient.[51] Some letters can even go straight to the point without giving the names of senders and recipients at all, thus omitting polite opening formulae entirely.[52]

---

[43] With some possible exceptions, see LAS II A pp. 26-27, especially p. 27 n. 2.

[44] On the literacy of officials in general, see Parpola (1997A) 319-22.

[45] A good example of the use of a scribe is to be found in SAA V 250 r.24e-25e. This letter is signed alone by a high military official (name lost). However, a characteristic stylistic trait of this and many other letters is that exclusive of the introductory formula, the military official uses the 1st person plural in his report, i.e. he also speaks on behalf of his subordinates. The same phenomenon is typical of royal letters: the king often addresses his letter to a high official but his words are addressed to a group of people.

[46] On the use of the literary style in a petition letter of a scholar, see Parpola (1987B) 271-74.

[47] See e.g. idem (1984) 204 n. 24.

[48] See 1.5.1 n. 23.

[49] LAS II no. 124 discussion section and Deller (1969) 48-49.

[50] LAS II 437-43. On page 438, the orthographically varying forms used in writing */bēlī'a/* "my lord" which essentially belongs to the opening formula, are listed.

[51] Ibid. ad no. 121:24.

[52] See Salonen (1967) 82, also Jursa and Radner (1995/1996) 96, particularly ibid. n. 37, and Jas (1990) 3-5. In some of these cases, the letter may be a sequel to the first part which was written on another tablet.

Typical stylistic variation also involves avoiding tautologies.[53] Many scribes alternate between the syllabic and the logographic way of writing a word in consecutive lines of the same letter.[54] Thus they did not have to repeat the same sign(s) line after line. The difference between the number and inventory of syllabic and logographic signs used by different scribes can be considerable.[55] In addition, certain words could be written with different logograms in the same context. Typical examples are the use of logograms LUGAL = MAN and/or ŠEŠ = PAB almost side by side in the same texts. This kind of stylistic variation is also widely attested in units smaller than words proper and is obviously related to the avoidance of tautology. Variation between different spellings of suffix morphemes often occurs even within the same text (i.e., <*-ia*> : <*-iá*>, <*-šu*> : <*-šú*>, <*-ša*> : <*-šá*>, and so on).[56] Nevertheless, the scribes tended to have clear-cut orthographical conventions, which they rather consistently applied.

The choice between the two different masculine (*šû* and *šūtu*, of which the former is much more common)[57] and feminine (*šî* and *šīti*) forms of the third-person singular independent personal pronoun may also belong under stylistic variation.

Sometimes individual scribes can be identified by their stylistic features. For instance, in otherwise uncertain cases, as in badly broken letters with the sender's name lost, the occurrence of certain rare cuneiform signs or reading values as clearly stylistic devices may help assign the letter to a definite sender.[58]

1.5.10 Prosodic variation

The prosody[59] of an extinct language is not an easy subject for research. The matter becomes even more difficult if the language in question is transmitted to us only through a complicated writing system, as is the case with Neo-Assyrian. Thus it is no surprise that prosody has not been one of the most researched domains in Neo-Assyrian studies. Nevertheless, the analysis of prosodic features should be taken seriously in the study of Neo-Assyrian, since prosodic analysis is crucial to an elaborate phonological interpretation of any language, and prosody unquestionably played a central role in the grammatical system of Neo-Assyrian.

---

[53] Cf. Parpola (1988B) 80.

[54] Ibid. p. 78 n. 2 gives an example of variation of one word by using both the syllabic and logographic way of writing in one text. Notice also ibid. the n. 7 of the page 80 in which there are two examples of more than one reading of logograms.

[55] E.g. Adad-šumu-uṣur, chief exorcist of the king, used syllabic writing exceptionally extensively, see Deller (1969) 48.

[56] For one example, the well-known scholar Adad-šumu-uṣur and his son Urdu-Gula both had a changeable orthography, cf. LAS II A pp. 28, 44 and (1987B) 269.

[57] Deller (1965B) 74.

[58] One example of a case in which stylistic factors play a significant role in the confirmation of the writer's identity, see LAS II no. 124 discussion section.

[59] On prosody in general, see e.g. Crystal and Quirk (1964).

The prosodic[60] features of a language normally include length, which is distinctive, stress, which may or may not be distinctive, and intonation.[61]

1.5.11 Chronological variation

The Neo-Assyrian letter corpus[62] currently covers a period of about 200 years, from Adad-nerari III until the collapse of the Neo-Assyrian empire (c.800-600 BCE), but the texts are not evenly distributed within this time period. Most of them stem from the end of the 8th century and the first half of the 7th century BCE.[63]

It would considerably further the research if the development of the language could be followed both synchronically and diachronically, and if the evidence from these complementary research methods could then be compared with one another.[64] Unfortunately, as no letters are available from the early part of the Neo-Assyrian period, the opportunities for a diachronic study over a long time period are rather limited.

The study of diachronic variation within an individual's writings might succeed in certain cases but the difficulty in dating letters accurately imposes severe restrictions in this respect. Therefore, I have not made a serious effort here to go into the chronological variation of an individual scribe or scribes in general.

Neo-Assyrian letters are roughly presented in chronological order in the SAA series. This means, in practice, that the letters are assigned to three different Neo-Assyrian kings (Sargon II [721-705], Esarhaddon [680-669], Assurbanipal [669-630]). The dates assigned to the letters must be treated with due caution, because the methods of dating them, even approximately, cannot always be watertight. In particular, it is extremely difficult to determine the dates of the numerous tiny fragments that no longer contain enough distinctive chronological data. However, it cannot be stressed too much here that referring to the SAA editions of letters gives a marked advantage in any chronological study of NA letters if compared with references to ABL and CT 53 copies. The main body of edited Neo-Assyrian letters are chronologically distributed in the following way:

Tiglath-pileser III	CTN V
Sargon II	SAA I, V, XV and part of the CTN V letters
Esarhaddon	SAA X, XIII, XVI
Assurbanipal	SAA X, XIII and more or less all ABL references in this book

---

[60] See Reiner (1966) 35.

[61] Parpola (1975) 2.

[62] See 2.1.

[63] See Parpola (1981) 118ff.

[64] See Paunonen (1973) 299 for arguments of why synchronic and diachronic aspects should be analysed together.

1.5.12 Semantic variation of logograms

The correct interpretation of word signs, logograms, in many cases depends on the context. For instance, the possessive suffix of the first person singular was normally left unmarked when a word in the nominative case was written logographically.[65] Depending on the context, the logogram EN, for example, could thus mean either *bēlu*, "lord," or *bēlī*, "my lord." In some cases, EN could also stand for *adi* "(together) with."

1.5.13 Scribal slips

Variation could also occur unintentionally. I have included a collection of scribal slips in Section 3.6. However, these writings are often rendered problematic by our lack of competence in correctly evaluating the writings of the ancient scribes. Thus many suspected mistakes have turned out to be definitely not mistakes at all, and, conversely, seemingly correct writings have turned out to be erroneous. Actually, classifying the many different types of errors correctly is difficult in practice (it is no coincidence that the majority of errors listed in 3.6 are missing cuneiform signs), and there is a real danger that an actual scribal error may mistakingly be taken for a grammatically correct form, and in this way obscure the reality. In view of this, one always has to pay careful attention to the frequency of all kinds of differences and oddities. Nowadays, with the help of computers, we have better facilities at our disposal to classify and analyze Neo-Assyrian than ever before. This enables us to recognize grammatical errors in Neo-Assyrian more clearly and at the same time deepen our knowledge of Neo-Assyrian grammar.

[65] See Parpola (1987B) 278 n. 24.

2 EVIDENCE

2.1 Description of the evidence

The whole available Neo-Assyrian letter corpus forms the basis of my study and provides the primary evidence for it.[66] I have made this choice because one may assume that letters[67] give the most reliable information on the spoken language of the Neo-Assyrian period.[68]

The Neo-Assyrian letters may roughly be classified as follows:

(1) Royal letters (from the king)
(2) Political letters (Assyrian domestic affairs and foreign policy)
  (a) Letters from Assyrian home provinces and foremost Assyrian cities
  (b) Letters from distant provinces (governors reporting on the current situation, etc.)
  (c) Letters from foreigners (foreign kings, vassals, city-lords, emissaries)
  (d) Intelligence reports (including military movements, etc.)
(3) Scholarly letters (from the capital and other Assyrian cities with many-sided topics)
(4) Priestly letters (esp. from Assur, Calah, Arbela and Nineveh: relating to the religious cult and the maintenance and construction of temples)

---

[66] See Appendix A on the Neo-Assyrian letter corpus at the end of this volume. Cf. also Parpola (1981) 117-34, as well as ibid. chart 1 (giving the situation on 15.6.1980, which has changed relatively little for 23 years) at the end of that article. Furthermore, very recommendable is Pedersén's (1997) pithy survey of the Neo-Assyrian textual evidence, including information (pages on Neo-Assyrian are 143-49 + table in pp. 151-52) on the number of letters (in addition to other text types) and their findspots. Cf. also n. 72 below.

[67] I will not discuss the external features of the letters or envelopes and the variation of those features. For these matters, see e.g. Radner (1995) 71f, 76 nn. 17, 20. Generally speaking, the more private letters are often slightly oval shaped, as distinct from the high and right-angled, official letters, see Fadhil and Radner (1996) 420f who also list all the preserved envelopes of the Neo-Assyrian letters. On the envelopes and the customary sealing of letters, see also SAA I p. xv.

[68] Cf. e.g. Reiner (1966) 22.

(5) Official letters of a private nature (petitions to the king and other letters relating to the royal court may, together with denunciations, belong to this category or they may also be "political")
(6) Private letters (including letters touching upon private business)

The Neo-Assyrian letter corpus consists principally of the royal correspondence from Nineveh published, or to some extent still to be published, in the SAA series produced by the State Archives of Assyria Project. The published letters from Nineveh are to be found in SAA I, SAA V, SAA X, SAA XIII, SAA XV and SAA XVI; some 60 letters from the reign of Assurbanipal and some 200 fragments that cannot be assigned to any particular king remain unpublished, but I have been able to use them through the database of the SAA Project. In addition, many Neo-Assyrian letters have been published outside the SAA series. The most important of these are the so-called Nimrud Letters (NL), which likewise form part of the Neo-Assyrian royal correspondence and can mainly be attributed to the reign of Tiglath-pileser III (744-727 BCE) and to the early part of the reign of Sargon II (721-705). These letters have also recently been edited.[69]

The largest part of the Neo-Assyrian royal letter corpus is formed by the correspondence of King Sargon II.[70] Next in size comes the correspondence from the last years of Esarhaddon's rule (672-669) and the first years of Assurbanipal (669-665), which includes the scholarly (SAA X), priestly (SAA XIII), political letters to Esarhaddon (SAA XVI), as well as the remaining correspondence of Assurbanipal (mainly from the period around the civil war of 652-648).[71]

Neo-Assyrian letters have been found at several archaeological sites: Nineveh (Kuyunjik), Assur (Qal^cat Širqāṭ), Kalhu (Nimrud), Guzana (Tell Halaf), Dur-Šarrukin (Khorsabad), and recently at Tušhan (Ziyaret Tepe).[72] Only relatively few of them actually originated in these cities, however; most of them were written in other cities of the Neo-Assyrian empire, some even outside its borders.

---

[69] H.W.F. Saggs, *Nimrud Letters, 1952,* Cuneiform Texts from Nimrud V (London 2001). The book contains a total of 244 documents, which includes more than 200 Neo-Assyrian and 29 Neo-Babylonian letters and letter fragments. The rest are not letters. In this work I have used the abbreviation NL for those Nimrud Letters which were originally published in the journal *Iraq* (1955-1974). In that case, the old NL number is always given first together with the new CTN V reference (numbers there refer to the page numbers of the volume). Note that all the letters having a NL number are now published in CTN V. Other letters in CTN V carry an ND (field number) + CTN V reference. This rather complicated way of quoting the letters from Nimrud was chosen because of the unfortunate lack of any consecutive numbers in CTN V.

[70] See SAA I pp. xi and xvi-xvii on the extent of Sargon's correspondence. All in all, the letters and letter fragments extant from the reign of Sargon number ca. 1,300.

[71] Cf. Parpola (1981) 119ff.

[72] In addition, one Neo-Assyrian letter (SAA X 295) originates in Sippar; cf. Parpola (1981) Chart 1. The "Neo-Assyrian" letter from Hamath mentioned ibid. is actually Neo-Babylonian, see ibid. 257-65. One can find a clear outline of all the Neo-Assyrian archives and libraries in Pedersén (1998) 130-81. The locations of cities and towns in the Neo-Assyrian period are now easy to find in Parpola and Porter (2001). The letters found at Ziyaret Tepe have not yet been published.

Naturally, I have used other kinds of sources as well, in particular the collection of Neo-Assyrian treaties and loyalty oaths of the kings published in SAA II. This group of texts is especially important for the present study because the large tablet known as "Esarhaddon's Succession Treaty" (SAA II 6), with its many manuscripts, offers an excellent source for the study of variation. On the other hand, I have made only limited use of the Neo-Assyrian legal documents (SAA VI and XIV, ND, TH, documents from Assur, etc.). I have left aside royal inscriptions,[73] literary (e.g. myths), administrative and economic texts, trade documents, astrological reports[74] and oracle queries because they contain a more conservative linguistic form than the one attested in letters. Therefore, few quotations from the aforementioned texts are found in this book.

It is important to keep in mind the chronological distribution of the material if one wants to study some diachronic developments more accurately. The oldest material I have utilized in this study originates from the reign of Adad-nerari III (810-783 BCE) and the most recent material comes from those two decades which followed the reign of Assurbanipal (i.e. ca. 630-610 BCE).

---

[73] For grammatical variants and analyses based on the royal inscriptions of the two "early-Neo-Assyrian" kings (= Tukulti-Ninurta II [888-884] and Assurnasirpal II [883-859]), see Deller (1957A + B).

[74] Many astrological reports written in Assyrian (SAA VIII nos. 1-243) contain comments and remarks in a language style that is not distinct from the one used in letters (see SAA VIII xvif). Hence this study includes some quotations from astrological reports.

3 GRAPHEMIC VARIATION AND ORTHOGRAPHIC PECULIARITIES

Neo-Assyrian texts were written by impressing cuneiform signs on clay tablets with a stylus. The signs were both syllabic and logographic. The cuneiform syllabary had independent signs for all the (primary) vowels (*a*, *u*, *i*; *e*), but in practice, vowels were more often expressed by syllabic signs also including a consonant or consonants (mainly of the type VC or CV, more rarely CVC). Contrary to our alphabetic writing, word boundaries were not systematically indicated by blank spaces left between individual words or by other conventions.[75]

In order to understand cuneiform writing better, it is necessary to compile a graphemic inventory that includes all the signs used in recording cuneiform script. Moreover, it is also necessary to clarify the possible compatibility of graphemes with other graphemes that may either follow or precede them in writing. This kind of graphical study is called graphotactics (the study of the sequence of graphemes).

A familiarity with graphotactics, combined with a correctly founded grammatical theory, helps us to determine clearly all the possible morphographemes of the language.[76] Using the knowledge of the alternation of morphographemes,[77] we can put forward theories about the phonetic nature of a language, though we cannot absolutely establish that our reconstruction of the phonemes of an extinct language is in every respect correct or accurate.

There are in principle two basically different modes of interpretation that can be applied to texts written in cuneiform: (1) the orthographic explanation and/or

---

[75] The fact that the cuneiform signs are often densely packed on tablets or partly even overlapping, because of the shortness of the lines or for some other reason, is not essential in this context.

[76] Cf. Reiner (1973) 43-45.

[77] For the morphographeme as a concept in the light of examples, see Gelb (1970A) 73-77. The word "morphographeme" means a graphic realization of a morpheme (or usually a part of a morpheme in the syllabic cuneiform script) in writing. In its morphographemic use, a graphic morpheme (or part of it) is not entirely correspondent with a linguistic (read: with phonetic) reality, e.g. <*a-mat-su*> > /*amassu*/.

(2) the phonetic explanation.[78] The basic problem is, how accurately can the Neo-Assyrian cuneiform script be assumed to reflect the phonology and grammatical structure of Neo-Assyrian, in particular the spoken language? In this respect, the theories of some modern scholars deviate considerably from one another.[79] In actual fact, neither of these possible modes of explanation can be applied as such without paying attention to the other.

3.1 Graphical mergers[80]

Occasionally scribes used signs considered to be wrong from the viewpoint of the standard rules of Neo-Assyrian grammar. Nevertheless, these "wrong" signs are similar to the expected sign both in their graphical appearance and phonetic interpretation. Thus it is difficult to decide whether they should really be interpreted as errors, as small inconspicuous slips of the stylus, or as intentional "graphic variants":

TÚ = TE/TE = TÚ

(*egirtu*)	*ša e-gír*-TÚ (gen.) SAA XV 131 r.8, Rfdn 17 28 r.8 ~ *ša e-gir/gír-te* SAA I 154 r.7/SAA X 283:9; *i-gír*-TE (nom.) SAA XV 217 r.6′ ~ *e-gír-tú* SAA V 52 r.11, SAA V 63 r.7 and passim
(*kunnu*)	*uk*-TÚ-*i-ni* SAA I 97:11 ~ *uk-te-en* SAA XIII 45:3′
(*pānāt*)	*ina pa-na*-TE-*šu-nu* SAA XV 115 r.10′[81] ~ (*ina*) *pānātū-/u-* + poss.suff. passim

E = IA/IA = E

(*pānu*)	*ina* IGI-E (suff. 1st sg.) *šu-nu* "I have ..." SAA I 241 r.7[82] ~ *ina* IGI-*ia* passim
(Eburaiu)	^{m}IA-*bu-ra-a-a* CTN I 3 i 20 ~ ^{m}*e-b*[*u*]-*ra-a-a* CTN I 2 r. ii 7[83]

---

[78] The ancient scribes already applied the two conflicting orthographic tendencies in their orthographies: (1) a phoneticizing one approximating the actual pronunciation of the word, as in <*ri-in-ku*> (*rimku* "bath, ablution," < *ramāku*), or (2) a phonemicizing one approximating the phonemic and morphological shape of the word (in this respect a more approximate tendency regarding the phonetic accuracy), as in <*ri-im-ku*>, see e.g. Parpola (1975) 4. Cf. also the phonological rule (which concerns the <*ri-in-ku*>/<*ri-im-ku*> example) given by Reiner (1973) 38 n. 47.

[79] E.g. Deller (1962B) 194 claims that Neo-Assyrian orthography is arbitrary as far as vowels are concerned. And because of this, he suggests an orthographic interpretation rather than a phonetic one for the vowels, which appear more troublesome for analysis, ibid. 195.

[80] See LAS II 71 n. 139.

[81] Cf. n. ad SAA XV 115 r.10.

[82] Cf. n. ad SAA I 241 r.7.

[83] Cf. Eburaiu in PNA 1/II p. 393.

AH/EH = *e'/a'*[84]

(*ma'du*) *dul-⸢lu ma⸣*-AH-*du šu-ú* (Nabû-nadin-šumi) SAA X 276 r.6 ~ *dul-lu ma-a'-du* / [*šu-ú*] SAA X 252 r.11′-12′

(*pe'ettu*) *pe*-EH-*n*[*a-a-ti*] (<*eh* = *ah*>) SAA II 6:533A ~ *pe-e'-na-a-ti* ibid. manuscripts G, B

3.2 Signs and lines for separating elements

Occasionally scribes used either a colon (:) or three dots (:.) to separate words and clauses more clearly from one another and to avoid possible misunderstandings in otherwise ambiguous passages. Of these two punctuation marks, the colon is much more commonly found in the texts. There is no difference in meaning, however, between the use of the colon and the three dots. In separating clauses, they may have functioned as prosodic signs hinting at an intonation pause. The typical use of a colon in administrative, legal and economical documents as a ditto sign is not pertinent to letters. Thus we find:

mutki ina pānīki lū paqid / bābu la uṣṣā : asseme mā "'Let your husband be in your custody – he may not go outdoors!' I have heard that ..." (: between the clauses) SAA X 348 r.17-18

PN *: ēqu / ša bēt-ilānīšu / ša rēš Ṣidūni / ittikis : mā ana Ṣurri / lantuh* "'PN has cut down the *ēqu*[85] of the temple of his gods on the hill of Sidon, saying 'I shall pick it up to Tyre'" (1.: between the words, 2.: between the clauses) NL 13:8-12 (CTN V 154f)

issēt : abutu ša ṭābtīj[*a šī*] "The first token of m[y] favour [is]: ..." (: between the words) SAA X 182:24

āpiu (= LÚ*.NINDA) *ša šakinte / ittalka :. iqṭibia* "The baker of the harem manageress came, (and) he said to me" (:. between the clauses) NL 81:5-6 (CTN V 232f)

ina muhhi :. pê (=KA-*e*) */ ša bēlīja* "according to my lord's instructions" (:. between the words) GPA 198:9-10

At least two scholars, Nabû-ahhe-eriba[86] (SAA X 72:10, 19, r.9 and in astrological reports) and Balasî (SAA X 51:13, r.9, unless the writer of this letter is Nabû-ahhe-eriba too),[87] also separate, however seldom, words from one another by means of the specific separation mark, |. E.g.

tu-kal-la | ITI *an-ni-⸢ú⸣* SAA X 72 r.9

Scribes can also separate the introductory formula (or part of it) containing the names of the recipient and sender (sometimes with their titles and a short greeting) from the other contents of a letter with a horizontal dividing line. Thus we find:

---

[84] LAS II ad no. 205 r.6, cf. also Lipiński (1997) § 19.9.

[85] A religious cult-object of which the exact meaning is uncertain.

[86] For his handwriting, see LAS II A p. 37 (paragraph D. Characteristic features).

[87] See LAS II 71f.

a-na LUGAL *be-lí-ia*
ARAD-*ka* PN
lu DI-*mu a-na* LUGAL EN-*ia*
(main contents of letter)
....

Preserved examples of this practice are at least:

ND 2373 (CTN V pl. 49)
ND 2395 (CTN V pl. 43)
ND 2401[88] (CTN V pl. 46)
ND 2427 (CTN V pl. 22)
ND 2439 (CTN V pl. 23)
ND 2464 (CTN V pl. 49)
ND 2604 (CTN V pl. 44)
ND 2613 (CTN V pl. 18)
ND 2669[89] (CTN V pl. 46)
ND 2698 + ND 2702 (CTN V pl. 58)
ND 2736 (CTN V pl. 30)
ND 2772 (CTN V pl. 29)
NL 24 (ND 2449[90] = CTN V pl. 39)
NL 25 (ND 2643[91] = CTN V pl. 49)
NL 26 (ND 2725 = CTN V pl. 6)
NL 29 (ND 2720[92] = CTN V pl. 28)
NL 35 (ND 2452[93] = CTN V pl. 5)
NL 45 (ND 2673 = CTN V pl. 27)
NL 47 (ND 2463 = CTN V pl. 22)
NL 52 (ND 2355 = CTN V pl. 38)
NL 62[94] (ND 2367 = CTN V pl. 21)
NL 64 (ND 2683= CTN V pl. 57)
NL 67 (ND 2666 = CTN V pl. 41)
NL 71 (ND 2771 = CTN V pl. 58)
NL 74 (ND 2648 = CTN V pl. 28)
NL 75 (ND 2448 = CTN V pl. 24)
NL 78 (ND 2379 = CTN V pl. 11)
NL 81 (ND 2703 = CTN V pl. 44)
NL 97 (ND 2434 = CTN V pl. 22)
NL 102 (ND 2660[95])
NL 103 (ND 2617 = CTN V pl. 39)
NL 104 (ND 2769 = CTN V pl. 42)
SAA I 131[96] (ABL 842)
SAA I 132 (ABL 841)
SAA I 191 (ABL 132)
SAA I 222[97] (ABL 938)
SAA I 223 (CT 53 87)
SAA I 224 (ABL 888)
SAA I 232 (CT 53 864)
SAA I 258 (ABL 860)
SAA XV 292 (CT 53 71)
SAA XV 385 (CT 53 743)

[88] ND 2401 and ND 2604 are certainly written by Inurta-belu-uṣur who also wrote ND 2683 and ND 2769 (all these letters have a horizontal line after the greeting formula of three lines).

[89] Possibly the same Aššur-ila'i also wrote ND 2379 (NL 78). Note, however, EN-*a* for *bēlī'a* in ND 2379, whereas EN-*ia* regularly for *bēlī'a* in ND 2669.

[90] ND 2449 and ND 2464 are by Aššur-šimanni. See CTN V 268 ad l. 2 (the edition renders the name "Aššur-išmeani") as grounds to take the same person as the author of both letters.

[91] ND 2355, ND 2643, ND 2725 are by Aššur-matka-tera (he is as regular in the marking of the dividing line as Inurta-belu-uṣur).

[92] ND 2720 and ND 2666 are by Duri-Aššur (cf. his other letters NL 28 = ND 2799 [CTN V pl. 24] and NL 49 = ND 2784 [CTN V pl. 18] which do not have a dividing line).

[93] In this table, ND 2452, ND 2703 and probably also ND 2617, are by Ašipâ (other letters of Ašipâ, but without a dividing line are NL 11 = ND 2365 [CTN V pl. 3], NL 36 = ND 2623 [CTN V pl. 5]) and NL 91 = ND 2418 [CTN V pl. 5]). His way of using a dividing line and blessing formula is not as regular as Inurta-belu-uṣur's and Aššur-matka-tera's (cf. above).

[94] Published also as SAA V 74.

[95] The dividing line is not seen in the new copy (CTN V Pl. 40), but is in the latest transcription ibid. p. 207 and in the previous copy in Iraq 36 (1974) Pl. XXXVI.

[96] SAA I 131-32 are by Ahu-lurši.

[97] SAA I 222-24 are by Samnuha-belu-uṣur.

Though all these letters containing a horizontal line after the introductory formula originate from the reigns of Tiglath-pileser III and Sargon II, it is not so obvious that we have a real chronological trait here. However, the high frequency of such a line in the Nimrud letters is remarkable. Perhaps it is only by chance that no extant Assyrian letters were written after Sargon's reign using a horizontal ruling. But this fact may underscore the different nature of the letters we have available from the reigns of Tiglath-pileser and Sargon – mostly letters from governors and high (military) officials from provinces – compared to the preserved correspondence of Esarhaddon and Assurbanipal, which are mainly scholarly, priestly and other types of letters from Assyria.

A horizontal line within a letter may equally well separate different topics, sections or other elements (see e.g. SAA I 202-203) from each other. E.g.

NL 46 (ND 2608 = CTN V pl. 24)[98]	SAA X 55[101]	SAA X 184
SAA I 134	SAA X 58[101]	SAA X 295
SAA I 202-203[99]	SAA X 64[101]	SAA XIII 27
SAA V 171	SAA X 67[102]	SAA XIII 29
SAA X 8[100]	SAA X 74[102]	SAA XIII 157
SAA X 20[100]	SAA X 79[102]	SAA XIII 160
SAA X 30[100]	SAA X 84[103]	SAA XIII 202
SAA X 33[100]	SAA X 94-95[103]	SAA XV 283
	SAA X 100-101[103]	A 3660

While the use of this kind of dividing line is more common in texts of other types than letters, such as administrative texts, astrological reports, etc., letters which include astrological reports routinely use the dividing line to separate the report section from the other parts of the letter. Moreover, the end of a letter can be indicated by a horizontal "end line." Thus, for instance:

NL 66 (ND 2494 = CTN V pl. 2), SAA I 202, SAA I 258, SAA V 77, SAA XIII 157, SAA XIII 166.

At least the reverse side of one letter has separate sections of writing without any dividing lines, see CTN V 175ff, Pl. 35 (ND 2644 = NL 23).

All these dividing lines are purely non-grammatical features, but they illustrate how it was possible to segment the different parts of a letter into individual sections which were subjected to their own rules.

---

[98] A letter by Sennacherib, edited also as SAA I 32, but the line on the reverse side of the tablet is missing from the SAA edition.

[99] Nabû-pašir writes about the measurements of doorposts (202) and doors (203). Except for the greeting formula in 202 (ll. 1-6) and the introduction of the topic (ll. 7-8), these "letters" only give the above-mentioned measurements.

[100] By Issar-šumu-ereš.

[101] By Balasî.

[102] By Nabû-ahhe-eriba.

[103] By Akkullanu.

3.2.1 Glosses

Lastly, the so-called "glosses" used as explanatory notes in letters must be mentioned. These glosses were added as small-sized syllabic writing between the lines to clarify the reading or interpretation of a syllabogram or logogram (often a rare one) in a particular context. Glosses are only attested in the letters of the already above-mentioned scholars Nabû-ahhe-eriba and Balasî.[104] E.g.

ina ši-id-di KASKAL "along the roadside" SAA X 70 r.15
hu-u-li (gloss)

3.3 Splitting a word over two separate lines

In Neo-Assyrian, words are very rarely split over two separate lines.[105] I only know of the following seven examples in the entire letter corpus. The only common denominator in them seems to be the lack of space at the end of the line:

ka-/[ni]-ik StAT 1 53:5-e.6
ina IGI URU. ŠÀ-URU-*/a-e* StAT 1 54 r.3-4
ip-ta-/ṭa-ru-ni-šú SAA XIII 27 s.2-3
iš-ku[n]-/a-ni-ni : NL 43 r.16-17 (CTN V 130ff) (note also the use of colon after the word)
ze-/ez StAT 1 55:5′-6′,
and possibly: ^{d}*ša-at-ru*[106] / ^{d}INNIN (= Šatru-Issar, nevertheless, this case is not entirely comparable to the above-mentioned) SAA XIII 149:1-2 and
A.ŠÀ *ina* IGI ^{m}*di-di-i-/a ra-am-me* "Release the field for the use of Didia!" CTN III 28 r.1-2

3.4 Number of graphemes used by scribes

The number of graphemes used by individual scribes could vary considerably. For instance, the scholar Mar-Issar used at least 225 graphemes in his correspondence, whereas Sîn-na'di (a writer of SAA XV 17) possibly mastered approximately 112 graphemes, provided he knew all the most common syllabograms and logograms of Neo-Assyrian.[107] These two figures (225 and 112) can in a way be taken to illustrate the two extremes of scribal competence; the former figure represents the skills of a master or expert scribe, whereas the average literate citizen could manage with slightly more than one hundred signs.

---

[104] LAS II A pp. 37-38 and LAS II 13, 71-72.

[105] For some additional examples outside the letter corpus, see Jursa and Radner (1995/1996) 100 n. 47.

[106] ^{d}Šatru, see e.g. LAS II 158f.

[107] See Parpola (1997A) 321 n. 17.

However, this does not necessarily mean that scribes had problems in understanding each other's letters. The scholarly specialists, particularly those in Nineveh who belonged to the "inner circle" when the city was the Assyrian capital in the seventh century, were a class apart, who mainly communicated with the king, the royal family, some high administrators, and with themselves. They often formed solid working teams with colleagues in their field of expertise and co-authored letters to the king.[108] If more ordinary scribes had problems in reading the signs on a tablet they had been sent or which otherwise had come into their hands, they surely had some sources available to consult or at least knew someone to turn to in order to ask for an explanation. Misunderstandings were more likely to occur if a non-specialist or an apprentice had to interpret or read something that was beyond his competence. Thus we find:

> "Perhaps there are, on the other *side*, sign-forms that he does not understand; I will explain to him all that I know ... Now then, let them [sel]ect a Babylonian writing-board ..."[109]

3.5 "Abnormal syllabification"

Normally the syllabification of Neo-Assyrian words (as in Akkadian in general) observes either the syllable or morpheme boundaries in a word.[110] Abnormal syllabification correspondingly breaks these boundaries.

Examples of abnormal syllabification (the pattern (C)VC-VC is considered to be exceptional[111]) are as follows:

(*alāku*) *ni-tal-ak* SAA I 147 r.11 ~ *ni-ta-lak* SAA X 3:11
(*epāšu*) *e-tap-áš* SAA I 124 r.8, SAA I 204 r.5, SAA I 251:7, ABL 1364:6′, SAA XIII 11 r.5′, SAA XV 108:4′, SAA XV 129 r.1, KAV 214 r.8 ~ *e-ta-pa-áš* SAA X 222:14, SAA XVI 34:6, NL 12 r.6 (CTN V 155ff)
(*gamāru* Dtt) *ug-da-ad-am-mar* SAA X 74 r.21 ~ *ug-da-dam-*[*mar* SAA V 176:7′
(*garāru* Ntn) *it-at-na-ag-ra-ra* SAA XVI 20 r.5′
(*habātu*) *ih-tab-at* NL 48:15 (CTN V 116ff) ~ *ih-ta-bat* NL 2 r.7′ (CTN V 22ff), [*i*]*h-ta-bat* SAA V 145 r.19e
(*hakāmu*) *tah-ti-ik-im* SAA XVI 10:3′ ~ *ih-ti-kim* SAA X 29 r.3

---

108 This is especially the case with Balasî and Nabû-ahhe-eriba. For the co-authored letters, see Appendix B.

109 SAA X 384:4-7, r.1-2. Cf. also SAA X 60.

110 See LAS II ad no. 247:10. For another example, ibid. ad no. 224:13 in which the syllabification following syllable boundaries gives a decisive hint to the predicate in question.

111 Reiner (1966) 29. The list here does not include the frequent (C)VC + VC spellings at morpheme boundaries (i.e. *iš-pur-an-ni*, etc. passim, or rather rare forms of nouns with an auxiliary vowel before the last consonant of the root, followed by a possessive 1st sg. suffix: *ina ṣu-pur-ia* SAA XV 129 s.4, *a-na* ⸢LÚ*⸣.*mi-hir-ia* SAA XV 194:7′, *ina* UGU *ki-ṣir-iá* BM 132980 r.9′). For these nouns, cf. n. 417. On observing morpheme boundaries in writing, cf. Hämeen-Anttila (2000) 3. On the cases of ventive + possessive suffix of the type CVC + VC (like *a-sa-bar-áš-šú* SAA V 32 r.5), cf. Deller (1959) § 39n.

(*kammusu*)	*kam-mu-us-at* StAT 1 55:3′ cf. e.g. ⸢*ka*⸣*-mu-*⸢*sa*⸣*-ak* NL 36:12 (CTN V 34f)
(*karābu*)	*ak-tar-ab-ka-*⸢*a*⸣ StAT 1 57 =[112] StAT 2 248:5; *ak-tar-ab-ki* KAV 215:4 cf. *ak-tar-ba* StAT 1 51:6, SAA X 198:13; *ak-ta-rab* KAV 213:5
(*mahāru*)	*ni-ta-ah-ar* SAA XIII 188:14; *mah-ir-u-ni* SAA XV 131 r.6
(*matāhu*)	*an-ta-at-a*[*h*] SAA XV 107:2′; *im-at-tah* SAA XV 117 r.9′
(*pahhuru*)	*up-*⸢*t*⸣*a-ah-ir* SAA XV 63 r.2′ ~ *up-ta-hi-ir* SAA I 160 r.7
(*qabû*)	*iq-ab-bu-ni* (presumably a prosodic syllabification, cf. 3.7) SAA XVI 90 r.5 ~ *i-qab-bu-u-ni* SAA V 40 r.1, SAA V 294:8′, SAA XIII 66 r.6′, SAA XVI 211 r.4′, ABL 1148:3′
(*šahāṭu*)	*is-sa-ah-aṭ* SAA X 75:9
(*šakānu*)	*šá-kan-at* StAT 1 9 r.2; *as-sa-ak-an-šu* SAA X 212 r.12 ~ *šak-na-at* SAA XV 362:7′, NL 67:9 (CTN V 215ff); *a-sa-kan-šú* SAA I 191 r.7, NL 64:17 (CTN V 290ff)
(*šamû*)	*áš-am-me* SAA I 29 e.34, SAA X 328:14 ~ *a-šá-me* SAA V 144 s.1
(*šapāru*)	*as-ap-ra* SAA XIII 18 r.6; *a-sap-ár-šu* SAA V 217 r.2 ~ *a-sa-ap-ra*, *as-sap-ra*, *a-sap-ra* all passim; ⸢*i*⸣*-sa-ap-ar* CT 53 660:5′; *i-sap-ár* SAA XV 74 r.1
(*šētuqu*)	*us-se-et-iq* SAA VIII 47:5 ~ *us/ú-se-ti-iq* SAA X 247 r.4, 10/SAA X 362:10′, SAA X 363:11
(*zaqāpu*)	*i-zaq-up-a-ni* VAT 5602:13 (VS 1 95)
(*zâru*)	*zir-at* SAA X 184 r.6

In any case, (C)VC-VC is repeatedly used for the glottal stop (aleph) in (*l*)*iš-al*(*-šú/šu/šunu*), *la-áš-al*(*-šu*) (< *ša'ālu* "to ask").[113]

Non-verbal examples (some of the cases follow the model [C]VC-V[C] [at the end of a word] which is quite conspicuous):

(Ariawāte)[114]	URU.*ar-ia-u-a-te* SAA I 63 r.9 ~ URU.*a-ri-a-ú-a-ti* TH 3:4
(*atâ*)	*at-a* SAA I 96:7 ~ *a-ta-a* passim
(*burallu*)	NA_4.*bur-al-*[*li*] SAA X 323 r.12 ~ NA_4.*bu-ra-al-li* ibid. r.10
(*ispillurtu*)	*is-píl-ur-tú* SAA X 30:3, 4 (*-ur*!!-), r.1
(*issēniš*)	1*-en-iš* StAT 1 53 r.4 ~ *i*(*s*)*-se-niš* passim
(*itussu/ittussu*)	*it-us-si* ABL 1385 r.5 cf. *it-tu-sa-te* ibid. l. 16
(*karaphu*)	[*k*]*ar-ap-hi-šú-nu* SAA XV 187 r.12 and passim in legal texts (e.g. in SAA VI)
(*kurangu*)	ŠE.*kur-an-gu* GPA 207 r.1′
(*lumnu*)	*lu-um-an-šú* SAA X 347 r.13′
(*mešlu*)	*meš-il píl-*[*ki-šú*] "half of [his work ass]ignment" SAA I 159 r.14 ~ *mi-šil/ši-il* SAA X 187:11/SAA X 196 r.5; *me-šil*(*-ma*) SAA I 181 r.8, 9
(*mīlu*)[115]	*mi-il-u* SAA X 361 r.14 ~ *mi-i-li* SAA X 226:11. Note also *mì-il-'a-a-ni* (' = C) SAA I 36 r.7′

---

[112] A 2199.

[113] Cf. Hämeen-Anttila (2000) 13.

[114] This example may not be very telling because of the consonantal nature of <*ia*> = /'*a*/, /*ja*/. However, several (foreign) place-names were syllabified by using the VC-VC pattern. Cf. e.g. URU.*am-an-te* SAA I 104:8; URU].*ap-al-la-a* SAA XV 186 r.1; URU.*el-iz-za-da/u* SAA V 86:6/12, URU.*el-iz-ki* SAA I 41:19, ND 2487:9 ([-⸢*ki*⸣] CTN V 120ff), URU.*el-iz-kun* ibid. l. 9, r.9 (⸢URU⸣.*e*[*l-iz-k*]*un*; for the spellings see ibid. p. 123 ad 9,13); KUR.*hu-ub-uš-ki-a* SAA V 44 r.3′; KUR.*kar-al-l*[*a* SAA XV 75 r.2 and URU.*ṭu-ur-uš-pa-a* passim in the glossary of SAA V.

(*pānu*) *ina pa-an-ia* SAA XV 125:5′ (although on the morpheme boundary, this syllabification is exceptional) ~ *ina pa-ni-ia/iá* passim
(*qarābu*) *qar-a-bi* SAA XV 113:18, SAA XV 130:14, 22; *qar-a-bu* ibid. 20 ~ *qa-ra-bu* SAA XV 69:14; *qa-ra-bi* SAA V 3 r.4, SAA X 84 r.12
(*šaknu*) LÚ.*šak-an-šú* SAA VI 82:8′ ~ LÚ*.*šá-kan-šú-nu* SAA I 240:4′
(*tarṣu*) *ina tar-iṣ* RN SAA VI 257 r.18 ~ *ina tar-ṣi* passim

Note that examples other than Ariawāti and perhaps also *mīlu* have nothing to do with expressing aleph.[116] What is peculiar to nearly all of the enumerated syllabification examples is the rare (mentioned above) pattern (C)VC-VC instead of the more common patterns, (C)V-CV-CV and (C)V-VC-CV-VC.[117]

3.6 Scribal errors

Cf. 1.5.13, 3.8, 6.4 and 6.5.

Most of these examples involve a missing sign. In these examples, the missing signs have been added in round brackets. Other types of errors and oddities listed here are inadvertent omission of words, contextually wrong signs (!! marks emended signs), superfluous signs, and some odd metatheses.

(*aiāka*) (*a*)-*a-ak-ka* SAA XV 118 r.4
(*akanni*) *a-ka-an-ni-u* [[]] (superfluous *u* before erasure) StAT 2 163 r.9
(*alāku*) *lil*-(*li*)-*ku-ni* SAA V 32 r.15; *it*-(*ta*)-*la-ka* SAA V 53:19; *il*-(*lu*)-*ku* "they go" SAA X 56 r.2; *li-lil-ka* SAA XIII 128 r.9 normally *li*(*l*)-*li-ka* passim
(*ammāka*) *am*!!-*ma-kam-ma* SAA V 83 r.7e[118]
(*ana*) [*l*]*u* DI-*mu a*-(*na*) LUGAL EN-*ia* SAA I 93:4; IM (*a-na*) PN SAA V 213:1, SAA V 214:1; DI-*mu* (*ana*) PN / DI-*mu* (*ana*) PN_2 / DI-*mu* (*ana*) É *gab-bu* StAT 2 248:6-8
(*-annāšīni*) *iš-pu-ra-na-ši-an-ni* (i.e. no ground for *-an-* after *-annāši*)[119] SAA XVI 137:7
(*-anni/-āni*) *i-sa-pa-ra-an*-(*ni*) SAA XV 54 r.5; *iš-pur-an*-(*ni*) SAA X 227 r.15

---

[115] Kaufman (1974) 72 calls attention to a possible Aramaic influence in the form *mil'u*. See also GAG § 15b and Gelb (1955) 100 sub § 15b.

[116] For the aleph expressed by means of syllabification, see Reiner (1964) 169-70.

[117] Reiner (1966) 29.

[118] The tablet reads QAR-*ma-kam-ma*, cf. n. ad SAA V 83 r.7. For other emended readings in the letter volumes of the SAA series, see, e.g., SAA I 11:14, 110:15, 125 r.2, 176:4, 183 r.9; SAA V 15 r.12, 37 r.10, 12, 64:13, 91:12, 215:6 (need no longer be emended since the copy is now improved in CTN V 128ff and pl. 26 [copy of ND 2631]), 7, 13 (cf. the remark ad ibid. l.6), r.6, 233:6, 8; SAA X 20:11, 21 r.5, 30:4, 33 r.11, 52:13, 74:22, 185:23, 215:11, 217:11, 227 r.11, 238:12, 316:21, 325:9, 327 r.6, 354 r.13; SAA XIII 18 r.15, 20:11, 88 r.4 (cf. l. 16!), 114:3, 125 r.8, 166:19; SAA XV 163:9, 221 r.5, 279:6′, 342:3; SAA XVI 5 r.5, 21 r.12, 121 r.11, 126 r.22.

[119] Cf. the sequential order of endings in Hämeen-Anttila (2000) 93.

(*anniu*) *ak* (*an*)-*ni-im-ma* SAA XVI 112 r.15; (*an*)-*ni-u* StAT 1 51:11

(*annurig*) *an-nu*-(*rig*) SAA XVI 32 r.10; StAT 2 163:3

(*āšibu*) *a*-(*ši*)-*bu-te* "(great gods) dwelling (in Assyria and Akkad)" SAA X 227:8

(Balasî) ^{m}*ba*-(*la*)-*si-i* SAA X 276:7[120]

(*emūqu*) *la e*-(*mu*)-*qa-a-a* SAA XV 260 e.15′

(*gamāru*) *li-gi*-(*ma*)-*ru-ku-nu* SAA II 6:629frg

(Illil) ÍD.*pat-ti*–^{d}BI (^{d}BI > ^{d}BE) SAA I 210:15[121] ~ ÍD.*pa-a-ti*–^{d}BE SAA XV 166 r.4

(*ina*) *ina ina* ŠU.2 (i.e. one superfluous *ina*) StAT 1 52 r.6

(*karābu*) *lik-ru*-(*bu*) VAT 9770:4

(*-kunu*) LÚ.*e-mu-qi-ku*-(*nu*) "your (pl.) troops" SAA V 164 r.8

(*lū*) (*lu*) DI-*mu a-na* LUGAL *be-lí-ia* SAA XIII 31:3

(*madādu* D) *bir-te* IGI.2 *la ú*-(*ma*)-⌜*di*⌝-*du-u-ni* (common idiom *birti ēni maddudu*: to make s.th. clear to so.") SAA XV 15 r.12′

(*matāhu*) *in-ta*-(*at*)-*ha* CTN III 3 r.9

(*memmēni*) *me-me*-(*ni*) *la-šu* "there is nothing" SAA V 227 r.20

(*muhhu*) TA* (UGU) LÚ*.*hu-ub-te* "As to the captives" SAA V 242:5

(*Mullissu*) ^{d}NIN.(LÍL) StAT 1 51:4

(*nēsupu*/*nensupu*) *in-né-ep-su* (probably nondeliberate metathesis: *sp* > *ps*) SAA XIII 134:21′[122]

(*pahāru*) *up*-⌜*t*⌝*a-ah*-(*hi*)-*ir* SAA XV 63 r.2′ (cf. 3.5)

(*palhu*) *pa*-(*al*)-*hu-te* SAA X 354 r.13

(*pānīu*) LÚ.ERIM.MEŠ *pa-ni*-(*u*)-*te* SAA V 52 r.2

(*pānu*) *ina pa*-(*né*)-*e-a* SAA XV 226:9; TA *pa*-(*an*) ÍD NL 35 r.4 (CTN V 33f)

(*pašāhu*) *ip-ta*-(*áš*)-*ha* SAA X 213:7

(*qabû*) *i-iq-ṭí-bi* (not really erroneous but the spelling is extraordinary) SAA V 164 r.7 ~ *iq-ṭí-bi* passim

(*raddû*) *u-ra-du-ni-ni* (*u*- instead of *ú*-, see *šērubu* below) NL 12:16 (CTN V 155ff)

(*sahāru*) *ú-sa-ah*-(*ha*)-*ra* SAA XVI 115 r.9

(*ṣabātu*) *la* (*i*)-*ṣi-bu-tú la i-di-nu* "they did not arrest (him) and hand (him) over" SAA V 53 r.8; (D) *u-ṣa-bi-ta* (*u*- instead of *ú*-, see *šērubu* below) NL 12 r.11 (CTN V 155ff)

(*ša*) LÚ.EN.NAM / *la* KUR.*bar-hal-zi* "the governor of Barhalzi" (i.e. *la* > *ša*!!)[123] SAA X 173:12-13; (*ša*) LUGAL *be-lí iš-pur-an-ni* SAA X 278:7

(*šakānu*) *ni-iš-ku*-(*nu*)-*u-ni* SAA V 53 r.8

(*šērubu*, *erābu* Š) *u-se-rib* (should be *ú*-, because <*u*> does not occur at the beginning of a finite verb form.[124] This error is repeated four times in

---

[120] See n. ad SAA X 276:7.

[121] Cf. n. ad SAA I 210:15.

[122] Cf. n. ad SAA XIII 134:21.

[123] See LAS II ad no. 114:13.

[124] This principle is reflected in the SAA series in the forms of the verb *udû* "to know". In particular, these occur in forms which are interpreted as so-called prefixed statives (see GAG § 78b, § 106q). The forms of *udû*, in which <*u*> immediately follows the *lū*-particle (cf. 4.11) are always written together, e.g. *lu-u-da* SAA I 179:20, SAA X 37 e.7′; *lu-u-di* SAA XIII 70 r.9, 126 r.13′; ⌜*lu*⌝-*u-di-ú* SAA V 117:16. Correspondingly the forms in which <*ú*> is combined with *lū* are written separately, e.g. *lu ú-da* SAA V 74 r.1; *l*]*u ú-di-u* (oath) SAA X 8:12 and *l*]*u-u ú-di-i-u* SAA X 365 r.6. The last of these examples seems to insinuate that *lū* and *udû* are to

	the same letter, cf. examples above) NL 12 r.14 (CTN V 155ff); *u-še-rab-šú-nu* ibid. r.22; possibly *i-se-ri-b*[*u*?]-⌜*šú*?*-nu*?⌝ (*i-* > *ú-*) NL 45 r.8′ (CTN V 136ff)
(*ubālu* Š)	*la u-še-ba-la* (*u* > *ú*) SAA XV 288:10
(*urdu*)	*ar-ka* (*ar* > ARAD) KAV 133:3; ARAD-(*ka*) NL 35:2 (CTN V 33f)

Some other orthographic oddities, which cannot result from either phonological or morphological alternation, are nothing more than blunders of scribes.[125] However, these kinds of errors are not easy to perceive in a dialect we cannot reconstruct with absolute accuracy. Thus, it is not surprising that scholars have had many conflicting views in interpreting questionable writings. Some scholars see the deviations as mere errors of the scribes, while others explain these rare orthographic phenomena in some other way, e.g. phonetically.[126]

3.7 Graphemic consonantal gemination?[127]

When examining finite verb forms, one can rather often observe the gemination of a consonant that appears to be merely graphemic. The term used is graphemic because the gemination is difficult to explain through any obvious grammatical (morphological) motive. Despite non-morphological motivation, some of the examples below may be termed morphographemic gemination (mg.).[128] Nevertheless, for most of these examples, a phonological ("non-grammatical") explanation appears most plausible, or more accurately, a prosodic (which is synonymous with the emphatic stress[129] in this context) or a coordinative explanation (coordinating clauses, most commonly to be taken as "and" between two clauses). However, every example should be analysed separately. For that reason, I have first tried to evaluate all the examples below in the light of each context and then added in parentheses the explanation which seems (to me) the most probable for the consonantal gemination.

The scribes' typical manner of observing the syllable boundaries rather than the morpheme boundaries in their writing may have had its own influence, at least in

---

be interpreted as separate elements. Notwithstanding, for this last type of writing, in my opinion, it would be clearer to read all the forms as combined (as *lu-u-da*, *lu-ú-di* etc.), since I do not see any real difference in meaning between the forms of *udû* following the *lū*-particle, exclusive of the orthographic (<*u*> vs. <*ú*>) one.

[125] Cf. e.g. Reiner's remark (1973) 54 (bottom of a page).

[126] As an example of the interpretative differences of opinion: cf. the so-called "broken writings". For these writings, see von Soden (1948), (1983) 93-95, Gelb (1955) 97-98 sub § 8c, (1970B) 535-36 and Groneberg (1980).

[127] See Deller (1959) § 39a-d, who gives several examples. For literature on the (exceptional) consonantal length in Akkadian, see Mayer (1992) 47.

[128] As in e.g. Parpola (1974) 10 n. 10, from which I have extracted many examples of the item /-*ā*/. On the concept morphographeme (and morphographemic), see n. 77.

[129] Cf. Parpola (1987B) 274-75.

cases interpreted to be morphographemic. In such cases, the gemination of a consonant would be a kind of hybrid writing caused by the collision of these two different principles.[130] On the other hand, the interpretation of these verb forms may be complicated by the idiosyncracies of some individual scribes. In any case, these kinds of geminated forms are, on the whole, distributed among several scribes.

In the light of the examples, the gemination of a consonant is extremely frequent at a morpheme boundary, mostly immediately before the subjunctive or ventive, as well as before the suffixes of the second- and third-person plural.[131] E.g.

/-a/

(ʾlk) *lal-lik-ka* (pros.) "should I come?" SAA V 62:5; *la-al-lik-ka* (coord.) "I'll go and ..." SAA V 126:6; *la i-lak-ka šú-nu l*[*a* ...] "they cannot [depart] (because of ...)" (coord.) SAA V 126 r.5

(dūl) *a-du-al-la* (coord.) SAA XV 288:6

(hrṣ) *a-ha-ra-aṣ-ṣa* (pros./coord.) SAA I 29:19; *ni-ih-ru-uṣ-ṣa* (broken cont., presumably pros.) SAA XVI 204 r.8

(pūg) *ip-tu-ag-ga* (pros.) SAA XVI 42 e.15

(shr) *i-sa-hur-ra* (coord.) SAA XV 60 r.6′

(škn) *a-sa-kan-na* (coord.) SAA XV 60 r.14′

(špr)[132] *a-sa-par-ra* (pros.) SAA V 126 r.15, (pros.) SAA X 290 r.12e; *i-sa-par-ra* (broken cont., presumably coord.) SAA I 251:11!!; *iš-pur-ra* SAA I 260 r.9 (interrogative int.); *liš-pur-ra* (pros.) SAA XV 60 s.1; *l*⌜*i-i*⌝*š-pur-ra* (pros./coord.) SAA V 244 r.8′; *la taš-pur-ra* (pros.) SAA X 202:7

(tdn) *la a-dan-na* (coord.) SAA V 56 r.4; *id-din-na-šú-ni* (pros.) SAA II 6:90A /-*aššu*/

(wbl) *nu-bal-la-šú-nu* (coord.) SAA XV 98 r.12′ /-*aššunu*/

/-anni/

(ʾmd) [*l*]*e-mi-id-da-an-ni* (pros.) SAA XV 260:14′

(hlq) *ú-hal-laq-qa-ni* (pros.) KAV 199 r.10′e; *la tu-hal-laq-qa-a-ni* (pros.) SAA II 6:141E, 161A, 256A, B

(pqd) [*i-pa*]*q-qid-dan-ni* (probably mg.) SAA XIII 112:10′; *ip-qid-da-ni* (pros./mg.) KAV 133 r.5; *ip-qid-da-ni-ni* (pros.) SAA XVI 112 r.5

(špr) [*i*]*š-pur-ra-a*[*n-ni*] (broken cont.) CT 53 645:2′; [*i*]*š-pur-ra-ni-ni* (mg. or coord.) SAA V 198 r.4′

/-ā/

(dmq) *tu-dam-mì-iq-qa* ABL 561:15′ (mg., 2nd pl.)

(nṣr) *ta-na-*⌜*ṣar-ra*⌝*-ni* (mg., 2nd pl. + the subjunctive marker of oath) SAA II 6:65W ~ *ta-na-ṣar-a-ni* ibid. ms. A

(nšʾ) *iṣ-ṣa* (imperat. > pros., both 2nd pl.) SAA X 348 r.6, SAA XV 179:15 ~ *i-ṣa* (all 2nd sg.) SAA V 202:8, SAA V 203 r.11′, SAA I 236 e.14′

(ṣbt) *tu-šá-aṣ-bat-ta* (mg., 2nd pl.) SAA II 6:85A ~ *tu-šá-aṣ-ba-ta* ibid. ms. I cf. also *tu-šá-aṣ-bat-a-ni* SAA II 6 passim

(škn) *ša-kan-na* (pros., rhetorical question) SAA XIII 80 r.11

---

130 See Parpola (1972) 25.

131 LAS II ad no. 247:10. Cf. also GAG § 83d-e.

132 However, see LAS II ad no. 223 r.12′.

(tdn) *ta-*⌜*dan*⌝*-na-a-ni* SAA II 6:213frg (mg., 2nd pl. + the subjunctive marker of oath) ~ *ta-dan-a-ni* ibid. Je, frg, *ta-da-na-a-ni* ibid. C, frg

/-ū/

('br Š) *ú-še-bar-ru-šu-nu-u-ni* (coord. or mg.) SAA V 100 r.13
('kl) *e-kul-lu* (coord.) SAA I 241 r.13, (pros./coord.) SAA XIII 33 r.1
('mr) *e-mur-ru*[133] (pros.) SAA XVI 21:19 ~ *em-mu-ru* SAA X 220 r.1, SAA XIII 1:17; *e-mu-ru* SAA X 151 r.2, NL 3 r.3′ (Face A in CTN V 64ff)
('pš) *e-pu-uš-šú* (coord.) SAA I 96 r.6
('rb) *ú-še-rib-bu* (pros.) SAA X 328:12
('tq Š) *ú-še-tu-uq-qu* (coord.) SAA X 278 r.6; *še-tu-uq-qi* (coord.) SAA X 278 r.4
(blṭ D) *lu-bal-liṭ-ṭuš* (shift of stress along with the apocope, pros.) SAA XIII 58:10
(krb) *lik-ru-ub-bu* (mg.) SAA XIII 139 r.8
(kšd) *uk-taš-ši-*⌜*id-du*⌝ (probably pros.) SAA X 354 r.10
(mgr) *la/*[*l*]*a-a i-ma-gúr-ru* (both coord.) SAA I 143 r.10/SAA I 260 r.16; *l*]*a im-ma-gúr-ru* (broken cont., presumably coord.) SAA XVI 155:9′
(mhṣ) *ú-ta-hi-iṣ-ṣu* (coord. or pros.) SAA V 53 r.5; *us-sa-an-hi-iṣ-*[*ṣu* 0] (pros.) ABL 879:6
(nšr) *li-iš-šur-ru* (coord.) SAA X 177 r.4
(pqd) *lip-qid-du* (pros.) SAA X 134 r.2, SAA X 135 r.2; *li-ip-qid-du* (pros.) SAA XVI 39 r.3
(š'l) *i-sa-al-lu* (assimil., see 4.2.1) SAA XV 101:10; *liš-ul-lu* (coord./pros.) SAA V 85:5, (broken cont.) SAA XV 84 r.8′ (CTN V 134ff); *li*[*š-a*]*l-lu-šú-nu* (coord./pros.) SAA XIII 128 r.13
(škn) (*li*)*-iš-kun-nu* (coord.) SAA XIII 80:15; *iš-kun-nu* (mg.) SAA VI 19:1; *iš-kun-ni-ni-ši-n*[*i*] (broken cont.) CT 53 167:2′ cf. 4.3.1
(špr) *liš-pur-ru* (broken cont.) SAA XV 132 r.4′; *iš-pur-ru-šu-u-ni* (coord.) SAA XV 125 r.4
(tdn) *lid-din-nu* (mg.) SAA XVI 106:12 ~ *li*(*d*)*-di-nu*(*-u/ú-ni*) passim
(ṭīb) *l*]*i-iṭ-ṭib-bu* (pros.) SAA X 294:10
(wbl) *ú-bal*[!!]*-lu-ni-šú*[134] (pros./coord.) NL 37 r.8′ (CTN V 84f)
(znn) *i-za-nu-un-nu* (pros./coord.) SAA XV 100 r.16′

/-ūni/

('kl) *a-kul-lu-u-ni* (pros., oath) ABL 390 r.12′
('lk) *lu i-lik-ku-u-ni* (pros.) SAA XV 54:16′; *ár-hiš lil-lik-ku-u-ni* (pros.) BaM 27 419 r.2 (IM 132409)
('pš) *e-*[*p*]*a-áš-šú-u-ni* (pros.) SAA V 56:12
(hlq) *ih-liq-qu-u-ni* (pros.) SAA XV 54:12′, (broken cont.) ibid. s.1 cf. *akī* ... *ih-li-qu-u-ni* ibid. 20′
(mhṣ) *ma-hi-iṣ-ṣu-*⌜*ni*⌝ (pros.) SAA X 294 r.12 (bis)
(mrṣ) *im-ra-aṣ-ṣu-ni* (mg.) SAA X 316:10
(pqd) *ip-qid-du-ni* (pros.) SAA XIII 150:8; *pa-qid-du-u-ni* (coord./mg.) SAA XIII 161:19′; *ip-qid-du-šú-u-ni* (mg.) SAA II 6:45E ~ [*ip*]*-qi-du-šú-u-ni* ibid. ms. A
(qbī) *iq-ab-bu-ni* (pros.) SAA XVI 90 r.5
(škn) *iš-kun-nu-ú-n*[*i* 0] (pros.) SAA XV 61 r.6′

---

[133] Cf. Parpola (1972) 25. The gemination of this form is most probably to be construed as phonetic in nature. On the basis of the context, there is clearly an element of excitement in this passage. For an alternative explanation, see Hämeen-Anttila (2000) 3, 5.

[134] *ú-*TI*-lu-ni-šú* (sic) must be a scribal mistake.

(tdn) *id-din-nu-ni* (pros.) SAA XV 181 r.1; [*l*]*a i-din-nu-u-ni* (pros., however cont. is pretty broken) SAA XV 267 r.5′; [*lid*]*-din-nu-u-ni* (pros.) ibid. r.7′
(wbl) *ub-bal-lu-ni* (coord.) SAA I 66 s.2

/-āku/
(mṣ') *ma-aṣ-ṣa-ku-ni* (pros.) SAA X 294 r.28
(nš') *na-aṣ-ṣa-ku-u-ni* (pros.) SAA X 354:10

As for the secondary gemination of the middle radical in perfect forms, the following occurs:

('lk) *i-tal-lak* (3 x coord.) SAA V 86:7, 9, SAA V 87 r.2, (broken cont.) SAA V 95:2′, (mg.) VAT 8670:10′; *it-tal-lak* (broken cont.) CT 53 512 r.7 (perhaps reign of Sargon II)
('mr) *a-tam-mar* (broken cont.) SAA XV 334 r.6′ ~ *a-ta-mar* passim; *e-ta-am-m*[*a*]*r-šú* (pros.) SAA V 53:23 ~ *e-ta-mar-šú* SAA XIII 134:14′
('pš) *e-tap-pa-šu* (according to other manuscripts mg., otherwise coord./pros. seems totally possible) SAA II 6:166M ~ *e-tap-šu/ú* ibid. manuscripts ES/P; *e-tap-pa-*[*áš* ibid. 200frg ~ *e-ta-pa-aš* ibid. ms. J; commonly *e-tap-šú/šu* and *e-ta-pa-áš* passim
(gṣṣ) *ag-du-uṣ-ṣu-uṣ* (pros.) SAA X 294:25
(nṣr) *at-ta-aṣ-ṣar* (pros.) SAA X 294:20, 21
(šdd) *as-sa-ad-da-ad*[135] (pros. or rather a haplological pf form of the Gtn-stem) SAA X 294:28
(šm') *a-sem-mi* (pros.) SAA XIII 28 r.11 ~ *as-se-me* SAA X 305 r.2, ABL 943:5, SAA XVI 54:4, *a-se-me* ABL 426:10
(špr) *a-sap-par* (both coord.) SAA XV 118:11′, r.1 ~ *a-sa-par/bar* passim
(hdū) *ah-tú-ud-du* (1. broken cont., 2. pros./coord.) CT 53 908:12, r.5 ~ ⌈*ah*⌉*-tu-d*[*u* CT 53 968 r.7′

Gemination of the first radical of a verb:

(bšī) ⌈*ib*⌉*-ba-áš-ši* (pros.) SAA X 274 r.5 (Nabû-nadin-šumi)[136]
(dbb) *ad-da-bu-ub* (pros., in cases like this, the secondary lengthening of a syllable preceding the stress cannot be excluded) SAA XVI 78:7; *lu* [*l*]*a id-da-ab-bu-ub* (pros.) SAA X 278 r.2 (Nabû-nadin-šumi)
(dgl) *id-da-gal-an-ni* (pros.) SAA XVI 78 r.4
(gmr) *ug-ga-mar* (pros./coord.) SAA XIII 187 r.13′
(hlq) *ih-hal-li-qu-ni* (pros./coord.) SAA V 52 r.4
(qbī) *iq-qab-bi* (pros.) SAA X 277 r.9 (Nabû-nadin-šumi); *i*]*q-qa-bi* (pros.) SAA X 90 r.7′; *iq-qab-bu-u-ni* (pros.) SAA XIII 133 r.3
(šm') *iš-šá-me* (pros.) SAA I 231 r.4

Non-verbal forms:

(*ēpišānu*) *e-piš-šá-nu-te* (mg. or pros.) SAA II 6:159S ~ *e-pi-šá-nu-ti* SAA II 6:136A; 147A; 159A; 145frg; *e-piš-a-nu-ti/te* SAA II 6:159EP/136Et
(*kala*) *ša kal-la*[137] (pros.) SAA X 327 r.6; *kal-la* UD-*mu* (pros.) SAA XVI 21 r.2

---

[135] Parpola (1987B) 276. Cf. also 4.9 (end).

[136] See LAS II ad no. 203 r.9 and LAS II A p. 39.

[137] This may be construed orthographically, cf. Hämeen-Anttila (2000) 3, 5 (for *e-mur-ru*).

(*kūdunu*) É–*ku-din-ni* (mg.) CTN I 4:20, CTN I 8:16, CTN I 9:10, CTN I 16:9 ~ É *ku-din* CTN I 6:11; LÚ*.*ša*–É–*ku-din* SAA V 79:4, 13, r.1; É–*ku-di-ni* ND 2646:4 (Iraq 23 40); ANŠE.*ku-din* (pl.) passim; ANŠE.*ku-din*.MEŠ passim; *ku-din*.MEŠ SAA XIII 100 r.2

I by no means claim to have interpreted the examples above correctly and in the only possible way in every single instance, since finding the right tone of each passage is very difficult in practice. Still, it is startling to notice how the use of geminated consonants in NA closely corresponds to the present-day use of exclamation (or question) marks. Namely, geminated consonants are often attested in, for example, the stressed precatives, which are used in assurances under oath, in explanations or excuses made up under pressure, in emphatic denials, in enthusiastic and exciting reports, in the hour of fear and despair, as well as in rhetorical questions. Could the desired message not be expressed emphatically enough by forms of the "normal orthography"? Undoubtedly, but I believe that the "non-grammatically" geminated consonants of the writing strived for the tone and emphasis of the phonetic reality. Perhaps the typical Neo-Assyrian way of forming questions by adding vowel(s) to create interrogative intonation is related to the matter of geminated consonants. Maybe some individuals experimented with the language and tried to create meaningful innovations by following the example of the interrogative intonation. Actually I wonder whether the motivation behind our own manner of using several exclamation marks, particularly in informal situations, is very different from the Neo-Assyrian use of geminated consonants.

Furthermore, the secondary gemination[138] of a consonant may lead to the development of an anaptyctic vowel. In this case, the result is an additional syllable. The purpose of such an additional syllable is apparently the avoidance of a row of consecutive, short, open syllables.[139] E.g.

(*šaṭrāni*) *šá-aṭ-ṭa-ra-a-ni* "the [...]s (f.) are written" SAA X 60:11
ṣil-li-ba-a-ni SAA X 241:5-6 ~ *ṣi-il-ba-ni* SAA X 315 r.9.

In addition, the secondary gemination of a consonant after a short vowel often occurs in free variation with a long vowel + a single consonant.[140] This phenomenon is called metathesis of quantity[141] (see 4.14).

[138] For statistics on the consonantal gemination (as far as morphological, phonological as well as other grounds are concerned) in an exceptional letter (SAA X 294, Urdu-Gula) compared to the Neo-Assyrian letters in general, see Parpola (1987B) 273 n. 14, as well as ibid. pp. 274-75.

[139] LAS II ad no. 39:11.

[140] See Deller (1959) § 38.

[141] See e.g. Parpola (1988B) 79 with the examples of n. 4 on the same page (note that n. 4 should be 3 and vice versa) in particular.

3.8 Defective writings

Cf. also 3.6 and 4.13.

The most common type of defective writing is the omission of the /*u*/ belonging to the subjunctive (= *-ū...ni*). Probably the marking of this <*u*> was an optional feature in writing but nevertheless, it may have been pronounced.[142] In addition, the vowel belonging to the ventive is missing from many writings. I cannot rule out the possibility that in many of the examples below, the purpose was to imitate the pronunciation of the fast, spoken language.

The following are examples of defectively written verb forms:

('br) *li-bir-né-e* /*lībirūnê*/ (prc 3rd pl. + vent. + interrogative int.) NL 78 r.6′ (CTN V 245f)

('lk) *il-lik-ni-ni* /*illikūninni*/ SAA XV 118 r.6; ('lk) *tal-lak-ni-ni* /*tallakanni*/ SAA II 6:179S

('pl) *e-pal-ka-ni* /*eppalūkanni*/ SAA V 115 r.3 ~ *ep-pa-lu-ka-a-n*[*i* SAA V 280 s.1

(glī) *ú-ša-gal-na-ši-ni* /*ušaggalūnāšīni*/ SAA I 190 r.6′

(hbl) *ih-bil-šú-ni* /*ihbilūšūni*/ SAA XVI 29:8

(nkr) *tu-nak-kar-šú-u-ni* /*tunakkaraššūni*/ SAA II 6:55A, 69A

(nṣr) *ta-na-ṣar-šú-u-ni* /*tanaṣṣaraššūni*/ SAA II 6:50A, E, 168A; *ta-na-ṣar-šá-n*[*u-ni* SAA II 3:6′; *ta-na-ṣar-šú-nu-u-*[*ni*] SAA II 6:100frg /*tanaṣṣaraššunūni*/

(škn) *áš-kun-ka-a-ni* /*aškunūkanni*/ SAA V 3:17; *i-šá-kun-šú* /*išakkanušu*/ (dissimil., 3rd pl. + obj. 3rd sg.) SAA I 22 r.5

(šlm) *tu-šal-lum-ni* /*tušallamūni*/ (dissimil.) SAA V 227 r.24

(špr) *iš-pur-ni-ni* (sg.) /*išpurūninni*/ or /*išpurannīni*/ ABL 1385:12, SAA I 148:5, SAA XVI 15:6 ~ *iš-pur-u-ni-ni* (pl.) SAA XIII 77:7, SAA XV 129 s.3; *išpurannīni* (sg.) passim
áš-pur-ka-a-ni CT 53 974:6 (Gula-eṭir); *la áš-pur-ka-ni* /*ašpurūkanni*/ StAT 1 51 e.14; *a-šap-par-kan-ni* /*ašapparūkanni*/ or /*ašapparakkanni*/ SAA V 3 e.20; *áš-pur-*[*k*]*e-e-ni* /*ašpurūkinni*/ CT 53 974 r.5 (Gula-eṭir);
iš-pur-šu-u-ni /*išpurūšūni*/ SAA XVI 21:16, SAA V 227:22; *i-šap-par-šá-nu-ni* /*išapparūšunūni*/ (dissimil.) SAA XV 4:16; *iš-pur-ni* /*išpuranni*/ SAA I 104:5, SAA I 76:8, SAA I 77:11; *taš-pur-ni* /*tašpuranni*/ SAA V 95:5

(šrk) *liš-ru-uk-nik-ka* /*lišrukūnikka*/ SAA XIII 137:4′

(šṭr) *liš-ṭur-*⸢*ni*⸣ /*lišṭurūni*/ (prc 3rd pl. + vent.) SAA X 285 r.1′

(tkl) *ú-tak-kil-*(*u*)*-ka-ni* (both 3rd pl. and subj.) SAA X 333 r.2

Omission of a root or stem vowel:[143]

('lk) *lil-*(*li*)*-ku-ni* SAA V 32 r.15

(hrp) *tah-ru-ba* /*taharrupā*/ SAA I 98:8

(kl') *la tak-la-a* /*takallā*/ SAA II 6:91I; *ak-tal-šú-u* /*aktalašû*/ (interrogative intonation may cause the syncope) "Could I hold him back?" SAA V 147 r.9

(krr) *ak-ra-ra* /*akarrara*/ NL 48:5, 7 (CTN V 116ff)

(nṣr) *iṣ-ru-ka-nu-u-*[*ni*] /*iṣṣurukunūni*/ (dissimil., presumably the syncope is due to the shift of stress) SAA XV 90 r.4

[142] See idem (1972) 24.

[143] With root vowel, the vowel between the first and second radical of a verbal root is meant, whereas the stem vowel is the vowel between the second and the third (last) radical.

(qrb) *i-qar-bu-u-ni-ni* /*iqarribūninni*/ SAA V 64 r.2
(rks) *tar-kás* /*tarakkas*/ "You set/bind" SAA X 298:9, 17
(špr) *áš-par* /*ašappār*(*a*)/ SAA V 217 s.1, SAA XVI 65 r.14′;[144] *as-par* /*assapār*(*a*)/ SAA XIII 20 r.13e, 22 r.5; *as-par-šú-nu* SAA XIII 20 r.4
(tdn) *lid-nu-ni* /*liddinūni*/ SAA I 150 r.15, SAA XIII 144 r.15

3.9 <*a* + *a*> and <*i* +*a*> signs

The word initial <*a*+*a*> is either to be read /*aj*/ (as a diphthong), /*a'*/ or /*aja*/ (disyllabic[145]), e.g.

(*aiu*/*a'u*) *a-a-'u-ú-ti*[146] SAA X 259 r.4, 6; *a-a-ú* SAA X 227:26, SAA X 280 r.2, NL 80[147] r.16′ (-⸢*ú*⸣, broken cont.) (CTN V 104ff); *a-a-ú-ti* SAA X 259:12; [*a-na*?] *a-a-e* (*gen.*) SAA V 194 r.6′; *a-a-i* SAA XVI 126 r.21′; ⸢*a*⸣*-a-im-ma* (broken cont.) SAA XVI 237 r.3 cf. orthographic variation: *a-i-ú* SAA X 52:12; *a'-u* SAA I 125:14; *a-iu-ú* NL 41:9 (CTN V 208ff)

(*aiāši*) *a-na a-a-ši* SAA I 181:9, SAA XIII 38 r.6, SAA X 334 r.8, SAA X 182:31; *a-a-ši* SAA I 236 s.1, SAA V 46 r.2, SAA X 295:3 and passim ~ (*ijāši*) *a-na ia-a-ši* GPA 1:5, SAA XVI 99 r.5; *an–ni-ia-ši*[148] SAA X 194 r.14′; *ia-ši* SAA X 39 r.5; *ia-a-ši* SAA XIII 1:5, SAA I 205 r.9, SAA XVI 4:2, NL 54:6 (CTN V 13f) and passim

In the middle of a word, <*a*+*a*> is either a diphthong /*aj*/, /*a'a*/ or /*ja*/. E.g.

(*ahāiš*) *a-ha-a-a-iš* NL 65:6 (CTN V 45f); (*aššūrāiu*) [*aš*]*-šur-a-a-te* SAA I 56:9; (*daiālu*) LÚ*.*da-a-a-li* SAA V 87 r.4, SAA V 246:6 cf. LÚ*.*da-ia-a-li* SAA V 105:17; (*kaiamānu*) *ka-a-a-ma-nu* passim; (*ka''unu*) *lu-ka-a-a-*⸢*en*⸣ SAA I 236:8′; (*pa''uṣu*) *up-ta-a-a-ṣi* SAA I 236 r.6 cf. *up-te-ii-ṣi* SAA XVI 63 r.21; (*taiāru*) *ta-a-a-ar-šú* SAA XIII 39:12; *ta-a-a-ru* SAA XIII 134:21′; (*uzuzzu* Š) *ú-sa-za-a-a-zi* SAA X 358 r.6 cf. *us-sa-zi-ii-zi* ABL 1022:27; (Waisi) URU.*ú-a-a-si* SAA I 29:27, 29, r.4 cf. URU.*ú-a-si* SAA I 30 e.8′, SAA V 164:7; URU.*ú-e-si* SAA I 29 r.2, SAA V 87:14; *ú-e-si* SAA V 89:10

The nisbe adjective at the end of a word usually informs us either of the geographical origin of an individual, or of the particular group an individual

[144] See n. ad SAA XVI 65 r.14.

[145] See Gelb (1970B) 540.

[146] See LAS II ad no. 163 r.4 and n. 294 on the same page. However, the letter in question is the only one I know in which <' + V> sign is written after the <*a*+*a*> sign. On the other hand, for the complete rejection of the <*a*+*a*> sign as a diphthong at the beginning of a word, see Gelb (1970B) 541. According to Gelb, the sign may possibly occur as a diphthong in interpreting some foreign words. On the supposed diphthongs of foreign languages occurring in Akkadian, see also Reiner (1964) 171 n. 8.

[147] Now NL 80 + ND 2396, see CTN V 106.

[148] See LAS II ad no. 151 r.14′.

belongs to. This adjective is regularly written -<*a-a*>, regardless of the case (nom. = gen./acc.) in both singular and plural masculine forms.[149] For instance,

> URU.*ṣi-du-na-a-a* (pl.) NL 12:17 (CTN V 155ff); URU.*ar-pad-da-a-a* (sg.) SAA I 2:4′

The uniform way of writing may also hint at a uniform way of pronunciation which may have been diphthongal /*-ai*/[150] or /*-aia*/.[151] Exceptions to the normal orthography are the following "marked" writings:

> KUR.URI-*a-a-e* ... / *li-din* (*-āi* > *-aê* due to interrogative intonation) "Would the king of Urarṭu give ...?" SAA V 34 r.21-22
>
> LUGAL E[N] *a-na* KUR.*š*[*u*]*b*-⌜*ri*⌝-*ia-a-e liš-pur* "Should the king, my lord, send a message to the Šubrian?"[152] NL 45 r.14′ (CTN V 136ff)
>
> LÚ*.*ku-ma-a-a-e* (pl.)[153] "the Kummeans" SAA V 105:13, 16

Cf. also

> *ina* IGI URU.ŠÀ–URU-/*a-e* (sg., interrogative intonation) "... before a man from the Inner City?" StAT 1 54 r.3-4
>
> LÚ*.*i-tú-'a-a-a-e-a* / 20 LÚ*.*i-tu-a-a-e-a* (pl. + suff. 1st sg.) "my Itu'aeans/20 Itu'aeans of mine" SAA I 93:6; KUR.*ú-tu-u-a*-⌜*e/ú*⌝ (pl.) "the Itu'aeans" NL 60 e.12′ (CTN V 241f)

It seems safe to claim that the marked spellings in these examples are well grounded (perhaps except for the last example) since they have a clear morphological function that marks interrogative intonation, emphasis, or the possessive suffix.

Some nominative forms with the 1st person singular possessive suffix might lend support to the interpretation of a diphthongal /*-ai*/ pronunciation:[154]

> *hi-ṭa-a-a* /*hiṭ(ṭ)ai-*/ (*hiṭ'u* + *ī*) SAA I 8 r.14, SAA X 182 e.35, SAA X 317 r.6′, SAA X 334:13, ABL 390:8, 11, r. 7′, 18′, ABL 543:10, ABL 1108:7′; *hi-iṭ-ṭa-a-a* SAA XVI 34 r.17
>
> DINGIR-*a-a* /*ilai-*/ (through Aramaic *ilāhī* ~ *ilāh*) SAA XVI 127 r.17 and passim in personal names as, e.g., ᵐ*aš-šur*–DINGIR-*a-a*[155]
>
> DUMU-*a-a* /*mar'ai-*/ (*mar*[*a*]' + *ī*) SAA X 226 r.10, SAA X 294 r.25, SAAB 1 66:7, SAA XVI 30:8, ABL 896 r.13, SAA XVI 63:10 ~ *i-na* UGU *ma-ar-i-šú*

---

[149] See Hämeen-Anttila (2000) 84, sub (b) Gentilic ending.

[150] See LAS II 152 n. 294.

[151] Deller (1959) § 22h. See also the monosyllabic reading values: ja_x, je_x, ji_x, ju_x proposed by Gelb (1970B) 540. Here the theory of Ea names is relevant, too, including a predominant <*a-a*> spelling at the end of names, see PNA 1/I p. xxvif.

[152] Or "... to the Šubrians?," cf. p. 137. With such orthography, the clause is probably a rhetorical question. For a different interpretation, see CTN V 138.

[153] Marked spellings here are probably due to emphasis, cf. the rhetorical question in SAA V 105:12 and the stressed clause (with the enclitic *-ma*), ibid. l. 20.

[154] Cf. Hämeen-Anttila (2000) 83.

[155] Cf. PNA 1/I p. 188. All the names with DINGIR-*a-a* are transcribed *ilā'ī* in PNA. For the reading see, e.g., Lipiński (1994) 238. On the rules of affixing possessive suffixes to nouns, see 5.4 p. 139 below.

(genitive + poss.suff.) "... for the benefit of his son" SAA X 222:13; *a-na* ⸢DUMU⸣-*ia* SAA I 220:3

The 1st person singular possessive suffix is written in the same way (-<*a*>-<*a*>) in dual forms (in the first place, this concerns some paired parts of the body):

(*emūqu*)	*la*(-)/(*e-*)*mu-qa-a-a* passim
(*kinṣu*)	*kin-ṣa-a-a* SAA IX 5:2
(*naglubu*)	*nag-ga-la-pa-a-a* SAA IX 9:18
(*qātu*)[156]	*a-na-ku qa-ta-a-a*/ŠU.2.MEŠ-*a-a* SAA V 32 r.8/SAA XV 182:3′
(*rittu*)	*rit-ta-a-a* SAA IX 9:17

In at least two instances the last sign is <*iá*> and thus, the ending, should probably be read as /-*āia*/, though <*iá*> could also, for instance, be taken for /-*iu*$_x$/:

^{m}*ár-ba-iá* ABL 273 r.2 (Assurbanipal)
URU.*nu-uh-ba-iá* ABL 307 r.10′ ~ URU.*nu-hu-ba-a-a* ibid. l. 2

and the gentilic ending can also have a sequence of <*a*> + <*ú*> /-*āiu*/:

LÚ.*ar-ma-a-ú* SAA XVI 123:8′ (unkn., cf. also ibid. l.2′)
aš]-*šur*.KI-*a-a-ú* Iraq16 197 viii 10′ (ND 3406)

The <*i+a*> at the beginning of a word is most likely to be interpreted as a disyllabic: /*i'a=ija*/, /*i'u=iju*/, /*i'e=ije*/, /*i'i=iji*/, since the protosemitic **ja* presumably changed into *i*/*e* already in an early phase of Akkadian.[157] Therefore, it would mean that all words beginning with [*j*] were foreign to Akkadian (and thus also to Neo-Assyrian). Actually, the word initial [*j*] appears in Akkadian owing only to the influence of loanwords from other languages, mainly from Aramaic.[158]

Cf. an interesting variant in this respect *i-*⸢*mut*⸣*-tú* "each" SAA I 223 r.9′ ~ *ia-mu-tú* SAA V 34 r.24, SAA V 48:13, SAA I 31 e.28; *ia-mu-tu* SAA I 45:11, SAA I 153 r.5; *ia-mut-t*[*u* SAA I 40:8′; *i*]*a-mu-ut-tum* SAA V 113:16; *ia-a-mut-tu/ú* SAA V 210 r.2, 12/SAA X 354 r.2. /*īmuttu*/ may reflect the actual pronunciation of Neo-Assyrian but this once attested variant of *iāmuttu* does not orthographically differ from prs 3rd pl. of *muātu*, cf. e.g. *i-mut-tú* "they will die" SAA V 126:3, SAA V 226 r.19, ABL 302 r.3.

When it appears in a place other than word initial position, <*i+a*> is to be read monosyllabically as *ia/ie/iu/ii*. E.g.

ia: (*ajāši*) *an–ni-ia-ši* SAA X 194 r.14′; (Ariawāti) URU.*ar-ia-u-a-te* SAA I 63 r.9; (Awiānu) ^{m}*a-ú-ia-a-ni* SAA XVI 59 r.13′, (*bašû*) possibly *ib-ši-ia-a* NL 74 r.13′ (CTN V 132ff); (*biādu*) *a-bi-ia-ad* CT 53 168 r.5; (*daiālu*) LÚ*.*da-ia-a-li* SAA V 105:17; (*dintu*) *di-ia-ti-ia* SAA XIII 158 r.10′; (*elû*) *e-te-*⸢*li*⸣*-ia-a* NL 96:15 (CTN V 49ff), etc. -*ia* is passim at the end of a word.

---

[156] For the specific adverbial meaning of *qātā* + the suffix of the 1st sg., see p. 142 below and Hämeen-Anttila (2000) 56.

[157] See GAG § 22c, Gelb (1955) 102 sub § 22c and idem (1970B) 537-39.

[158] See Gelb (1970B) 537 and LAS II 139 n. 278.

ie: (*ammiu*) *am-me-ie-e* NL 41:15 (CTN V 208ff); (*anniu*) *a-ki an-ni-ie-*⌜*e*⌝ SAA X 326:4′; (*kalliu*) *ka-li-ie* SAA V 227:4; (*mār nagî*) DUMU–*na-gi-ie-e* NL 41 r.5, 14 (CTN V 208ff)

ii: (*ahāiš*) *a-he-ii-ši* SAA V 227 r.14, *i-sa-ha-ii-ši* SAA XV 101:13; *a-ha-ii-ši* ibid. 14; (*damāqu*) *de-ii-qi* SAA X 325 r.1′, SAA XIII 60:14; (*kunnu*) *lu-ki-ii-ni* SAA XVI 44 r.5′; (*pa''uṣu*) *up-ta-ii-iṣ* SAA I 235:13; (*ṣuddu*) *nu-ṣi-ii-di* SAA XIII 28:5′, SAA XIII 29:10

iu: (*aiu*/*a'u*) *a-iu-ú* NL 41:9 (CTN V 208ff); (*ammiu*) *am-mì-iu-u* SAA V 163 r.12; (*anniu*) *an-ni-iu-u* passim; (*ba''û*) *lu-ba-'i-iu-u* SAA X 265:9; (*hadû*) *ha-di-iu-u* SAA X 334 r.9; (*kalliu*) *ka-li-iu-u* SAA V 227:6, 19; (*šabbû*) *lu-šab-bi-iu-u* SAA XIII 126:7, etc.

The <*a* + *a*> and <*i* + *a*> signs occur in the letter corpus as variant forms in either free or dialectal variation at the beginning of a word, at least in the oblique pronoun of the 1st person singular *aiāši*/*ijāši* "to me, me" (examples above), in the personal names of Aia (see PNA 1/I pp. 89-94) and possibly in the interrogative pronoun *aiāka* "where." /*ijā*/ is developed from /*ajā*/ (*ajā-* > *ijā-*). The original form is **a'āši*.[159]

(*ijāka*) *ia-a-ka* SAA XV 69 r.14, *ia-a-k*[*a*?] SAA V 146:6, [*i*]*a*?*-a-ka* SAA V 225:9 ~ (*aiāka*) *a-a-ka* passim

3.10 /*e*/- and /*i*/-signs

See also 4.3.3.

In Neo-Assyrian, <*e*> and <*i*> were not in opposition to one another. They did not form any minimal pair when both are written as single (short) vowels. Thus, they are in free variation.[160] Nevertheless, when they are stressed (regularly written as being long), they form a minimal pair in one case.[161]

Thus, the opposition is:

a-ke-e "how" e.g. SAA X 14:13, SAA X 316:11, 14, SAA X 322:13; SAA XVI 54:7, SAA XVI 36:13′; BM 103390:8; possibly once as short *a-ke* (interpretation uncertain, translated "why") SAA I 232:8 ~ *a-ki-i* "when, as, like" e.g. SAA V 92:8, 10, SAA V 218 r.7, NL 12 r.5 (CTN V 155ff), SAA X 276 r.7, SAA X 286 r.2′, SAA XIII 31:16, r.12

Usually the consecutive [*i*] and [*e*] vowels are marked uninterrupted in writing (C*i* + *i*C/C*e* + *e*C).[162] However, at least in certain contexts, it is possible to discern

---

[159] LAS II ad no. 151 r.14′.

[160] E.g. Parker (1997B) 50.

[161] For the status of /*e*/ in Akkadian, as a secondarily developed allophone of /*i*/ from [*a*] and [*i*], and as a variant of [*i*], see GAG § 8b, as well as Reiner (1973) 45-47, who would like to mark the <*e*> in interrupted vocalic contexts (as e.g. *ši-te-i-ni* SAA I 29 r.7), for the sake of clarity, as <*i*>; arguing that the orthographic practices do not reflect the allophonic alternation regularly enough.

[162] In that case, one CVC syllable is "split" into two ($CV_1 + V_1C$). A long vowel is written as a plene ($CV_1 + V_1$).

the mutual interchangeability of the *i*- and *e*-signs from the occurring interrupted (C*e* + *i*C/C*i* + *e*C) writings. Alternatively, the interrupted *i* + *e*/*e* + *i* contexts can also be "solved" by assigning high index numbers to some of the signs, e.g. *te* = *ti*$_{7}$, *iš* = *eš*$_{15}$. Concerning orthography, this kind of practice, which would facilitate the phonetic interpretation, is rather questionable.

As mere vocalic markers, *i* + *e*/*e* + *i* can follow one another only when the first vowel occurring alone functions as a glide, as e.g.

(*anniu*) *an-ni-i-e* SAA V 3:8 and passim, but also:
(*damāqu*) *de-e-i-qi* SAA VIII 1 r.4 (*dē'īqi* < *dē'iq* < *dā'iq* < **damiq*)

Nevertheless, as far as nouns (and adjectives) are concerned, there was an obvious orthographic tendency to follow one prevailing way of writing Assyrian. This led to a fairly consistently observed grapheme selection, hence the number of interrupted writings remains rather insignificant.

Examples of the "interchangeability of a reading value" regarding *i*- and *e*-signs:

<MI> = [*me*] (= ***mé***)
MI-MI-*e-ni* (=transliteration according to the signs) SAA XIII 134:15′, r.3, 6, 16, 28, SAA V 118:8, SAA X 289:12 (*mé-mé-e-ni* = phonetic transliteration)

<TE> = [*ti*] (= ***ti***$_{7}$)
it-TE-*ši* SAA XIII 138:11
ni-TE-⸢TE-*zi*⸣ NL 65:5 (CTN V 45f)
LÚ*.*ba*-TE-*qu* NL 81 r.5 (CTN V 232f)
mi-nu ši-TE-*ni* KAV 213 r.14
ši⸣-TE-*i-ni* VAT 9875 r.9

<TI> = [*te*] (= ***te***$_{9}$)
a-bi-TI-*e* SAA X 30 r.2
me-e-TI SAA XVI 127 r.15
TI-*pu-šu-ni* SAA XIII 43:2

<ŠE> = [*ši*] (= *ši*$_{x}$)
lu-ŠE-*bi* SAA XV 219 r.10′
i-di-na-na-ŠE SAA XVI 40 r.7
ú-še$^{?}$]-*ra-ba-na*-ŠE-[*ni*] SAA X 299:11

<ŠI> = [*še*] (= *še*$_{20}$)
ú-ŠI-*la* SAA V 150:12
[*ú*]- ŠI-*šá-bu-u-n*[*i*] SAA II 6:153H

<EL> = [*il*] (= *il*$_{5}$)
ni-EL-*lak* SAA X 212 r.4

<I> = [*e*]
I-*gír-tú* KAV 213 r.12

The graphemical sameness and opposition of the most common *e*- and *i*-signs:[163]

(Explanatory notes: the reading to the left of ≠ is included in sign lists, the reading to the right is not; ~ both reading values; > however, the *x*-reading value is given in sign lists)

'e/e' ~ *'i/i'*	*hi* ~ *he*	*ir* ~ *er*	*pi* ~ *pe*	*ṭè* ≠ *ṭi* (> *ṭi*$_{5}$)
be ≠ *bi*	*ib/p* ~ *eb/p*	*iš* ≠ *eš* (> *eš*$_{15}$)	*ri* ~ *re*	*ṭi* ~ *ṭe*
bi ~ *bé*	*id/ṭ/t* ~ *ed/eṭ/t*	*iz/ṣ/s* ~ *ez/ṣ/s*	*si* ~ *se*	*ṭí* ~ *ṭé*
di ~ *de*	*ig/q/k* ~ *eg/q/k*	*ki* ~ *ke*	*ṣi* ~ *ṣe*	*zi* ~ *ze*
el ≠ *il* (> *il*$_{5}$)	*ih* ~ *eh*	*li* ~ *le*	*še* ≠ *ši*	

[163] Both vowels have their own sign(s) when occurring alone: *e* ≠ *i* and *i* ≠ *e*. But as far as CVC-signs are concerned: in case C*i*C occurs, then also C*e*C, see n. 181.

en ≠ *in*	*il* ~ *él*	*me* ≠ *mi* > *mì*	*ši* ≠ *še* (> *še*$_{20}$)
eš ≠ *iš* (> *ìš*)	*im* ~ *em*	*mi* ≠ *me* > *mé*	*te* ≠ *ti* (> *ti*$_{7}$)
gi ~ *ge*	*in* ≠ *en*	*ni* ~ *né*	*ti* ≠ *te* (> *te*$_{9}$)

3.11 Signs for half-vowels and glottal stop

As independent phonemes neither [*w*] nor [*j*] exist in Neo-Assyrian.[164] They function as the allophones of aleph (or of a zero morpheme) in an intervocalic position. In writing, they are manifested either in "additional" vowels, <*u/ú*> may correspond to [*w*][165] and <*i*/IA> (= sign for ligature) to [*j*], or alternatively are not marked at all. To be "not marked/unmarked" means in practice that the additional vowel was not always written between heterogeneous vowels. E.g.

"marked" *an-ni-i-u* SAA V 2 r.8, SAA X 361 r.2 ~ "unmarked" *an-ni-u/ú* passim

The allophonic status of half-vowels turns up explicitly as a free variation between marked and unmarked forms. The marked form can replace an unmarked one, and vice versa.[166]

Since aleph was often left out in Neo-Assyrian writings, aleph can also be interpreted as an allophone of a zero phoneme.[167] Moreover, the complete absence of the written aleph at the beginning of a word, as well as the numerous sandhi writings, seem to suggest the loss of aleph at the word-initial position.[168] Nevertheless, within as well as at the end of a word, the explicitly written aleph was optional.[169] In fact, with certain verbs, the aleph is lexical (cf. 4.2.2 and 5.8).

The marked aleph in the middle of a word:

(*hasā'u*) *ih-ta-as-'u* SAA I 240:9′
(*ma'ādu*) *ma-'a-ad* passim; *in-ta-a'-da* SAA V 260:12′ ~ *ma-a-da* GPA 197 r.3′; NL 26:8 (CTN V 92f), NL 101:8, 10 (CTN V 292ff)

The written aleph at the end of a word:

(*mazā'u*) [*m*]*a-a-zu-u'* SAA I 97:10; *ma-zu-u'* SAA I 63:13′; *ma-zu-u*[*'* SAA XV 352:4′
(Munu') URU.*mu-nu-u'* SAA I 90 r.10, 13e

---

[164] Cf. e.g. Hämeen-Anttila (2000) 11f. See also Lipiński (1997) § 11.12, who interprets [*w*] phonetically, but due to the Sumerian influence, [*w*] is graphically defectively marked in writing.

[165] See LAS II ad no. 224:15 with examples.

[166] See Reiner (1964) 174-79. Reiner stresses that the basic function of the signs used ('A, *u*, *ú*, *i*, IA, 0) between heterogeneous vowels is the marking of syllable boundaries. Generally this marking should be done with aleph /'/, ibid. 176-79.

[167] See e.g. Lipiński (1997) § 19.9.

[168] Hämeen-Anttila (2000) 12. However, note e.g. the foreign toponym KUR.*'a-ta-a-a* SAA V 295 r.18. Perhaps KUR was read in this name as well as in the name Mazamua (KUR-*za-mu*(-*u*)-*a* passim).

[169] Cf. Hämeen-Anttila (2000) 12-14.

(*mušēṣiu*) *mu-še-ṣi-i'* KUG.GI SAA XIII 128:15
(*parā'u*) *pu-ru-u'* SAA XV 100 r.13′
(*sabā'u*) *a-sa-ab-bu-u'* SAA XVI 32 r.12

Examples of [*w*] are the following:

(*duāku*) *du-u-a-ki-šú-nu* SAA II 6:139A
(*duālu*) *a-du-ú-a-la* SAA XIII 190 r.21 ~ *a-du-al* SAA XV 240:4; *a-du-al-la* SAA XV 288:6; *i*]*-du-al* SAA V 35:14
(*karmu*) *ka-ru-a-ni-ia*[170] SAA I 264 r.3; [*k*]*a-ru-*⌜*a*⌝*-*[*ni*] ibid. r.8
(*muātu*) *i-mu-u-at* SAA XVI 70 r.1 ~ *i-mu-at* SAA XVI 40:10, SAA X 235 r.7; *a-mu-'a-at* SAA XVI 31 r.5′; *a-mu-at* passim; *m*]*u-ú-a-te* SAA X 289:15 ~ *mu-a-ti/te* SAA I 56 r.5/SAA X 226:21; cf. also *mu-'a-a-tu* SAA X 294 r.24
(Nabû'a) ᵐ*na-bu-u/ú-a* SAA VIII 126 r.1, SAA VIII 128 r.2, SAA VIII 129 r.1/SAA VIII 130 r.1, SAA VIII 131 r.1
(Nīnua) *ina* URU.*ni-nu-u-a* SAA XVI 63 r.16, SAA VI 142:8 cf. common URU.*ni-nu-a* SAA X 279:10, SAA V 100:14, NL 52:11 (CTN V 193f) and passim; URU.*ni-nu-ú* (See 4.4) BM 135586 r.16
(*nuāhu*) [*i*]*t-tu-ú-ah* SAA V 249:15′ ~ *it-tu-a-ha* SAA X 309:8′; *it-tu-ah-ma* ibid. r.3; *ta-at-tu-ah* SAA X 207:15
(*pānāt*) *pa-na-tu-u-a* (+ suff. 1st sg.) SAA XIII 138:14, SAA XVI 112 r.17e, SAA XVI 45 r.1 ~ *pa-na-tu-ia* SAA I 52 r.3′
(*pūtu*) *ina pu-tu-u-a* (+ suff. 1st sg.) SAA X 39:7, NL 17 r.7 (CTN V 283f); *ina pu-tú-u-a* SAA V 254 r.10; *i–pu-tú-u-a-a* SAA V 217 r.9; [*ša*] *pu-u-tú-u-a* SAA V 2:8 ~ *ina pu-tú-ia* SAA I 29 r.1
(*raqqūtu*) *ra-qu-ú-a-te* SAA VII 163 i 5; *ra-qu-a-te* ibid. r. ii 2′
(Šērū'a) ᵈ*še-ru-u-a* passim; ᵈ*ši*-EDIN-*ú-a* SAA II 14 ii 19′, also ibid. i 28′

As for foreign names:

(Que) KUR.*qu-u-a-a* SAA I 1:5, 19 (CTN V 188ff); KUR.*qu-u-e* NL 41:22 (CTN V 208ff)
(Hur-waṣi) ᵐ*hur-u-a-ṣi* KAV 189 r.6′, StAT 1 11 r.9e[171]

Examples of [*j*] are:

(*anniu*)[172] *an-ni-i-u* SAA V 2 r.8, SAA X 351:15; *an-ni-i-e* SAA VIII 98:7; *an-ni-iu-ma* SAA V 98 r.8; *an-ni-iu-u* SAA X 315:9, r.2, SAA X 324:12, r.3; *an-ni-i-ú* SAA VIII 95 r.1, SAA V 3 r.9, SAA X 42 r.16, SAA X 61 r.9 ~ *an-ni-'u-u* SAA XIII 76:14, SAA XIII 77 r.1
(*pānat*) see above
(*pānīu*) *pa-ni-iu-u-te* SAA I 250 r.6; *pa-ni-iu-te* SAA V 64:5
(*pūtu*) see above
(*rammû*) *lu-ra-am-mì-i-u* SAA X 349 r.10 (Mar-Issar)[173]
(*šarrû*) *ú-sa-ar-ri-i-u* SAA X 349 r.17
(*urkīu*) *ur-ki-iu-u* SAA V 163 r.9 cf. *ur-ki-ú* CT 53 820 e.2′

---

[170] Here <*u*> (= [*w*]) is the allophone of [*m*], see SAA I n. ad no. 264 r.3.

[171] See PNA 2/I p. 481f s.v. Hur-waṣi (with more examples).

[172] On the genitive forms of *anniu*, see Deller (1965B) 76 n. 1.

[173] Deller and Parpola (1966A) 67: remark on <*i*> in the non-assimilated III-weak verb forms of the third-person masculine plural, a feature typical only of Mar-Issar. Cf. also 4.4.

Note especially the neutralized forms of the above examples (as *pānāt* and *pūtu*). Cf. also the following writings:

(Aššur-hamatu'a) ^{m}*aš-šur–ha-mat-u-a* SAA XIII 140:2, SAA XIII 141:2 (2. ^{m}]) ~ ^{m}*aš-šur–ha-mat-ia* SAA XIII 138:2, SAA XIII 139 r.6′

(Aššur-mukin-pale'a) ^{m}*aš-šur–mu-kin*–BALA-*u-a* SAA X 320:8, SAA X 299:7 (^{m}*aš-šur*]-); ^{m}*aš-šur–mu-kin*^{in}–BALA-*u-a* (3. *kin*-[^{in}–BA]LA-*u-a*) SAA X 298 r.3, SAA X 300 r.5, SAA X 298:6 ~ ^{m}*aš-šur*–GIN–BALA.MEŠ-*ia* SAA X 207:7; ^{m}*aš-šur–mu-kin*–BALA.MEŠ-*ia* SAA X 296:6, SAA X 320 r.11; ^{m}*aš-šur–mu-kin*–BALA-*ia* (4. -*k*]*in*–BA[LA-*i*]*a*) SAA X 53:10, SAA X 70 r.8, SAA X 74 r.13, s.2 cf. also ^{m}*aš-šur*–GIN–B]ALA.MEŠ-*a* SAA X 208 r.2′

(*ba''û*) *ú-ba-'a* SAA X 240:26 ~ *ú-ba-ia* (Sennacherib) SAA I 35 r.12e

3.12 Syllabic V-signs and their usage (see n. 176 below)

SIGN		POSITION				REFERENCES
Number	Reading	1.	2.	3.	alone	
a 579	a	x	x	x		
á 334	á	x				*1.* É]–⸢*á*⸣*-ki-it SAA I 188:9*
e 308	e	x	x	x		
i 142	i	x	x	x		
ì 231 (NI)	ì		x			2. KÁ-*ì-lí* ABL 896:8, 18; ^{m}*sa-ì-lí* SAA I 118:4, r.7
u 411	u	x[174]	x	x	x	
ú 318	ú	x	x	x		
ù 455	ù				x	
u_8 494	u_8	x	x[175]			1. *u_8-u-a* SAA IX 1 i 26′, *u_8-a* SAA IX 2 iii 31′; 2. ^{md}*pa-u_8-a* SAA VI 247 r.6

3.13 VC- and CV-signs and their usage (see n. 176 below)

SIGN		POSITION			REFERENCES
Number	Reading	1.	2.	3.	
a' 397	a'	x	x	x	1. *a'-u* SAA I 125:14
	'a	x	x	x	1. KUR.*'a-ta-a-a* SAA I 179 e.26
	i'		x	x	
	'i		x	x	
ab 128	ab	x	x	x	
	ap	x	x	x	
ad 145	ad	x	x	x	
	at	x	x	x	
	aṭ		x	x	

174 The attestations of initial *u* can be considered erroneous, cf. p. 30.

175 Passim in royal inscriptions.

ag 97	ag	x	x	x	3. *puāgu*
	ak	x	x	x	
	aq	x	x	x	3. *i*]*r-ti-aq* SAA XVI 97:11
ah 398	ah	x	x	x	
	eh	x	x	x	1. *eh-hu-zu* SAA X 226:18; 3. *lu-*[*s*]*a-me-eh* NL 2:17' (CTN V 22ff)
	ih	x	x	x	
	uh	x	x	x	
ak see ag					
al 298	al	x	x	x	
am 170	am	x	x	x	
an 13	an	x	x	x	
	ìl		x	x	
ap see ab					
aq see ag					
ar 451	ar	x	x	x	
ár see ub					
as, aṣ see az					
aš 1	aš	x	x		2. see *našpantu* in SAA II 6:465, 489 and *šaggaštu* ibid. 456frg
	in_6	x		x	1. *in*$_6$*–ni-ri-te* SAA V 164 r.9; *in*$_6$*-ni-du-ú-*[*a* SAA I 20:3', r.1; 3. *mìn*^{in6} SAA XIII 190 r.25e
áš 339	ás		x		2. *la-ás-hu-ra* SAA X 202 r.15'
	áš	x	x	x	
at, aṭ see ad					
az 131	as	x	x	x	
	aṣ	x	x	x	1. *ṣabātu*
	az	x	x	x	
ba 5	ba	x	x	x	
ba_4 233 (GÁ)	ba_4		x	x	2. *i-ba*$_4$*-ia-la* KAV 215:13
be 69	be	x	x		2. *li-be-el* ABL 839 r.14; *ta-be-*⌜*e*⌝ SAA XV 179:4; *i-be-lu*$^?$*-šu*$^?$*-nu* SAA XV 167:3'
bé see bi					
bi 214	bé	x	x		
	bi	x	x	x	
bu 371	bu	x	x	x	
	pu	x	x	x	
da 335	da	x	x	x	
	ṭa	x	x	x	
dà 230 (GAG)	dà	x	x	x	2. KUR.*kal-dà-a-a* SAA V 59:5; LÚ.*kal-dà-a.a* SAA XVI 155:2', 5'; 3. URU.*ar-pad-dà* SAA XVI 48 e.13
de see di					
di 457	de	x	x	x	3. *ú-de* CTN III 3 r.9; *bé-e-d*[*e*] SAA XV 223 r.10; [*bé*$^?$]- ⌜*e*⌝*-de* SAA XV 186 r.6
	di	x	x	x	
	ṭe	x	x	x	3. *he-e-ṭe* StAT 1 56 r.3; *ta-*⌜*še*$^?$⌝*-ṭe* NL 71 r.5 (CTN V 312f)
	ṭi	x	x	x	1. *ṭi-bi-ih* SAA X 42 r.3; *ṭi-bu-te* SAA XVI 16:4'; *ṭi-bu* SAA XVI 82 r.5
du 206	du	x	x	x	

du$_6$ see dul$_6$					
du$_8$ 167 (DUH)	du$_8$		x	x	^{m}⌜*ba-du*$_8$⌝-*du*$_8$ SAA VI 130 r.5
eb see ib					
eg see ig					
eh see ah					
ek see ig					
el 564	el	x	x	x	2. *né-me-el-šú-nu* SAA X 207 r.5; *ni-el-lak* SAA X 212 r.4; *ú-še-el-la-a* SAA XIII 78 r.8
él see il					
em see im					
en 99	en	x	x	x	
ep see ib					
eq see ig					
er see ir					
es, eṣ see iz					
eš 472	eš	x	x	x	
et see id					
ga 319	ga	x	x	x	
	qá		x		2. *ú-pa-qá-da* SAA X 222 r.9
ge see gi					
gi 85	ge	x	x		1. *ge-*⌜*en-ti*⌝ SAA X 59:7
	gi	x	x	x	
gu 559	gu	x	x	x	
ha 589	ha	x	x	x	
he see hi					
hi 396	he	x	x	x	1. *he-e-ṭe* StAT 1 56 r.3 (obvious Babyl.)
	hi	x	x	x	
hu 78	hu	x	x	x	
i', 'i see a'					
ia 142a	ia	x	x	x	
	ie	x	x	x	1. Iēri (GN) SAA I 45 r.1, SAA V 162:5, 10; 2. (and 3.) mainly in foreign GNs and PNs
	ii		x		
	iu		x	x	3. *i-na-á*]*š-ši-iu* SAA XV 129:11; *am-ma*$^?$*-iu* Rfdn 17 28:7
iá 598a	iá	x	x	x	1. *iá-bu-tú* SAA XVI 60 r.7; Il-iada' (PN); 2. Karduniaš (GN); *me-me-ni-iá-ma* SAA I 194 r.4
ib 535	eb	x		x	1. *eb-ra-a-ni* CT 53 372:12; *eb-ra-ni* NL 5 r.2 (CTN V 25f); 3. *ú-se-še-eb* SAA XVI 95:7
	ep	x	x	x	3. *še-ep* SAA XV 30 r.9
	ib	x	x	x	
	ip	x	x	x	
id 334 (Á)	et	x	x	x	
	id	x	x	x	
	it	x	x	x	
	iṭ	x	x	x	1. *iṭ-hu-u-n*[*i*] SAA X 350:12'; *i*[*ṭ-ṭi*]*-ab* SAA X 182 r.3

ig 80	eg		x		2. *te-eg-gi* SAA X 8:26
	ek	x	x	x	2. *sa-me-ek-tú* ABL 879:24; *dēktu*; 3. *us-sa-am-me-ek* ABL 1148:10'; *lu-sa-am-me-ek* ABL 1148:11'
	eq		x	x	2. *e-te-eq-q[u-u-ni]* SAA XVI 150 r.1; *te-eq-te* StAT 1 53 r.5; 3. *tu-dam-me-eq* ABL 523 r.6
	ig	x	x	x	3. *a-nu-ri-ig* NL 28:9 (CTN V 148f)
	ik	x	x	x	
	iq	x	x	x	
ih see ah					
ik see ig					
il 205	él		x	x	2. *né-me-él-šú* SAA X 54 r.5'; 3. *[n]é-me-él* SAA X 31:2'; *né-me-él* SAA X 233 r.1
	il	x	x	x	
ìl see an					
im 399	em	x	x	x	3. ⸢*a*⸣*-se-em* SAA XV 222:11'
	im	x	x	x	
in 148	in	x	x	x	
in_6 see aš					
ip see ib					
iq see ig					
ir 232	er	x	x	x	
	ir	x	x	x	
is, iṣ see iz					
iš 212	iš	x	x	x	
it, iṭ see id					
iz 296 (GIŠ)	es	x	x		1. *es-pu* SAA XV 182:9'
	eṣ	x	x		1. *eṣ-ma-a-ti* SAA X 242:11; *eṣ-ra* SAA I 72:8'; 2. *še-eṣ-ṣu-ú* SAA X 294:26
	is	x	x	x	
	iṣ	x	x	x	
	iz	x	x	x	
ka 15	ka	x	x	x	
ke see ki					
ki 461	ke	x	x	x	3. *de-e-ke* SAA I 30 e.9′, SAA X 96 r.14, NL 65:10, 11 (CTN V 45f), SAA XVI 30:7
	ki	x	x	x	
	qé	x	x	x	2. KUR–LÚ.GAL–*šá-qé-e* SAA X 58 r.9; *e-mu-qé-e-ni* ABL 1116:16′; 3. *né-me-qé* SAA X 174:9
	qí	x	x	x	
ku 536	ku	x	x	x	
la 55	la	x	x	x	also independently
lá 481 (LAL)	lá		x		2. *[b]a-lá-ṭu* SAA X 252:8
le see li					
li 59	le	x	x	x	3. *šu-me-le* SAA X 358 r.6'; *ke-e-le* SAA XV 48:11; *uk-te-le* SAA X 279:12
	li	x	x	x	
lí see ni					
li_8 420 (ÁB)	li_8			x	*be-li*$_8$ SAA XVI 52 r.4; *be-li*$_8$*-ia* ibid. r.1, 7; *be-li*$_8$*-iá* ibid. r.8
lu 537	lu	x	x	x	also independently
lu_4 565	lu_4			x	3. rare in verbal forms, otherwise see lum

ma 342	ma	x	x	x	also independently
me 532	me	x	x	x	
	mì	x	x	x	3. *šu-mì* SAA XVI 34:6, CT 53 908 r.10; *ú-kal-li-mì* SAA X 293:23'; *k*]*a-ri-mì* CT 53 663 r.3'
mé see mi					
mi 427	mé	x	x		2. *mé-mé-e-ni* SAA X 289:12; *šu-gu-mé-*[*e*] SAA X 327 r.15
	mi	x	x	x	
mì see me					
mu 61	mu	x	x	x	
na 70	na	x	x	x	
né see ni					
ni 231	lí		x	x	
	né	x	x	x	
	ni	x	x	x	
nu 75	nu	x	x	x	
nú 431 (NÁ)	nú	x			1. *n*[*ú-š*]*e-ši-bu-šú-ni* SAA X 12 r.3
pa 295	pa	x	x	x	
pe see pi					
pi 383	pe	x	x		
	pi	x	x	x	
pu see bu					
pú 511 (TÚL)	pú		x		2. *šal-pú-tim* SAA X 100:26
qa 62 (SÌLA)	qa	x	x	x	
qá see ga					
qe see qi					
qé see ki					
qi 538 (KIN)	qe	x	x	x	
	qi	x	x	x	
qí see ki					
qu 191 (KUM)	qu	x	x	x	
ra 328	ra	x	x	x	
re see ri					
ri 86	re	x	x	x	
	ri	x	x	x	
ru 68	ru	x	x	x	
sa 104	sa	x	x	x	
sà see di					
sa_{16} see ud					
se see si					
si 112	se	x	x	x	1. *se-e-*⸢*re*⸣ SAA XV 94 r.7; ^{m}*se-e'–ra-hi-i* SAA XVI 55:4; (1. and) 2. ^{m}*se-e-se-e* CTN III 46:3, r.1; 3. *an-te-se* SAA XVI 242 r.7'
	si	x	x	x	
su 7	su	x	x	x	
ṣa see za					
ṣe see ṣi					
ṣi 147 (ZÍ)	ṣe	x	x	x	3. *e-ṣe* SAA X 257:9, SAA XV 317 r.6
	ṣi	x	x	x	
ṣu 555 (ZUM)	ṣu	x	x	x	

ša 353	ša	x	x	x	also independently
šá 597 (NÍG)	šá	x	x	x	also independently
šà 384	šà	x			1. *šà-ṭir* SAA X 6 r.13, SAA X 8 r.15, SAA X 20:2
še 367	še	x	x	x	
ši 449 (IGI)	ši	x	x	x	
šu 354	šu	x	x	x	
šú 545	šú	x	x	x	
ta 139	ta	x	x	x	
te 376	te	x	x	x	
ti 73	ti	x	x	x	
tí 396	ṭé	x	x		1. *ṭēmu*; 2. *mu-ṭé-e-šú* NL 97:11 (CTN V 111f)
	ṭí		x	x	3. *ah-ti-ṭí* SAA V 2 r.4; *un-*⸢*ta-ṭí*⸣ SAA I 176:14 (CTN V 169ff)
ti$_7$ see 3.10 above					
tu 58	tu	x	x	x	
tú see ud					
ṭa see da					
ṭe see di					
ṭé see tí					
ṭè 172 (NE)	ṭè	x	x	x	3. *in-ti-ṭè* SAA XV 125 r.7
ṭi see di					
ṭí see tí					
ṭu 595 (GÍN)	ṭu	x	x	x	
ub 306	ár	x	x	x	
	ub	x	x	x	
	up	x	x	x	
ud 381	tú	x	x	x	
	ud	x	x	x	
	ut	x	x	x	
	uṭ	x		x	1. *uṭ-ṭa-bi-hi* SAA XV 168:13'; 3. ⸢*i*⸣*-ba-al-lu-uṭ* SAA X 326 r.3
	sa$_{16}$	x			1. ^{m}*sa*$_{16}$*-gab* SAA X 138 r.4
ug 130	ug	x	x		2. *du-ug-li* SAA XIII 76:9; [*nu*]*-u*[*g-d*]*a-mir* SAA I 143:2'; *nu-ug-da-mir* SAA X 63 r.10
	uk	x	x	x	
	uq	x	x	x	3. *mu-ru-uq* SAA XVI 5:16
uh see ah					
uk see ug					
ul 441	ul	x	x	x	
um 134	um	x	x	x	
un 312	un	x	x	x	
up see ub					
uq see ug					
ur 575	ur	x	x	x	
úr 203	úr		x		2. GIŠ.*nu-úr-me* SAA I 227 s.1
us, uṣ see uz					
uš 211	uš	x	x	x	
ut, uṭ see ud					

uz 372	us	x	x	x	
	uṣ	x	x	x	
	uz	x	x		2. *uz-za-uz-zu* SAA X 294:33
za 586	sà			x	3. DAM-*sà* SAA VI 288 r.13 (Babyl.)
	ṣa	x	x	x	
	za	x	x	x	
ze see zi					
zi 84	ze	x	x		
	zi	x	x	x	
zu 6	zu	x	x	x	

3.14 CVC-signs and their usage

The syllabic CVC-reading values in the Neo-Assyrian letter corpus:

bab	bak	bal	ban	bar	bat	bil	bíl	bir	bìr
biš	bit	bul	bur	buš	dab	dáb	dag	dak	dàk
dal	dàl	dam	dan	dáp	daq	dàq	dib	dil	dim
dím	din	dip	dir	diš	duk	dul	dul$_6$	dun	dup
duq	dur	gab	gal	gàl	gam	gan	gap	gar	gaṣ
gaš	gat	gíl	gim	gir	gír	giš	gít	gul	gúl
gup	gur	gúr	hab	had	hal	hap	har	haš	hat
haṭ	haz	hir	hír	hiš	hiz	hub	hul	hum	hup
hur	kab	kad	kak	kal	kàl	kam	kám	kan	kán
kap	kaq	kar	kas	kás	kaš	kàt	kel	ken	ket
kib	kid	kik	kil	kim	kin	kín	kip	kir	kír
kis	kiš	kit	kub	kul	kun	kur	kúr	kut	lab
lad	lah	láh	làh	lak	lal	lál	lam	lap	laq
lat	laṭ	lem	let	lib	lid	lig	lih	lìh	lik
lil	lim	lip	liq	lis	liš	lit	liṭ	lub	lud
luh	lul	lum	lup	lut	luṭ	mad	mah	mal	mám
man	mar	maš	mat	med	mer	meš	mid	mil	mìn
mir	mis	miš	mit	mug	muk	muq	mur	mus	muš
mut	nab	nag	nak	nam	nap	nar	nàr	nat	neš
nid	nig	nik	nim	nin	niq	nís	niš	num	nun
pad	pah	pal	pan	paq	par	pat	paṭ	peš	pet
pik	pil	píl	pir	pír	piš	pit	pur	qab	qal
qàl	qáp	qaq	qar	qid	qil	qin	qip	qir	qiš
qit	qit$_4$	qud	qul	qúl	qur	qut	rab	rad	rag
rah	rak	ram	rap	raq	raš	rat	rém	rib	rid
rig	ríg	rik	rim	rím	rin	rip	riq	ris	riš
rit	rum	ruq	sab	sad	sag	sah	sak	sal	sam
san	sap	sar	sat	sek	sih	síh	sik	sím	sin
sip	sir	sír	sis	suh	suh$_4$	suk	sur	ṣab	ṣal
ṣap	ṣar	ṣib	ṣil	ṣip	ṣir	ṣur	šab	šad	šag
šah	šáh	šàh	šak	šal	šam	šap	šaq	šar	šár

šat	šaṭ	šèr	šib	šid	šik	šil	šim	šin	šip
šiq	šir	šìr	šit	šub	šud	šuk	šul	šum	šúm
šup	šur	tab	tah	táh	tak	tàk	tal	tam	tan
tap	taq	tar	tas	taš	ter	tik	til	tim	tin
tiq	tir	tub	tug	tuh	tuk	tum	tùm	tup	tuq
tur	tuš	ṭáh	ṭak	ṭar	ṭém	ṭib	ṭil	ṭir	ṭùl
ṭup	ṭur	ṭuš	zab	zak	zal	zar	zar_4	zib	zip
ziq	zir	ziz	zuk	zur					

CVC-signs in context:[176]

Sign		Position			References
Number	Reading	1.	2.	3.	
bab 60 (PAB)	bab		x		2. *da-bab-ti* SAA II 6:386A, D
	kúr		x		2. [KUR].*nu-kúr-ti* SAA X 210 r.7

[176] These numbers are according to Borger (1986[3]), whereas the manner of representation imitates the one by von Soden and Röllig (1967[2]). In practice, this means that after the most common reading value, I have used the order of von Soden and Röllig in listing the other reading values of the signs. However, a deviation from their list is the study of the position of CVC-signs within words. I have classified the occurrences of CVC-signs into three different categories: CVC-sign 1. (at initial position), 2. (at medial position) and 3. (at the end of a word). If a written word is a mixture of syllabic and a logographic writing, as e.g. in the case of LÚ*.GAL-*kal-lab*.MEŠ, I have classified *lab* in the category of reading values in the medial position, supposing that the <MEŠ>-sign replaces the end part of the word which is not written syllabically. In addition to the marking of the position of signs, the attested substitution is sometimes recorded, i.e. a CVC-sign is often substituted by the CV + VC-signs in similar forms. These substitution examples are here just to point out the possibilities of such a chart, if given in an extended form.

How to read the chart: I have mainly included rare reading values in the references column. My rule of thumb has been that if I have found either three or even fewer textual references to evidence of a reading value, then I have included all these source references in the references column. Only in a few cases have I enumerated more source references than three. In case a reading is attested in more than three references, I have only marked the position of the reading value (1., 2. or 3.) in the inner context of a word. In addition to references to sources, sometimes generalizations are given, e.g. in connection with the reading value *kas* the word *kaspu* is written in the references column. This means that the sign <*kas*> is often found in writings of the word *kaspu*.

If either the name or principal reading of a sign does not have a CVC value (at least not in Neo-Assyrian), then I have put the name of the sign in brackets after the Borger number. I have not listed theoretically probable reading values which are not attested in the tablets known up to the present; e.g. *mad* and *mat* values are to be found under the KUR-sign, but the reading value *maṭ* is not, because I have not found such an example. However, cf. Gelb (1970B) 519.

In this connection, I would like to point out that the list is still in a preliminary state with all its weaknesses, inclusive of Babylonianisms, for instance. However, one could easily proceed with this draft to cover the distribution of all the CVC-signs. At the least, all of the SAA-database information could be used. In fact, it would become much better and perhaps it could even lead to a study of all the signs used in Neo-Assyrian in the inner context of words.

The information of this chart is based mainly on the letter corpus part of the Neo-Assyrian Text Corpus Project's database, with some additions from other types of Neo-Assyrian documents.

bak see paq					
bal 9	bal	x	x	x	
	pal	x	x	x	
ban see pan					
bar 74	bar	x	x	x	
bat 69 (BAD)	bat	x	x	x	
	med			x	3. URU.*né-med–la-gu-du* SAA XIII 190:11, Nemed-Issar (GN)
	mid	x		x	1. *mid-bar* SAA I 13:15′; 3. *e-mid* SAA XV 84 r.13′ (CTN V 134ff), SAA XIV 104:11, *us-sa-am-mid* SAA X 294:30)
	mit	x	x	x	1. *mit-hu*[*r*$^?$-*r*]*u*$^?$ SAA XVI 5:8; 3. *māmītu*
	til	x	x		2. *pi-til-ti/e* SAA II 6:607A/frg, *a-ga-nu-til-la-a* SAA II 6:522I)
	ziz			x	3. *li-iz-ziz* SAA X 257 r.16 ~ *li-iz-zi-iz* SAA XVI 27 r.3′)
	šum$_4$	x			1. *šum$_4$-mu* S.U. 51/44 r.10e
bet see bit					
bil 172 (NE)	bil	x	x	x	1. *bil-te* SAA VIII 232:5
	pil	x	x	x	1. *pilku*; 2. *ú-sa-pil-šú* SAA X 361 e.18′, *iš-pil-u-ni* SAA X 187:9; 3. *lu-šá-pil* SAA X 182 r.8, *šá-pil* SAA X 226 r.6, SAA X 328 r.2, 5 ~ *šá-pi-il* SAA X 363 r.2
bíl 173	bíl		x	x	
	píl	x	x		1. *pilku*; 2. *ispillurtu*
bir 400	bir	x	x	x	
bìr see pír					
biš see gir					
bit 324 (É)	bit	x	x	x	
	bet		x		*er-bet-ti/te* SAA XIII 123:1/SAA X 321 r.6
	pit	x	x		2. *la-pit-u-ni* SAA X 275 r.3
	pet	x			
bul 515	bul	x	x		
bur 349	bur	x	x	x	
	pur	x	x	x	1. *pur-se-e* SAA XIII 48:10′
dab see dib					
dáb see tab					
dag 280	dag		x		2. *dagālu*
	dak		x		
	daq		x		2. *šaddaqdiš*
	ṭak			x	3. *mar-ṭak* SAA X 242:9
dak see dag					
dàk see tàk					
dal 86 (RI)	dal		x		
	tal	x	x	x	3. *kutallu* st. cstr.
dàl see dil					
dam 557	dam	x	x		
dan see kal					
dáp see tab					
daq see dag					
dàq see tàk					

dib 537	dib	x		x	
	dip		x		2. *id-dip-u-ni* SAA X 21 r.10′
	ṭib		x		2. *l*]*i-iṭ-ṭib-bu* SAA X 294:10, ⸢*ú*⸣-[*ṭ*]*ib-bu* SAA X 364:8′
	dab		x		
dil 1 (AŠ)	dil	x			1. Dil(i)bat
	rum			x	
	dàl	x	x		1. ^{m}] ⸢*i*?⸣*-ra–dàl-a* SAA XV 70:5; 2. *Kandalanu* (PN)[177]
	ṭil			x	3. *ni-ṭil* SAA II 6:423, SAA XII 96 r.7
dim 94	dim	x	x		1. URU.*dim-maš*?*-qa* SAA XIII 87:11; 2. ŠE.*ku-dim-me* SAA V 242 r.2
	tim	x	x	x	1. *tim-ra-a-ni* SAA X 263:5, *tim-me* SAA I 66:6, SAA IX 3 i 25
dím see gim					
din 465	din		x	x	
	tin		x	x	2. *etinnu*, *qatinnu*; 3. LÚ.*qa-tin* StAT 1 22 r.23
dip see dib					
dir 123	dir		x	x	
	ṭir		x	x	2. *e-ṭir-an-ni* StAT 1 56 r.2, *ša-ṭir-ú-ni* SAA X 276 r.12, *sa-ṭir-*[*u-ni*] SAA X 276 r.4′, Babyl.
diš 480	diš		x	x	2. ŠE.*kur-diš-šu* SAA I 105 r.3
duk 309 (DUG)	duk	x	x	x	1. *duk-šu*? ABL 1352:3′
	duq	x			1. GIŠ.*duq*⸣*-di* SAA I 226 r.1
	lud	x			1. URU.*lud-din*–DINGIR/*-a-a* SAA XIII 19 r.10/SAA XIII 20:8
	lut		x	x	2. *al-lut-te* SAA II 6:619frg; 3. *be-lut* SAA II 6:298A; *tillutu*
	luṭ			x	3. *bu-luṭ* SAA X 92:7, SAA XIII 78 r.11
dul 459	dul	x			1. *dullu*
dul$_6$ 459a (DU$_6$)[178]	dul$_6$	x			1. *dullu*
	ṭùl	x			1. *ṭùl-lu-ma-a* SAA IX 2 ii 17′(Aramaic loanword)
dun see šul					
dup 138 (DUB)	dup		x		2. *šanduppu* SAA X 41 r.3, 5
	ṭup	x	x		1. *ṭuppu*, *ṭupšarrūtu*; 2. *qar-ṭup-pi* SAA X 336:3
	tub	x			1. *tub-ki-ni* SAA II 2 iv 16
	tup	x			1. GIŠ.*tup-ni-nu* SAA I 158:4, 6, 13, *tup-šik-ki* SAA X 143 r.4
duq see duk					
dur 108	dur		x		2. URU.*mu-dur-na*(*-a-a*) SAA V 53:4-5
	ṭur	x			1. *ṭur-ri* SAA X 241 r.3; 2. *la-ap-ṭur-šú-nu* NL 22 r.3 (CTN V 180f), *šaṭāru*; 3. *šaṭāru*
dúr 536 (KU)	dúr			x	3. ^{m}ÙŠ–*a-dúr* StAT 1 12 r.4
	tuš		x		2. *it-tuš-bu* SAA XIII 48 r.1
	ṭuš		x	x	2. *ub-tal-li-ṭuš-šú* SAA X 333 r.3; 3. *lu-bal-liṭ-ṭuš* SAA XIII 58:10
gab 167	gab	x		x	3. ^{m}*sa*$_{16}$*-gab* SAA X 138 r.4
	gap	x	x		1. *x*]*x gap-pi ša* SAA XIII 47:3′, *gap-šu-ti* SAA X

177 See PNA 2/I p. 600f s.v. *Kandalānu*.

178 Instead of dul$_6$, the reading value du$_6$ is used in the transliteration of SAA I.

					226:12; 2. *a-gap-pi* SAA I 51:5, *a-gap-pi-ia* SAA IX 2 iii 27′
	qab	x	x		
	tuh			x	3. *la-an-tuh* ABL 896:11; *pu-tuh* StAT 1 11 r.1
	ṭáh	x			1. *ṭáh-du-ú-ti* SAA X 226:11
	táh		x		2. *i-ma-táh-u-ni* SAA II 6:192Y
gal 343	gal	x	x	x	
	qal	x	x		1. *qal-lu* MAss 67 r.14, [LÚ].*qal-lu-lu* SAA X 72:9; 2. *i-qal-lil* SAA X 56:10, r.3
gàl see qàl					
gam 362	gam	x	x		
	gúr	x	x	x	1. *gúr-sím-mu* ABL 1244:2′, ^{m}*gúr-di-i* SAA I 76:7
gan 143	gan			x	3. É–*da-gan* SAA XIII 17 r.3′, ^{d}[*d*]*a*-⌜*gan*⌝ SAA II 2 vi 21
	kan	x	x	x	
	kám[179]	x	x		1. *kám-mu-su* SAA XIV 108 r.2, SAA XV 167:8′ (-[*su*]), *kám*-[*mur* SAA VI 288:21; 2. *an-na-kám-ma* SAA X 101:11
gap see gab					
gar 597 (NÍG)	gar	x	x		1. Gargamis; 2. *pa-gar-šú* SAA I 100 r.13
gaṣ 192 (GAZ)	gaṣ	x			1. GIŠ.É–*gaṣ-ṣe-te* BM 103390:10, *gaṣ-ṣi* SAA II 2 i 9′
gaš see kaš					
gat 90 (GAD)	gat	x			1. *gat-ta-ka* SAA IX 2 iv 21′
	qit_4		x		2. *mì*-⌜*qit*$_4$[180]⌝-*ti* SAA X 69 r.7
	kad	x	x	x	
gíd see sír					
gíl see kil					
gim 440	gim	x			1. *gim-lu* SAA XIII 139:12, SAA II 6:459A, k, KUR/LÚ.*gim-ra-a-a* SAA X 100:14/27
	kim		x	x	2. *hakāmu* G/Š; 3. *hakāmu* G/Š/N
	dím		x		2. *ši-dím-ma* ABL 302:9
	ṭém		x		2. *eṭemmu* SAA X 188 r.5, 7
gir 346	gir		x	x	
	qir	x		x	1. *qirsu*; 3. *kaq-qir* SAA IX 8 e.9
	kir	x	x	x	1. *kir-ka-niš-šú* SAA I 18 s.1; 2. KUR.*zi-kir-ta-a-a* SAA V 45 r.6′, *ta-na-kir*-[*a-ni*] SAA II 6:244frg; 3. *maš-kir* SAA I 128:14, NL 11 r.13e (CTN V 31f)
	piš		x	x	
	peš			x	3. *e-peš* ABL 896 r.16, SAA XIII 100:7
	biš			x	3. *labāšu* N
gír 10	gír	x	x	x	1. *gír-ru-tú* SAA V 113:18; 3. *un-ta-gír* SAA I 179:12
giš 296	giš	x		x	1. *giš-par-ri* SAA II 6:650U, frg; 3. *ag-giš* SAA II 6:475D
	nís	x			1. *nishu* passim in SAA VII

[179] Syllabic *kám* is a Babylonianism.

[180] On the published copy (=CT 53 146), the sign looks erased. Here *qit* could be a possible reading. The passage needs to be collated.

gít see sír					
gul 429	gul	x	x	x	
	qúl		x		2. *i-qúl-lu* SAA I 32:14 (CTN V 125ff)
	sún			x	3. ^{m}*aš-šur–bé-sún* StAT 1 22 r.10, SAA I 73:4
gúl see kul					
gup 206 (DU)	gup	x			1. GIŠ.*gup-ni* NL 5 r.4 (CTN V 25f)
	qup		x		2. *zaqāpu*
	kub	x			1. *kub-sa* ABL 543 r.15, ABL 1244 r.5 ~ *ku-ub-sa* ABL 1108 r.13
gur 111	gur	x	x	x	1. *Gurru, gu*]*r-ṣip-ti* SAA IX 3 iii 24; 2. *im-ma-gur-u-ni* SAA X 96:7, URU.*šú-gur-a-a* SAA I 142 r.2, *en-gur-a-ti/te* SAA IX 7 r.3, 4/5; 3. *i-ma-gur* SAA XV 32:9, SAA XV 280:10′
	qur	x	x	x	3. [*li-i*]*s-qur* SAA X 285 r.1′, *ú-qur* SAA X 316 r.19
gúr see gam					
hab see kil					
had 295 (PA)	had	x			1. *had-du-ú-te* ABL 523 r.13
	hat	x			1. KUR–*hat-ti* SAA X 351 e.24, SAA II 2 iii 5′
	haṭ	x	x		1. GIŠ.*haṭ-ṭu* SAA XIII 34 r.3; 2. *i-haṭ-ṭ*[*u-u-ni*] SAA II 11 r.6′
hal 2	hal	x	x		
hap see kil					
har 401	har	x	x	x	
	hur	x	x	x	
	hír		x	x	2. ⸢*ú*⸣*-šam-hír-u-ni* ABL 1022:11; *ma-hír-tú* SAA XIII 35:9; 3. *šam-hír* SAA X 212 r.13, ^{md}UTU–*ú-pa-hír* SAA I 146:2
	mur	x	x	x	1. *murṣu, mur-din-nu* SAA IX 7 r.1
	kín		x	x	
haš see tar					
hat, haṭ see had					
haz see tar					
hir see šir					
hír see har					
hiš see tam					
hiz see tar					
hub 89	hub	x			1. ⸢*hub*⸣*-tu* SAA X 24 r.11
	hup			x	3. URU.*iš-ta-hup* SAA I 32:8 (CTN V 125ff)
hul 456	hul	x			1. *hul-lu-qí* SAA II 8 r.8, *hul-lu-qi-šú*(*/-nu*) SAA II 6:134A, t/O, Babyl.
hum see lum					
hup see hub					
hur see har					
kab 88	kab	x	x	x	3. *ú-šar-kab* SAA V 47:10
	kap	x	x		2. *a-kap-pi* SAA V 293:7, SAA IX 2 ii 6′, *ta-kap-pu-d*[*a-a-ni*] SAA II 10 r.6′
	qáp			x	3. *iz-za-qáp* SAA X 227 r.25
kad see gat					

kak 230 (GAG)	kak	x			1. *kak-kab-tú* SAA IX 11 r.7, 11; ^{m}*kak-ku-su* StAT 1 22 r.11
	kaq	x			
	qaq	x			1. *qaq-qa-ru* SAA X 100:29
	kàl	x			
kal 322	kal	x	x	x	
	rib		x	x	
	rip			x	3. *zarāpu*
	lab	x	x	x	2. LÚ*.GAL-*kal-lab*.MEŠ SAA V 88:5, LÚ*.*ka*]*l-lab*.MEŠ SAA XVI 231:1′, *labbušu*
	lap	x	x	x	1. *lap-lap-tu* SAA II 6:653U, *lap-tú-te* SAA I 100 e.20, r.8; 2. *šelappāiu*, *nahlaptu*; 3. *kallāp*(*u*) [*šipirti*]
	dan	x	x	x	
	tan		x	x	
kàl see kak					
kam 406	kam	x	x		
kám, kan see gan					
kán 105 I (GÁN)	kán		x		2. É–*na-k*[*án-te*] MAss 17a:2′
kap see kab					
kaq see kak					
kar 376*	kar	x	x	x	
kas 166 (KASKAL)	kas	x	x	x	1. *kaspu*; 2. GIŠ.*mar-kas-ši-na* SAA II 5 iv 11′; 3. *rakāsu*
	raš		x		2. *it-tah-raš-ši* SAA XVI 95:1, *a-šap-pa-raš-šú-nu* SAA I 40:5′, *a-sap-raš-šú* SAA XV 190 r.10′, *a-sap-raš-šú-nu* Sm 911:10
	buš		x		2. Hubuškia, Hubuškāia
kás see kaš					
kaš 214 (BI)	kaš	x	x	x	3. *la-a ú-kaš* SAA XVI 64 e.12
	kás		x	x	2. *ta-rak-kás-a-ni* SAA II 6:376frg
	gaš	x		x	1. *šag-gaš-tú* SAA II 6:456g, Babyl.; 3. ^{m}*um-man-ni-gaš* ABL 1385:13
kàt 63c (KÀD)	kàt	x	x	x	1. *kàt-mu* SAA X 353 r.5; 2. *nabalkutu*; 3. *par-kàt* SAA X 247 r.4
kel see kil					
ken see kin					
ket see kid					
kib 228	kib	x	x		2. *us-sa-ar-kib-šú* SAA X 24 r.4, *ik-kib-ku-nu* SAA II 6:489D, frg
	kip	x		x	3. *a-ti-kip* SAA XVI 63 r.32e, outside letters often in the verb *sakāpu* and its derivations
	qip		x	x	2. *ta-qip-u-ni* SAA X 37:3′, e.6′; 3. *it-ta-qip* SAA X 37:5′
kid 313	kid	x			1. –*kid-mu*(*r*)-*ri/a*, e.g. SAA X 197:11, SAA X 294 r.23
	kit	x	x	x	2. *nikittu*; 3. [*nu*]-⌜*sa*⌝-*bal-kit* SAA I 78:7
	ket	x		x	1. *ket-tu/ú/e/i* passim; 3. *u*]*r*$^{?}$-*ket* SAA X 20 r.3
	qid		x	x	
	qit		x	x	2. *piqittu*; 3. *maš-qit* SAA X 336:1

	sah	x	x	x	1. *sah-ru* SAA X 104 s.1; 3. (*nasāhu*)
	šàh		x		2. *i-šàh-hu-*⌜*ṭu*⌝ SAA X 368 r.7′
	suh$_4$			x	3. *ni-suh*$_4$ SAA X 206 r.3′
	síh	x		x	1. [DU]G.*síh-ha-ru* SAA IX 11 r.9; 3. *li-in-ni-s*[*íh*] SAA X 284 r.9
kik 446 (GIG)	kik		x		2. *sa-kik-ke-e-šú* SAA X 315:12
kil 483 (LAGAB)	kil	x	x	x	
	kel[181]		x		2. *ina e-kel-ti* SAA XVI 29:5
	qil		x		2. *ki-qil-li-ti* SAA X 294:15
	gíl		x	x	2. GIŠ.*su-pur-gíl-lum* SAA I 226 r.2
	rim	x	x	x	1. É–*rimki* ~ *ri-im-ki* SAA XIII 159:5′; 2. *ik-rim-u-ni* ABL 302:12, *e-rim-tú* SAA II 5 iii 29′, MÍ.*ha-rim-tú* SAA II 2 v 9, 10, *ta-ṣa*[*r*]-*rim-a-ni* SAA II 10 r.7′; 3. *ab-ti-rim* SAA XIII 157:14′, *ka-rim* KAV 214:6
	rin	x			1. É–*rin-ki* SAA X 352:18, SAA X 97:6′ ~ *ri-in-ku* SAA X 93:8, ABL 864+:4; *ri-i*]*n-ku* SAA X 189:13; *ri-in-ki* SAA X 312:1′, ABL 864+:6)
	hab	x	x		
	hap		x		2. *hapû* prs
kim see gim					
kin 538	kin	x	x	x	1. *kin-ṣa-a-a* SAA IX 5:2
	ken			x	3. *liš-ken* SAA X 74:20
	qin	x		x	1. *qinnu*; 3. *ú-sa-at-qin* KAV 197:36
kín see har					
kip see kib					
kir see gir					
kír 424	kír		x		2. *ta-na-kír-a-ni* SAA II 6:244frg
kis see kiš					
kiš 425	kiš	x	x	x	2. *ka-kiš-a-ti* SAA IX 1 v 3; 3. *ú-tu-uk-kiš* SAA X 104 r.3, SAA X 362 r.1
	kis	x	x	x	1. *ša la kis-pi* SAA XVI 52 r.3; 2. LÚ*.*mu-šár-kis*.MEŠ-*ni* SAA V 119:6
	qiš		x	x	2. *a*]-*a i-qiš-ku-nu* SAA II 6:416A, Babyl.; 3. *ta-qiš* SAA X 97:5′, SAA X 233:10
kit see kid					
kub see gup					
kul 72 (NUMUN)	kul	x	x	x	1. URU.*kul-la-ni-a* SAA X 96:15, SAA XIII 86 r.11
	qul	x	x		1. (ŠEM.)*qul-ku-la-ni* SAA X 298:12, 15; 2. *aq-qul-lu* SAA IX 3 ii 21
	gúl			x	3. *lid-gúl*!![182] NL 65:14 (CTN V 45f)
	zir	x	x		1. *zir-at* SAA X 184 r.6
	zar$_4$	x	x	x	1. stat. of *zarāpu* passim in legal texts; 2. *U/unzarhu* (i.e. also as PN), *pazzuru* SAA II 6:80G, x; 3. *a-zar*$_4$–*ia-u* SAA VII 118 r. ii 3, SAA XI 183 e.6

[181] Concerning a reading *CeC* being presumed for all the *CiC*-signs, see Gelb (1970B) 534. This list provides a separate *CeC*-reading alongside a *CiC*-reading only if such a reading has been used in the SAA series, or if it is otherwise well grounded, for instance lexically.

kun 77	kun	x	x	x	
kur 366	kur	x	x		2. *maš-kur-ru* VAT 9770 r.3, *iz-kur-u-ni* SAAB 1 66:5, 11, SAA XVI 61:4
	mad	x	x		2. *tu-šal-mad-a-ni* SAA II 6:388A, s
	mat	x	x	x	1. *mad/mat-a-a* passim, *mat-nat* SAA II 6:482D
	nat			x	3. *mat-nat* SAA II; *šik-nat*–ZI-*tim* SAA II; *šak-nat* StAT 1 11:4
	lad			x	3. *ul-lad* SAA X 188 r.9
	lat	x	x	x	1. *lat-tú/te* SAA I 34:10/20; 2. *gul-gu-lat-ku-nu* SAA XVI 88:13
	laṭ		x	x	2. *ba-laṭ-ka-ni* SAA II 2 v 2, *tab-laṭ-an-ni* ABL 523:12
	šad	x	x	x	3. *kašādu*
	šat	x	x	x	1. *šattu*; 3. *ep-šat* ABL 879:20, SAA XVI 62:11, *kiš-šat* SAA X 294:10, *rap-šat* SAA IX 1 i 2′
	šaṭ	x	x		1. *šaṭ-ru* CT 53 330:3′, *šaṭ-r*[*u*?] SAA I 72:10′; 2. *šaṭāru*
	sad	x			1. *sad-rat* VAT 9744:12, *sad-ru-te* ibid r.6, *sad-ru* SAA I 129:10
	sat		x	x	2. ⸢*ú*⸣-*sat-bi-šu* SAA V 35:15, ⸢*us-sat*⸣-*pi* SAA I 251:9!!; 3. TÚG.*dáp-pa-sat* SAA XVI 53:9
kúr see bab kut see tar lab see kal lad see kur lah see tam láh see pír làh see luh					
lah$_4$ 206a	lah$_4$			x	3. ^{m}*pí-lah$_4$–aš-šur* StAT 1 9 r.5
lak see šid					
lal 481	lal	x	x	x	
lál 482	lál			x	3. *a-da-lál* SAA XIII 187 r.13′
lam 435	lam	x	x	x	1. *lam-ma-du-u-ti* SAA XV 199 r.3
lap see kal laq see šid lat, laṭ see kur lem see lim let see lid lib see lul					
lid 420 (ÁB)	lid	x	x		2. KUR.*me-lid-a-a* SAA XIII 98 r.3
	lit	x	x	x	2. *te-lit-ka* VAT 8688 r.3, *talittu*
	let		x		2. *ek-let-te* SAA II 6:424c
	liṭ		x	x	2. *balluṭu*; 3. ⸢*i*⸣-*šal-liṭ* SAA XIII 134:15′, *balluṭu*
	rém	x			1. common in personal names, *rém-ni-tum* SAA XIII 48:7′
	rím	x			*rimku*

[182] Admittedly the sign looks like a good DIN, and accordingly the form is read as *lid-din* in CTN V (2001) 45f, Pl. 8. On the other hand, (*ina*) *pān* X *dagālu* "to wait for s.o." is a common Neo-Assyrian idiom, but *pān*(*ī*) X *tadānu* is not.

lig 575 (UR)	lig	x			1. *lig-ma-ru-ku-*⌜*nu* SAA II 6:629G, *lig-ru-ru* SAA X 369 r.15
	lik	x	x	x	
	liq	x	x	x	1. *qabû* prc; 2. *halāqu*; 3. *halāqu* G/D
	taš	x	x		
	tas	x			1. *tas-sap-ra* ABL 879:7, *tas-hu-up* SAA X 97:1′, URU.*tas-ti-a-te* SAA I 150 r.8, SAA I 120 r.4′
lih see tam					
lìh see luh					
lik see lig					
lil 336	lil	x	x	x	
lim 449 (IGI)	lim	x	x	x	
	lem	x			1. *lemnu*
lip see lul					
liq see lig					
lis see liš					
liš 377	liš	x		x	
	lis	x	x	x	1. *lis-di-ru* SAA X 325 r.2′, *lis-ki-pu* SAA X 294:8, *lis-ru-qu* SAA X 352 r.18; 2. KUR.*pi-lis-ta-a-a* SAA I 155:4; 3. *lu-u tap-pi-lis* SAA XIII 132:7
lit, liṭ see lid					
lub see lul					
lud see duk					
luh 321	luh		x		
	làh		x	x	
	lìh		x	x	2. *up-ta-lìh-an-ni* SAA V 15:11; 3. *ú-du-lìh* SAA X 273 r.15, *pa-lìh* SAA XVI 48 r.4, SAA XVI 15:10
	rah			x	3. *it-ta-aṣ-rah* SAA X 302 r.5
lul 355	lul		x	x	2. *i-ha-lul-u-ni* SAA II 6:637A, *tal-lul-tú* SAA X 24:14, *tal-lul-u-ni* ibid. 15; 3. *la-ad-lul* SAA XVI 31 r.3′, ^{m}*ga-lul* SAA XIII 128 r.11, *tah-lul* SAA XIII 29 r.9
	lib	x	x		2. *ug-da-lib-šú* SAA X 96 r.7, *ú-gal-lib-u-ni* SAA X 97:6′
	lip	x	x	x	2. *lu-u-hal-lip-šú-*[*nu*] SAA II 11 r.11′, *diliptu*
	lub	x			1. *lub-bi* SAA X 315 r.15, SAA XVI 65 r.15′
	lup		x		2. ANŠE.*ha-lup*.MEŠ SAA XVI 88:9
	pah	x	x	x	1. *pah-hi-ra* NL 86:11 (CTN V 239f); 2. É.*pa-pah-hu* SAA XIII 164 r.2′, 4′; 3. É.*pa-pah* SAA XIII 162:17, SAA XIII 168:14, *na-pah* SAA II 6:6A
	nar	x	x		1. GI]Š.*nar-kab-tu* SAA V 252 r.4′, *narmaktu*; 2. *ig-da-nar-ru-ru* NL 54 e.18 (CTN V 13f)
lum 565	lum	x	x	x	1. *lum-*[*n*]*a-a-ni* SAA XVI 62:10; 2. *dul-lum-ma* SAA XIII 3:7′, *tu-šal-lum-ni* SAA V 227 r.24, *su-lum-mu-u* BM 132980 r.17′
	hum	x	x		1. ^{m}*hum-bé-e* SAA I 15:14′, ^{m}*hum-ba-re-eš* SAA II 6:3H, ^{d}*hum-hum-mu* SAA II 2 vi 14; 2. URU.*ha-ri-hum-ba* SAA X 42:6, 14
lup see lul					
lut, luṭ see duk					
mad see kur					

mah 57	mah	x	x	x	3. ⌜*nu-sa-ta*⌝*-mah* NL 2:9′ (CTN V 22ff)
mal 233 (GÁ)	mal	x	x	x	1. *mal-'u-ni* SAA XV 341 r.1, *mal-ṭi-ri* SAA X 321 r.16e ~ *ma-al-ṭu-ru* SAA X 358 r.2′; 3. *gammalu*
mám see sal					
man 471	man	x	x	x	3. *ka-a-a-man* SAA XVI 29:9, ⌜URU$^{?}$.*ku*⌝*-lu-man* SAA I 73:8, LÚ.GAL–*kar-man* SAA X 96:18, *si-man* SAA XV 156 r.16
	mìn	x		x	1. [*i*]*na* UGU *mìn*^{in6} SAA XIII 190 r.25e; 3. *si-mìn* SAA XIII 158:5′ ~ *si-mì-in* SAA I 227:7, SAA X 359 r.5′; *si-mi-in* NL 79:12 (CTN V 178f)
	niš		x	x	
	neš		x		2. [*lu*]*-še-ti-iq-ú-neš-šú-*[*nu*] SAA X 72 r.5, *iṣ-ṣab-tu-neš-šú* SAA X 24 r.5
mar 307	mar	x	x	x	
maš 74	maš	x	x	x	
mat see kur					
med see bat					
mer see mir					
meš 533	meš	x		x	3. *ahāmeš*
mid see bat					
mil 212 (IŠ)	mil	x		x	3. Nabû-gamil SAA X 238 r.17, SAA X 291:11, SAA X 308:1; ^{md}ÌR.RA–*ga-mil* SAA I 204:4
mìn see man					
mir 347	mir		x	x	
	mer			x	3. *i-tam-mer* SAA X 263 r.12
mis 314 (MES)	mis		x	x	2. URU.*gar-ga-mis-a-a* SAA XVI 105 r.8, SAA I 183:10′; 3. (Gargamis)
	miš		x	x	2. *ú-ta-miš-ú-ni* SAA XV 65 r.5, *ú-na-miš-u-ni* SAA V 14:8; 3. *ut-tam-miš* SAA I 132 r.9′, *it-te-*⌜*miš*⌝ SAA X 10 r.4′, [^{d}]*a-ra-miš* SAA II 6:466frg
	rid		x	x	2. ⌜*ha-rid*⌝*-du-ú-ni* ABL 1121:6
	rit	x		x	1. [*ri*]*t*$^{?}$*-ta-a-ti* SAA XIII 47 r.7, *rit-ta-a-a* SAA IX 9:17
	riṭ			x	*i-ta-*[*am-r*]*iṭ* SAA XVI 100:15
miš see mis					
mit see bat					
mug 3	mug				LÚ.GAL–*mug*$^{!}$*-gi* SAA VI 247 e.9
	muk	x	x	x	1. and 3. =*muk* passim; 2. *Bīt-Amukāni*
	muq		x		2. *emūqi*
muq, muk see mug					
mur see har					
mus see muš					
muš 374	muš	x			
	mus	x			1. Musku
	ṣir		x	x	
mut 81 (MUD)	mut		x	x	3. *la-mut* SAA XIII 158 r.12′ ~ *la-mu-ut* SAA X 227 r.11
nab 129	nab	x	x		1. *nabnītu* SAA II 6:437; 2. *ubālu* Gtn
	nap	x	x		

nag 35	nag	x			1. *nag-ga-la-pa-a-a* SAA IX 9:18
	nak	x	x	x	
	naq	x	x		1. *naq-bar-ku-nu* SAA II 6:484D; 2. *mu-naq-qi-te* SAA X 336:4
nak see nag					
nam 79	nam	x	x		
nap see nab					
naq see nag					
nar see lul					
nàr 325 (NIR)	nàr	x	x		1. GIŠ.*nàr-an-tu* SAA IX 8:7, DUG.*nàr-ma-ka-a-te* VAT 9744:1, DUG.*nàr-ma-ka*.MEŠ NAIT. r.13; 2. *i-nàr-ru-ṭu* SAA X 72 r.18
nat see kur					
neš see man					
nid 211 (UŠ)	nid	x			1. *nid-ri* SAA X 253:18
nig 563	nig	x			1. *nig-da-mar* SAA X 349:25
	nik	x	x	x	1. *nikkassu*; 2. ventive, *ka-⌜ni⌝k-u-ni* SAA II 6:408A; 3. *ka-nik* SAA X 82 r.3′
	niq		x		2. *mu-še-ni[q]-ta-ka* SAA IX 1 iii 17′, *ú-sa-niq-šú* SAA X 355 r.7′, *sa-niq-šu* TH 7:5
nik see nig					
nim 433	nim		x	x	
	num			x	3. Anum
nin 556	nin		x		
niq see nig					
niš see man					
num see nim					
nun 87	nun		x	x	2. ^{m}*ka-nun-a-a* SAA V 14 r.8′, ^{d}*a-nun-na-ki* SAA X 188 r.10, *zanānu*; 3. *⌜i⌝-za-nun* SAA V 272 r.2
	ṣil	x			1. *ṣil-li-ba-a-ni* SAA X 241:6, ^{m}*ṣil*-^{d}PA CTN III 1:2, *ṣil-li* SAA XIII 154:15
pad 469	pad		x		2. Arpadda
	pat	x	x	x	1. ÍD.*pat-ti*–^{d}BI SAA I 210:15
	paṭ	x			1. *paṭ-ru-u-ni* SAA X 294 r.9
	šuk	x			1. *šuk-na* SAA XVI 156:5′
pah see lul					
pal see bal					
pan 439	pan		x	x	2. *ta-sa-pan-a-ni* SAA II 6:413A, *našpantu* SAA II; 3. *i-sap-pan* SAA IX 8 r.1
	ban		x	x	3. URU.*za-ban* SAA V 199:10, SAA V 259 r.1
paq 78 (HU)	paq	x	x	x	1. *⌜paq-da⌝-šú-nu* SAA V 9:1′, *paq-du* SAA I 11:8, *paq-d[u* SAA XV 320 r.2; 2. *ta-paq-qi-da-a-ni* SAA I 16 r.5′, *⌜ú⌝-paq-qí-du-ni* SAA X 97 r.7; 3. ^{m}*ú-paq*–^{d}*šá-maš* SAA V 163:2
	bak		x		2. *i-bak-k[i-u]* SAA X 199 r.3′; *[li]q-bak-ka* SAA I 8 r.14 ~ *liq-<u>ba-ak</u>-ka* SAA X 228 r.9

par see tam
pat, paṭ see pad
peš see gir
pet see bit
pik see sik
pil see bil
píl see bíl
pir see tam

pír 393	pír		x		2. *tak-pír-tu* TH 5 r.4
	bìr	x			1. *bìr-me* SAA XVI 84 r.12
	láh	x	x		1. *lahhinu*[*tu*]; 2. KUR.*ha-láh-hi* SAA I 106:7

piš see gir
pit see bit
pur see bur
qab see gab
qal see gal

qàl 49*	qàl	x			
	gàl		x		2. *ú-gàl-lu-du* SAA XV 241 r.6′

qáp see kab
qaq see kak

qar 333 (GÀR)	qar	x	x	x	3. *kaqquru* st. cstr., URU.*ba-qar* SAA V 142:5′, SAA I 170:8

qid see kid
qil see kil
qin see kin
qip see kib
qir see gir
qiš see kiš
qit see kid
qit$_4$ see gat
qud see tar
qul see kul
qúl see gul
qur see gur
qut see tar

rab 149	rab	x	x	x	1. URU.*rab-la-a* SAA I 180 e.12′
	rap	x	x		1. *rap-šat* SAA IX 1 i 2′; 2. *ár-rap-ha* ABL 1244:10′, *šarāpu* N SAA II 6:608
rad 83 (ŠITA)	rad	x	x	x	1. *rad-di-u* SAA XVI 5 r.7; 3. *ú-rad* SAA X 196 r.18e, SAA X 275 r.7, *qar-rad* SAA II 6:455frg
	rat		x	x	

rag see sal
rah see luh
rak see sal

ram 183 (ÁG)	ram	x	x		1. *ram-ni-šú* SAA I 205 r.14, *ram-ni-*[*šu*] SAA X 167:7; 2. *rammû*, *harammāma*

rap see rab					
raq see sal					
raš see kas					
rat see rad					
rém see lid					
rib see kal					
rid see mis					
rig see šim					
ríg 555 (ZUM)	ríg			x	3. *an-nu-ríg/[rí]g* SAA I 191 r.6/SAA V 81:5
rik see šim					
rim see kil					
rím see lid					
rin see kil					
rip see kal					
riq see šim					
ris, riš see sag					
rit, riṭ see mis					
sab see šab					
sad see kur					
sag 115	sag		x		2. Esaggil
	sak	x	x	x	1. URU.*sak-ku-a-na-a-a* SAA V 42 r.4, *sak-ku-uk-ku-tú* ABL 972:10′, *sak-ru* SAA XIII 61 e.18, 19; 3. *šan/msuku*
	šag	x	x		1. *šaglû* subst./adj., *šaggaštu*, Babyl.; 2. *ú-šag-ga-lu-na-ši* SAA XV 221:3′, r.8, [*ú*]-*šag-la-na-ši* SAA I 261:4′
	šak	x	x		
	šaq		x		2. [*i-š*]*aq-qu-a* SAA X 9:13
	san			x	3. *hu-ur-san* SAA XV 295:10
	riš	x	x	x	1. UR]U$^{?}$.*riš-te-*⌜*a*⌝-[*na*$^{?}$] SAA XV 58:2′; 2. *pi-riš-te* SAA XIII 163 r.2; 3. *le-r*[*iš* SAA V 7 r.2′, *e-ta-nar-riš* SAA IX 9:20 ~ *a-na da-ri-iš* SAA XIII 187:9
	ris			x	3. *pa-ris* SAA X 263 r.10, *ad-di-ris* SAA X 235 r.15, URU.⌜*sik*$^{?}$⌝-*ris* SAA I 23:3′
sah see kid					
sak see sag					
sal 554 (MUNUS)	sal	x	x		1. [UZU.*sa*]*l-qa* SAA XIII 46:7′, *sal-me-šú* SAA II 6:112frg
	šal	x	x		
	rag			x	3. *an-nu-rag* NL 72:8 (CTN V 246ff)
	rak	x	x	x	
	raq	x	x		1. *raq-qa-*⌜*aq*⌝ SAA X 21 r.8′; 2. *i-ma-raq-u-ni* SAA X 321 r.11
	mám	x			1. *mám-ma*-MEŠ-*šú-nu* SAA I 183:9′, *mám-ma* StAT 1 55 r.4 and often in legal documents
sam see šam					
san see sag					
sap see šab					

sar 331e	sar	x	x	x	2. *ú-s[ar-ri]* SAA V 249:13′, *tu-sar-pi-di* SAA IX 1 v 20, LÚ.*sar-sar-a-ni* SAA IX 3 ii 10; 3. *ú-ta-sar* SAA VIII 168:3
	šar	x	x	x	
sat see kur					
sih see šah					
síh see kid					
sik 592 (SIG)	sik	x	x		1. *sik-ra* ABL 273:11, ABL 543 r.14, ABL 1108 r.12, ABL 1244 r.4, Sikris; 2. LÚ*.*na-sik*.MEŠ SAA V 3 r.15
	šik	x	x		1. *šik-n[i* SAA X 182:18, LÚ*.GAL–*šik-na-ni* SAA I 72:5′; 2. *tup-šik-ki* SAA X 143 r.4
	šiq			x	3. *našāqu* G/D
	pik			x	3. *ši-pik* SAA X 294:11
sím see šúm					
sin 472 (EŠ)	sin	x	x		1. *sin-niš ak-li* SAA X 31:7′, archaism; 2. *i-sin-nu* SAA X 20:1, *[ku]r-sin-nu-šu* SAA II 2 i 26′
sir see šud					
sír 371 (BU)	sír			x	3. *e-sír* ABL 1186:10′
	gíd	x	x		1. Gidgidanu see SAA I; 2. ^{m}*gíd-gíd-dà-ni* BM 122698:13
	gít	x			1. *gít-ma-lu* SAA II 12:6
sis 331 (ŠEŠ)	sis		x	x	2. *tu-šah-sis-a-ni* SAA X 93 r.6; 3. *ha-sis* SAA XIII 31:15, r.11; *ú-šah-sis* SAA X 93 r.2 ~ *ú-sa-ah-si-is* SAA X 87 r.10′
suh 102 (MÚŠ)	suh		x		2. *sahāru*
suh$_4$ see kid					
suk 522 (SUG)	suk	x			1. *suk-ki* SAA XIII 135:11′, e.13′
	zuk	x			1. *zuk-ra* ABL 945 r.3′
sún see gul					
sur 101	sur	x			1. *sur-re-e* SAA I 238:7, *sur-ri* SAA X 376:10, *surrāti*
	šur		x	x	
ṣab 393 (ERIM)	ṣab	x	x		1. and 2., *ṣabātu* G and D
	ṣap	x	x		1. ANŠE.*ṣap-pu* SAA I 219:13; 2. *aṣappu*, Raṣappa
	zab	x	x		1. ^{m}*zab-bu-u-a* SAA I 24:6; 2. *zabālu*
ṣal see zal					
ṣap see ṣab					
ṣar see zar					
ṣib see zib					
ṣil see nun					
ṣip see zib					
ṣir see muš					
ṣur see zur					

šab 295k	šab		x	x	3. *ušābu*
	šap	x	x		
	sab		x		2. *ú-sab-ši-il* SAA X 323 r.11, *is-sab-bu* SAA X 226 r.1
	sap		x	x	2. *šapāru*, *i-sap-pan* SAA IX 8 r.1; 3. *ik-ta-sap* SAA I 181 r.8, *i[t-t]ak-sap* SAA XVI 25:11
šad see kur					
šag see sag					
šah 53 (ŠUBUR)	šah	x	x	x	3. *ni-ip-šah* SAA XVI 105 r.18
	sih	x			1. *sih-hi* SAA X 323 r.12
šáh see šul					
šàh see kid					
šak see sag					
šal see sal					
šam 318 (Ú)	šam	x	x	x	3. [*ú-mi*]-⸢*šam*⸣ SAA X 228 r.15
	sam	x	x		1. *sam-ku-u-te* ABL 1002 r.11; 2. *ú-sam-ma-ak-ak-ku-nu-ni* BM 132980 r.20′
šap see šab					
šaq see sag					
šar see sar					
šár 396	šár		x		2. *mušarkisu*
šat, šaṭ see kur					
šèr see šir					
šib 532 (ME)	šib	x	x	x	1. *šib-ṭi* SAA II 4 r.26′, *šib-še-ti* SAA X 238:13; 2. *ú-šib-*[*u-ni* SAA I 132:6, *ušābu* Š
	šip	x			
	sip	x		x	1. *sip-par*.KI SAA X 364 r.7; 3. *bar-sip*.KI SAA X 350 r.6, SAA X 353:15, 18, r.3
šid 314	šid	x	x		1. *šiddu*; 2. *uk-ta*]-*šid-du-ú-šú* SAA I 123:6, *lu-šak-šid-su* ABL 896 r.5
	šit	x			1. *šit-qu-lu* SAA VIII 140:3, SAA VIII 141:3, SAA VIII 142:3
	lak	x	x	x	1. *lak-la-šú-nu* NL 78 r.7′ (CTN V 245f)
	laq	x	x		1. *laq-qi/í* passim in legal documents
šik see sik					
šil see tar					
šim 215	šim	x	x	x	2. ⸢*e-pa*⸣-*šim-ma* SAA X 255 r.16; 3. *ú-b*[*a*]-*áš-šim* SAA X 102:9′[183]
	rig			x	3. *annurig*
	rik	x	x	x	1. *riksu*; 2. *pa-rik-tú* SAA X 247 r.4; *ši-rik-ti* SAA X 294:5; 3. *ik-te-rik* SAA XVI 112 r.12, *lu-ur-rik* SAA XVI 60 s.2
	riq			x	3. *is-si-riq* SAA VI 265:4, *us-sa-*⸢*riq*⸣ SAA X 228 r.11
šin 8 (ŠEN)	šin	x			1. KUR.*šin-gi-bu-tú* SAA XV 69:11, *šinnu*
	ruq	x			1. *ruq-qu* SAA XIII 28:14′
šip see šib					
šiq see sik					

[183] This passage is a literary quotation and not proper Neo-Assyrian.

šir 71	šir		x	x	2. *a-šir-ta-šú-nu* SAA I 11 r.8, *ú-še-šir-u-ni* SAA X 217 r.5; 3. ^{md}AG–*pa-šir* passim SAA I, *i-ka-šir* SAA I 208 r.9′
šir 152 (EZEN)	šìr		x		2. *pišru, piširtu*
	šèr	x			1. *šèr-ti* SAA X 63 r.7
	hir		x	x	
šit see šid					
šub 68 (RU)	šub	x		x	1. Šubria, *šubtu*; 3. ^{m}*hu–te-šub* see SAA V glossary
	šup	x			1. *šapāru* imperative
šud 373	šud	x			1. *šud-d*[*a* 0] SAA XV 306:4′
	sir	x			1. *sirdu* passim in administrative texts
šuk see pad					
šul 467	šul	x			1. *šulmu, šulmānu*
	dun	x	x		*1./2.* Karduniaš, see SAA II 6:88
	šáh		x		2. *i-šáh-hu-ṭu* SAA X 355:7, 12 [1. -[*ṭu x*]
šum see tak					
šúm 164 (SUM)	šúm	x			1. *šumma/u*
	sím		x		2. *gúr-sím-mu* ABL 1244:2′
šum$_4$ see bat					
šup see šub					
šur see sur					
tab 124	tab	x	x		
	tap	x	x		
	dáb		x		2. *dabābu*
	dáp	x			1. TÚG.*dáp-pa-sat* SAA XVI 53:9
tah 169 (DAH)	tah	x	x	x	3. *matāhu*
táh see gab					
tak 126 (TAG)	tak	x	x		
	taq	x	x	x	3. *batāqu*
	šum	x		x	1. *šumma/u, šum-ú-du* SAA X 197 r.17, *Babyl.*; 3. ^{d}*i-šum* SAA XIII 72 r.3, SAA II 2 vi 14
tàk 229	tàk	x			1. *tàk-si* CTN III 3:12
	dàk		x		2. *madāktu*
	dàq		x		
tal see dal					
tam 381 (UD)	tam	x	x		
	pir	x	x	x	1. LÚ*.EN–*pir-ri* SAA V 87:13, *pir-ku* SAA I 191 r.4; 3. *ši-pir* SAA XVI 72:7′
	par	x	x	x	
	lah	x	x	x	1. *lahhinu*; 2. *tap-lah-i-ši-i-ni* SAA XIII 76:6
	lih	x			1. *lih-mu* SAA XIII 147 r.6
	hiš			x	3. *arhiš*

tan see kal
tap see tab
taq see tak

tar 12	tar	x	x	x	3. *ú-tar* SAA X 188 r.10, *ú-qa-at-t*[*ar*] SAA IX 1 iv 30, *tu-šá-tar* SAA IX 9:21
	ṭar	x	x	x	1. *ṭar-kul-la-ši-na* SAA II 5 iv 12′
	kut		x		2. *na-bal-kut-a-tu-u-ni* ABL 1127:5′, *šakuttu*, *na-kut-tú* SAA I 190 r.9′
	qud		x	x	2. LÚ*.*pu-qud-di* ABL 896:16; 3. *ni-ir-qud* SAA X 226 r.12
	qut	x	x	x	1. *qut*-PA SAA X 250:8′, SAA X 328:8, *qut-ru* SAA IX 1 iv 30; 2. *in-qut-u-ni* SAA V 227 s.4, *pa-qut-ti* SAA II 6:657frg; 3. *maqātu*
	haš	x			1. ŠE.*haš-la-te* SAA XIII 134:25′
	haz			x	3. *a-haz de-ni* SAA XIII 128 s.2
	hiz			x	3. *us-sa-hiz*[184] SAA X 182:21
	šil	x	x	x	1. GIŠ.*šil-ta-hu* SAA X 174:21; 2. *me-šil-ma* SAA I 181 r.9; 3. *mi/ešlu* st. cstr., *lu-ša-an-šil* SAA XVI 146:4′, *ú-sa-an-šil* ibid. 12′
tas, taš see lig					
ter see tir					
tik 106 (GÚ)	tik	x			1. *tik-pi* SAA V 291:2′
	tiq		x	x	2. *ba-tiq-tú* NL 75:12 (CTN V 115f); 3. *e-te-tiq* SAA XVI 145 s.1, *l*]*e-e-ti*[*q* CT 53 433 r.3′ ~ e.g. *né-ti-iq* SAA XIII 60 r.1
til see bat					
tim see dim					
tin see din					
tiq see tik					
tir 375	tir		x	x	2. *tuāru* D
	ter		x		2. *ik-ter-ru* SAA XVI 63:19
tub see dup					
tug see tuk					
tuh see gab					
tuk 574	tuk	x	x	x	1. *tuk-ka-ni* SAA V 149 r.11, SAA XIII 25 r.16e; 2. *bir-tuk-ku-nu* SAA II 8 r.20, *i*]*–da-tuk-ka* SAA V 8:7′; 3. *lil-tuk* SAA X 182 r.29, *lit-ta-tuk* SAA II 6:471D
	tug	x			1. *tug-dam-me-ra* SAA I 25:5
	tuq		x		2. *maqātu*
tum 207	tum			x[185]	
tùm 434	tùm	x			1. *tùm-ma-tú-nu* SAA II 2 vi 6, archaism
tup see dup					
tuq see tuk					
tur 144	tur	x	x		1. E.g. in *turtānu*, *targumānu*; 2. GIŠ.*kit-tur*.MEŠ VAT 9744:11, *ki-tur-r*[*a-te* CT 53 941:5′, *ti-tur-ra-a-te* SAA I 29 r.6, *i-tur-ru* SAA XIII 128 r.21e

[184] The reading value TAR = *hiz* is not to be found in sign lists, but because TAR = *haz* exists, TAR = *hiz* also seems to be a potential reading. Cf. e.g. DIB/*dip* = *dab/p* 537, *har* = *hír* 401, *làh* (LUH) = *lìh* 321, *man* = *mìn* 471, *par* (UD) = *pir* 381, *sah* (KID) = *síh* 313, etc.

[185] On the different possibilities of interpreting a CV*m*-sign at the end of a noun, see Reiner (1973) 27, cf. also Gelb (1970B) 535.

tuš see dúr
ṭáh see gab
ṭak see dag
ṭar see tar
ṭém see gim
ṭib see dib
ṭir see dir
ṭùl see dul$_6$
ṭup see dup
ṭur see dur
ṭuš see dúr
zab see ṣab

zag 332	zag	x			1. *zag-ru* SAA V 294 r.1
	zak	x	x		1. *zakkû*; 2. *zakāru*; LÚ.*za-zak-ku* SAA XIII 166 r.4
zak see zag					
zal 231 (NI)	zal		x	x	2. KUR.*i-zal-li* SAA I 141:5′; 3. *ì-zal* KAV 174 r.10, VAT 9777:8
	ṣal	x	x		
zar 491	zar	x	x	x	1. Zarpanītu, stat of *zarāpu* passim in legal texts; 2. *pazzuru*, *tu-šá-an*]-*zar-a-ni* SAA II 6:364z, *i-zar-ru-ni-šú* GPA 15 r.4; 3. *pazzuru*
	ṣar	x	x	x	1. *ṣar-hu* SAA X 318 r.11e, SAA X 328 r.10, *ṣar-ṣa-ri* SAA IX 3 iii 5, GIŠ.*ṣar-bu-tú* SAA V 253:6′
zar$_4$ see kul					
zib 395	zib		x	x	2. *ezābu* Š; 3. *ezābu* Š
	zip		x		2. *kuzippi*
	ṣib	x			1. URU.*ṣib-te* SAA I 97 r.5′, 7′, *ṣib-ti* CT 53 981:7, *ṣib-te* StAT 1 56 r.1, 2. *hi-ṣib-šú* SAA XIII 157:13′, URU.*na-ṣib-na* SAA I 247 e.11′, *a-ra-*⸢*ṣib-bi*⸣ NL 69 r.5′ (CTN V 164ff); 3. *a-ra-ṣib* SAA XV 113 s.4, ^{m}*na-ṣib*–DINGIR SAA V 63:4, r.14
	ṣip	x	x	x	1. ⸢*ṣip*⸣-*rat* SAA I 158:5, ⸢LÚ*⸣.UŠ.BAR–*ṣip-rat* SAA XVI 55:2, *ṣip-pir-ra-a-te* SAA X 274:9; 2. *ir-ṣip-u-ni* SAA I 179:11, *a-ra-ṣip-p*[*i*] SAA XV 107 e.6′, *gu*]*r-ṣip-ti* SAA IX 3 iii 24
zip see zib					
ziq 190 (ZIK)	ziq	x		x	3. *tu-un-*[*ta*]-*ta-ziq* SAA XIII 29 r.9
zir see kul					
ziz see bat					
zuk see suk					
zur 437 (AMAR)	zur		x		2. *pa-zur-ti* TH 4:4
	ṣur	x	x	x	1. *ṣur-hi* SAA X 261:12, *ṣurru*; 2. *kaṣāru*, *muṣurāiu*, *naṣāru*

CVC-signs replace, for instance, CV + CV-signs at the end of a word in those verb forms of the third-person plural in which the last vowel of the paradigmatically normal form is omitted from the writing.[186]

[186] Parpola (1972) pp. 24 (n. 9) and 27.

4 PHONOLOGICAL VARIATION

Consonantal and vocalic variation occurring in written texts can be interpreted orthographically and attributed to scribal conventions[187] if it can be shown, for example, that two different scribal schools consistently use diverging spelling conventions and the observed variation closely corresponds to the relevant conventions. However, more often the observed variation can be better explained in phonetic terms. Hence many slight orthographic variants bear witness to phonological variation.

4.1 Consonants

4.1.1 Variation between voiced and voiceless consonants: stops (*b* ~ *p*; *d* ~ *t*; *g* ~ *k*; *ṭ*, *q*)

In Neo-Assyrian, a voiceless stop may become voiced either in a voiced environment or when there are no lexical restrictions.[188] The voiceless and voiced stops[189] are thus in partial free variation. The voiced environments which create opportunities for voicing are: (a) a voiceless stop between vowels, (b) a voiceless stop immediately beside a voiced consonant, especially a sonorant (= liquids [*l*], [*r*], nasals [*m*], [*n*]). The environments (a) and (b) in the forms below refer to the environment of a voiceless consonant which has become voiced.[190] Thus, voicing

---

[187] I am not using disyllabic reading values (such as *tala* instead of *tal*, or *aka* instead of *ak* and so on) as ascribed to several Neo-Assyrian cuneiform signs by Deller (1962A) and (1962B) 186-88. These disyllabic readings are, in my opinion, distorting the reality by forcing the orthography to conform to morphologically desired forms and thus to the more "correct" grammatical interpretations.

[188] Parpola (1988A) 76, especially n. 13 with examples.

[189] According to Reiner, the Neo-Assyrian stops differ from each other only on the basis of two contrasting oppositions, such as voiced vs. non-voiced and emphatic vs. non-emphatic, see Reiner (1966) 51 and (1973) 23 n. 28.

[190] Cf. Garr (1986) 45-52. The rules of voicing postulated for Ugaritic by Garr are also valid in Neo-Assyrian.

is an assimilatory process based on strict rules. In this process, a voiceless stop is assimilated to the voiced phonetic environment which surrounds it or with which it has immediate contact.[191]

Examples of the alternation of <*d*> and <*t*>:

(*balāt*) (b) *a–bal-duk-ka* SAA XV 241:9 ~ *a–bal-la-tuk-ka* ibid. l.6

(*galādu*) *ig-ta-al-du* SAA V 202 r.8′; *ig-tal-du* (verbs in contact position: regular alternation; see e.g. *gamāru* G/D-perfect forms) NL 105 r.8 (CTN V 223f)[192]

(*kabātu* G/D) (a) *ka-bi-di* SAA X 316 r.19; *kab-bi-da* SAA II 6:335; *ú-ka-bi-du-šú-u-ni* SAA X 182 r.14 (b) *ka-ab-di* SAA X 182 r.11. Possibly **kbt* > *kbd* has been lexicalized in verb forms as distinct from the nouns *kabattu* and *kabtu*

(**natbā/aku*)[193] (a) [*n*]*a-da-*[*b*]*a-k*[*i*] SAA II 12:7; possibly *na-*⸢*da-ba*⸣-[*ki*] NL 93:5 (CTN V 233); *na-da-ba-ku* SAA XV 113 s.3. Probably it is lexicalized as *nad*(*a*)*bāku*. Note the established status of the auxiliary anaptyctic vowel *a* (regularly written with the sign DA).

(*tabāku* G/D) (a) *la ni-di-bu-ku-ni* SAA XIII 137 r.3; *la ni-id-di-bu-ú-ku* BM 132980:17; [*l*]*i-di-bu-ku* NL 93 r.3 (CTN V 233) (anaptyctic vowel *i* in all of them); *la ú-du-*⸢*bi*$^{?}$⸣*-ku* NL 35:7 (CTN V 33f)]; cf. cases in which the writing system does not distinguish between a voiced and voiceless consonant: (b) (*ad*=*at*) *it-ta-*AD*-bu-ku* SAA V 249:12′; *ta-*AD*-bu-ka-šu-nu-u* SAA I 14 s.2; (*lid*=*lit*) LIT*-bu-ku* SAA XVI 27 r.7′

(*tabû* G and Š) (a) *i-di-ba-ka-a-ni* SAA IX 1 i 6′;[194] *i-di-ba-kan-ni* ibid. ii 35′; *ú-sa-da-bi-šu* StAT 1 51 r.6; *nu-sa-da-bi-*[*šú-nu*] SAA XIII 208:2′; *ú-šá-da-ba* SAA V 58:9′ (for the anaptyctic vowel in all examples, cf. *natbā/aku* above)

(*tubāqu*) (a) *ina du-ba-qi* SAA II 6:582Dv ~ *ina tu-ba-qi* ibid. ms. b

There are no clear attestations of a voiced allophone of the emphatic *ṭ*.[195] However, one passage appears to be the exception that proves the rule:

(probably *maraṭu* N) *a-ki* BÀD *x*[*x x x x*] / *i-me-ri-du-n*[*i*$^{?}$ *x x x*] "When the city wall [...] / was damaged [...] SAA XVI 101 r.3′-4′ ~ mrṭ N in SAA XVI 100:9, 15

Examples of the alternation between <*g*> and <*k*>[196] are:

(*kuzippu*)[197] (a) *ša* TÚG.*gu-zip-pi*(*-ia/ni*) SAA X 294 r.28, 35, SAA X 289 r.10′; (b) *liš-kun* / [TÚ]G.*gu-zip-pi* SAA X 338:12-13; (uncertain) *x*] / [*x* TÚG.*g*]*u-zip-pi* SAA X 289 r.3′ ~ (TÚG.)*ku-zip-pi* passim

---

[191] Garr (1986) 50-51.

[192] Or *ik-tal-du* as in CTN V 223.

[193] See e.g. von Soden (1957) 122, Deller (1985-1986) 44 n. 10 and Radner (1999A) 171. See also Kaufman (1974) 76 and 139, who records *ndbk* in the biblical Aramaic, prophecies of Targum, and Mishnaic Hebrew.

[194] Cf. n. ad SAA IX 1 i 6.

[195] Cf. Hämeen-Anttila (2000) 16.

[196] See e.g. von Soden ibid. and Kaufman (1974) 139f, who gives evidence of the intervocalic alternation in loanwords which probably originated in Assyrian.

[197] Deller (1985-1986) 49. See also Lipiński (1997) § 18.4.

(*akappu*/*agappu*) *a-kap-pi* SAA V 293:7, SAA IX 2 ii 6′ ~ (a) *a-gap-pi* SAA I 51:5, *a-gap-pi-ia* SAA IX 2 iii 27′; also *a-qa-pu-šú* SAA IX 1 i 7′[198]
(*aggu*) *ha-an-ga-ru ak-ku* "an angry dagger" SAA IX 1 iv 7[199]

Some writings may suggest the pronunciation of a voiced /*q*/.[200] For instance,

ú-pa-qá-da (the value *qá* = GA is otherwise not attested in NA[201]) SAA X 222 r.9 (*akappu*/*agappu*, cf. the <*g*> and <*k*> alternation above)
(Gurru) LÚ*.*qa-mur-ra*[202] SAA XV 136 r.22; less clear is KUR$^{?}$.*qu-ra*$^{?}$*-a-a* in SAA VII 112 r.2 ~ LÚ$^{(*)}$.*gur-ra-a-a* and (LÚ$^{(*)}$).*gur-ru/ri* passim; LÚ.*gur-a-a* SAA XI 228 ii 9′

On the other hand, the alternation among *q*, 0 and *h* may point to pharyngalization (*ṡ́* > *ḍ* > ʿ).[203] Thus:

qu-di-i-ni[204] SAA I 30 e.9′ (words of Urzana, king of Muṣaṣir, quoted in a letter of Sennacherib) ~ *ú-di-*(*i-*)*ni/a* passim
KUR./URU.*mar-qa-si* SAA I 257:12/BT 128 r.2 (=:11); KUR.*ma*[*r-q*]*a-*⸢*sa*⸣*-a-a* NL 50:11 (CTN V 182ff); URU.*ma-ra-qa-si* BT 108 r.1 (=:8) ~ *a-na* LÚ*.*mar-ha-sa-a-a* SAA I 124:24

The replacement of [*k*] with [*h*] indicates the fricativization[205] of [*k*] in the verb *kanāšu* > *hanāšu*.[206] As it was, *hanāšu* was probably gaining ground against *kanāšu* in Neo-Assyrian, but contrary to Hämeen-Anttila (2000) 17, it is not so certain that *knš* was restricted to the meaning 'to assemble'. The word *knš* has the meaning 'to submit' in the following NA letters: SAA X 33 r.16 (Issar-šumu-ereš), SAA X 174:16 (Marduk-šumu-uṣur), SAA X 294:29 (Urdu-Gula), SAA XV 230:15 (according to SAA XV p. 148 n. ad no. 230 "Hand of Šarru-emuranni, governor of Babylon) and ND 2676:7′ (CTN V 179). Whereas *hnš* is attested in SAA V 78:9, 12, r.12 (Aššur-belu-da''in, possibly the governor of Halzi-atbar), SAA V 149:7 (unknown from eastern Kurdistan), SAA V 184:6′ (unknown, the letter fragment relates to Urarṭu) and the only, and rather uncertain, D-stem attestation of *hnš*: *ú-ha-an-ni-*[*šú-ni*] in SAA V 286:3 (the treasurer Ṭab-šar-Aššur?), though *hnq* D "to suffocate, throttle" could just as well be the correct restoration in this passage. On the strength of these attestations, it is true that

---

[198] Cf. n. ad SAA IX 1 i 7.

[199] See n. ad SAA IX 1 iv 7.

[200] See LAS II ad no. 142 r.8.

[201] Ibid.

[202] Apparently there are two typing errors in SAA XV 166 (LÚ*.*qur-mur-a-a* l. 21; LÚ*.*qur-mur-a-a-*⸢*e*⸣*-a* r.7; *qur* = *gur*), or these may be intentional. Cf. the remark ibid. n. ad 166:21.

[203] See Lipiński (1997) § 10.9 and Hämeen-Anttila (2000) 17.

[204] Probably of Aramaic influence: */ʿ*udīni*/ > *qudīni*.

[205] See Hämeen-Anttila (2000) 17, who also mentions an "inverse" example: *'*sh* > *ussuku* (NA).

[206] Lipiński (1997) § 18.5 and § 19.11. See also Deller and Finkel (1984) 87: *maksûtu* ~ *mahsûtu* and Deller (1961B) 352.

dialectal variation[207] exists between *hnš* (in the north and probably east, too) and *knš* (Babyl./literary contexts) in NA letters. First, although very likely, interpreting *knš* as a Babylonianism in scholarly letters (SAA X references above) is not the only possibility as long as we do not have any reliable non-scholarly attestations of *hnš* or *knš* from Assyria. Second, it should be emphasized that the spellings of *h*/*knš* with *h* are roughly about 40 years older (during the reign of Sargon II) than the ones containing *k* (Esarhaddon/Assurbanipal; except for ND 2676:7′ and the probable Babyl. of SAA XV 230:15). Thus, the diachronic evidence to support the spread of *hnš* at the expense of *knš* is, thus far, very vague in Assyria during the time of the Sargonids (note that the development: [*k*] > fricativized > defricativized [*k*][208] is also possible).

For the alternation of <*p*> and <*b*>, see Deller (1959) § 47.

In Neo-Assyrian, /*p*/ in voiced environment often becomes voiced.[209] Since the change does not involve a change in meaning, some scholars take it as evidence that Neo-Assyrian had only a single labial stop, realized as either [*b*] or [*p*].[210] However, at least one possible minimal pair comes to mind: *battu* "side" vs. *pattu* "canal, ditch."[211] E.g.

(’pš) (a) *e-ba-še* MAss 67:10 ~ *e-pa-ši* SAA XVI 62:8, SAA X 277 r.11, SAA X 325 r.5′; *e-pa-a-še* SAA X 221:12; (a) *e-ta-ba-áš* SAA XIII 31:9; NL 8 r.15′ (CTN V 26ff)[212] ~ *e-ta-pa-áš* passim; (D) *ú-ba-šu-u-ni* SAA II 6:8A ~ *up-pa-áš-u*/*ú-ni* ibid. ms. G, F/T, *up-pa-šú-u-ni* ms. H

(d’p) (a) *i-da-’i-bi* Rfdn 17 28:9 ~ *i-di-i-pi* SAA XIII 27 r.19

(hpī) (a) *ha-bé-e* SAA II 6:294C ~ *ha-pe-e* SAA II 6:294A, B, H, NL 5:8′ (CTN V 25f)

(rdp) (a) *ir-ti-di-bi* SAA V 53:19 ~ *ni-ir-ti-di-pi* SAA I 175 r.31 (CTN V 167ff); *ar-ti-di-pi* GPA 207:3′ and (a) *ra-da-bi* (infinit. gen.) SAA V 47:13 ~ *ri-di-pi* (imperat. 2nd sg.) SAA V 53:18 (cf. *ir-ti-di-bi* above, by the same writer)

(*līpu*) (a) *le-bu* (*bu* = *pu*) / *a-na le-e-bi* SAA XVI 96 r.4-5 ~ *a-na li-pi-i-ka* SAA XIII 92:15

(*qēpu*) (a) LÚ.*qe-ba-a-ni* SAA XVI 96:14 ~ LÚ*.*qe-pa-a-ni* SAA X 352 r.9

---

207 Cf. Hämeen-Anttila (2000) 17.

208 Cf. n. 205.

209 LAS II 255 n. 457 lists examples of the alternation between *p* and *b*. See also Parpola (1988B) 79, especially n. 3 with examples (note that n. 3 is 4 and vice versa), Kaufman (1974) 137 and Hämeen-Anttila (2000) 15f.

210 See, e.g., Lipiński (1997) § 10.8, § 11.4.

211 Radner, (1997) 270 n. 1488 and (1999B) 120 n. 75, writes that the word *būlu* "cattle" does not occur in Neo-Assyrian, however, I cannot explain the following passages otherwise than *būlu* "cattle": *bu-*⸢*ú*⸣-[*l*]*um* NL 67 r.10 and *ša bu-li* SAA V 47:14. In any case, if the word *būlu* really existed in Neo-Assyrian, then it is noteworthy that it formed a minimal pair with the word *pūlu* "limestone".

212 CTN V 27 reads *e-ta-na-rab*, but probably means that the last sign was GAL (= *ráb*). However, I cannot find such a reading value in any Neo-Assyrian letter. According to the copy ibid. Pl. 3 (ND 2663), the sign looks like a good ÁŠ which has the two lowest horizontal strokes missing owing to the surface damage of the tablet. On the other hand, the difference between the variants of the BA and NA signs is often very slight.

More difficult and confusing to interpret are the forms in which <*p*> appears instead of the etymological <*b*>. E.g.

(btq) *i-pa-tu-qu* KAV 197 r.25 ~ *i-bat-tu-qu* SAA I 110:12, 14 (CTN V 219ff); *i-b[a]-tú-qu* SAA XV 90:25; *i-ba-ta-q[u-ni x x x* SAA XVI 67:11´; (D) *ú-pa-ti-qu-u-ni* SAA II 6:627G, K ~ *ú-bat-ti-qu(-u)-ni* ibid. ms. L, frg, *ú-bat-tú-qu-u-ni* ibid. ms. F

(*abiktu*)[213] *a-pi-ik-te* PN SAA XV 1:22 ~ *a-bi-ik-tú* SAA V 92:10

(*libānu*) *ina li-pa-*⌜*ni*⌝*-k[a]* "*On* your *expense*" SAA I 83 r.3´ ~ *l]i-ba-a-ni* SAA XIII 162 r.14

(*naglubu*) *nag-ga-la-pa-a-a* SAA IX 9:18

(rkb Š) *ú-sa-ar-ki-pi* SAA I 119:8

(*sbk D) ⌜*ú*⌝*-sa-pa-ak* SAA IX 2 i 11´[214]

Before drawing any conclusions on the grounds of these writings, interpreting them either phonetically or orthographically, it is good to bear in mind that <*p*> instead of the expected <*b*> is attested noticeably less than the other way round.

A rather special case in the alternation of *p* and *b* is the use of the BAR sign:

(špr) *a-šab-*BAR SAA V 46:12´ (near by Tidu) ~ *a-šap-par* ABL 879:15, ABL 1385 r.11
*a-sa-*BAR SAA V 21 r.15 (Tidu), SAA V 34:7, SAA V 37:29, r.5 (3 x Tušhan), CT 53 819:6´ (unkn.); *[a-s]a-b*⌜*a*⌝*r* SAA I 148 r.2´ (unkn.) ~ *a-sa-par* passim
*a-sa-*BAR*-a-ka* StAT 1 51 r.11 (Assur); *a-sa-bar-ka* GPA 206:3´ (unkn.)
*a-sa-*BAR*-áš-šú* SAA V 32 r.5 (Tušhan)
*a-sa-*BAR*-šú-nu* SAA V 32:10 (Tušhan)
*i-sa-*BAR SAA V 31 r.24´, SAA V 33 r.17e, SAA V 37:20 (all: Tušhan) ~ *i-sa-par* passim
*a-sa-ta-*BAR SAA XV 151:15 (Šabirešu) ~ *a-sa-ta-par* SAA I 241 r.8

(*paršumu*) LÚ.BAR*-šá-mu-tu* NL 100:9 (Mazamua) (CTN V 118f) ~ LÚ.*par-šá/ša-mu-te* SAA II 5 iii 7/SAA X 226:16

(*siparru*) *si-*BAR*-ri* SAA I 191 r.7 (Harran) ~ *si-par-ri* SAA I 246 r.5´; *si-pa-ri* SAA V 35:28

(*ṣupru*) *ṣu-*BAR*-šú* SAA VI 1:1, SAA VI 7:1, SAA VI 289:1 (1. Nadî, Calah, 2. unkn., Calah, 3. Ṭab-šar-Nabû, Nineveh); *ṣu-*BAR*-šú-nu* SAA VI 100:2 (Nabû-ahhe-eriba, Nineveh) cf. *ṣu-pur-šú(-nu)* SAA VI passim

It may be a question of geography (note that in the examples above, the frequency of attestations from Tidu and Tušhan is conspicuous; the fortress town, Tidu, and the provincial capital, Tušhan, were situated very close to each other) or an otherwise explainable orthographic variation <*bar*> = /*par*/. Nevertheless, I consider voicing (**p* > *b*) to be a more probable alternative, cf. e.g.

a-sa-ba-ra-š[u] TH 4:6 (considerably older than the other examples, ca. 800 BCE)

---

[213] Cf. n. ad SAA IX 2 i 11.

[214] See n. ad SAA IX 2 i 11.

4.1.2 Nasals[215]

Intervocalic /*m*/ may alternate with /'/ or disappear totally. In the latter case, the two adjacent vowels, which were originally of a different colour, can be monophthongized into a single long vowel.[216] [*w*] can function as an allophone of /*m*/ in Neo-Assyrian.[217]

Examples of the alternation of *m*, ' and Ø are the following:

(*ahāiš*, note <*he* = *hi*>) *a-ha-meš* SAA II 6:156EH, SAA VIII 136:4 (Nabû'a, Assur), NL 79 r.3 (CTN V 178f) (unkn./*from the northwest*), *a-h*]*a-meš* SAA XIII 66 r.12′ (Calah, Urdu-Nabû); ⸢*a*⸣*-ha-mì-iš* SAA X 63:7 (Balasî) ~ *a-ha-a-a-iš* NL 65:6 (CTN V 45f); *a-ha-ii-ši* SAA XV 101:14; *a-ha-iš* SAA II 2 v 23′, SAA I 54 r.3, SAA V 3 r.16, SAA V 286:5′, SAA XIII 50:8′; *a-he-ii-ši* SAA V 227 r.14; *a-he-'i-*[*iš*] SAA X 252 r.14′; *a-he-iš* SAA II 6:156AP and passim; *ina* ŠÀ *a-hi-ši* SAA I 172:12 (CTN V 173ff)

(*damiq*, <*iq* = *eq*>)[218] *de-iq* SAA X 217 r.2, BM 103390:8; *de-e-iq* SAA XVI 34:7; *de-'i-iq* SAA X 241 r.5, SAA X 242 r.7; *de-e-qe* SAA XVI 3 r.2, SAA XV 4 r.9; *de-ii-qi* SAA XIII 60:14, SAA X 325 r.1; (*damiqtu*) *de-iq-tú/u* SAA II 6:108E/SAA X 227 r.1, 4

(**dimtu*) *di-ia-ti-ia* (pl.) SAA XIII 158 r.10′; *di-at* (pl.) TH 5:5

Seldom between a vowel and a sibilant:

(*maṣû* Š) *ú-šá-ṣu-u* SAA XV 27:8 ~ *ú-šá-an-ṣu-u* SAA X 14 r.5

(*ṭēmu*) *ṭè-šu-*[*nu*] SAA I 183:10′; *ṭè*]*-e-šú* SAA II 4 r.19′ ~ *ṭè-en-šú-nu* passim; *ṭè-en-šu/ú* SAA X 191 r.4, SAA XV 113:8/SAA I 177 r.15

For examples of complete and partial assimilation of *m*, see 4.2.1-4.2.3.

Intervocalic [*n*] correspondingly changes to '/Ø, at least in the verb *danānu* > *da'ānu*:[219]

da-an (stat 3rd sg.) SAA X 222:15, SAA XIII 38 r.2; *da-a-na* SAA I 147:15; SAA XV 60:12; *da-a'-na* SAA V 200:10; NL 100:7 (CTN V 118f)

4.1.3 Variation between sibilants

In Neo-Assyrian, written *s* was pronounced as [*š*] and written *š* as [*s*]. In other words, <*s*> = [*š*], <*š*> = [*s*].[220] Evidence for this alternation comes predominately from loanwords in Neo-Assyrian and, on the other hand, from Neo-Assyrian

---

[215] On the rare (but still possible) nasalization in Neo-Assyrian, see Deller (1985-1986) 48.

[216] Cf. e.g. Lipiński (1997) § 11.8 and Hämeen-Anttila (2000) 24.

[217] According to ibid. 11, [*w*] is not the allophone of *m*. However, see e.g. nn. 170 and 230.

[218] For the possible progression of the word within Neo-Assyrian up to the potential form *ahêš*/*ahîš*, see Deller (1965B) 76 n. 1. Cf. also 5.7.

[219] E.g. Lipiński (1997) § 17.2.

[220] Kaufman (1974) 140-41 and Parpola (1974) 2 and 4 n. 13.

words in other languages.[221] Because of this, I only list some examples which occur in Neo-Assyrian letters and thus in a Neo-Assyrian context. Nevertheless, the orthographies deviating from the standard Neo-Assyrian practice as far as the sibilants *s* and *š* are concerned point to Babylonian or at least to a Babylonian orthographic influence.[222] E.g.

(*arāšu*) *a-na a-ra-si* SAA XV 136:14 (Lahiru)
(*balāt* + *-šunu*) *ba-la-tu-us-šú-nu* SAA X 349 r.1 (Akkad)
(*bīt salā' mê*) É–*šá-la–me-e* SAA X 352:18 (Akkad) ~ É–*sa-la–me-e*[223] SAA X 219:11
(*epāšu*) *e-pa-sa-an-ni* SAA XV 115 r.6′ (Der); *e-ep-sa-at* SAA XV 125:4′, *ep-sa-*[*at*] ibid.l. 7′ (Der); *e*[*p*]*-sa-tu-ni* SAA XVI 127:14 (Phoenicia); *e-pu-su-nu*/*e-pu-su-su-nu* SAA XVI 126 r.18′/21′; *ep-pa-su-nu* ibid. r.23′ (Phoenicia); *e-pu-sa-ak-ki* (prs, Babylonian verb conjugation) SAA X 273:18 (Nabû-nadin-šumi quoting Šumaia)
(*esāku* D) *ú-tu-uš-si-ku* SAA X 348 r.8 (Akkad)
(*issi*) *i-še-e-a* SAA XV 17:7 (Arrapha)
(*kikkisu*) *ki-ik-ki-si* SAA X 210:8 (Nineveh) ~ Babylonian *kikkišu*[224]
(*laššu*) *la-a-si* SAA XV 17:8 (Arrapha)
(*nammušu*) [*l*]*a ú-na-me-sa* SAA XV 114:10 (Der)
(*paristu*) *pa-ri-iš-tú* SAA XV 173:1′ (Babylonia)
(*sahāru*) *iš-hu-ra-an-ni* SAA XV 118 e.21′ (Der)
(*sissiktu*) TÚG.*ši-ši-ik-ti-šú* (Nabû-naṣir, Nineveh) SAA X 298:17 ~ Babylonian *sissiktu*[225]
(*šapal*) *ina sa-pal* SAA XVI 126:18, SAA XVI 127:12 (Phoenicia)
(*šapāru*) *li-is-pu-ru* SAA XV 17:9, [*li*]*-*⸢*is*⸣*-pu-ru* ibid. r.4 (Arrapha); *as-pur-*⸢*an*⸣*-*[*ni* SAA XVI 129 e.16′; *ni-is-pur-an-ni* ibid. r.6 (Phoenicia)
(Šapiku PN) ^{m}*sa-pi-ku* SAA XV 199:1, r.16 (Darati) ~ ^{m}*šá-pi-ku* SAA VIII 491 r.13, SAA VIII 492 r.1, SAA VIII 493 r.6, SAA VIII 494 r.3, SAA VIII 496 r.1, SAA VIII 497 r.2′
(*šaṭāru*) *sa-ṭir-*[*u-ni*] SAA X 347 r.4′ (Akkad)
(Šumāia/Šumâ PN) ^{m}*su-ma-a-a* SAA X 291 r.1 (Nineveh) ~ ^{m}*šu-ma-a* SAA X 257 r.7, SAA X 273:13, SAA X 371:16
(*šumma*) *a–su-mu* SAA XV 17:10, e.12 (Arrapha)
(*ubālu* Š) *ú-še-bi-la-áš-šú* (pf /*š* + *t*/ > <*ss*>) SAA XV 301:5′, SAA XV 161 r.12′ (Babylonia)
(*ušābu* Š) *uš-še-si-i*[*b-šú-nu*] (pf) SAA XV 232:8 (Babylon)

For alternation of /*z*/ and /*s*/:[226]

(*i/uzuzzu*) in plural forms in which <*s*> or even <*ss*> is between <*ti*(*-i*)> and the vowel <*u*> or <*a*>: *i-ti-ti-su* SAA V 104:8, CT 53 230:11; [*i-t*]*i-ti-is-s*[*u* SAA V 196:12; *it-ti-ti-is-su* SAA XVI 34 r.14 ; *it-ti-ti-su* SAA X 289

[221] For examples of both of these groups, see Parpola (1974) 4 nn. 11-13.

[222] See Parpola (1997A), especially 318 n. 10 (from which most of my examples come), and Deller (1959) § 46h.

[223] See AHw 1014-15 *salā'u*(*m*).

[224] See AHw 475 A.

[225] Ibid. 1050-51.

[226] See Deller (1959) § 46j.

r.17′, SAA XIII 140:13 (all pf 3rd pl.); *i-ti-sa* SAA XV 90 r.10; [*i-ti-s*]*a* ibid. r.2; *i-ti-is-sa* ABL 543:7, ABL 561 r.15 (all imperat. 2nd pl.); as exceptions to the preceding forms: *it-t*[*i*]*-it-su* (pf 3rd pl.) SAA V 11 e.9; *i-zi-su-u-ni* (prt 3rd pl.) SAA XVI 62 r.7′

(*mazzāz pāni*) LÚ.*ma-za-si–pa-ni* SAA X 199 r.8′ ~ LÚ.*man-za-za–pa-ni* (Babyl.) SAA XVI 128 r.2′, SAA XVI 127 r.7; LÚ.*ma*]*-za-az–pa-nu-te* SAA XVI 91:5′; LÚ*.*ma-za-az–pa-ni-*⸢*šú*⸣ SAA I 12 s.3. Or does the word in the first example stand for the feminine noun *mazzassu*?

(zkr > sqr) [*li-i*]*s-qur* SAA X 285 r.1′; *is-qur-u-ni* SAA X 218:9 ~ e.g. *iz-kur-u-ni* SAAB 1 66:5, 11, SAA XVI 61:4

(*zibbutu*) *šá si-bat / né-ši* SAA XIII 45 r.3-4; *šá si-bat še-li-bi* ibid. r.5 ~ *zi-ba-te* SAA V 90 r.4

The examples in which *s* (i.e. in normal conditions [*š*]) was written instead of *z*, suggest the existence of an allophone [*ž*].[227] The following forms speak in favour of this interpretation, since they attest the variation, however, the other way round:

> Neo-Assyrian *siqqurrutu* vs. apparent Babylonianisms: *ziq-qur-rat* SAA XIII 161:13′; *ziq-qur-r*[*a-te*] SAA XVI 93 r.1, as well as (*sakru*) *zag-ru* SAA V 294 r.1

On the voiced allophone [*z*] of <*š*> = [*s*], see Hämeen-Anttila (2000) 10.

4.2 Consonantal assimilations

Consonantal assimilations are lexically restricted.

4.2.1 Complete regressive assimilation[228]

' + *l* > [*ll*] (š'l) *i-sa-al-lu* SAA XV 101:10 ~ *is-s*]*a-a'-lu-šú* SAA I 71:8; *i-sa-a'-lu-šú* SAA I 194 r.2

' + <*š*> > <*šš*> = [*ss*][229] (kl' + suff.) *kil-áš-šú* SAA XV 85:7

d + *n* > [*nn*] A special case (tdn) pf: *attanna* and *ittann*|*a*/*u* (> when pf + vent./pl. morpheme/suff.) passim

l + *k* > [*kk*] See n. 438.

l + <*š*> > [*ss*] (*šalšu*) *i–ša-šu-me* NL 74:5 (CTN V 132ff); *i–šá-šu-me* SAA XVI 216:9′, SAA I 99 r.3′; *iš–šá-šú-me* SAA XIII 137:7′; *šá-šu-ú-*⸢*me*⸣ NL 102 r.11 (CTN V 207f); *šá-šu-me* SAA I 177 r.8; *a–šá-šu-me* SAA XVI 173:3′ ~ *ina* ⸢*ša*⸣*-al-š*[*i* U]D*-me* SAA I 233:21; *ina šal-še*–U[D*-me*] SAA X 267:5

m + *'* > [*'*] (šm') *i-sa-ú*[230] (pf 3rd pl.) SAA X 228:12; *is-sa-ú* ibid. l.14; *i-sa-'u-šú* SAA XV 51:6′; *a-se-'*[*e-e*] SAA XIII 22 r.1 ~ *as/a/is-se-me* passim

---

[227] See Hämeen-Anttila (2000) 10.

[228] See Deller (1959) § 41 and Parpola (1984) 196 and 206f n. 39. By regressive assimilation, I refer here to the direction of an assimilatory process within a word that goes from the end to the beginning of a word (<). Correspondingly, the direction of progressive assimilation goes from the beginning of a word towards the end (>).

[229] See 4.1.3.

m + *h* > [*hh*] (mhr) *i-hu-ru-ni* NL 24:5 (CTN V 196f); *i-hu-ur* SAA I 237:5´;⌜*ih*⌝*-ha-ru-ni* ibid. r.15; *ih-har-u-ni* SAA XV 7:6, SAA XV 15 r.2´; *a-hu-ru-u-ni* SAA V 43:5, SAA V 260 r.6´; *a-hur-u-ni* SAA XVI 30:4; *a-hur* SAA I 183 r.6; *ah-hur* SAA XV 24:11; *li-hu-ru* ABL 75 r.4 (LAS 37); *li-ih-hu-ru* SAA X 198:15; (mhṣ) *i-ha-ṣu-u-ni* ND 3443:4 (Iraq 15 pl. 12); *na-hi-ṣi* NL 99 r.21´ (CTN V 109ff) ~ (mhṣ and mhr [with their derivatives]) *lim-ha-ṣu-ku-nu* SAA II 6:474D; *mu-šam-hi-iṣ-ṣu-u* SAA XVI 204 r.10; *šam-hi-ṣa* SAA II 6:342frg; *tu-šam-ha-ṣa-a-ni* SAA II 6:326C, c; *šam-hír* SAA X 212 r.13; ⌜*ú*⌝*-šam-hír-u-ni* ABL 1022:11; *tu-šam-hir-a-ni* BM 132980:3

m + *p* > [*pp*] *šelappāiu* passim, see p. 137.

m + *q* > [*qq*] (mqt) *l*[*u t*]*a-qut* SAA X 50 r.12 cf. *in-qu-ta* ABL 1121:7; *in-qut-u-ni* SAA V 227 s.4, see 4.2.3

m + *š* > [*ss*] (*ṭēmu*) *ṭè-šu-*[*nu*] SAA I 183:10´; *ṭè*]*-e-šú* SAA II 4 r.19´ ~ partial assimilations *ṭè-en-šú/šu*(*-nu*) passim

m + *ṣ* > [*ṣṣ*] (mṣ') *ú-šá-ṣu-u* SAA XV 61:8 ~ partial assimilation *ú-šá-an-ṣu-u* SAA X 14 r.5

m + *t* > [*tt*] (mth) *ni-ta-ta-ah* SAA X 361 r.15; *a-ta-ta-ha* NL 41 r.3 (CTN V 208ff); [*a*]*t-ta-at-ha* SAA I 58:10, SAA V 253:8´; (mqt) *i-tú-uq-tu* SAA V 227 r.19; *i-tú-qut* GPA 193 r.2; *at-tu-uq-ta* ABL 390 r.5´; *i-tuq-tu-u-ni* SAA V 202:7, SAA XVI 148 r.20e; (mhr) *i-tah-ru* SAA I 118 r.4´; *i-ta-ah-ru-šu* SAA V 35:26; *i-ta-har-šu* SAA V 149:16; *it/at/a-ta-har* passim; (*taklimtu*) *tak-li-ta-šú-nu* SAA X 352:14 ~ (mhr) *am-ta-ha-ár* NL 64 r.4 (CTN V 290ff); (mlk) *tam-ti-lik* ABL 1264:3´; (mth) *li-im-tu-*[*hu* SAA XVI 59:10; *la-am-tu-u*[*h*] NL 25 r.12e (CTN V 281ff); (mtq) *li-im-ti-iq* SAA II 6:569frg

n[231] + *b* > [*bb*] *nabalkutu* prs and prt; (bšī N); (nbī)

n + *h* > [*hh*] (hkm N); (hrd N); (hss N)

n + *k* > [*kk*] (kṣr N); (nks) prt; (kl' N); (krk N); (krr N)

n + *l* > [*ll*] (lbš N)

n + *m* > [*mm*] *namarkû*; (mgr N); (mhṣ N); (mlk N)

n + *p* > [*pp*] (pṭr N); (nph) prt/k; *naparkû*; (pršd N); (npl N); (pšr N); (pšš N)

n + *q* > [*qq*] (nqī); once (*unqu*) *ú-qu* GPA 199:4 ~ *unqu/i* passim

n + *r* > [*rr*] (rdī N); (rks N)

n + *s* > [*ss*] (nsh) (*l*)*issuh* passim; (spn N) *i-sap-pan* SAA IX 8 r.1

n + *ṣ* > [*ṣṣ*] (nṣr) (*l*)*iṣṣur* passim

n + *š* > [*ss*] (šṭr N); (nšq) *liš-šiq* SAA X 44 r.7´; (nšr) (*l*)*iššur*; (škn N); (šmī N); (šrp N); (nš') (*l*)*išši* passim

n + *t* > [*tt*] This is regular in the perfect forms of verbs (*n* + *t*-infix): (nš') *ittiši* passim, (nṣr) *ittaṣar* passim; in the noun *tidintu* as an exception, at least once: *ti-di-ti-ka* SAA I 183 r.8 ~ *ti-din-tu* SAA XVI 42:12; *tidintu* SAA II 6 passim. A completely unexpected spelling of *maddattu* is *ma-da-a'-tú* ND 2711:13, 15, 17, 18 and LÚ*.GAL–*ma-da-a'-ti* ibid. r.10 (*n [of tdn] > ') ~ *maddattu* passim.

---

[230] Possibly [*iššawwu*]. In that case, the original *m* would have been fricativized, see Parpola (1974) 3 n. 10. Note that *m* > ' > Ø is only realized in the intervocalic position, see LAS II 321 n. 590 and 4.1.2.

[231] All assimilations of *n* in verb forms are regular and, by nature, morphophonological. For a medial *n* and *n* before the feminine ending *-t* in nouns, cf. Hämeen-Anttila (2000) 20.

n + ṭ > [*ṭṭ*] (nṭū/') *li-ṭu-šú* SAA V 142 r.9

n + z > [*zz*] (zkr N); (*man/zzāzu, man/zzassu*) see Deller (1959) § 41m. [*zz*] is probably lexicalized(?), however *man-za-su* SAA VIII 107 r.2 (Akkullanu), [*ma*]*n-za-az* É.GAL SAA X 7:10 (Issar-šumu-ereš); *man-za-as-su* SAA VIII 70:4 (Nabû-ahhe-eriba), cf. also 4.1.3. Certainly these dissimilative <*nz*> examples by scholars are a result of a Babylonian influence.

p + m > [*mm*] *a-hu-lam-ma* SAA X 33 r.11 and Ahulamma PNA 1/I p. 80 (< *ahulap* + *-ma*)[232]

r + d > [*dd*] (*mardītu*) *ma-di-tú* SAA V 164 r.4 ~ *mar-di-tú* SAA V 117:14, SAA I 172 r.31 (CTN V 173ff)

r + s > [*ss*] (*šaršīru/šaršuru*) É–*šá-ši-ri* GPA 25:3[233]

r + t > [*tt*] (Zikirtu) KUR.*zi-ki-ti-a* SAA V 164:15 cf. KUR.*zi-ki-ra-a-a* ibid. l.6 ~ KUR.*zi-kir-ta-a-a* SAA V 45 r.6′; (*takpirtu*) *tak-pi-ti* SAA X 69 r.5 ~ *tak-pi-ir-ti* SAA X 279:6; *tak-pir-tu* ibid. l.8

t + q > [*qq*] (btq) *ib-ta-qu-ni* VAT 8699 r.3 ~ *ib-ta-at-qa* SAA X 294 r.21

4.2.2 Complete progressive assimilation[234]

b + ' > [*bb*] (tb') *it-ta-ab-bu* SAA I 240:14′, SAA XV 88:12; *it-tab-bu* SAA I 244 r.8; (šb') *is-sab-bu*[235] SAA X 226 r.1; (rab'u) *ra-ab-bi*[236] ("fourth") SAA X 68 r.3 (as a gloss)

d + ' > [*dd*] (d'p) *id-dip-u-ni* SAA X 21 r.10′

n + '/0 [*nn*][237] (*ina + irtu*) *in*$_{6}$–*ni-ir-ti-iá* SAA V 224:9, r.16; *in*$_{6}$–*ni-ir-ti-i-k*[*a*] ibid. r.8; *in*$_{6}$–*ni-i*[*r-ti-iá*] ibid. r.3; *in*$_{6}$–*ni-ri-te* SAA V 164 r.9 ~ *ina ir-ti* passim

r + t > [*rr*] (rgm) *ta-ru-gu-u*[*m*] /*tartugum*/ SAA XIII 144 r.7 (Nabû-reši-išši, Arbela)

s + t-infix of the perfect > <*ss*> > [*šš*], *issuhur* passim

ṣ + t-infix of the perfect > [*ṣṣ*], *iṣṣabat* passim

š + ' > [*ss*] (nš')[238] *naṣa*, *ittaṣu* and *iṣa* passim; (š'l) *liš-šá-al-šú* SAA XIII 128 r.19 ~ *liš-al-šú* passim; *liš-'a-al-šú* NL 81 r.8 (CTN V 232f)

ṭ + ' > [*ṭṭ*] (hṭ') *ih-ti-iṭ-ṭu-ú-nik-ka* ABL 879:4 (Umman-aldaš)

ṭ + t-infix of the perfect > [*ṭṭ*], *uṭ-ṭa-bi-hi* SAA XV 168:13′; *iṭ-ṭu-bu* SAA XIII 45 r.5

z + t-infix of the perfect > [*zz*], *iz-za-kar* SAA X 226:7; *iz-zak-ru* SAA X 364 r.6; *az-zu-ku* SAA X 29:2; *iz-zu-qu-pu* SAA V 45 r.7′; *iz-za-qáp* SAA X 227 r.25

---

232 See LAS II ad no. 15 r.11.

233 Postgate (1973) 60 n. 5.

234 These examples are mainly taken from Parpola (1984) 207. See also Hämeen-Anttila (2000) 13 for the assimilation of 'hamza'.

235 Deller (1967) 189.

236 LAS II ad no. 59 r.3f.

237 Cf. 4.10 and 4.11.

238 See Parpola (1974) 1-2 and examples pp. 6-9.

As a counterbalance to the assimilated forms of the aleph, cf. the non-assimilated aleph-forms. In these verbs, aleph has been lexicalized:

(hs') *i[h]-ta-sa-'u* SAA I 179:16, *ih-ta-as-'u* SAA I 240:9′, *[ih]-ta-sa-'u-šu* SAA XVI 76 r.3
(kl') *ik-ta-al-'u* SAA XIII 166:17
(mš')[239] *in-taš-'a* SAA I 244 r.7, *in-ta-áš-'a* SAA XIII 154:13, r.1

4.2.3 Partial assimilation[240]

Cf. n. 25.

d + *t*-infix of the perfect > [*dd*], *iddubub* passim
g + *t* > [*gd*][241] Regular: the perfect forms of the G/D-stems of verbs with *g* as their first root consonant, e.g. gmr (also Dtt-forms), gr', etc. Exception(s): *ig-ta-al-du* SAA V 202 r.8, *ig-tal-du* NL 105 r.8 (CTN V 223f)[242]
m + *d* > [*nd*] (mdd) *la-an-du-du* StAT 1 53 r.4; (*ṣimdu*) *ṣi-in-di* SAA X 335:4′; (*umdu*) *un-di* SAA X 318:8, r.12e
m + *g* > [*ng*] (*ušumgallu*) *šu-un-gal-li* SAA XIII 134:12′
m + *h* > [*nh*] (mhṣ N/Š) *at-ta-an-ha-aṣ* NL 72:5 (CTN V 246ff); *šá-an-hi-ṣa* SAA II 6:342F, frg ~ *šam-hi-ṣa* ibid. ms. frg; (mhr Š) *ú-sa-an-hi-ri* SAA XV 125:6′ ~ *tu-šam-hir-a-ni* BM 132980:3
m + *k* > [*nk*] (*ṭēmu*) *ṭe-en-ka* ABL 896 s.1 (Aia-zeru-qiša); (*šumu*) *šu-un-ku-nu* ABL 561:14′, r.13 (Assurbanipal); *rimku* > *rinku*. Cf. also CVC-signs of which interpretation, however, places restrictions: (*samku*) *sam-ku-u-te* ABL 1002 r.11 (Assurbanipal); (klm D) *ú-kal-lam-ka* SAA XVI 65 r.13′; (*šulmu*) *šu-lam-ka* SAA IX 2 ii 27′, StAT 2 248:9; (šlm D) *lu-šá-lim-ka* CTN III 1 e.10
m + *q* > [*nq*] (dmq) *da-an-qu* passim ~ *dam-qu* (ambiguous CVC-sign) passim; (mqt) prt *inqut* passim ~ *im-qu-ta-a-ni* SAA I 137:4; (Š) ⸢*lu*⸣-*šam-qit-[ku-nu]* (CVC-sign) SAA II 6:425c
m + *ṣ* > [*nṣ*] (mṣ' Š) *ú-šá-an-ṣu-u* SAA X 14 r.5; *nu-ša-an-ṣa* SAA V 295 r.21, SAA X 255:8; *ú-šá-an-ṣi* SAA X 96:8 ~ *ú-šá-am-ṣ[i]* SAA I 152:14
m + *š* > [*nš*] (*ṭēmu*) see 4.1.2; (*hamšu*) *ha-an-ši* SAA XIII 157 r.6; (*šumu*) *šu-un-šú-nu* SAA X 182 r.25; *šu-*⸢*un*⸣*-šú* NL 45:9 (CTN V 136ff); (*šulmu*) *šu-la-an-šu/ú* SAA XIII 158:9′/SAA X 320 r.12 ~ *šu-lam-šú* SAA XVI 122:6′; *šu-lam-ka* SAA IX 2 ii 27′, StAT 2 248:9
m + *t* > [*nt*] e.g. (mth) *in-ta-at-ha* SAA X 218:7, SAA XIII 157 r.1; *li-in-tu-hu* SAA I 118 r.12, NL 34 r.10′ (CTN V 266f); *la-an-tú-hu* ABL 390 r.18′ (Bel-iqiša); *la-an-tuh* ABL 896:11 (Aia-zeru-qiša) ~ *li-im-tu-[hu* SAA XVI 59:10; *la-am-tu-u[h]* NL 25 r.12e (CTN V 281ff); (mṭ' G/D) *in-ṭí-ú* SAA I 100 r.11; *un-ta-aṭ-ṭi* SAA X 294 r.32; *un-*⸢*ta-ṭí*⸣ SAA I 176:14 (CTN V 169ff); (m'd) *in-ta-a'-da* SAA V 260:12′; (ms') *an-te-se* SAA XVI 242 r.7′; (mš') *an-ti-ši-i* SAA X 39 r.11

[239] The aleph is firm in this verb, see GAG § 99c.

[240] Deller (1959) § 40a-d.

[241] Ylvisaker (1912) 7-8 § 2b and Deller (1959) § 42b.

[242] See n. 192 above.

m + *ṭ* > [*nṭ*] (**humṭu*) *hu-un-ṭu* SAA X 328:17; (mṭī) *in-ṭí-ú* SAA I 100 r.11; see also *ham/nṭu* SAA II 6:458

q + *t* > [*qṭ*][243] Regular in the perfect forms of verbs of which the first root consonant is *q*. Exceptions: (qbī) *ni-iq-te-bi* SAA XVI 97 r.10 (Assur); *iq-ti-bi-i* SAA XV 129 r.11; *aq-ti-bi* ibid. r. 32; *aq-ti-ba-áš-⸢šú⸣-nu* SAA XV 120 r.8 (all from Der). Also *iq-t*[*i-bu-u-ni*] ABL 1116:15′ (unkn.) but cf. ibid. l.13′; *iq-t⸢i⸣-bu* ND 2757:11 (CTN V 202f, Bel-abu'a). This assimilation does not have an effect on verbs in which *q* and *t* (*t* as a radical) are in contact with one another: (btq) *bat-taq-ti-ni* (stat) VAT 9875:11; (mqt often) e.g. *i-tuq-tu-u-ni* SAA V 202:7, SAA XVI 148 r.20e; *it-tuq-ta* SAA XV 95:5′; *at-tu-uq-ta* ABL 390 r.5′, etc. The assimilation is neither realized in feminine nouns and adjectives (e.g. *batiqtu*, *de'iqtu*, *maqtu*), nor in the adverb *piqtatti*.

4.2.4 Other assimilations

Reciprocal consonantal assimilations:

Possible Aramaic influence *l* + [*š*] > [*ś*][244] or [*šš*]. *–bé-|su-nu/sún /bēlšunu/* passim in personal names

l + *t* > <*ss*>[245] > [*šš*]. A regular assimilation. Exceptions in the perfect forms of the I-weak verbs: (lbī) [*i*]*l-ti-bi-ú-šu* SAA V 93:4′; *il-ti-⸢bi⸣-i* SAA XV 118:3′; (lpt) *il-ta-pat-su* SAA X 238:11 *il-ta-pat* SAA X 351:17; *ul-tap-pi-it* SAA X 347 r.12′; (lsm) *al-tu-s*[*um*] SAA X 260 r.2; (ltk) *lil-tuk* SAA X 182 r.29; *tal-tu-ku-ni* ND 2786:9 (CTN V 95); *al-tu-ku-ni* ibid. l. 13; (lūd) *al-tu-u-da* SAA XVI 63 r.30. Exceptional nouns are, for example, *akiltu* SAA XVI 183 r.12′, NL 71 e.15 (CTN V 312f), *i/ekeltu* SAA XVI 29:5, *kinaltu* NL 54:3 (CTN V 13f), *maqaltānu* (note that *-lt-* is not a feminine ending in the example) SAA XVI 63 r.10, *napšaltu* SAA X passim, *ṣaltu* TH 106:5, *šiltāhu* (cf. *maqaltānu*) SAA X 174:21, SAA II 6:425B, *tallultu*, *tēltu* SAA X 37:4′, CT 53 826:7′, *tukultu* SAA X 294 r.30, *u'iltu* SAA X 75 r.4, SAA X 76:7, SAA X 100 r.6, SAA X 182 r.30. In the plural and singular status constructus forms of nouns with *-lt-* ending, the *-lt-* combination breaks: (*hibiltu*) *hi-bi-la-te/hi-bil-a-te* passim; *nap-šal-a-ti* SAA X 328:8; *ú-ìl-a-ti* SAA X 76:12; (*bēltu*) *be-lit* passim. It is probable that after removing all the Babylonianisms and lexical restrictions from the exceptions above, few forms would be left.

ṣ + *š* (of suff.) > <*ss*> > [*šš*]. (mhṣ) *it-ta-ha-su* SAA XVI 149:3′; (mrṣ Š) *ša-am-ri-su* SAA I 18 r.9′; (*murṣu*) *mu-ru-us-su* SAA X 242 r.6

š + *š* > <*ss*> > [*šš*]. (lbš D) *ú-sa-bi-is-su* (pf + suff.) SAA I 29 r.21; *ú-sa-bi-su* SAA XV 91 r.2; [*ú-sa-b*]*i-su-nu* SAA XV 90:26; (*rēšu*) (+suff.) <*rēssu*(*nu*)> passim

š + *d* > may be <*ld*> presumably a Babylonian influence: (kšd) *ak-tal-da* SAA XV 32:10. Note the preserved <*šd*>: (*išdu*) *iš-di* SAA X 182 r.17, SAA X 294:11; (kšd) *ka-áš-du* SAA X 353:14, NL 65:11(CTN V 45f); *kaš-du-*

---

[243] When an emphatic consonant is in contact with the *t*-infix of the perfect, cf. Lipiński (1997) § 27.7. See also Ylvisaker (1912) 7 § 2a.

[244] See Hämeen-Anttila (2000) 10.

[245] See Deller (1959) § 43a-b.

tú CT 53 609:3′; (šdd) *l/nišdu/ad* passim; *iš-da-du-ni-ni* SAA XV 60:14. However, cf. also *-ld-* writings: (*balāt*, *l* + *tu*>) *a–bal-duk-ka* SAA XV 241:9; (gld) *ig-ta-al-du* SAA V 202 r.8; *ig-dal-du* NL 105 r.8 (CTN V 223f);[246] (*Kaldu*) KUR.*kal-di* SAA X 351 e.23; LÚ.*k*[*à*]*l-da-a-a* NL 1:9 (CTN V 19ff); LÚ*.*kal-da-a-a* SAA V 79 r.2, SAA V 80 r.3′, SAA V 172:5; KUR.*kal-da-a-*[*a* SAA V 14 r.4′; KUR.*kal-dà-a-a* SAA V 59:5 and passim

š + *t* > <*ss*>[247] > [*šš*]. Regular. The written <*št*>-exceptions can be explained mainly as Babylonianisms and foreign proper names.[248]

d, *t* + the <*š*>-suffix of the third person sg. and pl. > [*šš*]. Nevertheless, these kind of phonetic complete assimilations are often realized in writing as partial assimilations.[249] In Neo-Assyrian writings, three different models appear:

d: (1) (pqd) *ap-ti-qid-su* SAA I 12 r.1; *ip-ti-qid-su* SAA X 97:8′; (kšd Š) *lu-šak-šid-su* ABL 896 r.5

(2) rare: (pqd) [*ap-t*]*i-qid-šu-nu* SAA I 39:19′; (prd Š) *ú/tu*]*-šap-rad-šú-nu* ABL 1127 r.6

(3) (ʼmd) *e-ti-mì-si-na-ma* SAA V 295 r.4; *e-te-mì-is-su* SAA VI 265:5; *e-te-me-su-nu* TH 110:4′; (kšd) *tak-ta-šá-su-nu* SAA X 316 r.4; *ik-ta-šá-su* NL 47:7 (CTN V 119f); (pqd) *ap-ti-qi-su* SAA V 122 r.12, NL 14 r.5 (CTN V 160f), SAA I 236:4′; *ip-ti-qi-su* SAA X 96 r.16

t: (1) rather common, e.g. (*abutu*) *a-bat-su* passim; (ṣbt) *iṣ-ṣa-bat-su* SAA X 239:2′; *li-iṣ-bat-su* SAA X 226 r.20; (lpt) *il-ta-pat-su* SAA X 238:11

(2) rare: (ṣbt N/Š) *iṣ-ṣab-bi-it-šú-nu-ni* ND 2657:5 (Iraq 23 42 and pl. 22); *tu-šá-aṣ-bat-šá-*⸢*nu*⸣*-ni* SAA XVI 11:6′; (blkt Š) *nu-ú-šá-bal-*[*k*]*àt-šú* SAA I 103 r.9

(3) (*anūtu*) *a-nu-su* SAA X 387 r.2; (*bētu*) *bé-su-n*[*u*] GPA 199:11; (*dannutu*) *dan-na-*⸢*su*⸣ KAV 197 r.22; (*eṣidītu*) *e-ṣi-di-su-nu* NL 25 e.12 (CTN V 281ff); (*middutu*) *mi-da-as-su* SAA I 210 e.17; (*pānāt*) *pa-na-su-nu* SAA I 226 r.10; *pa-na-as-su* SAA X 29 r.10; (*qanītu*) *qa-ni-is-sa* SAA XIII 130:15; (*qinītu*) *qi-ni-s*[*u* SAA XV 246:2′; *qi-né-e-su* SAA XV 297 r.2; (*rēʼûtu*) *re-ʼu-us-si-na* SAA X 198:8, *re-ʼu-u-s*[*i-na* SAA I 134:7; (ṣbt G/Š) ⸢*i*⸣*-ṣa-ba-s*[*u-nu*] SAA V 116:6′; *lu-šá-aṣ-bi-su-nu* NL 22 r.4 (CTN V 180f); *šá-aṣ-bi-su-nu* NL 25:9 (CTN V 281ff)

Concerning *ṭ*, I know only one example:

(blṭ D): *ub-tal-li-su* SAA X 226:22

---

[246] See n. 192 above.

[247] Deller (1959) § 43c-e.

[248] See ibid. § 43e.

[249] Cf. Gelb (1970A) 74.

4.2.5 Loss of a final consonant[250]

This is only attested in the adverb *annurig*:

> *an-nu-ri* passim; *an-nu-ra* CT 53 947 r.6e; {*ú-ma*}*-a* {*an*$^{?}$*-nu*$^{?}$*-ra*} SAA V 152:21 ~ *an-nu-rig* passim, *an-nu-ríg* SAA I 191 r.6, SAA V 81:5;[251] *a-nu-ri-ig* NL 28:9 (CTN V 248f); *a-nu-rig* SAA I 260 r.2 ({*a*}-), SAA V 227 s.3, ND 2668:3, r.2′, 8′ (CTN V 177f); SAA I 233:25 (-{*nu-rig*}); *an-nu-rag* NL 72:8 (CTN V 246ff)

The exceptional spelling in NL 28:9 (with -CV-VC [see above] instead of CVC) by Duri-Aššur, governor of Tušhan, would appear to confirm the final *g* of the word. In spite of this, the status of the final *g* in *annurig* in the spoken language can be well contested.[252] It may be morphological and orthographically thus referring to its etymological origin.[253] Otherwise noteworthy are the spellings with the initial <*a*> which suggest a pre-tonic shortening of a syllable.[254] Hence the adverb may have been pronounced as /*anū́ri*/.

4.3 Vowels

4.3.1 Allophones of /*a*/

/*a*/ has as allophones[255] [*a*], [*o*] and possibly also [*ä*].[256] The existence of an allophone [*ä*] is sometimes concluded from cases in which <*i*/*e*> is written instead of the expected <*a*>.[257]

/*a*/ > /*i*/ / /*e*/, in closed syllables before /*r*/, /*l*/, /*n*/ and /*t*/:

(*athusu*)	10 *it-hu-su* NU.ÚR SAA XI 36 I 26 ~ 50 GIŠ.*at-hu-su ša* GIŠ.NU.ÚR.MA.MEŠ SAA XII 71:6; 50 GIŠ.*at-hu-su* : ibid. l.9
(**išpallurtu*)	*is-pi-lu-ur-te* SAA V 227 r.6; *is-píl-ur-tú* SAA X 30:3, 4, r.1; NA$_4$.*is-pi-lu-ur-te* SAA XVI 148 r.13; *is-pi-lu-rat* (pl., st. cstr.) SAA XVI 143 r.7′ (*ispillurtu* has been lexicalized)
(krr)	*ik-ter-ru* SAA XVI 63:19; *ik*$^{?}$*-te-r*[*u*$^{?}$ SAA XVI 8 r.1′ ~ *ik-tar-ru* GPA 188:6, SAA XVI 95:14; *i*]*k-ta-ru* SAA I 181 r.5

---

250 Cf. Deller (1959) § 45 a-b.

251 For a new hand copy of the tablet, see Radner, SAAB 11 (1997) 29, Abb. 8.

252 Cf. AHw 54 *annûri*(*g*) and Hämeen-Anttila (2000) 58.

253 For the probable etymology, see AHw loc.cit.

254 Cf. n. 344.

255 On the principles of allophonic alternation, see e.g. Reiner (1973) 43.

256 See Deller (1959) § 19-23d, as well as Hämeen-Anttila (2000) 26f. The status of [*o*] as an allophone of /*a*/ may be justified. It occurs in a phonologically predictable environment (see below). Reiner (1973) 47f, however, denies the phonological predictability of *o* and, therefore, also its possible allophonic status.

257 Cf. Deller (1959) §22a-zw, although Deller's examples can, for the most part, be explained in other ways.

(*nēmulu*) *né-me-él-šu/šú* SAA X 53 r.1/SAA X 54 r.5′; *né-me-el-šú-nu* SAA X 207 r.5 ~ *né-ma-al-šú* SAA X 73 r.3, SAA X 218:9; *né-mal-šu* SAA XVI 36 r.3; *né-e-ma-al-šu* SAA X 194:11; *né-ma-al-šú-nu* SAA X 185:16

(*pišru*) *pi-še-er-šu/šú* SAA X 100:8, SAA X 55:4′/SAA X 56 r.4, SAA X 94:11, SAA VIII 95 r.6 ~ *pi-šá-ar-šú* SAA VIII 186 r.4 (La-baši)

(*simunu*) *si-mì-in* SAA VIII 157 r.1, SAA X 359 r.5′ ~ *si-ma-an* SAA X 31 r.4, cf. also *si-man* SAA XV 156 r.16

/*a*/ > /*i*/ / /*e*/, in closed syllables which begin with *d*:

(*dātu*) *de-et* LUGAL (Aššur-reṣuwa, Kumme) SAA V 86:11; ⸢*de-et*⸣ *ha-ni-*⸢*e*⸣ "after this" (Gabbu-ana-Aššur, Kurbail) SAA V 121 r.10 ~ *i–da-at* passim (+ the other equivalent prepositional forms of *ina*)

/*a*/ > /*i*/ / /*e*/, in open syllables before stressed /*i*/:

(*dalīlu*) *di-lil* SAA X 92:10; *di-lil-šu-nu* ibid. l.6; *a-na di-li-li* SAA II 2 vi 5 ~ *dà-lí-lí* (pl.) SAA XVI 31 r.2′; *da-li-li-šú-nu* (pl. + suff. 3rd pl.) SAA X 277 r.6

(Kalzi) *ša* URU.*ki-li-zi* SAA X 144:3 ~ URU.*kàl-zi* SAA X 143:3, SAA X 96:14; URU.*kàl-zi-a-*(*a*) SAA X 6:7

(*ṣahittu*) *ṣi-hi-it-tu-šú* SAA X 351 r.3 (Mar-Issar, all the other examples of this word begin with *ṣa-*)

Others:

(*ahhūr*) *mì-nu i-hur* (note that all the other writings of *ahhūr* are with *ah–*, never *a-*) "What else?" SAA XIII 45 r.2

(*am–mē/īni*) *i-na mi-i-ni* "why?" SAA XIII 190 r.5; *ina mì-ni* StAT 1 54 r.3; *ina mi-i-ni* MAss 100 r.3 ~ e.g. *a-na mi-ni*; *a-na mì-i-ni*; *a-na mi-i-ni* all passim

(*harammāma* "later") *ha-ra-me-ma* SAA X 191 e.14, SAA X 101:7, SAA II 6:210J, frg, SAA XVI 92:9; *ha-ra-am-me-ma* SAA X 209 r.3; *ha-ram-me-ma* SAA V 160:3; *ha-ra-am-mi-ma* SAA XIII 158:10′ ~ *ha-ra-ma-a-ma* SAA II 6:210e; *ha-ra-ma-ma* SAA X 349:26, SAA I 233:17, SAA I 156 e.2′, NL 44 r.8 (CTN V 139f)

(*ra'su*) LÚ*.*re-e'-sa-ni ša* KUR.*kal-di* (NA) "the chieftains of Chaldea" NL 5:5′ (CTN V 25f) ~ LÚ.*ra-šá-a-nu ša* LÚ.*kal-du* NL 6:18′ (CTN V 14ff); LÚ.*ra-šá-ni šá* KUR.*kal-du* SAA XVIII 14 r.6; LÚ.*ra-šá-a-ni* ABL 518 r.7 (all these examples are NB)

(Šadikanni) URU.*še-di-kan-a-a* SAA I 223:5, SAA I 224:15, SAA I 225:3′ ~ URU.*šá-di-kan-ni* SAA VI 286:2, see also Parpola (1970) 329-30

(*šapal*) *šap-li qa-ti* "secretly" SAA V 172:7 ~ *šap-la qa-ti* ibid. l.12

(šlm) *ú-sa-al-lam* /*ussallim*/ (pf) GPA 96:8

(škn) *iš-kun-ni-ni-ši-n*[*i*] (?) /*iškunannāšīni*/ / /*iškunūnāšīni*/ CT 53 167:2′

<AŠ> = /*ina*/ > /*ana*/ passim e.g.

(*ana*) *ina* EN-*iá a-sa-par* SAA XV 288 r.4 ~ e.g. *a-na* LUGAL EN-*iá* / *a-sa-bar* "I wrote to the king, my lord" SAA V 21 r.14-15, *a-na* LUGAL EN-*ia as-ap-ra* SAA XIII 18 r.6 and passim; however, cf. the construction *ina* UGU EN-*ia* / *a-sa-pa-ra* NL 64:10-11(CTN V 290ff) and passim

(*ana*) *lu* DI-*mu ina* [LUGAL EN-*ia*] "Good health to the [king, my lord]" SAA XIII 146:2; *lu* DI-*mu ina* LUGAL EN-*ia* NL 44:3 (CTN V 139f); DI-*mu ina* É-*ku-nu*

StAT 1 51:7; DI-*mu ina* É StAT 1 52:4; DI-*mu ina* É / *a-na* UN.MEŠ SAA X 130 r.4-5; [*l*]*u-u* DI-*mu ina* AMA-*ia* KAV 215:3; [DI-*m*]*u* ⸢*ina*⸣ URU.*kal-ha* "The city of Calah is well" SAA I 115:5; DI-*mu* / *ina* KUR LÚ.GAL–KAŠ.LUL NL 55:6-7 (CTN V 147f); IM PN / *ina* É *gab-bi* KAV 199:1-2

(*ana*) *ni-ip-tu-hu*[*r*] / *ina* LÚ*.*tur-ta-ni ni-te-*⸢*te-zi*⸣ NL 65:4-5 (CTN V 45f)

(*ana*, as a marker of the accusative) *ina šá-a-šú* / *i-da-gul-šú* "... observing him ..." SAA XIII 31 r.8-9

(*ana*) *a-ki-i* ... / *ina kas-pi ta-da-nu-u-ni* "that ... have been sold" SAA XIII 31 r.12-13

Compare also:

(*akê*) *ik-ke-e la ni-la-ka* NL 5 r.7 (CTN V 25f)

(*-em-*) *an-nu-te-*AM-*ma* SAA XVI 62 r.7′

[*o*] is concealed in forms which have a <*u*> instead of the expected <*a*>.[258]

/*a*/ > /*u*/, in the closed stressed syllables *u*-DENTAL + *a* (mostly D pf I ʾ/dental):

(ʾhr) *ú-tu-hi-*⸢*ir*⸣ SAA X 362:7′

(ʾkš) *ú-tu-uk-ki-iš* SAA X 362 r.1; *ú-tu-uk-kiš* SAA X 104 r.3

(ʾlī) *ú-tu-li* SAA X 319 r.5; *ú-tu-li-u* SAA V 87:17 ~ *ú-ta-li* SAA V 203:9, SAA I 64 r.7′; *ú-tal-li* SAA XIII 46:13′, SAA XIII 134:12′; *ú-tal-li-u* SAA XIII 47:5′, r.8

(ʾmd) *nu-tu-me-di* SAA I 210:12 ~ *nu-ta-mi-i*[*d*] SAA I 126:8′

(ʾpš) *ú-tu-pi-*⸢*eš*⸣ SAA XVI 125 r.6′ ~ *ú-tap-pi-šu* NL 69:6 (CTN V 164ff)

(ʾsk) *ú-tu-si-i*[*k* SAA V 251 r.7 ~ *ú-ta-si-ik* SAA I 236 r.4 also *ú-tu-uš-si-ku* SAA X 348 r.8 ~ *ú-ta-si-ku* CT 53 385 e.4′

(dlh) *ú-du-lìh*[259] SAA X 273 r.15

(tbk) *ú-du-*⸢*bi*?⸣*-ku* NL 35:7 (CTN V 33f) (Ašipâ)

Cf.

(*kutallu*) *ku-tu-li-šú-nu* SAA V 249:4′ ~ TA* *ku-tal-*[*li-šú*] SAA X 294 r.11

URU.*ku-tú-li* ABL 449:3 ~ *a-na ku-tal-li* SAA X 8:18; *ša ku-tal-li* ABL 541:5′

/*a*/ > /*u*/, in closed syllables ending in *r* (often near a labial):

(ʾmr) *am-*MUR /*ammar*/[260] SAA X 79 r.6

/Arzūhina/ URU.*ur-zu-hi-na* passim ~ URU.*ar/ár-zu-hi-na* passim

/Barsib/[261] *ša* URU.*bur-si-*⸢*bi*⸣ SAA I 87:9; *ša* URU.DUL–*bur-si-bi* SAA I 184 r.7; URU.*til–bur-si-ib* ND 2619:26 (Iraq 23 38 and pl. 19); URU.DU$_6$–*bur-si-b*[*a*] SAA I 192:8; URU.*tur-bu-si-bi* ND 2684 r.6′ (Iraq 23 43 and pl. 23) ~ URU.*til–bar-si-b*[*a* Iraq 23 23 r. I 19; URU.*til–bar-si-ba* SAA I 32 r.13′ (CTN V 125ff); URU.*tar-bu-si-bi* SAA I 193 r.4, SAA XV 106 r.3′, SAA I 4:10′

---

[258] See Deller (1959) § 19-21.

[259] See LAS II ad no. 211 r.15.

[260] This interpretation is likely but uncertain, see ibid. ad no. 64 r.6.

[261] For a list of the various readings of Til-Barsib, see Parpola (1970) 353. Cf. also Dalley (1996-1997) 68-70.

(mšl[262]) statives: *mu-šu-ul* SAA X 56:17, SAA X 382 r.9; *muš-[la]* SAA X 380:4′; *muš-la-ni* SAA I 132:18; *muš-lu* SAA X 316 r.17 ~ *maš-la-ku* SAA XVI 66:2′
/*mukarrirtu*/ *mu-ku-ri-ir-tú* ND 2490 r.2 (Iraq 23 33f and pl. 17)
(phr[263]) pl. stative *puhru* passim
/*qarrūbu*/ *qur-ru-bu* SAA XV 61 r.10′ ~ *[q]a?-ru-bu* SAA XV 348:5′
(qrb[264]) *qur-bu* passim, note that there are no *qarbu* forms
/Sippar/ URU.*si-pur* SAA XV 226:8, SAA X 366 r.6′ ~ *sip-par*.KI SAA X 364 r.7, SAA XIII 166:4; URU.*sip-par* SAA XV 159 r.1; URU.*si-par* NL 35:9, r.2 (CTN V 33f), SAA I 84 r.5
/*targumānu*/ LÚ*.*tur-gu-ma-[ni* SAA V 108 e.30 ⸢LÚ*.*tur-gu*⸣*-ma-ni* NL 40:3 (CTN V 186f) ~ LÚ*.*tar-gu-ma-nu* SAA V 203 r.5′
/*tartānu*/[265] LÚ(*).*tur-ta(n)-nu/ni* passim ~ LÚ*.*tar-ta-ni* SAA I 110 r.17 (CTN V 219ff), TH 3 e.7, r.3; LÚ*.*tar-ta-nu* NL 15:3 (CTN V 140), NL 79:4 (CTN V 178f)

/*a*/ > /*u*/, in closed syllables ending in a labial:

/*napšutu*/ *nu-up-šu-tú* SAA XV 229:10′; *nu-up-[šá-t]e* SAA XIII 92:8 (Nabû-šumu-iddina); *nu-up-[šá-te]* SAA XIII 10 r.3; *nu-up-šá-te* SAA V 11 s.3 ~ *nap-šá-a-te* SAA XIII 78 r.11, 18 (NAB = *nup*?; Nabû-šumu-iddina); *nap-šá-a-ti* SAA X 294:25

/*a*/ > /*u*/, in long, open syllables:

/*anāku*/ *an-nu-ku* SAA XIII 45 r.9

4.3.2 Allophones of /*i*/

Sometimes an expected <*i*> is replaced by <*a*>. Then <*a*> may stand for *e*, that is, /*i*/ > /*a*/ = [*e*].

/*ālâte*/ *a-la-ta-ia* BaM 27 419:5 (IM 132409)
/*annuri*(*g*)/ *an-nu-ra* CT 53 947 r.6′ (Babylonian writer?), ⸢*ú-ma*⸣*-a* ⸢*an?-nu?-ra*⸣ SAA V 152:21; *an-nu-rag* NL 72:8 (CTN V 246ff) ~ *an-nu-ri/rig* passim
/*annūtimma*/ *an-nu-te*-AM-*ma* SAA XVI 62 r.7′ cf. 4.3.1
/*darāti*/ *šá da-ra-a*-TA (see 4.5) SAA XVI 29:13[266]
/Gimir(rai)/ KUR.*ga-mir* SAA I 31:9; KUR.*ga-mir-ra* SAA V 92:6, 9; [LÚ].⸢*ga*⸣*-me-ra-a-a* SAA V 145:4 ~ e.g. KUR.PAB-*ir* SAA I 31 r.10, SAA I 32:12

---

262 It is most probable that in these few roots which end in *r*/*l*, the stative form *purus* replaced the original *paris*(/*paras*) form. On the development of the [*u*]-form (through an intermediate [*o*]), see GAG § 87l and LAS II ad no. 229:3′f. Lipiński (1997) § 10.9 explains that the occurrence of <*u*> e.g. in the forms *qurbum* (not *qarbum*) and *inaṣṣur* (instead of *inaṣṣar*) might result from emphatic consonants (= *q*, *ṣ*) and assumes that pronunciation had thus been under the influence of pharyngealization or velarization similar to /*u*/. However, such a theory would explain no more than a minority of the above-listed examples.

263 LAS II ad no. 229:3′f.

264 Ibid.

265 On the etymology of the word, see Wilhelm (1970) 277-82.

266 For the commented edition of SAA XVI 29 (ABL 916), see Deller (1959) § 22o-q.

(CTN V 125ff); KUR.*gi-mir-a-a* SAA V 144:9 (KUR.*g*[*i*]-⸢*mir*⸣-[*a-a*), r.5′ and LÚ.*gi-mir-ra-a-a* passim

/hibilāti/ HA-*ba-la*-TA-*ia* SAA XVI 29:16 ~ *hi-bil-a-te-šú* ibid. l.17

(Idri-aha'u[267]) ^{m}*ad-ra–a-ha-ú/u* SAA XVI 140:7/r.18 ~ ^{m}*id-ri–a-ha-a-ú* SAA X 354:11; ^{m}*id-ri–a-ha-ú* SAA XVI 141 r.2

Allophonic */ina/* > */ana/* is theoretically possible. See, however, 7.1.

/Kidmūru/ É–*kad-mu-ri* SAA XIII 154:4, SAA XIII 129:3, r.2; É–*kad-mu-ru* SAA XVI 126:5 ~ É–*kid-mur-ra* SAA XVI 127:5; É–*kid-mur-ri* SAA X 294 r.23; É–*ki-di-mu-ri* SAA XVI 105:5; ^{d}GAŠAN–*ki-di-mu-ri* ibid. r.13, SAA XVI 106:6; ^{d}*šar-rat–kid-mu-ri* SAA X 197:11

/sahhira/ *sa*-HA$^{?}$-*ra*[268] SAA XVI 29:17 ~ *sa-hi-ra* SAA I 76 r.12, CTN III 3 r.12

/ṣīt/ *ṣe-e*-TA ^{d}UTU-*ši* SAA XVI 29:14

Many of these references come from scribes who were of demonstrably Babylonian origin (such as Mardî,[269] the writer of SAA XVI 29) or display noticeable Babylonian influence in their writing conventions.

4.3.3 Variation of */i/* and */e/*[270]

See also 3.10.

When */i/* and */e/* occur in word-initial position, they are usually distinguished from one another. Few exceptions to this are found in the data.[271]

<*i*> instead of the normal <*e*>[272]

At the beginning of a word in finite verb forms:

('kl) ⸢*i-ku*⸣-*ul* */ekkulū/* SAA V 225:12 (Adad-isse'a, cf. by the same writer: *a-li-i* SAA V 224:13 ~ *a*-⸢*le*⸣-*e* SAA V 215 r.4)

('lī) *i-lu-u-ni* */ēlūni/* or */ellūni/* SAA XV 156 r.22 (Il-iada')

('mr) *i-ma-ru-ni* */emmarūni/* SAA V 260 r.7 (unkn.)

('pš) *i-pa-áš* */eppaš/* SAA XIII 71 r.10 (Nergal-šarrani); *i-pu-šu-u-ni* */ēpušūni/* SAA X 56 r.11(Balasî), SAA XV 140 r.4′ (Nabû-balliṭanni); *ti-pu-šu-ni* */tēpušūni/* SAA XIII 43:2 (anonymous, Assur; theoretically <*ti*> = <*te*$_9$> at least in sign lists)

('rb) *i-ra-ab* */errab/* KAV 215:9 (Nabû-šulmu-ereš); *i-tar-ba*[273] */ētarba/* (pf 1st sg.) SAA X 60 r.5 (Balasî); *i-tar-bu* */ētarbū/* SAA XVI 40 r.17e (Blacksmiths), SAA X 293 r.4 (Urdu-Gula)

---

[267] See LAS II ad no. 284:11.

[268] See Deller (1959) p. 90 and idem (1987) 178. In SAA XVI 29:17, this imperative is read as *sa-ha-ra*, but see collation ibid. p. 219. I agree with Deller to read it as *sa*-⸢*hi*$^{!}$⸣-*ra*.

[269] See PNA 2/II p. 704 s.v. *Mardî* no. 10.

[270] See Deller (1959) § 25 for additional examples.

[271] Ibid. § 25a.

[272] See also Parpola (1984) 206 n. 35.

[273] Cf. LAS II ad no. 39 r.5.

('rš) *i-ru-šu* /*errušū*/ GPA 207 e.10 (unkn.) ~ *e-ru-šú* SAA V 289 e.8, r.2; *i-ru-šu-u-ni* /*ērušūni*/ SAA X 69:14 (Nabû-ahhe-eriba)
('ṣd) *i-ṣi-du* /*ēṣidū*/ BT 104:6 (Iraq 25 pl. 20) ~ *e-ṣi-du* ibid. l.5
('tq) *i-ti-te-iq* /*ētetiq*/ SAA XVI 201 r.2 (unkn.) ~ e.g. ⌜*e*⌝*-te-ti-i*[*q*] NL 97 r.10 (CTN V 111f); *e-te-tiq* SAA XVI 145 s.1

In nouns:

(*egirtu*) *i-gír-te* SAA XV 217 r.6′ (Šarru-emuranni); *i-gír-tú* KAV 213 r.12 (Atanha-ilu)
possibly (*ebissu*) *i-bi-su* SAA I 226:4, 6, 7, r.9 (Nabû-dammiq) cf. *e-bi-is-su/i* SAA I 26:3/4 (CTN V 213f)

In the middle of a word (see e.g. 4.7 > *issi*) and at the end of a word (in the genitive singular, and in the plural forms of nouns and adjectives), the alternation of /*i*/ and /*e*/ is much more common.[274] The alternation of /*i*/ and /*e*/ within a word is also attested in the indefinite pronoun *memmēni*:

(*memmēni*) *mi-i-mi-ni* SAA XVI 39 r.2 (unkn.); *me-mì-i-ni* SAA XIII 17:9′ (probably Marduk-šallim-ahhe, Assur); *mì-mì-i-ni* SAA XVI 128 r.11′ (Itti-Šamaš-balaṭu) ~ *me-me-e-ni* and *mi-mi-e-ni* (the sign MI = *mi*, *mé*) passim; *me-em-me-e-ni* SAA X 183 r.3; *me-e-me-e-ni* SAA XVI 176:2′ (Nabû-šumu-iddina). But also note the extraordinary *mé-e-mi-i-ni* SAA X 224 r.1 (Adad-šumu-uṣur) in which both vowels are written as long

<*e*> instead of the normal <*i*>.[275] At the beginning of a word, note the following:

(*issi*) *e-si-šú-nu* /*issēšunu*/ SAA XIII 43:7 (anonymous, Assur, cf. *ti-pu-šu-ni* above)
(tdn) *e-da-na-kan-ni* /*iddanakkanni*/ NL 23:5 (CTN V 175ff)

Within a word:

(tdn) [*di*]-⌜*e*⌝*-ni* SAA I 192:11 (Nabû-pašir, Harran) ~ /*dīni*/ passim

Presumably these rare writings give, at least from time to time, a hint of the actual pronunciation.[276] Otherwise they can be interpreted as exceptions from the more standard form of writing. This indicates an almost free variation of [*i*] and [*e*] in writing.

4.3.4 Allophones of /*u*/[277]

In the following forms <*i*> appears instead of expected <*u*>:

/*laššu*/ *la-a-ši* SAA VI 52 r.1 (scribe unkn.); *la-áš-ši* SAA XIV 96:3′ (unkn.), KAV 213 r.16e (Atanha-ilu; these examples are Babylonianisms)

---

[274] See Deller (1959) § 25d-e.

[275] Ibid. § 25a.

[276] See LAS II ad no. 39 r.5.

[277] See Deller (1959) § 24, whose examples are chiefly accounted for by means of progressive vowel assimilation (see 4.5).

('rb Š) perhaps *i-se-ri-b*[*u*$^{?}$]-⸢*šú*$^{?}$-*nu*$^{?}$⸣[278] NL 45 r.8′ (CTN V 136ff, unkn.)
(dbb Š) *i-sa-*⸢*ad*⸣*-bi-ib* /*ussadbib*/ (scribe unkn.) SAA XV 216:8′ ~ e.g. *ú-sa-ad-bi-ib-šú-nu* SAA X 348 r.21

When [*u*] is in contact with a sibilant (the verb forms above) and appears as <*i*>, the examples may bear evidence of an allophone [*ü*].[279] On the other hand, no adequate theory can be proposed on the basis of a handful of examples. It is therefore likely that the above-mentioned examples are scribal errors, of uncertain ('rb Š) or Babylonian influence.

4.4 Assimilated vs. non-assimilated vowels[280]

(a) According to the rules of Neo-Assyrian grammar, the last radical of final weak verbs (usually realized as *-i*) normally assimilates to the following *-ū* in subjunctive and ventive plural forms.[281] (b) However, in simple plural forms and in ventive singular forms, the vowel *-i* is not assimilated.[282] In other words: (a) (qbī) *iqbûni*, but (b) *i-ba-ki-ú*, *i-qab-bi-a*. Exceptions to this rule are:

/*i*/ is not assimilated to /*u*/:

(*ahiu*) *a-hi-ú-ti* SAA X 240:25, SAA X 245 r.15 ~ *a-hu-ú-*[*ti* SAA X 101:3; *a-h*]*u-ú-ti* ibid. r.3; but note (*bariu*) *ba-ri-ú-ti* SAA X 226 r.1 and regularly *makiūte/i*, *paniūte/i*, *šaniūte/i*, *urkiūte/i* all passim vs. (*ammiu*) *ammūte/i* (*anniu*) *annūte/i* both passim
('lī) *e-li-ú-ni* NL 45 r.5 (subj.) (CTN V 136ff, unkn.) ~ *e-lu-u-ni* ibid. r.10′
(bkī) *ib-ki-i-u-ni* SAA X 348 r.19 (Mar-Issar)
(bšī) *i-bi-ši-u-ni* (a rarity: prt, cf. *ib*$^{?}$*-ši-ia-a* NL 74 r.13′ [CTN V 132ff]) SAA X 227:24 (Adad-šumu-uṣur); *ib-ba-áš-ši-u-*[*ni* SAA II 6:383D ~ *ibaššûni* and *ibbaššûni* passim
(lq') *i-la-qi-u-ni* SAA XV 60 r.6′ (Aššur-belu-uṣur)
(pt') *ip-ti-ú-ni* SAA I 195 r.17′ (subj., Nabû-pašir) ~ *ni-ip-tu-ni* SAA XVI 97:14; *ap-tu-u-ni* SAA XIII 33 r.6
(qbī) *x*]*x-qab-bi-u-ni* SAA X 219 r.6′ (broken cont.) ~ *i-qab-bu-u-ni* passim; *iq-ṭí-bi-ú-ni* SAA V 3:9 (Nashir-Bel) ~ *iq-ṭí-bu-u-ni* passim; *iq-bi-u-ni* ND 2369 r.4 (CTN V 243, unkn.) ~ *iq-b*[*u*]*-ni* ibid. l.9′, *iqbûni* passim
(rbī) *ša i-ra-bi-ú-*[*ni* CT 53 486 r.4 (unkn.)
(rd') *i-ra-di-u-ni* SAA I 99 r.4′ (Ṭab-ṣill-Ešarra) ~ *i-rad-du-u-ni* SAA XIII 48:6′

---

[278] This reading is uncertain, cf. CTN V Pl. 27 (ND 2673). It looks as if the last two signs are in the middle of an erasure. Saggs reads the verbal form now as *i-si-tal-li-m*[*u*] in CTN V, p. 137. Theoretically, *issitallimu* seems a fine Gtn pf 3rd pl. form of *salāmu* "to make peace," but the problem is that I do not know of any attestations of *salāmu* Gtn. On the other hand, the Gtn-stem was productive in NA.

[279] Cf. e.g. Hämeen-Anttila (2000) 26, who rejects the potential allophones of /*u*/.

[280] See Deller's legion of examples (1959) § 26-34.

[281] See ibid. § 27a.

[282] Ibid. § 26a: "Im absoluten Auslaut (d.h. am Ende eines Wortes ohne Anfügung weiterer Bildungselemente) bleibt *e/i-a* und *e/i-u* in der überwiegenden Mehrzahl der Fälle unkontrahiert."

The nominatives *i* + *u* > *î/ê* (all the examples are similarly constructed with three syllables):

(*ammiu*) *am-mì-i* ABL 1385:14 (Šamaš-šumu-ukin to Assurbanipal), KAV 213 r.8 ~ *am-mi-u* GPA 191:5; *am-mi-ú* SAA X 387 r.1; *am-mì-ú* SAA V 199:9, SAA I 183 r.13

(*anniu*) *an-ni-i* SAA X 228 r.16, SAA X 238 r.13, SAA X 240:18, SAA X 241 r.1, SAA X 290 r.16e, SAA X 347 r.11′, SAA X 357:10, SAA X 359 r.5′, VAT 9875:9 ~ *an-ni-u*; *a-ni-ú*; *an-ni-ú*; *ha-ni-u*;[283] *an-ni-i-u*, etc. passim

(*darīu*) *da-ri-i* SAA X 96:16; UDU.⸢*da-ri-i*⸣ ibid. l.11; UDU.*da-ri-i* SAA XIII 133:6

(*hariu*) DUG.*ha-ri-i* ND 2097:3 (Iraq 23 18f and pl. 9)

(*mašiu*) *ma-ši-i* AfO 32 39 (BM 103389 r.6)

(*pānīu*) *pa-ni-i* SAA X 366 r.4′

(*supiu*) *su-pi-*⸢*i*?⸣ SAA XIII 168:17

(*šaniu*) LÚ.MAŠ.MAŠ / 2-*i*[284] SAA X 238 r.5-6

(*urkīu*) *ur-ki-i* SAA X 358 r.8′

The third person plural in the consecutive forms of the III-weak verbs:[285]

(l'ī) *šu-nu i-la-'i-i / i-kab-bu-su /ila''iū/* "They will be able to *tread* ..." SAA XIII 127 r.15-16

(lbī) *i-tal-ku-*[*ú*]*-ni* GN / *il-ti-*⸢*bi*⸣*-i /iltibiū/* SAA XV 118:2′-3′

(rmū) *ur-ta-mì-i ... / ih-tab-tu /urtammiū/* SAA XV 118:6′-7′

i + *u* > *û*:

(*anniu*) *la an-nu-u šu-u* SAA X 30 r.9; *an-nu-ú* SAA X 217 r.1

In the demonstrative pronoun *anniu*, the proportion of non-assimilated to assimilated forms is about 6:1.[286] From these assimilations, the model (nom.) *i* + *u* > *î* is much more common than (nom.) *i* + *u* > *û*.[287]

u + *i* > *û*:[288]

(ml') *šá ma-lu-u* SAA IX 1 iv 12 (**mallui*), the following forms come to my mind as the closest possible points of comparison: *a-na pu-ud-de-e* SAA X 89:5′; *a-na ul-lu-e* NL 12 r.8 (CTN V 155ff) and *ina* UGU ... / *ša-at-bu-*⸢*e*?⸣ "to *raise* ..." SAA V 297:11′-12′

(rd') *ra-ad-du-u* SAA X 103 r.3′ (**raddui, Akkullanu*)

---

283 The forms of the word *anniu*, which begin with *h*, are probably due to an Aramaic influence, see e.g. Lipiński (1997) § 19.9, § 36.33.

284 See LAS II ad no. 172 r.5 f.

285 Since these vowel assimilations are attested in consecutive clauses, they may have a syntactic, coordinative explanation, unless they simply reflect the spoken language and its intonation.

286 LAS II ad no. 152 r.1.

287 Ibid.

288 See ibid. ad no. 305 r.3′.

u + *a* > *û*:

(*Ninuwa) URU.*ni-nu-ú*[289] SAA XVI 21 r.16 ~ URU.*ni-nu-a* passim

4.5 Progressive vowel assimilation[290]

When the penultimate syllable of a word is long and stressed, it may cause the vowel of the last syllable to assimilate qualitatively to itself. This vowel assimilation is optional.

1. Vowel assimilation after stressed /*ā*/:

As found in nouns and adjectives:

(*dārāti*)	*da-ra-a-ta* SAA XVI 29:13 (Mardî), SAA XVI 128:7 (Itti-Šamaš-balaṭu[291]) ~ *da-ra-a-te/ti* passim
(Ubāru)	^m^*ú-ba-ra* SAA XV 181:8 (Aššur-belu-taqqin)

As found in the verb forms:

(*erābu*)	*a*]-⸢*na*⸣ *e-ra-ba* (infinit.) SAA X 74 r.11 (Nabû-ahhe-eriba, probably a careless mistake, cf. the correct *er-ra-ba* ibid. r.10) ~ e.g. *a-na e-ra-a-bi* SAA X 73:11 (also by Nabû-ahhe-eriba)
(*etāku*)	*ba-si lu et-ka-ka* (possibly *a* because of clausal coordination) "So I can be alerted" SAA XIII 97 r.9
(*kammusu*)	*kam-mu-sa-k*[*a* (stat 1st sg.)[292] ABL 390:14 (Bel-iqiša) ~ *kam-mu-sa-ku* SAA I 55 e.10′; ⸢*ka*⸣-*mu*-⸢*sa*⸣-*ak* NL 36:12 (CTN V 34f)
(*nakrāk*[*u*])	*na-ka-ra-ka* (stat 1st sg.) SAA V 260:7′
(*našû*)	*na-ṣa-ka* NL 85 r.10 (CTN V 100ff) ~ *na-ṣa-ku* SAA I 56 r.13
(*pahāru* D)	*pa-ah-hu-ra-k*[*a*] SAA X 233:15
(*quālu*)	*qa-a-la* (infinit.) *šakin* "There is an order to remain silent" SAA XIII 134 r.16 (unkn. from the temple of Nabû in Calah)
(*takālu* D)	*ta-ku-la-ka* SAA XIII 45 r.10 cf. *tak-ku-lak* SAA XVI 127 r.11; *ta-ku-la-ak* SAA XVI 128 r.10′

2. After stressed /*ī*/ or /*ē*/:

(*anīnu*)	*a-ni-ni* NL 1:11, 22, r.5, 10, 17 (CTN V 19ff), NL 102:9 (-[*n*]*i*) (CTN V 207f), CT 53 565 e.7′, SAA X 3:8, SAA XV 136 e.27, SAA XV 116 r.5′, 9′, 15′, SAA XV 130:21; [*a-n*]*i-ni-i-ni* SAA XV 136:12 ~ *a-ni*(*-in*)*-nu*(*-ma/ni*) e.g. SAA V 105:12, SAA V 149 r.21 and passim
(*dēnu*)	*de-e-ni* SAA V 213:4; *de*-⸢*ni*⸣ AfO 32 38:12 (BM 103389) ~ *de-e-nu* e.g. SAA VI passim
(*kēnu*)	*ke-e-ni* SAA XIII 92:13 ~ *ke-e-nu* e.g. SAA I 134:6, SAA XVI 126:1
(*lilissu*)	[*l*]*i-li-si* SAA X 341:8
(*līṭu*)	*li-ṭi* SAA XV 136 r.15

---

289 See Parpola (1972) 27 for further examples.

290 Deller and Parpola (1967) 337f.

291 See ibid. 338.

292 Cf. 5.9.2.

(*mētu*) *me-e-ti* SAA XVI 127 r.15, SAA XVI 128 r.15e (both by Itti-Šamaš-balaṭu); *mé-te* SAA X 309 r.4 (probably by Ana-Nabû-atkal[293]) ~ *mi-i-tu* SAA X 294:14

(*mīnu*) *mi-i-ni* SAA XV 90:30 ([*mi-i*]-), r.2, SAA XV 100 r.9′, SAA XV 370:5′, SAA XVI 127 e.27, r.1, SAA X 3 r.13′, SAA XIII 28 r.6, SAA XVI 21:11; *mi-ni* SAA XV 129 s.6, SAA XV 183:2′; *mì-ni* SAA V 210 r.19e, SAA I 227 r.10′, SAA XV 71 r.2′, SAA XV 100 r.11′ ~ *mi/ì/*(*-i*)-*nu*(*-um-ma*) passim

(*nēmēqu*) *né-me-qe* SAA X 218 r.13

(*rēšu*) *re-e-ši* SAA X 298:18, SAA XVI 31:7 ~ *re-e-šú* SAA X 245 r.17, SAA X 255:13 and passim

(*rību*) *ri-i-bi* SAA X 203:14, SAA VIII 37:6

(*šumēlu*) *šu-me-le* SAA X 358 r.6′ (Mar-Issar)

(*tamlītu*) *tam-li-ti* SAA X 364:10′ (Mar-Issar)

(*ṭēmu*) *ṭè-e-me* SAA V 210 r.20e, SAA XVI 148 r.8, SAA XV 368:6′; *ṭe-e-me* SAA X 45 s.2; *ṭè-me* SAA V 29 r.1, 105 r.10; *ṭè-mi* SAA XVI 26:12, SAA XV 158:7, SAA XV 161:7 (the last two examples by the same writer) ~ *ṭè-*(*e-*)*mu* passim

(*udīna*) *ú-di-i-ni* SAA I 29:19, e.34, SAA I 31 r.15, SAA I 145 r.8e, SAA XIII 81 r.4, SAA XIII 118 r.4, SAA XIII 122 r.3; *ú-din-ni* SAA XV 60:19; *ú-di-ni* passim ~ *ú-di-na* passim (on the whole, *ú-di-ni* is a bit more common); *ud-di-ni* SAA X 349:9, SAA XVI 16 r.2; *qu-di-i-ni* SAA I 30 e.9′

(*urkītu* "later [on], afterwards, thereafter") *ur-ki-te* SAA X 329 r.6, NL 12:21, r.6 (CTN V 155ff); *ur-ki-ti* SAA V 6 r.6′, SAA XIII 131 r.16, SAA XV 40 r.6′, SAA XV 162 r.9 cf. *ur-ke-e-et* SAA X 74 r.24e, SAA X 76 e.16. Probably *urkīti* is lexicalized. Its behaviour is in a way analogous to some other temporal adverbs which, however, often use prepositional constructions (prep. omitted in the case of *urkīti*) as e.g. *ina pānīti*, *iddāt*, *immatīma*, *ina šiāri*, etc. all passim

3. After stressed /*ū*/:
Genitives in the singular:

(*ša*) *a-ši-pu-tú* SAA X 352:19
(*ina*) *bu-bu-tú* SAA XIII 190 r.19
^d^15 *ša* É–*kad-mu-ru* "Ištar of the Kidmuri temple" SAA XVI 126:5 ~ ^d^15 *ša* É–*ki-di-mu-ri* SAA XVI 105:5
(*a-na*) LÚ*.GAL–*ki-ṣir-u-tú* "the rank of cohort commander" SAA XVI 115:9
(MAN) KUR.*ku-u-su* SAA X 351 r.6 ~ *ša* KUR.*ku-u-si* SAA X 24:14
(*ša*) LÚ*.GAL–*mu-gu* SAA I 205:15 ~ *pa-an* LÚ*.GAL–*mu-gi* SAA I 160:12
(*ša*) *muš-ke-nu-tú* KAV 197:22
(*ša*) LÚ.*qur-bu-tú* passim (LÚ = *ša*) ~ LÚ*.*qur-bu-te/i* passim
(*a-du-ú*) *ru-ú-bu* SAA XVI 126:14
(*ba-ra-ar*) *ṣa-hu-ra-nu-tú* SAA X 290 s.1
(GIŠ.GU.ZA) LUGAL-*ú-tú* SAA XVI 29:10 ~ LUGAL-*ú-ti* passim
(*ma-qa-at* /) *šá-ru-ru* SAA X 104 e.13-14, 16′ ~ *ba-'i-il* / *šá-ru-ri na-a-ši* SAA X 48:10-11
(*ina* UGU) *ta-hu-mu* SAA X 349 r.22 ~ *ta-hu*(*-ú/u*)-*me/i* passim

[293] Cf. Appendix B.

(*ša*) *ṭup-šar-ru-tú* SAA X 352:20 ~ e.g. *ša ṭup-šar-ru-ti* SAA X 30 r.9; *ša ṭup-šar-u-te* SAA X 351:11
(*a-na*) LÚ*.*zu-ku* SAA I 11:6

Adjectives in the plural:

(*ammiu*) *am-mu-u-tu* SAA XIII 190 r.18 ~ *am-mu*(*-ú*)*-te/ti* passim
(*anniu*) *an-nu-tu* SAA XIII 190:14, 17, r.3; *a-nu-tú* AfO 32 39:16 (BM 103389); *an-nu-tú* SAA V 150 r.4′, Rfdn 17 28:7, SAA I 205 r.14; *ha-an-nu-tú* SAA I 72:6′ ~ (*ha-*)*an-nu-*(*u-*)*ti/e* passim
(*arku*) *ar*]*-ku-*⌜*ú*⌝*-tú* SAA XIII 114:1′ ~ *ar/ár-ku-te* passim
(*āšibu*) *a-ši-bu-tu* SAA XIII 186:7; *a-ši-bu-tú* SAA I 130:8 ~ *a-ši-bu-te/ti* e.g. SAA I 128:5/SAA X 197:15, 16
(*kabru*) *kab-ru-tu* SAA X 353:19
(*ma'du*) *ma-a'-du-tu* SAA X 296:16 ~ *ma-a'-du-te/i* passim
(*maqtu*) LÚ*.*ma-aq-tu-tú* SAA V 245:13 ~ LÚ(*).*ma-aq-tú/tu*(*-u*)*-te* SAA I 181 r.7, NL 98:8 (CTN V 272), SAA XVI 148:17, r.19, SAA XVI 136:6, r.5
(*mērešu*) *mi-ri-šu-tú* SAA X 226 r.3
(*ṣalmu*) *ṣal-mu-u-tú* SAA XIII 118:9
(*šaklulu*) [*šak-l*]*a-lu-tu* SAA V 238:5; GUD.*šak-la-lu-tú* SAA X 353 e.25 ~ GUD.*šak-la-lu-te* ibid. l.23
(*šakrānû*) *šá-ak-ra-nu-tú* SAA XVI 115 r.5
(*ṭābu*) *ṭa-bu-tú* ABL 943:4 (Tammaritu) ~ e.g. *ṭa-bu-u-ti* SAA XIII 12:15, r. 10, SAA XV 159:7′; *ṭa-bu-te* SAA XVI 154 r.6

In the subjunctive and ventive forms:[294]

('lk) *i-la-ku-nu* BT 104:5 (Iraq 25 pl. XX); *il-la-ku-nu* SAA XV 223 r.11 (Šarru-emuranni); *it-tal-ku-nu* SAA XVI 49 r.4,[295] SAA V 245 r.5′ (Zabaiu), SAA XV 226:9 (Šarru-emuranni); *lil-li-ku-nu* NL 67 r.13 (CTN V 215ff) (Duri-Aššur)
('pš) *ep-pa-su-nu* SAA XVI 126 r.23′; *e-pu-su-nu* ibid. r.18′; *e-pu-su-su-nu* ibid. r.21′ (Itti-Šamaš-balaṭu)
('rb) *e-ra-bu-u-nu* SAA XV 90:4 (Mannu-ki-Ninua)
(nph) *i-nap-pa-ha-an-nu*⌝ SAA XVI 128:10 (Itti-Šamaš-balaṭu)
(nš') *ta-na-áš-šú-nu* SAA XV 181 r.10 (Aššur-belu-taqqin)
(prk) GIL-*u-nu* AfO 32 38:15 (BM 103389)
(rb') *i-rab-bu-ú-nu* SAA XVI 127:11; *i-rab-bu-un-nu* SAA XVI 128:11 (both by Itti-Šamaš-balaṭu)
(škn) *iš-kun-u-nu* SAA XVI 129:13′ (possibly by Itti-Šamaš-balaṭu)[296]
(tdn) *i-di-nu-u-nu* SAA XVI 128 r.4′ (Itti-Šamaš-balaṭu); *id-di-nu-u-nu* SAA XVI 127 r.8 (Itti-Šamaš-balaṭu); *ta-di-nu-nu* NL 81 r.3 (CTN V 232f) (Ašipâ)
(*dullu*) *ma-ri dul-lu*!!*-nu* "all the work" SAA XVI 126 r.22′ (Itti-Šamaš-balaṭu) ~ *am–mar dul-lu-ni* SAA XVI 79:8
(*kēnu*) *ke-nu-u-nu* SAA XVI 126:10 (Itti-Šamaš-balaṭu)

---

294 Cf. Deller (1959) § 24c-d.

295 *Sarai* (f.), the author of the letter, has a West Semitic name (cf. PNA 3/I p. 1092 s.v. *Saraia*) and her letter contains many Babylonianisms: *iš-šu-ú* r.1, *qi-bi-i'* r.5, *a-du-u* r.6, *...-na-ši-na* r.7. See also the gods (ll. 3-5) invoked in the greeting formula.

296 See SAA XVI p. 115 n. ad no. 129.

(*ṭēmu*) *ṭè-⌜en⌝-ša-nu-nu* NL 1 r.7[297] (CTN V 19ff, Šamaš-bunaia and Nabû-eṭir) ~ *ša ṭè-en-šú-ni* SAA I 1:15 (CTN V 188ff)

Most of these cases are pure Babylonianisms.

Other cases:

(*issurri*)	*i–su-ru* SAA XV 131 r.21e, s.1 (Nabû-duru-uṣur) ~ *i(s)–su(-ur)-ri* passim
(*kettu*)	*ket-ti* SAA XV 181 r.2 ~ *ke-e-tu*/*ket-tu*/*ú* passim
(*libbu*)	ŠÀ-*bi ša* SAA X 301:10, SAA XV 4 r.10; ŠÀ-*bi* (+ *šaškunu* "to encourage") SAA V 210:14
(*šumma*)	*šum-mu* ABL 896 r.3 (Aia-zeru-qiša*)*, SAA X 245 r.8, SAA X 255:14, SAA X 257:9, SAA X 258 r.6, SAA X 261:10, SAA V 54 r.4, SAA V 182 r.8′ (all the SAA X examples: Marduk-šakin-šumi), otherwise *šúm-mu* passim ~ *šúm-ma* passim
(*tūra*)	*tu-ú-ru* SAA X 300:5′ ~ *tu-(u/ú)-ra* passim
(*ūdi*)	*ú-du* (3rd sg.) SAA XVI 127:14, r.6, 14. Note also the alternation of the same verb (*udû*) in plural forms, e.g. *l*]*u-u-du-u* SAA V 178 e.12′; *lu-ú-du-ú* SAA I 132:15; ABL 390 r.7′ ~ *lu ud-di-ú* SAA X 29:3, ⌜*lu*⌝*-u-di-ú* SAA V 117:16

4.6 Regressive vowel dissimilation: /*u*/ > /*a*/

In Neo-Assyrian,[298] the short and unstressed /*u*/ of an open syllable can be replaced by /*a*/ before a stressed (short or long) /*u*/.[299] This dissimilation is optional.[300] For example:

(qbī) *iq-ba-ka-nu-u-ni* SAA II 6:102 (occurs in several manuscripts; dissimil. *-kunu-* > *-kanu-*), but ~ *qa-ba-šú-nu-u-ni* SAA I 260 r.15 (*-šunu-*)

Some words (*unūtu* > *anūtu* "utensils, tools, implements," *šukuttu* > *šakuttu* "jewellery, decoration,"[301] *ukultu* > *akussu* and *ukullû* > *akullû* "food," for the examples of the two last-mentioned, consult dictionaries) confirm that this dissimilation not only occurred just before subj./vent./pronominal endings, but that *a* was apparently widely replacing *u* on the lexical level too in word-initial position.

---

[297] The interpretation given in CTN V is ungrammatical.

[298] Already in Middle Assyrian, cf. Mayer (1971) 12-13 and Postgate (1974) 274. Neo-Assyrian examples are given by Deller (1959) § 39j-m.

[299] See Parpola (1972) 23.

[300] LAS II ad no. 166:14. As a rough estimate, it appears that subjunctival verbs and nouns with disyllabic infixes/suffixes (dative/accusative and possessive suffix) of the second- and third-person plural are considerably rarer written without dissimilation than with dissimilation. E.g. in SAA II 6 there are numerous *iq-ba-ka-nu(-u)-ni* forms (also in the present tense: *iqabbakkanūni*), but not a single *iqbakkunūni* form.

[301] See Parpola (1972) 23.

Dissimilation in nominal stems:

(*abutu*)	*a-ba-tu-ni* SAA XVI 127 r.1; *a-bat-u-ni* SAA V 52 r.19 ~ *a-bu-tu-u-ni* SAA XVI 105 r.6
(*hubullu*)	*ha-bul-li* SAA I 159 e.20, r.6, 11; *ha-bu-ul-li* CTN III 1 e.10; *ha-bul-le-ia* BM 103390 r.8; *ha-bul-li-k[a]* SAA I 159:7; *ha-bu-li-ni* SAA I 147 r.12
(*mu'un/ttu*)	*ma-'u-tú* ND 10009 r.36 (CTN III 87 [edition], CTN I pl. 47 [copy]); *ma-'u-te* (sg.) NL 24 r.10 (CTN V 196f); *ma-'u-ti* BT 107:6, Iraq 23 51:8; *ma-'u-ta-a-[ti]* NL 52:5 (CTN V 193f)
(*qubūru*)	*qa-bu-ra-ni* BT 106:5 (Iraq 25 91)
(*šukuttu*)	*ša-kut-tum* SAA XIII 134 r.3; *šá-kut-tú* SAA X 349:26 ~ *šu-ku-ut-tu* SAA XIII 59:10
(*ubussu*)	*a-bu-sa-a-te* SAA XIII 71 r.3; *a-bu-sa-te* CT 53 302:2′
(*unūtu*)	*a-nu-tú* SAA XVI 139:6; *a-nu-ti* SAA XIII 50:4, e.11; *a-nu-ut* SAA XIII 154 r.6, SAA XV 362:5′; *a-nu-ti-šú* SAA XVI 141:3′; *a-nu-su* SAA X 387 r.2; *a-nu-su-nu* SAA V 97:9 ~ *ú-nu-tú* SAA II 6:276 cf. also 1 GIS.*ú-nu-tú* NL 17 e.11 (CTN V 283f)
(*uruthū*)	*aruthē*, see Deller and Finkel (1984) 82-83

However, in one special case,[302] the change of /*u*/ into /*a*/ is clearly grammatically conditioned: the masculine forms of the third-person plural and singular can be distinguished from each other by the vowel dissimilation in the subjunctive (and ventive) forms of the present and preterite tense of the basic stem and in the stative forms of the D- and Š-stems. In these cases, the dissimilation is thus reserved for marking the plural form. This dissimilation is particularly often observed in complicated clause structures, as well as in cases where singular and plural forms are close to one another. It thus contributes to the interpretation of passages which would otherwise possibly remain obscure. The dissimilation is regular in contexts that involve an activity of the king.[303]

Examples of the dissimilation in connection with the ventive and subjunctive endings.

The preterite forms (all the forms are 3rd pl., unless otherwise mentioned):

('gr)	*e-ga-ru-ni-ni* SAA XV 2:6
('kl)	*e-kal-u-ni* SAA X 107 s.2, SAA II 6:332B (*[e-k]al-*) ~ *e-kul-u-ni* (3rd sg.) SAA X 43:11
('mr)	*e-ma-ru-u-ni* SAA XV 88:10, SAA VIII 21 r.8 ~ *e-mur-u-ni* SAA XIII 187:15
('pš)	*e-pa-šú-u-ni* SAA X 221:14, ABL 1148 r.7 ~ *e-pu-šú-ni* (3rd sg.) SAA I 8 r.10
(gld)	*ig-la-du-u-ni* SAA V 202 r.12
(kṣr)	*lik-ṣa-ru-ni* SAA I 148 r.11e
(mhr)	*ih-ha-ru-ú-ni* SAA I 190:10 ~ *i-hu-ur-ú-[ni]* (3rd sg.) SAA I 118:5
(mqt)	*in-qa-tu-ni-⸢ni⸣* SAA XV 43:3′ ~ *in-qut-u-ni* SAA V 227 s.4
(mrṣ, *a/a*)	*i]m-ra-ṣu-ni* SAA X 200 r.3′; *im-ra-aṣ-ṣu-ni* SAA X 316:10 cf. *am-ra-ṣu-ni* (1st sg.) StAT 1 52:7

[302] See Fabritius (1995) 51-55.

[303] Ibid. 55.

(mth) *in-ta-hu-u-ni* SAA XV 119 r.5; *li-in-ta-h*[*u-ni* SAA XIII 2 r.4′
(nsh) *li-is-sa-hu-u-ni* SAA X 55 r.5
(shr) *is-ha-ru-ni* NL 45 r.10′ (CTN V 136ff) ~ *is-hur-u-ni* (3rd sg.) SAA XIII 157:12′
(ṣbt, *a/a*) *iṣ-bat-*⸢*ú*⸣*-ni* (here, the subjunctive ending neutralizes vowel harmony) SAA XVI 21 r.4 cf. e.g. *li-iṣ-*[*b*]*u-tu* SAA I 246:11; (*i*)*-ṣi-bu-tú* SAA V 53 r.8
(šdd) *liš-da-du-*[*u-ni*] SAA I 102:7; *is-da-du-ni-ni* SAA XV 60:14
(škn) *iš-ka-nu-ni* SAA X 221 e.18; *iš-ka-nu-u-ni* SAA X 98 r.3 ~ *iš-kun-u-ni* BM 103390 r.3
(špr) *iš-pa-ru-niš-šú* SAA XV 1:21; *liš-pa-ru-ni* SAA X 245 r.10, SAA I 33:18; *liš-pa-ru-u-ni* SAA I 177:19, NL 50 r.14 (CTN V 182ff), SAA XV 36 r.16; *l*]*i-iš-pa-ru-u-ni* SAA V 144 s.2′; *liš-pa-ru-*[*né*]-⸢*e*⸣ SAA XV 151 r.9; *liš*]*-pa-ru-niš-šú-nu* SAA X 361 r.9
(šṭr) *áš-ṭa-ru-u-ni* (1st sg.) SAA V 121:12

Statives (D-stem):

(gmr) *gam-mar-u-ni* SAA XIII 108 r.9, SAA X 109 r.3; *gam-ma-ru-ni* SAA XIII 88:11; *gam-ma-ru-u-ni* SAA XIII 88:14, SAA XIII 86 r.14; *gam-ma-ru-ú-ni* SAA XIII 103:9, 12
(kms) *kam-ma-su-u-ni* SAA V 53 r.10; *kam-ma-su-ni* NL 10:12 (CTN V 43ff) ~ e.g. *kam-mu-su-u-ni* SAA X 277 r.6, SAA XVI 121:8
(ksp) *ka-sa-pu-ni* SAA I 77 r.7

Cf. present forms (all pl.; another matter is if it is desirable to call these forms dissimilations or not):[304]

---

[304] According to Fabritius ([1995] 55), in the present, it is theoretically possible to separate plural and singular verb forms of the third-person masculine from one another by vowel dissimilation. He gives two examples in which the plural subject is unambiguously in the present and which include vowel dissimilation /*u*/ > /*a*/: *i-da-ba-bu-u-ni* 4R^2 61 v 5 (SAA IX 1) and ⸢*i-sa-ha*⸣*-r*[*u*]- ⸢*ni*⸣ ABL 1041 r.11′ (SAA XV 157) (while the example with *qarāhu* is less certain, see Fabritius (1955) 53, example no. 7 [ABL 531 = SAA XIII 127]). Thus, the dissimilation also works in practice, and not only in theory, on the verbs *dabābu* and *sahāru*, because both of them belong to the *u/u* class of verbs. However, in the present tense this distinction between plural and singular forms by vowel dissimilation does not work out in other verb classes where the shift /*u*/ > /*a*/ cannot either be treated as a dissimilation or where the dissimilation just does not happen. Therefore, this distinction concerns only a minority of verbs in the present (*u/u* class), whereas most of the Neo-Assyrian verbs belong to the *a/u*-class. Other classes are rare *a/i* (although including, e.g., all the original primae-*w* verbs and few very common Neo-Assyrian verbs: *tadānu, alāku*) and *i/i*. Hence the differentiation between plural and singular forms by vowel dissimilation remains almost only theoretical. On the other hand, if we consider the present plural forms of the *a/u* and *a/i* classes having -*aCūni* as dissimilation, we get of course many more dissimilated forms. However, Fabritius rejects this possibility, ibid. 53, by reasoning that /*a*/ is not a dissimilated /*u*/, but non-assimilated /*a*/ in those verb forms. An alternative approach may still be justified, and a theory can be developed stating that vowel harmony would originally have been realized in forms of *a/u* and *a/i* classes: *ekkal* + *ū* > *ekkulū*/*ekkūl* (and *illak* + *ū* > *illukū*/*illūk*), but adding the subjunctive ending to these forms would have caused a dissimilation of the same quality as the original *a* (of a singular form): *ekkulū*/*ekkūl* + *ūni* > *ekkalūni* (and *illukū*/*illūk* + *ūni* > *illakūni*). In that case, the added subjunctive (or some other stressed morpheme at the end of a word) would either restore the original vowel or prevent the realization of vowel harmony. Note that the Neo-Assyrian vowel harmony is an assimilatory process that takes place between the second to

('kl) *e-ka-lu-u-ni* SAA I 10:6 ~ *e-ku-lu* passim
('lk) *il-la-ku-u-ni* passim; *il-la-ku-ú-né-e* SAA XIII 102 r.3
('pš) *e-pa-šú-u-ni* SAA I 147:5, SAA IV 322 r.4; *e-[p]a-áš-šú-u-ni* SAA V 56:12; *e-pa-šu-niš-šu-un-ni* SAA II 6:169M (also other manuscripts with *e-pa-*... but manuscripts I and P have forms with *e-pu-*..., cf. the textual variants of SAA II 6:169 in the critical apparatus of SAA II, p. 35)
('rb) *e-ra-bu-u-nu* SAA XV 90:4
('rš) ⸢*e*⸣*-ra-šu-u-ni* SAA XVI 86 r.12′
(mth) *i-ma-ta-hu-né-e* (interrogative int.) "Should they be picked up?" SAA I 33:15
(rgm) *i-ra-ga-mu-ni* StAT 1 51 r.8
(špr) [*i-š*]*ap-par-u-ni* SAA VIII 63 r.7
(tdn) *i-da-nu-ni* SAA V 100 r.11, ABL 75 r.2 (LAS 37); *id-da-nu-u-ni* SAA XVI 86:15, 16; *id-da-nu-ni* SAA XVI 84:11; *i-da-nu-ni-šú-nu* SAA V 257 r.1; *i-da-nu-na-ši-ni* NL 26 r.4 (CTN V 92f); *id-da-nu-na-ši* SAA XVI 84 r.7; *i-da-nu-ši-na-a-ni* SAA I 33 r.3
(wbl) *ub-bal-lu-ni* SAA I 66 s.2; *ú-ba-lu-ni* SAA I 33:16, SAA XIII 17:8′
(wšb) *uš-ša-bu-ni* SAA XIII 168:13.
(wšr) *ú-šá-ru-ni* SAA VIII 157 r.7

Pronouns:

(*attunu*)*at-ta-nu-u-ni*[305] SAA I 25:9 ~ *at-tu-nu-u-ni* SAA X 228:16
(*šunu*) *ša-nu-u-ni* SAA XV 54:5′; *šá-nu-u-ni* NL 86:10 (CTN V 239f) ~ *šu-nu-u-ni* SAA X 293:22′, SAA I 183:21′

Suffixed pronominal forms:

(*-kunu-*):
(*bēlu*) EN-*ka-nu-u-ni* SAA II 6:191
(*dēnu*) *de-en-ka-nu-ni* StAT 1 54 r.10
(*šarru*) LUGAL-*ka-nu-*[*ni* SAA II 6:191
('pš) *ep-šá-*(*a*)*-ka-nu-ni* BM 132980:6, r.4′ (Assurbanipal)
(glī Š) *ú-šá-ga-lu-ka-nu-ni* ABL 541 r.4 (Assurbanipal)
(klm D)*ú-kal-lim-u-ka-nu-ni* SAA II 6:63, 93 cf. e.g. ~ (smk D) *ú-sam-ma-ak-ak-ku-nu-ni* BM 132980 r.20′ (Assurbanipal)
(kpd Š) *ú-šak-pa-du-ka-nu-u-ni* SAA II 6:322N, 336frg (see also ibid. other manuscripts for the lines 322, 336)
(qbī) *iq-ba-ka-nu-*(*u*)*-ni* SAA II 6:64, 102, 125; *i-qab-ba-*(*ak*)*-ka-nu-*(*u*)*-ni* SAA II 6:323; *iq-qa-ba-kan-u-ni* SAA II 6:323N
(shr D) *ú-sa-ha-ru-ka-nu-*[*ni*] ABL 541 r.6 (Assurbanipal)
(tdn) [*i*]*-ta-nu-ni-ka-nu-u* (question) "Did they [g]ive ...?" SAA XVI 67:8′; SUM-*ka-nu-ni* SAA V 264:6′

---

last and the last vowel of a word only, and that any additional morpheme, such as the subjunctive, may correspondingly "confuse" the stress of the whole word and cause dissimilation.

305 Cf. Lipiński (1997) § 36.5. Contrary to his interpretation, the "original vowel" (= *a*) of the second syllable of the pronoun *attunu*, attested in the form *attanūni*, has been specifically restored by dissimilation caused by the stress of the following syllable. Since the vowel *a* can be accounted for by this rule, it does not have to be an original vowel.

(**-*šunu***):

(*hašaddu*) *ha-šad-da-šá-nu-u-ni* SAA XIII 78 r.17 cf. e.g. *a-hi-ta-te-šú-nu-u-ni* SAA II 5 iii 26′
(*pû*) *pi-i-ša-nu-ú-*[*ni*] SAA XV 42:12
(*ṭēmu*) *ṭè-*⸢*en*⸣*-ša-nu-nu* NL 1 r.7 (CTN V 19ff)
(’šr) *a-šur-ú-šá-nu-ni* SAA I 195 r.2
(’tq Š) [*ú-š*]*e-ta-qu-ni-šá-nu-u-ni* NL 86:16 (CTN V 239f) cf. e.g. *ú-š*]*at-ba-šú-nu-u-ni* SAA V 57:6; (’br Š) *ú-še-bar-ru-šu-nu-u-ni* SAA V 100 r.13
(dūk) *ta-du-ka-a-šá-nu-ni* SAA II 6:140
(klm) *ú-ka-la-mu-šá-nu-ni* SAA I 82 r.3
(qbī) *iq-ba-áš-šá-nu-u-ni* SAA XVI 63:10
(rmū) *ú-ra-mu-šá-nu-u-ni* SAA XVI 62 r.6′
(sīq) *i-si-qa-áš-šá-nu-ú-ni* ABL 561 r.10 (Assurbanipal)
(slm D) ⸢*ú*⸣*-sa-li-mu-šá-nu-*⸢*ni*⸣ SAA XV 90:9
(ṣbt) *ta-ṣab-bat-a-šá-nu-ni* SAA II 6:139
(škn) *iš-ka-nu-šá-nu-u-ni*[306] SAA XVI 21:14
(špr) *a-šap-par-áš-šá-nu-u-ni* ABL 543:13 (Assurbanipal); KIN-*áš-šá-nu-u-ni* ABL 1108:10′ (Assurbanipal); *i-šap-par-šá-nu-ni* SAA XV 4:16
(wbl Gtn) *ta-ta-nab-bal-a-šá-nu-u-ni* SAA II 6:98frg ~ *ta-ta-na-bal-a-šú-nu-u-ni* ibid. ms. I

Before other enclitic endings:

(*-ma*) *is-se-e-šá-nu-ma* SAA XV 90:9; *ka-šá-nu-*⸢*u*⸣*-ma* SAA XVI 63 r.1
(*-šina*) *li-in-ta-hu-ši-na* SAA V 295 r.6
(*-šunu*) (pṭr) *i-pa-ṭa-ru-šú-nu* NL 12 r.16 (CTN V 155ff); (š’l) *li*[*š-a*]*l-lu-šú-nu* SAA XIII 128 r.13 (the pronominal ending neutralizes vowel harmony: *ipaṭṭuru; liš’ullu*, e.g. *liš-ú-lu* passim)

Before interrogative intonation or other sort of stressed *-u*:

(question): *il-la-ku-ú* SAA XVI 27 r.4′; *it-taq-qa-nu-u* SAA I 239:6; *i-da-nu-ni-šá-nu-ú* SAA I 257 r.5 ~ possibly e.g. *iš-ku-nu-u-*[*ni*] (ending not certain in a broken cont.) SAA XVI 33 r.2′
(*-û*) *ik-ka-nu-ú* SAA XV 69:13; *iš-šá-nu-ú* ibid. e.24, SAA VIII 11 r.2 (*-n*[*u-u*) ~ *i-šu-nu-u* SAA I 182:11′

Before the plural and abstract ending *-ūt*:

(*paršumu*) LÚ.*par-šá-mu-te* SAA II 5 iii 7′; LÚ.*par-ša-mu-te* SAA X 226:16; LÚ*.*par-šá-mu-ti* SAA XV 24 r.16
(*rakkusu*) *rak-ka-su-te* SAA XIII 88 r.8
(*šahsusūtu*) *šah-sa-su-te* SAA X 96 r.17
(*šaklulu*) GUD.*šak-la-lu-te* SAA X 353:23; GUD.*šak-la-lu-tú* ibid. e.25

306 *iš-ka-nu-šá-nu-ni* is an interesting form, since the dissimilation is realized twice in it before two different (primarily and secondarily) stressed syllables. Therefore, in appearance, the form looks like a dissimilated masculine plural form, but the context of the passage is so clear that one cannot be mistaken in identifying the subject (= the king).

4.7 Marking the stressed syllable, shift of stress and opening of an overlong syllable

In Neo-Assyrian writings, the stressed syllable is expressed by (1) the auxiliary vowel (at the end of a word) and (2) the gemination of a consonant. The vowel of the stressed syllable can also be written as long (3).

(1) */dīn/* <*dīni*>, */muk/* <*muku*>, */nuk/* <*nuku*>
(2) */laqe/* <*laqqe*>
(3) */taddin/* <*tādin*>

Case (1) is rather common in monosyllabic words of the type (C)V̄C. Owing to the auxiliary vowel, the words in question change into disyllables.

Examples of the addition of an auxiliary vowel to a stressed (mono)syllable (for the group in question, see 4.8.2):

(*muk*) *mu-ku* (quotation particle) passim ~ *muk* passim; *mu-uk* passim
(*nuk*) *nu-ku* (quotation particle) passim ~ *nu-uk* passim
(*bēt*) *bé-te* (subordinating particle) SAA V 25 r.5, 6
(*šīt* < not in NA) *šīti* ("she" f.), e.g. *ši-i-ti* SAA V 74:6 (CTN V 103f), SAA I 247 r.5; *ši-i-ti-i-[ma]* SAA XVI 181 r.3
(*šūt* < not in NA) *šu-u-tú* ("he") passim

Syllabic spellings may give a hint of changes in stress and syllable boundary, as in forms of the preposition *issi* "with" followed by monosyllabic possessive suffixes (all suffixes in question are either singular or 1st pl.). In these forms, the first syllable of the preposition is often written <*i-*> instead of <*is-*>. Thus, it can be assumed that the addition of the possessive suffix shifted the stress in these forms onto the penultimate syllable, with a concomitant weakening of the geminated consonant (*issi* + *ka* > *isēka*):[307]

(2nd sg.) *i-si-ia* passim; *i-se-e-a* SAA I 124:17, SAA XV 24 r.17; *i-še-e-a* SAA XV 17:7 ~ *is-si-ia* passim; *is-se-e-a* SAA I 205:14, SAA X 354:5, 10, e.27; *iš-se-e-a* NL 96 r.14 (CTN V 49ff)
(2nd sg.) *i-se-ka* passim; ⸢*i*⸣*-se-e-ka* NL 27:10 (CTN V 286f) ~ *is-se-ka* passim; *is-se-e-ka* CT 53 908 r.2 (Assurbanipal)
(3rd sg.) *i-se-šú* passim; *i-si-šú* SAA V 2 r.6, SAA I 124 r.13; *i-se-e-šú* SAA I 29:31, SAA I 35 r.3′, SAA I 124:22, SAA X 369:12, SAA XVI 43 r.8, VAT 9855:6′ ~ *is-se-šú passim*; *is-se-e-šú* SAA I 4:13′, SAA XIII 134 r.4, 6, SAA X 97 r.8; *is-[se]-e-šú* SAA X 353 r.7; *is-si-šá* SAA XVI 78 r.11
(1st pl.) *i-se-ni* passim; *i-si-ni* SAA I 92 r.10, SAA XVI 62 r.6′; *i-se-e-ni* SAA I 210 r.14 ~ *is-se-ni passim*; *is-*⸢*si-ni*⸣ SAA I 1:18 (CTN V 188ff), SAA XV 92 r.10′; *is-se-e-ni* SAA XVI 21:10, SAA XV 90 r.20; *is-se-en-ni* SAA XV 131:9

---

[307] See Parpola (1997A) 317 n. 6.

By contrast, the substitution of <*i-*> for <*is-*> is quite rare in corresponding forms with the second- and third-person plural possessive suffixes:

(2nd pl.)	*i-si-ku-nu* SAA I 172:6 (CTN V 173ff), NL 1 r.11 (CTN V 19ff) ~ e.g. *is-si-ku-nu* SAA X 290 r.5′
(3rd pl.)	*e-si-šú-nu* SAA XIII 43:7; *i-si-šú-nu* NL 100:10 (CTN V 118f), NL 99 r.21′ (CTN V 109ff) ~ *is-si-šú-nu* SAA V 78 r.14, SAA XV 95:10′, SAA XVI 21:18, r.5; *is-se-e-šú-nu* SAA X 354:13, SAA XV 95:12′

In interrogative intonation, the pitch rises sharply on the last syllable of a word and causes the lengthening of the last syllable. However, this does not always appear in the plene writing of verbal forms. If the last syllable was a closed syllable ending in a consonant, then an anaptyctic vowel was usually added to the form. The anaptyctic vowel always follows the colour of the preceding vowel.[308]

Of the examples below, the first (*amāru*) and fourth (*epāšu*) cannot be interpreted as verb forms of the third-person plural. This is because the vowel which followed the original last syllable (a closed syllable ending in a consonant) of these examples is only opening the closed syllable, which is an auxiliary vowel that eases the syllable structure of the verb form.[309] E.g.

(*amāru*)	[*e*]-*mu-u-ru* (prt 3rd sg. + interrogative int.) "[Has he s]een ...?" SAA I 260 r.12
(*dabābu*)	*issi libbīka* / *lā ta-ad-bu-ú-bu*!! (prt 2nd sg. + interrogative int.) "Have you not said to yourself?" SAA I 11:13-14
(*elēlu*)	⸢*i*⸣-*te-li-li* (pf 3rd sg. + interrogative int.) "Did he become clean?" SAA X 184 r.9
(*epāšu*)	*le-e-pu-u-šu* (prc 1st sg. + interrogative int.) "Should I perform (these rites)?" SAA X 274 r.8 ~ (not interrogative int.) *le-pu-uš* SAA V 2 r.1; *le-e-pu-uš* SAA XVI 34:19, SAA XVI 35 r.4′; *le-e-pu-šú* CT 53 169 r.1 (coord.)
	ep-pa-a-šá (prs 1st sg. + interrogative int.) "Shall I perform (the ritual)?" SAA X 258:7′
(*sadāru*)	*la-as-de-e-re* (prc 1st sg. + interrogative int.) // *ina ši-a-ri* "Should I array them tomorrow?"[310] SAA XIII 95:14-r.1, *ina kal-la-ma-a-ri* ANŠE.KUR.RA.MEŠ / *la-as-de-e-re* "Should I array the horses early in the morning?" SAA XIII 100 r.9-10 ~ (not interrogative int.) *la-as-dir* SAA XIII 92 r.12; *la-*[*as-d*]*ir* SAA XIII 123 r.2′
(*šapāru*)	*ni-iš-pu-u-ru* (cohort. 1st pl.) "Shall we send word ... ?" SAA V 139:7

Thus sometimes interrogative intonation cannot be recognized as such from the way the original last syllable is written, but only from the added anaptyctic vowel:

at-ta la te-⸢*ra*⸣*-b*[*a*[311] (prs 2nd m.sg.) "Will you not enter?" SAA X 246:4′

[308] Deller (1965A) 38.

[309] LAS II ad no. 208 r.8.

[310] Translated in SAA XIII 95 "I will array them tomorrow".

[311] LAS II ad no. 187:4′.

Examples of interrogative intonation in third-person plural verbal forms are:

(*alāku*)	*il-la-ku-ú* "Should they go?" SAA XVI 27 r.4′; *il-la-ku-ú-né-e* "Are they coming in?" SAA XIII 102 r.3
(*bašû*)	*ib*?*-ši-ia-a* (prt 3rd f.pl., *nusāhi*) NL 74 r.13′ (CTN V 132ff)
(*ebāru*)	*li-bir-né-e* (prc 3rd pl. + vent. + interrogative int., syncope: *-u-* > 0) NL 78 r.6′ (CTN V 245f)
(*epāšu*)	*ep-pa-šu-ú* "Are they to perform ...?" SAA XIII 46:6′
(*šamṣû*)	*im–ma-ti ú-šá-an-ṣu-u* "When can they do it?" SAA X 14 r.5

The use of the perfect in questions marked by intonation is only limited to clauses for which a yes/no-answer is expected, i.e. so-called "echo questions."[312] Some of these examples seem to be chiefly rhetorical in nature.

Examples of the use of the perfect in questions:

('lk)	*i-tal-ku-u* (3rd pl.) "Are they going?" KAV 214:8 (for the perfect referring to the future, see 6.3)
('rb)	LÚ*.2-*u* / *ša* LÚ*.*tur-ta-ni* / *e-tar-ba-a* "Has the commander-in-chief's deputy come in?" SAA XIII 81 r.1-3; *te-tar-ba-*[*a*] "Has it come in?" SAA XIII 118 r.3
(kl')	*ak-tal-šú-u* "Could I hold him back?" SAA V 147 r.9
(qbī)	TA* IGI *ri-i-bi* / *iq-ṭi-bi-i* "Is it because of the earthquake that he has said: ...?" SAA X 203:8-9
(škn)	LUGAL *be-lí uz-nu is-sa-ka-a-na* "Has the king, my lord, paid attention [to this]?" SAA X 90 r.12′

Orthographically marked lengthening of a stressed syllable:

/dari/	*da-a-ri* (stat 3rd sg.) SAA X 357:10
/da'iq/	*lu-u de-e-iq* SAA XVI 34:7; *de-e-i-qi* SAA VIII 1 r.4 ~ *de-iq* passim
/gamir/	*ga-a-m*[*ir* SAA X 4 r.1
/hadi/	*lu ha-ad-di* SAA X 185 r.20
/hasi/	*ha-a-si* SAA X 96 r.10
/mala/	*ma-a-la* SAA X 315 r.11, SAA XVI 86:8
/maṣi/	*ma-aṣ-ṣi* SAA X 294 r.9, SAA XIII 7 r.9 ~ *ma-ṣi* passim
/maṭi/	*ma-aṭ-ṭi* SAA XVI 139 r.2, SAA X 349:11; *ma-aṭ-ṭi-ia-at* ibid. l.13
/naši/	*na-a-ši* (stat 3rd sg.) SAA X 48:11, *na-a-*[*ši*] SAA X 52 r.11
/pati/	*pa-a-te* SAA VIII 82:9; *pa-a-ti* SAA X 253 r.5
/qabi/	*qa-a-bi* SAA VIII 52:6
/qibi/	*qi-i-bi* SAA X 2:18
/raṣip/	*ra-a-*[*ṣip*] SAA X 4:6′
/raši/	*ra-áš-ši* SAA I 190 r.9′
/šaṭir/	*šá-aṭ-ṭir* SAA XIII 12:17
/tadin/	*ta-a-din*, see n. 376 below.

Emphatic shift of stress (note its marking with an additional vowel or with an additional consonant):[313]

(*abutu*)	*ina* UGU *a-bé-e-te* CT 53 974:5

---

[312] Ibid. ad no. 148:9.

[313] LAS II ad no. 252 r.10.

(*arhiš*)	*ár-hi-ši ár-hi-ši* KAV 214:12; *ár-hi-ši* VAT 9770 r.14 ~ *ar-hiš* SAA I 29 r.9; *ár-hiš* SAA I 22:9, SAA V 45:5, SAA V 115 r.4, SAA X 151 r.3, SAA X 236:8 and passim; *ar-hi-iš* SAA V 298:13′, SAA V 7 r.5′; *a-na ar-hi-iš* SAA I 24:8; [*a-n*]*a ár-hiš* SAA XIII 158:5′
(*laššu*)	*la-a-šú la-a* ... *la-a-áš-šu* SAA I 245:5′, 8′
(*nagiu*)	*i-na* KUR *ma-ti-ia* / *i-na na-gi-ia-a la tú-ra-da* "Do not come down to my country and my district!" SAA V 260:8′-9′
(*nahnāhutu*)	*ina* UGU / *na-ah-na-he-e-te* SAA X 322 r.9-10 ~ *na-ah-na-hu-tú* ibid. r.11
(*naššuqu*)	*nu-ú-na-áš-*⸢*šiq*⸣ SAA I 133 r.9′; *lu-u-na-*⸢*áš*⸣*-šiq* ibid. r.3′

Lengthening of a vowel or a consonant before a possessive suffix:

1st sg.	(*dāmu*) *da-me-e-a* SAA XV 30:13
	(*emūqu*) LÚ*.*e-muq-e-a* SAA XV 30 r.9
	(*mihru*) *ina qa-ni mi-ih-re-e-a* SAA XV 30:15
	(*issi*) *i-se-e-a* SAA XV 24 r.17, SAA I 124:17
2nd sg.	(*duāku*) *du-a-ki-i-ka* SAA XVI 10:4′
3rd sg.	(*pānu*) IGI-*e-šú* StAT 1 51 r.7
1st pl.	(*dullu*) *dul-li-in-ni* (cf. 1st pl. forms in the paragraph 5.4) SAA X 215 r.1, SAA XV 100:7
2nd pl.	(*dullu*) *dul-la-ku-nu* NL 12:25 (CTN V 155ff), SAA XV 344:4′
	(*pilku*) *pi-il-ka-ku-nu* SAA I 235:21
3rd pl.	(*dullu*) *dul-la-áš-*[*šú-nu*] SAA XV 100 r.3
	(*pānu*) IGI-*e-šú-nu* StAT 1 54 r.1
	(*pilku*) *pil-ka-šú-u-nu* SAA XV 156 r.9 cf. *pi-il-ka-šu-nu* SAA I 235:20; *p*[*i*]*l-ku-šú-nu* SAA V 56:6

In perfect forms:

('mr)	*ta-ta-ma-a-ra* "Did you see ...?" SAA XVI 5 r.22
(pt')	*ip-ti-e-ti* "it departed (from it)" SAA VIII 55 r.12e
(rbī)	*ir-ti-i-bi* "(the sun) set" SAA VIII 47:4

The change of a vowel in a stressed syllable (*i* > *e*):

/*ašpurūkīni*/	*áš-pur-*[*k*]*e-e-ni* CT 53 974 r.5
/*bulṭīšu*/	*bul-ṭe-e-šú* SAA X 315:10
/*din*/	[*di*]-⸢*e*⸣-*ni* SAA I 192:11
/*hīṭ*/	*he-e-ṭe* StAT 1 56 r.3
/*issī'a*/	*i-se-e-a* SAA XV 24 r.17, SAA I 124:17; *i-še-e-a* SAA XV 17:7; /*issīka*/ ⸢*i*⸣-*se-e-ka* NL 27:10 (CTN V 286f); /*issīšu*/ *i-se-e-šú* passim; /*issīni*/ *i-se-e-ni* SAA I 210 r.14
/*līpi*/	*le-e-bi* SAA XVI 96 r.5
/*nagî*/	*na-ge-e* NL 87:8, 10 (CTN V 225ff)
/*pānīšu*/	IGI-*e-šú* StAT 1 51 r.7; /*pānīšunu*/ IGI-*e-šú-nu* StAT 1 54 r.1
/*sakikkīšu*/	*sa-kik-ke-e-šú* SAA X 315:12
/*tīr*/	*te-e-re* SAA XV 186 r.8
/*uttīr*/	*ut-te-e-re* SAA XIII 126 r.9′

4.8 Anaptyctic vowels[314]

Cf. also 4.7.

Anaptyctic vowels always follow the quality of the preceding vowel. They occur both in nouns and in finite verb forms. In Neo-Assyrian, these vowels are to be interpreted phonetically, not orthographically.[315] Presumably their main function in nouns was to balance the syllabic structure and thus to keep the rhythm of the language undisturbed.[316] However, in finite verbal forms they had other functions as well. Many verbal forms with anaptyctic vowels can be explained only with reference to syntax, and in these cases the vowels in question will have served primarily to indicate relationships between larger syntactic structures, such as phrases, clauses and sentences.

The following functions of anaptyctic vowels can be distinguished (the numbering of the functions of anaptyctic vowels continues in spite of the division of sections [4.8-4.8.3]):

(1) In interrogative intonation,[317] the anaptyctic vowel marks the rising pitch (for examples, see 4.7).

(2) The additional vowel, placed between consonants, can separate two consecutive and potentially stressed syllables from one another when the stress had possibly either shifted from its original position, or had fallen on the latter of the two syllables. Then an added vowel gives a hint as to the position of the stress on a word. This is also related to the sometimes discernible secondary gemination of a consonant instead of the mere adding of an anaptyctic vowel (in this case, a complete syllable [as model CV] is added to a form). The purpose of this probably was to hinder the development of consecutive, short, open syllables (CVC + CV-syllabification instead of the CV + CV).[318] The anaptyctic vowels in nouns belong to this group. Sonorants seem to produce these anaptyctic vowels in many of the following examples.[319]

---

[314] Cf. Deller (1959) § 8-17. Usually in the scientific literature, these vowels are either called schwa, epenthetic or anaptyctic vowels. In the German-speaking literature of Assyriology, "überhängende" and "Sprossvokale" are the corresponding established terms in use.

[315] Certainly some of the writings are scribal errors.

[316] See Parpola (1975) 2.

[317] Ibid., as well as the examples of paragraph 2 at the end of this unpublished article.

[318] LAS II ad no. 39:11.

[319] On sonorants – especially on the similarity between liquids [*r*, *l*] and vowels, and their ability to develop and modify vowels, as well as being the "carriers" of intonation, etc., see Matouš and Petrácek (1956) 5-7 and 12 in particular. As a matter of fact, in reality there is a lot of dispersion in the phonetic realization of anaptyctic vowels, and all the transitional stages from an ultra short schwa, to a schwa with the length of a short vowel, are even possible in one idiolect. It may also be difficult to determine whether an "additional" vocalic segment is really audible or not. Usually schwa is adopted more easily in environments which have a very strong sonority, see Itkonen (1970) 428-30, 436. Bearing all this in mind, it is not really surprising that in Neo-Assyrian (often conservative) orthography the marking of phonetic anaptyctic vowels is by no means systematic.

4.8.1 Anaptyctic vowels before the stress

Examples are arranged according to sonority: nm > lr > bdg > hz > ṭqṣ > ptk > sš; in the examples, the additional vowel is the one which occurs between the consonants (marked in parentheses)

(br) *e-⸢ta⸣-ba-⸢ru⸣-ni* NL 41:28 (CTN V 208ff)
a-sa-par-ak-ka SAA XV 186 r.10; *a-sa-bar-a-ka* KAV 215 r.11 ~ *a-sap-rak-ka* SAA I 1:13 (CTN V 188ff), NL 37 r.9 (CTN V 84f); *a-sa-ap-rak-ka* SAA I 11:19; *as-sap-rak-ka* SAA XIII 40:11, r.5; *as-sa-pa-rak-ka* MAss 100:8

(mr) KUR].*ha-mar-a-na-a-a* SAA I 90:11

(pr) *ši-pir-a-ti* SAA IV 302:1; ^{m}⸢*si-par*⸣*-ra-a-nu* (note that the additional vowel is of a "different colour" than the vowel preceding it) GPA 35 r.4; *ṣip-pir-ra-a-te* SAA X 274:9; *i-sa-par-u-ni* SAA XV 136:24, SAA I 31 r.25, SAA I 58:4, SAA I 221:4, NL 12:21 (CTN V 155ff); *i-sa-pa-ru-ni* ibid. r.7; *i-sa-pa-ru-u-ni* SAA V 202 r.14e; *i-sa-pa-ra-an-(ni)* SAA XV 54 r.5

(ṭr) *ši-ṭi-ri-šá* SAA V 295 r.24; *šá-aṭ-ṭa-ra-a-ni* SAA X 60:11; *ip-ta-/-ṭa-ru-ni-šú* SAA XIII 27 s.2-3

(tr) *ú-tú-ru-te* SAA XVI 96:12

(gr) *na-ga-ru-ti-ni* (cf. *kr* below) "the enemies (+ subj.)" SAA XVI 126:17; *i-gi-*⸢*ru-ú-ni*⸣ SAA V 37:28

(kr) *na-ka-ra-ka* SAA V 260:7′

(hr) *ṣe-he-ri-ia* SAA X 187:8; *mì-hi-ri-šu* SAA XVI 115 r.8; *i-ta-ha-ru-šú* StAT 1 51 s.1; *i-su-hu-ru-u-ni* SAA XV 90:6; *i-su-*⸢*hu-ru*⸣*-ni* NL 29 r.4 (CTN V 143f); *ta-ha-ru-pu* SAA V 199:5; *i-hi-ru-pu* NL 44 r.5 (CTN V 139f) ~ *ih-ru-up* SAA XVI 150:6′

(zr) *ma-za-ru-te* GPA 33:3

(šr) *pi-šìr-a-ti* SAA X 245 r.11, SAA X 246:12′

(bl) *hi-bi-la-te-ka* SAA V 260 r.2′; *hi-bi-la-te-ia* ibid. r.4′; *hi-bil-a-te-šú* SAA XVI 29:17; *hi-bil-a-te-šú-nu* SAA XVI 43 r.9; *ha-ba-la-ta-ia* SAA XVI 29:16

(pl) *šap-a-lu-*[*a*$^{?}$] SAA XVI 70 r.3; *šá-pa-lu-*[*uš-šú*] SAA XVI 68 r.12′

(gl) *di-gi-li-ia* SAA IX 11 r.6, SAA X 361 r.2 ~ *di-ig-lu* SAA X 294 r.32
šá-ga-lu-ti ABL 541:4′; LÚ*.*šá-ga-l*[*u-te*] SAA XV 41:14′ ~ LÚ.*šag-lu-u-te* SAA I 257:5; LÚ*.*šag-lu-te* SAA I 219:13, 16, SAA XIII 157:10′
ša-ga-la-ni NL 5:12′ (CTN V 25f); *ú-šá-ga-lu-šú-nu* SAA V 105:23; *ú-šá-ga-lu-ka-nu-ni* ABL 541 r.4; *ú-sa-ga-li-ia* SAA I 234:12; *ú-sa-ga-li-uš* SAA I 204 r.11; *ú-šá-gal-u-šú-nu* SAA V 112 r.2; *ú-šá-gal-na-ši-ni* SAA I 190 r.6′; *ú-šag-ga-lu-na-ši* SAA XV 221:3′, r.8

(ql) *ma-qa-lu-tú* SAA X 212 r.7, SAA XIII 57 r.4′; *ma-qa-lu-a-te* SAA VIII 102 r.10 ~ *ma-aq-lu-a-ti* SAA XIII 72 r.5; *ma-aq-lu-a-te* TH 5 r.2

(hl) ⸢*ú*⸣*-sa-ha-li-qu-šú-nu* NL 85:9 (CTN V 100ff); *ú-ša-ha-li-qu-šú-n*[*i*] ibid. r.14

(ṣl) *m*]*u-ṣu-la-li* SAA X 131:6

(bn) NA$_4$.*a-ba-na-ti* SAA I 141:4′

(dn) *ta-da-nu-u-ni* (stat) SAA XIII 31 r.13, SAA XV 268:6′

(ṭn) GIŠ].*bu-ṭu-na-te* ND 10009 r.39 (CTN III 87 [edition], CTN I pl. 46-48 [copy])

(qn) *iq-qi-nu-u-n*[*i*] SAA II 6:274B ~ *iq-nu-u-ni* ibid. A, frg

(zn) *i-zi-nu-nu-*[*ni*] SAA V 26 e.11′; *tu-šá-za-na-a-ni* SAA II 6:265F, i; *tu-šá-za-a-na-a-ni* ibid. B ~ *tu-ša-az-na-a-ni* ibid. I

(šn) *ú-sa-ša-ni-ú* SAA XV 42:7 ~ *us-sa-áš-ni-ú* SAA XIII 134 r.17

(mn) URU.*ta-ma-nu-n*[*i*] GPA 128:9
(dm) ^{d}GAŠAN–*ki-di-mu-ri* SAA XVI 105 r.13, SAA XVI 106:6; ^{d}15 *ša* É–*ki-di-mu-ri* SAA XVI 105:5 ~ É–*kid-mur-ri* SAA X 294 r.23; ^{d}*šar-rat–kid-mu-ri* SAA X 197:11; É–*kid-mur-ra* SAA XVI 127:5
(gm) *ir-tu-gu-mu-ni-šú* SAA I 194 r.1; *li-gi-*(*ma*)*-ru-ku-nu* SAA II 6:629frg ~ *lig-ma-ru-ku-*⸢*nu*⸣ ibid. G, *li-ig-mur-u-ku-nu* ibid. K
(šm) [*nu*]*-sa-šá-me-šú-nu* SAA V 105:10; *iš-ši-mu-u-ni* SAA XV 88:11
(rṣ) ^{m}*ta-ra-ṣi-i* SAA XVI 63 r.12, 23 ~ ^{m}*tar-ṣi-i* ibid. 5, r.14, 16, 18, 26
(bs) *qa-ba-si-ú* SAA XIII 193:9; *qa-ba-sa-a-t*[*i* SAA X 385:4; *qa-ba-sa-a-te* SAA XIII 71 r.4
(db) *na-da-ba-ku* SAA XV 113 s.3; perhaps *na-*⸢*da-ba*⸣*-*[*ki*] NL 93:5 (CTN V 233); [*l*]*i-di-bu-ku* NL 93 r.3 (CTN V 233); *ni-id-di-bu-ú-ku* BM 132980:17 (Assurbanipal); *la ni-di-bu-ku-ni* SAA XIII 137 r.3; *i-di-bu-u*[*b-u-ni*] SAA V 95 r.2; *id-di-bu-ub-u-ni*[320] SAA V 91:6; *ta-da-bu-bu* SAA V 108:24 (prt), SAA V 260:6′, SAA XVI 59 r.4′ (prs); *ú-šá-da-ba* SAA V 58:9; *ú-sa-da-bi-šu* StAT 1 51 r.6; *nu-sa-da-bi-*[*šú-nu*] SAA XIII 208:2′; *la-da-bu-ub* SAA V 78 r.14, SAA V 133 s.2
(gb) *na-qa-ba-a-te* SAA X 352:20; *na-qa-bi-ia-te* SAA X 351:11; *a-qa-bu-u-ni* (prt) SAA XVI 43:14, SAA XVI 63 r.31e, NL 57 r.2 (CTN V 294), SAA I 75:9, SAA V 232 r.5′; *la a-qa-ba-áš-šú-nu* (prt) SAA XV 4:15; *a-qa-ba-kan-ni* (prt) SAA V 213:6; *ta-qa-bu-u-ni* (prt) StAT 1 51:10; *i-qi-bu-ni* (prt) SAA V 199 r.8′; *i-qi-ba-an-ni* (prt) ND 2682:9 (CTN V 289f); *i-qi-b*[*a*]*-u-ni* (prt) ibid. l.7; [*l*]*i-qi-bu-nik-ku-nu* SAA I 14:5′; [*l*]*i-qi-ba-áš-šú-nu* SAA V 63 r.12; *li-qi-ba-áš-šú* GPA 194:23; *l*]*i-qí-bu-ni-šú-nu* SAA V 203 s.1; *ú-sa-qa-bi-šú* SAA X 351:12
(kb) *a-ka-bu-su-ni* (prt) NL 87 r.10′, 11′ (CTN V 225ff); *i-ki-bu-su-ni* ABL 307 r.9′
(tb) *ba-ta-ba-ti-ia* SAA V 79:7; [*b*]*a-ta-ba-ti* SAA V 67:6′; *ba-ta-ba-tu-šú-n*[*u* 0$^{?}$] NL 99:12 (CTN V 109ff)
(zb) *ša-za-bu-su* SAA I 234:17; *ša-za-bu-sa-*[*te*] ibid. l.16; *i-zi-bi-lu-u-ni* SAA XIII 50 r.5
(ṣb) *la-ṣa-ba-ta* SAA XIII 43 r.2; *ta-ṣa-bat-ú-ni* KAV 198:4; *iṣ-ṣi-bat-tu* SAA II 6:24frg ~ *iṣ-*⸢*ba-tu*⸣ ibid. A *ú-ša-ṣa-bat* CT 53 868:2′; *ú-sa-ṣa-bit-ma* SAA I 227 r.2′
(lb) *ṣil-li-ba-a-ni* SAA X 241:6 ~ *ṣi-il-ba-ni* SAA X 315 r.9
du-lu-ba-ni SAA XV 283:7′
(rb) *iq-ṭa-ra-bu-u-ni* SAA V 64:8
(hb) URU.*nu-hu-ba-a-a* ABL 307:2 ~ URU.*nu-uh-ba-iá* ibid. r.10′
(bd) KUR.*la-ba-du-da-a* SAA XV 121:5
(rk) *pa-ra-ak-at* SAA XIII 34 r.4 ~ *par-kàt* SAA X 247 r.4
(rg) ^{m}*na-ra-ge-e* SAA V 91:3
(rq) URU.*ma-ra-qa-si* BT 108:8 (Iraq 23 pl. XXI)
(qd) *pa-qa-da-a-ni* (stat.) SAA XVI 148:11
(ht) *ú-hu-ta-bi*[*l* SAA XV 330:3′; *ú-hu-ta-ri-du-šú-nu* SAA V 217:12
(qt) *m*[*a*]-⸢*šá*⸣*-qí-it* SAA X 294 r.1
(pq) *a-pa-qi-du-ni* (prt) SAA I 82 r.7

[320] For the possible special function of an anaptyctic vowel in such writings, see Fabritius (1995) 54.

4.8.2 Anaptyctic vowels after the stress

(hr) *i-su-hu-ra* SAA XVI 45 r.2; *ni-is-su-hu̱-ra* SAA XV 94:9
(gr) *li-gi-ru-ru* SAA V 203 s.1
(kr) *na-ka-ri* (back formation from the plural form) SAA XV 54 r.11
(tr) NA$_4$.*ni-ti-ru* SAA XVI 82 r.9
(ṣr) *i-ta-ṣa-ru* SAA X 145:4′
(bl) *i-tu-bu-lu* SAA XV 59 r.13′
(dl) UZU.*me-di-li* SAA XIII 18 r.8
(hl) *ši-hi-li* CTN III 113:2;[321] *ši-hi-lu* SAA XV 119 r.19
(pl) *ki-pi-li* SAA XV 184:7
(bš) *ha-ba-šu* (this form is exceptional and possibly to be interpreted as a D-stem stative + a coordinating vowel: *habbuš* + *u* > [including a shift in stress?] *habbāšu*?) SAA X 224 r.4
(mn) *šá-me-ni* BT 128:7 (Iraq 25 pl. XXVI)
(ṭn) GIŠ.*bu-ṭu-ni* CT 53 230:7
(pt) *a-pa-ta-làh* (if *ap-* is necessarily the stressed syllable?) SAA I 160 r.3
(qt) *ba-ti-qí-tú* SAA V 164 r.11, 13; *bu-ti-qe̱-te* SAA XIII 30:5
(kn) *i-sa-ka-nu* SAA I 179 r.8, 9, SAA X 309:8′, r.3
(rd) *i-tu-ru-du* NL 41 r.11 (CTN V 208ff)
(qp) *i-zu-ku-pu* SAA V 53 r.3
(lq) *ih-ta-*⸢*la*⸣*-qu* SAA I 23:4′ however, cf. *ih-ti-li-qu* (= *ihtalqū* > *ihtilqū* or a back formation from *ihtiliq*?) SAA XIII 33 s.2

Opening of a closed final syllable after the stress by means of an anaptyctic vowel ([C$\bar{\text{V}}$C > C$\bar{\text{V}}$ + CV]):

(*ahîš*) *i-sa-a-hi-ši* SAA I 182:8′ ~ *a-hi/e-iš* passim
ina ŠÀ *a-hi-ši* SAA I 172:12 (CTN V 173ff), *a-hi-ši* SAA I 175:13 (CTN V 167ff)[322]
(*ahā'iš*) *i-sa-ha-ii-ši* SAA XV 101:13; *ša a-ha-ii-ši* ibid. l.14
a-he-ii-ši SAA V 227 r.14
(*bēt*) *bé-te* SAA V 25 r.5, 6 ~ *bé-et* passim
(*hur*) *ah–hu-ru* SAA V 147:15; *a-na hu-ru* SAA V 235 r.2′ ~ *ah–hur* passim; *a-na hur* SAA I 52 r.6′, SAA X 43 r.6
(*issēt*) 1-*te* SAA XVI 63 r.29 ~ 1-*et* passim; note also É–1-*te* SAA XVI 100 r.15; *ša* É–1-*te* ibid. r.6; 1-*te* HAR KUG.U[D] SAA XVI 53 r.2
(*kūm*) *ku-mu* S.U. 51/44:7 ~ *ku-um* passim; note also *ina ku-mi* SAA I 240 r.4; *ina ku-me* SAA XVI 78:9; *i–ku-me* SAA XVI 36:6′
(*manzāz*) *man-za-za–pa-ni* (*ana pāni*?) SAA XVI 127 r.7, SAA XVI 128 r.2′ cf. [*ma*]*n-za-az* É.GAL SAA X 7:10
(*muk*) *mu-ku* passim ~ *mu-uk* passim; *muk* SAA V 46:12′, SAA V 210 r.6, 11, SAA V 217 r.15, SAA V 297:8′; [mu]*muk* SAA V 217 r.16, SAA V 224:12; most of the writings are of the type *mu-uk*
(*nuk*) *nu-ku* SAA V 21 r.15, SAA V 32 r.5, SAA V 33:7, r.2′, SAA V 37:29, NL 3 r.8′, 9′ (Face A in CTN V 64ff) ~ *nu-uk* passim
(*pīt*) *pe-te* K[Á SAA X 356:7′
(*šīt*) *ši-i-ti* SAA V 74:6 (CTN V 103f), SAA I 247 r.5; *ši-i-ti-i-*[*ma*] SAA XVI 181 r.3; *ši-ti* SAA X 31:8′; *ši-i-te* SAA V 52 r.11, NL 80 + ND 2396 r.4′ (-

---

[321] Cf. n. ad CTN III 113:2.

[322] See CTN V 168 n. ad l. 13.

⸢*i-t*⸣*e*) (CTN V 104ff); (*mīnu* [*ša*]) *ši-ti-ni* passim; *ši-ti-i-ni* SAA X 42 r.18, SAA X 347 r.10′, SAA XVI 140 r.12; *ši-te-ni* KAV 213 r.14, *ši-te-i-ni* SAA I 29 r.7, VAT 9875 r.9

(*šūt*) *šu-tu* SAA XV 217 r.2′; *šu-tú* SAA I 1 r.66 (CTN V 188ff), NL 37 r.7′ (CTN V 84f), NL 41 r.28 (CTN V 208ff), SAA X 51 r.11, SAA X 241:10, SAA V 164 r.1; *šú-tú* CTN III 5 r.2, SAA I 191 r.14, StAT 2 123:6′; *šu-tu-ma* SAA X 56 r.11, SAA X 253 r.15, NL 54 r.2 (CTN V 13f); *šu-tú-ma* NL 55:11 (CTN V 147f), SAA X 319 r.11; *šu-tu-ni* SAA I 171 r.35 (CTN V 227ff), SAA X 206:7′; *šu-tú-ni* SAA I 235:11; *šu-u-tu* SAA V 98 r.8′, SAA XVI 53 r.8; *šu-u-tú* passim; *šú-u-tú* SAA V 52:9, r.8; *šu-ú-tú* SAA I 235:13; *šu-tú-u-ma* SAA I 31:24; *šu-tu-u-ni* SAA II 6:278B, SAA X 95:11, SAA X 265:18, SAA X 280 r.2, SAA X 298 r.4, SAA X 328:15, SAA XVI 63 r.14, KAV 213 r.9; *šu-tú-u-ni* SAA II 6:278A, SAA X 321 r.12, SAA XVI 96 r.14; *šu-tu-ú-ni* SAA XVI 196:11; *šu-ú-tu-u-*⸢*ni*⸣ SAA V 91 e.24

(*ṭūb*) *ṭu-bu* / ŠÀ-*bi* SAA X 329 r.9-10 ~ *ṭu-ub* passim

(Zāba) ÍD.*za-ba* NL 48 r.7 (CTN V 116ff), SAA I 62:5

Verbs:

Stative (of II-weak verbs):

(bēd) *bé-e-d*[*e*] SAA XV 223 r.10

(dār) *lu*(*-u*) *da-ra* SAA X 283:7, SAA XVI 34 r.3 ~ *lu-u da-a-ar* SAA X 345:7; *lu-u dà-ri* SAA XVI 36 r.12

(dēk) *de-e-ke* SAA I 30 e.9′, SAA X 96 r.14, SAA XVI 30:7, NL 11 r.11 (CTN V 31f), NL 65:10, 11 (CTN V 45f)

(ēṣ) *e-ṣe* SAA X 257:9; *e-ṣe-e* SAA X 43:9, SAA X 89:10′

(kūn) *ku-ú-nu* SAA X 363:13

(mēt) *mé-te* SAA X 309 r.4; *me-e-te* SAA X 97:9′, SAA XVI 31:2, SAA XVI 34 r.26e; *mé-e-te* SAA I 23:2′, SAA V 91 r.3, SAA XIII 157 r.8, SAA X 90 r.14′; *me-e-ti* SAA XVI 105:15, e.23, SAA XVI 127 r.15; *mé-e-ti* SAA XVI 95:3

(nēh) *né-e-hi* SAA I 55:5′

(qāl) *qa-a-la* SAA XIII 134 r.16, SAA X 72 r.17; *qa-la* SAA XV 288:4

(rēh) *re-e-he* SAA X 47 r.2′, SAA X 84 r.12, SAA I 194 r.3, 5, SAA XV 164 r.8′, NL 96:8 (CTN V 49ff); *re-he* SAA I 52 r.7′, SAA XIII 162 r.7

(ṭāb) *ṭa-a-ba* passim; *ṭa-ba* SAA X 70:10, r.3, 10, SAA X 222 r.3, SAA X 378:6′, SAA XIII 141:15, SAA XV 286:5′; *ṭa-ba-a*[323] (interrogative int.) SAA X 73:10, SAA X 190:8, SAA X 207:6 ~ *ṭa-ab* SAA I 138 r.17, SAA X 90 s.3, SAA XIII 50 r.1

Imperative (of II-weak verbs + tdn, wšb):

(tdn) *di-i-ni* passim; *di-ni* passim; [*di*]-⸢*e*⸣-*ni* SAA I 192:11; SUM-*ni* StAT 1 55 e.8′ ~ *di-in* SAA XVI 112:14

(hīṭ) *he-e-ṭe* StAT 1 56 r.3

(mūt) *mu-ú-tu* SAA XIII 158 r.11′

(wšb) *ši-i-bi* SAA I 7:8′; *ši-bi* SAA XVI 59 s.3

(tēr) *te-e-re* SAA XV 186 r.8; *te-re* SAA I 220 r.8e

[323] This interrogative intonation contains the lengthening which witnesses to the stability of the use of an anaptyctic vowel, see LAS II 58 n. 102.

Present (D/Š-stem of II-weak verbs):

(*ukâl*)	*ú-ka-la* SAA X 87 r.6′, SAA XIII 147:14, A. 2199 r.11, SAA XVI 63 r.18; *ú-kal-l*[*a*] SAA X 238 r.2; *nu-ka-la* SAA X 23:11, 12; *nu-ka-a-la* SAA VIII 3:4, SAA X 221 r.9, SAA X 241 r.13, SAA X 72 r.10; *nu-kal-la* NL 2:24′ (CTN V 22ff); *tu-ka-la* (sg./2nd pl.?) SAA X 23:10, *tu-kal-la* (sg./2nd pl.?) SAA X 72 r.9 ~ *nu-ka-al* SAA X 33 r.2
(*uktatâl*)	*uk-ta-ta-la* SAA X 363 r.17e; *uk-ta-ta-la-ma* ibid. r.12
(*ukân*)	*ú-ka-na* SAA I 77 r.11
(*upâq*)	⸢*ú*⸣-*pa-qa* SAA X 39 r.13
(*ušarâq*)	*nu-ša-ra-qa* SAA I 66:13
(*utâr*)	*ú-ta-ra* SAA V 105 r.10, SAA I 56:14, SAA XV 214 r.8; *ú-tar-ra* SAA VIII 47:7 ~ *ú-tar* SAA X 188 r.10

Perfect (of II-weak verbs):

(*iddūl*)	*id-du-lu* ABL 561:7′
(*irtūb*)	*ir-tu-bu* SAA XVI 100:7, SAA VIII 37:6; *ir-tu-bu-u-ma* SAA X 10 r.7′
(*uktīl*)	*uk-te-li* SAA X 279:12, SAA X 182:6 ~ *uk-ti-il* SAA X 322:12; *uk-ti-il*$_5$ SAA X 328:18
(*uktīn*)	*nu-uk-ti-ni* SAA I 236 r.12
(*uttēr*)	*ú-te-re* SAA V 142:10′, SAA I 226:11, SAA XIII 38:9 ~ *ú-tir* SAA XIII 128:18; *ut-te-e-re* SAA XIII 126 r.9′; *tu-ut-te-re* SAA I 8 r.12

Preterite (and precative of II-weak verbs):

(*idūl*)	*li-du-lu* (3rd sg.) SAA V 254:11′
(*ihīṭ*)	*li-hi-ṭi* SAA XIII 127:10
(*išīṭ*)	*ta-*⸢*še*?⸣-*ṭe* NL 71 r.5 (CTN V 312f)
(*utēr*)	*lu-te*⸣-*re* SAA I 220:5
(*uktatīn*)	*lu-uk-ta-ti-ni* "He should be tried" SAA V 163:10
(*ukein*?)	*lu-ki-ii-ni* SAA XVI 44 r.5′ (Iqbi-Aššur, Til-Barsib)

(3) Monosyllabic words of the type CVC/C$\overline{V}$C regularly take an anaptyctic vowel when they are stressed[324] (e.g. examples of the imperative above).

(4) Presumably, at least, a few "ventive" forms, such as *assapara, assaṭara and issuhura*, are "marked" and seldom-occurring alloforms of otherwise paradigmatically conjugated forms, such as *assapra*, etc.[325] These forms may, however, also be related to the cases of paragraph (5). On the whole, it is often difficult to separate the meaningful "ventive forms and the anaptyctic vowels from each other in Neo-Assyrian."[326] Thus, for instance:

(shr)	*i-su-hu-ra* SAA XVI 45 r.2, SAA V 164 r.6
(špr)	*a-sa-par-ra* SAA V 126 r.15, SAA X 290 r.12e; *a-sa-pa-ra* (3. [*a*]-; 5. -[*ra*]) SAA V 53:11, 14, SAA I 92 r.4, SAA I 123 r.6′, SAA V 260:3′, NL 64:11 (CTN V 290ff), NL 87 r.12′ (CTN V 225ff); *as-sa-pa-ra* SAA XVI 115

---

[324] LAS II ad no. 259 r.9f.

[325] LAS II ad no. 223 r.12′.

[326] On the "irregularity"of marking the ventive ending in *-a*, see Deller (1959) § 8a, x, § 9e-10 and idem (1971) 642 n. 10. Cf. also idem (1962B) 196.

r.12; *i-sa-par-ra* SAA I 251:11!!; *i-sa-pa-ra* NL 15:4 (CTN V 140); *is-sa-pa-ra* SAA XV 142:7′; *ni-sa-pa-ra* SAA XV 93:4′

(šṭr) *a-sa-ṭa-ra* SAA I 221:8 ~ *a-sa-ṭar* SAA I 192 r.4, SAA XV 89:10′, NL 3:14′ (Face B in CTN V 64ff)

4.8.3 Syntactic anaptyctic vowels

(5) The anaptyctic vowel has taken over the functions of the obsolete *-ma* particle in the verb forms (clause intonation).[327] (a) It coordinates clauses.[328] In this case, an anaptyctic vowel is marked on the first member of the two closely related predicates which usually also appear as consecutive predicates. The most appropriate translation of the anaptyctic vowel is then usually: "and," "but" (in clauses emphasizing their contrast nature), "but (also)," "that" or just the use of a comma coordinating clauses. It should be noted that clauses which are clearly contextually-interpreted coordinated clauses appear frequently asyndetically, without any auxiliary vowel. Therefore these two different types are in (partial) free variation with one another.

Examples of clauses coordinated by anaptyctic vowels (additional vowel in the first predicate):

('lk) *ina šaddaqdiš / issīja ana hūli lā* i-li-ki / *ṣābāni danqūti iktal'a* "Last year he did not go with me to the expedition but kept the best men (at home)" SAA V 200 r.5′-7′

(hrp) *iššiāri* DNf. / *issu* GN / ta-har-ru-pu *pān šarri tērab* "Tomorrow the DNf. will arrive early from GN and enter before the king" SAA XIII 149:1-3

(nrṭ) [*šarr*]*u bēlī lā* i-nàr-ru-ṭu / [*arh*]*iš lurabbīš* "The [kin]g, my lord, should not hesitate (but) promote him [at once]!" SAA X 72 r.18-19

(*uzuzzu*) *pān abulli Marduk* ni-it-ti-ti-zi / *issi* [*mār*]-*Bābili niddubub* "we stood before the Marduk-gate and discussed with the Babylonians" NL 1:6-7 (CTN V 19ff)

(zqp) *šinīšu ina muhhīšu* i-zu-qu-pu / [*d*]*ēktušu iddūak* "he has attacked him twice defeating him" OR alternatively with "... and defeated him" NL 48:13-14 (CTN V 116ff)

(b) The additional vowel expresses repetition and emphasis. It may also convey a possible secondary meaning. In this case, the added (phonetic) vowel is attached to the latter member of two syntactically closely related predicates. The interpretation "and" is also possible in this case, but mostly it is a question of emphasis.[329]

---

327 The enclitic *-ma* had fallen into disuse in Neo-Assyrian but was still used in the contemporary Neo-Babylonian. For the parallel type of early-Neo-Assyrian and Neo-Babylonian clauses (both with *-ma*) compared to (later) Neo-Assyrian clauses with an anaptyctic vowel, see Parpola (1975) examples of item no. 5.

328 See LAS II ad no. 18 r.8.

329 This interpretation broadly follows the theory proposed by Parpola (1975) 3ff although the terminology differs slightly. In any case, ample and systematic research on this topic is still lacking.

Often either a broken context or somewhat elliptically expressed clause(s) may obscure the exact nature of an additional vowel.

In the following examples, the additional vowel has an emphatic function:

('pš) *ūmâ / kī ša ina pān šarri / bēlīja* ma-hi-ir-u-ni / [le]-pu-u-šu "Nowadays it should be done as it (best) suits the king, my lord." SAA X 76 r.7-10

(pqd) *mannu ša ina pān šarri* / ma-hi-ir-u-ni / *šarru* ⌜*bēlī* lip-qi⌝-di "Let the king, my lord, appoint the one who is acceptable to the king, my lord." SAA I 75 r.6-8

(škn) *ūmâ anāku* 30 *bētāti* lu-šá-bi-šá *ina libbi* la-áš-ku-nu "Now, let me get together 30 families <u>and</u> place them there." SAA I 177:8-9

The following examples contain two consecutive clauses. Both clauses begin with a temporal adverb except for the penultimate example. The first adverbs of the examples refer to the past and the second ones to the present (always *ūmâ* "now"). These examples therefore indicate a sharp contrast between the first and second clause. The meaning of the anaptytic vowel in these clauses corresponds to the conjunction *u* "but":[330]

[... / *iš*]*šaššūme* ... / ... / ... *lā* a-⌜ka-ṣur⌝ / ú-ma-a "In the past days, ... I did not have to supply ..., <u>but now</u> ..." SAA I 99 r.2′-6′

iššaddaqdiš šaluššīni / ina pāni at-ti-ti-zi / *ú-ma-a* "Last year and the year before last, I stayed in the entourage (of the king), <u>but now</u> ..." ABL 1174:10′-12′

ina šaddaqdiš ... / ... / ... ap-ti-qi-di / ú-ma-a "Last year ... I assigned (them), <u>but now</u> ..." SAA XIII 18 r.5-10

ina šaddaqdiš / issī'a ... *lā* i-li-ki / ... / ú-ma-a "Last year he did not go with me ... (<u>But</u>) now" SAA V 200 r.5′-9′

ittimāli iššaššūme / ... // *lā* ú-na-ri-ṭi / ú-ma-a "Yesterday and the day before yesterday, I did not bother ..., <u>but now</u> ..." SAA XIII 137:7′-r.2

... *memmēni lā* iq-ri-bi / ú-ma-a "Nobody has gone near ... <u>But now</u> ..." SAA XVI 141:4′-5′

14 *šanāti* / ... / *memmēni issī'a / lā* id-di-bu-ub (note the added syllable: CV in the middle of the word) / ú-ma-a "For 14 years ... and nobody disputed it with me. (<u>But</u>) <u>now</u> ..." SAA X 173:8-12

4.9 Loss of end vowels (vocalic apocope)

Unstressed final vowels (both long and short) were probably regularly shortened in colloquial Neo-Assyrian. This phenomenon is occasionally also attested in writing as the loss of end vowels.[331] Nevertheless, forms without end vowels are rarer than forms with end vowels. Thus they are marked.

The apocope of /*a*/:

(*aiāka*) TA *a-a-ak* [*šu-n*]*u* "Where [are th]ey from?" SAA XIII 19 r.8

([*h*]*annāka* "here") *ha-na-ak* SAA XIII 17 r.4′, *an-na-ak* SAA XV 121 r.14, TA* *na-ak* "from here" SAA V 233:5

---

[330] See LAS II ad no. 246:12 with examples (which are now repeated here).

[331] Parpola (1972) 23-27.

(*aqṭibakka*)[332] *aq-ṭi-ba-ak* SAA IX 1 iii 31′
(*nāṣa*) PN ... / *un-qu* KUG.GI / *na-aṣ ina* UGU-*hi-ni* "PN ... brings us the (king's) golden stamp seal" SAA V 234:4′-6′
(*tuppašā*) *šúm-ma qa-ra-bu* / *tu-up-pa-áš*[333] *ep-šá* "If you (want to) fight, do so ..." SAA XV 69:14-15

The apocope of /*i*/:
After a stressed syllable in temporal adverbs (cf. proclitics 4.10 and metathesis of syllables 4.15):

(*aššiʾāri*) *a-sa-na-am-me a–še-ʾa-ar* / *ina* ⸢UGU⸣ *ku-u*[*s-si*]*-iá al-lak* "I listen and obey. Tomorrow I shall go *in my se*[*dan chair* ...]" SAA X 204:6-7
(*immati*) *im–ma-at* LUGAL *be-li* / *i-qab-bu-u-ni* "Whenever the king, my lord, says" SAA X 5 r.3-4; *im–ma-at* KUR.MEŠ / ... / *er-rab-u-ni* "When are the horses ... to come ...?" SAA XIII 97 r.5-7; *im–ma-at* (cont. broken) SAA XV 346:4; *im–mat* ⸢LUGAL *i*⸣*-qab-b*[*u-u-ni* "Whenever the king orders" SAA I 134 r.5
(*urkēte*) *ah–hur lu-šá-ad-g*[*i-il*] / *ur-ke-e-et* / *lil-li-ka* "(The king, my lord,) should still wait (for its emergence); thereafter PN may come" SAA X 74 r.23e-25e; *ur-ke-e-et* // *ina* UGU ÍD / ... / *i-sa-as-si* "Afterwards, he ... used to read ... on the river bank" SAA X 76 e.16-r.6
(Aššur-reši-išši, PN) ᵐ*aš-šur*–SAG–*iš* passim see PNA 1/I pp. 213-14.
(*bēlu*) LUGAL EN-in "the king, our lord" SAA XVI 76:5′ (in a broken context)
(*bīrtu* "fort") URU.*bi-rat* SAA V 21:5, SAA I 31:6 and passim ~ URU.*bi-ra-a-ti/e* SAA V 31:4/SAA V 80:4; *b*]*i-ra-a-ti* NL 50:6 (CTN V 182ff); URU.*bi-*[*ra*]*-ti* SAA I 36:6; *bi-ra-ti* NL 53:8 (CTN V 194); ⸢URU.*bi-ra-te*⸣ NL 101 r.5 (CTN V 292ff)

After a short unstressed syllable which is liable to vowel harmony:

(*abiti* "word, matter") *a-na a-bi-it an-ni-te* SAA XVI 62:5
(*kūdini* "mules")[334] É/ANŠE.*ku-din* e.g. SAA V 227:9, 11, 24 and passim

The apocope of /*u*/:
In nouns, adjectives and adverbs:

(*kaiamānu*) *ka-a-a-man ina* UGU LUGAL EN-*ia ú-ṣal-li* "I constantly prayed ... for the king, my lord" SAA XVI 29:9
(*ṣammuru*) *ṣa-mur ka-šá-du* "... the attainment of all he strives for" SAA XIII 128:9
(*šaplušu*) *šap-lu-uš* / *is-sa-kan* "He has subjected it to himself" SAA XVI 112 r.12-13
(*ṭābtušu*) *ki-ma ṭa-ab-tu-uš la* ⸢*e*⸣*-*[*pu-u*]*š* "If I didn't do him a favour ..." SAA X 182:28

---

[332] This interpretation is uncertain. See n. ad SAA IX 1 iii 31.

[333] Deller (1962C) 230.

[334] For an alternative, orthographic (pseudologographic) interpretation, see Hämeen-Anttila (2000) 4.

In first-person singular statives (with paradigmatic ending /*-āku*/; ≠ indicates the end of a clause):

(hlq) *hal-qa-ak* / TA* ŠU.2-*ki e-te-li* "I am lost and falling out of your (f.) hands" ABL 896 r.18-19 (Aia-zeru-qiša)

(mhr) *mah-ra-ak* / TA* *lib* É.KUR-*ri* / *ka-šu-da-ak* ≠ / DUMU–MAN *lip-qi-da* "I received/inherited ... (but now) I am (even) chased away from the temple. Let the crown prince take care of (this) ..." SAA XIII 154 r.12-14

(plh) *i-na pa-ni-šú šu-ú pal-ha-ak ša la* LUGAL / EN-*ia la a-ṣab-bat-si* "He is in his presence. I am afraid, I cannot seize him[335] without the king, my lord's permission" SAA XVI 127 r.5-6 (Itti-Šamaš-balaṭu, Phoenicia)

(qrb) *ina* ŠÀ *lā qur-ba-ak* ≠ *ki-i an-ni-i* "I am not involved in it ... thus ..." SAA XV 69:17

(tkl D) *a-na-ku ana* UGU LUGAL EN-*ia tak-ku-lak* ≠ / 1 GÍN ½ GÍN *a-na me-me-e-ni la ad-dan* "I (however) put my trust in the king, my lord. I don't give one shekel (or even) half a shekel to anybody ..." SAA XVI 127 r.11-12 (Itti-Šamaš-balaṭu, Phoenicia)

In verb forms ending in the third-person singular masculine suffix /*-šu*/:

(*lūballiṭūšu*) *lu-bal-liṭ-ṭuš* SAA XIII 58:10 ~ *ub-tal-li-ṭuš-šu* SAA X 333 r.3
(*iddukūšu*) *i-du-ku-uš* SAA XVI 105 r.9
(*lūgallibūšu*) *lu-gal-li-bu-uš* SAA X 97 e.13′
(*ussag*[*a*]*liūšu*) *ú-sa-ga-li-uš* SAA I 204 r.11
(*liklīšu*) *li-ik-liš* ABL 426:11 (Šamaš-šumu-ukin to Assurbanipal)
(*liṣṣurūšu*) *li-iṣ-ṣu-ru-uš* SAA X 70 r.17e
(*lūrabbīšu*) *lu-rab-bi-iš* SAA X 72 r.19

In third-person plural masculine verb forms with consecutive intonation (the last consonant of the verbal root either /*r*/ or /*l*/; *-*a*C*u* > -*u*C*u* [vowel harmony] > -*ū*C)

('kl) LÚ*.MAH.MEŠ-*ni ina* ŠÀ-*bi-šu šu-nu* / NINDA.MEŠ *ša ra-me-ni-šú-nu e-kul* ≠ / *i-ma-ta-hu-né-e* "The emissaries are there, eating their own bread ..." SAA I 33:13-15
šu-nu ŠE.NUMUN / [*e*]-*ta-ár-šú* TA* ŠÀ-*bi* ⸢*i-ku*⸣-*ul* / [TA*] ŠÀ-*bi* KUR.RA.MEŠ-[*šú-nu*] / ⸢*ú*⸣-*šá-ku-ul* "They, by contrast, having planted their seed, [e]at from it, feed [their] horses [fr]om it" SAA V 225:11-14
ina IGI-*ka lu š*[*u-nu*] / [NINDA.MEŠ *le*]-*kul* A.MEŠ *li-is-si-u* "T[hey] should stay with you and be provided with [foo]d and drink" SAA V 106:20′-21′ ~ [NINDA] *is-sa-he-iš* // *e-kul-lu* / GIŠ.GEŠTIN *i-šá-ti-u* "... eating [bread] together, drinking wine ..." SAA XIII 33 16-r.2

('mr) (PNN) ... SAG KUG.GI-*ma i-na-áš-ši-u* / *a-bu-ba-nim-ma am-mu-te em-mur* ≠ "They will make gold available; they will also inspect those Flood *monsters*" SAA XIII 7 r.5-6 however, cf. MUL.MEŠ *e-mur-ru* UDU.*pu-ha-da-a-ni* / *i-nak-ki-su* "They are observing the stars (and) dissecting lambs" SAA XVI 21:19-20

(dgl) LÚ.GAL.MEŠ *ina pa-ni-*[*ia*] / *i-da-gul* ≠ *ina* ITI.SI[G_4 0] "The magnates are waiting for [me]. ... (until) Siv[an] (III)" SAA V 298 r.2-3

---

[335] Scribal error "her," so also in r.4. The context does not support a feminine object, such as *eleppu* "boat," but a masculine object makes good sense here (cf. ll. e.24-r.5).

LÚ*.A.BA ... *šú-nu* / *mu-šu kal-la*–UD-*mu* AN-*e i-da-gul* ≠ / ⸢*ù*⸣ UN.MEŠ "They are astrologers, they watch the sky day and night. Moreover, ... the people ... SAA XVI 21 r.1-2

LÚ*.GAL.MEŠ / ... *ina šá-a-šú* / *i-da-gul-šú ba-aṭ-lu* / *i-šak-ku-nu* "The ... magnates, observing him, will also go on strike ..." SAA XIII 31 r.7-10

(gmr) *pil-ka-šú-u-nu* / ... *ú-pa-su-ku* / *i-ga-mur* ≠ "They are finishing up and clearing off their work assignment" SAA XV 156 r.9-11;

ma-a ina SAG.DU ITI *ú-ga-mur* [0] / *ma-a ú-ma-a* ITI.MEŠ ... / ... / *nu-uk* 3 GIŠ.MÁ.MEŠ / *ina* UD-1-KÁM *ša* ITI.BARAG *ú-ga-mur* / *mu-uk* 4-*tú ina* UD-1-KÁM *ša* ITI.G[UD] / *ú-ga-mur* ≠ *ú-ma-a* "They must be finished by the beginning of the month! Now ... months ... They will finish three boats by the 1st of Nisan (I), the fourth will be ready by the 1st of Iyyar (II) ..." SAA I 80:7-15 (passively used prs 3rd m.pl.)

(kṣr) *ma-a* DUMU–GÉME–É.GAL / *bat-qu i-ka-ṣur* / *ma-a ú-ri i-si-ru-šú* / *ma-a šúm-mu* GIŠ.ÙR // *ka-si-ip ma-a* / LÚ*.*ú-ra-si* ... / *bat-qu i-ka-ṣur* ≠ *ú-ma-a* "The sons of the palace maids will supply the materials needed and plaster its roof; if a beam is broken, the masons ... will supply the replacement ..." SAA I 77:16-r.4; *i-ka-ṣur* (cont. broken) SAA XVI 216:10′

(mgr N)[336] *la-a i-ma-gúr* / [LUGAL *b*]*e-li la i-pa-lu-hu* "They refuse to fear the [king], my lord" SAA XIII 19 r.3-4

la i-ma-gúr / *de-e-nu ša* É–EN.MEŠ-*šú-nu* / [*la*] *e-pu-šú* "They have refused to render justice to the household of their lord" SAA XVI 41:14-e.16

[*šu-nu la*] ⸢*i*⸣-*ma-gúr* [*a-na pi-i*]*r-ri* // [*la*] *e-ru-bu* "They re]fuse to come in [for the tax col]lection" SAA XIII 20 e.12-r.1

... *la* / *i-ma-gúr la i-du-*[*nu*] "They refuse to give" SAA XIII 21 r.9-10

la im-ma-gúr / *ina* É.GAL *la-a ú-ba-lu-na-ši* "They did not agree to bring us to the Palace." SAA V 104 r.10-11

KUR.*ku-mu-ha-a-a* (it is also possible to interpret this form as singular, see 5.3) *la im-ma-gúr* ≠ / *ma-a* ... "The Commageneans did not agree but ..." SAA I 33 e.22-23

UN.MEŠ KUR / ... / *la im-ma-gúr* / *a-na dul*$_6$-*l*[*i-i*]*a* / *la ú-*[*su-u-ni*] / ... / ⸢*a*⸣-*ni-*⸢*ni*⸣-[*e*] "The people of the country ... refuse to g[o forth] to my wor[k]" SAA V 118:7-e.13

la-a ⸢*i*⸣-*ma-gúr la-a i-šá-mi* / *a-ta-a in-nu-te ma-a* URU.MEŠ-*ni* "They have not agreed to this though, but are disobedient, saying: "Why should our villages ...?" SAA I 172:9-10 (CTN V 173ff)

⸢*la i*⸣-*ma-gúr ina* IGI-*ia* / [*la i-z*]*a-zu* "They refuse to stay with me" SAA I 155:8-9

liš-ši-ú la i-ma-gúr NL 9:6′ (CTN V 66f)

... PAB.MEŠ-*šú-nu* / *la i-ma-gúr* NL 22 r.4-5 (CTN V 180f)

[Š]E.NUMUN-*šú-nu la i-*⸢*ma-gúr*⸣ / *la i-ru-šu* GPA 207 e.9′-10′

~

[*l*]*a-a i-ma-gúr-ru* / [*l*]*a-a i-šá-mu-u-ni* "They refuse to listen to me" SAA I 260 r.16-17

la i-ma-gu-ru ma-a il-lu-ku / ... "They disagreed, saying: "(If) they go ..." SAA V 226 r.18-19

la im-ma-gu-ru la i-qab-bu-u-ni "They wouldn't tell me" SAA V 294:8′

---

336 The difference between the G- and N-stem of the verb *magāru* is not clear to me. Is it really the negated N-stem of *magāru*, which is frequently used with another verb in NA to express "to refuse to do sth"? Or could *im*(*m*)*agūr*(*u*)/*im*(*m*)*agur*(*ru*) be a stiff form of the G-stem?

[LÚ*].GAL.MEŠ *la i-ma-gúr-ru* / *la i-da-nu-na-ši* / ... "The magnates won't give it to us" SAA I 143 r.10-11

UN.MEŠ-*ku-[nu x x x x]* / *[la i-m]a-gu-ru dul-l[um la e-pu-šu]* "Your people [do not] agree [to do] the work" SAA I 237 r.16-17

ú-ma-a la i-ma-gu-ru la i-za-zu "Now they refuse to stand (there) ..." SAA XVI 88:10

la i-ma-gúr-ru / *la ú-še-ra-bu-šú-nu* NL 102 r.13e-14e (CTN V 207f)

la i-ma-gúr-⌜*ru*⌝[337] *la ú-ṣu-u-ni* NL 2:17′ (CTN V 22ff)

la i-ma!!*-gu-ru*[338] / DUMU.MEŠ ... *i-si-šú la il-lu-ku* NL 2 r.13′-14′ (CTN V 22ff), also e.g. NL 26 r.1-6 (CTN V 92f), SAA XV 91:5′, r.5, GPA 199 r.10-11

(nṣr) LÚ*.*e-mu-qi [šu-n]u* / *ša ina* IGI-*ia lu-ra-[mi-š]ú-nu* / *ú-la-a ma-*⌜*ṣar*⌝*-tú* [0] / *li-ṣu-ur* [0!] "Shall I relea[se] the troops at my disposal, or should they (continue to) keep the watch?" SAA V 78 r.7-10

LÚ*.EN.NAM / ... LÚ*.EN.NAM 2-*u* / *i-si-šú ina* GN / ... EN.NUN *i-na-ṣur* / *ma-a ... ul-lu-a-te sa-ad-ra* "The governor ... is keeping watch with the deputy governor in GN, ...; *levied* troops are positioned ... in battle array" SAA V 3:9-14

ú-ma-[a LÚ*.ERIM.MEŠ] / *ú-se-li i-na-ṣur* ≠ *šúm-ma ú-ṣa-bit-u-ni* ... / *ú-bal-u-ni-šú-nu* "I have now moved [troops] up to keep watch; if they catch them, they will bring them ..." SAA V 227 s.1-3

UD-2-KAM / DINGIR.MEŠ ... *i-na-ṣur ina ša-li-in-te* / *ina* [GN] *ni-qar-rib* "On the next day, the gods ... guarding, we shall safely arrive in [GN]" SAA I 54:6-8

LÚ*.*i-tú-'a-a-a-e-a* / ... / *ú-se-bir ina* GN / EN.NUN *i-na-ṣur* ≠ "I have moved my Itu'aeans ... to stand guard in GN" SAA I 93:6-9 however, cf. *a-ta-a* EN [[]] EN.NUN.MEŠ PN / *ina* ŠÀ-*bi la i-na-aṣ-ṣu-ru* TA *pa-an* / *a-bi-te šá ki-i an-ni-i* "Why don't the guards *and* PN keep watch there, on account of a matter like this?" SAA X 183:7-9

ma-a LÚ*.ARAD.MEŠ-*šú-nu a-ke-e is-se-šú-nu* / *i-da-li-pu* ... / *i-zab-bi-lu-šú-nu* ... / *a-ke-e i-na-ṣu-ru* "How did their servants sit up with them all nights and carry them ...! How (well) did they keep (watch over them)" SAA X 316:11-14

30 LÚ*.ERIM.MEŠ / [KUR.*š*]*i-ia-na-a-a ina* ŠÀ-*bi u-se-rib* / E[N.N]UN-*tú i-na-ṣu-ru* 30-*ma* LÚ*.ERIM.MEŠ / *i-pa-ṭa-ru-šú-nu* NL 12 r.13-16 (CTN V 155ff), but also *i-na-ṣar-ru* (probably a solemnly emphatic statement, the passage concerns the protection of the crown princes) SAA XIII 79 r.4′ (Nabû-šumu-iddina, Calah)

(phr) *ú-ma-a* LÚ*.GAL–ARAD.MEŠ / *ša* AD-*ka* / *ip-qi-du-u-ni* / *ina* UGU-*hi-šú-nu* / *ip-tu-hur gab-bi-šú-nu* / *up-ta-ti-iu-šu* "Now the chief of servants, whom your father appointed over them – they gathered and unanimously dismissed him" SAA XIII 143 r.1-6[339]

---

[337] The latest edition reads now *i-ma-gúr-u-[n]i*, which looks as possible as ...-⌜*ru*⌝ on the copy, but *-ūni* is grammatically unmotivated because the clause is not subordinated. See the parallel in NL 1:21-22 (CTN V 19ff).

[338] UD = *tam* on the copy (ND 2717 = CTN V Pl. 3), but *i-tam-gu-ru* is dubious since there are no parallels. The MA-sign is expected. Moreover, *lā* + pf would be grammatically incorrect, cf. Hämeen-Anttila (2000) 110.

[339] Cf. n. ad SAA XIII 143 r.5.

(shr) LÚ.GAL–50 *ú-ta-hi-iṣ-ṣu* / *is-su-hur ina* GN *e-tar-bu* "They wounded the commander-of-fifty. They turned back and entered GN." SAA V 53 r.5-6

(sqr) [*li-i*]*s-qur liš-ṭur-*⌜*ni*⌝ / *lu-še-bi-lu-né-eš-šu* "Let them recite it, write it down and send it to him" SAA X 285 r.1′-2′

The last consonant is either a sibilant or a nasal:

('pš) *ma-a* ... QÀL.MEŠ / *di-i-ni ma-a p*[*i*]*l-ku-šú-nu* ... / *le-pu-uš* ≠ 16 LÚ.TIN.MEŠ-*ni-ia* / ... / *dul*$_6$*-lu e-pu-uš* / 10 *ša* ... / *i-ra-ṣip-u-ni* "Give junior ones ..., so they can perform their work assignment ... ; (out of) my 16 master builders ... are working ..., and ten are engaged in bricking ..." SAA V 56:5-11
dul-la-šú-nu i-ba-ši ša dam-mu-qi / *e-pu-uš ú-da-mu-qu* "They are working on minor improvements in their finish" SAA I 77:8-9
LÚ*.UŠ.BAR.MEŠ / ... // LÚ*.*ú-ra-su-tú* / *e-pu-uš* ≠ "The ... weavers ... They are performing masonry-duty" SAA XIII 145:7-r.2
ṭè-e-mu ... / *ur-tam-mi-ú ša ra-ma-ni-šú-nu e-pu-uš* / PN ... "They have neglected the order ... (and) are acting on their own. PN ..." SAA XVI 21:14-16 cf. *an-nu-rig ú-bal* / *ina* ŠÀ-*bi ú-šá-áš-kan-šú-nu* / *e-pu-uš-šú* ≠ / 1-*en* LÚ*.NAGAR.MEŠ ... "I am bringing and settling them there right now, and they are going to do it ..." SAA I 96 r.4-7

('rš) ŠE.NUMUN.MEŠ *e-ru-uš* / *ú-ri i-si-r*[*u*] "They cultivate the seed and plaster the roof(s)"[340] ND 2423:6-7 (CTN V 257f)

('ṣṣ) *i-ša-ú-lu* / *ú-ṣu-uṣ a-na* LUGAL / *a-šap-par* "(I am now sending [spies]) to inquire and investigate, and shall write (again) to the king, my lord." SAA V 91 r.8-10 cf. *a-sa-'a-al ú-ta-ṣi-ṣi* passim

(škn) 2-*ta li-gi-na-a-te* / *ša ṣa-a-ti* / *li-iš-šur-ru* / 2-*ta ša ba-ru-te* / *liš-kun* 2 UDU.NITÁ.MEŠ / ... / *le-pu-*[*š*]*u* "Two 'long' tablets containing explanations of antiquated words should be removed, and two tablets of the haruspices' corpus should be put (instead). Two rams should be sacrificed ..." SAA X 177 r.2-9

When the last consonant is /*b*/:

(krb) *aš-šur* ^{d}UTU ^{d}EN ^{d}PA *a-na* LUGAL / EN-*iá lik-ru-ub* ≠ PN ... "May Aššur, Šamaš, Bel (and) Nabû bless the king, my lord. PN ..." SAA XVI 65:1-2 cf. *aš-šur* ^{d}15 *a-na* LUGAL / *lik-ru-ub-bu* "May Aššur and Ištar bless the king" SAA XIII 139 r.7′-8′

(dbb) (LÚ.EN.NAM.MEŠ) *dul-lu* / ... *e-pu-šú* / *i-da-bu-ub* : *ma-a* "(the governors) are doing service ... They say ..." SAA V 147:11-13

When the last consonant is /*k*/:

('sk) *i-su-*[*u*]*k* SUM-*u-ni* (= *issūk*[*u*] *iddanūni*) GPA 180 r.8′

In III-weak verb forms:

(l'i) *šu-nu i-la-'i-i* / *i-kab-bu-su* "They will be able to *tread* ..." SAA XIII 127 r.15-16

(lwī + rmū D) *i-tal-ku-*[*ú*]*-ni* URU.[GN] / *il-ti-*⌜*bi*⌝*-i a-k*[*i* UD-*mu*] / *im-me-ra-an-ni ina* UG[U *x x*] / URU.MEŠ LÚ*.*ra-mu-ú-*[*ti*] / *ur-ta-mì-i* UN.MEŠ GUD.MEŠ *g*[*a*]*b-*[*bu*] / *ih-tab-tu* "They came and besieged [GN]. At [day]break, they

---

340 Saggs interprets this passage differently in CTN V p. 257f. For *ūru siāru*, cf. SAA I 77:18, SAA VI 21 e.10, NL 67 r.1 (CTN V 215ff).

let their released troops go to the [...] and towns, and they plundered all the people and oxen" SAA XV 118:2′-7′

(nš') *i-ti-ši* / *ur-ta-mi-ú-šu-nu* "... they let them go" SAA V 91:19-20

Possibly a syllable disappeared from *as-sa-ad-da-ad* (< **aštatantad, šadādu* Gtn perfect 1st sg.) SAA X 294:28.[341]

4.9.1 The plural dissimilation *a* > *u*

For examples, see 4.9 apocope of /*u*/.

This special case of the *a* > *u* dissimilation is attested in the third-person plural forms. The development of this dissimilation has possibly gone through vowel harmony and vowel apocope. As such, it may be a question of a substitute lengthening of the last changed syllable (-C*u* > -C*u*C), expressed by apocope, and of the shift of stress onto this syllable, or at least a shift of stress to the last syllable without any lengthening.

In Neo-Assyrian, stress and vowel are closely correlated. In numerous cases, stress also causes the development of an anaptyctic vowel, the latter resulting, e.g., from the lengthening of the preceding stressed syllable (for examples, see 4.7-4.8). Realized apocope would correspondingly hint at the possible lengthening of a syllable. Then the whole process could be (including vowel harmony): **éppašū* > *éppušū* > *éppušu* > *eppúš*/*eppű̄š* (prs 3rd pl.). Nevertheless, as consecutive verb forms indicate, plural dissimilations were apparently also strongly connected to sentence stress.

4.10 Proclitics

Cf. also 4.11.

Short unstressed or very weakly stressed prepositions, such as *ana* and *ina* in particular, may often merge with the following word.

Proclitic forms of /*ina*/ are:

(*bētu*) *i*–É /*ib* + *bēti*/ KAV 170:4

(*dātu*) *i–da-at* passim; *id–da-at* passim; *i–da-a-ti* SAA VIII 84 r.2, SAA XIII 149:4, 6; *id–da-a-ti* SAA X 221 r.10, SAA X 256 r.2, 5; *i–da-te* SAA I 155 r.3′, SAA X 322:12, SAA I 63 r.13, SAA XVI 56 r.7′; *i–da-a-te* SAA X 293 e.32′, SAA I 12:12′: *id–da-te* SAA XVI 34 r.8; *id–da-a-te* SAA I 250 r.9′, ABL 879:7, SAA XVI 85 r.4′ + (numerous /*id* + *dāt*/ + *-um* + forms with personal suffixes) cf. *ina da-at* SAA V 180:3, ABL 1244 r.6

(*harammēma*) *ih–ha-ra-me-ma* SAA XV 27 r.5′

(*harpūtu*) *i–har-pu-u-te* SAA XVI 86 r.19′

(*harru*) *i–ha-ri* SAA V 166:2′

(*hur*) *i–hur* SAA XIII 45 r.2

[341] Parpola (1987B) 276.

(*idu*)	*in*$_6$*-ni-du-ú-a* SAA I 20:3(-[*a*), r.1
(*irtu*)	*in*$_6$*–ni-ir-ti-iá* SAA V 224:9, r.16; *i–ni-ir-ti-šú-nu* SAA V 223 r.2; *in*$_6$*–ni-ri-te* SAA V 164 r.9; *ni-ri-it* SAA XII 25 r.26, SAA XII 26 r.26
(*kal* + *ūmu*)	*ik–kal–*UD*-me* SAA XIII 48 r.2
(*kê*)	*ik–ke-e* NL 5 r.7 (CTN V 25f)
(*kūmu*)	*i–ku-me* SAA XVI 36:6′; *ik–ku-me-iá* ABL 1264 r.5
(*libbu*)	*il–li-bi-ni* SAA V 105:7
(*mati*)	*im–ma-at* SAA X 5 r.3, SAA XIII 97 r.5, SAA XV 346:4; *im–mat* SAA I 134 r.5; *im–ma-ti* SAA X 14 r.5, SAA X 255:10, KAV 197 r.6, SAA X 263 r.11; *im–ma-te* SAA X 320 r.9, SAA I 66:8, r.3, SAA X 90 r.16′, SAA XVI 176:6′, KAV 197 r.7
(*nagiu*)	*i–na-gi-e* SAA V 84:6
(*namāru*)	*in–na-ma-ri* SAA X 147 r.3
(*pānu*)	*i–pa-ni-šú* SAA V 84 r.8
(*pānātu*)	*i–pa-na-tú-šú* SAA V 133 r.10; *i–pa-na-tú-šú-nu* SAA V 227:9
(*pittu*)	*ip–pi-it-ti* SAA XV 35:7; *ip–pi-ti-im-ma* SAA X 275:12 ~ *ina pi-te* SAA I 65 r.10; *ina pi-ti* CT 53 167 r.3; *ina pi-it-te* SAA XIII 37 r.14, SAA XVI 143:11; *ina pit-ti* SAA X 235 r.3, SAA XIII 149:8; *ina pi-it-ti* SAA X 183 r.8, SAA X 294:24, CT 53 169 e.11′
(*pūtu*)	*i–pu-tú-u-a-a* SAA V 217 r.9 ~ *ina pu-tú-u-a* SAA V 254 r.10; *ina pu-tú-ia* SAA I 29 r.1
(*surru*)	*i–su-ri* passim; *i–su-ru* SAA XV 131 r.21e, s.1; *i–su-ur-ri* SAA X 315 r.1, 14, SAA X 316 r.19, s.1, SAA V 52:10, SAA X 325 r.3′; *is–su-ri* passim; *is–su-ur-ri* SAA V 52:6, SAA X 63 r.11, SAA X 216:9, SAA XVI 148:19; *is–su-ri-*⸢*i*⸣ (interrogative int.) StAT 1 52:6 ~ *ina sur-ri* SAA X 376:10; *ina sur-re-e* (interrogative int.) SAA I 238:7
(*šaddaqdiš*)	*i–šá-daq-di-iš* ABL 1174:10′; *iš–šad-*[*daq-diš*] SAA V 170:4 ~ *ina šá-dàq-di-iš* SAA V 28:7; *ina šad-dàq-diš* SAA I 128 r.3; *ina šá-daq-diš* SAA XIII 18 r.5; *ina šad-daq-diš* BM 132980:18, SAA XVI 201 r.2
(*šalšūmi*)	*i-ša/šá-šu-me* NL 74:5 (CTN V 132ff)/SAA XVI 216:9′; [*i*]*-šá-šu-me* SAA I 99 r.3′; *iš–šá-šú-me* SAA XIII 137:7′ ~ *ina* ⸢*ša*⸣*-al-š*[*i* U]D*-me* SAA I 233:21; *ina šal-še–*U[D*-me*] SAA X 267:5; *ina* 3–UD*-me* NL 64 r.5 (CTN V 290ff)
(*šaluššīni*)	*i–šá-daq-di-iš*(–)*šá-lu-ši-ni* (no need to repeat the preposition *ina* neither assimilated nor unassimilated, esp. as the first adverb ends in -*iš*) ABL 1174:10′ ~ *ina šal-še-ni* SAA V 52:17; *ina ša-lu-še-ni* SAA I 204 r.1; *ina ša-lu-ši-ni* SAA XV 83:15 (CTN V 102ff)[342]
(*ši'āri*)	*i–ši-a-ri* SAA I 47 r.10, SAA I 143:14′, SAA I 172 e.19 (CTN V 173ff), SAA XIII 149:1 *i–ši-'a-a-ri* SAA XIII 71 r.10; ⸢*i*⸣*–ši-a-ru-ma* SAA I 41 r.8; *iš–ši-a-ri* SAA X 7 r.2, ABL 972 r.4, SAA XIII 187 r.14′, SAA X 210:6, SAA XVI 137 r.14; *iš–ši-ia-a-ri* SAA XIII 130:8 ~ *ina še-a-ri* SAA X 202 r.13′; *ina ši-a-ri* passim; *ina ši-'a-a-ri* SAA X 222 r.5; *ina ši-ia-a-ri* SAA X 324 r.5′; *ina ši-i-a-ri* SAA XIII 70:6
(*šulmu*)	*i–*⸢DI⸣*-me* SAA I 41:15 ~ *ina* DI*-me/mu* passim
(*timāli*)	*i–ti-ma-li* SAA XIII 137:7′, SAA X 98:6, SAA V 291 r.12, NL 74:4 (CTN V 132ff); *it–ti-ma-li* SAA X 12 r.5, SAA XVI 25:6, NL 64 r.4 (CTN V 290ff) ~ *ina ti-ma-li* SAA X 96:9, SAA X 235 r.10, SAA X 255:6, SAA X 322 r.5, SAA X 324:10, SAA XIII 88 r.3; *ina ti-ma-a-li* SAA I 240 r.10, SAA XVI 94:4′

[342] ND 2359 is joined with ND 2777 by S. Parpola in SAA XV 83, but the joining is "not confirmed physically," cf. ibid. p. 56 n. ad no. 83.

(*udē*) *in-nu-di-šu* "to *him alone*" SAA XVI 91:9′

Proclitic forms of /*ana*/ are:

(*balāt*) *a–bal-la-tuk-ka* SAA XV 241:6; *a–bal-duk-ka* ibid. l.9
(*bēt*)[343] *a–bé-e-ti* SAA V 146:5, r.4
(*danniš*) *a–da-niš* SAA V 145 r.8, NL 5:11′ (CTN V 25f), Rfdn 17 29 r.6; *a–da-ni-iš* GPA 197 r.3′; *a–dan-niš*[344] passim; *ad–dan-niš* passim
(*dāt*) *a–da-at* SAA I 92:10, SAA V 53 r.7
(*gammuru*) *a–ga-am-mu-ri* SAA XV 107 r.1
(*hur*) *ah–hur* passim: *ah–hu-ur* SAA X 227:17, 21, SAA V 291:8; *ah–hu-ru* SAA V 147:15 ~ *a-na hur* SAA I 52 r.6′, SAA X 43 r.6; *a-na hu-ru* SAA I 235 r.2′
(*aiāši/ijāši*) *an–ni-ia-ši*[345] SAA X 194 r.14′ ~ *a-na a-a-ši* SAA I 181:9, SAA XIII 38 r.6, SAA X 182:31, SAA X 334 r.8; *a-na ia-a-ši* GPA 1:5, SAA XVI 99 r.5 (cf. also 3.9)
(*kīma*) *a–ki-ma* SAA XIII 184 s.1, SAA XVI 78 r.15, SAA XV 115:9, SAA XV 118 r.11, SAA XV 119 s.4, SAA XV 163 r.6, SAA XV 201:5′
(*mar*) *am–mar/a–mar* passim cf. *mar* passim
(*mati*) *am–ma-te* SAA X 70 r.5 ~ *a-na ma-a-ti* SAA X 23 r.12; *a-na ma-ti* NL 96 r.19 (CTN V 49ff)
(*ši'āri*) *a–še-'a-ar* SAA X 204:6; *a⌉–š[i-i]a-ri* SAA X 54 r.1′ ~ *a-na ši-a-ri* SAA X 260:8, SAA X 322 s.1; *a-na ši-ia-a-ri* SAA X 278:8, SAA XVI 114 r.9e
(*šummu*) *a–su-mu*[346] SAA XV 17:10, e.12

/*ina*/ > /*ana*/ in proclitic forms (cf. also the semantic variation of prepositions in 7.1)

(*balāt*) *a–bal-la-tuk-ka* ("without you") SAA XV 241:6; *a–bal-duk-ka* ibid. l.9 ~ *ina ba-lat* SAA II 6:334
(*dātu*) *a–da-at* ("after") SAA I 92:10, SAA V 53 r.7 ~ *i/id–da-at* passim
(*mati*) cf. above
(*ši'āri*) cf. above

Proclitic forms of /*adi*/*u*/:

a-da-kan-ni "up to now" SAA V 245 r.6′; *a-da-kan-ni-ma* "up until now" SAA I 229:10; *a-da-ka-an-ni* SAA XVI 62:3; *a-da-ka-a-ni* NL 43:10 (CTN V 130ff); *ad-da-kan-ni* SAA XVI 138:7; *a-di-na-ka-ni* (*adi ana akanni*) KAV 213:11; *a-du-na-kan-ni* (*adu ana akanni*) SAA I 220 r.5, SAA X 230 r.5 (-*k*[*an-ni*]), SAA X 349 r.13, SAA X 353:21; *a-du-na-k*[*a-ni* SAA XVI 7:2′; *a-du-na-kan-an-ni* SAA XVI 55:5 ~

[343] However, see n. ad SAA V 146:5.

[344] The consonantal gemination between the first and second syllable is often shortened (e.g. usually not <*ad–dan-niš*> = /*addanniš*/ but *a–dan-niš* = /*adanniš*/) before the stressed syllable. /*addanniš*/ is morphologically justified but phonologically less likely. Thus gemination occurs regularly in connection with the stressed syllable only: /*adánniš*/, cf. Parpola (1987B) 273 n. 14 and (1980) 178 n. 22. Nevertheless, it is true that, for example, Urdu-Nanaia repeatedly writes <*ad–dan-niš*>, see the letters of Urdu-Nanaia: SAA X 314-27.

[345] See LAS II ad no. 151 r.14′.

[346] However, cf. Parpola (1997A) 318 n. 9.

a-du a-kan-ni SAA I 233:13, SAA XIII 19:6; *a-di a-kan-ni* SAA X 95 r.23e, SAA X 89 r.1

Proclitic forms of /*akī*/:

la ak an-ni-e ... / *áš-pu-ra* ABL 390 r.15′-16′ (Bel-iqiša) ~ *la-a ki-i an-ni-e* ... / *áš-pu-ra* "Did I not write ... like this" SAA I 80:11-12
ak (*an*)-*ni-im-ma šul-ma-na-te* / *i-ti-din* "In the same way he has given out gifts ..." SAA XVI 112 r.15-16e (probably another Bel-iqiša, cf. SAA XVI p. xliv)
a-kan-ni-i[347] NL 9:4′ (CTN V 66f), SAA X 294 r.6

Proclitic forms of /*libbu*/:

TA* lib É.KUR-ri /(*is*)*su libbēkurri*/ "from the temple" SAA XIII 154 r.12

4.11 Sandhi[348]

Changes that occur in two consecutive words closely connected with each other (such as compound words) are cases of external sandhi. Here the effect is either on the end of the first word or at the beginning of the second word. In Neo-Assyrian, these phonological changes are possible in compound nouns or phrases which can merge. Prepositions, in particular *ina* and *ana* (see 4.10),[349] are often the first elements of these mergings. A merging, including sandhi, may occur in at least four different ways: (1) the last vowel of the first word is dropped and the first vowel of the following word is concomitantly lengthened, (2) the first vowel of the second word disappears and the consonant of the first word first loses the gemination of the consonant, and in the end, the whole first syllable of the first word disappears[350] (cf. 4.12), (3a) the last vowel of the first word disappears and the remaining consonant at the end of that word assimilates to the first consonant of the second word, (b) if the latter word begins with a vowel, the last consonant of the first word remains in the resultant composition, and (4) the words merge with one another.

Aphesis (4.12) may also be related to this phenomenon. Sandhis and their source phrases are in free variation[351] with one another. Possibly sandhi spellings were considered to be more colloquial and the longer (non-assimilated) forms correspondingly to be more correct and literary.[352]

---

347 Parpola (1987B) 277 ad r.6.

348 Cf. e.g. Hämeen-Anttila (2000) 37f. Besides, Parpola (1984) 190-91 lists several sandhi examples.

349 Already Ylvisaker (1912) 16 § 11b.

350 See Parpola (1988A) 75-76 regarding the first two cases and for the listing of the syllabically spelled attested variants of the prepositional phrases with *issu*/*issi* as the first component: *issi ahāiš* "together," *issu annaka* "from here," *issu ammaka* "from there" and *issu pāni* "because of, in view of".

351 Parpola (1984) 191.

352 See ibid. 204 n. 24.

Examples of sandhi and its non-assimilated variants are the following:

(*issi ahāiš*) (1)	*i-si a-ha-iš* SAA V 286:5 TA* *a-he-iš* SAA I 14:12′, SAA I 18:10′ *is-sa-he-iš* SAA I 250:7′, SAA X 207:10 *i-sa-a-hi-ši* SAA I 182:8′
(*issu annaka*) (2)	TA* *an-na-ka* NL 2:15 (CTN V 22ff) TA-*un-na-ka* CT 53 598:3 *su-na-ka* CTN III 5 r.4 TA*-*na-ka* SAA V 166:4′, 5′
(*ina timāli*) (3a)	*ina ti-ma-li* SAA X 322 r.5, SAA X 324:10 *i–ti-ma-li* SAA XIII 137:7′ *it–ti-ma-li* SAA X 12 r.5
(*ina šiāri*) (3a)	*ina ši-a-ri* SAA X 240 r.1, SAA V 104 r.5 *iš–ši-a-ri* SAA X 7 r.2, ABL 972 r.4
(*ina irti*) (3b)	*ina ir-ti* SAA I 261:2′ *in*$_6$*–ni-ir-ti-iá* SAA V 224:9, r.16 *i–ni-ir-ti-šú-nu* SAA V 223 r.2
(*alik alkā*)[353] (4)	*li-kal-ka* "Go!" SAA XV 34:6′, NL 10:8 (CTN V 43ff), NL 15:8 (CTN V 140), SAA I 25:16, SAA I 96 r.14; *l*]*i-kal-ka* NL 10:4 (CTN V 43ff); *lik*˺*-al-ka* SAA I 29:16 ~ *a-lik al-ka* SAA V 210 r.11
(*kal* + *amāri*)	*ina ka-la-ma-ri* "in the morning" SAA V 243 r.14; *ina kal-la-ma-ri* SAA X 183 r.2, SAA XIII 98:12, SAA XIII 157 r.4, NL 34:9 (CTN V 266f); *ina kal-la-ma-a-ri* SAA XIII 88 r.6, SAA XIII 100 r.9
(*kal* + *ūmu*)	*ik–kal–*UD-*me* SAA XIII 48 r.2; *kal–*UD-*me* SAA X 263 r.9
(*in*(*a*) + *idū'a*)	*in*$_6$*-ni-du-ú-a* SAA I 20:3(-[*a*), r.1[354]
(*in*(*a*) + *udēšu*)	*in-nu-di-šu* "to *him alone*" SAA XVI 91:9′

(*issi* + *ahāiš*):

i-sa-he-iš	SAA V 150 r.12′, SAA I 221 r.8
i–sa-a-hi-iš	SAA X 354 r.11
i-sa-a-hi-ši	SAA I 182:8′
i-sa-ha-ii-ši	SAA XV 101:13
is-sa-he-'i-iš	SAA X 233 r.2, SAA X 238 r.14, SAA X 244 r.5
is-sa-he-iš	passim
is-sa-a-he-e-iš	SAA X 73 r.15

(*šalši* + *ūmi*): (cf. 4.2.1):

i–ša-šu-me NL 74:5 (CTN V 132ff); *i–šá-šu-me* SAA XVI 216:9′, SAA I 99 r.3′ ([*i*]–); *iš–šá-šú-me* SAA XIII 137:7′; *šá-šu-ú-*˹*me*˺ NL 102 r.11 (CTN V 207f); *šá-šu-me* SAA I 177 r.8; *a–šá-šu-me* SAA XVI 173:3′

(*aššutu* + *abī'a*):

áš-ta-bi-ia StAT 1 51 r.3[355]

---

[353] Parpola (1984) 191 finds it possible that *a-lik al-ka* and *li-kal-ka* were in complementary distribution, but, based on other evidence, these two forms are more probably free variants with a distribution conditioned both by prosodic and stylistic factors.

[354] Cf. n. ad SAA I 20:3, r.1.

(*iṣa* + *alka*):

i-ṣal-ka "Get (and) come!" SAA V 14:13 ~ *i-ṣa al-ka* SAA I 128 r.2, SAA I 235:17, *i-ṣa al-ka-a-ni* (2nd pl.) SAA I 29:18; *i-ṣa al-k*[*a-ni*] (2nd pl.) SAA I 15:11′; *is-se-niš iṣ-ṣa al-ka* "Take it along as well and come!" StAT 2 315 r.9

Crasis:
la/*lā* + vowel:

(*emūqu*, see aphesis below)
(mgr) *la* + *ammaggur* > *a-na-ku* TA* *pa-ni* / *la-ma-gu-ru la e-pa-áš* "I myself do not agree with this and I will not fashion (it so)" SAA XIII 34 r.7-8
la + *immaggur* > *le-ma-gúr-ru* / *la i-da-na* "He will not agree to give (them) to me" SAA I 149:8-9; *man-nu* ... / *le-ma-gúr* "Who ... is disagreeable?" SAA XVI 65 r.12′-13′
(ml') *la* + *imalla* > *lu la-mal-la* CTN III 4 r.5
(mth) *la* + *imattuhū* > *ú-di-ni* / *le-ma-tú-hu* "they cannot be picked up yet" SAA V 105 r.6-7
(qbī) *la* + *aqabbi* > *la mu-qa-a-a la-qa-bi* "I am unable to tell" SAA XVI 63:25
(tdn) *la* + *addan* > *la-da-na* "Should I not give ..." SAA I 124 r.4

lu(/*lū*) + vowel (cf. GAG § 81c):

lu + *aprus* > *laprus* passim
lu + *iprus* > *liprus* passim
lu + *ēpuš*/*ēmur* > *lēpuš*/*lēmur* passim
lu + *āmur* > *lāmur* passim
lu + *uparris* (D) > *luparris*/*lūparris* passim
lu + *ušapris* (Š) > *lušapris*/*lūšapris* passim

Cases in which *lu* is exceptionally written *lu-u*/*ú*-...:

(*balluṭu*)	*lu-u-bal-li-ṭu* SAA XIII 144:9 (Nabû-reši-išši, Arbela); ⸢*lu*⸣-*ú-bal-liṭ-ṭa* SAA IX 9 r.3′ (Arbela)
(*hallupu*)	*lu-u-hal-lip-šú-*[*nu*] SAA II 11 r.11′ (treaty of Sîn-šarru-iškun)
(*kallumu*)	*lu-ú-kal-li-mu* SAA X 18 r.9
(*kunnu*)	*lu-u-ki-nu* NL 41 r.17 (CTN V 208ff)
(*maddudu*)	*lu-u-ma-di-du* SAA V 169:15
(*nammuru*)	*lu-u-nam-mir* SAA X 29:6
(*na''udu*)	*lu-u-na-'i-id* SAA X 30 r.2 cf. *lu-u na-'i-id* ibid. r.11
(*naššuqu*)	*lu-u-na-*⸢*áš*⸣*-šiq* SAA I 133 r.3′
(*pallušu*)	*lu-*⸢*ú*⸣*-pal-li-šu* SAA II 6:598h
(*qarrubu*)	*lu-u-qar-ri-b*[*u*] SAA I 139 r.1
(*rummu*)	*lu-u-ri-ma-ka* SAA I 236 r.9
(*sahhuru*)	*lu-u-sa-hi-ru* SAA XIII 144 r.14 (Nabû-reši-išši, Arbela); [*l*]*u-u-sa-hi-ri* SAA V 163 e.14; *lu-ú-sah-*⸢*hi*⸣*-ri* SAA XV 337 r.4′
(*šakšudu*)	*lu-u-ša-ak-ši-di* SAA V 298 r.6
(*šatbû*)	*lu-ú-šat-bi-u* SAA X 14 r.10
(*šēbulu*)	*lu-u-še-bi-l*[*u-u-ni*] SAA XV 10 e.8′; *lu-u-še-bi-la* GPA 192 r.5′

---

[355] See Radner (1999A) 170-71, but note that it is not necessary to read the sign ÁŠ as *áša*. It may rather be a question of a writing representing, or trying to represent, a phonetic reality: the unstressed open syllable <*ša*/*u*> may be intentionally omitted from the writing.

(*šētuqu*)	*lu-u-še-ti-iq* SAA XIII 73 r.12; *lu-u-še-ti-qu-u-ni-šú* SAA V 218 r.8; *lu-u-še-t*[*i-qu*] SAA XV 37:6′
(*ubālu*)	*lu-ú-bi-lu*$_4$/*lu* SAA X 20 r.9/SAA XVI 6 r.5; *lu-ú-bi-lu-niš-šu* SAA XV 168 r.7; *lu-u-bi-lu-u-ni* KAV 213 s.3
(*udû*)	*lu-u-da* SAA I 179:20, SAA X 37 e.7′; *lu*/*ú-u-di* passim
(*uṣû*)	*lu-u-ṣi* SAA XV 368:5′
(*zummû*)	*lu-u-za-am-me* SAA II 11 r.10 (treaty of Sîn-šarru-iškun)

This exceptional length results from the combination *lu*/*lū* + *u*- (D- and Š-stems, I-*u*-verbs).

4.12 Aphesis[356]

Aphesis in the strict sense means the loss of a short unstressed vowel at the beginning of a word. It principally occurs in nouns, pronouns and adverbs. Nevertheless, in Neo-Assyrian, the phenomenon is not restricted to single words only, but also works on the phrase level. In particular, phrases forming a solid continuous unit and having only one main stress can become subjected to aphesis and other phonetic changes.[357] In that case, an entire unstressed syllable at the beginning of the phrase (e.g. the proclitic forms of the prepositions *ana*, *ina*, *issi* and *issu*, or even the whole preposition) may be dropped. Concomitantly with aphesis, other phonetic changes, such as sandhi[358] (4.11) and assimilation, may also occur.

The longer "normal forms" and the shorter aphesis forms are in free variation with each other but stylistically the "normal forms" were probably more appreciated.[359] E.g.

(*adu*/*i an* + *akanni*) see 4.10	
(*agūsi*)	> /*gūsi*/ see PNA 1/I p. 56.
(*akanni*)	> ⸢*ka*⸣*-a-ni* SAA V 146:8
(**alahhinu*)	> LÚ.*lah*/*láh-hi-nu* passim
(*alik alka*)	> *li-kal-ka* NL 15:8 (CTN V 140), SAA I 96 r.14 ~ *a-lik al-ka*[360] SAA V 210 r.11
(*ammāka*, TA* = *issu*)	> TA* *ma-ka* SAA V 92:11, SAA I 1 r.49 (-[*k*]*a*) (CTN V 188ff); TA* *ma-ak-ka* SAA V 100 r.4; *š*]*a ma-ka* SAA X 350:8′ ~ TA* *am-ma-ka* SAA X 211:10, SAA XV 25:13
(*ammar*)	> *mar* passim
(*ana mala*)	> ⸢*n*⸣*am–ma-la* SAA V 88:10 ~ *a-na ma-la* SAA I 31:11, r.11, SAA XV 198:7′, TH 6:5, SAA XV 84 r.14′ (CTN V 134ff)
(**an*/*ddurāru*)[361]	> *du-ra-ru* SAA V 203 r.17′; *du-ra-ri* GPA 248 r.2′

---

[356] On aphesis in Semitic languages in general, see Tropper (1992) 448-53; in Neo-Assyrian, e.g. Ylvisaker (1912) 16 § 11a, Deller (1959) § 37 and Hämeen-Anttila (2000) 37.

[357] See Parpola (1984) 187, 190-91, 203-204 (n. 15).

[358] Ibid. 190f. See also examples in idem (1988A) 75f.

[359] Cf. 1.5.9 and 4.11.

[360] *alik alkā*, for more examples see 4.11.

(*anīnu*) > *né-e-nu* SAA I 133 r.7′ ~ *a-ni-nu*, etc. passim

(*annāka*) > TA* *na-ka* SAA V 166:4′, 5′, SAA I 1 r.49 (CTN V 188ff); TA* *na-ak* SAA V 233:5; *su-na-ka* CTN III 5 r.4; T]A*-*un-na-ka* CT 53 598:3 ~ TA* *an-na-ka* SAA XVI 95 r.3′, SAA XVI 140 r.3, NL 2:15′ (CTN V 22ff); [T]A *an-na-ka* SAA XIII 47 r.6, SAA XV 37:11′ ([*x* T]A); T]A *an-na-kám-ma* SAA X 101:11

(*aṣappu*) > ANŠE.*ṣap-pu* SAA I 219:13 ~ (ANŠE).*a-ṣa*(*p*)-*pu* passim

(*egirrû*) > *gi-ir-ru-u* SAA X 59 r.4

(*emūqu*, probably aphesis is due to the assimilation of *a* + *e* => *ā*. Hence this item could as well be put under sandhi, cf. 4.11) > *la mu-qa-a-a* SAA V 37:11, NL 71:6 (CTN V 312f), SAA XVI 60:12, SAA XVI 63:25, NL 79:7 (CTN V 178f); *la mu-qa-šá* SAA XIII 76 r.7; ⸢*la*⸣-*mu-qa-a-šú* SAA X 60 r.13; *la-mu-qa-ni* SAA V 95 e.17′, SAA XVI 40:7 *la mu-qa-an-ni* SAA XIII 161 r.6 ~ *la e-mu-qa-a-a* SAA X 349 r.1, SAA XIII 33 r.11, SAA XVI 88 r.7′; [*l*]*a e-mu-qa-šú* SAA I 65:11; *la e-mu-qa-a-ni* SAA XVI 140 r.9; *la e-mu-qu-ši-na* SAA I 119:9

(*igigallūtu*) *i-na gi-gal-lu-ti* RIMA 2 A.0.101.40:33 ~ *ina igi-gál-lu-ti* Ash AsBbA1R012, [*u* IG]I.GÁL-*ú-ti* PKTA 27 13

(Inūrta) > /Nūrta/. See PNA 1/I p. xxv (3) Inūrta and ibid. n. 38. See also ibid. xxv Issār.

(**ikkillu*) > *kil-lu* SAA II 6:637A, frg; *ki-il-lu* SAA X 348 r.11, SAA XVI 36:14′; *kil-lum* SAA X 19 r.1

(*ina irti*) > *ni-ri-it* (see *ina* + *irtu* 4.10)

(*issu* + *pānu*) *su-pa-ni-ia* SAA I 29 r.13

(**ningallu*/*niggallu*)[362] > *in-gal*.MEŠ NAIT:4; *in-gal-li-šú-nu* NL 13 r.10 (CTN V 154f); ⸢*in*⸣-*qal-a-te* GPA 155 iv 18, *x*]*x in-gal-lu* SAA XV 26:13; possibly also GIŠ.*in-gal-lu*[363] SAA V 295 r.24

(Upūmu) > URU.*pu-u-me* SAA V 31 r.6′, 13′

(*ušumgallu*) > *šu-un-gal-li* SAA XIII 134:12′

4.13 Syncope[364]

For more examples, see 3.8.

Syncope affects the structure of a word by shortening it and shifting its stress. There were at least two different types of syncope operative in Neo-Assyrian: (1) one eliminating an open unstressed short syllable within a word (e.g. C*ara*C*u* > C*ar*C*u*, in practice > *e-tam-ru* passim, *a-tab-ka* SAA V 117:14, etc.), in order to prevent a sequence of three consecutive unstressed syllables in a word; and (2) one eliminating the geminated radical of perfect forms of Dtt(/Gtt)-stem(s) and the vowel which precedes it. As a result of syncope, the stress of a word shifts one

[361] However, cf. Deller (1959) § 37 d.

[362] For "sickle," see Deller and Finkel (1984) 83-84. Note also (*n*)*indabû*, which is mentioned in the same connection.

[363] However, see ibid.

[364] See GAG § 12, § 93e.

syllable forward from its normal position to the following syllable.[365] The latter type differs from the former mainly because of the special character of Dtt-perfects: if the perfect forms of the Dtt-stem were fully realized according to a paradigm analogous to other stems, then these Dtt-perfects would have been extremely cumbersome with their many t-sounds. The following examples illustrate the two types of syncope:

Type (1):

(*balāt*)	*a–bal-duk-ka* SAA XV 241:9
(*battibatti*)	*bat-bat-ti* SAA XV 136:13; *bat-bat-*[*ti* SAA XV 139:1′; *bat-bat-te-šu/šú-nu* SAA XVI 148:18/SAA XV 136:9 cf. [*b*]*a-ta-ba-ti* SAA V 67:6′; *ba-ta-ba-ti-ia* SAA V 79:7; *ina bat-ta-bat-t*[*e* SAA XIII 114 r.2; *ša ba-te-ba-tu-ka* NL 99 r.19′ (CTN V 109ff); ⌜*ša*⌝ *ba-ta-ba-tu-šú-n*[*u* 0?] ibid. l.12; *ba-tu-ba-ti-ni* SAA XVI 97:12
(*ṣummurāt*)	*ṣu-um-rat* ŠÀ-*bi* SAA X 123:7 ~ *ṣu-um-mu-rat ša* LUGAL EN-[*ia* "the wishes of the king, [my] lord" SAA XVI 132:9
('lk)	*lil-*(*li*)*-ku-ni* SAA V 32 r.15 (however, cf. 3.8)
(kl')	*ak-tal-šú-u* SAA V 147 r.9
(qrb)	*i-qar-bu-u-ni-ni* SAA V 64 r.2

Type (2):

Dtt in the perfect forms:[366] (examples 3rd pl., unless otherwise mentioned)

(gmr)	**ugdatámmiru* = *ug-da-ta-mir* (sg.) NL 17 r.11e (CTN V 283f) > *ugdátmiru* = *ug-da-at-me-ru* SAA I 80:9 ~ *ug-da-ta-me-ru* ND 2761:11 (CTN V 41)
(ktm)	*uk-ta-at-ti-mu*[367] SAA X 226 r.3
(šmn)	*us-sa-at-mi-nu*[368] SAA X 226 r.2

Gtt in the perfect (analogous to Dtt-forms[369]):

ittatákku > *ittátku*

('lk)	*i-ta-at-ku* "They went (off/away)/left" SAA V 32:11, SAA V 217:9; ⌜*i*⌝*-ta-at-k*[*u x*] SAA V 18:7 ~ *i-ta-*⌜*ta*⌝*-ku* SAA V 36:4′; *it-ta-ta-ku* NL 92:11 (CTN V 281); *i*[*t-t*]*a-ta-ku* SAA XV 59:10; *it-ta-tak-ku* SAA XV 172:3′; *it-ta-tak-k*[*u*] SAA V 19 r.7′; *i-ta-ta-ku-ú-ni* NL 60:7′ (CTN V 241f)

4.14 Metathesis of quantity[370] ($C_1\bar{V} + C_2 = C_1VC_2 + C_2$)

The metathesis of quantity describes a relatively often-attested alternation between the gemination of a consonant and the lengthening of a vowel.

---

[365] Parpola (1984) 199.

[366] Cf. Parpola (1984) 208 n. 51 and von Soden (1950) 391-93.

[367] Deller (1969) 53.

[368] Ibid. as well as idem (1967) 189.

[369] Parpola (1984) 199.

[370] See e.g. Deller (1959) § 38, Reiner (1966) 45f, GAG § 20d-e and Parpola (1988B) 79 and ibid. n. 4 (note that n. 3 is 4 and vice versa). See also 4.7.

4.14.1 A long open syllable replaces a closed syllable

Sometimes a long vowel appears instead of the expected gemination of a consonant in some finite verb forms, but a long vowel can also occur in words belonging to other parts of speech.[371] This variation is not very common. Nevertheless, these two different types of syllable appear to be in free variation with one another.

For example, consider:

In nouns and adverbs:

/adi/u + akanni/	*a-da-ka-a-ni* NL 43:10 (CTN V 130ff) ~ *a-da-kan-ni* "up to now" SAA V 245 r.6′; *a-da-ka-an-ni* SAA XVI 62:3
/ahulla/	*a-hu-u-la* SAA I 80 r.4
/dibbī/	*di-i-bi an-nu-te* StAT 1 51 r.10 ~ *dib/di-ib-bi* passim
/kēttu/	*ke-e-tu* SAA I 124:8, 11, 17, SAA X 302:9, CT 53 826:11′, SAA XVI 243:7′; *ke-e-tú* SAA V 295:23, SAA XIII 44 r.5, SAA X 316 r.5; *la ke-e-te* NL 80 + ND 2396 r.9′ (CTN V 104ff); *ki-i-tu* SAA I 110:23 (CTN V 219ff) ~ *ket-tu/tú* passim
/kuṣṣu/	TA *pa-an ku-ú-ṣi* SAA XV 61 r.10′ ~ *ku-uṣ-ṣi* SAA X 236:5 and *ku*(-*uṣ*)-*ṣi/u* passim
/mazzassu/	*ma-za-a-su* SAA II 6:369z ~ *m*]*a-za-s*[*u* ibid. frg; *ma-za-as-su* SAA XVI 34 r.12; *ma-az-za-as-su* SAA X 294:28
/memmēni/	*me-e-me-e-ni* SAA XVI 176:2′; *mi-i-mi-ni* SAA XVI 39 r.2 cf. *me-me*(-*e*)-*ni* passim; *me-em-me-e-ni* SAA X 183 r.3
/pitti/	*pi-i-te* SAA V 202:6 ~ *pit/pi-it-ti/te* passim
/qannu/	*ina qa-a-ni* SAA I 180 e.12′ ~ *qa-an-ni* passim
/ṣassu/	*ṣa-a-su* SAA XV 84 r.18′ (CTN V 134ff), NL 99 r.8′ (CTN V 109ff), SAA VIII 83:7

In verb forms:

('mr)	*/nemmar/ né-e-mar* SAA I 63 r.14 ~ *né-em-mar* SAA X 42 r.19, SAA V 287:5′(*n*]*é*-); *né-em-mar-u-ni* SAA I 210 r.1; *la né-em-ma-ra* SAA X 79 e.19
('pš)	*/neppaš/ né-e-pa-áš/*[*áš*] SAA X 349:26/SAA X 281 r.4′; *n*]*é-e-pa-*⸢*áš*⸣ SAA I 126:9′ ~ *né*(-*ep*)-*pa-áš* passim
('rb)	*/terrab/ te-e-rab* SAA XIII 76 r.8, SAA XIII 130:18, SAA XIII 149:3, 6 ~ *te-rab* SAA I 54 r.8, *te-ra-b*[*a*] (+ vent.) SAA XIII 118 r.5
(dūl)	*/idullū/ i-du-u-lu* SAA I 154 r.4 cf. *i-du-lu* SAA V 119:7, SAA I 153 r.4, SAA XIII 20 r.3, 9, SAA XIII 24 r.7′ (all these forms are prs 3rd m.pl.)
(jšū)[372]	*/laššu/ la-a-šú* SAA V 69:15, SAA V 113:18, SAA I 82 r.7, s.1, SAA I 194 r.4, SAA XV 108:8′, SAA XIII 28 r.6, CT 53 831:4′, SAA XVI 40 r.5, NL 85 r.6 (CTN V 100ff), *l*]*a-a-šú* SAA VIII 3 r.5; *la-a-š*[*ú* SAA I 35 r.10e; [*l*]*a-a-šú* SAA I 144 e.11′; *la-a-šu* SAA I 233:18, 20, *la-a-*[*šu* SAA V 259:5′; *la-a-šu-u* (interrogative int.) SAA I 80:10; *la-a-ši* SAA VI 52 r.1; *la-a-si* SAA XV 17:8 ~ *la-áš-šú* passim; *la-áš-šu* SAA V 120 r.4, SAA V 295 r.20

---

[371] For literature on exceptional vowel length in Akkadian, see Mayer (1992) 47. For examples of different "quantitative" variations (both consonantal and vocalic) in Neo-Assyrian, see Deller (1959) § 38.

[372] Cf. Parpola (1997A) 317 n. 7.

Note also *la-a-šú* ... *la-a-áš-šú* (2. emphasis) SAA I 245:5′-8′

(nš') */naššal na-a-ṣa* SAA XV 272:5′

(qbī) */iqabbi/ i-qa-a-⌜bi⌝* NL 29:10 (CTN V 143f) ~ *i-qab-bi* passim

(rmū D) */ramme/ ra-a-me* ND 2487:6 (CTN V 120ff) ~ *ra-am-me* SAA V 32 r.6, CTN III 28 r.2,[373] *ra-(am)-me-a* (pl.) passim

(tdn)[374] */taddin/* (prt 2nd m.sg./3rd f.sg.)[375] *ta-a-din*[376] SAA XIII 144 r.11 (Nabû-reši-išši) ~ *ta-din* SAA I 124:21, SAA X 187:12, KAV 199 r.8′ ~ *ta-ad-din* SAA I 52:5, SAA XIII 130 r.9; */laddin/ la-a-din* SAA I 240 r.4 ~ *la-ad-din* SAA XVI 83 r.6′, SAA XVI 34:19; note also *la-a-di-na-šú* SAA I 99 r.19′

(wd') */tudda/ ⌜tu⌝-u-da*[377] NL 86 r.1 (CTN V 239f); *tu-ú-da* BaM 27 419:5 (IM 132409); */nudda/ nu-ú-da* SAA V 40:10, SAA X 259 r.9

(wṣ') */ušeṣṣa/ ú-še-e-ṣa* NL 33 r.8 (CTN V 206f)

(wšb) */tuššab/ tu-ú-šab* SAA XIII 130:12, 20

/-annāši/

(kl') *ik-ta-na-la-a-na-ši* "He holds us up continually ..." SAA V 234:7′

(qbī) *iq-ṭi-ba-a-na-a-ši* "He gave us ..." SAA V 217 r.4

/-anni/

(hss) *tu-šah-si-sa-a-ni* SAA X 94 r.13′ cf. also *tu-šah-sis-a-ni* SAA X 93 r.6

(mqt) *im-qu-ta-a-ni* SAA I 137:4

(nmš) *ú-na-me-šá-a-ni-ni* "(The very day that) he ... ordered me to depart ..." SAA V 217 r.12

(shr) *ú-sa-hi-ra-a-ni* "He turned me back ..." SAA V 126:10

(snq) *ú-sa-ni-qa-a-ni* "He interrogated me" SAA XIII 154:11

(wrd) *ú-še-ra-da-a-ni* NL 12:10 (CTN V 155ff), SAA XVI 63 r.27

---

373 Cf. n. ad CTN III 28:4.

374 On the alternation of infinitive forms of the verb *tadānu* in legal documents, see Deller (1962C) 229.

375 Note that the spellings do not distinguish *taddin* of the prt 2nd m.sg./3rd f.sg. (*lū taddin* prc 3rd f.sg.) from the paradigmatic *tadin* of the stat 3rd m.sg. The distinction can only be concluded from the context. In legal documents, the stat 3rd m.sg. is often written as *ta-ad-din* (in hendiadys with *gmr* D: *kaspu gammur tádin/taddin/tādin* "The money is paid completely"; for the hendiadys *kaspu gammur tadin*, see Radner [1997] 349f) or even *ta-din-ni* and *ta-di-ni* (both passim), i.e. *tadinni/tadīni*, but never as **ta-ad-din-ni* or **ta-ad-di-ni*. These latter attested forms are illustrative because they elucidate well how the stress in NA can shift from the first syllable onto the second syllable when a word becomes trisyllabic (*tádin*, *táddin*, *tā́din* > *tadínni*, *tadī́ni*). Undoubtedly this shift is due to the emphasis of the hendiadys construction.

376 The form *ta-a-din* is attested in legal documents for the stat 3rd m.sg. in SAA XIV 29:11; SAAB 12 70:2′ (copy ibid. p. 78; Si. 660 = Div. 124); Rfdn 17 4:10; BaM 24 11:15; StAT 2 137:5′; StAT 258:8′; SAAB 9 73:16; SAAB 9 103:10′, VAT 19495:10, and in every case in hendiadys with *gmr* D, cf. the previous note. Our mistake in Verbal paradigms (Hämeen-Anttila [2000] 160 n. 20) needs to be corrected: *ta-a-din* SAA XIII 144 r.11 stands for the prt 2nd m.sg, not the stative.

377 Or *⌜tu⌝-u-da-⌜a⌝*, as in CTN V 239 r.1, cf. ibid, Pl. 43 (ND 2356). Perhaps *⌜a⌝* is only an erasure at the end of the line.

4.14.2 A closed syllable replaces a long open syllable

/*-āni*/

(*emūqu*)	*la mu-qa-an-ni* SAA XIII 161 r.6
(mṣ’)	*ma-ṣa-an-ni* ABL 1385 r.6 (Šamaš-šumu-ukin to Assurbanipal)
(Nergal-šarrāni)	^{md}U.GUR–LUGAL-*an-ni* SAA XIII 74:2, SAA XIII 75:2; ^{md}U.GUR–MAN-*an-ni* SAA XIII 71:2, SAA XIII 73:2, SAA XIII 76:2
(qbī)	*iq-ba-a*[*n-ni*] (3rd f.pl. + subj.) SAA X 284 r.5
(ṭīb)	*ṭa-ba-kan-ni* SAA XVI 127:23

/*-īni*/

(*ahu*)	*a-hi-in-ni* SAA X 289 r.9′, s.1
(*bēlu*)	EN-*in-ni* SAA X 147:3′
(*ēnu*)	*e-ni-in-ni* SAA X 68 r.1, SAA X 50 r.11
(*dullu*)	*dul-li-in-ni* SAA X 215 r.1, SAA XIII 64 r.5′, SAA XV 100:7; *dul*$_6$*-li-in-ni* SAA XV 94:14
(*issi*)	*is-se-en-ni* SAA XV 131:9
(*libbu*)	*lib-bi-in-ni* SAA X 185:15
(*muātu*)	*mu-a-tin-ni* SAA II 2 v 1
(*zittu*)	*zi-it-ti-in-ni* SAA X 48:18
(Urkittu-remini)	MÍ.^{d}*ur-ki-*⸢*tu–re*⸣*-mì-in-ni* SAA XIII 65 r.9
(špr)	*taš-pur-in-ni* SAA XVI 2:7

/*-ūni*/

(’pš)	*e-pa-šu-niš-šu-*⸢*un-ni*⸣ SAA II 6:169M; *e-pa-šú-ni-šú-un-ni* ibid. E ~ *e-pa-šú-ni-šú-u-ni* ibid. A; *e-pa-áš-šu-ni-šu-u-ni* ibid. S; *te-(ep)-pa-šá-niš-šú/u-un-ni* ibid. 233X, N, *te-pa-šá-a-ni-niš-šu-un-ni* ibid. f, *te-ep-pa-šá-niš-un-ni* ibid. 264F ~ *te-ep-pa-šá-ni-šú-u-ni* ibid. 68A, 233A
(btq)	*bat-qu-un-ni* SAA X 349 r.6
(mrṣ)	*mar-ṣa-áš-šú-un-ni* SAA II 6:208frg, *mar-ṣa-šu-un-ni* ibid. J, *mar-ṣa-šu-un-ni* SAA XVI 82:6 ~ *mar-ṣa-šu-u-ni* SAA II 6:208u, *mar-ṣa-šú-u-ni* ibid. O
(qbī)	*iq-bu-niš-šú-un-ni* SAA XV 104 r.13′
(rabû)	*i-rab-bu-un-nu* SAA XVI 128:11
(špr)	*x*]*-par-áš-šu-un-ni* SAA XV 120 r.10
(tdn)	*ad-din-áš-šu-un-ni* SAA XV 24:15
(*dullu*)	*dul-lu-un-ni* SAA X 277:8
(*eššu*)	*eš-šú-un-ni* SAA X 21 r.7′
(*gabbu*)	*gab-bu-un-ni* SAA X 289 r.6′
(*nakru*)	LÚ.KÚR-*un-ni* ABL 943:7 (Tammaritu)
(*ṭēmu*)	*ṭè-mu-un-ni* SAA XV 30 r.17, SAA XV 131 r.28, SAA XV 45:8

/*-ūtu*/

(*abbūtu*)	*ab-bu-ut-ti* SAA X 226 r.19
(*hardūtu*)	*ha-ar-du-ut-te* SAA V 152:7 ~ *har-du-u-te* ABL 945:7, 9
(*šalputtu*)	*šal-pu-ut-ti* SAA X 362:11′

/-*ītu*/

(*pānītu*)	*pa-ni-it-ti* SAA X 198:3; *p*]*a-ni-it-t*[*i*] SAA XVI 230 e.1′; *pa*⌉-*ni-it-tim-ma* SAA X 294:25; *pa-ni-it-t*[*e*] SAA I 15:15′ ~ *pa-ni-ti* passim
(*šanītu*)	*šá-ni-it-tú* SAA X 74 r.4 ~ *šá-ni-ti* SAA V 104:15, MAss 100:11

/-*i* + *ma*/

(*ammāka*)	*am-ma-kam-ma* SAA I 33 r.1
(*ammūti*)	*am-mu-te-em-ma* SAA X 199 r.15′
(*annūti*)	*an-nu-te-am-ma* SAA XVI 62 r.7′; *an-nu-tim-ma* SAA X 258 r.1, NL 96:9 (CTN V 49ff)
(*dibbī*)	*di-ib-bi-im-ma* SAA X 90 r.21′
(*immati*)	*im–ma-te-em-ma* SAA X 48:12
(*libbu*)	ŠÀ-*bi-im-ma* SAA XV 24 r.7
(*pānīūti*)	*pa-ni-ú-tim-ma* SAA X 6:17
(*šiddu*)	*ši-id-di-im-ma* SAA X 361 r.3

/-*ū* + *šu*/

(blṭ)	*ub-tal-li-ṭuš-šú* SAA X 333 r.3

/-*ū* + *naši*/

(rd')	*lu-rad-du-un-na-ši* "Let them *add* (more gold) to us" SAA V 294:19′

In (verb) patterns:

(*parāsu*)[378]	*ha-ra-aṣ-ṣi* SAA I 137:7
	ṣa-bat-ti-šú SAA II 6:306B ~ *ṣa-ba-ti-šú/šu* ibid. A/C; *ṣa-ba-te-*⌈*šú*⌉ ibid. frg
	ta-qa-an-nu ABL 1262 r.5′
(*pārisu*)[379]	[L]Ú.*par-ri-ṣu* SAA X 72:10; LÚ*.*par-ri-ṣu-te* SAA X 316:20; [*par-r*]*i-ṣu-te* SAA X 338 r.7;
	LÚ.*ra-ag-gi-mu* SAA X 294 r.31 ~ LÚ.*ra-gi-me* SAA II 6:116frg; ⌈LÚ.*ra*⌉-*gi-mu* SAA IX 3 iv 31
/*ušākal*/	*ú-šak-kal-šú* CT 53 501:7′
/*ušānah*/	*ú-šá-an-na-ah* SAA X 23 r.4
/*ušērab*/	*ú-še-er-ru-bu* SAA X 76 e.15
/*ušēṣi*/	~ *ú-še-e-ṣa* (prs) NL 33 r.8 (CTN V 206f)
/*ittūru*/	*i-tur-ru* SAA XIII 128 r.21e
/*ittūṣi*/	*it-tu-uṣ-ṣi* SAA X 349 s.1, SAA I 152 r.12, SAA V 204 r.5
/*lūṣūni*/	*lu-uṣ-ṣu-u-ni* SAA X 259 r.12 ~ *lu-ṣu-u-ni* ibid. r.1
/*lūdi'ū*/	*lu ud-di-ú* SAA X 29:3

Adverbs, pronouns and nouns:

(*aiāka*)	(*a*)-*a-ak-ka* SAA XV 118 r.4 ~ *a-a-ka* passim
(*anīnu*)	*a-ni-in-nu* SAA X 259 r.8, SAA X 289:9, SAA VIII 163:6; *a-nin-nu-ma* SAA X 241:9; *a-né-en-nu* SAA XVI 140 r.5, SAA X 289 r.9′; *a-né-en-nu-ni* ibid. r.14′
(*annāka*)	*an-na-a*[*k-k*]*a-a* SAA XIII 190 r.6

---

[378] Concerning infinitives, see Deller (1962C) 226, 229 who also lists several examples from legal texts.

[379] See GAG § 55l-m; for *parriṣu*, see Deller (1961A).

(*būnu*)	*bu-un-ni* SAA XIII 34 r.9
(*emūqi*)	LÚ.*e-muq-qi* SAA V 86:10, SAA I 250:10′, ABL 273:7 (Assurbanipal); *e-muq-qi* ABL 543 r.12, ABL 1108 r.9, ABL 1244 r.2 (all three by Assurbanipal); LÚ*.*e-m*]*uq-qi-ku-nu* SAA I 40:7′; LÚ*.*e-muq-qi-šú* SAA V 147:6; LÚ*.*e-muq-qe-e-šú* SAA XV 173:10′
(*hīṭu*)[380]	*hi-iṭ-ṭa-a-a* SAA XVI 34 r.17; *hi-iṭ-ṭi* SAA I 244 r.16; *hi-iṭ-ṭa-šú-nu* SAA XVI 63:10
(*māka*)	TA* *ma-ak-ka* "from there" SAA V 100 r.4
(*turtānu*)	LÚ].*tur-tan-nu* SAA XIII 105:12; LÚ*.*tur-tan-ni* SAA XIII 93 r.3, SAA XIII 97:8, SAA XIII 112:4′, r.3 ~ LÚ*.*tar-ta-a-ni* GPA 199:7
(*udīni/a*)	*ú-din-ni* SAA XV 60:19

4.15 Metathesis of syllables (CV́ + CVC ~ CV́C + CV)

The open syllable at the beginning of a word can change into a closed syllable, and the other way round. For instance, the paradigmatic imperative *purus* is sometimes replaced by the variant form *pursu*. These two forms are apparently in free variation with each other.[381] However, their alternation may be related to the stress of Neo-Assyrian in a larger context and thus also to prosody.[382]

> *ša* LUGAL EN / *iš-pur-an-ni ma-a di-ib-bi* / DÙG.GA.MEŠ *is-si-šú-nu* <u>*du-ub-bu*</u> / *ka-a-a-ma-nu di-ib-bi* DÙG.GA.MEŠ / *is-se-e-šú-nu* <u>*a-da-bu-ub*</u> "... about whom the king, my lord, wrote to me: 'Speak kindly with them!' – I constantly speak kindly with them" SAA XV 95:8′-12′, in which: *du-ub-bu* = *dubub* (imperat.),[383] not *dubba* since *a-da-bu-ub* has no ventive.

Note the difference between the imperative *pursu* and the imperative + ventive *pursa*:

> *nu-uk* <u>*šu-up-ru*</u> / UGU PN // [*m*]*a a-ta-a* LÚ*.ERIM.MEŠ-*ni* / *tu-ṣa-bi-ta nu-uk* / *mi-nu ša e-pal-ka-ni* / *ár-hiš* <u>*šup-ra*</u> "Write to PN: 'Why have you seized our men?' and quickly write me what he replies" SAA V 115:12-r.4; i.e. *šu-up-ru* UGU PN = "write to PN" ~ *šup-ra* = "write (to) me"

Examples of metathesis of syllables. Undeclinables and nouns:

(*birti*)	*bir-te* SAA V 92:6, SAA V 200:9, SAA XVI 43:12; *bir-ti* SAA X 51 s.1, 2, SAA XV 30 r.7, ABL 879:5, 6, ABL 1364 r.8, SAA XVI 148:14, SAA XV 30:6, SAA X 95 r.13′, SAA II 6:326C, N; *ina bir-ti* SAA X 226 r.21, SAA II 6:326B, c; *bi-ir-ti* SAA I 137:9, 11 ~ *ina bi-rit* SAA X 33:7, 13 (*ina* > *kīma*)

---

[380] Or *hiṭṭu*, Deller (1965A) 38.

[381] Parpola (1972) 24-25 n. 11 and LAS II ad no. 151 r.15′.

[382] Idem (1972) 24f n. 11.

[383] In a way this is a poor example, because I do not know of a Neo-Assyrian imperative of *dabābu* of the pattern *purus*. All the attested imperatives of the verb are *dubbu* or *dubbā* (pl.). Thus the alleged "free variation" between the patterns *purus* and *pursu* may not be supported by the data, especially in the case of geminate verbs, such as *dabābu* (*dbb*, the second and third radicals being the same), which seem to favour the *pursu* imperative.

(*irtu*)	*in*(*a*) *ir-ti* passim ~ *ni-ri-it* SAA XII 25 r.26, SAA XII 26 r.26
(*mi/ešli*)	*meš-li* (st. cstr.) SAA I 64:8, SAA I 107:9, SAA I 235:19, NL 70:8, r.2′ (CTN V 161ff) ~ *meš-il* SAA I 159 r.14; *me-šil* SAA I 181 r.8; *mi-šil* SAA X 187:11, *mi-ši-il* SAA X 196 r.5 cf. *me-šil-ma* SAA I 181 r.9, but also *a-n*[*a*] *meš-li-ma* NL 70 r.4′ (CTN V 161ff) ~ *a-na me-š*[*il*] StAT 1 53 r.3
(*šapla*)	*šap-la qa-ti* (st. cstr.) "secretly" SAA V 172:12; *šap-la* SAA X 33:9, r.4, 14, SAA X 363 r.9, CT 53 168 e.8′, SAA X 289:14, SAA I 66:6, SAA X 6:22; *ina šap-la* SAA V 146 r.10, SAA X 51 r.6, SAA XIII 135:10′, SAA XVI 59 r.6′; TA* *šap-la* SAA I 255 e.6′; *šap-li qa-ti* "secretly" SAA V 172:7 ~ *šá-pal* SAA V 4 r.8, SAA XIII 125 r.4, SAA X 359:6, SAA V 218 r.11 (SU.2); *ina šá-pal* SAA X 69 r.15; *ina sa-pal* SAA XVI 127:12, SAA XVI 126:18
(*tarṣi*)	*tar-*[*ṣ*]*i* SAA X 364:7′; *ina tar-ṣi* SAA I 132:17, SAA X 226:15, SAA X 246:11′
(*uznu*)	*uz-nu* (st. cstr.) SAA X 90 r.12′ ~ *ú-zu-un* SAA XIII 34 r.1; *ú*]*-zu-un-šú* SAA X 89:14′

In verb forms:
Stative (*pari/as*):

(blṭ)	*ba-al-ṭa* SAA V 91 r.3 ~ *ba-la-aṭ-u-ni* SAA X 8 r.24
(d'n/dnn)	*da-a'-na* SAA V 200:10, NL 100:7 (CTN V 118f), SAA X 104 e.17′, SAA X 60 r.1; *da-a-na* SAA I 147:15, SAA XV 60:12 ~ *da-an* SAA X 222:15, SAA XIII 38 r.2; KALAG-*an* NL 29 r.2 (CTN V 143f), SAA I 93:11, SAA V 105 r.6
(dmq)	*de-e-qe* (coord.) SAA XV 4 r.9, SAA XVI 3 r.2 ~ *de-iq* passim; *de-e-iq* SAA XVI 34:7; *de-'i-iq* SAA X 241 r.5, SAA X 242 r.7
(gmr)	*ga-am-ri* SAA XIII 150:9 ~ *ga-mir* SAA XIII 39:9, SAA X 17 r.1, SAA X 368:7
(kbr)	*kab-ra* SAA V 294:15′
(kbt/d)	*ka-ab-di* SAA X 182 r.11
(krm)	*la kar-me* SAAS V 54 e.6′ (ND 2095) ~ *ka-rim* KAV 214:6; *ka-ri-im* SAA I 79:15, SAA XV 30 r.12, SAA XV 164 r.10′
(krr)	[*k*]*a-ár-ri* SAA V 118:6
(m'd)	*ma-a'-da* passim; *ma-a-da* GPA 197 r.3′, NL 26:8 (CTN V 92f), NL 101:8, 10 (CTN V 292ff) ~ *ma-'a-ad* SAA V 292:5, SAA I 11 r.1, SAA X 30:11, 12, SAA X 235:11, SAA VIII 207:7
(mhr)	*mah-ri* SAA XVI 78:16 ~ *ma-hir* e.g. SAA X 96 r.21, SAA X 97 e.12′ and passim; *ma-hi-ir* e.g. SAA X 291 r.4, SAA X 308 r.8′ and passim
(n'd)	^{m}*aš-šur–na-a'-di* SAA XIII 30:2; ^{m}*na-a'-di–*DINGIR SAA V 291 r.3
(qrb)	*qur-bu* SAA X 203 r.8 ~ *qu-ru-ub* SAA X 95 r.22′, SAA XVI 125:9′
(šlm)	*šá-al-me* SAA X 290 r.14e
(zrp)	*za-ar/ár-pi* SAA VI 154 r.5, SAA VI 219:8′/SAA VI 213:4′ ~ *za-rip* passim in legal documents

Imperative:

(*itiz*)	*it-zi* SAA V 63 r.5 ~ *i-ti-iz* ABL 523 r.10, SAA I 132:8
(*dubub*)	*du-ub-bu* SAA V 203:13, SAA I 2:5′, SAA X 276:7, KAV 213:8, SAA XV 95:10′, CTN III 3 s.2
(*dulul*)	*du-ul-lu* SAA XIII 187 r.12′
(*huruṣ*)	[*hu*]*-ur-ṣu* SAA V 128:9

(*kurur*) *ku-ur-ru* SAA I 235 s.1; *kur-ru* SAA XIII 161:9′, SAA I 57 r.5′, SAA V 216 s.2, SAA XVI 21:17, SAA XVI 5:18

(*mutuh*) *mu-ut-hu* SAA XV 123 r.2′, NL 27:10 (*-h*[*u*]) (CTN V 286f) ~ *mu-tu-uh* SAA XV 275:3′

(*ṣabat*) *ṣa-ab-ta* SAA XV 85:7, KAV 198:5, SAA I 29:16; *ṣab-ta* SAA X 187 e.22 ~ *ṣa-ba-at* TH 1 e.8; *ṣa-bat* SAA I 179:18, SAA I 204:9, CT 53 282 r.7′, StAT 1 54 r.8

(*ša'al*) *šá-a-la* SAA V 265:5; *šá-*⌜*a*⌝*'-la* GPA 188:11 ~ *šá-'a-al* SAA V 34:6, SAA I 71:7, SAA X 9:10, SAA XVI 84:10; *ša-'a-al* SAA X 280:8, SAA I 21:10′; *ša-al* SAA I 21 r.3, Rfdn 17 28:10; *šá-al* SAA XV 90:4, SAA XVI 136:10, VAT 9770 r.9

(*šudud*) *šu-du* SAA XV 123 r.3′

(*šukun*) *šu-u*[*k*]*-nu* SAA XV 90 r.20 ~ *šu-kun* SAA X 185 e.27, SAA I 18 r.10′, SAA XIII 41:15, SAA XVI 120 r.4

(*šupur*) *šu-up-ru* SAA V 115:12, SAA I 246:10, SAA X 194 r.15′; *šup-ru* SAA XV 238:9, SAA XVI 65 r.17e ~ *šu-pur* SAA X 255 r.4, SAA I 102:7, SAA I 103:8, SAA I 245:2′, SAA XVI 17:8, SAA XV 252:11′

Relatively many of these examples include either an *r* or *l* which functions as the nucleus of a syllable and can thus also manipulate the syllable stress. Geminate verbs are common in this group too (*dbb*, *dll*, *krr*, *šdd*).

Perfect:

(*ētakal*) *e-tak-la* SAA V 32:16 ~ *e-ta-kal* SAA X 96 r.9, SAA X 107 r.6

(*ētamar*) *né-ta-am-ra* SAA VIII 21 r.2, SAA X 185:13 ~ *né-ta-mar* SAA X 126 r.1, SAA X 147 r.5

(*ātanah*) ^{m}*a-tan-ha*(–DINGIR/^{d}UTU) passim, see PNA 1/I pp. 231-32 ~ ^{m}*a-tan-ah*–DINGIR SAA XVI 81 r.4′; ^{m}*a-ta-na-ah*–DINGIR(.MEŠ) see PNA 1/I p. 232

(*ētapaš*) *e-tap-šá* SAA V 147 r.10; *te-ta-*⌜*ap*⌝*-šá* SAA I 179:22 ~ *e-tap-áš* SAA I 251:7, SAA XV 108:4′, ABL 1364:6′, KAV 214 r.8; *e-ta-pa-áš* passim

(*ētapal*) *e-tap-la* (f.pl.) SAA X 347:9 ~ *e-ta-pal* SAA XVI 63 e.34

(*ētarab*) *e-tar-ba* SAA I 64 r.3′, 6′ (the final *a* is not ventive[?], cf. ibid. r.17e) ~ *e-ta-rab* SAA X 8:23, SAA X 351:10, SAA XVI 64 r.7, SAA XVI 45 r.6, SAA I 110:6 (CTN V 219ff), SAA XV 113:9

(*i/a/ni*|*ttitiz*) *a-ti-it-zi* SAA XVI 45:5′, GPA 194:12 ~ *at-ti-ti-iz* SAA XIII 134 r.25, SAA X 294:20
⌜*i*⌝*-ti-it-zi* SAA V 256:10′; *it-ti-it-zi* SAA I 235:15, SAA VIII 68:7, SAA VIII 71:3, SAA X 104 r.3, SAA XVI 10:7′; *it-te-et-zi* SAA X 193:10; *ni-ti-it-zi* SAA XVI 41:13 ~ *ta-ti-ti-iz* ABL 523 r.4; *it-ti-ti-iz* SAA VIII 101:8

(*ibtataq*) *ib-ta-at-qa* (vent.?) SAA X 294 r.21 ~ *ab-ta-taq* SAA I 58:9, SAA IX 8:7

(*iddubub*) *id-du-ub-bu* SAA X 354 r.12, SAA XVI 10:2′; *ni-du-ub-bu* StAT 1 54 r.2 ~ *ni-id-du-bu-ub* NL 1:7, 19 (CTN V 19ff), SAA X 43 r.9; *ni-du-bu-ub* NL 5 r.5 (CTN V 25f)

(*iddi'in*) ⌜*i*⌝*-di-i'-ni* (cont. broken) SAA XIII 135:11; *i-di-i-ni*[384] SAA V 145 r.12

(*iddi'ip*) *i-di-i-pi* SAA XIII 27 r.19 ~ [*i*]*d-di-'i-ib* SAA I 138:12; *ta-ad-di-ib* SAA XIII 29 r.4′; *ta-ad-dib* SAA XIII 28 r.12

[384] Usually aleph disappears between two similar vowels, LAS II ad no. 206:8.

(*iddimiq*)	*⸢i⸣-di-im-qi* SAA XV 50 r.4′ ~ *i-d*]*i-mì-iq* ibid. r.6′; *id-di-mì-iq* SAA X 69:10
(*a/iktarab*)	*ak-tar-ba* StAT 1 51:6, SAA X 198:13; *ik-tar-ba* SAA I 188 r.7; *ni-ik-*[*t*]*ar-ba* SAA X 185:14 ~ *ak-ta-rab* KAV 213:5; *ni-ik-ta-rab* SAA XIII 143:13
(*iktarar*)	*ik-tar-ra* SAA X 217 r.7 ~ *ik-ta-ra-ar* SAA X 75:11, SAA X 96 r.13; *ik-ta-ra-ár* KAV 197 r.23, NL 64 r.3 (-*á*[*r*]) (CTN V 290ff)
(*iptaras*)[385]	*ip-tar-sa* BaM 15 227:13
(*assuhur*)	*a-su-uh-ru* (coord.) SAA V 146:13 *ni-su-uh-ru* (coord.) SAA XV 116 r.10′ ~ *i-su-hur* SAA V 129:3′; *is-su-hur* SAA X 8 r.4, 14; *ni-su-hur* NL 10:9 (CTN V 43ff)
(*a/iṣṣabat*)	*a-ṣa-ab-ta* NL 12 r.6 (CTN V 155ff); *a-ṣab-ta* SAA XIII 25 r.3; *i-ṣab-ta* SAA XIII 154:11 ~ *iṣ-ṣa-bat* SAA I 205 e.19, SAA X 24 r.2, SAA XIII 134:8′, SAA XIII 138:13, SAA XVI 29:6; *iṣ-ṣa-ba-at* SAA I 31:15; *a-ṣa-bat* NL 85:16 (CTN V 100ff); *aṣ-ṣa-bat* ABL 879:8, ABL 1148:6′. However, it seems that these metat. forms of *ṣbt* are connected with clausal coordination. Therefore, they cannot be considered as occurring in completely free variation with their non-metat. variants)
(*assa'al*)	*a-sa-a'-la* SAA V 163 r.1 ~ *a-sa-al* passim; *a-sa-'a-al* SAA I 66:10, r.2 *as-sa-a*[*l*] SAA X 99:8; *as-sa-'a-al* SAA XIII 125:11, SAA X 9:11, SAA XVI 84:13, r.6; *áš-sa-al* NL 96:7 (CTN V 49ff)

II-weak verbs:

(bīl)	*i-pi-la* Tell Billa 72:2
(dūk)	*i-du-ka* SAA I 171 r.19 (CTN V 227ff), SAA V 53:5 ~ *i-du-ak* SAA XVI 127:21, SAA XVI 95 s.1, SAA XIII 70 r.4 *ni-du-ka* SAA I 221 r.6, 8 ~ *ni-du-ak* NL 65:9 (CTN V 45f)
(mūt)	*i-mu-ta* NL 71:12 (CTN V 312f) ~ *i-mu-at* SAA XVI 40:10; *a-mu-at* passim
(nīl)	*i-ti-i-la* SAA XVI 64:10
(pūg)	*ip-tu-ga* ABL 307 r.11′ ~ *ip-tu-ag* SAA X 173:16, SAA X 368 r.9′, 12′
(rīq)	*a-ri-qa* SAA X 320 r.10 ~ *i*]*r-ti-aq* SAA XVI 97:11
(tūr)	GUR-*ra* SAAB 1 66f: 8, r.3; [*ta-tú*]*-a-ra* SAA XIII 66:18 ~ *a-tu-ar* SAA XVI 34:22; *i-⸢tu-ar⸣* SAA I 1:34 (CTN V 188ff); *it-tu-ar* ibid. l.10
(zūz)	*ú-za-zi* SAA XVI 112 r.14

[385] See Deller (1971) 642 for examples, and especially n. 10 on the same page: the ventive ending in -*a* is not strictly distinguishable from forms of which -*a* is missing.

5 MORPHOLOGICAL VARIATION

5.1 Pronouns[386]

Discernible variation[387] occurs in the following pronouns (note that the variation, for instance, between the third-person pronouns, both masc. and fem., is frequent, while some spellings in the list, such as *a-ta* and *an-nu-ku*, are exceptional):

Independent personal pronouns:

3rd m.sg. *šû* / *šūtu*[388] Both passim
3rd f.sg. *šî* / *šīti*[389] Both passim
2nd m.sg. *atta* > *at-ta* passim; *a-ta* BaM 27 419:5 (IM 132409)
1st sg. *anāku* > *an-nu-ku*[390] SAA XIII 45 r.9; *an-na-ku* (cont. broken) SAA XVI 56 r.13′; *a-na-ku/ana-ku* passim
3rd m.pl. *šunu* > *šu/šú-nu* passim, *šá/ša-nu-u-ni* (+ subj.) NL 86:10 (CTN V 239f) /SAA XV 54:5′
2nd m.pl. *attunu* > *at-tu/tú-nu* passim; *at-tu-ú-ni* SAA V 81:13
1st pl. *anīnu* > *an-ni-nu* SAA V 53 r.7, SAA I 172 r.32, 36e ([*a*]*n*-) (CTN V 173ff); *a-ni-in-nu* SAA X 259 r.8, SAA X 289:9, SAA VIII 163:6, [*a-ni*]-*in-nu* SAA X 289:14; *a-ni-in-nu-ma* SAA X 241:9; *a-né-en-nu* SAA X 289 r.9′, SAA XVI 140 r.5; *a-né-en-nu-ni* SAA X 289 r.14′; *né-e-nu* SAA I 133 r.7′ ~ *a-ni-nu/ni* (*a-ni-ni*, see 4.5) passim

Independent oblique forms of the personal pronouns:

3rd f.sg. *šāša* ~ *šāši* (*a-na šá-a-šá* NL 3 r.4′ [Face A in CTN V 64ff] ~ [*a*]-*na ša-ši-ma*[391] SAA V 108:16)
1st sg. *aiāši* ~ *ijāši*, see 3.9

---

[386] In this study, I have only included a brief review of the NA pronouns. For more on them, see Hämeen-Anttila (2000) 43-54.

[387] Irrespective of the fact that the variation in pronouns is chiefly of a phonological nature.

[388] For the differences of the use of these forms, see Hämeen-Anttila (2000) 45-47.

[389] Ibid.

[390] An emphatically marked form, cf. the prosodically marked forms in 3.7. See Ylvisaker (1912) 13 § 7c, 17 § 12, cf. Hämeen-Anttila (2000) 43.

[391] Not a masculine form as given in Hämeen-Anttila (2000) 44.

3rd m.pl. *šunāšunu* (*a-na šú-na-šú-nu* SAA V 52:20, *a-na š*]*u*?*-na-šú-nu* NL 8:5 (CTN V 26ff), cf. the land grant texts of Adad-nerari III: *šu-na-tu-nu* SAA XII 7 r.14, SAA XII 8:23) ~ *šāšunu* (*a-na šá-a-šú-nu* SAA XV 257:12′ cf. e.g. Adad-nerari III: *ša-tú-nu* SAA XII 1 r.2′; *šá*?*-tu-nu* VAT 5602:10 [VS 1 95] 625 BCE)
2nd m.pl. *kanāšunu* (*a-na/ana ka-na-šú-nu* NL 1:25 [CTN V 19ff]/KAV 199:3) ~ *kāšunu* (*a-na ka-a-*⸢*šu*⸣*-nu* SAA V 34:20, *a-na ka-šá-nu-*⸢*u*⸣*-ma* SAA XVI 63 r.1, *a-na ka-šú-nu* [NB] CT 53 664:3′)

Independent possessive pronouns:[392]

3rd sg. **iššû*
2nd sg. *ik-ku-u* SAA X 90 r.16′, SAA XVI 183:11
1st sg. *ijû* (m. *ia-ú/u* passim), f. *ijātu* (*ia-a-tú* SAA I 94:6), possibly pl. *ia-u-ti* GPA 205:4, 9 (cont. broken)
3rd pl. *iššanû* ~ *iššunû* "theirs," see 4.6. Possibly in SAA V 36:2′: *iš* ⸢*x*⸣*-nu-ti* > *iš-*⸢*šú*⸣*-nu-ti*, but because of the broken context, this is not certain.
2nd pl. *ik-ka-nu-ú* URU.MEŠ*-ni-ku-nu* "your towns" SAA XV 69:13
1st pl. *innû* "ours" > *in-nu-u/ú* (sg.) SAA X 89:10′, SAA X 84:15/SAA X 48:17; *in-nu-te* (pl.) SAA I 172:10 (CTN V 173ff)

The rarely attested independent possessive pronouns (except 1st sg.) offer some traces of gender and number inflection (1st sg., 3rd pl., 1st pl.). The use of these pronouns is probably mainly emphatic (note the stress which appears exceptionally on the last syllable) and stylistic since they may be used together with possessive suffixes (cf. 2nd pl. above). E.g.

ia-u mi-i-nu / hi-iṭ-ṭa-a-a "What is my fault?" SAA XVI 34:16, cf. ABL 390:8, 11-12
*ia-ú / ṣi-it–*ŠÀ*-bi-ia /* EDIN *tu-sar-pi-di* "But you have made my own offspring roam the steppe" SAA IX 1 v 18-20

Demonstrative pronouns:[393]

Near deixis	m.	f.
sg.	*anniu* passim (⸢*a*⸣*-ni-ú* SAA V 162 r.5; *a-ni-e* [gen.] ibid. r.6) ~ *hanniu* passim (for the forms with h, cf. n. 283), *ha-ni-u* SAA V 53:15, SAA V 154 r.6′, SAA X 319:10; *ha-ni-e* (gen.) SAA V 121 r.10 (-⸢*e*⸣), SAA V 199:13 ~ *annû*, see 4.4	(*h*)*annītu* (passim) *a-ni-tú* SAA XV 288 r.2, *ha-ni-tu* StAT 2 315 r.3
pl.	(*h*)*annūti/e* (passim) *a-nu-ú-te* NL 45 r.3′ (CTN V 136ff), *a-nu-te* SAA XIV 464:14, *ha-nu-te* SAA I 99:6, SAA I 176 r.38 (CTN V 169ff), SAA V 121 r.19, TH 14:5; *ha-nu-u-te* SAA V 121:8 ~ (*h*)*annūtu*, see 4.5	(*h*)*annāte/i* (passim) *ha-na-a-te* MAss 67 r.2

392 Hämeen-Anttila (2000) 48f.

393 Cf. ibid. 50.

Far deixis	m.	f.
sg.	*ammiu* (passim)	*ammī/ēti/e* (gen.[394] passim)
pl.	*ammūti/e* (passim) *a-mu-te* SAA V 202:6 ~ *am-mu-u-tu* SAA XIII 190 r.18	*ammāti/e* (passim) *a-ma-te* CTN III 5 e.10 ~ *šuātu/i/e* (passim in legal documents, this pronoun refers to both gender [m. and f.] and number [sg. and pl.])

Interrogative pronouns:[395]

Contrary to Hämeen-Anttila (2000) 64f, *aiu/a'u* (sg.) ~ *aiūti/a'ūti* (pl.) "what?, which?, (the one) who?"[396] is often constructed with *ša* to form subordinate clauses, and then almost exclusively adjectivally: *aiu* + noun + *ša* (...) + verb in the subjunctive.[397] E.g.[398]

a-a-i dul-lu ša LUGAL *be-lí e-pu-su-su-nu* ... "What work has the king, my lord, done ...?" SAA XVI 126 r.21

[*a*]*i-'u šá-a-ru ša i-di-ba-ka-a-ni* "What wind has risen against you?" SAA IX 1 i 6′

a-a-ú-ti URU.MEŠ-*šú* / *ša ina* NAM-*at* GN *áš-šu-u-ni* "What towns of his have I taken in the province of GN?" SAA XV 24:8-9

Sometimes the difference between *aiu/a'u* and *mannu* can be very slight, e.g.

man-nu LUGAL *šá a-ki an-ni-i a-na* LÚ.ARAD.MEŠ-*šú* / SIG$_5$-*tu e-pu-uš-u-ni ù a-a-ú* / EN–DÙG.GA *šá a-ki an-ni-i* / *a-na* EN–DÙG.GA-*šú ṭa-ab-tu* / *ú-tir-ru-u-ni* "Who is the king that has done such a favour for his servants, and what friend has returned a kindness in such a manner to his friend." SAA X 227:25-e.29

at-ta-ma ša-'a-al // LÚ *la ú-da* / *a-a-ú šu-tu-u-ni* / *a-na man-ni la-áš-al* / LÚ *lu-šah-*⸢*kim*⸣*-u-ni* / *la-áš-al-šu* "You ask (him)!" – I don't know who this man is – whom should I ask? Let the man be pointed out to me, (then) I will ask him." SAA X 280:8-r.5

Indefinite pronouns:[399]

memmēni (passim) ~ *mamma* (TA* *mám-ma* StAT 1 55 r.4, otherwise passim in legal documents)

Quantifying pronouns:[400]

Note that *gabbu* "all" also has the adjectival meanings "whole, entire" when used with a noun in the singular, e.g.

UD-*mu gab-bi-šú* / ... / MI *gab-bi-šú* "the whole day ... the whole night" NL 56:4′-6′ (CTN V 197ff)

---

394 I do not know of any nominative form of the feminine singular.

395 In general, see Hämeen-Anttila (2000) 51f, 64f.

396 Cf. the examples in 3.9.

397 Cf. GAG § 48h.

398 Cf. also SAA IX 1 i 15′-16′, ii 34′-35′, SAA X 27 r.10-12 (though broken), NL 41:9-10 (CTN V 208ff).

399 For the use of indefinite pronouns in NA, see Hämeen-Anttila (2000) 52f.

400 See ibid. 53f.

EDIN URU *gab-bi-šu* "The outer town in its entirety" SAA XVI 100:8
BÀD *ša* EDIN URU *gab-bu* "the whole wall of the outer city" ibid. l.10
nap-tu-nu gab-bu "the entire meal" SAA XIII 10 r.10

gabbu/*gabbi*- can be used independently:

gab-bi-šú-nu ⌜*a*⌝-[*na* GN] / *lil-li-ku* "All of them should go t[o GN]!" SAA V 298:8′-9′
UD-15-KÁM *li-kar-ku* / *lil-lik-ú-ni* / *gab-bu am-ma-ka* / *ki-i a-he-iš* / *ina* ŠÀ-*bi a-de-e le-e-ru-bu* "Let them reconvene on the 15th, come here and all enter the treaty in the said place at the same time." SAA X 6 6-10
gab-bu sa-ak-lu-te šú-nu "They are all common men." SAA XIII 152:6′

As an exception, *gabbu* may even be used before a noun:

gab-bi / *nu-uh-šú* / [*x x x x*]-*šú a*-⌜*da*?-*na*?⌝ "I will (then) give total abundance [to] his [...]." SAA XIII 144 r.16e-s.1

In this example, however, the broken context makes the interpretation uncertain. Perhaps *gabbi* should be understood independently here as "all (of it)" or possibly the scribe has failed to use it in a grammatically correct way.

5.2 Adverbs[401]

Interrogatives:

aiāka ~ *ijāka*, see 3.9
akê (*a-ke-e* passim) ~ *ik–ke-e* NL 5 r.7 (CTN V 25f), see 4.10
alê "where?" (*a-le-e* passim) ~ *a-le-e'* SAA II 6:332B ~ *a-li-i* SAA V 224:13 ~ *a-li-ma (+ -ma)* SAA XVI 105 r.21e, SAA XVI 52 e.9
ammēni (passim) ~ *ammīni* (passim) ~ *ana mīni* (passim) ~ *ina mīni* SAA XIII 190 r.5, StAT 1 54 r.3, MAss 100 r.3
immati/e ~ *ammati* ~ *ana māti*, see 4.10 and 7.1
mannu (passim) ~ *ma-a'–at-tú-nu* SAA I 33 e.23, *m*]*a–at-ta-a* NL 5:5′ (CTN V 25f, sandhi spellings: *mannu* + *attunu/atta*)

5.3 Variation of plural forms of nouns

The plural has only one case in Neo-Assyrian. Nonetheless, there are altogether four different plural endings of nouns in use:

(1) *-āni*,[402] e.g. *ṭuppu* > *ṭup-pa-a-ni* SAA X 245 r.13 and passim
(2) *-āti*,[403] e.g. *ṭābtu* > *ṭa-ba-a-te* ABL 1022 r.21

---

[401] For a full treatment of adverbs, see Hämeen-Anttila (2000) 54-65.

[402] In professional titles *-āni* is the more common plural than *-āti*, see Deller and Parpola (1966A) 69. Note also ibid. *mušarkis*(*u*) which might have had two different plural forms: *-āni* passim ~ LÚ.*mu-šar-kis-te* ND 2706:4, possibly to be read *mušarkisūti* (the word in ND 2489 i 3 [Iraq 23, pl. 16] = NWL 35 may not refer to *mušarkisu*).

(3) -*i/e*,[404] e.g. *ṣupru* > [*ṣ*]*u-up-ri* SAA X 210 r.1; *ummânu* > *ummâni* passim
(4) -*ūti*, (with substantivated adjectives and participles) e.g. *maqtu* > LÚ.*ma-aq-tú-te* NL 98:8 (CTN V 272)

Words that are masculine in form may have any of these four different plural types, including the only plural ending of feminine nouns (-*āti*). For example,

(*ekurru*) É.KUR-*ra-a-te* SAA I 133:7

In addition to the four above-mentioned plural endings, there is still the ending -<*a-a*>, which can be considered as the fifth ending of a noun in the plural. The morpheme -<*a-a*> also functions as a singular ending, and thus there is no morphological distinction between the plural and singular when using -<*a-a*>. However, the use of this ending is strictly restricted to make the (place of) domicile or the place of origin of people known (cf. 3.9). But in at least two cases, the ending in -<*a-a*> has developed into a professional title, although these professional titles may have a geographical background:

(*šelappāiu*)[405] 5 LÚ*.*še-lap-pa-a-a* "five *architects*" SAA I 95 r.1
(*hundurāiu*)[406] LÚ.*hu-un-du-ru-a-a* (pl.) SAA XIII 41:6

Some words have two different plural endings:[407]

(*appatu*) LÚ*.*mu-kil*–PA-*a-te* SAA VI 328:10′; LÚ*.DIB–*a-pa-te* SAA VI 323 r.8; LÚ*.*mu-kil*–KUŠ.*a-pa-te* SAA VI 335:11′ ~ LÚ*.*mu-kil*–KUŠ.*a-pa-a-ni* SAA XVI 63:21
(*bību*) *bi-ba-a-ni* SAA X 168 r.3, SAA XIII 162 r.8 ~ *bi-bi*[408] NL 67:11 (CTN V 215ff)
(*dullu*) *dul-la*(-*a*)-*ni* passim ~ *du*$_6$-*la-ti* SAA I 132:15; *dul-la-te-šú* SAA I 12 r.2

403 According to some scholars, the final feminine *t* disappeared from pronunciation after /*a*, *ā*, *ē*/ at the end of a word. The evidence for this is based on Aramaic parallels to words, especially place names, which also occur in Neo-Assyrian, see e.g. Lipiński (1997) § 27.28, § 30.4, cf. also Millard (1980) 49f and Dalley (1996-1997) 70 n. 19. If the findings corroborate the theory, then, for example, the feminine plural ending -*āti/e*, regularly attested in cuneiform writing, would no longer reflect the phonetic reality but would be merely an archaizing conditioned writing. However, this interpretation does not appear very likely. In any case, see also Kaufman (1974) 145, 151.

404 The plural forms ending in -*i/e* merit a study of their own. At least at the moment, it is often rather unclear to me if this is a question of a genuine -*i/e* plural form or if, for example, it concerns a collective word.

405 For the etymology (= Šallim-pî-Ea) of the word, see Freydank (1985) 362-64.

406 As for the several different theories proposed for this professional title, see e.g. Postgate (1995) 405f.

407 See Deller and Parpola (1966A) 69 for words also having two plurals: *ṭuppū -āni*/*-āti*, (*ša pān*) *dēnāni*/*dēnāti*). For the latter, see also Deller (1971) 652f.

408 Unless *bi-bi* is sg. (with progressive vowel assimilation, see 4.5) used as a collective referring to all the drainage pipes of the garrison? Cf. also Parker's interpretation ([1997A] 79f).

(*etinnu*)	LÚ.TIN.MEŠ-*ni-ia*[409] "my master builders" SAA V 56:7; LÚ.TIN.MEŠ-*ni* SAA V 56 r.9 ~ LÚ.*e-tin-na-ti* SAA I 138:13
(*hazannu*)	LÚ*.*ha-za-na-te* SAA I 77:12, SAA I 263:4′; LÚ.*ha-za-na-ti* SAA XVI 97:2, r.11 ~ LÚ.*ha-za-nu-*⌜*ti*⌝ (scribal error or an allophone of *a*?) ibid. r.4
(*hillānu*)	É.*hi-il-la-na-ni* SAA I 66:12 ~ É.*hi-il-la-na-te* ibid. 7
(*hīṭu*)	*hi-ṭa-ni-šú-nu šani'ūte* "their other crimes" SAA XVI 63:8 ~ *hi-ṭa-a-te* (both by the same anonymous scribe) SAA XVI 62:11
(*mīlu*)	*mi-i-li* SAA X 226:11 ~ *mì-il-'a-a-ni* SAA I 36 r.7′
(*nasīku*)	LÚ*.⌜*na-si*⌝*-ka-a-te* SAA X 354 r.11; LÚ*.*na-si-ka-*[*t*]*i* NL 96:7 (CTN V 49ff); ⌜LÚ*.*na-si-ka*⌝*-a-ti* NL 96:10 (CTN V 49ff) ~ LÚ*.*na-si-ka-ni* NL 87 r.7′ (CTN V 225ff), LÚ*.*na-si-ka-a-ni* SAA XV 130:16
(*riksu*)	*ri-ik-sa-a-ni* SAA XVI 98 r.4′ (Babyl.) ~ *ri-i*[*k-s*]*a-t*[*i*] SAA XVI 99:2′
(*ṭēmu*)	*ṭè-ma-a-ni* SAA V 152:6; *ṭè-ma-ni* SAA XVI 62 r.9′ ~ *ṭè-ma-te* SAA I 177 r.15
(*ūmu*)	*ši-it-ta ú-ma-ti* "two days" SAA X 196 r.3; *ú-ma-a-t*[*i* SAA X 255 r.14; UD.MEŠ-te passim; 3 UD.MEŠ-ti SAA X 92:13 ~ UD-*me-ni*[410] (for *ūmāni*?) SAA V 206 r.6′

Exceptional forms:

(*epšutu*)	*ep-še-e-tu* SAA X 380:3′; *ep-še-e-ti* SAA X 351 r.4; *ep-še-ti-ia* SAA X 294:24; *ep-še-te-ka* SAA III 21:8′, SAA XVI 72:7′ (all pl.) ~ *ep-šat* ARAD.MEŠ (st. cstr.) ABL 879:20

⌜LÚ*⌝.*ziq-na-nu*[411] (pl.) SAA X 257 r.12, cf. *ša–ziq-ni* (sg.) SAA X 294:21 ~ *ša–*⌜*ziq-ni*⌝ (pl./koll., context: between two other plural forms) ibid. l.30.

When the MEŠ-logogram is attached to nouns, they do not always behave predictably. Usually this logogram simply expresses the plurality of a noun, but MEŠ seems to carry such a strong distinctive characteristic in itself that the syllabified form of a word does not have to be written accurately according to the correct and expected phonetic form in writing. This may be due to the desire to simplify the writing and to refrain from repeating information, which was very self-evident both to the writer and the reader of a letter. The writer's purpose must have been to keep his letters short and pithy, making himself and his main point(s) understood clearly by the recipient of a letter and, as a consequence,

---

409 Possibly TIN is not a logogram here. For the different theories of TIN, see Deller and Parpola (1966A) 68-69.

410 I would prefer to read this UD.ME-*ni*. Also UD-*me*(-) > UD.ME(-) in SAA I 20 e.9′, SAA X 73 r.2, SAA X 352:10, SAA XIII 12:9 (cf. SAA XIII 9:11, SAA XIII 10:11, SAA XIII 13:10 by the same writer) and so on, cf., e.g. UD.ME DÙG.GA.ME SAA X 379:5′, 8 UD.ME ibid. r.1, ITI UD.ME StAT 2 298:5. At least it would be clearer to mark the explicit plural forms always as UD.ME and the genitive spellings as UD-*me*, even though there is, of course, no difference between these writings on tablets. Moreover, it is difficult to determine how scribes themselves interpreted this matter. Further complications are naturally that ME = *mì* and that ME is used, all in all, much more rarely than MEŠ as a plural marker. However, note an interesting orthographic fact that the spelling UD-*mi* is not used in Neo-Assyrian letters for the plural (gen. e.g. UD-*mi* in SAA V 263:3′, SAA X 196:14, NL 10:13). Thus it may seem doubtful to postulate an *-ī/ē* plural ending for *ūmu* in NA, but some probable Babylonianisms are a completely different matter.

411 LAS II ad no. 174 r.12, and ibid. n. 313 on the same page.

information of secondary importance was certainly often omitted from these letters.[412] The use of MEŠ is quite common in connection with syllabically written nouns which take a determinative.[413]

E.g.

LÚ.EN–*pi-qit-ta-a-te*.MEŠ SAA XVI 86:13; DUG.*šap-pa*-MEŠ VAT 8699:7; ŠE.*nu-sa-hi*.MEŠ GPA 196:8; UZU.*dà-ri-i*.MEŠ KAV 197 r.13; ANŠE.*gam-mal*.MEŠ e.g. in SAA XV 257:8′, SAA XVI 5:9.

Much rarer with nouns without determinative, e.g.

a-ṣap.MEŠ SAA V 119:8; *e-gír-*⌜*te*⌝.MEŠ SAA V 52:21.

Some plural forms of *ūmu* "day" belong to the same category, e.g.

am–mar UD-*mu*.MEŠ SAA V 217 r.6; *ina* ŠÀ-*bi* / UD-*mu*.MEŠ *ša* LUGAL "in the time of the king" SAA XV 184:13-14; 6 UD-*mu*.MEŠ SAA XV 201:2′; 2 UD-*mu*.MEŠ SAA I 105:6′, SAA VI 201 r.15.

The function of <*mu*> may be somewhat difficult to determine in the plural, without the MEŠ-sign, and in the genitive singular, but <*mu*> might be a sort of fixed complement (UD.MU[? 414]). However, in the genitive singular, the phonetic complement *-me* is normally used.[415] E.g.

(*ūmu*) UD-*mu* GÍD.DA.MEŠ "long days" SAA XVI 126:6, SAA XVI 128:6 (.GÍ[D.D]A.); UD-*mu ar-ku-u-te* SAA XIII 27:5

A phonetic complement may follow MEŠ in words, which are otherwise written syllabically (as well as in words written logographically: LÚ*.GAL–10.MEŠ-*te* SAA V 257:5′; UD.MEŠ-*te* passim). E.g.

É–*kar-ra*.MEŠ-*ni* NL 12:6 (CTN V 155ff); ANŠ[E].⌜*ú*⌝-*ra*.MEŠ-*te* GPA 199 r.7; LÚ*.*mu-šár-kis*.MEŠ-*ni* SAA V 119:6. The same holds true for ME: *ki-ṣir*.ME-*ni* KAV 133 r.3.

5.4 Main word and the affixed possessive suffix[416]

In the genitive, the ending *-i* remains before possessive suffixes. This is why genitive forms are not included under this heading: only nominative-accusative forms with possessive suffixes are discussed here.

---

412 It is also likely that more shorthand or layout-influenced types of documents, such as administrative lists, sometimes exerted strong influence on the writers of letters. Still, that influence did not have to be realized arbitrarily.

413 Deller and Parpola (1966A) 70.

414 Cf. Hämeen-Anttila (2000) 32.

415 On the use of the phonetic complement in general, see Leichty (1970) 27ff, especially the so-called "pseudo-logographical" complements on p. 29.

416 See e.g. GAG § 65, Deller (1959) § 35h-k and Hämeen-Anttila (2000) 82f.

Nouns ending in two identical consonants have an auxiliary vowel that tends to undergo vowel harmony before the possessive suffixes of the second- and third-person singular. In these cases, the consonantal gemination of a noun is preserved after a suffix is attached (> *ṭuppaka*, *ṭuppiki*, *ṭuppušu*). On the other hand, with the so-called segholate nouns[417] – originally nouns ending in two different consonants which have taken an auxiliary vowel between the second and the third radical – the position of the auxiliary vowel may alternate and the contact of the consonants may disappear when adding a suffix to the main word: e.g. (*amtu*) *amtušu* ~ *amassu*.[418] In the forms of *pirs*-nouns, the auxiliary vowel is *i* (or *a*, e.g. *kiṣru* ⸢*ki-ṣar*⸣*-ka* SAA V 69:5, *pišru pi-šá-ar-šú* SAA VIII 186 r.4), of *pars*-nouns *a* and of *purs*-nouns *u* or *a*. This also applies to plural possessive suffixes.

A suitable point for comparison is the alternation in position of an auxiliary vowel with forms having the enclitic *-ma*: *me-šil-ma* SAA I 181 r.9 ~ *meš-lu-ma* SAA I 107:11, SAA I 235:19, NL 70:10 (CTN V 161ff), as well as some status constructus forms: *me-šil* ŠE.*ki-si-te* "half of the fodder" SAA I 181 r.8 ~ *meš-li* LÚ.ERIM.MEŠ "half of the men" SAA I 235:19.

When adding possessive suffixes, the vowel of the last syllable disappears in noun stems ending in one consonant:

> *ahu* "arm" *ah-šú* SAA X 283 r.4′ (however, cf. *abu* and *ahu* "brother" below), CT 53 820 r.2; *dabābu da-ba-ab-šú* SAA XVI 63 s.1, 2.

Nouns ending in a stressed long vowel, marked invariably with the circumflex *-û*, take a long *ā* as their auxiliary vowel in connection with possessive suffixes:

> (*elû*) *la e-la-šú* SAA XIII 138 r.18e; (*egirrû*) *e-gi-ra-šú* SAA X 305 r.2; (*uṣû*) *ú-ṣa-a-šú* SAA I 29 r.4.

Examples of nouns with a possessive suffix are:

3rd m.sg.

(*anūtu*)	*a-nu-su* SAA X 387 r.2
(*aqappu*)	*a-qa-pu-šú* SAA IX 1:7′
(*bētu*)	É-*su* NL 3 r.12′ (Face A in CTN V 64ff), SAA XV 219 r.8′, SAA I 244 r.8
(*dannutu*)	*dan-na-*⸢*su*⸣ KAV 197 r.22
(*dullu*)	*dul-lu-šú* SAA XIII 134 r.15
(*hiṣbu*)	*hi-ṣib-šú* SAA XIII 157:13′
(*ilku*)	*ša il-ka-šú-ni* // *il-ku-šu* "those obliged to provide labour ..." SAA V 78 e.17-r.1
(*kaspu*)	*kas-pu-šú* SAA V 150:7
(*kurummutu*)	*ku-ru-ma-at-su* SAA X 74:13 (as a gloss)
(*lumnu*)	*lu-um-an-šú* SAA X 347 r.13′
(*madāktu* or *mādaktu*[419])	*ma-dak-tú-šú* SAA I 31 r.14

---

[417] For the definition and behaviour of these nouns in Hebrew, see Joüon and Muraoka (1991) 293-301 § 96A. Cf., regarding biblical Aramaic, Rosenthal (1974[4]) 27-28, paragraph 51.

[418] See Parpola (1988A) 74.

[419] One spelling, *ma-a-dak-tu* in SAA XV 60 r.15′ (cf. also the less certain [*ma*]-⸢*a*!-*dak*!⸣-*t*[*u* in SAA XV 119:11), may convey the correct reading of the word.

(*maddattu*)	*ma-da-tú-šu* NL 44:10 (CTN V 139f)
(*middutu*)	*a-di mi-da-as-su* (pl.) SAA I 210 e.17
(*mihru*)	*mi-hir-šú* SAA XV 256:3′
(*miksu*)	*mi-ik-si-šú* NL 12:11 (CTN V 155ff)
(*murṣu*)	*mu-ru-us-su* SAA X 242 r.6
(*napšutu*)	*nap-šat-su* CT 53 493:6′
(*nēmulu*)	*né-ma-al-šú* SAA X 73 r.3, SAA X 218:9; *né-e-ma-al-šú* SAA X 194:11; *né-mal-šu* SAA XVI 36 r.3; *né-me-él-šu/šú* SAA X 53 r.1/SAA X 54 r.5′
(*pagru*)	*pa-gar-šú* SAA I 100 r.13
(*pišru*)	cf. 4.3.1
(*qassu*)[420]	A.ŠÀ GIŠ.BAN-*šú* "his bow field" SAA V 16:6
(*qinnu*)	*qi-in-nu-šú* ABL 896:15 (Aia-zeru-qiša)
(*sartinnu*)	LÚ.*sar-tin-nu-šú* SAA X 90 r.14′
(*ṣupru*)	*ṣu-pur-šú* SAA VI passim; *ṣu-bar-šú* SAA VI 1:1, SAA VI 289:1, SAA VI 7:1
(*šulmu*)	examples see 4.2.3
(*ṭābtu*)	*ṭa-ab-tu-uš* SAA X 182:28
(*uznu*)	*ú*]*-zu-un-šú* SAA X 89:14′

Exception: *ṭé-mi-i-šú* (nom. + suff.) LUGAL *be-lí* / *a-na hi-iṭ-ṭi-ia liš-kun* SAA I 124:15-16 (an error or pl. [however, see 5.3] + suff. or some kind of a specific nuance?) ~ *ṭēnšu*(*nu*) passim

3rd f.sg.

(*ahātu*)	NIN-sa SAA XVI 28:6
(*dullu*)	*dul-la-šá* SAA XIII 134 r.5
(*eṭemmu*)	*e-ṭém-ma-šá* SAA X 188 r.5
(*gabrû*)	*gab-ra-a-šá* SAA XV 35:5
(*mar'utu*)	DUMU.MÍ-*sa* SAA XVI 53:6, 13
(*milku*)	*mi-i*]*l-ka-ni-šá* (pl.) SAA X 29 r.3
(*qanītu*)	*qa-ni-is-sa* SAA XIII 130:15
(*ramanu*)	*ra-man-ša* SAA XIII 28 r.12, SAA XIII 29 r.4′
(*rupšu*)	*ru-up-šá-šá* SAA XVI 81 r.2′
(*šīru*)	*ši-ir-šá* SAA X 297:10, r.4′
(*tapqirtu*)	*tap-qí-ir-ta-šá* SAA X 30 r.7

2nd m.sg.

(*amāru*)	*a-ma-ár-ka* SAA X 294 r.33
(*ebhu*)	*e-b*[*i*]-⌜*ih*⌝*-ka* SAA I 1 r.50 (CTN V 188ff)
(*kāribu*)	*k*[*a*]*-rib-ka* SAA X 186:4
(*milku*)	*mì-li*[*k-ka* 0] SAA V 46:12′
(*muātu*)	*mu-at-ka* SAA II 2 v 1
(*mušēniqtu*)	*mu-še-ni*[*q*]*-ta-ka* SAA IX 1 iii 17′
(*nashuru*)	*na-as-hur-ka* SAA X 294 r.33
(*nikittu*)	*ni-kit-ta-ka* SAA I 1 r.42 (CTN V 188ff)
(*rā'iūtu*)	⌜LÚ.SIPA-*ut-ka*⌝ SAA X 294:10
(*šarrūtu*)	*šar-ru-ut-ka* SAA XIII 78 r.20
(*ṭābtu*)	*ṭa-ab-ta-ka* SAA XVI 32 r.21

420 Parpola (1988A) 74.

2nd f.sg.

(*ṭuppu*) *ṭup-pi-ki* SAA XVI 28:3

The possessive suffix *-ī* of the first-person singular is added to the last consonant of a noun. In the plural, the suffix *-ia* is added to the last vowel *-i* of the form. For the 1st person examples of a noun + -<*a-a*>, as *hi-ṭa-a-a,* DINGIR-*a-a*, etc., see 3.9.

1st sg.

(*abu* "father")	AD-*u/ú-a* passim and (*ahu* "brother") ŠEŠ/PAB-*u/ú-a* passim, ŠEŠ-*u-iá* GPA 189:6, are always written long with the *u*-vowel before the suffix,[421] whereas AD-*ia* (nom. + suff.) SAA XVI 53:12 and *a-na* (...) PAB-*u-a* (gen. + suff.) SAA V 81:2, 4 (but correct [nom.] ibid. r.5) are incorrect spellings. Moreover, we may expect to find <*u/ú*> with interrogative intonation in the clause *la-a* ŠEŠ-*a-a* ⸢*at*⸣-*ta-a* "Are you not my brother?" ibid. r.3 because we may have a good parallel: *šu-tú* ŠEŠ-*u-a-a* /*ahwai*(?)/ "(But) isn't he my brother?"[422] ND 2682 r.13′ (CTN V 289f)
(*ahu* "arm")	*a-hi* NL 12 r.8 (CTN V 155ff)
(*bēlu*)	*be-lí* passim ~ *be-lí-iá/ia* (nom. + suff. 1st sg.) SAA I 205:5/SAA XVI 15:4; *be-lí-ia/iá* SAA XVI 25:12/SAA XVI 34:16; see also SAA XIII 187:14, SAA XVI 119:5. I would interpret these writings as scribal errors under the influence of *ša* (although it is not the genitival *ša*) in the first two examples. A few errors like these would not be surprising at all, especially when we consider the high frequency of *bēlu* both in the nominative and the genitive in the NA corpus
(*de'iqtu*)	*de-iq-ti* SAA I 183 r.11
(*dintu*)	*di-ia-ti-ia* (pl.) SAA XIII 158 r.10′
(*hādiānu*)	*ha-di-a-nu-te-ia* (pl.) SAA X 226 r.22
(*maškunu*)	TÚG.*maš-ki-ni* SAA I 55:9′
(*qātu*)	*qa-ti* SAA X 361 r.1 ~ *qa-ta-a-a* (specific adverbial meaning "personally") SAA V 32 r.8
(*ṣahittu*)	*ṣa-hi-it-ti* CTN III 2 r.1
(*ṭābtu*)	*ṭa-ab-ti* SAA X 228 r.12, SAA XVI 32 r.20
(*urû*)	*ú-ra-a-a* SAA V 74 r.4, 12 (CTN V 103f)

The disyllabic possessive suffixes of the second- and third-person plural are connected to a noun having a stem that ends in two consonants (e.g. *dullu*, *pilku*), usually with the help of an auxiliary vowel *a*. In these forms, *a* can be interpreted as being stressed:[423] *dullá̆šunu*, but some writings, such as *pil-ka-šú-u-nu,* an alternative variant *ṭa-ab-tu-ku-nu*, the third-person singular *il-ka-šú-ni* (above) and so on, also suggest the possibility of interpreting the form in another way: *dullašūnu*. For the latter interpretation, cf. the regressive vowel dissimilation 4.6.

---

421 Cf. Hämeen-Anttila (2000) 83.

422 The clause is not interpreted as a question in CTN V, p. 290. In my opinion, the clause is a (rhetorical) question, especially if the sign following the latter A-sign is really : (which separates words and clauses, see 3.2).

423 Cf. GAG § 65h.

In nouns ending in one consonant (e.g. *dēnu*, *dilīlu*, *markāsu*), the vowel at the end is normally dropped, but in at least one case it has remained unchanged (see *ebūru* below). In plural forms with possessive suffixes (*-āti* + suff.), the unstressed vowel that precedes a possessive suffix may remain unchanged or disappear (cf. e.g. *nap-šá-te-ku-nu* ~ *nap-šat-ku-nu*):

3rd m.pl.

(*dilīlu*) *di-lil-šu-nu* SAA X 92:6
(*dullu*) *dul-la-áš-*[*šú-nu*] SAA XV 100 r.3′; *dul-la-šú-nu* passim; [*dul*]*-lu-šú-nu* SAA XIII 141:8
(*ebūru*) ŠE.*e-bu-ru-šú-nu* SAA I 219:11
(*hīṭu/hiṭṭu*) *hi-ṭa-šú-nu* SAA XVI 63:12
(*maddattu*) *ma-da-tú-šú-*[*nu*] SAA I 15:13′
(*mešlu*) *meš-lu-šú-nu* SAA I 95 e.12′
(*nēmulu*) *né-ma-al-šú-nu* SAA X 185:16; *né-me-el-šú-nu* SAA X 207 r.5;
(*pilku*"work assignment") *pil-ka-šú-u-nu* SAA XV 156 r.9; *pi-il-ka-šu-nu* SAA I 235:20; *p*[*i*]*l-ku-šú-nu* SAA V 56:6
(*qassu*)[424] GIŠ.BAN-*šú-nu* ABL 1400:12 (Tammaritu)
(*ṣupru*) *ṣu-bar-šú-nu* SAA VI 100:2; *ṣu-pur-šú-nu* SAA VI passim
(*ṭābtu*) DÙG.GA-*ta-šú-nu* SAA II 6:271F
(*ṭuppu*) *ṭup-p*]*a-šú-nu* SAA X 101 r.4
(*uznu*) *ú-zu-un-šu-nu* SAA XV 121 r.10

3rd f.pl.

(*markāsu*) GIŠ.*mar-kas-ši-na* SAA II 5 iv 11′
(*re'ûtu*) *re-'u-us-si-na* SAA X 198:8
(*ṭarkullu*) *ṭar-kul-la-ši-na* SAA II 5 iv 12′

2nd pl.

(*dēnu*) *de-en-ku-nu* SAA XVI 41:12
(*dullu*) *dul-la-ku-nu* NL 12:25 (CTN V 155ff), SAA XV 344:4′
(*eṭemmu*) *e-ṭém-ma-ku-nu* SAA II 6:452frg, 477D
(*gulgullu*) *gul-gu-lat-ku-nu* (pl.) SAA XVI 88:13
(*kaqquru*) *kaq-qar-ku-nu* SAA II 6:528A, F
(*kidinnu/kidinnūtu*) LÚ*.*ki-di-nu-ut-ku-nu* NL 1:17 (CTN V 19ff)
(*mašqītu*) *maš-qit-ku-nu* SAA II 6:491D, frg
(*napšutu*) *nap-šá-te-ku-nu* (pl.) SAA II 6:268i; *nap-šat-ku-nu* (pl.) ibid. A, 651frg; *nap-šat-kun* (pl.) SAA II 6:651U
(*naqbaru*) *naq-bar-ku-nu* SAA II 6:484D
(*nikittu*) *ni-kit-ta-ku-nu* SAA I 14:3′
(*piššatu*) *pi-šat-ku-nu* SAA II 6:491D
(*tāmirtu*) *ta-me-ra-a-ti-ku-nu* (pl.) SAA II 6:441g, 532B; *ta-me-ra-ti-ku-nu* (pl.) SAA II 6:532G; *ta-me-rat-k*[*u*]*-nu* (pl.) SAA II 6:532A
(*ṭābtu*) ⌜*ṭa-ab*⌝-[*t*]*a-ku-nu* CT 53 968 r.4′; *ṭa-ab-tu-ku-nu* ABL 561:16′
(*ugāru*) *ú-ga-ar-ku-nu* TH 5 e.8

When the possessive suffix of the first person plural (*-ni*) is added to a singular word, the main word in the nominative-accusative does not differ from the

424 Parpola (1988A) 74.

corresponding genitive: the stem of the main word + *ī/in* + *ni*.[425] A possible explanation for the *ī* preceding the suffix could be that the plural form, *bēlī/ē* of the word *bēlu* "lord," was used as a model for the whole paradigm. In that case, other nouns would have followed the example of *bēlu* analogously.[426] Another possibility is that the end vowel of the singular main word is first subjected to vowel harmony in connection with the suffix <*-ni*> after which it becomes stressed.

Examples:
1st pl.

(*bēlu*)	*be-li-ni* SAA X 205:6; *be-lí-ni* SAA X 259:9, r.3; *be-lí-i-ni* SAA V 105:11; EN-*i-ni* SAA XVI 117:11, r.3, KAV 197 r.26, SAA X 25:10; EN-*e-ni* SAA XV 230:13; EN-*in-ni* SAA X 147:3′
(*dullu*)	*dul-li-in-ni* SAA X 215 r.1, SAA XV 100:7, SAA XIII 64 r.5′; *dul*$_6$*-li-in-ni* SAA XV 94:14 (*habullu*) *ha-bu-li-ni* SAA I 147 r.12
(*libbu*)	*lib-bi-in-ni* SAA X 185:15
(*zittu*)	*zi-it-ti-in-ni* SAA X 48:18

5.5 Suppletive stems

In a few instances, the paradigms of the noun (declensional) and verb (conjugational) have been put together from different stems:

abutu (sg.) "word, matter" > *dibbī* (pl.)

The stem (wšb) *ušābu* "to sit" forms the paradigm except for the stative, for which the stem (kms) *kammus* is used.[427] It is possible that the verb *našû* "to take, bring" was replaced by the verb *matāhu* in the meanings "to lift (up), raise." However, this kind of interpretation is partly unclear.[428]

Suppletive stems may be part of morphological variation but, strictly speaking, they concern word formation and are thus lexical phenomena. However, it is important to mention these few suppletive stems, because they reflect well the inclination towards language change. As to the chronology, diachronic description confirms, for example, that the (wšb) stem was still used for the stative in Middle Assyrian but had become obsolete in Neo-Assyrian.[429]

---

[425] Deller and Parpola (1966B) 121-22.

[426] Ibid. 122.

[427] LAS II ad no. 185 r.18.

[428] Parpola (1974) 10 n. 18 and (1984) 209 n. 57.

[429] Cf. LAS II ad no. 185 r.18.

5.6 Dtt- and Gtt-stems

The Dtt-stem is a speciality of Neo-Assyrian. The following forms are attested in the letter corpus (+ one attestation from SAA VIII and two from treaties [SAA II]):

('dr) *ú-ta-da-ar*[430] (prs) SAA X 196 r.6; *ú-ta-a[d-du-ru]* (prs) SAA XIII 155:8
(gmr) *ug-da-dam-[mar* (prs) SAA V 176:7; *ug-da-ad-am-mar* (prs) SAA X 74 r.21; *ug-da-da-mar-u-⸢ni⸣* (prs) SAA I 47 r.13; *la ug-da-ta-mu-[ru-u-ni]* (prs) SAA XVI 150 r.2; *ug-da-ta-mir* (pf) NL 17 r.11e (CTN V 283f); *ug-da-at-me-ru* (pf) SAA I 80:9; *ug-da-ta-me-ru* (pf) ND 2761:11 (CTN V 41)
(ktm) *uk-ta-at-ti-mu* (pf) SAA X 226 r.3
(kūl) *uk-ta-ta-la-(ma)* (prs) SAA X 363 r.12, 17e; *la uk-ta-la* (defective prs form) SAA VIII 98:6
(kūn) *lu-uk-ta-ti-ni* (prc) SAA V 163:10
(mzq) *lu-un-ta-ta-zi-qu* (prc) SAA I 229 r.5′
(nzm) *ut-ta-ta-zu-mu* (prs) SAA X 353 r.4
(phr) *up-ta-at-hu-ru* (prs) SAA V 227 s.1
(pršm) *[tu-up]-ta-tar-šá-am*[431] (prs) SAA X 185 r.23; *up-ta-tar-šu-mu* (prs) SAA XIII 56 r.16
(pṣd) *up-ta-ta-ṣi-[d]i* (pf) SAA XVI 100:16
(smh) *⸢ú⸣-sa-ta-mah-⸢u-ni⸣* (prs) SAA II 6:282A; *ú⸣-sa-ta-a-mah-u-ni* (prs) SAA II 6:282B; *⸢nu-sa-ta⸣-mah* (prs) NL 2:9′ (CTN V 22ff)
(šmn) *us-sa-at-mi-nu* (pf) SAA X 226 r.2
(špl) *ú-sa-ta-pu-lu* (prs) SAA I 82 r.5

The meaning of the Dtt-stem is identical with the common Akkadian Dt-stem,[432] and thus could as well be called a Dt-stem, because all the Dtt-perfects are syncopated (cf. 4.13).[433] In the present tense, the sequence of three consecutive alveolar stops is also avoided.[434] The Dtt-paradigm is, in fact, on the whole defective, since we do not know of any Dtt-stem stative, infinitive, participle, imperative, or verbal adjective; nor is even one single, real preterite form attested (note that the ostensible preterites function as the perfect forms[435] of the paradigm).

Note that the partial assimilation (*gt* > *gd*) may go beyond the following vowel as far as the following *t* in the forms *ug-da-da-mar-u-⸢ni⸣* and *ug-da-dam-[mar* (unless one wants to read DAM.QAR > *tám*-QAR; however, *dam* = *tám* is not Neo-Assyrian). The partial assimilation of the second *t* is not necessarily real in the forms *ug-da-ad-am-mar* and *ug-da-ad-me-ru* because <*ad*> = <*at*>.

---

430 See ibid. ad no. 143 r.6.

431 See Deller (1969) 57.

432 On the Dt- and Dtt-stems, see GAG § 93.

433 For a discussion on the Dtt-stem with examples, see Parpola (1984) 199 and 208 nn. 48-49, 51.

434 LAS II ad no. 143 r.6.

435 Cf. GAG § 93e.

The Dtt-stem is analogous to the Gtt-stem, of which the paradigm also appears to be defective. This latter stem is only attested in the verb *alāku*.[436]

The meaning of these Neo-Assyrian *alāku* Gtt-forms corresponds to the Gt-forms of other Akkadian dialects: "to go off/away."[437]

Most of the *alāku* Gtt-forms are perfects of the third-person masculine plural:

> (’lk) *i-ta-at-ku* SAA V 32:11, SAA V 217:9; ⌜*i*⌝*-ta-at-k*[*u x*] SAA V 18:7; *i-ta-*⌜*ta*⌝*-ku* SAA V 36:4′; *it-ta-ta-ku* NL 92:11 (CTN V 281); *i*[*t-t*]*a-ta-ku* SAA XV 59:10; *it-ta-tak-ku* SAA XV 172:3′; *it-ta-tak-k*[*u*] SAA V 19 r.7′; *i-ta-ta-ku-ú-ni* NL 60:7′ (CTN V 241f); for the variation *ittatakku*[438] ~ *ittatku*, see 4.13

Other Gtt-forms are singular forms of the perfect (expect one or two of these examples):

> *i*[*t*]*-ta-at-lak* SAA I 29 r.3; *it-ta-at-lak* SAA XV 37 r.4′; [*it-t*]*a-at-lak* SAA XVI 205 r.10; *a-ta-a*[*t*]-⌜*lak*⌝ or *a-ta-t*[*a*]*-lak* NL 69:9 (CTN V 164ff); *li-it-ta-at-lak* (prc) SAA XV 24 s.1; *i-ta-ta-ka* SAA V 163 r.14; *a*⌜*t*!!⌝*-ta-ta-ka*[439] NL 64:19 (CTN V 290ff); *i-si-ia a-*[*t*]*a-*[*k*]*a-ni* (imperat. 2nd pl. + vent.) NL 2 r.12′ (CTN V 22ff)

5.7 D-stem: strong vs. weak conjugation; exceptions of the I-weak verbs

The variation between the so-called strong ("Assyrian") and weak ("Babylonian") conjugation in the II-weak verb forms of the D-stem is, to some extent, discernible in Neo-Assyrian.[440]

The best example of this variation is the verb *ka’’unu/kunnu*:[441]

(pf)	*uk-tú-i-ni*[442] SAA I 97:11 (Ṭab-ṣill-Ešarra, Assur); *uk-ta-in* SAA I 64:13 (Ṭab-šar-Aššur), SAA X 294:24 (Urdu-Gula, Nineveh) ~ *uk-te-en* SAA XIII 45:3′ (unkn., Assur); *uk-ti-i-nu* SAA XVI 1:12 (Esarhaddon to the king of Elam)
(prc)	*lu-ke-’i-in* SAA X 185:22 (Adad-šumu-uṣur, Nineveh); *lu-ka-a-a-*⌜*en*⌝ SAA I 236:8′ (Taklak-ana-Bel, Naṣibina), *lu-ka-a-a-in* SAA XV 24

[436] See Parpola (1984) 197-99.

[437] Ibid. 198-200.

[438] For the regressive assimilation *l* + *k* > [*kk*] in the form **ittatalkū*, see Parpola (1984) 196f.

[439] The first sign is clearly I but the vertical wedge that distinguishes I from AD may be lacking at the end of the sign because of the TA-sign that follows very closely. Cf. CTN V 5 Pl. 57 (ND 2683).

[440] These few forms cannot explain this alternation exhaustively; the purpose is simply to exemplify such an alternation. It is somewhat premature to draw conclusions from these writings.

[441] Deller (1965B) 76 n. 1 maintains that the conjugation of the II-weak verbs in the perfect was analogous to the development of the adverb **ahāmeš* (cf. 4.1.2 and n. 218). On the conjugation of "hollow" II-weak verbs in the D-stem, see also von Soden (1950) 392f n. 7.

[442] For the unexpected <*tú*>, see 3.1 above.

r.19 (Nabû-belu-ka''in[443]) ~ *lu-kin* NL 74:11 (CTN V 132ff, Šarru-emuranni, Isana); *lu*]*-u-ki-in-šú* SAA XIII 134 s.3 (unkn.); *lu-ki-in-ma* SAA XVI 78 r.5 (Mannu-ki-Libbali); *lu-ki-na-a-ni* SAA XVI 43 r.9 (unkn.); *lu-ki-ii-ni* SAA XVI 44 r.5′ (Iqbi-Aššur, Kar-Šalmaneser); scribal error?: *lu-ka-ni-i*[*n*] (> *luka''in*) ABL 307 s.2 (see Appendix A)

(imperat.) *ka-in* SAA I 64:12 (Ṭab-šar-Aššur)

Note also e.g.

lu-ke-'i-il SAA X 235:9, 12 (Marduk-šakin-šumi, Nineveh) ~ several *kullu*-forms and (*ṭa''ubu/ṭubbu*) *lu-ṭa-i-*[*bu*] SAA V 146 r.13 (Urzana, Muṣaṣir) ~ [*lu-ṭ*]*i-ib-bu* SAA XVI 72 r.2 (unkn.) cf. also *l*]*i-iṭ-ṭib-bu* SAA X 294:10 (Urdu-Gula, Babyl.)

As distinct from strong verbs, the verbs having a weak first radical do not have *a* but *u* in the infinitive, imperative, verbal adjective and stative as the vowel of the first syllable of the D-stem. For instance:

(*abālu* D) *ub-bu-lu-ti* (verb.adj. pl.) SAA X 226 r.2 ~ *rak-ka-su-te* SAA XIII 88 r.8

(*aḫāzu* D) *a-na uh-hu-zi* (infinit.) SAA XIII 166:2; *uh-hu-zu* (stat) SAA X 349:14, 15, 22

(*akāšu* D) *ú-ku-šú* (stat) NL 35 r.8 (CTN V 33f) ~ *ṭa-hu-da* (stat 3rd f.pl.) SAA X 226:14

(*amāru* D) *ú-mu-ru* (verb.adj. sg.) SAA V 204:16, SAA X 253 r.14

(*elû* D) *ul-li/ú-li* (imperat.) SAA XVI 20 r.7′/SAA V 203:7; *a-na ul-lu-e* (infinit.) NL 12 r.8 (CTN V 155ff) ~ *a–ga-am-mu-ri* SAA XV 107 r.1

(*epāšu* D) *ú-pu-šú* (stat) SAA X 353 r.11

(*eṣādu* D) *uṣ-ṣi-di* (imperat.) Rfdn 17 29 r.7 ~ *ṣab-bi-ta* (imperat. 2nd pl.) NL 54:13 (CTN V 13f)

(*ubālu* D, I-w) *ub/ú-bíl* (imperat.; this oddity, which is analogous to the D-stem is, however, derived from the G-stem)[444] SAA II 6:365frg/ibid. another frg

(*uṣṣuṣu* only D) *ú-ṣi-ṣi* (imperat.) SAA V 68:7, SAA I 21:2′, 10′; GPA 188:11

5.8 III-weak verbs – Babylonian vs. Assyrian model

The last radical of almost all the originally III-weak verbs is contracted owing to Babylonian influence. Almost all III-weak verbs are therefore of the model *našû*, *manû*, *rabû*, etc., with some rare exceptions:

hasā'u, *mašā'u*, *mazā'u* (also D), *parā'u*, *rapā'u*, *sabā'u*, note also the doubly weak verb *qiā'u*[445]

Moreover, the finite forms of *kalû* are sometimes uncontracted: *lu ka-la-'u* SAA V 106:23′; *ik-ta-al-'u* SAA XIII 166:17; *ik-ta-al-'u-šú-*[*nu*] NL 50 e.17 (CTN V 182ff); *kil-áš-šú* SAA XV 85:7

---

[443] See PNA 2/II pp. 815-17.

[444] For the different interpretations of the form, see Deller (1965D) 261 and Watanabe (1987) 187 n. ad line 365.

[445] See LAS II ad no. 152:8 ff.

5.9 Irregular, exceptional and rare verbs

Some verbs have irregular forms that form an exception to the rule.

alāku "to go, come":

(1) /*(a)lik alkā*/ (see examples in 4.11). In this non-ventive imperative of the second-person plural, /*alik*/ functions as a prefix distinguishing the form from the second-person singular imperative in the ventive: /*(a)lik alkā*/ "go!" (pl.) ~ /*alkā*/ "come!" (sg.).[446] This morphological innovation was necessitated by the loss of mimation and the shortening of unstressed final vowels; it provided a means of differentiating the ventive singular and non-ventive plural imperatives and shows how loss of phonological distinctions can lead to compensation in the morphology. Cf. the analogy with *ana* which functioned as a marker of the accusative (see 6.6 and 7.1 below).[447]

(2) Gtt-forms, see 5.6

udû "to know":[448]

> *ú-da-kan-ni*[449] (undeclinable stat. + dat. 2nd sg. + subj.) "(whom) you know" i.e. "(who are) known to you" SAA X 9:10 (Issar-šumu-ereš)
>
> *a-na* LUGAL *bé-li-ni* / *lu ud-da-áš-šú* (stat + dat. 3rd sg.) "May it be known to the king, our lord ..." SAA XVI 42 r.2 (Ṣallaia and Asalluhi-ereš)

napāhu "to ignite, light up; to rise":

> *nap-ha-ta-ni* SAA X 31:3′; *nap-ha-ta*[450] (both are stat 3rd f.sg. + ventive [+ subj.]) ibid. r.5 (Issar-šumu-ereš)

In the case of *napāhu*, the ventive gives a specific, lexicalized meaning, when speaking of heavenly bodies, "to shine, clear up." Thus the syllabification of the form is neither prosodic nor orthographic, nor is an "inverse spelling"[451] applicable.

(d'n) *ki-i da-a'-nu-tú-*[*ni*] (stat 3rd f.sg. + subj.) SAA X 46:13 in which *da'nut* occurs instead of the expected *da'nat*. However, vowel harmony did not usually have an effect on the syllable before the stress. The root *d'n* (as stat 3rd f.sg. *da'na/ut*) was in free variation with the more common root *dnn* (stat 3rd f.sg. dannat e.g. *dan-na-at* SAA VIII 21:2, SAA X 351 r.13 and passim).[452] E.g.

> (d'n) *da-a'-na* (2. -[*na*]) SAA X 104 e.17′, SAA X 60 r.1, SAA V 200:10, NL 100:7 (CTN V 118f); *da-a-na* SAA I 147:15, SAA XV 60:12 ~ (dnn) *da-an* SAA X

---

[446] See Parpola (1984) 191.

[447] Ibid. 192.

[448] See Hämeen-Anttila (2000) 102f.

[449] See LAS II ad no. 4:10. Also GAG § 78b and § 106q.

[450] LAS II ad no. 11 r.5′.

[451] Deller (1959) § 17i and more extensively idem (1962B) 188-96.

[452] See LAS II ad no. 42:13.

222:15, SAA XIII 38 r.2; KALAG-*an* NL 29 r.2 (CTN V 143f), SAA I 93:11, SAA V 105 r.6

(qbī) the finite form *ta-qa-tab-bi* (or *ta-qa-ṭab-bi,* cf. gmr Dtt in 5.6) SAA X 30 r.4 is possibly Gtn prs 2nd sg., since in addition to the regularly conjugated Gtn-forms (prs *iptanarras*, pf *iptatarras,* prt *iptarras*), the present of the stem may have been conjugated according to the pattern **iptanras*. Cf. e.g. *la it-tal-la-k*[*u-u-ni*] (Gtn prs 3rd sg. + subj., **i'tanlak-ūni*) SAA X 285 r.8′. Thus, *ta-qa-tab-bi* may have developed in the following way: **taqtanbi* > **taqṭabbi* > *ta-qa-t/ṭab-bi*.[453]

The verb *tadānu* "to give" may have had, possibly owing to Aramaic influence, a variant root *ntn* as two precative forms of the third-person plural indicate:

> *li-te-nu-ni*[454] SAA V 17 r.1 (Nashir-Bel, Amidi), SAA XV 50:6′ (unkn.) ~ *li*(*d*)-*di-nu*-(*u*)-*ni* passim

(*ša'ūdu*)[455] *âdu* Š "to inform." Apparently this is a question of analogy to the verb *udû* "to know." The known forms include:

> *ú-šá-ad* (prs 1st sg.) SAA I 132:13; *lu-šá-id-du* (prc 3rd pl.) SAA X 259 r.11; *us-sa-ta-'i-da-ni* (Štn/t pf 3rd sg. + obj. 1st sg.) SAA XVI 78:19 cf. *ú-šá-'i-id-du* (prt 3rd sg. + subj.) SAA X 161:7 (NB); *ú-šá*]-*'i-du* (prt 3rd pl. + subj.) ibid. r.5

The II-weak verbs are rare in the Š-stem:

> *šadūlu* (*duālu* Š): *lu-šá-di-lu* (prc 3rd pl.) SAA II 6:575D; *lu-šá-di-il-lu* SAA II 6:575Q (see also SAA II 6:620)
> *šarūqu*[456] (*riāqu* Š): *ú-šá-ra-qu* (prs 3rd pl.) SAA I 66:8; *ú-šá-r*[*a-qu*? SAA XIII 54:8′; *ú-šá-ra-qu-m*[*a*] SAA I 66 e.17; *nu-ša-ra-qa* (prs 1st pl.) ibid. l.13; *us-sa-*⌜*riq*⌝ SAA X 228 r.11

i/uzuzzu[457]

prs	*iz-za-az* e.g. SAA X 363 r.10; *ta-az-za-az* (2nd sg.) ABL 1174:9′; *iz/i-za-zu* (3rd pl.) e.g. SAA I 244 r.12/NL 1:11 (CTN V 19ff); *iz-za-a-zu* (interrogative clause) SAA X 246:10′
prt	*ta-az-zi-*[*iz* (3rd f.sg.) SAA X 293 r.3; *az-zi-zu-u-ni* (1st sg.) SAA X 222 r.2; *i-zi-zu-u-ni* (3rd pl.) SAA X 353 r.7 cf. *i-zi-su-u-ni* SAA XVI 62 r.7′

---

[453] Ibid. ad no. 318 r.4.

[454] See Parpola (1979) 27 sub *nadānu*.

[455] Cf. CAD Š/3 (w'd) 418 a, GAG § 107p, von Soden (1952) 175-76, AHw 14 a and Tropper (1997) 201 n. 32.

[456] See LAS II ad no. 206 r.10

[457] As to the interpretation of the verb (= **nazāzu*), I would rather prefer to follow Tropper (1997) 204-207 and Ylvisaker (1912) 38-39 than von Soden (1952) 163-69, GAG § 107a-j and Poebel, Studies in Akkadian Grammar: III. The Verb *uzuzzu* AS 9 (1939) 75-196. I have only become acquainted with the latter through secondary references (von Soden [1952] and Tropper [1997]). The regular conjugation of the verb in Š-stem **šanzuzu* > *šazzuzu* would also support the *nazāzu*-interpretation. For examples of the Š-stem, see e.g. Hämeen-Anttila (2000) 99f.

pf [*a*]-*ti-te-zi* (1st sg.) SAA I 160:6; *at-ti-ti-iz* SAA XIII 134 r.25, SAA X 294:20; *ta-ti-ti-iz* (2nd sg.) ABL 523 r.4; *it-ti-ti-iz* SAA VIII 101:8; *ni-ti-ti-zi* (1st pl.) SAA X 39 r.2 ~ (metat. forms) *a-ti-it-zi* SAA XVI 45:5′, GPA 194:12; ⸢*i*⸣-*ti-it-zi* SAA V 256:10′; *it-ti-it-zi* SAA I 235:15, SAA VIII 68:7, SAA VIII 71:3, SAA X 104 r.3, SAA XVI 10:7′; *i-te-et-zi* SAA V 149 r.4; *it-te-et-zi* SAA X 193:10; *ni-ti-it-zi* SAA XVI 41:13; *ni-it-te-et-*[*zi*] SAA V 8 r.2′ cf. also *ta-ti-ti-sa* (2nd pl.) SAA X 39:8; *it-ti-ti-is-su* (3rd pl.) SAA XVI 34 r.14; *it-ti-ti-su* SAA X 289 r.17′, SAA XIII 140:13; *it-t*[*i*]-*it-su* (possibly the metathesis which took place in singular *ittitiz* > *ittitzi* created an analogical plural form *ittitissu* > *ittitsu*) SAA V 11 e.9; *i-ti-ti-su* SAA V 104:8; CT 53 230:11; [*i-t*]*i-ti-is-s*[*u x* SAA V 196:12

(so-called prefixed) stat[458] [*i*]-*za-zu-u-ni* SAA X 24:17; *iz-za-az* SAA X 363:8

infinit. is not attested in the letter corpus

imperat. *i-ti-iz* SAA I 132:8, ABL 523 r.10 ~ *it-zi* SAA V 63 r.5; *i-ti-sa* (2nd pl.) SAA XV 90 r.10; *i-ti-is-sa* (2nd pl.) ABL 543:7, ABL 561 r.15 (both by Assurbanipal)

prc *la-zi-iz-ma* (1st sg.) SAA X 198 r.3; *li-zi-iz* NL 70 r.16′, 18′ (CTN V 161ff); *li-iz-zi-iz* SAA XVI 27 r.3′; *li-iz-zi-iz-zu* (3rd pl.) SAA X 289:6

The present and preterite are to be interpreted as being analogous to *tadānu* (*iddan*, *iddin*). However, the imperative (*z* > *t*) might be morphologically "marked" in distinction to the preterite. The variation *z* > <*s*> = [*š*] that occurs between vowels can possibly be explained sometimes as an allophone [*ž*].[459] The consonantal cluster -*ts*- found in the writing of *it-t*[*i*]-*it-su* (cf. above) may correspond to cases such as *iṣ-ṣa-bat-su* /*iṣṣabassu*/ SAA X 239:2′, *ap-ti-qid-su* /*aptiqissu*/ SAA I 12 r.1. However, in the latter cases there is admittedly a morpheme boundary involved. In any case, as an analogy to -*ts*- clusters, perhaps all -*tz*- -forms could be read as /*zz*/.[460]

5.9.1 Variation of the stem vowel

In a few passages we find the "wrong" stem vowel in a verb:[461]

(mnū *u/u*[462]) "to count, recite": *i-man-ni-u* SAA X 321 r.4, 13 (Urdu-Nanaia); *lim-ni-i-u* SAA X 348 e.22 (Mar-Issar)

---

[458] See LAS II ad no. 29:17 and GAG § 78b, § 107e. Perhaps this is a matter of taste, but I would prefer to call this, e.g., habitual present of the past instead of prefixed stative, cf. 6.3 below. In the case of *uzuzzu*, the meaning "to be (present)" is a later, secondary development in addition to its primary meaning "to stand". Cf., e.g., the use of the Dutch verbs liggen "to lie; to be situated," staan "to stand; to be" and zitten "to sit; to be". All these Dutch verbs, as *uzuzzu* in NA, are always normally conjugated.

[459] See Hämeen-Anttila (2000) 99.

[460] For the development of the perfect of the verb: *ittiziz* OA, Hecker (1968) 174 § 100c. According to the Middle Assyrian grammar by Mayer (1971) 95 § 82.5, the perfect form is not attested in Middle Assyrian. Presumably the form went through a dissimilation at some point. Thus the later development could possibly be reconstructed as: *ittišiz* MA > *ittiṯiz* [ø] (*ṯ* > *t*) MA > *ittitiz* NA (S. Parpola, personal communication).

[461] LAS II ad no. 139 r.1f.

(šqū *u/u*) "to be(come) high, move upward": *li-iš-qi-a* SAA X 209 r.2, *i-šá-qi-a* SAA X 225:11 (both by Adad-šumu-uṣur)

5.9.2 Stative of the 1st sg.

Three different stative forms of the first-person singular are attested (the statives with the subjunctive are not included):

(1) Normal paradigmatic statives ending in *u*: *ah-*⌜*za*⌝*-ku* SAA X 294:31; *bal-ṭa-ku* SAA XIII 121 r.3′, 147 r. 11; *ha-ab-la-ku* ABL 449:4; *hal-qa-ku* SAA XVI 30 r.4; *kam-mu-sa-ku* SAA I 55 e.10′; *mar-ṣa-ku* SAA XIII 66:18; *na-ṣa-ku* SAA I 56 r.13; *né-ha-ku* SAA V 26 r.5; *pa-al-ha-*[*ku*] SAA XV 59 r.6′; ⌜*pa-al*⌝*-ha-ku* SAA X 324 r.10; *pa-làh-ku* SAA I 149:10, SAA XV 62:10 (metat. of syllables); *pa-aq-da-ku* SAA I 124 r.9; *ṣab-ta-ku* Rfdn 17 29 r.18e

(2) Apocopated forms without paradigmatic *u* (cf. 4.9): *ep-šá-ak* SAA X 294:24; *ga-am-rak* SAA XIII 190 r.24e; *hal-qa-ak* ABL 896 r.18 (Aia-zeru-qiša); ⌜*ka*⌝*-mu-*⌜*sa*⌝*-ak* NL 36:12 (CTN V 34f); *ka-ra-ak* SAA X 182 r.13, CT 53 169 e.10′; *kar-rak* SAA X 242:9, SAA XVI 29:15; *ke-nak* SAA I 179 r.12; *mah-rak* SAA X 294 r.31; *mar-ṣa-ak* SAA V 217 r.16; *mar-ṭak* SAA X 242:9; *pa-al-ha-ak* SAA XIII 73 r.5; *ta-ku-la-ak* SAA XVI 128 r.10′

(3) Forms ending in *a*. Here the first-person singular stative forms are equal to the second-person singular stative forms (i.e. the distinction of the two different forms is no longer morphologically marked; the pattern of the 2nd sg stative is *parsāka*):

et-ka-ka SAA XIII 97 r.9 ~ *et-ka-ka* (2nd sg.) SAA V 200:6
kam-mu-sa-k[*a* ABL 390:14 ~ *kam-mu-sa-ka* (2nd sg.) SAA I 107:8
na-ka-ra-ka SAA V 260:7′; *na-ṣa-ka* NL 85 r.10 (CTN V 100ff); *pa-ah-hu-ra-k*[*a*] SAA X 233:15; *ta-ku-la-ka* SAA XIII 45 r.10; *za-ku-ka* (according to the context pros., though I would expect the form to be *zakkūku*) NL 74 r.16e (CTN V 132ff). For the interpretation of forms with a final *a*, see 4.5.

---

[462] However, *i/i* is often attested in Neo-Babylonian, thus our exceptions here are probably due to Babylonian influence, cf. AHw 604f.

6 SYNTACTIC VARIATION

6.1 Typical word order

The order of the main constituent parts of a sentence in Neo-Assyrian is either SOP or OSP.[463] The OSP order is used when emphasizing and stressing a topic. Temporal adverbs occur at the beginning of a sentence and can be preceded only by particle(s), other adverbs or an emphasized subject.[464] Other adverbs than temporal may occur at the end of a sentence as well. However, the position of adverbs in a sentence is less strictly regulated than the position of the main constituent parts of a sentence.

The position of interrogatives also alternates within a clause; e.g. *atâ* "why?" and *mannu* "who?" are usually at the beginning of a clause, e.g

a-ta-a / LÚ*.EN.NAM *ša* URU.*ar-rap-ha* / *meš-li* KÁ.GAL *ina* IGI-*šú ú-ram-me* "Why has the governor of Arrapha left half of the gate to him (= to the governor of Calah)?" SAA I 64:6-8

ù a-ta-a ina ŠÀ URU.*ak-ka-di ú-še-ši-bu* "And why did they enthrone (it) in Akkad?" SAA X 90:10

a-ta-a LUGAL / *la ta-pal-la-ha* "Why do you not fear the king?" SAA XIII 20 r.5-6

TA* *man-ni* / IGI.MEŠ-*šú šak-na* "On whom are his eyes fixed?" SAA X 86 r.3′-4′

man-nu EN DÙG.GA *la i-ra-am* "Who does not love his benefactor" SAA X 198 r.9

cf. in an emphasized clause: LÚ : *man-nu šu-ú-tú* "Who is this man?" SAA I 238:6

On the other hand, *aiāka* "where?" (*issu aiāka* "whence?") may be placed either at the beginning of a clause or at the end of a clause just before a predicate. Even so, it is to be noted that *aiāka*-clauses, as interrogative clauses in general, are often very short:

ṣa-hi-ta-a-te an-na-te (obj.) TA* *a-a-ka* / *i-na-šu-ni* "where they *fetch* these valuables?" SAA V 100 r.10-11

---

[463] See Parpola (1984) 205 n. 29. O = object, S = subject, P = predicate. OSP is the "marked" word order compared to SOP. The predominant word order type may be OSP in some languages of the Amazon region in South America but otherwise it is not attested as a basic word order type in the languages of the world, whereas SOP is a very common word order type, see Comrie (1989^2) 35.

[464] LAS II ad no. 39:11.

a-ni-in-nu / *a-a-ka nu-u-da* "Whence would we know?" SAA X 259 r.8-9
The predicative copula at the end of a clause: [*la*] *ú-da a-a-ka šú-u* "I [do not] know where it is" SAA I 72:11′ and an elliptic predicate (or an idiomatic clause): TA* *a-a-ka* KASKAL.2-ka "From where have you come?"(/"Where does/has your road [come from]?") SAA XIII 157:19′ however, cf. LUGAL KUR.NIM.MA.KI / (*a*)-*a-ak-ka* "Where is the king of Elam?" SAA XV 118 r.4

The separately mentioned subject of a predicate may also come after *aiāka*:

a-a-ka GIŠ.NÁ *te-rab* "Where will the bed enter?" SAA I 54 r.8; the subordinating conjunction of a clause after *aiāka*:
ù [*a*]-*a-ka* É *i-za-z*[*u-u-ni*] "and (also) the place where they should stand" SAA X 13:11.

The interrogative *alê* "where?" is usually at the end of a clause:

LÚ.ERIM.MEŠ / *a-le-e* "(and asked them) where the men are" SAA V 103:8′-9′
1-*me*-20 GIŠ.ÙR⌉.MEŠ / *ša* LUGAL *a-le-e* "Where are the king's 120 logs?" SAA V 129:1′-2′
ŠEŠ-*ka a-le-e* "(I asked him) where his brother was" SAA I 245 r.3
re-[*e*]*h-te e-mu-q*[*i*] *a-le-e* "Where are the rest of the troops?" SAA V 215 r.4 (CTN V 128ff), but when emphasized also *a-le-e mì-li*[*k-ka* 0] "Where is [your] sense?" SAA V 46:12′

6.1.1 Mutual order of main and subordinate clauses

Usually subordinate clauses precede the main clause but relative clauses immediately follow the main word (in a main clause) which they qualify.[465] Thus relative clauses are placed in the middle of a main clause or between two main clauses. Syntactically, subordinate clauses have the same position as temporal adverbs.

6.2 Exceptional word order

6.2.1 Numeral following the main word

Normally a numeral precedes its main word:

50 TÚG.GADA.MEŠ "50 tunics" SAA I 34:9
22 LÚ*.NAGAR.MEŠ "22 carpenters" SAA I 95 e.11′
3-*me*-72 GIŠ.ÙR.MEŠ KALAG.MEŠ "372 heavy beams" SAA I 100:14
13-*lim*-1-*me*-57 / *lap-tú-te* KÚ.MEŠ "13,157 damaged or burnt (here the main word "beam" is given only after the first entry, cf. l. 14)" ibid. e.19-20
3 LÚ*.EN.NAM.MEŠ "three governors" SAA V 21:11
2 LÚ*.SAG.MEŠ-*ia* / TA 6 LÚ*.ERIM.MEŠ "my two eunuchs and the six soldiers" SAA V 32 r.1-2
50 LÚ*.ERIM.MEŠ "50 men" SAA I 97 r.8′

---

[465] Cf. e.g. Hämeen-Anttila (2000) 126.

50 ANŠE.GÌR.NUN.NA "50 mules" SAA V 35:25
10/40 LÚ*.ERIM.MEŠ "10/40 soldiers" SAA V 35 r.2/4
16 LÚ.TIN.MEŠ "16 master builders" SAA V 56:11
1-*en* UD-*mu* SAA X 43:9; 5 UD.MEŠ SAA X 362 e.19′, 40 UD.MEŠ ibid. r.1 PAB 1-*me*-64 ANŠE.KUR.RA.MEŠ "a total of 164 horses" SAA XIII 84 r.3′
47 KUR.MEŠ *ša* BAD-HAL-*li* "47 cavalry mounts" SAA XIII 93 r.4, etc.

In the following examples, the change of word order suggests that the interpretation deviates from the normal one:

(1) ITI.MEŠ-*ni an-nu-ti* 2 / *na-ah-ri-di* "For these two months, be attentive ..." SAA XV 156:8-9
(2) UD.MEŠ 5 *ina* URU.*d*[*e-r*]*i* / [*kam-m*]*u-su* "They [sta]yed five days in D[e]r" SAA XV 37:16′-17′ cf. e.g. 5 UD.MEŠ *ina* URU.[*x x*] "5 days in the city [...]" SAA V 19 r.8e
(3) *ina* ŠÀ UD.MEŠ / 5 6 *re-e-šú ni-*[*i*]*t-ti-ši* "It took us 5 to 6 days" SAA X 255:12-13
(4) *a-du* UD.MEŠ 5 6 MUL.AL.LUL *i-kaš-šá-ad* "Until the 5th or 6th she (= Venus) will reach Cancer" SAA VIII 175:6
(5) *a-du* UD.MEŠ 7 8 *i-ba-laṭ* "He will be cured in 7 or 8 days" SAA X 319 s.1

The first example is surely emphatic, because /*nahrīdi*/ is an imperative. On the other hand, Examples (2)-(3), and (5) are all probably estimates (the numbers are mostly given in pairs), and not to be taken literally, cf. e.g. (3) "(it ...) took us about/approximately 5 to 6 days." In (2), the marked word order hints at a different, approximate interpretation, whereas in (4), the two numbers refer to the exact calendar days, giving two alternatives "either on the 5th or 6th." Of course it is likely that any of the examples having pairs of low figures as estimates cannot deviate much from the accurate figures.

The numerals of Example (6) are also consecutive and likewise refer to the approximate number of people purchased by the writer. This approximate interpretation of a numeral also appears to be the best alternative in Examples (7)-(17). However, round figures are characteristic of these examples: tens, hundreds and even thousands (cf. e.g. the normally accurately stated number: 1-*lim*-1-*me*-19 LÚ*.ERIM.MEŠ KALAG.MEŠ [1,119 *ṣābāni dannūti*] "1,119 able-bodied men" SAA I 11:2). Thus the use of numerals in round figures is slightly emphatic, and presumably also suggests exaggeration (or underestimation) in some of the examples. Note that with hundreds and thousands, no consecutive pairs are given.

(6) LÚ.ZI.MEŠ 5 6 *aq-ṭu-nu* "I have purchased (some) 5 or 6 souls" SAA X 294 r.23
(7) [LÚ*.ER]IM.MEŠ 1-*me i-ba-ši ina* URU.GN / [*a-n*]*a* EN.NUN *kam-mu-su* "100 men standing guard in GN" SAA I 97 r.5′-6′
(8) ERIM.MEŠ 30 T[A*] / GN 50 TA* GN$_2$ "Some 30 men from GN and some 50 from GN$_2$" SAA XV 116:9′-10′
(9) LÚ*.⌜ERIM⌝.MEŠ 50 *ina* GN / [*ina pa-ni*]-*ia i-ta-al-ku-u-ni* "Some 50 men came [to] me to GN" SAA XV 54:3′-4′
(10) ERIM.MEŠ 2-*me i*-[(*ṣābāni* 200 *i*[) SAA XV 104:4 cf. e.g. 5-*me* LÚ*.[ERIM].MEŠ / *ut-ru-te i-ba-ši* / *šu-nu* "There is a surplus of 500 men" SAA V 21 r.16-18
(11) LÚ*.ERIM.MES 2-*me x*[*x* "200 soldiers" SAA V 130:6′
(12) [ERIM.ME]Š 2-*lim i-ba-áš-ši* LUGAL / [*it-ti-d*]*in-ni* "The king did [giv]e (me) 2,000 [men]" SAA XV 54 r.16-17
(13) UDU.MEŠ 10-*lim* / *ša* PN *ih-tab-tu-u-ni* NL 2 r.9′-10′ (CTN V 22ff)

(14) *ina* UGU UDU.NITÁ.MEŠ *li-mi* / *ša* LUGAL *be-lí iš-pur-an-ni* "As to the 1,000 rams about which the king, my lord, wrote me" SAA V 263:6′-7′

(15) *ṭup-pa-a-ni* 30 40 / SIG$_5$.MEŠ "the 30 to 40 canonical tablets" SAA X 245 r.13-14

(16) *ṭup-pa-a-ni* / *ma-a'-du-ti lu* 20 *lu* 30 / SIG$_5$.MEŠ *a-hi-ú-ti* "numerous – 20 to 30 – canonical and non-canonical tablets" SAA X 240:23-25

(17) [GIŠ.KI]N.GEŠTIN.MEŠ *lu* 20 *lu* [30 ANŠE] / ⸢*a*⸣*-mar nu-še-rab-u-ni* "grapes, 20 or [30 homers], as much as we bring in ..." SAA I 179 e.27-28

6.2.1.1 Expressing indefiniteness

No real definite or indefinite articles were used in Neo-Assyrian.[466] When a plural noun (or a plural pronominal suffix, attached to a compound preposition, and referring to a plural noun mentioned earlier) is used with the numeral one /*issēn*/, then *issēn* corresponds by and large with the use of an indefinite article: "one (out) of many" > "a/an/any/some/something/someone/somebody" (sometimes known from the context, sometimes not). This kind of use is apparently a borrowing from Aramaic.[467]

(*ina libbi* +)[468] /*issēn*/ "one" (+ *ina*/*issu libbi*[-]) + (pl. poss.suff./) main word in the plural:

ŠEŠ.MEŠ-*šú ša* PN / ... / ... [*šú*]*m-mu* 1-*en* TA* ŠÀ-*bi-šú-nu* / ... *it-tu-uṣ-ṣi* "the **brothers** of PN ... if even **one of them**" SAA I 152 r.9-12

i-se-en TA* ŠÀ LÚ*.GAL.[MEŠ] / *i-si-šú-nu ár-hiš lil-li-*[*ki*] "**one of the magnate[s]** should quickly go with them" SAA I 163 e.6′-7′ cf. LÚ.A.ZU 1-*en* // *lil-li-ka* "(that) a physician should come" SAA XVI 26:13-r.1

1-*en ina* LÚ.*ki-na-ta-ti-ku-nu* / *is-sap-ra* "**one of your colleagues** wrote to me" SAA X 23:7

ina ŠÀ-*bi* 1-*en* URU.MEŠ-*ni-ia* / *pa-da-ku ip-te-te* "he opened a *silo* in **one of my villages**" SAA I 181:12-13

1-*en ina* ŠÀ-*bi* LÚ*.ARAD.MEŠ-*šú-nu la-*[*šú* "none (= not even **one**) **of them** are their **servants**" SAA I 183:5′

[*ina* ŠÀ] 1-*en* URU.ŠE.MEŠ-*ia lu-šib* ["(Any)one who [......] may live [in] **one** of **my villages**" SAA XV 33:13′

1-*en* LÚ*.NAGAR.MEŠ TA ŠÀ-*bi-šú-nu* / ... / *i-ta-al-ka* "**one carpenter** from their ranks ... came" SAA I 96 r.7-9 (note that the clause is not expressed e.g. as: *issēn ina/issu libbi naggarānišunu*. Word order seems to be rather free in cases like this)

1-*en* LÚ*.SAG.MEŠ *lu-ṣi-a* "Let **one** of **the eunuchs** come out" SAA XVI 90:4′ (elliptical: when the compound preposition is omitted, alternatively the singular may be used: *issēn ša-rēši lūṣīa* "Let one eunuch come out")

/*issēn*/ can also be placed after its main word (*issēn* + main word in singular):

ŠEŠ-*šú* 1-*en* "a brother of his" SAA XV 169:9; the same word order also, e.g., in SAA I 1 r.62 (CTN V 188ff), SAA I 183:7′-8′, SAA XIII 31 r.1-2, SAA XV 368:3′ ~ 1-*en* UD-*mu* "one day" SAA I 26 r.10 (CTN V 213f), SAA X 60 r.3, [*ša*] 1-*en*

---

[466] See Hämeen-Anttila (2000) 79.

[467] See Degen (1969) 104 § 72. Cf. also the later, biblical Aramaic, Rosenthal (1974⁴) 24 § 46 and p. 32 § 64.

[468] Brackets indicate that the place and use of these items is partly optional.

LÚ*.GAR-*ni* "[of] a single prefect" SAA I 143:10′, 1-*en* / LÚ*.*ki-ṣir* "a cohort" SAA I 177:11-12, 1-*en* [L]Ú*.*ma-ki-su* "a toll collector" SAA I 179 r.7

6.2.2 Subject or object following the verb[469]

An object may follow a verb in complicated constructions. In this context, by placing an object after a verb form, the awkwardness of a clause can often be avoided. In addition, changing word order is a means of emphasizing the out of place subject matter. However, this does not mean that this shift in word order to emphasize a subject or object necessarily leads to a permanent change in the normal word order of the language. Deviations from word order may also hint at an inclination to change the structure of the language in a larger context. This inclination towards change in word order is, in the case of Neo-Assyrian, possibly caused by language contact with the West Semitic languages, especially with Aramaic, but it may also be partly an internal Assyrian tendency or a combination of the two.

(1) TA* *a-a-ka* / *ni-iš-ši-a ig-re-e* (obj.) *ša am–mar* LÚ.TUR-*šú* / *a-ni-nu la ma-aṣ-ṣa-ni-ni* "Whence are we supposed to get (our) wages, we who have not (even) as much money as a pupil of his?" SAA X 289 r.11′-13′

(2) *i-tu-ru-du* / *ša* PN (subj.) *ša da-a-ni* URU.ŠE [*š*]*a*[470] / *ina* ŠÀ-*bi i-ṣa-ab-tú* "Those of PN came down and seized the village there by force" NL 41 r.11-13 (CTN V 208ff)

(3) *ina ma-ti-me-ni la a-mur* PN (obj. which becomes the subject of a clause following the verb *amāru*, and this latter clause is subordinate to *amāru*) / GÌR.2-*šú ina* ŠÀ-*bi* A.ŠÀ *am-me-ie-e* / *la um-me-di* "I have never seen PN to set foot in that field" NL 41:14-16 (CTN V 208ff)

(4) *ina* ŠÀ-*bi a-ta-lak a-ta-ta-ha* / IGI.2.MEŠ-*ia* (obj.) URU.ŠE *a-ta-mar* "I went there, lifted my eyes and examined the village" NL 41 r.3-4 (CTN V 208ff)

(5) *la-áš-*[*šú*] / [U]DU.MEŠ (obj.) *ina* UGU-*hi-iá* TH 106:9-10

(6) [*lu-bi*]*l-u-ni ku-zip-*[*pi*] / [*š*]*a* SÍG KUŠ.E.[SÍR.MEŠ] (obj.) / [*ú-l*]*a-a an-na-ka* / *ku-zip-pi* "[Let] them [brin]g me woolen garments and leather san[dals]; [o]r ... clothes here" SAA X 87 r.2′-5′

(7) *i-se-niš* ANŠE.KUR.RA.ME / *ga-mu-zu* / *lip-šu-hu* / *bur-ba-a-ni* (subj.) "*All the same*, the horses have been *heavily pressed*; the *foals* should rest out" SAA V 64 r.3-6

---

469 On the object following a verb, see LAS II ad no. 304 r.2′f. If an OSP/SOP language does not have a case system separating the nominative from the accusative, then the potential interpretative confusion, which may be due to this lack of a case system, can be avoided by placing the verb between subject and object, thus causing the word order to change into SPO, see Comrie (1989²) 214.

In practice, contact with another language may change the word order of a language in a short time, see ibid. 208f in which Amharic is given as an example. In the case of Neo-Assyrian, naturally Aramaic comes into question. Owing to the influence of language contact, the sound-meaning correlations may go through a quick change, ibid. 209. For examples of the partial change of a typology, see Clyne (1999) 444-63.

470 Instead of [*š*]*a*, the edition reads *š*[*ú*]-*tu*.

(8) [*ha*]-*ra-me-ma a-na* LUGAL EN-*iá as-sap-ra pi-še-er-šu* (obj.) "I am subsequently sending the relevant interpretation to the king, my lord" SAA X 100:8

(9) *u ina* ŠÀ-*bi-ma* / *ana-ku a-ta-a a-šam-me* / *la ta-pal-làh* GUR-*šu* (obj.) / ZI-*ka* GÁL-*ši ina* IGI-*iá* "And in the middle of it, why would I listen to it? Do not fear his return; your life is with me" ABL 523:14-17

(10) [LUGAL] *liš-al a-na* EN *pi-qit-ti* (obj. + subj. of the following clause)/ [*š*]*a* URU.*ar-rap-ha-a-a* / [*ša*] *re-ha-a-ti na-aṣ-ṣa-an-ni* "[The king] should ask the official [o]f the Arrapheans [who] brings the leftovers" SAA X 108 r.7′-9′

(11) LUGAL *be-lí liš-al-šu* / *mì-nu ša di-bi-šú-u-ni* (obj.) "Let the king, my lord, ask him what he has to say" SAA V 241:13-14

(12) *šú-tú i-se-me* / [*ša*] *pi-šú* (obj.) "he heard his statement" SAA I 191 r.14-15

(13) *x x ša* LU]GAL ... *liš-pur-an-ni am–mar* 2 *ú-ma-a-me* (obj.) "... the kin[g's ...] ... and may he at least send me the two beasts" SAA X 294 r.34

(14) *ina* GIŠ.MI-*šú la-mur nu-ú-ru* "May I see light under his protection!" SAA XVI 29:11

6.2.3 *adi*-adverbial clause following a verb[471]

On the basis of the large number of *adi/u*-clauses following a verb, it seems that this clause type was already deeply rooted in Neo-Assyrian.

i-si-ia a-na / *ma-ṣar-ti li-zi-zu* / *a-di* GIŠ.ÙR.MEŠ *an-nu-te* / *ú-še-ṣu-u-ni* "... should ... stand guard with me, until those beams are brought out" SAA V 32 r.15-18

ina UGU ÍD-*ma ni-bi-ad* / EN.NUN-*šá ni-na-ṣar a-di mi-nu* / *ša* LUGAL *be-lí i-šap-par-an-ni* "We shall also spend the night on the river and keep watch over it, until the king, *our* lord, sends me instructions." SAA I 54 r.14-16

ina UGU ÍD *kam-mu-sa-ku* EN.NUN *a-na-ṣar* / *a-di* ŠÀ UD-*me ša ú-nam-maš-u-ni* "I am staying on the river and keeping watch until the day I depart." SAA I 55 e.10′-11′

ú-la i-ti-iz EN.[NUN-*ka*] / *ú-ṣur* EN KUR *ta-a*[*t-qa-nu-ni*] "Alternatively, stay (there) and keep [your] wat[ch] until the country has been put in order" ABL 523 r.10-11

EN.NUN-*k*[*u-nu*] ⌜*lu*⌝ [*d*]*an*-⌜*na*⌝-*a*[*t*] / *a-du bé-e*[*t*] *a-qar-r*[*i-bu-ni*] NL 54 r.12-13 (CTN V 13f)

na-ah-ri-di EN.NUN-*ka lu dan-nat* / *a-di* É *ana-ku al-lak-an-ni* "Be attentive and keep your guard strong, until I come!" SAA XV 156:9-10

le]-*e*-[*k*]*u-la* / A.MEŠ *li-is-si-a a-d*[*i*] ⌜É *a*⌝-[*na*]-⌜*ku*⌝ *al-lak-an-ni* "should be given (bread) to eat and water to drink until I come." SAA I 10 r.12-13

ERIM.MEŠ / ... *pi-iq-da* / *li-ir-'u-ú-šú-nu* / *a-di* PAB.MEŠ-*ku-nu* / *il-lak-u-ni-ni* "Appoint ... men ... to graze them, until your brothers come" SAA V 257:8′-e.12′

ina É-*ia* ... / *lu ṣab-bu-t*[*u*] / *a-du* LUGAL *re-su-*[*nu*] / *i-na-áš-šu-u-ni* "Let them be held in my house ... until the king summons them" SAA X 99 r.4′-7′

[IT]I.GUD UD-26-KÁM *a-ta-mar a-du iš-qa-an-ni* / [*ha*]-*ra-me-ma* ... "I saw it on the 26th of Iyyar (II) when it had (already) risen high and (I am) subsequently ..." SAA X 100:7-8

[471] For the varying position of a subordinate temporal clause in relation to the main clause, cf. LAS II ad no. 147 r.7′.

ina UGU *pi-qit-tú* / *ša* É PN / *la-a iq-bu-u-ni* / *ki-i ina* ŠÀ-*bi a-na-ku-u-ni* "They did not tell me about the charge of the house of PN, when I was there" SAA X 202 r.4′-7′

6.2.4 Other adverbial clauses following a verb[472]

(*abāku*) 2 *mar-di-*⸢*a*⸣-[*te*] / *e-tab-ku-u-ni a-di* UGU-*hi-ia* / *a-na-ku a-na ú-di-ia* / 3 *mar-di-tú a-tab-ka* "They have hauled (the beams) to me (over a distance of) two stag[es], while I had to haul them for the third stage alone!" SAA V 117:11-14

(*alāku*) *an-nu-te* LÚ.MAH.MEŠ-*ni* / *ša il-lik-u-ni-ni a-na te-gír-te* "These emissaries who came to *bargain* ..." SAA V 52 r.7-8

ina GN / *kam-mu-su ù is-su-hur* / *it-ta-lak a-na* É–AD-*šú* "(PN ...) spending ... in GN, and returned to his father's house" SAA I 205 r.19e-21

ina UGU *ta-hu-m*[*e*] / *ša* KUR.*man-a-a i-tal-ku* / *a-na ma-ṣar-te* / KUR.URI-*a-a* / *ina* GN *šu-u* "They have gone to the Mannean border, to guard (it). The Urarṭian is in GN" SAA V 84 r.1-5

UD-29-KÁM *ú-na-mu-šú* / *al-lak ina* GN / *ú-še-bir-šú-nu* "They will set out on the 29th. I shall go and bring them across (the river) to GN" SAA V 64:10-12

LUGAL *be-lí* [[*ut-ta-mì-ši*]] / *il-la-ka a-na-ku lal-lik-ka* / *a-du* GN / *ina* GABA LUGAL *be-lí-ia-*⸢*a*⸣ "The king, my lord, has set out and is coming, should I come as far as GN to meet the king, my lord?" SAA V 62:4-7

lal-li-ka ina pa-an LUGAL / EN-*ia* TA* LÚ *ha-ni-u* / *la-ad-bu-ub* "Let me come and speak with this man in the king my lord's presence" SAA V 154 r.5′-7′

ma-a šum-ma i-tal-ku-u-ni / *ina pa-ni-ka ma-a* ⸢*i*⸣*-ṣa* "If they come to you, get them ..." SAA V 203 r.10′-11′

x]*x al-la-ka ina* UGU-*hi-ka* / [*ana-ku*] *aq-ṭi-ba-áš-šu mu-uk* "I shall march against you." [I] told him: "... SAA I 250:2′-3′

UN.MEŠ *an-na-ka šu-nu* / *it-tal-ku-nu ina* UGU-*hi-ia* / *ma-a* ... "The(se) people are here. They have come to me, saying ..." SAA XVI 49 r.3-5

ŠEŠ-*ka a-le-e* / *ma-a la il-li-kam-ma ina* UGU-*hi-ia* / *an-nu-rig ina* UGU ... "(I asked him) where his brother was, and he (answered): "He did certainly not come to me." ... now ... to ..." SAA I 245 r.3-5

mu-uk al-ka is-si-ia / *ina* UGU *ka-ra-ri ša* URU$_4$ / *ma-a la-áš-šú* ... "I told him: 'Come with me to lay the foundations,' but he said: 'there is no way ...'" SAA XIII 161:20′-22′

le-ti-qu lil-li-⸢*ku*⸣ / *i-si-ka* "they may go straight away with you." SAA I 195 r.13e-14e

an-nu-rig / *ú-ta-mi-šu i-lu-ku* / *la-li-ki i-si-šu-nu* / *mi-i-nu ša* LUGAL EN / *i-qa-bu-ú-ni* "Now then they have set out and are going. Should I go with them? What is it that the king, my lord, commands?" SAA XV 34:6′-10′

at-ta-lak is-si-šú-nu "I went with them" SAA XV 94:7

[472] Cf. LAS II ad nos. 214 r.3′ and 247:16ff.

(*dagālu*) TA* *mar* / [TA*] IGI LUGAL EN-*ia* / [*a*]*l-li-kan-ni a-da-gal* // [*ina* I]GI-*šú-nu la-áš-šu la i-li-ku-ni* "I have been waiting for them ever since I came back from the king my lord's presence, but they have not come." SAA I 241 e.4′-r.1

(*ebāru*) [*l*]*i-bi-ru-u-ni ina* URU.*ni-nu-a* / [*e*]-*gír-te gab-ru-u ša e-gír-te* / LUGAL *be-lí liš-pu-ru* "They should cross over to Nineveh. Let the king, my lord, send a letter in reply to (this) letter" SAA XIII 83 r.8′-10′

(*elû*) *ta-a-ba a–dan-niš ana e-le-e* / *ina pa-an* LUGAL *be-lí-ia* "it is really auspicious to go (now) to the king, my lord." SAA X 207:16-17

ú-la-a LÚ.ERIM.MEŠ *la* DÙG.GA *ana* E$_{11}$ / *ina* ŠÀ-*bi* ÙR *šá* É–DINGIR *ina kal-la-ma-ri* "Alternatively, if it is not good to let the men go to the roof of the temple at dawn ..." SAA X 183 r.1-2

(*erābu*) *gul-gul-la-te* / *ši-na šá ina* ŠÀ-*bi dul-li* / *qa-bu-u-ni* / *nu-še-ri-ba-a* / *ina qir-si* // *ku-zip-pi* "May we bring these skulls prescribed in the ritual into the *qirsu*, ... garments" SAA X 264:6-r.1

(*ibašši*) GI.AMBAR.MEŠ / *mar i-ba-šú-ni* / *a-na ma-te-ni* "Whatever reed there is in our country ..." SAA V 120:3-5

ZI-*ka* GÁL-*ši* / *ina* IGI-*ia* "Your life is with me" ABL 523:17

(*kallumu*) GIŠ.MÁ.MEŠ / ... *ša ina* ÍD *kar-ra-ni* / *uk-ta-lim a-na* LÚ*.MÁ.DU.DU.MEŠ / *iq-ṭí-bi-u ma-a* "... boats which had been launched on the river. I showed them to the boatmen, but they said: "..." SAA I 56:8-11

(*karābu*) *aktarabka* / *ina pān Mullissi* "I have blessed you before Mullissu" CT 53 974:3-4 ~ *ina pān Aššur Mullissi* / *aktarabkā* StAT 2 248:4-5 (= StAT 1 57)[473]

(*kunnu*) *al-ka píl-ka-ni-ni* / *ina bir-tu-ni ka-in at-ta-lak* / *uk-ta-in ina bir-tu-šú-*⌜*nu*⌝ / *i–su-ri* "Come and settle our work allocation between us!" I went and settled it between them. Perhaps ..." SAA I 64:11-14

(*laššu*) *ma-a* LÚ-*ma la-a-šú* / *ina pa-ni-ia* NL 85 r.6-7 (CTN V 100ff)

la-áš-[*šú*] / [U]DU.MEŠ *ina* UGU-*hi-iá* TH 106:9-10

(*mahāru*) *ú-ma-a* / *šum-ma ma-hir ina* IGI LUGAL EN-*ia* / *lu-gal-li-bu-uš* "Now, if it is acceptable to the king, my lord, let them shave him" SAA X 97 e.11′-13′

ù [*ina* UGU] ŠEŠ-*ia* / *ša* ... / *la-a ma-hi-ir ina pa-ni-šú-nu* / *ina* É-*ka la iz-zaz* "And [concerning] my brother about whom ... he is not to their liking. (Therefore) he does not serve in your palace" SAA X 308 r.6′-9′

li-di-⌜*na*⌝*-áš-šú-nu* / *šum-ma ma-hi-ir pa-an* LUGAL / *e-gír-tú ina* UGU PN / ... *liš-pa-ru-u-ni* "Let him give them (fields and gardens). If it is acceptable to the king, my lord, let them send a letter to PN ..." SAA I 177:16-19

ù ina UGU LÚ.*ú-ra-si* / ... / *šum-ma ma-hi-ir ina* IGI [LUGAL EN-*ia*] / *ú-*⌜*x*⌝ "And regarding the *brick masons*, ... if it is acceptable to the [king, my lord]" SAA XVI 90:6′-e.13′, see also SAA XVI 36 r.14-15, SAA XVI 92:11-12 and SAA XVI 131 r.6e-7e.

(*nakāru*) *a-ta-a* UGU LÚ*.ARAD.MEŠ-*ni* / *ša* LUGAL *ta-da-bu-bu* / *ma-a na-ka-ra-ka i-si-ku-nu* / *ma-a i-na* KUR.*ma-ti-ia* / ... *la tú-ra-da* "Why do you plot against the king's subjects? I am at war with you, do not come down to my country!" SAA V 260:5′-9′

---

[473] For other attestations of this blessing formula, typical of letters from Assur, see StAT 1 p. 170 ad l. 4.

(*nammušu*) LÚ*.ERIM.MEŠ-*šu* / *ú-ta-mi-šu-ma* / *a-na* GN / *a-se-me ma-a* ... "His troops have also set out towards GN. I have heard that ..." SAA V 88 r.2-5

ša nam-⸢*mu*⸣*-ši* / *a-na ma-šar-te* / PN ... / *un-qu* KUG.GI / *na-aṣ ina* UGU-*hi-ni* "... to set out for the review, *but* PN ... brings us the (king's) golden stamp seal ..." SAA V 234:2′-6′

UD-*mu ša* LÚ*.KIN.A.MEŠ / *e-mu-ru-ni* / *ú-ta-mì-ši* / *ina* GN "The day he saw the messengers he set out to GN" SAA V 164:12-15

(*našû*) PN LÚ*.GAL–*ki-ṣir* / *un-qu* KUG.GI / *na-aṣ ina* UGU-*hi-ni* / *ik-ta-na-la-a-na-ši* / *ma-a* ... "PN, the cohort commander, brings us the (king's) golden stamp seal and holds us up continually, saying ..." SAA V 234:4′-8′

(*palāhu*) *liš-ṭur-*⸢*ni*⸣ / *lu-še-bi-lu-né-eš-šu* / *i-pa-lah* TA* *pa-an* LUGAL / *i-šam-me ú-la-a* "Let them write it down and send it to him; he will get afraid of the king and obey. Otherwise ..." SAA X 285 r.1′-4′

(*paqādu*) *ú-ma-a* LÚ*.GAL–ARAD.MEŠ / *ša* AD-*ka* / *ip-qi-du-u-ni* / *ina* UGU-*hi-šú-nu* "Now the chief of servants, whom your father appointed over them ..." SAA XIII 143 r.1-4

(*parāsu*) *ú-ma-a ap-ta-ra-as ina bir-tu-šú-*[*nu*] / [*ia*]*-mut-tú* "I have now arbitrated between them ..." SAA I 64 s.1-2

TA* *a-ha-a-a-iš* / *ni-id-bu-ub* ⸢LUGAL⸣ *lip-ru-us* / *ina bir-tu-un-ni* "Let us litigate with each other, and let the king decide between us" SAA XV 24 r.19-21

(*qabû*) *šu-ú mi-i-nu i-qab-bi* / *ina* UGU-*hi-ka* "What could he say against you?" ABL 523:13-14

⸢*x x*⸣ / *aq-ti-bi a-na* PN / *a-ki ša* LUGAL *be-lí iq-ban-ni* "I spoke to PN as the king, my lord, had told me" SAA XVI 20 r.1′-3′

ù ša LUGAL *be-lí iq-bu-u-ni* / *ina* UGU DUMU.ME ⸢EN⸣.ME-*ka ma-a* "And as to what the king, my lord, said to me about the sons, your lords: ..." SAA X 187:16-17

(*šapāru*) *ša áš-pur-an-ni* / *a-na* ŠEŠ-*ia mu-uk* "... about which I wrote to my brother: ..." ABL 1385:8-9

ki-i ina IGI LUGAL *ma-hi-ir* / *la-áš-pur a-na* É–*a-muk-a-ni* / *šum-mu* PN *ina* ŠÀ-*bi*?-*šú*? "If it is acceptable to the king, I will write to Bit-Amukani (and) if PN is there"[474] ABL 896 r.1-3 (Aia-zeru-qiša)

LUGAL *li-is-pu-ru* / *a–su-mu a-na* LÚ*.EN.NAM / *ša* GN / ⸢*a*⸣*–su-mu* // ⸢*a*⸣*-na* PN "Let the king direct either the governor [o]f GN or PN ..." SAA XV 17:9-r.1

ip-ta-al-hu / *i-sa-pa-ru-u-ni* / *ina* UGU-*hi-ia e-da-nu* / *a-sa-kan-šú-nu* "They got afraid and wrote to me, and I imposed a deadline upon them" SAA V 202 r.13′-16e

[TA* É.GAL] *i-sa-par-u-ni* / *ina* UGU-*hi-ia ma-a* 1-*me*-50 / *e-bir-tú* ... "They wrote to me from the palace: "(Let them cut out) 150 (basalt) steps" SAA I 58:4-6

UN.MEŠ ... EN–*ta-hu-me-šú-nu* / *a-šap-par ina* UGU-*hi-šú-nu* ARAD.MEŠ-*ia* / *šá ih-ṭu-ú-nin-ni* ... *ú-ba-ʾu-*[*u*] "I shall send people who live in the same region to them to call my servants who sinned to account" ABL 879:14-16

---

[474] For ABL 896, see Frame (1992) 172f. Note here the Babylonian *kî*, which equates with the Assyrian *šumma*; *šumma ina pān šarri bēlī'a mahir*, e.g., in SAA XVI 141:5′-r.1 (SAA XVI 34:15-16 has *šumma pān mār šarri mahir*) and passim in SAA X. Cf. also *mahāru* above.

LÚ*.NU.GIŠ.SAR *šu-ú* / ... / *a-sap-ra ina* UGU-*hi-šú* / *ma-a lu-ú-bi-lu-niš-šú* "I sent a gardener ... to him, saying: 'Let him be brought here'" SAA XV 168 r.4-7

⌜a⌝-sa-ap-ra :. *ina* UGU / [L]Ú*.*šá*–UGU–É *ša* L[Ú*.EN.NAM] / [*š*]*a* GN "I have written to the household overseer of the [governor o]f GN" SAA V 254:12′-14′

nu-uk šu-up-ru / UGU PN // [*m*]*a a-ta-a* "Write to PN: 'Why ...'" SAA V 115:12-r.1

(*ṭiābu*) UD-*mu an-ni-ú la ta-ba* / *a-na a-la-ki* "It is not good to go today" SAA X 222 r.3-4. See also sub (*elû*) above (SAA X 183 and SAA X 207).

(*uzuzzu*) *ina* UGU UDU.SISKUR.MEŠ *ša* LUGAL / ... / *al-la-ka a-za-za ina* IGI UDU.SISKUR.MEŠ / *ú-la-a* ... "Concerning the king's sacrifices ... shall I go and supervise the sacrifices? Or ..." SAA X 94 r.6′-9′

ma-a de-en-ku-nu / *ep-pu-šú ni-ti-it-zi* / [*ina*] *pa-ni-šú-nu la i-ma-gúr* "'They do justice to you' – we have stood before them, but they have refused ..." SAA XVI 41:12-14

ANŠE.KUR.RA.MEŠ / *ša* ... / ... / *e-rab-ú-ni* / *i-za-zu-ú* / *ina* ŠÀ É.GAL *ma-šar-te* / *ú-la-a ú-ṣu-ú* "Will the ... horses which will come ... stay in the Review Palace, or will they leave?" SAA XIII 98 r.2-9

(*zabālu*) *ma-a* ŠE.PAD.MEŠ / *zi-ib-la* // *a-na* GN / *mì-nu ša* LUGAL *be-lí* ... "'Bring barley rations to GN!' What does the king, my lord ...?" SAA V 234:8′-r.2

Exceptions

Expressing cause (*issu, issu pān*):

('lk) *i-ta-al-ka* / *ma-a al-lak* / TA *pi-i ša* LUGAL-*⌜ma⌝* / *ma-a* LUGAL *iq-ṭí-b*[*a-na-ši*] "(one carpenter) came (to me) saying: "I am going by the order of the king himself; the king told [us] ..." SAA I 96 r.9-12

(nkl) *ni-ik-lu me-em-me-e-ni lu nak-la* / TA *pa-an* MUŠEN TA *pa-an me-me-ni a-hu-la* "Some expedient must be formed on account of the bird (and) anything beyond it" SAA X 183 r.3-4

(plh) *ù pa-lìh* TA* *pa-an* / EN-*iá* "... and one who reveres my lord" SAA XVI 48 r.4-5

(špr) LÚ*.*qur-bu-te* / [*is*]-*si-ia* / [*liš*]-*pu-ru* / [TA*] *pa-an* / [*par-r*]*i-ṣu-te* "A bodyguard [should be] sent with me because of [the tr]aitors" SAA X 338 r.3-7

Expressing finality (*ana*):

(šhṭ) *i–ši-a-ri ina* ŠÀ *mi-i-ni* / SIG$_4$.MEŠ *i-šá-hu-ṭu* / *a-na píl-il-ki-šú-nu* "By means of what will they *glaze* bricks for their work-quota tomorrow?" SAA I 143:14′-16′

Local clause (*ina*):

(qbī) *ma-a um-mi šap-ra-at ta-ta-l*[*ak*] / *la taq-bi ina* É.GAL *ma-a ina pa-an* PN / ... *taq-ṭè-bi* "My mother was charged to go, (but) she did not tell (anything) in the palace. (Instead) she spoke in the presence of PN ..." SAA X 199 r.11′-13′

(škn) *ina šá-a-šú* / *i-da-gul-šú ba-aṭ-lu* / *i-šak-ku-nu ina* É–DINGIR.MEŠ-*ni-ka* / *ma-a* LUGAL *lu-u ha-sis* "(They) ... observing him, will also go on strike against your temple(s). Moreover, the king should bear in mind ..." SAA XIII 31 r.8-11

Temporal clause:

(nš') GIŠ.*pi-laq-qu šu-u-tú / a-na* ᵈ*dil-bat* *a-na-áš-ši* / 3 UD.MEŠ-*ti* // LUGAL *be-lí lu ú-di* "It is the spindle (symbol); I carry it three days for Venus. The king, my lord, should know ..." SAA X 92:11-r.1

(sdr) 25 *ú-ra-a-te* / ... / *it-tal-ka-a-ni* / *la-as-de-e-re* // *ina ši-a-ri* / *mi-i-nu* / *ša* LUGAL ... "25 teams have arrived ... Should I array them tomorrow? What is it that the king ...?"[475] SAA XIII 95:7-r.3

(ṭīb) See sub (*elû*) above (SAA X 183).

Others:

(*šūtu*) *ú-ta-mì-ši* / *ina* GN // *šu-tú* *a-di* / *e-mu-qi-šu* "he set out to GN, he himself with his troops" SAA V 164:15-r.2

(blṭ) *ana-ku la ud-da-a šá* / ... *tab-lat-an-ni* *ina* UGU É–EN.[MEŠ-*ka*] "Don't I know what ... you have lived for the house of [your] lords?" ABL 523:8-12

(nš') *pu-tu-hu* *ta-na-áš-ši-ia-a* / *ina* UGU AN.MI ᵈ*šá-maš* "Will you assume the responsibility for the eclipse of the sun?" SAA X 216:7-8

6.2.5 Relative clause following a verb

('lk) LÚ*.SAG *ša* LUGAL EN-*iá lil-li-ka* / *ša ke-e-tu* TA* LUGAL EN-*iá i-da-bu-ub-u-ni* "Let a royal eunuch who will tell the king my lord the truth come ..." SAA I 124:10-11

(dmq) SIG₅-*iq a–dan-niš* / *bé-et* LUGAL *be-lí* / *iq-bu-ú-ni* "What the king, my lord, said is quite right" SAA X 191:8-10

ina [UGU] LÚ.É–*a-muk-a-na-a-a* / *ša* [KIN-*an*]-*ni* SIG₅ É *te-pu-šú-ni* "Concerning the Bit-Awukaneans about whom [you wrote], what you did is good" ABL 945:3-4

ù de-e-qe / *ša taš-pur-an-ni* "But it is good that you wrote to me" SAA XVI 3 r.2-3

SIG₅ *a–dan-niš* / *ki-i ša taq-bi-ni* "It is fine indeed, as you said" SAA XVI 2 r.2-3

6.3 Unusual use of tenses

The perfect is used only a few times to refer to the future[476] (note that the perfect is often used in conditional *kīma* and *šumma* clauses), yet the use of the "epistolary" perfect describing the epistolary acts themselves (e.g. *ūmâ annurig assapra* "I am writing right now") is very common in Neo-Assyrian letters.[477] In the examples below, however, it may be a question of some type of analogy (as e.g. omitted *kīma* or *šumma*), or emphasis:

---

475 Cf. p. 99 above.

476 See LAS II ad no. 34 (+) 49:8.

477 For the epistolary verbal usage in Akkadian, see Pardee and Whiting (1987).

Examples

(*alāku*) *an-nu-ri ka-rim* / *i-la-ka* LÚ*.UŠ.MEŠ / *a-na e-ṣa-di i-tal-ku-u* (pf) "(the way)[478] is now blocked, (but) is it possible that the drivers went to the harvest (later on)?" (On the perfect in questions marked by intonation, see p. 100 above) KAV 214:6-8. Alternatively, *i-tal-ku-u* could be interpreted as the present of the Gt(t)-stem.

(*uzuzzu*) *ina ha-ra-am-me ina pu-tu-u-a* / *ta-ti-ti-sa* (pf) "From now on you (pl.) will stay in my entourage" SAA X 39:7-8 cf. *ina ha-ra-am-me* / *ina pu-tú-ú-a* / *ta-za-az* (prs) "From now on you (sg.) will stay in my entourage" SAA X 68:9-10

ina pu-ut L[UGAL] / *ni-ti-ti-zi* (pf) "we stand in front of the k[ing]" SAA X 39 r.1-2 cf. *a-ke-e ina pu-ut* / LUGAL EN-*ia* / *la az-zaz* "how would I not stand in front of the king, my lord?" SAA X 68:14-e.16

The present can be used aspectually in describing an action occurring repeatedly in the past:[479]

[*na-mu*]-⌜*r*⌝*a-te-šú a-mah-mar-šú* TA* LÚ.ERIM.MEŠ SIG$_5$.MEŠ-*ti šu-mi* [*i*]*z-zak-kar* / [*re*]- ⌜*e*⌝-*ha-ti ma-a'-da-a-ti ak-kal* "I got to receive (repeatedly) gifts from him, and my name was mentioned among men of good fortune. I used to enjoy generous 'leftovers,'[480] intermittently." SAA X 294:16-17

ù MU.AN.NA-*ia* KUG.UD 1 MA.NA 2 MA.NA *a-kaš-šad* / [UD.MEŠ] *ša* DUMU–LUGAL *be-lí-ia* TA* LÚ.MAŠ.MAŠ.MEŠ-*šú re-ha-a-ti a-mah-har* "and yearly I earned a mina or two of silver. (And) [in the days] of my lord's crownprincehood I received 'leftovers' with your exorcists (lit. "with his exorcists")." ibid. 18-19

LÚ*.ARAD.MEŠ-*šú-nu a-ke-e is-se-šú-nu* / *i-da-li-pu ina* ŠÀ-*bi* GIŠ.NÁ.MEŠ / *i-zab-bi-lu-šú-nu ma-ṣar-ta-šú-nu* / *a-ke-e i-na-ṣu-ru* "How did their servants sit up with them all nights and carry them on litters! (And) how (well) did they keep watch over them!" SAA X 316:11-14

ina É–*rin-ki er-rab* "(perhaps) he took care of the ablution chamber" (liter. in SAA X: "he used to enter the ablution chamber") SAA X 97:6′

TA* *be-et* .../ .../ *ma-ṣar-tu ša* LUGAL EN-*ia* / *a-na-ṣar* "Ever since ..., I have been keeping the watch of the king, my lord." SAA XVI 98 r.7′-10′

i–ti-ma-li] / [*i*]–*šá-šu-me ki-i* ⌜AD-*šú*⌝ [*ša* LUGAL EN-*ia*] *i-ra-di-u-ni* "In the past days, when *the father of* [*the king my lord*] was leading ..." SAA I 99 r.2′-4′

tab-lu ú-tab-bu-lu ú-sa-hu-ru "They used to commit thefts and cover them up" SAA XIII 138 r.4

ina IGI AD-*šú ša* LUGAL / EN-*ia ú-ìl-a-ti* / *ša* LÚ.A.BA UD–AN–$^{d+}$EN.LÍL / *gab-bu i-mah-hu-ru* / *ú-še-er-ru-bu* "they used to receive and introduce all astrological reports into the presence of the father of the king, my lord." SAA X 76:11-e.15, see also ibid. r.6

ki-i ina UGU / LUGAL EN-*ia a-la-ka-a-ni* "when I was *about to come* to the king, my lord" NL 43 r.4-5 (CTN V 130ff)

---

[478] This clause without a subject is elliptical, but cf. SAA I 97:15, SAA V 79:14-15, SAA V 199:9, SAA XV 30 r.12.

[479] Parpola (1987B) 275.

[480] "Leftovers" do not mean anything to be belittled or despised, on the contrary, see Oppenheim (1964) 189 and Parpola (1987B) 275.

ŠE.*nu-sa-hi ša* ⌜*i*⌝*–ti-ma-li* / *i–ša-šu-me ša* PN / *ša* PN_2 *ša ni-na-sa-hu-ni* / *ú-ma-a* "(Concerning) the earlier corn-tax of PN and PN_2 which we used to extract, (but) now ..." NL 74:4-7 (CTN V 132ff)

See also SAA I 12:9′-12′, SAA I 92:10-13, SAA I 160:6-9, SAA V 53:6-9, SAA V 165:5-9, SAA VIII 21:8-r.2, SAA X 304:10-13, SAA X 363:7-8, SAA XIII 33:9-r.4, SAA XIII 186 r.6′-10′, SAA XVI 78:13-14, SAA XVI 82:13-15, ABL 1148:3′-4′, NL 2 r.7′-8′ (CTN V 22ff).

The preterite is often used as a positive past tense in legal documents. In that case, it is apparently a question of an archaism favoured by this specific genre.[481] A comparable use of the preterite is not attested in letters: the perfect is the tense of the past in the positive main clauses, apart from some possible, but very rare, exceptions:

⌜*ù*⌝ *mu-ru-uṣ* ŠÀ-*bi-ia uk-tam-me-ra a-na* LUGAL EN-*ia áš-pu-r*[*a*] "but I (only) heaped up the grief of my heart, *writing* to the king, my lord"[482] SAA X 294 r.4

6.4 Ellipsis

In most cases ellipsis probably concerns prepositions, although *ša* can be substituted for a missing preposition. However, here I only provide a few examples of clauses from which a noun is omitted. Ellipsis often occurred when the subject matter was well known to both the writer and the recipient of a letter. Of course, the omission of a noun or other part of speech involved the risk of misunderstanding, but as it is often attested, it presumably only rarely prevented the recipient from understanding the message correctly. Elliptical examples:

(*lumnu*) *ú-ṣa* <u>*la me-me-ni*</u> / *ina qa-ab-si*[483] "... there is nothing (wrong) ..." SAA X 48 r.2-3 cf. ⌜HUL⌝ *ina* ŠÀ É.GAL *la me-me-ni* "There is no evil inside the palace" SAA X 42:13

(*murṣu*) *ú-ma-a ki-i* LUGAL *in-na-šar-u-ni*[484] "Now that (the illness of) the king is being taken away" SAA X 199 r.16′ cf. [*a-ki*] $^{d+}$EN *mur-ṣ*[*i*] MAN ⌜*iš*⌝*-šur-u-ni* "[When] Bel took away the illness of the king" SAA X 200:10

(*dullu*/*namburbû*) *ina* UGU-*hi* (d./n.) *ša iz-bi*[485] "Concerning the *izbu* (= anomalous birth) omen [or: "ritual"]" SAA X 276 r.9; *a-na-ku šá ha-liq-ti* UZU "I (shall perform one) against "Loss of Flesh" ..." (*dullu* is mentioned on line 9) SAA X 212:12; (*dullu*) UD-*mu ep-pu-šu* UD-*mu ú-ra-am-mu-u*[486] "(but) one day they do the work, (whereas) the next day they leave it" SAA X 349 r.18

---

[481] On the archaisms, as well as for the alternating use of past tenses in legal documents, see Postgate (1997) 162-63.

[482] See Parpola (1987B) 276f.

[483] LAS II ad no. 45 r.2.

[484] Ibid. ad no. 133 r.16′.

[485] Ibid. ad no. 205 r.9.

[486] Deller (1961B) 350.

(*ūmu*)[487] *a-na šal-ši* LUGAL "The day after tomorrow the king ..." SAA X 275 r.6; *a-na šá-al-še ina* ŠÀ-*bi šu-u* "he (will) be there on the third (day)" (in SAA V: "it takes him three days to get there") SAA V 199:11 cf. *a-na* 3-*ši* UD-*me-š*[*ú*] / *i-tal-ka* "Two days later he came (again) ..." SAA I 191 r.2-3

(*hūlu* "road") *ši-id-di-im-ma*[488] "Along (the roadside)" SAA X 361 r.3 cf. *ina ši-id-di* KASKAL (+ gloss: *hu-u-li)* "along the roadside" SAA X 70 r.15; *ina* UŠ KASKAL "alongside the road" SAA XV 137 r.7′ and similar types of clauses passim

(*pišru* "interpretation")[489] *la-áš-šú la in-na-sa-*[*ha*] "it (= *pišru*) will not be excerpted at all" SAA VIII 98 r.3 cf. *pi-šir-šu a-na-sa-ha* "... and I extract the (relevant) interpretation" SAA X 202:12

6.5 Contamination of cases[490]

In the Neo-Assyrian letter corpus, the nom./acc. *-u* and the gen. *-i/e* were carefully set apart from one another. Nevertheless, such developments as the use of the preposition *ana*, combined with a syntactically specialized word order,[491] as a marker of the accusative, suggest that the language may have been moving towards the use of a single case.[492]

This list of examples of the contamination of cases does not include the forms that are under the influence of progressive vowel assimilation (see 4.5) because those forms are not valid in this connection. Nevertheless, they do support the presumable development towards the use of one case.

The nominative <*u*> instead of the expected genitive <*i/e*>:

(*anniu*) TA* *pa-an da-ba-bi an-ni-iu-u* "Because of this speech" SAA X 316:19 (Urdu-Nanaia, Nineveh)
ina UGU *ṭè-e-me an-ni-u* NL 54:9 (CTN V 13f, *abat šarri*)
ki-i an-ni-u SAA XVI 73:5′ (unkn.)
TA* LÚ *ha-ni-u* "with this man" SAA V 154 r.6 (Aššur-alik-pani, from the northeastern boundary of Assyria)

(*batqu*) *a-na bat-qu* SAA I 205 e.19 (Zeru-ibni, Raṣappa)

---

[487] *ana/ina šalši ūmi* clauses may refer to the future as well as to the past, see LAS II ad no. 210 r.6. For some more possible elliptical clauses, see ibid. ad nos. 223:9ff, 289:18′f, r.1, 290 r.11, 298:13, 309:9, 325 r.2.

[488] Ibid. ad no. 294 r.3. See also Luukko, SAAB 9 (1997) 33 n.8.

[489] *pišru* is often omitted, see LAS II ad no. 325 r.3.

[490] Contrary to Lipiński's ([1997] § 32.21) claim, cases were marked with concern as to their syntactic function in NA. Thus: *-u* = acc./nom. and *-i/e* = gen. However, it is true that this otherwise carefully observed system was not applied in proper names. Moreover, many Babylonian scribes (or other non-native Assyrians) who wrote NA letters did not follow this rule as systematically as the native Assyrian scribes.

[491] On the relation of word order to the functional case system from the viewpoint of language universals, see Comrie (1989[2]) 213-15.

[492] See Lipiński (1997) § 52.11.

(*dannu*) [*ina* UGU K]Á *ša* É–*ra-m*[*a-ki*] / [*ša*] É–*hi-la-ni dan-nu* "[As to the g]ate of the bathroom [of] the big *hilānu* palace" SAA I 67:4-5 (Ṭab-šar-Aššur)

(*dī'u*) [*né-p*]*e-še ša di-hu* "rites against malaria" SAA X 351 r.14 (Mar-Issar, Akkad)

(*duāku*) TA* *pa-ni du-a-ku* (only one wedge separates *ku* from the *ki*) "because of killing" ABL 1364 r.4 (unkn.)

(*dullu*) *a-na dul-lum* SAA I 248 r.5 (possibly Taklak-ana-Bel, Naṣibina)

(*egirtu*) *ṭè-e-mu* / *ša e-gír-tú* (for TÚ = TE/TE = TÚ see 3.1) "the report included in the letter" SAA XV 131 r.7-8 (Nabû-duru-uṣur, Der)

(*gišru*) *ina* UGU / *gi-iš-ru* "on the bridge" SAA I 47 r.15-16 (Ṭab-šar-Aššur)

(*guhaṣṣu*) *ki-i gu-ha-ṣu* "like a wire cable" SAA X 382 r.10 (unkn.)

(*gusīgu*) *ina* UGU NA$_4$.*gu-si-gu* "concerning the *gusīgu*-jewelry" SAA X 348:5 (Mar-Issar)

(*hīṭu*) EN *hi-i-ṭu šu-ú* "He is a criminal" SAA V 210:16 (Nabû-hamatu'a, Mazamua)

(*hubtu*) TA* LÚ*.*hu-ub-tu* [*ha-an-ni-i*] "with [these] captives" SAA I 10 r.6 (*abat šarri*, Sargon II)

(*ildu*/*išdu*) *a-ki il-du* "like a base" SAA X 316 r.18 (Urdu-Nanaia)

(*kāru*) *ina*/*a-na ka-a-ru* SAA XVI 127:16/20 (Itti-Šamaš-balaṭu, Phoenicia); *ka-a-ri* (st. cstr.) É.ZI.DA SAA X 364:15′ (Mar-Issar)

(*kaspu*) *ina kas-pu* SAA XV 181:25 (Aššur-belu-taqqin, near the Babylonian border)

(*kuṣṣu*) *ina dan-ni-te šá ku-uṣ-ṣu* "at (the time of) the severest cold" ABL 302 r.1 (Assurbanipal); *ina ku-uṣ-ṣu* ibid. r.3

(*līmu* "thousand") *i-na li-mu mu-ta-ni* "(from) a thousand pestilences" SAA XVI 127 r.16 (Itti-Šamaš-balaṭu, Phoenicia)

(*nagiu*) *ina na-gi-u* NL 86:9 (*abat šarri*, Tiglath-pileser III or Sargon II) (CTN V 239f); [*ina* UGU *ṭè*]*-e-mu ša* KUR.*na-gi-u* "[Concerning the n]ews of the district" SAA XV 69:5 (Marduk-šarru-uṣur, Šingibutu)

(*nibzu*) *ina* UGU *ni-ib-zu* "on the tablet" SAA X 365:12′ (Mar-Issar)

(*piqittu*) *ina* UGU *pi-qit-tú* "about the charge" SAA X 202 r.4′ (Adad-šumu-uṣur, Nineveh)

(*raddû*) *ša ra-ad-du-u* / *lu-ra-ad-di-i-u* "let them add what is to be added" SAA X 103 r.3′-4′ (possibly Akkullanu, Assur)

(*ṣehru*) TA* ŠÀ-*bi ṣe-he-ru* "from childhood" SAA XVI 126:14 (Itti-Šamaš-balaṭu, Phoenicia)

(*šaklulu*) TA* ŠÀ-*bi* GUD.*šak-lu-lu ša ka-ri-bi* "of the blesser's ungelded bull" SAA X 353 r.1 (Mar-Issar)

(*šammu*) *ina* UGU-*hi* / *šam-mu* "concerning the drug" SAA X 191:5-6 (Adad-šumu-uṣur)

(*šipṭu*) T[A] *pa-an ši-ip-ṭu* "because of punishment" SAA X 353 r.21 (Mar-Issar); TA* IGI *šip-ṭu* "because of punishment" SAA XV 181 r.7 (Aššur-belu-taqqin, near the Babylonian border)

(*šulmānu*) *a-ki-lu-ti* / *ša šul-man-nu* ... / *e-kal-u-ni* "(all those) who have enjoyed gifts ..." SAA X 107 r.14e-s.2 (Akkullanu)

(*šulmu*) *a-na* DI-*mu* SAA XIII 26:8 (Sîn-na'di, Assur); *ina* DI-*mu* SAA X 351:9 (Mar-Issar); (*i-na*) SAA I 188:12 (Nabû-pašir, Harran)

(*ṭēmu*) *ina* UGU *ṭè-e-mu* (cf. *nagiu* above) SAA XV 69 r.11 (Marduk-šarru-uṣur) (*ūmu*)[493] *la-ba-ri* UD-*mu* (*ūmu* is here problematic, cf. 5.3) "old age" SAA X 348:20 (Mar-Issar); *ina kal* UD-*mu* SAA V 211 r.9; *kal-la*–UD-*mu* SAA XVI 21 r.2; *ša* UD-*mu* SAA I 8 r.9; *ina* ŠÀ UD-*mu* SAA V 217 r.11, SAA XV 19:2′ (*in*]*a*), SAA XV 101 r.8, SAA XV 192 r.5; *ina* Š]À UD-*mu* SAA XV 281 r.3; *x* UD-*m*]*u an-ni-i* SAA XV 115 r.4′; *ina* UD-*mu an-ni-i* SAA X 193:11; *a-na* 1-*en* UD-*mu* SAA X 60 r.3; *ina* UD-*mu ša* StAT 2 228 r.1

Genitive <*i/e*> instead of the expected nominative/accusative <*u*>:
This type of confusion is extremely rare in Assyrian letters. In any case, it should be stressed that the examples from scholarly letters (SAA X) in particular are often a result of Babylonian influence (i.e. they are mostly Babylonianisms).

(*aiu*) *a-a-i dul-lu ša šarru* ... "What work (has) the king ..." SAA XVI 126 r.21′ (Itti-Šamaš-balaṭu, Phoenicia)

(*egirtu*) *i-gír-te* / *a-na* É.GAL *us-se-bi-la* "I sent the letter to the Palace" SAA XV 217 r.6′-7′ (Šarru-emuranni, Babylon)
EN-*ia e-gír-ti* / ... / ... *ú-se-ṣi-ia-a* "my lord ... He forwarded me the (attached) letter ..." SAA V 210:6-8; *e-gír-ti liš-pu-ru* "Let him ... send a letter ..." SAA V 213:9 (both by Nabû-hamatu'a, Mazamua)

(*išātu*) *lu-u i-šá-ti* / *mì-im-ma ú-qa-al-li* "or if fire burns anything" SAA X 42 r.4-5 (Balasî, Nineveh)[494] ~ [*i*]-⌜*šá-tú* ibid. obv. 7

(*kalbu*) *kal-bi me-e-ti a-na-ku* "I am (but) a dead dog" SAA XVI 127 r.15, SAA XVI 128 r.15e (both by Itti-Šamaš-balaṭu, Phoenicia); *kal-bi mé-te* / [*a-na-ku x*]*x* SAA X 309 r.4-5 (Ana-Nabû-atkal, Nineveh)

(Kaldu) *ù* KUR.*su-tu-u šá-niš* / KUR.*kal-di* "... and the nomad land or, according to another tradition, Chaldea" SAA X 351 e.23 (Mar-Issar)

(*kettu*) *ù ket-ti ina* ŠÀ-*bi* "However, there is definitely ... among ..." SAA XV 181 r.2 (Aššur-belu-taqqin, near the Babylonian border)

(*kusāpu*) *la ku-sa-pi ta-kal* "She does not (even) eat bread" SAA XVI 26:10 (Šamaš-metu-uballiṭ, *Nineveh*) ~ *ku-sa-pu la e-kul-u-ni* "(who) does not eat bread" SAA X 43:11 (Balasî)

(*libbu*) ŠÀ-*bi ša* LUGAL SAA XV 4 r.10 (Issar-duri, Arrapha), SAA X 296:9, SAA X 301:10, SAA X 305:9, (all Nabû-naṣir, Nineveh); ŠÀ-*bi liš-ku-nu-šú-nu* "They should be encouraged" SAA X 354 r.14 (Mar-Issar, Akkad); ŠÀ-*bi ú-sa-áš-kin-šú-nu* "I encouraged them" SAA V 210:14 (Nabû-hamatu'a, Mazamua)

(*qātu*) 1 *qa-ti* SAA I 64 r.10′ cf. 3 ŠU.2.MEŠ ibid. r.9′ (Ṭab-šar-Aššur)

(*raggintu*) [M]Í.*ra-gi-in-ti*[495] *tar-tu-gu-mu* "A prophetess has prophesied ..." SAA X 352 e.23 (Mar-Issar)

(*šāru*) *šá-a-ri* / ... *i-na-sa-ha* "and the wind ... will be quoted" SAA X 26 r.8′-9′ (Issar-šumu-ereš, Nineveh)

(*šībūtu*) *ši-bu-ti lit-tu-tu* SAA XIII 60:10 (*Urdu-Nabû*, Calah)

---

[493] Alternatively, these examples can also be interpreted to include the progressive vowel assimilation, see 4.5 above.

[494] Note that this passage is a non-verbatim quotation from Šumma Ālu Tablet LV (and thus not really proper Neo-Assyrian), cf. LAS II ad no. 38 r.1-8.

[495] LAS II ad no. 280:23 (Mar-Issar).

-i instead of the expected -Ø:

/mar/	*ma-ri na-ga-ru-ti-ni* "all the enemies" SAA XVI 126:17; *ma-ri dul-lu*!!-*nu* "all the work" ibid. r.22′ (Itti-Šamaš-balaṭu, Phoenicia)
/labār/	*la-ba-ri* UD-*mu* SAA X 348:20 (Mar-Issar)

6.6 Marking the object

The preposition *ana* is used to mark the object in contexts in which there would otherwise be confusion between the subject and the object of the clause.[496] Thus, the following occur:

LÚ.GAL–50-*ia šú-u ša* LÚ.*gur-ra-a-a* URU.*mu-dur-na-a-a / a-na* LÚ.*ha-za-ni ša* URU.*mu-dur-na i-du-ka* "A commander-of-fifty of mine, of the Gurrean (troops) from *Mēturna*, killed the mayor of *Mēturna*" SAA V 53:4-5

LÚ*.EN–MUD.MEŠ *ša a-na /* LÚ*.GAL–URU.MEŠ-*ni i-du-ku-u-ni* "The avengers who killed the vilage managers ..." SAA XV 98 r.7′-8′

a-na PN *a-di* LÚ.TUR.[MEŠ]-⌜*šú*⌝ / *id-du-ku* "They killed PN along with his attendants ..." SAA I 244:11-12 ~

la-áš-šú mi-mi-ni ina ŠÀ-*bi-šú-nu / la i-du-ku* "none of them got killed" SAA V 53 r.4-5

LÚ*.ARAD.MEŠ-*ni / ša* LUGAL *be-lí-ia* É *i-ma-ru-ni / i-du-ka* "he has been killing the king my lord's servants wherever he sees them" SAA V 260 r.6′-8′

LÚ *i-du-ku* "they killed the man" SAA XV 73 r.6′

Also e.g.

PN PN_2 / *a-na* PN_3 *lu-šá-ki-lu* "PN and PN_2 are to support PN_3!" SAA I 172:7-8 (CTN V 173ff)

In these examples, the preposition */ana/* has been added to clauses in which the gender and number of the subject and object are the same, and thus, without this marking, confusion could arise. In the other examples above, */ana/* is not used, since the subject and object are declined in a different number. However, the use of */ana/* was not merely restricted to necessary contexts, but was possibly spreading and becoming the general marker of the accusative in Neo-Assyrian. Obviously, pressure was greater for such a change when the marker of the accusative case was lost after the Middle Assyrian period.[497] In addition, certain verbs, such as *šamû* "to hear, heed" and *ša'ālu* "to ask, enquire," regularly mark their direct object with */ana/*.[498] For example:

LUGAL *a-na* PN / *liš-al* "May the king ask PN" SAA XVI 71:5′-6′

ša a-na LUGAL EN-*ia la a-šam-*[*m*]*u-ni a-na man-ni-ma ah–hur la-áš-me* "If I did not obey the king, my lord, whom else would I obey?" SAA XV 30:8-9

---

[496] Parpola (1984) 192 and 205 n. 29 from which the examples (above) have been taken.

[497] Ibid. 205 n. 29.

[498] Ibid.

Normally an object is not repeated in consecutive clauses; if the object is the same in both clauses, then it is normally mentioned only in the first clause:

UD-20-KÁM / UD-22-KÁM / UD-25-KÁM / *a-na ša-ka-ni* / *ša a-de-e* / *ṭa-a-ba* / *im–ma-at* LUGAL *be-li* / *i-qab-bu-u-ni* / *nu-šá-aṣ-bi-it* / *liš-ku-nu* "The 20th, the 22th and the 25th are good days for concluding the treaty. We shall undertake (that) they may conclude it (i.e. the treaty, *adê*, which is not mentioned again in the following clause) whenever the king, my lord, says" SAA X 5:8- r.6

The practice of not repeating the object naturally has far-reaching consequences, e.g., when reconstructing broken passages. Hence, occasionally we need to guess the most likely object on the basis of a particular verb. For example:

ina muhhī'a šupr[*anni kî adê*] / *issīšunu taškuna*[*nni* "Write me ... [when] you have concluded [a treaty] with them" SAA I 14 r.11-12

This reconstruction appears very probable here since the phrase *adê šakānu*[499] "to conclude a treaty" is often attested, and besides, in this particular case, the historical context is quite well-known.[500]

Instead of the normal object-marking practice, a slightly different case is attested when the object is only a personal suffix in the latter part of a conditional clause:[501]

šúm-ma ú-ṣa-bit-u-ni ina IG[I LUGAL EN-*ia*] / *ú-bal-u-ni-šú-nu* "if they catch them, they will bring them (= -*šunu*) t[o the king, my lord]." SAA V 227 s.2-3 (Šamaš-belu-uṣur). However, it is noteworthy in this connection that the object ("them," i.e "criminals") of the sentence is easy to infer from the context since the word (*parriṣu*) already occurs both as a subject and an object several times earlier in the letter (as LÚ*.LUL.MEŠ on r.15, 22 and LÚ*.*pa-ri-ṣu-u-te* r.25) and still later on in line s.3 (LÚ*.LUL.MEŠ-*te*). The three different ways of writing the plural of *parriṣu* in this letter also gives a clear idea as to how important it was for some writers to avoid writing a word always the same way.

It is not obligatory to repeat an object suffix in consecutive clauses, but it is often repeated.[502] Thus we find:

TA* UGU PN LÚ*.DAM.QAR / *ša* LUGAL EN *iš-pur-an-ni* / *šá-pal* ŠU.2 *a-šap-pa-r*[*a*] / *ú-bal-u-ni-šú ina* U[GU LUGAL EN-*iá*] / *ú-še-bal-a-šú* "As to PN, the merchant about whom the king, my lord, wrote, I shall secretly send word that they bring him to me, and I shall (then) send him t[o the king, my lord]. SAA V 218 r.9-13.

A good example of this practice of repeating object suffix(es) in consecutive clauses is SAA I 245, which lacks the beginning and the end. For this reason, we

---

[499] For examples, see Watanabe (1987) 15ff.

[500] Even though the letter itself is very fragmentary, see, e.g., PNA 1/I p. 143 s.v. Ašpa-bara.

[501] See Deller (1961A) 250, who stresses that the marking of an object suffix – either once or twice – is connected to the subject, depending probably on the position of the subject: whether it is different or the same in the earlier and the later part of a complex sentence.

[502] Cf. Deller (1961A) 250. The example given by Deller, ND 2700:9-10 = NL 3 = CTN V 64ff, is now rendered very differently in the edition. However, this rendering does not appear convincing because it involves grammatical difficulties.

do not know the identity of the man (his name probably being given only once right at the beginning of the letter) whom the king wants to be brought to him.

6.7 Giving orders and prohibiting

Orders are given either by using the imperative or the present tense.[503] The imperative can only be used in positive sentences.[504] E.g.

ṣi-ir-ma dam-me-qa ep-šá "Apply yourselves and do a good job!" SAA XIII 40 r.3

The imperative could even be addressed to the king:

ŠÀ-*ba-ka ṣab-ta* / *qab-le-e-ka ru-ku-us* "Take hold of yourself, prepare for everything!" SAA X 187 e.22-23 (Adad-šumu-uṣur)

or to a superior official by an inferior official:

a-na URU.NINA.KI / *e-ru-ub pa-ni ša* ᵈAG / *pa-ni ša* LUGAL / *ina* DI-*me a-mur* "Enter Nineveh in good spirits and see the face of Nabû (and) the face of the king in peace!" (Tabnî to the palace scribe, his lord) SAA XVI 48:7-10
ú-ma-a ṭè-mu te-re ... "Now send a notice ...!" (Arihu to Nabû-duru-uṣur, his "lord") SAA I 220 r.8e

The construction: *lū lā* + a third- or first-person form of the present[505] is used in negative wishes, i.e. as a vetitive, such as:

PN / *lu la-a i-ka-šir* ... "May PN not succeed ..." SAA I 208 r.8′-9′
1-*en lu-u la-a* / *i-ma-ṭi* / GPA 190:7- e.8, 1-*en lu la i-ma-ṭí* VAT 9744 r.14, 1-*en lu la* LAL "not a single one should be missing" StAT 1 56 r.6
lu la ni-qar-ri-ib/i-qar-ri-ib "May we not arrive"/"He should not advance" SAA XVI 121 r.20e/SAA XVI 77 r.5
me-me-ni / Á-*šú ina dul-li* / *lu la ú-ba-la* "Nobody may take part in the service ..." SAA V 147 r.5-7
lu la a-mu-'a-at "May I not die" SAA XVI 31 r.5′; *lu la a-mu-*[*a*]*t* SAA XVI 127 r.18

lū lā + second-person forms are prohibitives. However, the use of *lū* is not binding in the prohibition construction, but optional. In reality, prohibitions rarely have *lū*:[506]

PI.2-*ka lu la ta-sa-hu-r*[*a* "Do not turn away your attention" SAA XVI 61 r.4′
lu l[*a t*]*a-bat-taq* "You should not cut off" SAA I 1:14 (but cf. CTN V 191)

but

la te-pa-áš "Don't do it!" SAA V 3:18; *la ta-kal-la* SAA I 1:23 (CTN V 188ff); *la ta-pa-làh* "Have no fear!" SAA XVI 60 r.14′; *la ta-pal-la-ha* (2nd pl.) "Fear not!"

---

503 See Hämeen-Anttila (2000) 112.

504 See Lipiński (1997) § 54.6.

505 Ibid. § 47.9 and § 54.6.

506 Cf. Deller (1965C) 79.

e.g. ABL 1186:8′, ABL 541 r.9; *la ta-ši-ṭa* (2nd pl.) “Don’t be negligent!” SAA XIII 40 r.2, SAA XVI 148:16, ABL 623 r.1′

Moreover, the construction *lū lā* + the stative is possible:

LÚ*.EN–*ṭa-ab-ti-ka ù* [LÚ*.EN–KÚR.MEŠ-*k*]*a* / *lu la pa-ri-si* “Your friend and [enemy] should not be treated differently!” SAA XV 91:16′-17′
... *lu la-a hal-*[*qa-ku*] “May I not perish ...” SAA XIII 118 r.9

6.8 Other syntactic variation

Syntactic (as well as semantic) variation also includes, among other things, the study of hendiadys-structures.[507] In Neo-Assyrian, as in the other dialects of Akkadian, these structures include two separate verb forms which combine their meanings to present a single idea. Normally, only one of the two verbs functions as a proper predicate, while the other one can usually be interpreted as an intensifying adverb for the predicate.

A study of all the different clause types, especially the conditional clauses, is a central part of syntactic variation. However, such a detailed study is beyond the scope of this work. However, moving forward in the study of syntactic variation in Neo-Assyrian, among the recently published articles is one on the manifold usage of *maṣi* (in appearance either the stative or status absolutus of the verb *maṣû*).[508] Hopefully, other articles or monographs will also be written about specific syntactic questions in Neo-Assyrian in the not-too-distant future.

[507] Two different explanations for hendiadys-structures based on Old Babylonian are to be found: Kraus (1987), who presents the subject in a more traditional way of grammatical interpretation, though not by the use of terminology, and Buccellati (1995) 377-80, who has a liking for a more modern and linguistical manner of presenting the subject.

[508] See Parker (1997B).

7 SEMANTIC VARIATION

7.1 Semantic merging of the prepositions *ana* and *ina*

Cf. also 4.3.2 and 4.10.

Based on numerous examples, the prepositions *ana* and *ina* were almost completely interchangeable in most Neo-Assyrian contexts. The occurrences of the preposition *ana* in temporal and spatial usage (below), for instance, serve as proof of this merging. Nevertheless, only the preposition *ana* was used as a marker of the accusative (see 6.6). Thus *ana* may be interpreted as being the more marked preposition.

A phonological difference possibly remained between the two prepositions [*ana*] vs. [*ina*]. A clear problem here arises out of the difference between the spellings of these prepositions; *ana* was quite invariably written syllabically <*a-na*>, whereas *ina* almost always appeared only with the AŠ-sign. However, AŠ is ambiguous since it can also be read as *àna*.[509]

The following are some examples in which the expected <*a-na*> has been replaced by <*ina*> = *àna*.[510] These spellings are orthographically unusual in the passages and quite many of them originate from Assur:

ina mi-i-ni "why?" MAss 100 r.3; *ina mì-ni* StAT 1 54 r.3; exceptionally *i-na mi-i-ni* SAA XIII 190 r.5 ~ *a-na mi/ì-i-ni* passim

ina a-hi-te-šú SAA V 90 r.1 ~ *a-na a-*⸢*hi*⸣*-t*[*i-šú* ibid. l. 4′

IM PN / *ina* É *gab-bi* ("the letter of PN to the whole household") KAV 199:1-2 ~ *lu-u* DI-*mu a-na ka-na-šú-nu* ibid. l.3

[DI-*m*]*u* ⸢*ina*⸣ URU.*kal-ha* "the city of Calah is well ..." SAA I 115:5 ~ *lu* DI-*mu a-na* LUGAL EN-*ia* / ⸢DI⸣-*mu a-na* É.KUR.MEŠ ibid. l.3-4, [DI-*mu*] *a-na* MÍ.É.GAL / [DI-*mu*] *a-na* LÚ*.QAL.MEŠ-*te* ibid. l.6-7

DI-*mu ina* É / *a-na* UN.MEŠ "The palace and the inhabitants are well" SAA X 130 r.4-5

lu-u DI-*mu ina* EN-*iá* CTN III 3:4

lu-u DI-*mu ina* [LUGAL EN-*iá*] "Good health to the [king, my lord]" SAA XIII 146:2

[*lu-u*] DI-*mu ina* [*x x x x*] / [*lu*]-*u* DI-*mu a-na* MÍ-*ia* [*x x*] StAT 2 30:3-4

DI-*mu ina* StAT 1 51:7, KAV 215:3, StAT 1 52:4 ~ DI-*mu a-na* passim

---

[509] See LAS II ad no. 39 r.3.

[510] Cf. Hämeen-Anttila (2000) 69f.

/ina/ > */ana/*:
In spatial use:

a-na UGU É.SIG$_4$ "As to the wall" CT 53 319:7′
a-na UGU UN.MEŠ "As to the people about ..." SAA I 258:6
a-na UGU ^{m}*x*[*x* "As to [PN]" SAA V 265:3
a-na UGU *ṭè-e-me a-sa-al-šú* "I asked him about the news" (probably the choice of a prep. is influenced by the verb *ša'ālu* which regularly marks its direct object with *ana*, see p. 169 above) SAA I 45:9
a-na UGU LUGAL [EN-*ia*] / *ú-se-bi-la-*[*šú-nu*] "I am (herewith) sending [them] to the king, [my lord]." SAA V 116 r.3′-4′
a-na URU.*ar-rap-ha* "in Arrapha" NL 72:4 (CTN V 246ff)
a-na ŠÀ-*bi ta-hu-me* "within the area" SAA I 98 r.7′
a-na ma-te-ni "in our country" SAA V 120:5

In temporal use (*ina* originally "at, in, on, during" and *ana* "for"):[511]

a-na ba-a-di "in the evening" SAA XIII 70:6, SAA I 41:11 ~ *ina ba-di-šú* "that evening" SAA XIII 157 r.3; *ina ba-*⸢*a*⸣-[*di* SAA X 2 e.19
a-na ma-a-ti "when?" SAA X 23 r.12 ~ *im-ma-te/ti*, etc. passim
a-na ma-hi-ir-te "*previously*" SAA V 203 r.16′ cf. several temporal expressions, e.g. *ina pānīti*, etc.
a-na si-man ... "at the time of ..." SAA XV 156 r.16
a-na ITI.ZÍZ "in Shebat (XI)" SAA I 77 r.10
a-na šá-al-še (alternatively this could be translated:) "the day after tomorrow" SAA V 199:11; *a-na šal-ši* SAA X 275 r.6; *a-na* 3-*ši* UD-*me-š*[*ú*] "two days later" SAA I 191 r.2
a-na ši-a-ri "tomorrow" SAA X 260:8, SAA X 322 s.1; *a-na ši-a-*[*ri*] SAA XVI 162 r.4′; *a-na/ina ši-ia-a-ri* SAA X 278:8/SAA XVI 114 r.9e; *a–še-'a-ar* (procl.) SAA X 204:6 ~ *iš–ši-a-r*[*i*] SAA X 260:11, *iš/i–ši-a-ri* passim and *ina ši-a-ri* passim; *ina ši-i-a-ri* SAA X 61 r.12
a-na 1-*en* UD-*mu* "on the first day" SAA X 60 r.3
a-na UD-2-KÁM ⸢*ša*⸣ ITI.AB "on the 2nd of Tebet (X)" SAA X 255 r.10 ~ *ina* 2-*i* UD-*me* "on the second day" SAA XIII 157:13'
a-na ha-an-ši UD-*me-šú* "on the fifth day" SAA XIII 157 r.6
a-na UD-7-KÁM-*im-ma* "on the 7th day" SAA X 260 r.5 ~ *ina* UD-29-KÁM SAA X 138:11
a-na UD-24-KÁM[512] "by/on the 24th day" SAA X 255:7
a-na-ku a-na 10 UD.MEŠ / *ina* IGI-*ki a-na-ku* "I will be in your (f.) presence (with)in ten days" CT 53 974 r.12-13 ~ *a-*[*n*]*a-*⸢*ku*⸣ *a-di* 10 UD.MEŠ / *ina* IGI-*ka a-na-ku* "I will be in your (m.) presence (with)in ten days" ibid. obv. 11-12

---

[511] See the table on temporal adverbs, including *ana* and *ina*, in LAS II 146.

[512] See ibid. ad no. 173:7.

7.2 "Exceptional" meanings of some graphemes and words

Normally the MEŠ[513]-sign indicates the plural (of a noun, but it can also denote the plural in verbs,[514] as, e.g., KÚ.MEŠ TH 3 r.2; DU.MEŠ-*ni* SAA XV 84 r.21′ (CTN V 134ff);[515] SAA XV 116 r.11′, ABL 1210:11′; ÍL.MEŠ[516] ABL 1244:3′; ÚŠ.MEŠ[517] passim). In addition to this, MEŠ can function as a marker of a long vowel both in the genitive singular forms (e.g., EN.MEŠ-*šú* = *bēlīšú*),[518] and as a rebus for the first-person singular possessive suffix (homophonic with the plural morpheme -*ī*).[519]

LÚ.ERIM.MEŠ normally represents *ṣābāni* "men, troops, army," but possibly it stands in one instance (SAA X 76 r.2) for *ummânu* "master, scholar, expert" (note the homophony with the word *ummānu* "army, troops"), unless the word for "man" was *ṣabû* in NA.[520]

In some contexts, the meaning of the preposition *ana* is clearly comparative.[521] Thus:

> *a-na* [d]UTU / LUGAL DINGIR.MEŠ / *man-nu* ⌜*id-du-ru*⌝ "Who (now) stays in the dark much longer than Šamaš, the king of the gods?" SAA X 196 e.17-19
>
> *ma-qa-at šá-ru-ru a-na* / AN.MI *da-a'-na* "loss of radiance is (even) more dangerous than an eclipse" SAA X 104 e.16′-17′

But note also:

> *šu-nu-ú ina* UGU-*hi-ku-nu ma-a'-du* "Were they (supposed to be) more numerous than you?" ABL 1186:7

The (pseudo) compound logogram KI.TIM in Neo-Assyrian was read as *kaqquru*, not *erṣetu*.[522]

---

[513] In general, it was possible to manipulate the syllabic readings of a logogram within the same Akkadian lexical root, see Parpola (1998) 322 n. 32 with references and examples. Though MEŠ as a sign for the plural is a special case, and thus not well suited to be compared with logograms signifying lexical roots, its use was certainly as flexible and manipulative as with other signs.

[514] But this usage is by no means typical of verbs in the NA letters.

[515] According to the recent copy, CTN V Pl. 25 (ND 2655), SAA XV 84 r.21′ should be corrected: i.e., no -*u*- before -*ni*.

[516] See p. 178 below.

[517] However, ÚŠ.MEŠ is more often nominal "death; dead (people/animals)," than verbal.

[518] LAS II ad no. 223:9ff and Fales (2000) 232.

[519] See PNA 1/I p. xxiii.

[520] See LAS II ad no. 60 r.2. Sometimes a phonetic complement was used in order to mark the correct reading in cases where the reading of a logogram deviated from its most common value, cf. Leichty (1970) 29.

[521] LAS II ad no. 143:17ff.

[522] Ibid. ad no. 129:6, 21.

Apparently, the logogram LUGAL = *šarru* "king" should be read as *etellu* when the personal name Aššur-etel-šamê-erṣeti-muballissu is written as ᵐaš-šur–LUGAL–AN–KI–TI.BI.[523]

The logogram EN, *bēlu* "lord," had an allograph BE[524] (cf. 7.4). DUMU, *mar'u* "son, boy" can stand for (*am*)*mar* "as much as."[525]

As far as professional titles are concerned, the determinative pronoun *ša* is clearly in free variation with the determinative LÚ (= *amēlu* "man," or probably *a'īlu* in NA). It is important to note the common *i*/*e* ending of the profession *ša-qurbūti* "bodyguard" in particular, when LÚ begins the word.[526] Sometimes both LÚ and *ša* simultaneously appear in the same word. But from time to time, only one or the other is marked, or sometimes neither of them is. Yet the occurrence of *ša* is often concealed behind the abundant use of LÚ(*).[527]

Examples[528] (LÚ.*ša*- ~ LÚ. ~ *ša*-):

(*ša-akussīšu*) LÚ*.*ša–a-ku-si-šú* CTN III 87:22 (copy: CTN I pls. 46-48) ~ *ša–a-ku-si-šú* ibid. r.43

(*ša-bēt-kūdini*) LÚ.*ša*–É–*ku-din* SAA V 79:4, 13, r.1 and passim ~ *ša*–É–*ku-din*(*-ni*) passim in texts from Nimrud (CTN I and CTN III)

(*ša-halluptīšu*) LÚ*.*ša–hal-lu-up-ti-*⌜*šú*⌝*-nu* SAA XII 83 r.14 ~ *šá–hal-lu-up-ti-šú-nu* SAA VII 115 r.i 8

(*ša-lišāni*) 1 LÚ.*šá*–EME SAA XVI 148 r.21e ~ LÚ.EME SAA V 55:5

(*ša-maṣṣarti*) LÚ(*).*ša*–EN.NUN passim ~ *šá–ma-ṣar-ti* StAT 1 20 and StAT 2 238 r.10′ (same text: A 338)

(*ša-pēthalli*) e.g. LÚ*.*šá–pet-hal-la-ti* SAA V 32 s.1; L]Ú*.*šá*–BAD.HAL-*a-te* SAA I 30 r.3; LÚ*.*ša*–BAD-HAL-*lum* SAA XV 129 s.5; *ša*–LÚ*.BAD.HAL-*li-a-ti* SAA XV 118:10′ and *ša*–LÚ*.BAD-HAL SAA V 246 r.7′ (examples of [un]intentional metat.?) ~ 10 LÚ*.ERIM.MEŠ *ša*–BAD.HAL-⌜*a*⌝-[*te* (possibly the repetion of LÚ*. is avoided) SAA V 35 r.2; *šá–pet-hal-li* SAA II 2 iii 21′ ~ also ANŠE.*ša*–BAD-HAL-*la-ti* SAA I 11:11

(*ša-qurbūti*) LÚ*.*qur-bu-ti/e* SAA I 10:12, SAA I 224:10, SAA V 104:7, r.9/SAA I 10:3, SAA I 99 r.17′ and passim

(*ša-ṣallīšu*) LÚ.*ṣal-li-šú-nu* SAA VII 115 r.i 5

(*ša-ziqni*) LÚ*.*šá–ziq-ni* ABL 307:3 and passim; LÚ*.*ša*–SU$_6$.MEŠ SAA V 91:11 ~ ⌜LÚ⌝.*ziq-na-nu* SAA X 257 r.12 ~ *ša–ziq-ni* SAA X 294:21, 30 and passim; *šá*–SU$_6$.MEŠ SAA IX 7:4

---

[523] See ibid. p. 117f with n. 249 and PNA 1/I p. 184f s.v. Aššur-etel-šamê-erṣeti-muballissu.

[524] Parpola (1972) 25.

[525] See n. ad SAA XV 288:13.

[526] Note that the word is also frequently spelled LÚ(*).*qur-bu-tú* (LÚ(*).*qur-bu-tú* SAA XV 236:10) but mainly these spellings are Babylonianisms.

[527] LAS II ad nos. 174 r.12, 294 r.4. Note also the name of an important lexical series: lú = *ša*. B. Landsberger. E. Reiner and M. Civil (eds.), The Series lú = *ša*: A Reconstruction of Sumerian and Akkadian Lexical Lists. MSL 12 (Rome 1969).

[528] For more examples of the alternation LÚ.*ša*– ~ *ša*–, see Radner (1999B) 122, sub *ša husunnīšu*; 123: *ša kubšīšu*; 124: *ša pūlīšu* and *ša zizibīšu*.

<TA*> = /*ana*/, /*ina*/

(1) PN *ša* TA* (= *ana*) LÚ*.3.U$_5$.MEŠ / *ka-a-(a)-ma-nu-te* / LUGAL *be-lí ú-še-lu-u-ni* "PN whom the king, my lord, promoted to the rank of permanent 'third man'" SAA XVI 115:11-13

(2) PN / *ša* TA* (= *ana*) LÚ*.*qur*-ZAG.MEŠ / LUGAL BE *ú-še-lu-u-ni* "PN whom the king, my lord, promoted to the rank of bodyguard" ibid. r.1-3 (Bel-iqiša),

but cf.

(3) PN ... / *ša a-na* LÚ*.GAL–*ki-ṣir-u-tú* / LUGAL *be-lí ú-še-lu-u-ni* "PN whom the king, my lord, promoted to the rank of cohort commander" ibid. ll. 8-10.

In Example (3), an individual is promoted to the high office of *rab-kiṣri/kiṣir*, while in Examples (1) and (2), individuals are also promoted, but along with their promotion, these individuals ended up in a "group of third men/bodyguards." An alternative interpretation would be "from the rank of (permanent) "third man"/bodyguard to something," which does not appear likely on account of (3). The use of TA* in Examples (1) and (2) does not necessarily have to be completely comparable with (3). However, it is difficult to determine if these slight differences in meaning between (1-2) and (3) would really bring about a change in preposition.

TA* UGU (e.g. SAA I 230:5, SAA V 218 r.9, NL 2 r.19′ (CTN V 22ff), NL 3 r.7′ (Face A in CTN V 64ff), NL 12:3, r.3 (CTN V 155ff), NL 43:4, r.15 (CTN V 130ff), NL 95:4 (CTN V 319f), SAA XVI 119:4) ~ *ina muhhi* "As to/Concerning" passim

MAN *be-lí* LÚ*.*qu*]*r-bu-tú* / TA* (*ana*) LÚ.GAR–UMUŠ *u* LÚ*.[ŠÀ.TAM *ša*] GN *i-sap-ra* "[The king, my lord], sent a [bo]dyguard to the commandant and the [prelate of] GN" SAA X 353:14-15

TA* (*ina*) ŠÀ UD-*me an-*[*ni-e*] "presently" SAA X 51 r.5

It is important to bear in mind that *ina* also had the meaning "from, out of." This meaning is otherwise rare, but is common in *ina* ŠÀ(*-bi*) + pl. poss.suff./noun which alternates with TA* ŠÀ(*-bi*) + pl. poss. suff./noun.

2-*a-a* ERIM.MEŠ / *ina* ŠÀ-*bi-šú-nu pi-iq-da* "Appoint two men each from among them" SAA V 257:8′-9′

1-*en ina* ŠÀ-*bi-šu-nu* / *la ú-še-zib* "Not even one of them escaped" SAA XVI 105 r.10-11

1-*en ina* ŠÀ LÚ.TU–É *e-ta-mar-šú* "One of the clergymen saw him" SAA XIII 134:14′-15′ ~

4 LÚ*.ERIM.MEŠ / TA ŠÀ-*bi-šú-nu* / *a-na mu-da-bi-r*[*i*] / *ih-tal-qu-n*[*i*] "Four men from among them ran away to the desert" SAA XV 53:10-e.13

ERIM.MEŠ TA* ŠÀ-*šú-nu de-e-ku* "Some of the men were killed" SAA XIII 128 s.1

<TA*> = /*issi*/ is normally "with" but can sometimes be interpreted as "and":

a-na-ku / TA* PN *ni-sa-al-lam* "I *and* PN are making peace" SAA XVI 17 r.10′-11′. On the other hand, *issi* is obligatory with *salāmu* "to make peace with s.o."

a-ta-a a-na-ku TA* PN / *ina bir-tu-šú-nu ik-ki-ni ku-ri lib-bi-ni* / *šá-pil* "Why then must I and PN, amidst them, be restless and depressed?" SAA X 226 r.4-6

ši-i TA* *am-mu-te-em-ma mé-e-tú* "She and the others died" SAA X 199 r.15′

šu-u TA* [md]PA–*še-zib* / EN–MUN *ša* LUGAL KÁ.DINGIR.KI *šú-nu* "He and Nabû-(u)šezib are friends of the king of Babylon" ABL 896:5-6 (Aia-zeru-qiša)

DUMU–MAN TA* [md]GIŠ.NU_{11}–MU–GI.NA / ... / *a-na qa-an-ni la ú-ṣu-u* "the crown prince and Šamaš-šumu-ukin should not go outdoors ..." SAA X 314:7′-9′

LÚ.GAL–50 TA* LÚ.ERIM.MEŠ-*šú* / ... / ... *e-ta*[*r*]-*bu* "The commander-of-fifty and his soldiers ente[r]ed ..." SAA V 53:20-22

LÚ.GAL–50-*ia* TA* 1-*me* L[Ú.ERIM.MEŠ] // ... / *i–da-at* PN *it-tal-ku-u-ni* "My commander-of-fifty and 100 ... [ho]plites went after PN ..." SAA V 53 e.27-r.2

ma-da-tú TA* ANŠE.*ku-din* / ... *pa-aq-du* "the tribute and the mules are entrusted ..." SAA I 33:11-12

<*a-du*> = <*issi*> "with" > "and"

šu-u-tú a-du ⸢PAB⸣.MEŠ-*šú* / [*ip-ta*]*l-hu a–dan-niš* "he and his brothers had become very scared" SAA I 39 r.3′-4′ cf.

LÚ*.2-*ú* ... / 9 LÚ*.ERIM.MEŠ *i-si-šú ina* ŠÀ GIŠ.BAN / *ma-hu-ṣu* "The deputy ... and nine of his soldiers were struck down by a bow" SAA V 3 r.5-7

LÚ*.EN.NAM / ... LÚ*.EN.NAM 2-*u* / *i-si-šú* ... / ... *i-na-ṣur* (dissimil. 3rd pl.) "The governor ... and his deputy governor are keeping watch" ibid. obv. 9-12

ša / *šá* "that/since/because"[529]

(1) SAA X 39:14, (2) SAA X 217 r.3, (3) SAA X 218 r.17e, (4) SAA X 228:22 [(1) and (4) an ellipsis for: *ina muhhi ša*; (2) and (3) *nēmel*/TA$^{(*)}$ *pa-an*]

<ÍL> = /*elû*/

la [ŠU.2 MAN] / *la* ÍL.MEŠ "may they not fall out of [the hands of the king]" ABL 1244:2′-3′ (Assurbanipal) cf. TA* ŠU.2 LUGAL / [*la-a e*]*l-li-ú* ABL 1108:16′-17′ (Assurbanipal. This phrase is more frequent in NB)

Here MEŠ is perhaps a kind of "syllabical logogram" *il*-MEŠ$^{?}$ = *el-li-ú*. Moreover, another interesting variation appears in these examples: *la* [ŠU.2] ~ TA* ŠU.2. The *la* of the first example is not the negative *lā* but corresponds to the preposition TA* = *issu*; an Aramaism which had possibly spread to Neo-Assyrian through Babylonian.[530] Cf.

la ŠÀ LUGAL U-*ia la el-li* "I must not become estranged from the king, my lord." SAA XIII 174 r.6; *la* [ŠU.2] LUGAL EN-*iá* / [*l*]*a el-li* "May I not drift apart from the king, my lord!"SAA X 166 r.9-10 (both examples are NB)

7.3 Homonym DUMU/*mar'u* "son," exceptionally "lord"

Due to Aramaic influence, the logogram DUMU, normally in NA *mar'u* "son, boy," may be taken as "lord."[531] There is at least one case (1) in a NA letter in which the interpretation "son, boy" does not make sense. Apparently in this case, the geographical origin of the writer of the letter was decisive. The sender had a

---

529 LAS II ad no. 125:22.

530 Cf. Lipiński (1997) § 48.7.

non-Akkadian name (Arihu[532]) and his letter was possibly sent from the province of Laqê (cf. SAA I 261:2′-6′), located in the middle Euphrates region.

(1) *a-na* ^{md}PA–BÀD–PAB / IM ^{m}*a-ri-hi lu* DI-*mu* / *a-na* ⸢DUMU⸣-*ia* "A letter from Arihu to Nabû-duru-uṣur. Good health to my lord!" SAA I 220:1-3. Note ⸢EN⸣ = *bēlu* "lord" on l. 5.

cf.

(2) [*a-na*] ^{md}PA–BÀD–PAB / [I]M ^{m}DINGIR-*a-a*–EN / [*lu*] DI-*mu a-na* EN-*ia* "A letter from Ila'i-Bel [to] Nabû-duru-uṣur. [Good] health to my lord!" SAA I 215:1-3

(3) *a-na* ^{md}PA–BÀD–PAB EN-*ia* / ARAD-*ka* ^{m}*ri-mu-te* / *lu* DI-*mu a-na* EN-*ia* "To Nabû-duru-uṣur, my lord: your servant Rimutte. Good health to my lord!" SAA I 221:1-3

It is crucial to interpret these three examples according to the normal letter hierarchy. According to the usual letter hierarchy, the higher ranking person is always mentioned first, and it makes no difference if he/she is the sender or the receiver of the letter:

IM/*ṭuppi* ... [sender: a superior official]	*ana* ... [receiver: superior]
ana ... [receiver: an inferior official]	IM/*ṭuppi*/ARAD-ka ... [sender: inferior]

Thus, only after the name of the individual with the higher status was mentioned, would the name of the person with the lower position in the Assyrian official machinery follow.

7.4 Synonymous logograms[533]

Adad "(God) Adad" > ^{d}IM (passim) = ^{d}10 (passim in personal names)

[531] The same semantic variation, as a result of phonetic similarity between the Neo-Assyrian *mar'u* and the contemporary Aramaic **mar'e* (or similar form) "lord," is attested in some personal names such as Mar-larim, see Fales (1977) 49 no. 24 (and PNA 2/II s.v. Mar-larim 3.d., p. 740), who labels this phenomenon "improper encoding." Cf. also PNA 2/II s.v. Mar-bi'di (p. 702), Mar-lihia (p. 740), Mar-nuri (p. 741) and Mar-suri (p. 741) whose Aramaic "[The] Lord ..." names have also occasionally been written with the DUMU sign in Neo-Assyrian sources.

[532] PNA says, 1/I p. 131, in the etymological section of the name *Arihu*: "(mng. unknown); Sem."

[533] The list does not include logograms that differ only graphically from their variant, such as TA ~ TA* or LÚ ~ LÚ*. In case no other discernible difference is found, slight variants with or without mainly optional determinatives (e.g., ANŠE, DINGIR, DUG, GIŠ, KUR, KUŠ, LÚ, MÍ, MUL, MUŠEN, NA_4, ŠE, ŠEM, SÍG, TÚG, Ú, UDU, URU, UZU, ZÍD) are not listed. In addition, some of the words on the list can hardly be called synonyms since the logograms themselves are the same in these words, but one (optional) element is omitted from some writings, e.g., ANŠE.KUR.RA ~ ANŠE.KUR, etc. Nevertheless, I have included these cases in the list.

A quite similar type of list of synonyms, in a wider Akkadian context, is published by von Soden and Röllig (1967) 75-76.

ahu “arm” > Á.2 (passim) = Á (e.g. ⸢Á⸣-*šú-nu* SAA V 294:2′; Á-*šú* SAA V 147 r.6, SAA I 210 r.11, SAA XIII 34 r.5)

ahu “brother” > ŠEŠ (passim) = PAB (passim), variation even within one letter, e.g. *ana* PAB-*iá* StAT 1 51:3 ~ *ana* ŠEŠ-*iá* ibid. l.6

Akkad > KUR–URI.KI (passim) = A.GA.DÈ.KI (A.GA.[DÈ.KI] SAA X 352:6)

aladlammû “bull colossus” > (NA$_4$.)^{d}ALAD.^{d}LAMA (passim) = NA$_4$.^{d}LAMA.^{d}ALAD ([N]A$_4$.^{d}LAMA.⸢^{d}⸣[ALAD SAA I 166:7) = NA$_4$.^{d}LAMA.ALAD (passim in SAA XV 283)

alpu “ox, bull” > GUD (passim) = GUD.NITÁ (passim). E.g. GUD(.MEŠ) SAA X 294:33 ~ GUD.NITÁ ibid. l.18

aplu “heir” > DUMU.UŠ = A. Both passim in personal names

atānu “mare” > MÍ.ANŠE.KUR.RA (SAA V 47:9, 15; cf. also URU.BÀD-MÍ.ANŠE.MEŠ-*te* SAA V 227 r.13) = ANŠE.MÍ.HÚB (ANŠE.MÍ.HÚB.MEŠ SAA V 122 r.4) = KUR.MÍ.HÚB (KUR.MÍ.HÚB.MEŠ SAA V 171:11)

Bābili “Babylon” > (URU.)KÁ.DINGIR.RA.KI (passim) = (URU.)KÁ.DINGIR.KI (passim) = KÁ.DINGIR (SAA V 293 r.3, SAA XIII 56 r.7) = (URU.)KÁ.DINGIR.RA (SAA I 33:15, SAA X 50 e.13)

balāṭu “life” > TI.LA (passim) = TI (for instance *a-na* TI SAA X 218 r.6 and in personal names, e.g. ^{m}PA-TI-AŠ StAT 1 13:3 ~ ^{m}PA–TI.LA–AŠ ibid. e. 6 [env.])

bēltu “mistress, lady” > GAŠAN (e.g. SAA X 359:4, SAA II 2 v 12; GAŠAN-*ia* SAA X 348:13) = NIN (SAA II 2 vi 15, 16; ⸢^{d}⸣NIN.⸢É⸣.GAL SAA X 368:8). See the Belet– personal names in PNA 1/II pp. 296-98. Cf. also DINGIR.MAH = *bēlet ilī* (SAA II 6:19U, A, 29A, frg)

bēlu “lord” > EN = BE = BE.LUM = U. BE is a geographical variant of EN.[534] EN passim; BE SAA XIII 33:6, SAA VIII 140 r.2 (both: Assur), SAA XV 121:1, 3, 6, 14, SAA XV 122:1, 3, r.7′; SAA XV 125:3′, 5′, e.8′; SAA XV 126:3, 6 (all: Der), SAA XVI 21:20 (Babylon), SAA XVI 115 r.3 (Bel-iqiša), SAA V 146:3, 4, 18; SAA V 168:2, 4, r.8e (from eastern Kurdistan); SAA V 105:15 (Kumme), SAA XVI 41:1, 6, 8, 9, r.5; CT 53 176:1 (unkn.); BE.LUM SAA V 238:6; U-*iá* SAA XVI 19:3, 4 (Assurbanipal), StAT 2 317:2, 4 (unkn.); ^{md}PA–U–PAB (Nabû-belu-uṣur) SAA I 258:2.

da'ānu/danānu/dannu “(to be) strong” > KALAG (passim) = KALAG.GA (e.g. KALAG.GA.MEŠ SAA I 98:10)

damqu “good” SIG$_5$ (passim) = SIG (SAA VI 206:1)

Ēa “(God) Ea” > ^{d}É.A (passim) = ^{d}60 (SAA II 2 vi 8, SAA XVI 88:5; ^{d}60–MAN SAA XIII 45:9′) = $^{d+}$EN.KI (SAA X 345 r.10, cont. broken)

ebūru “harvest” > (ŠE.)BURU$_{14}$ (passim) = GURUN.BURU$_{14}$ (SAA V 97 r.2′) = ŠE.GÁN (SAA XV 286 r.8′) = ŠE.ŠIBIR (SAA XV 63:11′)

ekallu “palace” > É.GAL (passim) = KUR (LÚ$^{(*)}$.A.BA KUR SAA I 34 r.19′, SAA X 130:1, LÚ.600–KUR KAV 213:7; KUR–*ma-šar-ti* SAA XVI 21 r.15; LÚ*.*šá*–IGI–KUR SAA V 295 r.11)

Elamtu “Elam” > (KUR.)NIM.MA.KI (passim) = KUR.NIM.KI (SAA IX 7 e.14, SAA X 355 r.14; NIM.KI-*a-a* SAA X 185 r.6)

eqlu “field” > A.ŠÀ (passim) = A.ŠÀ.GA (rarer), cf. A.ŠÀ.GA SAA I 233:19, r.12 ~ A.ŠÀ ibid. 24, 25, r.13

ēreš < *erāšu* “to request, desire”) > KAM/KÁM = APIN (all of them passim in personal names, usually together with the phonetic complement -*eš*)

[534] See Parpola (1997A) 318 n. 10.

	almost synonyms?: *(bēt-)erš|i/u* (GIŠ.NÁ passim; É–GIŠ.NÁ passim SAA XIII) ~ *bēt-maiāli* (É–KI.N[Á] SAA XIII 200 r.3, [*x x x* É$^{?}$–K]I$^{?}$.NÁ ibid. r.6, É–KI.NÁ.MEŠ SAA X 263 r.6) "bedroom"
gallābu	"barber" > LÚ.ŠU.I ([LÚ].ŠU.I SAA X 210:13) = LÚ.ŠU.U.I (SAA X 211 r.1)
Gula	"(God) Gula" > ^{d}ME.ME (passim, see PNA 1/II pp. 428-30) = ^{d}ME (SAA II 2 vi 11, CT 33 15a r.6, SAA XIV 78 r.14e, CT 53 974:1, r.3)
hūlu	"road, way" > KASKAL = KASKAL.2. Both passim
Illil	"(God) Enlil" > ^{d}BE (passim) = $^{d(+)}$EN.LÍL (e.g. SAA X 174:1, SAA X 212 r.1, SAA X 237 r.7′, SAA X 294 r.26, SAA II 3 r.3′, SAA II 6:16G, 26A, frg, 659frg. These examples may be interpreted as Babylonianisms.)
imāru	"donkey" > ANŠE (e.g. ANŠE.MEŠ SAA I 244:18, SAA II 6:277A, B, Y, frg, SAA V 52 r.13) = ANŠE.NITÁ (e.g. SAA I 26:5 [CTN V 213f], SAA II 6:491D)
Inurta	"Ninurta" > ^{d}MAŠ (passim) = ^{d}NIN.URTA (SAA IX 5:6, SAA X 197:12, SAA X 227:6, SAA X 228:5, SAA X 329:7, SAA X 334:5)
Issār	"(Goddess) Ištar" > ^{d}15 (passim) = ^{d}INNIN (SAA XIII 149:2, 6, r.1, 3; SAA II 2 vi 16; $^{d+}$INNIN–GIŠ.TUK SAA I 141 r.2) = ^{d}IŠ.TAR[535] (e.g. SAA XIII 154:5, SAA II 5 iv 2′; SAA II 6:264B, i, 453A, g, l, 459frg, SAA V 146 r.7)
KÁM	= KAM (as marker of numbers, especially of ordinal numbers)
kunāšu	"emmer" > ŠE.ZÍZ.ÀM.MEŠ SAA XI 28:6 = ŠE.ZÍZ.MEŠ SAA XVI 5:12
lē'u	"writing board" > GIŠ.ZU (e.g. SAA I 128:18, SAA X 101 r.8; SAA X 202:10, 11; SAA X 295:4, SAA XIII 39:14) = GIŠ.DA ([GIŠ].DA *ša* MUL.APIN SAA X 62:13) = GIŠ.LI.U_5.UM (SAA XVI 139:11, SAA XVI 5:19, SAA I 192 r.4, SAA X 384 r.1, SAA XIII 100:8); once also GIŠ.U_5.LI *x*[*x* ABL 1022:23 (Assurbanipal)
lēšir	(< *ešāru* "to be/go well, prosper") > SI.SÁ = GIŠ. Both passim in personal names. E.g. Nabû-zeru-lešir: ^{md}PA–NUMUN–SI.SÁ SAA X 2:2 ~ ^{md}PA–NUMUN–GIŠ SAA X 3:2
libbu	"heart" > ŠÀ (passim) = ŠÀ.2 (ŠÀ.2.MEŠ-*šú* SAA X 91:8)
manû	"mina" > MA.NA (passim) = MA (1 MA SAA I 52 r.6′, ½ MA ibid. r.7′, StAT 1 55:4′)
Marduk	"(God) Marduk" > ^{d}AMAR.UTU (passim) = ^{d}ŠÚ (SAA XVI 88:5, SAA V 127:4, SAA X 351:2, SAA X 358:2, SAA XIII 134 r.2, Rfdn 17 28:5) = ^{d}MES (at least in SAA I 128:4, SAA XIII 19:4, SAA XIII 127:4, SAA VIII 126:4, SAA X 127:4, SAA XVI 48:4 and often in personal names)
mār šipri	"messenger" > LÚ.A.KIN (passim) = LÚ.KIN.A(.MEŠ) SAA V 164:5, 6, 12
mar'u	"son, boy" > DUMU (passim) = A (A PN, e.g. SAA I 230:8, 10, r.2; SAA XV 295:4, r.7; StAT 1 55:5′, r.5. Both in the same text, e.g. DUMU PN Grayson [1991] 1:2 ~ A PN ibid. 7, 25)
masennu(/*rab–māsiāni*)	"treasurer" > LÚ.IGI.DUB (passim) = LÚ.GAL.TUG.UD[536]
maṣṣartu	"watch, guard" > EN.NUN = EN.NUN.NA. Both passim

[535] In Neo-Assyrian *<*š* + *t*> is normally <*ss*>. Perhaps the writing ^{d}IŠ.TAR is to be interpreted as a frozen, conservative spelling.

[536] It is unclear if LÚ.GAL–TÚG.UD really refers to the *masennu*, but it is not at all excluded. See Radner (1999A) 49-52.

Māt Amurrî "Westland" > KUR–MAR (SAA X 100:13, r.14) = KUR–MAR.TU (SAA X 351:19) = KUR.MAR.TU.KI (SAA X 26 r.4′; SAA X 75 r.2; SAA X 347 r.13′; SAA X 351:16, 17)

mātāti (pl.) "countries" > KUR.KUR (passim) = KUR.MEŠ (e.g. SAA X 174:14, SAA V 79:11, cf. *sissû*)

MEŠ = ME (as plural markers) alternate sometimes even in the same letter, e.g. URU.MEŠ SAA I 172:12 (CTN V 173ff) ~ URU.ME-*šú-nu* ibid. l.13; URU.ME SAA I 182:9′ ~ [U]RU.MEŠ-*ni* ibid. r.10; SIG_4.ME SAA V 291:13′, r.8 ~ SIG_4.MEŠ ibid. r.4, 5

Nabû "(God) Nabu" > ^{d}AG = ^{d}PA. Both passim

nāgir ekalli "palace herald" > LÚ(*).ŠÚ.NIGÍR–É.GAL (SAA V 227 r.27e) = LÚ.600–KUR (KAV 213:7, SAA I 170:6, SAA V 149:20); LÚ.600–É.GAL (passim) = LÚ.NIGIR/NIGÍR–É.GAL (both passim)

nāgiru "herald." The same variants are attested as in the first element of the compound *nāgir ekalli*, i.e. LÚ$^{(*)}$.|600/NIGIR/NIGÍR (passim) and LÚ*.ŠÚ.NIGÍR.MEŠ (SAA XV 222 r.4)

Nergal "Nergal" > ^{d}U.GUR = ^{d}MAŠ.MAŠ = ^{d}ŠEŠ.GAL. The first two writings passim. ^{d}ŠEŠ.GAL SAA VI 87 r.4

niqiu "offering"> (UDU.)SISKUR.SISKUR(.MEŠ)(passim) = (UDU.)SISKUR(.MEŠ) (passim)

nukaribbu "gardener" > LÚ*.NU.GIŠ (SAA I 128:15) = LÚ*.NU.GIŠ.SAR (SAA I 179:8, SAA I 216:4)

pāhutu "governor; province" > LÚ.EN.NAM (passim) = LÚ.NAM (passim) = NAM (SAA I 36 r.5′, SAA I 97:9; SAA V 250 r.14′) "province"

qātu "hand" > ŠU.2 (passim) = ŠU (e.g. SAA I 87 e.17, SAA V 116:2′, 4′; SAA IX 3 ii 1)

saharšuppû "leprosy" > SAHAR.ŠUB.BA (SA]HAR.ŠUB.B[A] SAA X 327:1, SAHAR.ŠUB.BA-*a* SAA II 4 iv 5) = SAHAR.ŠUB (SAHAR.ŠUB-*pu* SAA II 6:419, SAA II 11 r.11′)

Sîn "(Moon god) Sin" > ^{d}30 (passim) = $^{d(+)}$EN.ZU (SAA I 188 r.1; $^{d+}$EN.[ZU$^{?}$] SAA XIII 156:5)

sissû "horse" > ANŠE.KUR.RA = ANŠE.KUR = KUR.RA = KUR (all of these passim, KUR, cf. *mātāti*)

ṣarrāpu "goldsmith" > LÚ.SIMUG.KÙ.GI = LÚ.KÙ.DÍM[537] = KÙ[538]

šaknu "governor; prefect" > (LÚ.)GAR = LÚ.GAR.KUR. Both passim. LÚ.GAR always$^{(?)}$ with a complement: LÚ.GAR-*nu*/*i*

Šamaš "Šamaš" > ^{d}UTU (passim) = ^{d}GIŠ.NU/GIŠ.NU_{11} (both GIŠ.NU and GIŠ.NU_{11} common e.g. in the name Šamaš-šumu-ukin)

šamnu "oil" > Ì.MEŠ (passim) = Ì.GIŠ (SAA II 10:9′, SAA X 108 r.11e, SAA X 294:10, SAA XIII 76:12) = Ì (SAA X 318 r.3, SAA X 323 e.15, 16) = Ì.GIŠ.MEŠ (SAA X 315 r.4, SAA X 316 r.8)

šarru "king" > LUGAL = MAN. Both passim

šat urri "morning watch" > EN.NUN–UD.ZAL.LI (e.g. SAA X 78:7′, SAA X 137 r.1) = EN.NUN–UD.ZAL (SAA X 149:4′) = EN.NUN–UD.ZAL.LA (see SAA VIII, cf. also a gloss: *e-nu-un ú-*⌜*za-al*⌝*-la* SAA X 78:5′)

---

[537] Possibly KÙ.DÍM is to be read syllabically as *kuttimmu* "goldsmith". However, such a syllabic writing has not been attested, see Radner (1999A) 42f. It is actually not entirely clear whether *ṣarrāpu* and *kuttimmu* are really synonyms, see Kwasman, AfO 48/49 (2001/2002) 222.

[538] Radner loc.cit.

šattu	"year" > MU.AN.NA (passim) = MU (as a Babylonianism: MU.MEŠ SAA X 283:4, SAA IX 1 iv 16)
šēpu	"foot/feet" > GÌR.2 (passim) = GÌR (at least: GÌR-*šú* SAA XIII 70 r.2, GÌR-*ia* [cont. broken] SAA X 254:14′, GÌR [cont. broken] SAA X 308:8 cf. also 2 GÌR.MEŠ SAA I 243:3′ and 1-*et* GÌR-*šú-nu* SAA I 244 r.12)
Šihṭu	"Mercury" > ^{d}GUD.UD (e.g. SAA X 152 r.2, SAA X 224:12, MUL.GUD.UD SAA X 51 s.1) = (MUL.)UDU.IDIM.GUD.UD (e.g. SAA II 6:14A, SAA X 197:10, SAA XIII 72:10 and passim)
šuillakku	"hand-lifting (prayer)" ŠU.ÍL.LÁ.KAM (SAA X 240:22 + MEŠ ibid. 5, r.10; SAA X 206 r.4′) = ŠU.ÍL.KAM (ŠU.ÍL.KAM.MEŠ SAA X 296:17, ŠU.ÍL.KAM-*ni* SAA X 277 r.1)
tadānu	"to give" > AŠ = SUM, (in personal names), e.g. ⸢*a-na* ^{md}PA–NUMUN–SUM-*na*⸣ StAT 1 52:1 (env., left edge) ~ *a-na* ^{md}PA–NUMUN–AŠ ibid. 1 (the inner tablet). Essentially, all the SUM-writings are Babylonianisms. Note also the rare way of writing: ^{md}15–MU–A for Issar-nadin-apli SAA VI 314 r.24. However, in Neo-Assyrian the logogram MU was normally reserved for the word *šumu* "name."
ṭāb(a/u)	(< *ṭiābu* "to be good") > DÙG.GA = DÙG. Both passim
ṭuppu	"(clay) tablet" > IM (passim) = DUB (DUB.MEŠ SAA X 101:2, 3, 10; SAA X 102 r.6′. Cf. also DUB.IM SAA VI 23 r.12)
ṭupšarru	"scribe" > LÚ.A.BA (passim) = LÚ(*).DUB.SAR (SAA X 98 r.12; SAA X 225 r.11; SAA X 349 e.28, SAA XVI 98:2 obvious Babylonianisms)
ukīn, kēn	(< *kuānu* "to be true," *kunnu* D "to establish, confirm") > GIN (passim) = GI.NA (passim) = GI = GIN.NA. The two last-mentioned ones e.g. in the place-name Dur-Šarrukin: URU.BÀD–^{m}MAN–GIN.NA SAA V 119:4; URU.BÀD–LUGAL–GI SAA V 133:4
ušburrudû	"anti-witchcraft magic" > UŠ$_{12}$.BÚR.RU.DA (passim) = UŠ$_{12}$.BÚR.DA (UŠ$_{12}$.BÚR.D[A.MEŠ SAA X 316 r.21)

MUL is *kakkubu* "star," but when writing about gods, referring to their astral forms of existence, then also ^{d}(= DINGIR) + a proper name is possible. See, for example, the following variation: MUL.*dil-bat* ~ ^{d}*dil-bat* and MUL.SAG.ME.GAR ~ ^{d}SAG.ME.GAR in the glossary of SAA X.

Some geographical names contain an alternation between the determinatives URU "city" and KUR "land, country":[539]

> KUR.*hi-in-za-ni* SAA I 82 r.2 ~ URU.*hi-in-za-ni* ibid. 14; URU.*am-pi-ha-bi* SAA X 361 r.7 ~ KUR.*am*$^{!!}$*-pi-ha-a-bi* SAA V 233:6; KUR.*hu-buš-ki-a* SAA V 135:7, SAA V 194:4 ~ URU.*hu-bu-u*[*š-ki-a*] SAA V 195:2′. However, the distinction between the city proper and the area surrounding it is often made in this sort of writing.

In the so-called nisbe-adjectives, which express geographical origins, the determinative LÚ can sometimes be used instead of URU or KUR, and the combination of two different determinatives is also possible:

> LÚ*.*ak-kad-u-a* SAA X 352 r.7, LÚ*.URU.*ak-kad-u-a* SAA X 368 r.6′; KUR.*kal-dà-a-a* SAA V 59:5, LÚ*.*kal-da-a-a* SAA V 79 r.2; SAA V 80 r.3′, SAA V 172:5; KUR.*mu-ṣur-a-a* SAA XIII 13:14, LÚ*.*mu-ṣur-a-a* SAA XIII 144 r.10; LÚ*.UNUG.KI-*a-a* SAA X 349:6, LÚ*.URU.UNUG.KI-*a-a* SAA XV 138:6; LÚ.KUR.*pil-la-ta-a-*[*a*] SAA VII 60 r. i 6′.

---

[539] Cf. Kataja, SAAB 1 (1987) 67 n. 9.

The combination LÚ.KUR + GN (+ *-a-a*) is not used in NA letters, but it occurs several times in royal inscriptions and in NB letters.

7.5 Gender variation of nouns[540]

Some nouns may occur in Neo-Assyrian both as masculine and feminine. This fluctuation of gender can be observed by studying (a) the agreement of a noun with its adjectival attribute, (b) a subject's concord with its conjugated verb form, and (c) the predicative agreement in a nominal phrase as, for instance, the use of the masculine pronoun *šû*. E.g.

(GISKIM[541] = *ittu* "sign, omen") (m.) GISKIM-*šú la i-lap-pa-*[*at*] SAA VIII 98 r.2; *šu-u* GISKIM *ka-a-a-ma-nu* ibid. r.7; GISKIM *la-ap-tu* SAA X 2:15 ~ (f.) GISKIM-*šú* // *la-ap-ta-at* SAA X 104 e.17′-r.1; GISKIM.MEŠ ... / *am–mar ši-na-ni* SAA X 2:6-7; *it-tum ul ta-lap-pat* SAA VIII 307 e.6

(*martu*[542] "gall [bladder], bile") (m.) *mar-tu* / ... / *it-tu-šib* SAA X 217 e.13-15 ~ (f.) *ki-i šá mar-tu mar-rat-u-ni* "Just as gall is bitter ..." SAA II 6:646

The gender of the planet Venus (*Dilbat*) probably alternated at least partly according to its position in relation to the sun: as the morning star, Venus was masculine, the evening star was feminine.[543] E.g.

(f.) [MUL].*dil-bat* / ... / ... *nap-ha-ta* SAA X 31 r.3-5 (cf. also ibid. ll.2′-3′); M]UL.*dil-bat nam-rat* SAA X 72:7 ~ (m.) MU[L.*dil-bat*] / [*la*] *in-n*[*a-mar*] SAA X 72 e.22-23; [*ki-m*]*a* MUL.*dil-bat it-ta-mar* SAA X 74 r.15; [MU]L.*dil-bat pa-ni-šú* / ... *is-sa-kan* ibid. r.17-18; MUL.*dil-bat a-na* MUL.AB.SÍN / *i-kaš-šad* SAA X 224:10-11; ^{d}*dil-bat* / ... *i-kun* SAA X 23 r.10-11

Note also an extraordinary stative form:

(*kizirtu*) *ki-zir-tú šá-kin* SAA X 30:6 (i.e. masculine stative for a word that looks feminine)[544]

Some words appear masculine but are in fact feminine[545] (or in some cases both masculine and feminine), such as:

abullu, *ekallu*, *ekurru*, *eleppu*, *eršu*, *gulgullu*, *kanīku*, *liginnu*, *lišānu*, *nādu*, *niqiu*, *qarnu*, *qinnu*, *ubānu*, *ūmu*, *unqu*, *urpu*, *urû*, *uznu* and so on.

---

[540] On the phenomenon in Semitic languages in general, see e.g. Lipiński (1997) § 30.5. For example, a psychological or sociological reason may be decisive but still hidden in the background of the gender change of a word, cf. Paddock (1991) 29-46.

[541] LAS II ad nos. 30:15, 325 r.2.

[542] Ibid. ad no. 152:13ff.

[543] See ibid. ad no. 69 + 71 r.4′, as well as about the hermaphrodite nature of the planet, e.g. ibid. 77 n. 157.

[544] For a discussion about the meaning and gender of *kizirtu*, see LAS II ad no. 318:3.

[545] Cf. GAG § 60a, d.

As an indication of the occasional wavering between masculinity and femininity, at least on a psychological level, note that it was, for instance, possible to address Queen Naqi'a using the masculine form:[546]

> *a-na* AMA–LUGAL EN-*ia/iá* "To the queen mother, my 'lord'" SAA XIII 76:1/5, *a-na* AMA–MAN EN-*iá* ibid. l. 3, *ša* AMA–MAN *be-lí iš-pur-an-ni/i-qab-bu-u-ni* ibid. l. 10/r.9-10; however, cf. the use of the second-person feminine singular possessive suffix referring to Naqi'a in ARAD-*ki* ibid. l. 2, ŠU.2-*ki* ibid. l. 7 and *taq*-[*bu-u-ni* ibid. r.2.

See also SAA X 16, SAA X 200,[547] SAA XIII 77, SAA XIII 188; NB letters: SAA X 313; SAA XVIII 10, SAA XVIII 85).

One of the many possible explanations[548] is that the prestigious "lord" refers to the mental and physical qualities of the queen mother which were actually not "inferior to those of the male gods." Note the queen mother "whose verdict is as final as that of the gods ..."[549] or "the queen mother is as able as (the sage) Adapa!"[550] However, this theory is neither supported nor undermined by the following address:

> ⌜*a*⌝-*na* MÍ.GAŠAN–⌜GIŠ EN⌝-*iá* / ARAD-*ki* ᵐᵈPA–PAB–AŠ "To (the lady) Balti-lešir, my lord: your (f.) servant Nabû-ahu-iddina" SAA XVI 56:1-2.

Be that as it may, it would not be surprising if this otherwise unknown lady, Balti-lešir,[551] was, in fact, a *šakintu* or some other high female official serving the queen mother at the royal court.

---

546 See Hämeen-Anttila (2000) 115, cf. LAS II 147 n. 286.

547 In l. 7, EN-*ia* might theoretically be interpreted ambiguously as referring either to the king or to the queen mother, but the latter is preferred (cf. SAA X 244:11f, albeit in this passage the use of the periphrastic genitive "the mother of the king" instead of "the queen mother" in the English translation does not convey the nuance of Assyrian very well).

548 See also Hämeen-Anttila loc.cit.

549 SAA X 17 r.1ff.

550 SAA X 244 r.7-9, cf. Melville (1999) 32f.

551 PNA 1/II s.v. Belet-lešir, p. 297.

8 CONCLUSIONS

Introduction

In the first half of the first millennium BCE, the Neo-Assyrian dialect underwent substantial grammatical changes. This dialect grew apart from Middle and Old Assyrian, its forerunners. It should be noted that in the case of Middle Assyrian this may be partially untrue since there are far fewer extant Middle Assyrian letters than Neo-Assyrian. Moreover, many Middle Assyrian letters have only quite recently been excavated (especially letters from Dur-Katlimmu), and the entire Middle Assyrian letter corpus has not been the subject of a single comparative study (however, see Cancik-Kirschbaum [1996] 49-71). In any case, the grammatical structure of Neo-Assyrian became simultaneously both more simple and more complicated. Some grammatical constructions disappeared, while others reappeared. In practice, newer and older variants confirm changes in almost every grammatical category of the Neo-Assyrian dialect.

Originally I anticipated adding the name of a sender and the geographical origin of a letter to all of the "marked" forms wherever possible. I abandoned this idea because it turned out to be rather cumbersome in practice. However, in view of the absence of these details, the conclusions regarding individuals and geographical factors still seem to me to be very premature. It is certain that one could still acquire a deeper understanding of the Neo-Assyrian dialect used by the individual scribes through a closer scrutiny. Naturally, the same is valid for geographical factors.

Evidence

Grammatical variation is attested in all languages of the world. Some of the variation results from an internal process within the language, some is due to external pressure. However, the number and intensity of language contacts may be decisive for the amount of grammatical variation.

Thus, it is no surprise that grammatical variation can be shown in every main point of Neo-Assyrian grammar. Especially Neo-Assyrian contacts with Aramaic (but also with other West Semitic languages) and Neo-Babylonian reciprocally changed and enriched all these languages. In this connection, one should not forget that the Neo-Assyrian empire was bilingual with Assyrian-Babylonian and Aramaic as the co-official languages. Thus, the juxtaposition of Neo-Assyrian and Aramaic is rather artificial, especially if one wants to examine differences between them. The interaction between the two languages was based on day-to-day contacts in addition to occasional encounters.

The well-attested free variation in Neo-Assyrian particularly indicates that the dialect was going through a remarkable process of change. However, the existence of variation does not always prove to be a process of change, e.g., the motivation for the use of archaisms may be based on other reasons. In addition, a recurrent process of change can cause a strong counteraction because the language does not always unambiguously undergo a transformation, even if sporadic innovations are to be found.

Graphemic variation

With regard to the use of graphemes, clearly discernible differences in writing occasionally point to the phonetic reality. However, the more phonemic and thus more approximate type of writing was the prevalent norm in general. Therefore, Neo-Assyrian is, in many respects, strikingly conservative and loyal to the earlier forms of the Assyrian dialect.

Thus far, my research has not gone deep enough to answer the following important question: Are the above-mentioned writings which "stress" the phonetic reality distributed among several scribes "at random," or do some individuals have such an exceptional sense of their language, its phonetic nature in particular, that their share in the development of writing should be underlined more clearly?

Phonological variation

What information do the letters give about Neo-Assyrian phonology? In Neo-Assyrian, there is a tendency for voiceless consonants to become voiced in a voiced environment or when no lexical restrictions apply. Additionally, the vowel dissimilation (*u* > *a*) is very systematically realized. The phonological processes observed in writing, e.g., sandhi (including proclitic forms of prepositions) and aphesis, often hint at the real spoken Neo-Assyrian dialect.

Numerous assimilations suggest changes in Neo-Assyrian phonetics. However, as I am not diachronically comparing Neo-Assyrian to Middle Assyrian in this study, the significance and extent of the genuinely Neo-Assyrian sound changes have to be clarified elsewhere. The evidence on assimilations assembled in this work may help in such a study. For the simplification of Neo-Assyrian phonetics, extensive assimilations, anaptyctic vowels, metatheses, apocope, aphesis and syncope indicate this simplification process.

Morphological variation

Some morphological innovations are easy to observe, for instance, in pronouns and in many special forms of verbal conjugation. Several Neo-Assyrian morphological paradigms differ in many details from the corresponding paradigms of the Middle Assyrian period. The same holds true when comparing the Neo-Assyrian paradigms with the Neo-Babylonian ones. Ample variation can be observed in the plural forms of masculine nouns in particular.

Of the morphological features treated in this study, those suggestive of language change are the variants in word formation (especially the above-mentioned plural forms) and, as rarer, but attested, phenomena, suppletive stems and the gender variation of some nouns. Cf. syntactic variation below.

Syntactic variation

The two Neo-Assyrian cases (nominative-accusative and genitive) were clearly contaminated by Babylonian influence. The reaction against such contamination is not known, but while the Assyrians probably tried to keep their case system intact, pressure from outside was likely to cause it to deteriorate.

The alternation of tenses is closely connected to very specialized syntactic clause types. The use of tenses strictly follows their rules but some departures from the normal Neo-Assyrian use are observed in the aspectual use of tenses, probably owing to Aramaic influence.

It is clear that the word-order typology was subjected to great pressure to change. Rather numerous variants strongly suggest this transformation process. Hints provided by the Neo-Assyrian case system even indicate that there was pressure for the language to move towards a single case. Typologically (note that language typology was originally part of morphology in linguistics), Assyrian gradually changed from a more synthetic dialect to a very analytic dialect.

Semantic variation

In practice, the semantic difference between the prepositions *ana* and *ina* was blurred in most of the places.

When analysing Neo-Assyrian, one real challenge is to distinguish the vast interference of the Babylonian language on Neo-Assyrian. In order to assess what is really Neo-Assyrian, one has to filter out the Babylonian features. It is necessary to be aware of the fact that many scribes who wrote Neo-Assyrian were not native Assyrians but were Babylonians or belonged to some other ethnic group. For these people, Assyrian was a second (for some scribes, a third or fourth) language. Some of these originally foreign – non-Assyrian, non-Babylonian – officials and scribes were probably educated in both NA and NB. From time to time the Neo-Assyrian dialect they wrote included features from their own native language. However, in the Neo-Assyrian period, influences other than Babylonian are much more difficult to track down in practice. Nevertheless, the spread of Aramaic and other West Semitic features into Neo-Assyrian is conceivable, for example, in loan words (not treated in this study), phonology and word order.

Connected, but still partly another matter, is the influence of Babylonian on the scholarly language. Although most of the scholars in Sargonid Nineveh and elsewhere in Assyria (at least those whose letters are extant) were probably native Assyrians, they had a tendency to season their language with Babylonianisms which mainly came from the technical literature which they regularly studied and used.

The Babylonian influence in Assyrian letters is due to: (a) Babylonians (and presumably to a certain degree other non-native Assyrians) writing in Assyrian, (b) Scholars often preferring Babylonian terminology, (c) Babylonian scribes serving Assyrian officials in the border areas of the Neo-Assyrian empire, especially in the southwest, or these Assyrian officials or their Assyrian scribes being themselves otherwise under the influence of Babylonian.

Assyrian scholars often resorted to Babylonian because Babylonian was highly esteemed, e.g., in literature and Mesopotamian sciences. It must be remembered that Neo-Assyrian royal inscriptions were generally written in the Babylonian literary language. Therefore, in addition to the scholars, royal scribes responsible for writing these inscriptions were surely trained in both Babylonian and Assyrian.

But despite the prestige of literary Ba bylonian, there is no reason to doubt the existence of a standard Neo-Assyrian. The ample evidence points to a strong motivation for writing good Neo-Assyrian, but because of the background of many scribes, their writings were not always impeccable or flawless.

Unfortunately, we rarely know concrete facts about the background of those people who wrote the Neo-Assyrian letters. Their affiliation is mostly unknown; their place of origin not mentioned; and, except for the scholars, the professional expertise of scribes is rarely touched upon in the letters. Nor is there much evidence for the training of scribes. I assume that the scribal skills were often first passed from father to son or in the temple or administrative schools where advanced scribes guided their inexperienced colleagues.

The internal Neo-Assyrian causes for language change may be sought in linguistic mechanisms and functional aspects that operate to keep the balance between the tension of articulatory simplification and morphological differentiation. However, many changes that are observed in Neo-Assyrian must be based on external influence, but because this study is based only on Neo-Assyrian sources, conclusions are presented in the same vein. Extragrammatical factors, such as geography and idiolects, must have played a considerable role in language change, but their real extent and importance and how decisive they were is difficult to determine.

In general, it is certain, and extensively exemplified in this work, that Neo-Assyrian as a dialect was in the process of structural change in all grammatical categories. But diachronically, we cannot even follow up these changes to the end of the Assyrian era to find out which forms prevailed and whether others really died out or continued to coexist as variants of the more frequent forms.

APPENDIX A: NEO-ASSYRIAN LETTER CORPUS[1]

ABL 1	SAA X 222
ABL 2	SAA X 226
ABL 3	SAA X 191
ABL 4	SAA X 210
ABL 5	SAA X 196
ABL 6	SAA X 228
ABL 7	SAA X 197
ABL 8	SAA X 229
ABL 9	SAA X 218
ABL 10	SAA X 186
ABL 11	SAA X 256
ABL 12	SAA X 194
ABL 13	SAA X 204
ABL 14	SAA X 231
ABL 15	SAA X 209
ABL 16	SAA X 232
ABL 17	SAA X 257
ABL 18	SAA X 255
ABL 19	SAA X 241
ABL 20	SAA X 260
ABL 21	SAA X 264
ABL 22	SAA X 263
ABL 23	SAA X 240
ABL 24	SAA X 238
ABL 25	SAA X 261
ABL 26	SAA X 234
ABL 27	SAA X 344
ABL 28	SAA X 343
ABL 29	SAA X 339
ABL 31	SAA X 15
ABL 32	SAA X 24
ABL 33	SAA X 7
ABL 34	SAA X 10
ABL 35	SAA X 18
ABL 36	SAA X 13
ABL 37	SAA X 23
ABL 38	SAA X 26
ABL 39	SAA X 34
ABL 40	SAA X 35
ABL 41	SAA X 28
ABL 42	SAA X 98
ABL 43	SAA X 96
ABL 44	SAA X 91
ABL 45	SAA X 92
ABL 46	SAA X 90
ABL 47	SAA X 93
ABL 48	SAA X 99
ABL 49	SAA X 95
ABL 50	SAA X 94
ABL 51	SAA X 278
ABL 52	SAA X 279
ABL 53	SAA X 276
ABL 55	SAA X 280
ABL 56	SAA X 274
ABL 57	SAA X 273
ABL 58	SAA X 284
ABL 59	SAA X 285
ABL 60	SAA XIII 89
ABL 61	SAA XIII 104
ABL 62	SAA X 130
ABL 63	SAA XIII 101
ABL 64	SAA XIII 96
ABL 65	SAA XIII 78
ABL 66	SAA XIII 79
ABL 67	SAA XIII 102
ABL 68+[2]	SAA XIII 85
ABL 69	SAA XIII 91
ABL 70	SAA XV 138
ABL 71	SAA XIII 88
ABL 72	SAA XIII 106
ABL 73	SAA X 129
ABL 74	SAA X 42
ABL 75	LAS 37
ABL 76	SAA X 59
ABL 77	SAA X 53
ABL 78	SAA X 43
ABL 79	SAA X 47
ABL 80	SAA X 68
ABL 81	SAA X 80
ABL 82	SAA X 74
ABL 83[3]	SAA X 77
ABL 84	SAA XVI 112
ABL 85	SAA XVI 115
ABL 86	SAA XVI 117
ABL 87	SAA I 96
ABL 88	SAA I 84
ABL 89	SAA I 94
ABL 90	SAA I 76
ABL 91	SAA I 77
ABL 92	SAA I 100
ABL 93	SAA I 83
ABL 94	SAA I 91
ABL 95	SAA I 97
ABL 96	SAA I 88
ABL 97	SAA I 107
ABL 98	SAA I 90
ABL 99	SAA I 99
ABL 100	SAA I 47
ABL 101	SAA I 41
ABL 102	SAA I 65
ABL 103+[4]	SAA I 56
ABL 104	SAA I 42
ABL 105	SAA I 53
ABL 106	SAA I 71
ABL 107	SAA I 70
ABL 108	SAA X 322
ABL 109	SAA X 320
ABL 110	SAA X 318
ABL 111+[5]	SAA X 321
ABL 112	SAA V 145
ABL 113	SAA XIII 56
ABL 114	SAA XIII 61
ABL 115	SAA XIII 62
ABL 116	SAA XIII 63

ABL 117	SAA X 289
ABL 118	SAA X 290
ABL 119	SAA X 168
ABL 120	SAA XIII 162
ABL 121+[6]	SAA V 121
ABL 122	SAA V 119
ABL 123	SAA V 113
ABL 124	SAA V 120
ABL 125	SAA V 118
ABL 126	SAA XV 94
ABL 127	SAA XV 105
ABL 128	SAA XV 100
ABL 129	SAA XV 90
ABL 130	SAA I 202
ABL 131	SAA I 190
ABL 132	SAA I 191
ABL 134	SAA I 188
ABL 135	SAA I 200
ABL 136[7]	SAA I 146
ABL 138	SAA V 32
ABL 139+[8]	SAA V 31
ABL 140	SAA XVI 136
ABL 141	SAA X 123
ABL 142	SAA X 127
ABL 143	SAA XVI 120
ABL 144	SAA V 91
ABL 145	SAA V 96
ABL 146+[9]	SAA V 92
ABL 147	SAA V 97
ABL 148	SAA V 85
ABL 149	SAA XIII 37
ABL150	SAA XIII 25
ABL 151	SAA XV 17
ABL 152	SAA XIII 154
ABL 153+[10]	SAA XV 294
ABL 154	SAA I 205
ABL 155	SAA I 206
ABL 156	SAA I 207
ABL 157	SAA XV 4
ABL 158	SAA XV 1
ABL 159	SAA XV 3
ABL 160	SAA XV 9
ABL 161	SAA XV 11
ABL 162	SAA XV 5
ABL 163	SAA XV 8
ABL 164	SAA XV 13
ABL 165	SAA XV 53
ABL 166	SAA XVI 30
ABL 167	SAA I 128
ABL 168	SAA XV 24
ABL 169	SAA XV 35
ABL 170	SAA XV 36
ABL 171+[11]	SAA XV 25
ABL 172	SAA XV 39
ABL 173	SAA I 45
ABL 174	SAA XV 69
ABL 175	SAA I 153
ABL 176	SAA XIII 125
ABL 177	SAA XIII 126
ABL 178	SAA X 301
ABL 179	SAA I 135
ABL 180	SAA I 51
ABL 181	SAA X 176
ABL 182	SAA I 216
ABL 183	SAA X 211
ABL 184	SAA XIII 23
ABL 185	SAA XIII 39
ABL 186	SAA XVI 105
ABL 187	SAA XVI 106
ABL 188	SAA XVI 108
ABL 189	SAA XVI 107
ABL 190	SAA I 124
ABL 191	SAA I 125
ABL 192	SAA V 64
ABL 193	SAA V 71
ABL 194	SAA V 63
ABL 195	SAA V 66
ABL 196	SAA I 33
ABL 197	SAA I 31
ABL 198+[12]	SAA I 29
ABL 199	SAA I 38
ABL 200	SAA V 1
ABL 201	SAA V 16
ABL 203	SAA XIII 73
ABL 204	SAA X 333
ABL 205	SAA V 169
ABL 206	SAA V 104
ABL 207	SAA V 242
ABL 208	SAA V 210
ABL 209	SAA XIII 145
ABL 211	SAA XVI 78
ABL 212	SAA XV 181
ABL 213	SAA XIII 32
ABL 215	SAA V 45
ABL 216	SAA I 133
ABL 217	SAA XIII 35
ABL 218	SAA I 155
ABL 220	SAA XVI 49
ABL 221	SAA XVI 48
ABL 222	SAA XV 199
ABL 223	SAA X 2
ABL 224	SAA I 173
ABL 225	SAA I 174
ABL 226	SAA XV 65
ABL 227	SAA XV 66
ABL 230	SAA XV 67
ABL 231	SAA I 118
ABL 232	SAA I 115
ABL 233+[13]	SAA I 116
ABL 234	SAA I 117
ABL 235	SAA I 123
ABL 236+[14]	SAA I 112
ABL 237	SAA I 122
ABL 241	SAA XV 61
ABL 242	SAA XV 60
ABL 243	SAA V 126
ABL 244+[15]	SAA V 127
ABL 245	SAA V 79
ABL 246	SAA V 78
ABL 247	SAA V 80
ABL 248	SAA X 329
ABL 249	SAA X 331
ABL 250	SAA X 332
ABL 251	SAA V 53
ABL 252	SAA V 52
ABL 253+[16]	SAA V 56
ABL 257	SAA X 358
ABL 271	SAA V 293
ABL 273	(Asb)
ABL 298	SAA I 6
ABL 300	SAA XVI 4
ABL 302	(Asb)
ABL 303	SAA XVI 2
ABL 304	SAA I 11
ABL 305	SAA I 5
ABL306+[17]	SAA I 10
ABL 307[18]	(Sg)
ABL 308	SAA XVI 28
ABL 309	SAA V 246
ABL 310	SAA V 202
ABL 311	SAA V 199
ABL 312	SAA V 200
ABL 313	SAA XV 217
ABL 314	SAA XV 219
ABL 315	SAA XV 223
ABL 316	SAA XV 224
ABL 317	SAA V 243
ABL 318	SAA XV 239
ABL 319+[19]	SAA V 206
ABL 320+[20]	SAA XV 226
ABL 321	SAA V 201
ABL 322	SAA I 184
ABL 323	SAA I 185
ABL 325	SAA I 219
ABL 329	SAA I 137
ABL 330	SAA I 80

ABL 331	SAA I 230
ABL 332	SAA X 1
ABL 333	SAA XVI 121
ABL 337	SAA X 347
ABL 338	SAA X 357
ABL 339	SAA X 369
ABL 340	SAA X 348
ABL 341	SAA XVI 26
ABL 342	SAA V 217
ABL 343	SAA V 245
ABL 346	SAA X 143
ABL 347	SAA XVI 82
ABL 348	SAA X 242
ABL 351	SAA X 46
ABL 352	SAA X 61
ABL 353	SAA X 58
ABL 354	SAA X 52
ABL 355	SAA X 56
ABL 356	SAA X 48
ABL 357	SAA X 202
ABL 358	SAA X 227
ABL 359	SAA X 220
ABL 360	SAA X 215
ABL 361	SAA X 212
ABL 362	SAA X 221
ABL 363	SAA X 217
ABL 364	SAA X 259
ABL 365	SAA X 190
ABL 366	SAA XIII 70
ABL 367	SAA XIII 71
ABL 368	SAA XIII 76
ABL 369	SAA X 282
ABL 370	SAA X 277
ABL 371	SAA XIII 92
ABL 372	SAA XIII 86
ABL 373	SAA XIII 97
ABL 374	SAA XIII 94
ABL 375	SAA XIII 98
ABL 376	SAA XIII 87
ABL 377	SAA XIII 80
ABL 378	SAA X 233
ABL 379	SAA X 235
ABL 380	SAA V 88
ABL 381	SAA V 84
ABL 382	SAA XV 288
ABL 383env.[21]	SAA XV 289
ABL 384	SAA X 5
ABL 385	SAA X 33
ABL 386	SAA X 6
ABL 387	SAA V 203
ABL 388	SAA XV 238
ABL 389	SAA XVI 111
ABL 390	(Asb)
ABL 391	SAA X 315
ABL 392	SAA X 319
ABL 393	SAA XIII 108
ABL 394	SAA XIII 109
ABL 395	SAA XIII 110
ABL 396	SAA I 85
ABL 397	SAA I 101
ABL 398	SAA I 102
ABL 404	SAA X 41
ABL 405	SAA X 79
ABL 406	SAA X 70
ABL 407	SAA X 75
ABL 408	SAA V 227
ABL 409	SAA V 147
ABL 410	SAA V 163
ABL 411	SAA V 172
ABL 413	SAA XVI 84
ABL 414	SAA I 177
ABL 415	SAA XVI 42
ABL 417	SAA XVI 3
ABL 419	SAA XIII 33
ABL 420	SAA I 119
ABL 421	SAA X 173
ABL 423	SAA X 138
ABL 424	SAA V 3
ABL 425	SAA XVI 139
ABL 426	(Asb)
ABL 427	SAA XIII 58
ABL 428	SAA XIII 81
ABL 429	SAA X 107
ABL 431	SAA V 28
ABL 432	SAA X 137
ABL 433	SAA I 54
ABL 434	SAA XVI 148
ABL 435	SAA X 198
ABL 437	SAA X 352
ABL 438	SAA XV 184
ABL 439	SAA X 193
ABL 440	SAA XIII 95
ABL 441	SAA V 162
ABL 442	SAA XVI 96
ABL 443	SAA XV 16
ABL 444	SAA V 87
ABL 445	SAA XVI 69
ABL 446	SAA XVI 80
ABL 447≠	SAA XI 156
ABL 448	SAA V 139
ABL 449≠	
ABL 450	SAA X 298
ABL 452	SAA I 66
ABL 453	SAA X 245
ABL 455	SAA XV 30
ABL 457	SAA I 203
ABL 463	SAA V 260
ABL 464	SAA XIII 166
ABL 465	SAA X 324
ABL 466	SAA V 171
ABL 467	SAA V 295
ABL 470	SAA X 148
ABL 471	SAA XIII 161
ABL 473	SAA XVI 95
ABL 474+[22]	SAA XIII 190
ABL 476	SAA X 349
ABL 479	SAA XIII 38
ABL 480	SAA I 106
ABL 481	SAA I 109
ABL 482	SAA I 93
ABL 483	SAA I 78
ABL 484	SAA I 98
ABL 486	SAA I 64
ABL 487	SAA I 67
ABL 488	SAA I 43
ABL 489[23]	SAA I 50
ABL 490	SAA V 111
ABL 491	SAA V 94
ABL 492	SAA V 86
ABL 493	SAA XIII 128
ABL 494	SAA XIII 65
ABL 495	SAA XIII 64
ABL 502	SAA XV 162
ABL 503+[24]	SAA XV 156
ABL 504	SAA XV 158
ABL 505	SAA XV 169
ABL 506	SAA V 21
ABL 507	SAA V 25
ABL 508	SAA V 23
ABL 509	SAA V 24
ABL 510	SAA V 27
ABL 512	SAA XVI 50
ABL 513	SAA X 303
ABL 514	SAA XIII 187
ABL 515	SAA V 164
ABL 519	SAA X 8
ABL 522	SAA V 241
ABL 523	(Asb)
ABL 525	SAA X 334
ABL 526	SAA I 147
ABL 528	SAA XV 241
ABL 529	SAA V 224
ABL 531	SAA XIII 127
ABL 532	SAA XIII 31[25]
ABL 533	SAA XIII 143
ABL 534	SAA XVI 22

ABL 535	SAA XVI 24
ABL 536	SAA XVI 23
ABL 537	SAA XV 121
ABL 538	SAA XIII 99
ABL 541	(Asb)
ABL 543	(Asb)
ABL 544	SAA V 105
ABL 545	SAA XIII 100
ABL 546	SAA XIII 82
ABL 547	SAA I 82
ABL 548	SAA V 2
ABL 549	SAA X 201
ABL 550	SAA XV 295
ABL 551	SAA XIII 26
ABL 552	SAA XV 12
ABL 553	SAA X 275
ABL 554	SAA XVI 196
ABL 555	SAA XIII 45
ABL 556	SAA XV 54
ABL 557	SAA XVI 43
ABL 558	SAA XIII 124
ABL 561	(Asb)
ABL 562	SAA I 89
ABL 563	SAA I 241
ABL 564	SAA XV 168
ABL 565	SAA X 84
ABL 566	SAA V 294
ABL 567+[26]	SAA V 251
ABL 568	SAA I 34
ABL 569	SAA XIII 77
ABL 570	SAA X 323
ABL 572	SAA XVI 154
ABL 573	SAA I 239
ABL 574≠[27]	SAA XI 231
ABL 575	SAA XIII 111
ABL 577	SAA I 75
ABL 578+[28]	SAA I 114
ABL 579	SAA V 115
ABL 580	SAA XIII 7
ABL 581	SAA XV 123
ABL 582	SAA V 234
ABL 583	SAA XVI 163
ABL 584+[29]	SAA X 316
ABL 585	SAA I 247
ABL 586	SAA X 302
ABL 590	SAA V 103
ABL 591	SAA X 122
ABL 592	SAA XVI 197
ABL 593	SAA XVI 141
ABL 594	SAA X 314
ABL 595+[30]	SAA X 185
ABL 596	SAA V 223
ABL 597+[31]	SAA X 214
ABL 598	SAA XV 34
ABL 599	SAA V 228
ABL 600	SAA XV 236
ABL 601	SAA XIII 116
ABL 602	SAA XV 268
ABL 603	SAA XVI 72
ABL 604+[32]	SAA X 39
ABL 605	SAA XIII 137
ABL 606	SAA XIII 57
ABL 607	SAA XIII 3
ABL 608	SAA XV 159
ABL 609≠[33]	SAA VI 306
ABL 610	SAA I 240
ABL 611	SAA XIII 44
ABL 612	SAA X 340
ABL 613	SAA XVI 198
ABL 614	SAA X 188
ABL 615	SAA XIII 17
ABL 618	SAA X 51
ABL 619+[34]	SAA V 117
ABL 620	SAA XVI 36
ABL 621+[35]	SAA I 210
ABL 623	(Asb)
ABL 624+[36]	SAA V 68
ABL 625	SAA X 341
ABL 626	SAA I 144
ABL 628	SAA XVI 143
ABL 629+[37]	SAA X 351
ABL 630	SAA I 48
ABL 631≠	SAA XI 162
ABL 632≠	SAA XI 33
ABL 633+[38]	SAA XVI 63
ABL 634	SAA XIII 133
ABL 635	SAA V 229
ABL 636	SAA X 300
ABL 637+[39]	SAA XV 68
ABL 638	SAA XV 182
ABL 639	SAA I 236
ABL 641+[40]	SAA XV 25
ABL 642	SAA I 193
ABL 643	SAA I 136
ABL 644	SAA I 141
ABL 645+[41]	SAA XV 101
ABL 646	SAA V 90
ABL 647	SAA X 67
ABL 648	SAA XIII 72
ABL 649	SAA XIII 112
ABL 650	SAA X 205
ABL 651+[42]	SAA X 214
ABL 652	SAA X 207
ABL 653	SAA X 189
ABL 654	SAA X 195
ABL 655	SAA X 281
ABL 656	SAA X 199
ABL 657	SAA X 224
ABL 658	SAA X 213
ABL 659+[43]	SAA XIII 190
ABL 660	SAA X 200
ABL 661+[44]	SAA X 267
ABL 662	SAA X 252
ABL 663	SAA X 236
ABL 664	SAA X 243
ABL 665+[45]	SAA X 265
ABL 666	SAA X 266
ABL 667	SAA X 338
ABL 668	SAA XIII 67
ABL 669	SAA X 342
ABL 670	SAA X 9
ABL 671	SAA X 141
ABL 672	SAA X 32
ABL 673	SAA X 14
ABL 674	SAA X 25
ABL 675	SAA X 22
ABL 676	SAA X 12
ABL 677	SAA X 16
ABL 678	SAA X 106
ABL 679+[46]	SAA X 100
ABL 680	SAA X 87
ABL 681	SAA X 86
ABL 682	SAA XIII 103
ABL 683	SAA XIII 83
ABL 684	SAA XIII 93
ABL 685	SAA XV 136
ABL 686	SAA XIII 84
ABL 687	SAA X 45
ABL 688	SAA X 60
ABL 689	SAA X 40
ABL 690	SAA X 49
ABL 691	SAA X 57
ABL 692	SAA X 50
ABL 693+[47]	SAA X 62
ABL 694	SAA X 66
ABL 695	SAA XVI 181
ABL 696	SAA X 83
ABL 697	SAA X 82
ABL 700	SAA XVI 113
ABL 701	SAA I 195
ABL 703	SAA V 38
ABL 704+[48]	SAA V 34
ABL 705	SAA V 33
ABL 706+[49]	SAA I 204
ABL 707	SAA XV 6
ABL 708	SAA XV 7

ABL 709	SAA XV 15
ABL 710	SAA XIII 129
ABL 711	SAA XV 14
ABL 712	SAA XV 40
ABL 713	SAA XV 85
ABL 714	SAA XVI 83
ABL 715	SAA XV 70
ABL 719	SAA X 297
ABL 720	SAA X 306
ABL 722	SAA X 177
ABL 723	SAA I 217
ABL 724	SAA XIII 18
ABL 725	SAA XIII 24
ABL 726	SAA XIII 19
ABL 727	SAA XIII 20
ABL 728	SAA XVI 109
ABL 729	SAA V 62
ABL 730	SAA I 35
ABL 731	SAA I 36
ABL 732	SAA V 6
ABL 733	SAA XVI 98
ABL 734	SAA XIII 74
ABL 735	SAA XIII 75
ABL 737	SAA X 181
ABL 739	SAA X 330
ABL 740	SAA X 328
ABL 741	SAA V 55
ABL 742	SAA V 59
ABL 744	SAA X 363
ABL 745	SAA X 366
ABL 746	SAA X 359
ABL 756	SAA XVI 31
ABL 757	SAA V 47
ABL 758	SAA V 205
ABL 759	SAA XV 234
ABL 760	SAA XV 232
ABL 761	SAA V 207
ABL 762	SAA XV 220
ABL 763+[50]	SAA XV 218
ABL 766	SAA XVI 25
ABL 767	SAA XIII 107
ABL 768	SAA V 146
ABL 769	SAA V 83
ABL 770	SAA XVI 85
ABL 772	SAA XV 71
ABL 773	SAA X 175
ABL 775	SAA XVI 140
ABL 776	SAA XVI 144
ABL 777	SAA XVI 142
ABL 778	SAA XVI 86
ABL 779	SAA XVI 87
ABL 783	SAA V 161
ABL 784	SAA V 152
ABL 785	SAA V 159
ABL 786	SAA V 153
ABL 787	SAA V 154
ABL 788	SAA V 155
ABL 798	SAA XV 122
ABL 799+[51]	SAA XV 113
ABL 800	SAA XV 115
ABL 801	SAA XV 127
ABL 802	SAA V 233
ABL 809	(Asb)
ABL 810	SAA XV 27
ABL 812	SAA XIII 27
ABL 813	SAA I 226
ABL 814	SAA I 227
ABL 816	SAA X 128
ABL 817≠	SAA VIII 130
ABL 818	SAA X 124
ABL 819≠	SAA VIII 126
ABL 820≠	SAA VIII 131
ABL 821≠	SAA VIII 135
ABL 822≠	SAA VIII 136
ABL 823≠	SAA VIII 134
ABL 824≠	SAA VIII 138
ABL 825≠	SAA VIII 132
ABL 826≠	SAA VIII 137
ABL 827≠	SAA VIII 128
ABL 828≠	SAA VIII 129
ABL 829	SAA X 139
ABL 830	SAA XV 186
ABL 839[52]	(Asb)
ABL 840	SAA XIII 16
ABL 841	SAA I 132
ABL 842	SAA I 131
ABL 843	SAA I 160
ABL 845	SAA XVI 79
ABL 847	SAA XVI 81
ABL 858	SAA XIII 130
ABL 860	SAA I 258
ABL 861	SAA XIII 184
ABL 864+≠[53]	
ABL 867	SAA V 257
ABL 868	SAA XV 142
ABL 869	SAA X 78
ABL 870+[54]	SAA X 185
ABL 871	SAA I 105
ABL 872	SAA XVI 99
ABL 873	SAA X 291
ABL 874	SAA XVI 92
ABL 875	SAA XVI 91
ABL 876	SAA XIII 147
ABL 877≠	SAA XI 153
ABL 879	(Asb)
ABL 881	SAA X 135
ABL 882	SAA X 134
ABL 883	SAA XV 166
ABL 884	SAA V 226
ABL 885	SAA XVI 34
ABL 887	SAA XV 179
ABL 888	SAA I 224
ABL 889	SAA XIII 156
ABL 890	SAA V 133
ABL 891	SAA V 136
ABL 894	SAA X 225
ABL 896	(Asb)
ABL 902	SAA V 237
ABL 903	SAA V 238
ABL 904	SAA V 239
ABL 905	SAA V 240
ABL 908	SAA X 131
ABL 909	SAA X 133
ABL 910	SAA I 221
ABL 911	SAA XV 291
ABL 916	SAA XVI 29
ABL 918	SAA XVI 1
ABL 919+[55]	SAA XIII 36
ABL 921+[56]	SAA V 48
ABL 922	SAA V 49
ABL 923	SAA X 174
ABL 924[57]	(MB)
ABL 927	SAA XVI 119
ABL 929	SAA X 54
ABL 931	SAA V 134
ABL 932	SAA X 308
ABL 933	SAA I 215
ABL 934+[58]	SAA I 151
ABL 935+[59]	SAA I 210
ABL 936	SAA V 194
ABL 937+[60]	SAA I 223
ABL 938	SAA I 222
ABL 939	SAA XV 188
ABL 940	SAA XIII 191
ABL 941	SAA XIII 30[61]
ABL 943	(Asb)
ABL 945	(Asb)
ABL 946	SAA V 244
ABL 948	SAA XVI 35
ABL 950	SAA XVI 124
ABL 951	SAA XIII 134
ABL 952	SAA V 29
ABL 953	SAA I 178
ABL 955	SAA I 165
ABL 956	SAA X 253
ABL 957	SAA V 297

ABL 959	SAA XIII 117
ABL 962	SAA XV 214
ABL 966+[62]	SAA I 257
ABL 970	SAA X 247
ABL 971	SAA XIII 60
ABL 972	(Asb)
ABL 973	SAA XIII 113
ABL 975	SAA XIII 131
ABL 976	SAA XIII 155
ABL 977+[63]	SAA X 296
ABL 978	SAA V 132
ABL 979	SAA XIII 14
ABL 980	SAA I 238
ABL 981	SAA XVI 131
ABL 982	SAA X 136
ABL 983+[64]	SAA XV 68
ABL 984+[65]	SAA I 150
ABL 985+[66]	SAA I 56
ABL 986	SAA XVI 152
ABL 987	SAA V 75
ABL 988+[67]	SAA V 156
ABL 989+[68]	SAA I 192
ABL 990	SAA I 130
ABL 991+[69]	SAA XIII 34
ABL 992	SAA XVI 127
ABL 993≠[70]	SAA VIII 83
ABL 995	SAA I 108
ABL 996	SAA XV 351
ABL 997	SAA XIII 29
ABL 1001	SAA XVI 14
ABL 1002	(Asb)
ABL 1003	SAA XV 33
ABL 1004	SAA X 377
ABL 1005+[71]	SAA XV 177
ABL 1008	SAA XV 98
ABL 1009	(Asb)
ABL 1011+[72]	SAA XV 161
ABL 1012	SAA V 82
ABL 1014	SAA X 350
ABL 1015	SAA I 103
ABL 1017	SAA XIII 114
ABL 1018	SAA V 70
ABL 1019	SAA XV 317
ABL 1021	SAA X 361
ABL 1022	(Asb)
ABL 1023	SAA XIII 8
ABL 1024	SAA XV 189
ABL 1026+[73]	SAA XVI 15
ABL 1031+[74]	SAA XVI 60
ABL 1033	SAA I 246
ABL 1035	SAA V 284
ABL 1036	SAA I 162
ABL 1037	SAA X 144
ABL 1038+[75]	SAA I 49
ABL 1039	SAA XVI 162
ABL 1041	SAA XV 157
ABL 1042	SAA I 12
ABL 1043	SAA V 12
ABL 1044	SAA XV 116
ABL 1045	SAA XV 106
ABL 1046	SAA XV 95
ABL 1048	SAA V 148
ABL 1049	SAA I 58
ABL 1050	SAA XVI 73
ABL 1051+[76]	SAA XIII 34
ABL 1055	SAA XVI 199
ABL 1056	SAA XV 2
ABL 1057	SAA XV 180
ABL 1058	SAA V 218
ABL 1060	SAA XIII 132
ABL 1061	SAA XVI 39
ABL 1063	SAA XV 118
ABL 1064	SAA I 156
ABL 1065	SAA XV 280
ABL 1066	SAA XV 248
ABL 1068	SAA V 211
ABL 1069	SAA X 71
ABL 1070	SAA I 181
ABL 1071	SAA XV 155
ABL 1073	SAA I 194
ABL 1075	SAA X 249
ABL 1077+[77]≠	SAA VII 89
ABL 1078	SAA XIII 50
ABL 1079	SAA I 30
ABL 1080	SAA X 55
ABL 1081	SAA V 168
ABL 1082	SAA XV 42
ABL 1083	SAA V 11
ABL 1084	SAA XV 187
ABL 1085	SAA I 245
ABL 1086	SAA I 92
ABL 1087	SAA I 129
ABL 1088	
ABL 1092	SAA XIII 12
ABL 1093	SAA XV 131
ABL 1094	SAA XIII 59
ABL 1096	SAA X 76
ABL 1097	SAA X 19
ABL 1098	SAA XIII 140
ABL 1099	SAA X 262
ABL 1101	SAA XVI 41
ABL 1103	SAA XIII 152
ABL 1104	SAA I 59
ABL 1107	SAA XVI 33
ABL 1108	(Asb)
ABL 1110+[78]	SAA XVI 126
ABL 1115	SAA XVI 137
ABL 1116	(Asb)
ABL 1118+[79]	SAA X 203
ABL 1121	(Asb)
ABL 1122	SAA XIII 105
ABL 1126	SAA X 246
ABL 1127	(Asb)
ABL 1132+[80]	SAA X 72
ABL 1133	SAA XIII 66
ABL 1134	SAA X 104
ABL 1137	SAA X 125
ABL 1139	SAA XVI 200
ABL 1140	SAA X 379
ABL 1141+[81]	SAA X 44
ABL 1142	(Asb)
ABL 1143	SAA XIII 13
ABL 1144	SAA XVI 201
ABL 1145	SAA X 31
ABL 1147	SAA XIII 68
ABL 1148	(Asb)
ABL 1149	SAA XIII 158
ABL 1150	SAA X 346
ABL 1152	SAA XVI 179
ABL 1153	SAA XIII 118
ABL 1156	SAA X 126
ABL 1157+[82]	SAA X 327
ABL 1158	SAA XVI 202
ABL 1159	SAA XIII 122
ABL 1160	SAA XIII 11
ABL 1161	SAA XVI 16
ABL 1163	(Asb)
ABL 1164	SAA XIII 149
ABL 1166	SAA X 286
ABL 1167	(Asb)
ABL 1168	SAA X 254
ABL 1171	SAA XIII 9
ABL 1173	SAA X 283
ABL 1174	
ABL 1175	SAA XV 231
ABL 1176	SAA V 54
ABL 1177	SAA I 39
ABL 1178	SAA I 138
ABL 1179	SAA X 307
ABL 1180	SAA I 143
ABL 1181[83]	
ABL 1184	SAA X 251
ABL 1186	(Asb)
ABL 1187	SAA XV 274
ABL 1188	SAA XV 365
ABL 1190	SAA XV 82

ABL 1191	SAA XV 26
ABL 1192	SAA V 232
ABL 1193	SAA V 14
ABL 1194	SAA XIII 28
ABL 1196	SAA V 89
ABL 1197	SAA XIII 189
ABL 1199	SAA XVI 27
ABL 1201	SAA I 220
ABL 1202	SAA X 353
ABL 1203	SAA I 250
ABL 1205	SAA I 229
ABL 1206	SAA V 263
ABL 1209	SAA I 140
ABL 1210	(Asb)
ABL 1211	SAA XV 93
ABL 1212	SAA XIII 192
ABL 1213+[84]	SAA XV 218
ABL 1214	SAA X 364
ABL 1217+[85]	SAA XVI 59
ABL 1218	SAA XIII 15
ABL 1219	SAA XIII 163
ABL 1220	SAA X 383
ABL 1221	SAA XIII 46
ABL 1223	SAA I 201
ABL 1224	SAA XV 73
ABL 1225	SAA XV 258
ABL 1227+[86]	SAA I 189
ABL 1228	SAA XVI 132
ABL 1229	SAA XIII 160
ABL 1232	SAA I 252
ABL 1234	SAA XVI 44
ABL 1235	SAA XVI 150
ABL 1238	SAA XVI 97
ABL 1239+[87]≠	SAA II 8
ABL 1242	(Asb)
ABL 1243	SAA XIII 193
ABL 1244	(Asb)
ABL 1245	SAA XVI 65
ABL 1249	SAA XIII 139
ABL 1250	SAA XVI 32
ABL 1252≠[88]	
ABL 1254	
ABL 1257	SAA XVI 17
ABL 1262	(Asb)
ABL 1263	SAA I 244
ABL 1264	(Asb)
ABL 1265	SAA V 274
ABL 1267	SAA XV 203
ABL 1268	SAA XVI 203
ABL 1270	SAA XV 337
ABL 1271	
ABL 1272	
ABL 1273	SAA V 149
ABL 1276	SAA I 148
ABL 1277	SAA X 30
ABL 1278	SAA X 183
ABL 1280≠	SAA IX 8
ABL 1281	
ABL 1282≠[89]	
ABL 1285	SAA X 294
ABL 1287	SAA I 183
ABL 1288	SAA V 256
ABL 1289	SAA X 309
ABL 1290+[90]	SAA V 250
ABL 1291	SAA XVI 67
ABL 1292	SAA I 18
ABL 1294	SAA XV 103
ABL 1295	SAA V 179
ABL 1296	SAA XV 163
ABL 1297	SAA XIII 136
ABL 1298+[91]	SAA V 165
ABL 1299	SAA XVI 103
ABL 1300	SAA XV 363
ABL 1302+[92]	SAA I 237
ABL 1305	SAA V 272
ABL 1306	
ABL 1308	SAA XVI 62
ABL 1310	SAA XVI 204
ABL 1312	SAA XV 45
ABL 1314+[93]	SAA XV 119
ABL 1315	SAA XV 130
ABL 1318+[94]	SAA I 204
ABL 1324	
ABL 1325	SAA V 166
ABL 1328	SAA I 19
ABL 1332+[95]	SAA XV 113
ABL 1333	SAA XVI 122
ABL 1336	SAA X 365
ABL 1343	SAA XVI 123
ABL 1346	SAA XVI 8
ABL 1347	SAA X 305
ABL 1348	SAA XV 114
ABL 1349	SAA XV 117
ABL 1350	SAA XV 240
ABL 1351	SAA XVI 145
ABL 1352	(Asb)
ABL 1353	SAA XV 293
ABL 1354	SAA XVI 114
ABL 1357	
ABL 1358+[96]	SAA X 267
ABL 1359	SAA V 158
ABL 1360	SAA I 55
ABL 1362	SAA V 298
ABL 1364	(Asb)
ABL 1367≠	SAA IV 321
ABL 1368≠	SAA IV 322
ABL 1369	SAA XIII 43
ABL 1370+[97]	SAA X 316
ABL 1371	SAA XVI 45
ABL 1372	SAA XIII 157
ABL 1375	SAA X 27
ABL 1376	SAA X 3
ABL 1377+[98]	SAA XIII 21
ABL 1378	SAA X 21
ABL 1379	SAA XIII 90
ABL 1381	SAA X 132
ABL 1383	SAA X 73
ABL 1384	SAA XIII 10
ABL 1385	(Asb)
ABL 1388	SAA X 244
ABL 1389	SAA XIII 138
ABL 1390	SAA X 85
ABL 1391+[99]	SAA X 100
ABL 1392	SAA X 147
ABL 1396+[100]	SAA X 74
ABL 1397	SAA X 89
ABL 1399	SAA XVI 180
ABL 1400	(Asb)
ABL 1401	SAA X 206
ABL 1405≠	SAA VIII 231 (NB)
ABL 1407	SAA V 213
ABL 1407Aenv.[101]	SAA V 214
ABL 1408≠	SAA VIII 207
ABL 1409≠[102]	SAA VIII 224
ABL 1412	SAA XV 300
ABL 1413≠	
ABL 1414	SAA V 125
ABL 1415	SAA XIII 146
ABL 1416	SAA V 221
ABL 1417	SAA I 163
ABL 1418+[103]	SAA I 208
ABL 1419	SAA V 58
ABL 1421	SAA XVI 133
ABL 1422	SAA XVI 135
ABL 1423+[104]	SAA I 25
ABL 1426[105]	SAAVIII 163
ABL 1427	SAA XIII 119
ABL 1428≠	SAA VIII 140
ABL 1429≠	SAA VIII 141
ABL 1432	SAA I 235
ABL1433	SAA I 87
ABL 1434	SAA XV 221
ABL 1435+[106]	SAA X 216
ABL 1436	SAA XV 301

ABL 1438	SAA X 142
ABL 1441	SAA XV 346
ABL 1442	SAA I 159
ABL 1444	SAA X 149
ABL 1446	SAA I 139
ABL 1447≠[107]	SAA VIII 79
ABL 1449	SAA X 81
ABL 1450+[108]	SAA XIII 85
ABL 1451	SAA XVI 93
ABL 1452≠	SAA XII 88
ABL 1453+[109]	SAA XV 32
ABL 1454	SAA XV 91
ABL 1455[110]	SAA III 26
ABL 1458	SAA I 52
ABL 1462≠	SAA III 21
ABL 1463	SAA XV 209
ABL 1466	SAA V 135
ABL 1469	SAA I 16
ABL 1470	SAA I 249
ABL 1471+[111]	SAA XV 101
CT 53 1	SAA I 158
CT 53 2	SAA I 233
CT 53 3	SAA X 336
CT 53 4	SAA V 40
CT 53 5	SAA XV 164
CT 53 6	SAA XV 237
CT 53 7	SAA V 114
CT 53 8	SAA X 381
CT 53 9	SAA XVI 53
CT 53 10	SAA I 179
CT 53 11	SAA XIII 85
CT 53 12	SAA I 152
CT 53 13	SAA XVI 40
CT 53 14	SAA XVI 89
CT 53 15	SAA I 251
CT 53 16	SAA XVI 128
CT 53 17+[112]	SAA XVI 60
CT 53 18	SAA XIII 141
CT 53 19	SAA XV 25
CT 53 20	SAA I 192
CT 53 21	SAA X 316
CT 53 22	SAA I 62
CT 53 23	SAA X 326
CT 53 24	SAA I 150
CT 53 25	SAA XVI 125
CT 53 26	SAA XVI 20
CT 53 27	SAA XV 74
CT 53 28	SAA X 214
CT 53 29	SAA XV 172
CT 53 30	SAA V 290
CT 53 31	SAA X 185
CT 53 32+[113]	SAA I 56
CT 53 33	SAA V 56
CT 53 34	SAA X 355
CT 53 35	SAA V 117
CT 53 36	SAA V 281
CT 53 37+[114]	SAA V 108
CT 53 38	SAA V 291
CT 53 39	SAA XV 48
CT 53 40	SAA V 68
CT 53 41	SAA XIII 34
CT 53 42	SAA V 98
CT 53 43	SAA I 134
CT 53 44	SAA XVI 71
CT 53 45	SAA X 145
CT 53 46	SAA XVI 63
CT 53 47+[115]	SAA V 250
CT 53 48	SAA X 258
CT 53 49	SAA X 219
CT 53 50	SAA X 304
CT 53 51	SAA XIII 36
CT 53 52	SAA X 325
CT 53 53	SAA XVI 56
CT 53 54	SAA V 44
CT 53 55	SAA XV 62
CT 53 56	SAA V 204
CT 53 57+[116]	SAA V 31
CT 53 58	SAA V 48
CT 53 59	SAA V 150
CT 53 60	SAA XIII 164
CT 53 61	SAA XV 151
CT 53 62	SAA XV 104
CT 53 63	SAA V 127
CT 53 64	SAA XV 177
CT 53 65	SAA V 15
CT 53 66	SAA XV 108
CT 53 67	SAA XV 367
CT 53 68	SAA XV 161
CT 53 69	SAA X 187
CT 53 70	SAA XVI 138
CT 53 71	SAA XV 292
CT 53 72	SAA I 237
CT 53 73	SAA XVI 118
CT 53 74+[117]	(Sg)
CT 53 75	SAA X 354
CT 53 76	SAA I 13
CT 53 77	SAA XV 119
CT 53 78+[118]	SAA XVI 64
CT 53 79	SAA V 225
CT 53 80	SAA XVI 68
CT 53 81	SAA XV 110
CT 53 82	SAA I 44
CT 53 83+[119]	SAA XV 59
CT 53 84	SAA X 17
CT 53 85	SAA V 67
CT 53 86	SAA XV 370
CT 53 87	SAA I 223
CT 53 88	SAA X 192
CT 53 89+[120]	SAA XV 113
CT 53 90	SAA I 209
CT 53 91	SAA XV 216
CT 53 92	SAA XV 37
CT 53 93	SAA XV 92
CT 53 94	SAA I 208
CT 53 95	SAA V 34
CT 53 96+[121]	SAA I 260
CT 53 97+[122]	SAA X 293
CT 53 98	SAA V 107
CT 53 99	SAA V 173
CT 53 100	SAA XV 226
CT 53 101	SAA V 37
CT 53 102	SAA XV 150
CT 53 103	SAA XV 259
CT 53 104+[123]	SAA XV 32
CT 53 105	SAA X 321
CT 53 106	SAA X 368
CT 53 107+[124]	SAA XVI 60
CT 53 108	SAA I 149
CT 53 109	SAA XVI 205
CT 53 110+[125]	SAA XV 129
CT 53 111	SAA X 345
CT 53 112	SAA I 49
CT 53 113	SAA XVI 57
CT 53 114	SAA V 112
CT 53 115+[126]	SAA X 62
CT 53 116	SAA X 356
CT 53 117	SAA X 380
CT 53 118+[127]	SAA XVI 59
CT 53 119	SAA X 268
CT 53 120+[128]	SAA I 29
CT 53 121	SAA X 367
CT 53 122	SAA V 177
CT 53 123	SAA X 292
CT 53 124	SAA V 178
CT 53 125	SAA V 69
CT 53 126	SAA V 254
CT 53 127	SAA V 110
CT 53 128	SAA I 21
CT 53 129	SAA XIII 21
CT 53 130	SAA X 223
CT 53 131	SAA V 141
CT 53 132	SAA V 46
CT 53 133	SAA V 176
CT 53 134	SAA XVI 55
CT 53 135	SAA V 236
CT 53 136	SAA I 22

CT 53 137	SAA V 122
CT 53 138	SAA V 106
CT 53 139	SAA X 182
CT 53 140	(Asb)
CT 53 141	SAA XIII 190
CT 53 142	(Asb)
CT 53 143	SAA X 360
CT 53 144	SAA I 46
CT 53 145	SAA XV 176
CT 53 146	SAA X 69
CT 53 147	SAA XVI 19
CT 53 148	SAA XVI 126
CT 53 149	SAA X 97
CT 53 150	SAA XVI 90
CT 53 151	SAA XVI 88
CT 53 152	SAA X 265
CT 53 153	SAA X 203
CT 53 154	SAA X 384
CT 53 155	SAA X 29
CT 53 156	SAA I 63
CT 53 157	SAA X 317
CT 53 158	SAA XV 41
CT 53 159	SAA X 108
CT 53 160	SAA V 35
CT 53 161	SAA XV 55
CT 53 162	SAA XVI 186
CT 53 163	SAA V 36
CT 53 164+[129]	SAA V 121
CT 53 165	SAA XIII 52
CT 53 166	SAA XV 28
CT 53 167-69	
CT 53 170	SAA V 116
CT 53 171	SAA XV 165
CT 53 172+[130]	SAA V 95
CT 53 173≠	SAA XI 145
CT 53 174	
CT 53 175≠	SAA IV 302
CT 53 176	
CT 53 177	SAA X 37
CT 53 178	SAA XVI 70
CT 53 179	SAA XV 372
CT 53 180	SAA XV 321
CT 53 181	SAA XV 356
CT 53 182	SAA XVI 94
CT 53 183	SAA I 142
CT 53 184	SAA X 208
CT 53 185	SAA I 23
CT 53 186	SAA XV 200
CT 53 187	SAA X 101
CT 53 188	SAA V 296
CT 53 189	SAA XVI 206
CT 53 190	SAA XVI 149
CT 53 191	SAA X 230
CT 53 192	SAA V 138
CT 53 193	SAA XIII 159
CT 53 194	SAA V 190
CT 53 195	SAA XV 80
CT 53 196	SAA X 387
CT 53 197	SAA V 249
CT 53 198	SAA XV 373
CT 53 199	SAA I 180
CT 53 200	SAA V 271
CT 53 201	SAA V 299
CT 53 202	SAA XV 19
CT 53 203	SAA XV 353
CT 53 204	SAA V 170
CT 53 205	SAA XV 76
CT 53 206	SAA X 4
CT 53 207	SAA XV 302
CT 53 208	SAA I 196
CT 53 209	SAA XV 318
CT 53 210	SAA V 4
CT 53 211+[131]	SAA I 257
CT 53 212	SAA I 231
CT 53 213	SAA V 26
CT 53 214	SAA I 264
CT 53 215	SAA V 128
CT 53 216	SAA XVI 101
CT 53 217	SAA XV 18
CT 53 218	SAA XVI 178
CT 53 219≠	SAA IX 11
CT 53 220	SAA XV 78
CT 53 221+[132]	SAA I 10
CT 53 222	SAA XV 128
CT 53 223	SAA XIII 142
CT 53 224	SAA XV 374
CT 53 225+[133]	SAA V 206
CT 53 226+[134]	SAA XVI 15
CT 53 227	
CT 53 228	SAA XV 341
CT 53 229	SAA I 8
CT 53 230	
CT 53 231	SAA XV 357
CT 53 232	SAA XV 88
CT 53 233	SAA I 72
CT 53 234	SAA X 146
CT 53 235	SAA XIII 150
CT 53 236≠	SAA XI 12
CT 53 237	SAA XV 242
CT 53 238	SAA XV 230
CT 53 239	SAA XV 348
CT 53 240	SAA V 230
CT 53 241	SAA X 105
CT 53 242	SAA XV 250
CT 53 243	
CT 53 244	SAA XV 195
CT 53 245	SAA I 24
CT 53 246	SAA XIII 151
CT 53 247+[135]	SAA I 114
CT 53 248	(NB)
CT 53 249	SAA XVI 207
CT 53 250	SAA V 220
CT 53 251	SAA XV 22
CT 53 252	SAA XV 97
CT 53 253	SAA XVI 74
CT 53 254	SAA X 312
CT 53 255-56	
CT 53 257	SAA V 286
CT 53 258	SAA XV 375
CT 53 259	SAA XVI 208
CT 53 260	SAA XV 261
CT 53 261	SAA V 193
CT 53 262	SAA I 198
CT 53 263	SAA XVI 182
CT 53 264	SAA V 20
CT 53 265	SAA XV 254
CT 53 266	SAA XVI 171
CT 53 267	
CT 53 268	SAA V 300
CT 53 269+[136]	SAA I 259
CT 53 270	SAA XVI 209
CT 53 271	SAA V 219
CT 53 272	SAA V 188
CT 53 273	
CT 53 274	
CT 53 275	SAA XVI 46
CT 53 276	
CT 53 277	SAA XV 210
CT 53 278	SAA XVI 210
CT 53 279	
CT 53 280	SAA V 7
CT 53 281	SAA XIII 22
CT 53 282	(Asb)
CT 53 283	SAA V 43
CT 53 284	SAA I 234
CT 53 285	SAA XV 133
CT 53 286	SAA XV 63
CT 53 287	SAA XV 49
CT 53 288	
CT 53 289	SAA XVI 129
CT 53 290+[137]	SAA X 327
CT 53 291	SAA XV 350
CT 53 292	SAA XVI 211
CT 53 293	SAA X 150
CT 53 294	SAA XVI 212
CT 53 295	SAA XV 311

CT 53 296	SAA V 61
CT 53 297	SAA XIII 121
CT 53 298	SAA X 335
CT 53 299	SAA XV 339
CT 53 300	
CT 53 301	SAA XV 322
CT 53 302	
CT 53 303	SAA XV 376
CT 53 304	SAA I 86
CT 53 305	SAA V 277
CT 53 306	SAA XV 120
CT 53 307	SAA I 37
CT 53 308	SAA XV 290
CT 53 309	SAA XVI 184
CT 53 310	SAA XV 58
CT 53 311	SAA I 15
CT 53 312+[138]	SAA I 28/ SAA X 216
CT 53 313	SAA XV 207
CT 53 314	SAA XV 247
CT 53 315	SAA XV 109
CT 53 316	SAA XIII 194
CT 53 317	SAA XVI 185
CT 53 318	SAA XV 377
CT 53 319	
CT 53 320	SAA XV 96
CT 53 321≠	SAA XI 200
CT 53 322	SAA XV 38
CT 53 323	SAA V 289
CT 53 324	SAA V 269
CT 53 325	SAA XV 309
CT 53 326	
CT 53 327	SAA I 145
CT 53 328	SAA V 30
CT 53 329-30	
CT 53 331+[139]	SAA XV 156
CT 53 332+[140]	SAA XV 190
CT 53 333	SAA I 170
CT 53 334+[141]	SAA XV 294
CT 53 335	SAA V 18
CT 53 336	
CT 53 337	SAA X 376
CT 53 338	SAA XV 352
CT 53 339	SAA XV 124
CT 53 340	SAA I 7
CT 53 341	SAA XV 286
CT 53 342	SAA XV 235
CT 53 343	SAA V 253
CT 53 344	SAA I 242
CT 53 345	SAA XV 368
CT 53 346	SAA V 57
CT 53 348	SAA I 265
CT 53 349	SAA XIII 69
CT 53 350	SAA X 271
CT 53 351	SAA XVI 9
CT 53 352	SAA XV 333
CT 53 353	SAA XVI 37
CT 53 354	SAA XVI 213
CT 53 355	SAA XV 358
CT 53 356	SAA XV 29
CT 53 357	SAA X 239
CT 53 358	SAA XV 354
CT 53 359	SAA XV 222
CT 53 360	SAA XV 355
CT 53 361	
CT 53 362	SAA XV 306
CT 53 363	SAA XV 283
CT 53 364	SAA XV 173
CT 53 365+[142]	SAA V 93
CT 53 366	
CT 53 367	SAA XV 246
CT 53 368	SAA XV 366
CT 53 369	SAA XV 198
CT 53 370+[143]	SAA V 108
CT 53 371	SAA XV 262
CT 53 372	(Asb)
CT 53 373	
CT 53 374	SAA XV 140
CT 53 375	
CT 53 376	SAA XVI 146
CT 53 377	SAA XVI 214
CT 53 378	
CT 53 379	
CT 53 380+[144]	SAA I 56
CT 53 381	SAA XVI 215
CT 53 382+[145]	SAA XV 111
CT 53 383	
CT 53 384	SAA XV 331
CT 53 385	
CT 53 386+[146]	SAA V 17
CT 53 387	SAA V 282
CT 53 388	SAA XV 134
CT 53 389	SAA V 60
CT 53 390	SAA XIII 48
CT 53 391	SAA XVI 6
CT 53 392	SAA XV 107
CT 53 393	SAA I 225
CT 53 394	SAA V 109
CT 53 395	SAA XV 345
CT 53 396	SAA XV 244
CT 53 397	SAA XVI 11
CT 53 398	SAA V 261
CT 53 399[147]	
CT 53 400+[148]	SAA XV 129
CT 53 401	SAA I 243
CT 53 402	
CT 53 403	SAA V 279
CT 53 404≠[149]	SAA III 24
CT 53 405+[150]	SAA X 293
CT 53 406	SAA XIII 195
CT 53 407	SAA V 186
CT 53 408	SAA XV 208
CT 53 409	SAA V 196
CT 53 410	SAA XV 269
CT 53 411	SAA X 184
CT 53 412[151]	
CT 53 413	SAA XIII 148
CT 53 414	SAA V 137
CT 53 415	SAA V 192
CT 53 416	SAA XV 364
CT 53 417+[152]	SAA X 102
CT 53 418	SAA XIII 120
CT 53 419	SAA I 263
CT 53 420	SAA V 252
CT 53 421	
CT 53 422	SAA XV 57
CT 53 423	
CT 53 424	SAA V 42
CT 53 425	SAA XIII 196
CT 53 426+[153]	SAA XVI 64
CT 53 427	SAA V 187
CT 53 428	SAA XVI 51
CT 53 429+≠[154]	SAA XI 19
CT 53 430+[155]≠	SAA XI 19
CT 53 431	SAA XV 342
CT 53 432	SAA V 212
CT 53 433	
CT 53 434	SAA XIII 115
CT 53 435	SAA XV 183
CT 53 436	SAA XV 139
CT 53 437	SAA XVI 175
CT 53 438+[156]	SAA I 29
CT 53 439	SAA XV 361
CT 53 440	SAA V 124
CT 53 441	SAA I 214
CT 53 442	SAA V 280
CT 53 443	SAA XV 359
CT 53 444+[157]	SAA I 204
CT 53 445	SAA V 184
CT 53 446	SAA XV 229
CT 53 447	SAA XV 315
CT 53 448-49	
CT 53 450	SAA XV 279
CT 53 451	SAA I 166
CT 53 452	SAA XIII 197

CT 53 453	SAA XV 369
CT 53 454	SAA V 131
CT 53 455+[158]	SAA XV 129
CT 53 456	SAA XVI 216
CT 53 457	SAA XV 147
CT 53 458	SAA I 255
CT 53 459	SAA XV 266
CT 53 460+[159]	SAA XV 59
CT 53 461	SAA I 161
CT 53 462+[160]	SAA V 93
CT 53 463	SAA I 3
CT 53 464	SAA XV 284
CT 53 465	SAA I 164
CT 53 466	SAA I 120
CT 53 467	SAA XV 282
CT 53 468	
CT 53 469	SAA XVI 18
CT 53 470	SAA V 157
CT 53 471	SAA XV 338
CT 53 472	SAA I 40
CT 53 473	SAA V 288
CT 53 474	SAA XV 330
CT 53 475	SAA XVI 217
CT 53 476	SAA XV 344
CT 53 477	SAA X 36
CT 53 478	SAA V 5
CT 53 479	SAA XV 50
CT 53 480	SAA V 259
CT 53 481	SAA XV 10
CT 53 482	SAA XV 252
CT 53 483	SAA X 65
CT 53 484	SAA I 61
CT 53 485	SAA V 197
CT 53 486	
CT 53 487+[161]	SAA X 293
CT 53 488	SAA XVI 218
CT 53 489	SAA XV 167
CT 53 490	SAA XV 126
CT 53 491	SAA I 186
CT 53 492	SAA V 102
CT 53 493	
CT 53 494	SAA I 211
CT 53 495	SAA X 337
CT 53 496	(Asb)
CT 53 497	SAA XV 267
CT 53 498	SAA XV 185
CT 53 499	SAA XV 323
CT 53 500	SAA XIII 153
CT 53 501	
CT 53 502	SAA I 2
CT 53 503	SAA XV 20
CT 53 504	SAA XV 193
CT 53 505	SAA XVI 116
CT 53 506	SAA I 168
CT 53 507	SAA XV 149
CT 53 508	SAA X 378
CT 53 509	SAA V 140
CT 53 510	SAA I 95
CT 53 511	SAA XV 249
CT 53 512	(Sg)
CT 53 513+[162]	SAA V 247
CT 53 514	
CT 53 515≠	SAA XI 99
CT 53 516	SAA XIII 198
CT 53 517+[163]	SAA V 258
CT 53 518	SAA XV 312
CT 53 519	SAA V 183
CT 53 520	SAA XIII 2
CT 53 521	SAA XV 287
CT 53 522+[164]	SAA V 156
CT 53 523	
CT 53 524	SAA XV 285
CT 53 525	SAA I 157
CT 53 526	SAA XV 334
CT 53 527	SAA V 208
CT 53 528	SAA XVI 174
CT 53 529	SAA XV 174
CT 53 530	
CT 53 531[165]	
CT 53 532+[166]	SAA XV 111
CT 53 533	SAA V 198
CT 53 534	SAA XV 362
CT 53 535	SAA I 68
CT 53 536+[167]	SAA X 296
CT 53 537	SAA XV 56
CT 53 538	SAA XVI 38
CT 53 539	SAA XVI 219
CT 53 540	SAA XV 253
CT 53 541	SAA XVI 157
CT 53 542+[168]	(Sg)
CT 53 543	SAA XV 378
CT 53 544	SAA XIII 199
CT 53 545	
CT 53 546	SAA XV 205
CT 53 547	
CT 53 548[169]	
CT 53 549	SAA XV 340
CT 53 550+[170]	SAA XV 190
CT 53 551	SAA XVI 176
CT 53 552	
CT 53 553	SAA V 231
CT 53 554	SAA XV 44
CT 53 555-56	
CT 53 557	SAA XV 146
CT 53 558	SAA V 276
CT 53 559	SAA XIII 51
CT 53 560+[171]	SAA V 247/ SAA XV 379
CT 53 561	SAA XV 380
CT 53 562	SAA I 212
CT 53 563	SAA I 113
CT 53 564	SAA XV 305
CT 53 565	
CT 53 566	SAA XV 296
CT 53 567	
CT 53 568	SAA XV 141
CT 53 569	SAA V 255
CT 53 570	SAA XVI 187
CT 53 571	SAA XV 51
CT 53 572	SAA XV 251
CT 53 573	SAA V 50
CT 53 574	SAA XV 381
CT 53 575	
CT 53 576	SAA XV 144
CT 53 577	SAA XV 175
CT 53 578	SAA V 76
CT 53 579+[172]	SAA V 17
CT 53 580	SAA XV 314
CT 53 581	SAA V 195
CT 53 582+[173]	SAA X 39
CT 53 583	SAA V 174
CT 53 584	SAA V 22
CT 53 585	SAA V 222
CT 53 586	SAA V 181
CT 53 587	
CT 53 588	SAA XV 145
CT 53 589	SAA I 9
CT 53 590	
CT 53 591	SAA I 111
CT 53 592	SAA XV 382
CT 53 593	SAA X 11
CT 53 594-95	
CT 53 596	SAA XV 31
CT 53 597-98	
CT 53 599	SAA XV 320
CT 53 600	
CT 53 601	SAA XIII 200
CT 53 602	SAA XV 383
CT 53 603	SAA X 64
CT 53 604	SAA XV 303
CT 53 605	
CT 53 606	SAA XV 72
CT 53 607	SAA XV 297
CT 53 608	SAA X 272
CT 53 609	
CT 53 610	SAA I 126

CT 53 611	SAA XV 371
CT 53 612-13	
CT 53 614+[174]	SAA I 25
CT 53 615	SAA V 167
CT 53 616	SAA V 9
CT 53 617	SAA V 267
CT 53 618	SAA I 262
CT 53 619	(NB)
CT 53 620	SAA I 74
CT 53 621	SAA V 175
CT 53 622	SAA XIII 201
CT 53 623	SAA XVI 153
CT 53 624	SAA XV 310
CT 53 625	SAA V 19
CT 53 626	SAA XVI 155
CT 53 627	SAA XV 270
CT 53 628	SAA V 287
CT 53 629	SAA V 285
CT 53 630	SAA XV 43
CT 53 631	SAA V 8
CT 53 632	SAA XV 227
CT 53 633	
CT 53 634	SAA XV 206
CT 53 635	SAA XIII 169
CT 53 636	SAA I 20
CT 53 637	SAA V 151
CT 53 638	SAA XVI 147
CT 53 639	SAA I 81
CT 53 640	SAA XV 347
CT 53 641	SAA V 51
CT 53 642	SAA I 17
CT 53 643	SAA XVI 220
CT 53 644	SAA I 169
CT 53 645-48	
CT 53 649	SAA XV 204
CT 53 650	SAA XVI 189
CT 53 651	SAA V 266
CT 53 652	SAA XVI 194
CT 53 653	SAA XIII 202
CT 53 654	SAA XVI 221
CT 53 655	SAA XVI 222
CT 53 656	SAA V 99
CT 53 657	SAA XVI 195
CT 53 658	SAA V 283
CT 53 659	SAA XV 99
CT 53 660	
CT 53 661	SAA XV 79
CT 53 662	SAA XIII 203
CT 53 663	
CT 53 664	(NB, Asb)
CT 53 665	SAA XV 152
CT 53 666+[175]	SAA I 260
CT 53 667	
CT 53 668	SAA XV 307
CT 53 669	SAA XVI 223
CT 53 670[176]	
CT 53 671+[177]	SAA I 116
CT 53 672≠	SAA XI 47
CT 53 673	SAA XV 153
CT 53 674+≠[178]	SAA VII 24
CT 53 675	SAA XV 148
CT 53 676	SAA V 262
CT 53 677	SAA V 278
CT 53 678	
CT 53 679+[179]	SAA V 108
CT 53 680	
CT 53 681	SAA XIII 204
CT 53 682	
CT 53 683	SAA XVI 12
CT 53 684	SAA XV 324
CT 53 685	SAA XV 325
CT 53 686	SAA XV 77
CT 53 687	
CT 53 688	SAA XVI 224
CT 53 689	SAA XV 46
CT 53 690	SAA XVI 225
CT 53 691+[180]	SAA I 112
CT 53 692	
CT 53 693	SAA XVI 7
CT 53 694	
CT 53 695	SAA V 275
CT 53 696	SAA XVI 226
CT 53 697	SAA V 41
CT 53 698	SAA XVI 227
CT 53 699	
CT 53 700	SAA XV 211
CT 53 701	
CT 53 702+[181]	SAA X 102
CT 53 703	
CT 53 704	SAA XVI 166
CT 53 705	SAA XVI 228
CT 53 706	SAA XV 326
CT 53 707	SAA XV 327
CT 53 708	SAA V 10
CT 53 709	
CT 53 710	SAA XV 384
CT 53 711	SAA XV 273
CT 53 712	(Sg)
CT 53 713	SAA XVI 229
CT 53 714	SAA XVI 230
CT 53 715	SAA XVI 13
CT 53 716	SAA XV 201
CT 53 717	SAA XV 228
CT 53 718	SAA XV 170
CT 53 719	SAA XV 263
CT 53 720	
CT 53 721≠	SAA XI 152
CT 53 722≠	SAA XI 34
CT 53 723	
CT 53 724	SAA I 79
CT 53 725	SAA XV 319
CT 53 726	SAA V 39
CT 53 727	SAA XV 191
CT 53 728	
CT 53 729	SAA V 73
CT 53 730	SAA V 248
CT 53 731	SAA XVI 151
CT 53 732	
CT 53 733	SAA XV 265
CT 53 734	SAA I 199
CT 53 735	SAA XVI 231
CT 53 736	
CT 53 737+[182]	SAA XV 190
CT 53 738	SAA XIII 205
CT 53 739	SAA XV 196
CT 53 740	
CT 53 741	SAA XV 281
CT 53 742	
CT 53 743	SAA XV 385
CT 53 744	SAA XVI 232
CT 53 745	SAA XV 160
CT 53 746	
CT 53 747	SAA I 69
CT 53 748+[183]	SAA I 259
CT 53 749	SAA XVI 233
CT 53 750	
CT 53 751	SAA XVI 160
CT 53 752	SAA XVI 161
CT 53 753-54	
CT 53 755	SAA XVI 234
CT 53 756	SAA XV 308
CT 53 757	SAA XV 143
CT 53 758	SAA XVI 235
CT 53 759	SAA XIII 55
CT 53 760	SAA X 310
CT 53 761	SAA XV 277
CT 53 762-63	
CT 53 764	SAA XVI 236
CT 53 765	SAA XV 264
CT 53 766+[184]	SAA V 258
CT 53 767	SAA XV 212
CT 53 768	SAA X 153
CT 53 769	SAA XVI 190
CT 53 770	SAA XV 197
CT 53 771	

CT 53 772	SAA XVI 237
CT 53 773-75	
CT 53 776	SAA XVI 238
CT 53 777	SAA V 235
CT 53 778	SAA XV 278
CT 53 779	SAA V 209
CT 53 780	SAA XVI 177
CT 53 781	
CT 53 782	SAA XVI 159
CT 53 783-84	
CT 53 785	SAA XV 154
CT 53 786	SAA XV 329
CT 53 787≠	SAA XI 168
CT 53 788	
CT 53 789	SAA V 185
CT 53 790	SAA XV 47
CT 53 791	
CT 53 792	SAA XVI 239
CT 53 793+[185]	SAA V 165
CT 53 794	SAA XVI 102
CT 53 795	SAA V 273
CT 53 796	
CT 53 797+[186]	SAA V 251/ SAA XV 335
CT 53 798+[187]	SAA I 260
CT 53 799	SAA V 180
CT 53 800-801	
CT 53 802	SAA I 256
CT 53 803	SAA XV 171
CT 53 804	
CT 53 805	SAA XV 386
CT 53 806	SAA XV 52
CT 53 807	
CT 53 808+[188]	SAA V 156
CT 53 809	SAA XV 255
CT 53 810	
CT 53 811+[189]	SAA XIII 53
CT 53 812+[190]	SAA XIII 53
CT 53 813	SAA XVI 130
CT 53 814	SAA I 57
CT 53 815	SAA XVI 240
CT 53 816	
CT 53 817≠	SAA XI 35
CT 53 818	SAA I 127
CT 53 819-20	
CT 53 821	SAA XV 332
CT 53 822	SAA XV 87
CT 53 823	SAA I 14
CT 53 824+[191]	SAA XV 113
CT 53 825	SAA XV 192
CT 53 826	
CT 53 827	SAA V 270
CT 53 828	
CT 53 829	SAA I 154
CT 53 830-31	
CT 53 832	SAA XV 298
CT 53 833	SAA XV 272
CT 53 834	SAA I 4
CT 53 835	SAA XV 75
CT 53 836	SAA V 268
CT 53 837	SAA XV 257
CT 53 838	
CT 53 839	SAA I 197
CT 53 840	SAA V 142
CT 53 841	
CT 53 842	SAA XV 271
CT 53 843	
CT 53 844	SAA XV 256
CT 53 845	SAA XV 336
CT 53 846	SAA XIII 165
CT 53 847	SAA V 77
CT 53 848	SAA I 218
CT 53 849-50	
CT 53 851	SAA I 213
CT 53 852	SAA V 72
CT 53 853-54	
CT 53 855	SAA XVI 167
CT 53 856	SAA V 264
CT 53 857	SAA XV 313
CT 53 858+[192]	SAA V 95
CT 53 859	SAA V 123
CT 53 860	SAA XVI 241
CT 53 861	
CT 53 862	SAA XVI 158
CT 53 863	SAA I 261
CT 53 864	SAA I 232
CT 53 865	SAA XV 299
CT 53 866	SAA I 248
CT 53 867	SAA XV 81
CT 53 868	(Asb)
CT 53 869	SAA XV 233
CT 53 870	SAA X 250
CT 53 871	SAA XV 194
CT 53 872	SAA V 129
CT 53 873	SAA I 254
CT 53 874	SAA V 143
CT 53 875	
CT 53 876	SAA XIII 172
CT 53 877	SAA XV 213
CT 53 878	SAA I 253
CT 53 879	SAA XV 276
CT 53 880	SAA XV 215
CT 53 881	SAA XV 316
CT 53 882	SAA V 265
CT 53 883	SAA XV 225
CT 53 884	SAA XV 202
CT 53 885	SAA V 216
CT 53 886	SAA XV 135
CT 53 887	SAA XV 21
CT 53 888	SAA I 182
CT 53 889	SAA XV 89
CT 53 890	SAA XIII 54
CT 53 891	SAA V 182
CT 53 892	SAA XV 86
CT 53 893	SAA XV 112
CT 53 894	SAA XVI 58
CT 53 895	SAA XV 102
CT 53 896	SAA XIII 206
CT 53 897	SAA X 237
CT 53 898	
CT 53 899	SAA XIII 207
CT 53 900	SAA X 103
CT 53 901	SAA XIII 208
CT 53 902	SAA XV 23
CT 53 903	SAA XV 260
CT 53 904	SAA XV 125
CT 53 905	SAA XIII 171
CT 53 906	SAA XIII 47
CT 53 907	SAA I 187
CT 53 908	(Asb)
CT 53 909	SAA XIII 209
CT 53 910	SAA XVI 170
CT 53 911	SAA XV 349
CT 53 912	SAA V 189
CT 53 913	
CT 53 914	SAA V 160
CT 53 915	SAA X 151
CT 53 916≠	SAA VIII 234
CT 53 917	SAA XV 132
CT 53 918	SAA V 130
CT 53 919	SAA XV 243
CT 53 920	SAA XV 245
CT 53 921	SAA XIII 188
CT 53 922	SAA XVI 242
CT 53 923+[193]	SAA I 189
CT 53 924	SAA X 388
CT 53 925	SAA XIII 210
CT 53 926	SAA X 389
CT 53 927	SAA XV 328
CT 53 928	SAA X 269
CT 53 929	SAA X 287
CT 53 930+[194]	SAA XVI 5
CT 53 931	(Asb)
CT 53 932	SAA X 311

CT 53 933	SAA X 270
CT 53 934	SAA XV 304
CT 53 935	SAA XVI 243
CT 53 936	SAA XVI 134
CT 53 937+[195]≠	SAA II 4
CT 53 938	SAA XVI 61
CT 53 939	SAA X 385
CT 53 940	SAA XVI 192
CT 53 941[196]	
CT 53 942+[197]	SAA X 44
CT 53 943	SAA X 38
CT 53 944	(Asb)
CT 53 945	SAA X 152
CT 53 946≠	SAA IX 10
CT 53 947	
CT 53 948	
CT 53 949	SAA XIII 123
CT 53 950	SAA XVI 168
CT 53 951	SAA X 248
CT 53 952	SAA XVI 164
CT 53 953	(Asb)
CT 53 954	SAA XVI 75
CT 53 955	SAA X 299
CT 53 956+[198]	SAA X 327
CT 53 957	SAA XIII 211
CT 53 958	SAA XVI 77
CT 53 959	SAA XIII 167
CT 53 960	SAA XVI 110
CT 53 961	SAA XVI 104
CT 53 962	SAA X 288
CT 53 963	SAA XVI 169
CT 53 964	SAA X 375
CT 53 965	SAA XIII 135
CT 53 966	(Asb)
CT 53 967+[199]	SAA XVI 5
CT 53 968	(Asb)
CT 53 969	SAA XIII 144
CT 53 970	SAA XVI 183
CT 53 971	
CT 53 972	SAA XVI 156
CT 53 973	
CT 53 974[200]	
CT 53 975	SAA XV 275
CT 53 976	SAA XVI 66
CT 53 977	SAA XVI 10
CT 53 978	SAA XVI 244
CT 53 979	
CT 53 980[201]	
CT 53 981	
CT 53 982	
A 71	StAT 2 163[202]
A 2129	StAT 2 12

A 2199	StAT 1 57/
	StAT 2 248
A 2484	StAT 2 315
A 2493	StAT 2 85
A 2536	StAT 2 317
A 2538	StAT 2 63
A 2548	StAT 2 318
A 2629	StAT 2 30
A 2642	StAT 2 316
A 3177env.	StAT 2 249[203]
A 3660[204]	NABU 2002/90
ACh 2 Spl. 62	SAA X 362
ADD 91[205]	
ADD 867[206]	SAA VII 15
ADD 1136	SAA XV 64
BM 79099/SAAB 2 72	
	SAA XIII 186
BM 103390[207]	
BM 123358/Iraq 4 189	
	SAA XVI 100
BM 123359/Iraq 7 99	
	SAA V 65
BM 132980	(Asb)
Bu 91-5-9,149+[208]	
	SAA XVI 47
CTDS 9[209]	
CTN 3 1-5	
CTN 3 28	
CTN 3 46	
CTN 3 84	
GPA 180-200	
GPA 203	
GPA 205-11	
GPA 230	SAA I 228
GPA 240	SAA I 104
GPA 241	SAA I 121
GPA 242	SAA V 292
GPA 243	SAA V 144
GPA 244	SAA V 191
GPA 245	SAA I 167
HAV 256f	SAA X 140
IM 132409	BaM 27 419
Iraq 34 21f./BM 135586	
	SAA XVI 21
K[210] 496	SAA X 63
K 1273	SAA XVI 52
K 12992+/RCAE III 65	
	SAA V 92
K 15626	SAA XVI 173
K 16498	
K 16521	SAA XVI 172
K 16550	SAA XVI 245

K 16561	(Sg)
K 16570	
K 17607	SAA XV 387
K 17736	SAA V 101
K 18297	SAA XV 388
K 18474	SAA XV 389
K 19147	SAA I 73
K 19520	SAA XV 390
K 19544	SAA XV 360
K 19588	SAA XV 137
K 19621	SAA V 13
K 19673	SAA I 27
K 19683	SAA XIII 170
K 19787	SAA XVI 193
K 19931	SAA XV 343
K 19971	SAA XIII 49
K 19979	SAA XVI 188
K 19986	SAA XVI 165
K 19994	SAA I 60
K 20292	SAA XV 391
K 20565	SAA XVI 246
K 20906	SAA X 370
K 20907+	SAA X 351
K 22065	SAA XV 178
KAV 112	SAA XIII 41
KAV 113	SAA XIII 40
KAV 114	SAA XIII 1
KAV 115	StAT 1 51
KAV 120	
KAV 133	
KAV 170	
KAV 197-99	
KAV 206env.[211]	SAA XIII 42
KAV 213-15	
LAS 231	SAA X 382
LAS 343	SAA X 20
LAS 347	SAA X 386
MAss 17a[212]	
MAss 51	
MAss 51env.	
MAss 63	
MAss 63env.	
MAss 67	
MAss 100	
ND 2062	CTN V p. 236
ND 2064	CTN V p. 150
ND 2067	CTN V p. 236
ND 2087	CTN V p. 237
ND 2350	CTN V p. 47
ND 2351	CTN V p. 237
ND 2353	CTN V p. 239
ND 2361	CTN V p. 240

ND 2362	CTN V p. 241
ND 2363	CTN V p. 35
ND 2369	CTN V p. 243
ND 2373	CTN V p. 244
ND 2376	CTN V p. 245
ND 2384	CTN V p. 106
ND 2392	CTN V p. 248
ND 2394	CTN V p. 249
ND 2395	CTN V p. 251
ND 2399	CTN V p. 171
ND 2400	CTN V p. 72
ND 2401	CTN V p. 251
ND 2402	CTN V p. 107
ND 2404	CTN V p. 252
ND 2411	CTN V p. 76
ND 2413	CTN V p. 254
ND 2415[213]	CTN V p. 172
ND 2417	CTN V p. 151
ND 2420	CTN V p. 255
ND 2421	CTN V p. 59
ND 2422	CTN V p. 256
ND 2423	CTN V p. 257
ND 2425	CTN V p. 258
ND 2426	CTN V p. 259
ND 2427	CTN V p. 108
ND 2428	CTN V p. 260
ND 2429	CTN V p. 261
ND 2432	CTN V p. 262
ND 2436	CTN V p. 263
ND 2439	CTN V p. 113
ND 2444	CTN V p. 39
ND 2445	CTN V p. 114
ND 2455	CTN V p. 48
ND 2456	CTN V p. 82
ND 2459	CTN V p. 264
ND 2464	CTN V p. 267
ND 2467	CTN V p. 268
ND 2468	CTN V p. 269
ND 2469	CTN V p. 270
ND 2472	CTN V p. 265
ND 2473	CTN V p. 271
ND 2474	CTN V p. 271
ND 2481	CTN V p. 214
ND 2487	CTN V p. 120
ND 2488	CTN V p. 124
ND 2493	CTN V p. 60
ND 2604	CTN V p. 273
ND 2605	CTN V p. 273
ND 2610	CTN V p. 184
ND 2613	CTN V p. 275
ND 2614[214]	CTN V p. 238
ND 2615[215]	CTN V p. 275

ND 2616	CTN V p. 224
ND 2626	CTN V p. 87
ND 2627	CTN V p. 278
ND 2630	CTN V p. 28
ND 2639	CTN V p. 280
ND 2654	CTN V p. 284
ND 2657[216]	Iraq 15 Pl. 14/ Iraq 23 Pl. 22
ND 2658	CTN V p. 285
ND 2662	CTN V p. 153
ND 2668	CTN V p. 177
ND 2669	CTN V p. 229
ND 2675	CTN V p. 287
ND 2676	CTN V p. 179
ND 2682	CTN V p. 289
ND 2688	CTN V p. 320
ND 2698 + ND 2702	CTN V p. 295
ND 2704	CTN V p. 321
ND 2708	CTN V p. 296
ND 2709	CTN V p. 142
ND 2711	CTN V p. 297
ND 2713	CTN V p. 187
ND 2716	CTN V p. 158
ND 2718	CTN V p. 300
ND 2719	CTN V p. 200
ND 2723	CTN V p. 38
ND 2724	CTN V p. 303
ND 2729	CTN V p. 36
ND 2731	CTN V p. 201
ND 2733	CTN V p. 181
ND 2735	CTN V p. 304
ND 2736	CTN V p. 202
ND 2737	CTN V p. 166
ND 2740	CTN V p. 306
ND 2743	CTN V p. 306
ND 2746	CTN V p. 307
ND 2747	CTN V p. 271
ND 2749	CTN V p. 308
ND 2752	CTN V p. 308
ND 2753[217]	CTN V p. 321
ND 2755	CTN V p. 145
ND 2756	CTN V p. 309
ND 2757	CTN V p. 202
ND 2760[218]	CTN V p. 309
ND 2761	CTN V p. 41
ND 2763	CTN V p. 311
ND 2767	CTN V p. 163
ND 2770	CTN V p. 221
ND 2772	CTN V p. 146
ND 2775	CTN V p. 313
ND 2786	CTN V p. 95

ND 2793	CTN V p. 318
ND 2794	CTN V p. 318
ND 2795	CTN V p. 97
ND 2797	CTN V p. 78
ND 2801	CTN V p. 250
ND 2802	CTN V p. 320
ND 3410	Iraq 15 138, Pl.11
ND 3470[219]	Iraq 15 Pl. 13
ND 3471	Iraq 15 147, Pl.13
NL[220] 1-5	
NL 8-15	
NL 16	SAA I 110
NL 17	
NL 18	SAA I 171
NL 19	SAA I 175
NL 20	SAA I 176
NL 21-31	
NL 32	SAA I 26
NL 33-37	
NL 39	SAA I 1
NL 40-41	
NL 42	SAA XV 84
NL 43-45	
NL 46	SAA I 32
NL 47-60	
NL 61+	SAA XV 83
NL 62	SAA V 74
NL 63+	SAA XV 83
NL 64-81	
NL 85-87	
NL 88	SAA I 172
NL 89	SAA V 215
NL 90-105	
PBS 7 132	SAA X 295
Rfdn 17 28-29	
RMA 212A	SAA X 88
SAAB 4 5/K 992	SAA XVI 54
SÉ 152	AfO 42/43 96
TCL 9 67	SAA V 100
TCL 9 68	SAA V 81
TH 1-9	
TH 10 + 88	
TH 11-16	
TH 19[221]	
TH 115	
TIM 11 29	
VAT 8646	StAT 1 52
VAT 8650	StAT 1 53
VAT 8655[222]	StAT 1 49
VAT 8688	
VAT 8699[223]	

VAT 9770	VAT 15460	StAT 1 54	83-1-18,147	SAA XVI 191
VAT 9855[224]	VAT 15545	StAT 1 56	83-1-18,153	SAA XVI 76
VAT 9875	VAT 15580	StAT 1 55	83-1-18,742+	SAA XVI 47

ABL and CT 53 joins and the other notes to the table:

[1] This table includes all the ABL texts except the Neo-Babylonian letters. A list enumerating the Neo-Babylonian ABL letters is published in Woodington (1982) 339-344. Some of the ABL texts are neither Neo-Assyrian nor Neo-Babylonian letters (in the table marked with the symbol ≠). Documents of uncertain nature (maybe not letters) are marked with a footnote. These documents mainly consist of very small fragments. In addition to the Neo-Assyrian ABL texts, all the CT 53 texts are listed in the table. ABL and CT 53 letters form by far the majority of the Neo-Assyrian letters. The texts having an abbreviation other than ABL or CT 53 are recorded only if they really are letters. In every entry in the table, the publication number, museum number or archaeological find number is followed by the publication number in the SAA series (e.g., ABL 100 SAA I 47) – provided that the letter is already published in the series. The letters not (yet) published in the series may have a reference to another publication (i.e., if they are published in transliteration and translation elsewhere). This Appendix does not include the recently excavated letters from Tušhan (Ziyaret Tepe).

The non-bibliographical abbreviations in this table are:

Asb = the letter is either part of Assurbanipal's correspondence or possibly dates to his reign

Env. = Envelope

MB = Middle Babylonian

NB = Neo-Babylonian

Sg = the letter is either part of Sargon's (II) correspondence or possibly dates to his reign

[2] ABL 68 + ABL 1450 > CT 53 11 = SAA XIII 85.

[3] ABL 82 + ABL 1396 = SAA X 74.

[4] ABL 103 + ABL 985 (K 1166) > CT 53 32 + CT 53 380 (K 7482!) = SAA I 56.

[5] ABL 111 + K 7553 > CT 53 105 = SAA X 321.

[6] ABL 121 + CT 53 164 = SAA V 121.

[7] ABL 133 + ABL 989 > CT 53 20 = SAA I 192.

[8] ABL 139 + CT 53 57 = SAA V 31.

[9] ABL 146 + K 12992 (RCAE III 65) = SAA V 92.

[10] ABL 153 + CT 53 334 = SAA XV 294.

[11] ABL 171 + ABL 641 > CT 53 19.

[12] ABL 198 + CT 53 120 + CT 53 438 = SAA I 29.

[13] ABL 233 + CT 53 671 = SAA I 116.

[14] ABL 236 + CT 53 691 = SAA I 112.

[15] ABL 244 + K 12957 > CT 53 63 = SAA V 127.

[16] ABL 253 + K 1179 + K 1207 > CT 53 33 = SAA V 56.

[17] ABL 306 + CT 53 221 = SAA I 10.

[18] ABL 307 is not a proper letter but a royal decision. For ABL 307, cf. Watanabe (1985) 151. Note that the Neo-Assyrian royal letters regularly began with *abat šarri ana PN* "The king's word to PN" and not *abat šarri ina muhhi* PN, as in ABL 307, where the phrase should be interpreted as "The king's word concerning PN". ABL 307 has been erroneously interpreted as a letter in PNA.

[19] ABL 319 + CT 53 225 = SAA V 206.

[20] ABL 320 + Sm 320 > CT 53 100.

[21] Env. of ABL 382. A list of letters still preserved in their envelopes was given in Radner (1995) 76 n. 17 and Fadhil and Radner (1996) 420. In the meantime, the total number of envelopes has increased to 6 (4 listed by Radner + MAss 63 and A 3177. The last one is only preserved as a small fragment, loose from the tablet).

[22] ABL 474 (81-2-4, 67) + Bu 89-4-26, 17 (ABL 659) > CT 53 141 = SAA XIII 190.

[23] ABL 485 + K 7342 > CT 53 22 = SAA I 62.

[24] ABL 503 + CT 53 331 = SAA XV 156.

[25] Probably from the reign of Sargon II, see SAA XIII, p. 34, n. ad no. 31.

[26] ABL 567 + CT 53 797 = SAA V 251.

[27] ABL 574 = ADD 778 = SAA XI 231.

[28] ABL 578 + CT 53 247 = SAA I 114.

[29] ABL 584 + ABL 1370 > CT 53 21 = SAA X 316.

[30] ABL 595 + K 1915 + ABL 870 > CT 53 31 = SAA X 185.

[31] ABL 597 + ABL 651 > CT 53 28 = SAA X 214.

[32] ABL 604 + CT 53 582 = SAA X 39.

[33] ABL 609 = ADD 187 = SAA VI 306.

[34] ABL 619 + K 1543 + K 1917 > CT 53 35 = SAA V 117.

[35] ABL 621 + ABL 935 = SAA I 210.

[36] ABL 624 + K 14622 > CT 53 40 = SAA V 68.

[37] ABL 629 + K 21907 = SAA X 351.

[38] ABL 633 + K 11448 > CT 53 46.

[39] ABL 637 + ABL 983 = SAA XV 68.

[40] ABL 641, see ABL 171 above.

[41] ABL 645 + ABL 1471 = SAA XV 101.

[42] ABL 651, see ABL 597 above.

[43] ABL 659, see ABL 474 above.

[44] ABL 661 + ABL 1358 = SAA X 267.

[45] ABL 665 + 83-1-18, 167 > CT 53 152 = SAA X 265.

[46] ABL 679 + ABL 1391 = SAA X 100.

[47] ABL 693 + CT 53 115 = SAA X 62.

[48] ABL 704 (K 13008) + K 7336 + K 7391 > CT 53 95 = SAA V 34.

[49] ABL 706 + ABL 1318 + CT 53 444 (K 12968) = SAA I 204.

[50] ABL 763 + ABL 1213 = SAA XV 218.

[51] ABL 799 (K 7299) + ABL 1332 (K 5997) + K 7478 > CT 53 89 + CT 53 824 = SAA XV 113.

[52] ABL 839. Only the postscript is Neo-Assyrian, otherwise the letter is Neo-Babylonian, see Mattila (1987) 27-30.

[53] ABL 864 + 82-5-22, 162 is a cultic ritual.

[54] ABL 870, see ABL 595 above.

[55] ABL 919 (K 1555) + K 15409> CT 53 51 = SAA XIII 36.

[56] ABL 921 + K 5572 + K 7327 + K 15383 > CT 53 58 = SAA V 48.

[57] ABL 924 is Middle Babylonian written in (Neo-)Assyrian script.

[58] ABL 934 + K 15059 = SAA I 151.

[59] ABL 935, see ABL 621 above.

[60] ABL 937 + K 5581 + K 7550 > CT 53 87 = SAA I 223.

[61] Probably from the reign of Sargon II, see SAA XIII, p. 34 n. ad no. 30.

[62] ABL 966 + CT 53 211 = SAA I 257.

[63] ABL 977 + CT 53 536 = SAA X 296.

[64] ABL 983, see ABL 637 above.

[65] ABL 984 + K 1612 > CT 53 24 = SAA I 150.

[66] ABL 985, see ABL 103 above.

[67] ABL 988 + CT 53 522 + CT 53 808 = SAA V 156.

[68] ABL 989, see ABL 133 above.

[69] ABL 991 (K 1268) + ABL 1051 > CT 53 41 = SAA XIII 34.

[70] ABL 993 = SAA VIII 83.

[71] ABL 1005 + K 14600 > CT 53 64.

[72] ABL 1011 + K 5578 > CT 53 68.

[73] ABL 1026 + CT 53 226.

[74] ABL 1031 (K 7395) + K 1034 + K 11021 + K 9204 + K 10541 > CT 53 17 + CT 53 107.

[75] ABL 1038 (K 13095) + K 14586 > CT 53 112 = SAA I 49.

[76] ABL 1051, see ABL 991 above.

[77] ABL 1077 + ADD 1051 = SAA VII 89.

[78] ABL 1110 (83-1-188, 55) + Bu 91-5-9, 86 > CT 53 148.

[79] ABL 1118 + 83-1-18, 793 > CT 53 153 = SAA X 203.

[80] ABL 1132 + 81-2-4, 420 = SAA X 72.

[81] ABL 1141 + CT 53 942 = SAA X 44.

[82] ABL 1157 + CT 53 290 + CT 53 956 = SAA X 327.

[83] ABL 1181. A fragment with writing on five lines only. A letter?

[84] ABL 1213, see ABL 763 above.

[85] ABL 1217 + CT 53 118!

[86] ABL 1227 + CT 53 923 = SAA I 189.

[87] ABL 1239 + JCS 39 189 = SAA II 8.

[88] Published in Kohler and Ungnad (1913) 164, no. 212.

[89] ABL 1282, see Grayson (1972) 137f § 888, 892-896.

[90] ABL 1290 + CT 53 47 = SAA V 250.

[91] ABL 1298 + CT 53 793 = SAA V 165.

[92] ABL 1302 + K 4752 > CT 53 72 = SAA I 237.

[93] ABL 1314 + K 14085 > CT 53 77.

[94] ABL 1318, see ABL 706 above.

[95] ABL 1332, see ABL 799 above.

[96] ABL 1358, see ABL 661 above.

[97] ABL 1370, see ABL 584 above.

[98] ABL 1370 + Sm 1097 = CT 53 129.

[99] ABL 1391, see ABL 679 above.

[100] ABL 1396, see ABL 82 above.

[101] Env. of ABL 1407.

[102] ABL 1409 = SAA VIII 224.

[103] ABL 1418 + K 7345 + K 13136 > CT 53 94 = SAA I 208.

[104] ABL 1423 + CT 53 614 = SAA I 25.

[105] ABL 1426 = SAA VIII 163. I prefer to interpret this as an anonymous letter containing an astrological report.

[106] ABL 1435 + CT 53 312 = SAA X 216.

[107] ABL 1447 = SAA VIII 79.

[108] ABL 1450, see ABL 68 above.

[109] ABL 1453 + CT 53 104 + K 7488 = SAA XV 32.

[110] ABL 1455, ABL 1462 and CT 53 404 are written in literary Babylonian. Thus they belong to a different genre than the real Neo-Assyrian letters.

[111] ABL 1471, see ABL 645 above.

[112] CT 53 17, see ABL 1031 above.

[113] CT 53 32, see ABL 103 above.

[114] CT 53 37 + CT 53 370 + CT 53 679 = SAA V 108.

[115] CT 53 47, see ABL 1290 above.

[116] CT 53 57, see ABL 139 above.

[117] CT 53 74 + CT 53 542 (Sg).

[118] CT 53 78 + CT 53 426.

[119] CT 53 83 + CT 53 460 = SAA XV 59.

[120] CT 53 89, see ABL 799 above.

[121] CT 53 96 + CT 53 666 + CT 53 798 = SAA I 260.

[122] CT 53 97 + CT 53 405 + CT 53 487 = SAA X 293.

[123] CT 53 104, see ABL 1453 above.

[124] CT 53 107, see ABL 1031 above.

[125] CT 53 110 + CT 53 400 + CT 53 455 + K 7307 + K 9413 + K 9593 = SAA XV 129.

[126] CT 53 115, see ABL 693 above.

[127] CT 53 118, see ABL 1217 above.

[128] CT 53 120, see ABL 198 above.

[129] CT 53 164, see ABL 121 above.

[130] CT 53 172 + CT 53 858 = SAA V 95.

[131] CT 53 211, see ABL 966 above.

[132] CT 53 221, see ABL 306 above. There is a misprint in the index of SAA I (p. 251): CT 53 211+ > CT 53 221+ SAA I 10.

[133] CT 53 225, see ABL 319 above.

[134] CT 53 226, see ABL 1026 above.

[135] CT 53 247, see ABL 578 above.

[136] CT 53 269 + CT 53 748 = SAA I 259. SAA I, p. 252, CT 53 478+ should be CT 53 748+.

[137] CT 53 290, see ABL 1157 above.

[138] CT 53 312 = SAA I 28 (published before joining with another fragment), now ABL 1435 + CT 53 312 = SAA X 216.

[139] CT 53 331, see ABL 503 above.

[140] CT 53 332 + CT 53 550 + CT 53 737 = SAA XV 190.

[141] CT 53 334, see ABL 153 above.

[142] CT 53 365 + CT 53 462 = SAA V 93.

[143] CT 53 370, see CT 53 37 above.

[144] CT 53 380, see ABL 103 above.

[145] CT 53 382 + CT 53 532 = SAA XV 111.

[146] CT 53 386 + CT 53 579 = SAA V 17.

[147] CT 53 399 is a literary text, cf. SAA XVI, p. XLV.

[148] CT 53 400, see CT 53 110 above.

[149] CT 53 404, see ABL 1455 above.

[150] CT 53 405, see CT 53 97 above.

[151] CT 53 412 is an administrative text, cf. SAA XVI, p. XLV.

[152] CT 53 417 + CT 53 702 = SAA X 102.

[153] CT 53 426, see CT 53 78 above.

[154] CT 53 429 + CT 53 430 = SAA XI 19.

[155] CT 53 430, see CT 53 429 above.

[156] CT 53 438, see ABL 198 above.

[157] CT 53 444 = K 12968, see ABL 706 above.

[158] CT 53 455, see CT 53 110 above.

[159] CT 53 460, see CT 53 83 above.

[160] CT 53 462, see CT 53 365 above.

[161] CT 53 487, see CT 53 97 above.

[162] CT 53 513 + CT 53 560 = SAA V 247. A copy joining SAA V 247 to SAA V 248 is published, ibid. p. 265.

[163] CT 53 517 + CT 53 766 = SAA V 258.

[164] CT 53 522, see ABL 988 above.

[165] CT 53 531 is a legal fragment, cf. SAA XVI, p. XLV.

[166] CT 53 532, see CT 53 382 above.

[167] CT 53 536, see ABL 977 above.

[168] CT 53 542, see CT 53 74 above.

[169] CT 53 548 is an administrative text, cf. SAA XVI, p. XLV.

[170] CT 53 550, see CT 53 332 above.

[171] CT 53 560, cf. CT 53 513 above. Is CT 53 560 erroneously republished alone as SAA XV 379?

[172] CT 53 579, see CT 53 386 above.

[173] CT 53 582, see ABL 604 above.

[174] CT 53 614, see ABL 1423 above.

[175] CT 53 666, see CT 53 96 above.

[176] CT 53 670 is a fragment of an extispicy query, cf. SAA XVI, p. XLV.

[177]CT 53 671, see ABL 233 above.

[178] According to the SAA-database CT 53 674 belongs together with ADD 827 + ADD 0914 + ADD 1135 = SAA VII 24. But note that CT 53 674 is joined to the other fragments only after the publication of SAA VII.

[179] CT 53 679, see CT 53 37 above.

[180] CT 53 691, see ABL 236 above.

[181] CT 53 702, see CT 53 417 above.

[182] CT 53 737, see CT 53 332 above.

[183] CT 53 748, see CT 53 269 above.

[184] CT 53 766, see CT 53 517 above.

[185] CT 53 793, see ABL 1298 above.

[186] CT 53 797, see ABL 567 above.

[187] CT 53 798, see CT 53 96 above.

[188] CT 53 808, see ABL 988 above.

[189] CT 53 811 + CT 53 812 = SAA XIII 53.

[190] CT 53 812, see CT 53 811 above.

[191] CT 53 824, see ABL 799 above.

[192] CT 53 858, see CT 53 172 above.

[193] CT 53 923, see ABL 1227 above.

[194] CT 53 930 + CT 53 967.

[195] CT 53 937 + 83-1-18, 420 + Bu 91-5-9, 131 > JCS 39 187 = SAA II 4.

[196] CT 53 941 is possibly a fragment from a ritual text.

[197] CT 53 942, see ABL 1141 above.

[198] CT 53 956, see ABL 1157 above.

[199] CT 53 967, see CT 53 930 above.

[200] CT 53 974. This letter originates from Assur.

[201] CT 53 980 is probably a ritual text.

[202] This tablet includes two letters.

[203] Env. of VAT 8646 (StAT 1 52).

[204] It is not so certain whether this text should be classified as a memorandum, "an informal appeal to the governor" (cf. Donbaz [2002] no. 90) or an informal letter without address. In any case, this text has many features typical of letters, and could be filed under the category of anonymous denunciations.

[205] Not certain if a letter, cf. SAA XIV, p. XXIII.

[206] Perhaps a letter, cf. n. ad SAA VII 15.

[207] BM 103390 is published even three times: Fales (1983) 246-249, 253 (copy) and photo after p. 254; Deller (1986) 21-27; Neumann (1997) 281-293.

[208] 83-1-18,742 + Bu 91-5-9,149.

[209] A letter from Dur-Šarrukin.

[210] The Appendix does not include all the very small K (Kuyunjik) fragments which may prove to be letter fragments.

[211] Env. of KAV 112.

[212] MAss 17a. A letter fragment?

[213] Possibly a list of towns, cf. CTN V, p. 173.

[214] This text is not a letter.

[215] According to Saggs (CTN V, p. 276) this document is not a letter. Perhaps it is a school tablet overlapping two different exercise texts (?).

[216] ND 2657 and ND 3470 are possibly duplicates of the same written order.

[217] ND 2753. A letter? See Saggs, CTN V, p. 321.

[218] Possibly a literary text.

[219] ND 3470, cf. ND 2657.

[220] For the complete concordance between the NL and ND numbers and the CTN V page numbers, see CTN V, pp. 323-325.

[221] Uncertain if a letter.

[222] VAT 8655 is an anonymously written order.

[223] Cf. Deller (1984) 228f.

[224] VAT 9855 is presumably a ritual text.

APPENDIX B: WRITERS OF NEO-ASSYRIAN LETTERS

This Appendix is presented in table format. Its five columns contain the following information:

(1) NAME: the name of the sender/writer of the letter

(2) PROFESSION: the profession of the sender/writer (if known)

(3) LOCATION: the geographical location of the sender/writer (if known)

(4) LETTER(S) the letters sent by the person (mentioned in the first column). If this person is also co-authoring some letters: see (also) PN.

(5) OTHER REMARKS:

(a) If known, the recipient of a letter is given if he/she was somebody other than the king of Assyria.

(b) "Private letters." It should be stressed that the definition of private letter is not very strict. The letters referred to here as private letters generally come from private archives (Assur). These are rather informal letters between family members and/or business partners (some of these letters may be part of the more formal correspondence). What is characteristics of a private letter is, for instance, the oval tablet format,[1] and that the letter was, for instance, addressed to PN "my/his/our brother/mother/father/sister." Note that family relations are not marked in the table.

(c) References to PNA are given in an abbreviated form:

- PNA no. ...: reference to the number of this individual in PNA (if several persons in PNA are attested with the same name)
- s.v. + personal name (if the name referred to in PNA differs of the one given in the first column)
- no PNA reference is given if the individual in question is the only one so far attested in Neo-Assyrian cuneiform records with a certain name or if there is no entry (yet) for such a name in PNA (as for the names from Š to Z, which remained unpublished at the time of publication of this dissertation).

(d) Astrological reports (SAA VIII) and queries to the sun-god (SAA IV) (referred to only as "reports" and "queries") by the same person.

Note that conjectural suggestions are in italics.

Abbreviations used in the Appendix:

Adn	= Adad-nerari III
anon.	= anonymous(ly)
Asb	= Assurbanipal
Esh	= Esarhaddon
Sg	= Sargon II
Sn	= Sennacherib
Tgl	= Tiglath-pileser III
&	= (authored with ...)

NAME	PROFESSION	LOCATION	LETTER(S)	OTHER REMARKS
Abat-šarri-uṣur	Mannean emissary and Assyrian informant	Mannea	SAA V 172	–
Adâ	A ruler in the vicinity of Ukku	near Ukku	SAA V 168	PNA no. 2. To the vizier
Adad-ahu-iddina (a)	Recruitment officer(?)	Calah	GPA 199	PNA no. 3. To the governor of Calah
Adad-ahu-iddina[2] (b)	– (a temple official)	*Assur*	SAA XIII 37	PNA no. 4
Adad-dan	– (official active in the west)	–	SAA XVI 131-32	PNA no. 4
Adad-eṭir	– (subordinate of the governor of Calah)	(Letter sent from Daunanu)	GPA 195	PNA no. 2. To the governor of Calah
Adad-ibni (a)	– (official active in northern Syria	(near) Til-Barsib	SAA I 184-85	PNA no. 4
Adad-ibni (b)	– (official active on the Assyrian-Babylonian border)	Zaddi mentioned in the letter	SAA V 241	PNA no. 5, cf. nos. 3.-4.
Adad-isse'a	Governor of Mazamua *and Til-Barsib*	Mazamua *and Til-Barsib*	SAA V 215-25	PNA no. 2
Adad-nerari III	King of Assyria (810-783)	Calah	TH 1, 3-8	PNA no. 3. 1 to Ilumma-le'i, governor of Naṣibina; 3-8 to Mannu-ki-mat-Aššur, governor of Guzana
Adad-šumu-uṣur	King's exorcist	Nineveh	SAA VIII 163, SAA X 185-215, 217-32, SAA XVI 167 (assignation uncert.). (205 &	PNA no. 5. SAA VIII 163 anon. The text contains an astrological omen. SAA X

NAME	PROFESSION	LOCATION	LETTER(S)	OTHER REMARKS
			Nabû-mušeṣi and Issar-šumu-ereš; 209, 221, 231 & Marduk-šakin-šumi [see also Issar-šumu-ereš, Marduk-šakin-šumi, Nabû-nadin-šumi and Nabû-zeru-lešir]; 212 & Urdu-Ea; 232 & Urdu-Ea, Issar-šumu-ereš and Akkullanu)	186, 192, 195 to the (great) crown prince (of Assyria); 209-12, 221 to the "farmer"; 198 is a (anon.) continuation of no. 197. Reports: SAA VIII 160-62, 232 (assignation uncert.). Recipient of SAA X 216
Adda-hati	Governor of Hamat	Hamat	SAA I 173-76	PNA no. 2
Ah-abi ($^{(m)}$PAB-ba)[3]	– (official)	*Kilizi*	NL[4] 44	PNA no. 2
Ahi-suri	– (superior to Ahi-ramu)	Guzana	TH 115 (late 7th century)	PNA no. 3. Private letter to Ahi-ramu
Ahu-lamur	– (subordinate of the chief eunuch)	–	ND 2698 + ND 2702 = CTN V 295f	Not in PNA, cf. nos. 8-10. Letter to the chief eunuch
Ahu-lurši	Priest of the temple of Nabû in Dur-Šarrukin	Dur-Šarrukin	SAA I 131-32	PNA no. 1. Possibly a Babylonian priest, with a Babylonian name, cf. PNA ibid.
Ahunu	Goldsmith(?)	Assur	see Issar-na'di (b)	PNA no. 16
Aia-zeru-qiša[5] (*letter written by an Assyrian scribe*)	Chaldean chieftain	Bit-Amukani (but he was detained in Assyria)	ABL 896	Private letter to his mother Humbuštu
Akkullanu	Astrologer and priest of the Aššur temple	Assur	SAA X 84-108 (see also Adad-šumu-uṣur and Ṭab-šar-Sîn).	PNA no. 1. Reports: SAA VIII 100-12
Amar-ili	– (royal official)	*Arbela*	SAA I 135-39	PNA no. 1
Ammi-hatî see Mahdê				
Ana-Nabû-atkal[6]	Exorcist	Nineveh	SAA X 309	–
Anonymous informer	Servant of the crown prince, *scholar*	– (Harran in 71:6′)	SAA XVI 69-71	69-70 to the crown prince
Anu-eṭir	–	Calah	CTN III 46	Letter to Baqi-Amri
Aplaia (a)	– (official)	Laqê	see Išmanni-Aššur	PNA no. 8

NAME	PROFESSION	LOCATION	LETTER(S)	OTHER REMARKS
Aplaia (b)	Priest of Edurhenunna, the temple of Adad of Kurbail	Kurbail	SAA XIII 186	PNA no. 16
Aplaia (c)	Temple steward of Ištar of Arbela	Arbela	SAA XIII 143	PNA no. 22
Aqar-Aia	Diviner	Nineveh	See Marduk-šumu-uṣur.	PNA no. 2. Co-author of several queries
Ariazâ	Co-ruler of Kumme	Kumme	See Arije	–
Arihu	– (official)	Laqê (see SAA I 261)	SAA I 220	PNA no. 1. To his lord Nabû-duru-uṣur
Arije	King of Kumme	Kumme	SAA V 110 (& Ariazâ)	to the treasurer
Asalluhi-ereš	Scribe	–	See Ṣallaia	–
Assurbanipal (Aššur-bani-apli)	Crown prince of Assyria (king, see below)	Nineveh, Tarbiṣu	SAA XVI 14-20	Recipient of many letters
Assurbanipal (Aššur-bani-apli)	King of Assyria (669-630; cf. also above)	Nineveh	SAA XIII 1, 3, ABL 273, 302, 523, 541, 543, 561, 945, 972, 1002, 1022, 1108, 1121, 1186, 1210, 1242, 1244, 1262, BM 132980, CT 53 142, 282, 372, 496, 908, 931, 953, 968	SAA XIII 1 to Aššur-mudammiq, Aššur-šarru-uṣur and Aššur-hussanni, ABL 273, 543, 1108 and 1244 are duplicates of the letter to Nabû-ušabši,[7] governor of Uruk, also ABL 945 is to Nabû-ušabši; ABL 302 to Nabû-šar-ahhešu; ABL 523 and 1002 to Sîn-tabni-uṣur; ABL 541 to the men of [Gambulu?]; ABL 1022, CT 53 908 to Tammaritu; ABL 561 and 1186 by Asb(?) to the people of Nippur(?); ABL 972 to *the king of Elam*; ABL 1121 and possibly also

NAME	PROFESSION	LOCATION	LETTER(S)	OTHER REMARKS
				CT 53 372 to the people of Kissik; BM 132980 to the elders of Elam; ABL 1242 to the king of Urarṭu; CT 53 953 to the village managers of [Ba]šimu
Ašipâ (a)	Governor (in the north)	Possibly Tidu[8]	SAA V 21-30	PNA no. 3. Recipient of SAA I 5-6
Ašipâ (b)	Royal official in Babylonia	Babylonia	NL 11, 35-36, 81, 91, 103	PNA no. 1
Aššur-ahu-iddina see Esarhaddon				
Aššur-alik-pani	– (a high military official)	active on the north-eastern frontier	SAA V 152-61 (156-58 &Nergal-šarrani)	PNA no. 1
Aššur-balassu-iqbi/Aššur-balaṭu-iqbi	– (superior to Handabu and involved in business affairs)	Assur	StAT 2 315	PNA: in the section between nos. 9 and 10. Private letter to Handabu
Aššur-balliṭ	– (subordinate of the goldsmith Nabû-zeru-iddina)	Assur	StAT 1 52 (VAT 8646), StAT 2 249 (A 3177)	PNA no. 12. Private letter and its envelope to his lord Nabû-zeru-iddina
Aššur-balti-niše	Palace supervisor (title in SAA I 257)	– (sent by the king to different places)	SAA V 242	–
Aššur-bani	Governor of Calah (eponym of the year 713)	Calah	SAA I 111-23	PNA no. 5. 123 to the vizier
Aššur-bani-apli see Assurbanipal				
Aššur-bel-šarrani	– (*military* official)	in Babylonia (Sab[hanu] l. 5)	SAA XV 240	–
Aššur-belu-da''in	*Governor of Halzi-atbar*	*Halzi-atbar*	SAA V 78-80	–
[*Aššur*?]-*belu*-ka''in	*Governor (or deputy) of Tušhan*	*Tušhan*	SAA V 40	–
Aššur-belu-taqqin	Assyrian prefect in Babylonia	Babylonia	SAA XV 177-83	PNA no. 7, cf. nos. 4 and 6
Aššur-belu-uda''an	Governor(?)	Northern border of Assyria	SAA V 126-27	PNA no. 1
Aššur-belu-uṣur	Governor	in the east	SAA XV 59-64	PNA no. 10

NAME	PROFESSION	LOCATION	LETTER(S)	OTHER REMARKS
Aššur-da''inanni	Governor of Mazamua (eponym of the year 733)	Mazamua	NL 100; ND 2711 = CTN V 297ff[9]	PNA no. 4
Aššur-dur-pani'a	Treasurer	Province of the treasurer	SAA V 52-53, 55-61	PNA no. 1
Aššur-hamatu'a	Priest or other high functionary of the temple of Ištar	Arbela	SAA XIII 138-42	Obverse of 139 reports a prophecy, introductory formula is at the end of the letter
Aššur-ila'i	Governor(?)	–	NL 78, ND 2669 = CTN V 229ff	PNA no. 3
Aššur-le'i	– (military official)	active on the Urarṭian border	NL 75	PNA no. 3
Aš[šur-mat]ka-pahhir	– (official)	active in the west (governor of Guzana mentioned)	NL 95	PNA no. 1
Aššur-matka-tera	*Agent* of the king	–	NL 25-26, 52	PNA no. 2
Aššur-matu-taqqin (a)	Treasurer	Assur	Rfdn 17 29 (recipient of Rfdn 17 28)	PNA no. 5. Anonymous draft of a private letter
Aššur-matu-taqqin (b)	Gate guard and overland trader	Assur	MAss 63 + env., MAss 67, MAss 100 (63, 100 & Nabû-taqqinanni)	PNA no. 6. Private letters to "their/his" brothers Duri-Aššur and Ṭab-šar-papahi; 100 to Duri-Aššur alone
Aššur-na'di	*Deputy priest of the Aššur temple*	Assur	SAA XIII 30	PNA no. 1. Probably from the reign of Sargon II
Aššur-natkil	– (military official)	Northern border of Assyria	NL 99	PNA no. 2. Letter to the palace herald
Aššur-nirka-da''in	Governor of Assur[10] (eponym of the year 720)	Assur	ND 2795 = CTN V 97ff; ND 2682 = CTN V 289f	Cf. PNA no. 2. ND 2682 to his "brother" Nabû-nammir
Aššur-patinu	– (official)	active in Bit-Zamani	SAA V 48-51	
Aššur-remanni (a)	–	Assur	KAV 120	PNA no. 25. Letter to his "brother" Nabû-šumu-iškun

NAME	PROFESSION	LOCATION	LETTER(S)	OTHER REMARKS
[Aššur?]-remanni (b) (cf. Marduk/ Nabû-remanni below)	– (high official: governor?)	– (possibly somewhere in the northeast)	SAA V 132	Cf. e.g. PNA s.v. Aššur-remanni nos. 2, 9, 10
Aššur-reṣiwa	– (official subordinate of a deputy [governor])	–	SAA XV 288-89 (letter and its envelope)	PNA s.v. Aššur-reṣuwa no. 2.[11] To the deputy (governor)
Aššur-reṣuwa (a)	Intelligent agent reporting on Urarṭian activities	Kumme	SAA V 84-103	PNA no. 2
Aššur-reṣuwa (b)	Priest of the Ninurta temple	Calah	SAA XIII 128	PNA no. 3
Aššur-šallimanni	Governor of Arrapha (eponym of the year 735)	Arrapha	NL 10, 65, 90, 96; ND 2761 = CTN V 41f, ND 2350 = CTN V 47; ND 2455 = CTN V 48f	PNA no. 1
Aššur-šarru-ibni	– (official dealing with public works)	– (city in Assyria)	SAA I 149	PNA no. 1
Aššur-šimanni	– (high official: governor of Kilizi and eponym of the year 724?)	– (*Kilizi*)	NL 24; ND 2464 = CTN V 267f	PNA no. 1, cf. no. 2
Aššur-šittu-uṣur	– (official concerned with equids)	–	NL 71	–
Aššur-šumu-iddina	–	Assur	StAT 2 163	PNA no. 18. Tablet includes two private letters: (1) to Šumma-Aššur, (2) to Šumma-ussezib
Aššur-šumu-ka''in	– (official in charge of the bull colossi for Dur-Šarrukin)	*Calah*	SAA I 150	PNA no. 1
Aššur-taklak	– (subordinate of the governor of Calah)	Calah(?)	GPA 196	PNA no. 5. To the governor of Calah
Aššur-ušallim	– (military official: royal agent)	active at the eastern border of Assyria	SAA XVI 148	PNA s.v. Aššur-ukin no. 2
Aššur-zeru-ibni	– (high official)	active in northern or western Assyria	SAA V 81	PNA no. 1. Letter to his "brother" Nergal-eṭir

NAME	PROFESSION	LOCATION	LETTER(S)	OTHER REMARKS
Aššur-[...]	– (official: palace manager?)	*Assur*	SAA I 148	See n. ad SAA I 99
Atanha-ilu	Engaged in trade(?) with leather goods	Assur (letter sent from elsewhere to Assur)	KAV 213	PNA no. 8. Private letter to his master Kiṣir-Nabû
Atanha-Šamaš	– (high official)	active in eastern Kurdistan	SAA V 150-51	PNA no. 1
Babilaiu	– (official: royal bodyguard?)	– (active in Assyrian cities)	SAA XVI 118 (see also Bel-iqiša [a])	PNA no. 15, but cf. also nos. 16-20
Babu-šumu-iddina	Astrologer	Calah	SAA X 134-35	PNA no. 2
Balasî	Astrologer and *ummânu* of Assurbanipal	Nineveh	SAA X 39-66 (40-41, 43-44, 47, 50, 53, 62, 64, 66 & Nabû-ahhe-eriba; 63 &Bammaia)	PNA no. 3. Reports: SAA VIII 80-99
Bammaia	Astrologer	Nineveh	see Balasî	PNA no. 1. Reports: SAA VIII 168-74
Banî	Deputy of the chief physician	Nineveh	SAA X 333	PNA no. 8
Bel-abu'a	– (subordinate of the palace scribe)	Assur (l. 6)	ND 2757 = CTN V 202f	to the palace scribe
Bel-duri	Governor of Damascus	Damascus	SAA I 171-72, ND 2749 = CTN V 308	PNA no. 6
Bel-emuranni	– (intelligence officer)	active on the *north-eastern* frontier of Assyria	SAA V 246	PNA no. 7, cf. no. 6
Bel-eriba (a)	– (governor?)	active on the *south-eastern frontier*	SAA XV 72	PNA no. 1
Bel-*e*[*riba*] (b) (perhaps identical with [a])	*Governor*	–	NL 58	PNA no. 1. to the governor of Calah, "his bro[ther]"
Bel-iddina (a)	*King of Allabria*[12]	*Allabria*	SAA V 164-67	PNA no. 5, but cf. also nos. 4, 6, 8
Bel-iddina (b)	High functionary of the temple of Sîn	Harran	SAA XIII 187	PNA no. 17
Bel-iqiša[13] (a)	– (high official)	– (active in Assyrian cities)	SAA XVI 111-17 (117 &[NN] and Babilaiu)	PNA. no. 10. 116 to the crown prince
Bel-iqiša (b)	Leader of the Gambulu tribe	Gambulu (*but caught and held in captivity*)	ABL 390	PNA no. 7, ABL 390 s.v. no. 10 in PNA.[14]

NAME	PROFESSION	LOCATION	LETTER(S)	OTHER REMARKS
Bel-le'i	– (military official)	*Arrapha*	SAA XV 16	PNA no. 2
Bel-lešir	Governor	– (*in the west*)	NL 87	PNA no. 5
Bel-liqbi	Governor of Ṣupat	Ṣupat	SAA I 177-82	–
Bel-naṣir	– (official)	Arbela(?)	SAA XVI 121	PNA no. 14
Bel-šarru-uṣur	– (Temple functionary)	– (see n. ad SAA XIII 191)	SAA XIII 191	PNA no. 23
Blacksmiths	Blacksmiths	Nineveh(?)	SAA XVI 40	Letter without introductory formula
Borsippan women	–	Borsippa	SAA XVI 153	–
Chief eunuch	Chief eunuch	*Calah*	TH 12 (reign of Adn)	to Mannu-ki-mat-Aššur, governor of Guzana
Chief scribe	Chief scribe	*Nineveh* (conjectural as the date of the letter is unknown)	VAT 9875	to Babu-ahu-iddina, Babu-mušeṣi, Miqtu-adur and their colleagues
Chief victualler	Chief victualler	*Nineveh*/*Calah*	CT 53 230	–
City rulers working in Milqia	City rulers	from the east	SAA I 147	–
Commander-in-chief	Commander-in-chief	Province of the commander-in-chief/Calah	TH 9-10(+88) (reign of Adn)	to Mannu-ki-mat-Aššur, governor of Guzana
Commander-in-chief	Commander-in-chief	Province of the Commander-in-chief	ND 2361 = CTN V 240f	
Dadî (a)	– (high official of the Aššur temple)	Assur	SAA XIII 18-24	PNA no. 11
Dadî (b)	Priest of the Bet-Kidmuri of Ištar	Nineveh	SAA XIII 154 (Esh)	PNA no. 12. To the crown prince
Dadi-ereš	*Deputy priest of the Aššur temple*	Assur	StAT 1 56 (VAT 15545)	PNA no. 2. Private letter to *Mar*-[...]
Dinanu	– (official)	active on the north-eastern frontier	SAA V 170-71 (see also Nabû-belu-uṣur)	PNA no. 1. 171 an anon. letter without address
Duri-Aššur (a)	Governor of Tušhan (eponym of the year 728)	Tušhan	NL 28-29, 49, 67	PNA no. 2
Duri-Aššur (b)	– (involved in overland trade)	Assur	StAT 1 53 (recipient of Mass 51, 63, 67, 100)	PNA no. 9. Private letter to "his brother" Aššur-reṣuwa
Enigmatic anonymous writer	Scholar, informer	*Nineveh*	SAA XVI 62-68	–

NAME	PROFESSION	LOCATION	LETTER(S)	OTHER REMARKS
Esarhaddon (Aššur-ahu-iddina)	King of Assyria (680-669)	Nineveh	SAA X 216, SAA X 295;[15] SAA XIII 2, 7 (these two can also be by Asb), SAA XVI 1-13	PNA no. 7. SAA X 216 by the "farmer" to Adad-šumu-uṣur and Marduk-šakin-šumi, 295 to Urdu-Gula; SAA XVI 1 to Urtaku, king of Elam, 2 to the queen mother (Naqi'a), 3 to Issar-na'di, 4 to Ištar-[...], 5 to [...*l*]*î*
Gabbu-ana-Aššur	*Palace herald*	Kurbail	SAA V 113-25	PNA no. 1
Governor of Assur	Governor (possibly Adad-belu-ka''in or Aššur-nirka-da''in)	Assur	GPA 188-89	Letters to "his brother" Šarru-duri, governor of Calah
Governor of Calah	Governor	Calah	GPA 190	to Ṣil-šarri
Gula-eṭir	–	Assur	CT 53 974 (tablet includes two letters)	PNA no. 3. Private letters to Ribaia/ Riba-Aia and *Meia* (f.)
Hunanu	– (official)	–	GPA 180	PNA no. 2
Hunnî	Priest or scholar(?)	*Nineveh*	SAA I 133-34	PNA no. 1
Hu-Teššub	Ruler of Šubria, Assyrian vassal	Šubria	SAA V 44-45, ND 2439 = CTN V 113f	–
Ibašši-ilu	*pahhizu*	–	SAA XVI 30	PNA no. 2
Iddinaia(/ Nadin-Aia)	Priest of the Ninurta temple	Calah	SAA XIII 126 (See also Nabû-balassu-iqbi)	PNA no. 8.
Iddin-Aššur	– (official)	*Assur*	SAA XIII 31 (*reign of Sg*)	PNA no. 6
Iglî	– (official responsible for building activities)	*Dur-Šarrukin*	See Nabû-ušabši	PNA no. 1
Ikkaru	*Chief* physician	Nineveh	SAA X 328-32 (332 &[NN])	PNA no. 2
Ila'i-Bel	– (official)	in the south-west	SAA I 214-15	215 to his lord Nabû-duru-uṣur
Il-iada'	Governor of *Dur-Šarrukku*	Northern Babylonia	SAA XV 155-76	PNA no. 1. 169 to the vizier

NAME	PROFESSION	LOCATION	LETTER(S)	OTHER REMARKS
Ilu-iqbi	– (*member of the temple personnel*)	– (Dur-Šarrukin?)	SAA I 140-44	PNA no. 2
Ina-šar-Bel-allak	Treasurer of Dur-Šarrukin	Dur-Šarrukin	SAA I 128-30	PNA no. 2
Inurta-belu-uṣur	– (high official)	active in the north-west	NL 64, 104, ND 2401 = CTN V 251f; ND 2604 = CTN V 273	PNA no. 5. Recipient of NL 23?
Inurta-ila'i (a)	–	Guzana	TH 19 (not certain if a letter)	PNA no. 4
Inurta-ila'i (b)	*Governor of Naṣibina* (eponym of the year 736)	*Naṣibina*	NL 15, 34, 37	PNA no. 6. 37 to the palace scribe
Inurta-ila'i (c)	– (official)	Calah	GPA 193	PNA no. 8. To the governor of Calah
Inurta-ila'i (d)	– (official)	*active in the region of Til-Barsib*	SAA I 186 (SAA I 187 Inurta-ila'i or Nabû-pašir?)	PNA no. 10
Inurta- [...]	– (official)	–	SAA XVI 179	PNA no. 15
Iqbi-Aššur	Scribe of Kar-Šalmaneser	Kar-Šalmaneser (i.e. Til Barsib)	SAA XVI 44	PNA nos. 2-3
Issar-duri	Governor of Arrapha (eponym of the year 714)	Arrapha	SAA XV 1-15	PNA no. 9
Issar-na'di (a)	Mayor	Assur	see Mutakkil-Aššur	PNA no. 19
Issar-na'di (b)	Chief goldsmith	Assur	StAT 1 54 (& Nabû-zeru-iddina, Qibit-Aššur, Šulmu-mat-Aššur and Ahunu)	PNA no. 23. Private letter to Nabû-šumu-iškun and Aššur-kurubšunu
Issar-nadin-apli	Foreman of the scribal college of Arbela	Arbela	SAA X 136-42	PNA no. 5. 136 to the crown prince. 136-37 without his name but with his title
Issar-šumu-ereš	Chief scribe	Nineveh	SAA X 4-38, SAA XVI 80 (24 & Adad-šumu-uṣur and Marduk-šakin-šumi; 25 & Urdu-Ea and Marduk-šakin-šumi; see also Adad-šumu-uṣur and Nabû-zeru-lešir)	PNA no. 3. 16-17 to the queen mother; 26 to the "farmer", 30 anon. SAA XVI 80 is an anon. memorandum. Reports: SAA VIII 1-38. (3, 19 and 21 anon.)

NAME	PROFESSION	LOCATION	LETTER(S)	OTHER REMARKS
Issar-šumu-iqiša	– (official)	active on the north-eastern frontier	SAA V 169	PNA no. 4
Issar- [...]	Priest of Bet-Kidmuri	Calah	SAA XIII 129	PNA no. 26
Išmanni-Aššur	*Governor*	in the south-west	SAA I 216-19 (219 &Aplaia and Šarru-lu-dari)	PNA no. 2
Itti-Šamaš-balaṭu	– (royal agent)	Northern Phoenicia	SAA XVI 126-29	–
Kabar	– (official)	Assur	KAV 133	PNA no. 2. To the chief eunuch
Kabtî	Scribe in the house of the palace superintendent	Assur	SAA XVI 98	PNA no. 15, cf. nos. 8-11, 16
Kanunaiu	Deputy of the palace scribe	Nineveh	SAA XVI 79 (& Mannu-ki-Libbali)	PNA no. 16
Kenî	–	– (letter found in Calah)	IM 132409 (BaM 27 419)	PNA no. 31. Private letter to his father Nabû-šumu-iddina
Kinâ	– (*subordinate of the chief cook*)	*Arbela*	SAA XVI 120	PNA no. 4
King of Assyria[16] (Letters from Calah: Tiglath-pileser III or Sargon II)	King of Assyria	Calah; Nineveh/ Calah	NL 54, 86, ND 2404 = CTN V 252f; ND 2735 = CTN V 304ff; GPA 181-82, CT 53 168, 816	NL 54 to the clergymen, the congregation, leaders of [Der$^{?}$], and the citizens of Babylon, NL 86 to Aššur-belu-[...], ND 2404 to Madaia, ND 2735 to Aššur-remanni and the scribe Nabû-bel-ahhešu, GPA 181 to the governor of Calah, GPA 182 to Qat-ili-gabbu
Kiṣir-Aššur	Governor of Dur-Šarrukin	Dur-Šarrukin	SAA I 124-27	PNA no. 7
Kudurru	*Chieftain of Bit-Dakkuri* (son of Šamaš-ibni)	(in confinement in Nineveh)	SAA XVI 31	PNA no. 12
Kuškaiu	– (official: in charge of a town)	*in Mazamua*	SAA V 213-14 (letter and its envelope)	to his lord Nabû-hamatu'a, deputy governor of Mazamua

NAME	PROFESSION	LOCATION	LETTER(S)	OTHER REMARKS
Liphur-Bel see Nashir-Bel/Nashur-Bel				
Lu-teširi (f.)	– (*female official*)	Assur	KAV 170	*Private* letter to the woman Kabtaia
Magnates of Assurbanipal	Magnates of Assurbanipal	*Nineveh*	ABL 623, 1163	623 to the eunuch (of [...]) and the deputy [...] of the city [...], 1163 to the eunuch and [...]
Mahdê (Ammi-hatî)	Governor of Nineveh (eponym of the year 725)	Nineveh (but note that his letters relate to the north)	SAA V 74-77, possibly also ND 2436 = CTN V 263f	PNA no. 1
Mannî	– (official: *subordinate of* Isseme-Ili, palace manager of the Review Palace)	Calah	CTN III 2	PNA no. 7. To Isseme-ili.[17]
Mannu-ki-Adad	Governor of ...(?)	in the east	SAA V 237-40	PNA no. 7. Recipient of SAA I 11
Mannu-ki-Arbail	– (official)	active in the north-east	SAA V 194	PNA no. 3
Mannu-k[i-Aššur-le'i]	Governor(?) of Guzana	Guzana	SAA I 233-34	PNA no. 2, cf. no. 1
Mannu-ki-Libbali	– (*scribe* working under the palace scribe)	Nineveh	SAA XVI 78 (see also Kanunaiu)	PNA no. 2
Mannu-ki-mat-Aššur	Governor of Guzana (eponym of the year 793)	Guzana	TH 13-16 (recipient of TH 3-12)	PNA no. 1. TH 13 to Mušezib-Aššur, 14 to Šamaš-zeru-uṣur, 15 to [Bel] -ahhešu, 16 to Zeru-ukin
Mannu-ki-Nergal	– (high official)	*Dur-Šarrukin*	NL 94	–
Mannu-ki-Ninua	Governor of Kar-Šarrukin	Kar-Šarrukin	SAA XV 90-105	PNA no. 2, however, see no. 1 for SAA XVI 105
MAN[...]	– (official)	active in the west	SAA I 252	–
Mardî	– (Babylonian, subordinate of the governor of Barhalza)	Barhalza	SAA XVI 29	PNA nos. 10 and 5
Marduk-*bani*-[...]	– (official)	–	SAA XVI 180	PNA s.v. Marduk-ibni no. 8

Name	Profession	Location	Letter(s)	Other remarks
Marduk-remanni[18]	Governor of Calah	Calah	SAA I 110 (NL 16)	PNA no. 5
Marduk-šakin-šumi	Chief exorcist	Nineveh	SAA X 233-72 (256, 259 & Adad-šumu-uṣur. See Adad-šumu-uṣur, Issar-šumu-ereš and Nabû-nadin-šumi)	PNA no. 2. 270 anon. Recipient of SAA X 216
Marduk-šallim-ahhe	Scribe/priest of the Aššur temple	Assur	SAA XIII 8-15, 17 (17 uncert. See also Ṭab-šar-Sîn)	PNA no. 3
Marduk-šarrani	– (official)	active in northern Babylonia	SAA XV 187-88	PNA no. 1, cf. nos. 2 and 5
Marduk-šarru-uṣur (a)[19]	Governor of Šingibutu	Šingibutu	SAA XV 69-71,	PNA no. 5, cf. no. 6
Marduk-šarru-uṣur (b)	– (high official: Assyrian prefect in Babylonia?)	active in Babylonia	SAA XV 184-85	PNA no. 6, cf. nos. 5, 7-9
Marduk-šarru-uṣur (c)	– (official concerned with the textile industry)	Nineveh	SAA XVI 82-83	PNA no. 18, cf. nos. 14-15
Marduk-šumu-uṣur (d)	Chief diviner	Nineveh	SAA X 173-77 (176 &Naṣiru and Aqar-Aia, 177 & Naṣiru and Tabnî).	PNA no. 1, cf. no. 3. Co-author of several queries
Marduk- [...]	Priest/official of the Ištar temple	Arbela	SAA XIII 147	PNA no. 2
Mar-Issar (a)	– (official: subordinate of the governor of Calah)	Calah	GPA 197	PNA no. 15. To the governor of Calah
Mar-Issar (b)	Scholar, royal agent in Babylonia	Akkad	SAA X 347-70, SAA XVI 171	PNA no. 18
Mayors and elders of the Inner City	Mayors and elders of the Inner City	Assur	SAA XVI 96	–
Mayors, city scribe, the principals and the citizens of the Inner City	Mayors, city scribe, the principals and the citizens of the Inner City	Assur	SAA XVI 97	–
Mušallim-Adad	– (military official)	–	SAA V 244	PNA no. 2

NAME	PROFESSION	LOCATION	LETTER(S)	OTHER REMARKS
Mušallim-Aššur	Governor of Naṣibina[20]	Naṣibina	TH 11 (reign of Adn)	PNA no. 1. To Mannu-ki-mat-Aššur, the governor of Guzana
Mušezib-*ilu*	– (official)	active in Babylonia	NL 73	PNA no. 5[21]
Mušezib-ilu	– (military official)	active in Arrapha and northern Babylonia	NL 72	PNA no. 6
Mutakkil-Adad	– (official)	–	see Nabû-tukulti	PNA no. 1
Mutakkil-Aššur	Deputy priest of the Aššur temple	Assur	SAA XIII 32-33 (33 &Issar-na'di [a])	PNA no. 8
Mutaqqin-Aššur	– (linked with the treasurer Aššur-matu-taqqin)	Assur	see Urdî	PNA no. 9
Nabû'a	Astrologer	Assur	SAA X 122-27	PNA no. 38. Reports: SAA VIII 126-42
Nabû-ahhe-eriba (a)	Astrologer at the royal court	Nineveh	SAA X 67-83 (see also Balasî)	PNA no. 6. Reports: SAA VIII 39-79 (69 anon.)
Nabû-ahhe-eriba (b)	– (subordinate of Didia, involved in trading ventures)	Assur	KAV 214, VAT 9770	PNA no. 12. Private letters to his lord Didia
Nabû-ahhe-šallim	Scholar *at the royal court*	*Nineveh*	SAA X 153, SAA XVI 181	PNA nos. 5-6,[22] cf. also no. 11
Nabû-ahu-iddina	–	*Nineveh*	SAA XVI 56	PNA no. 55. *Private* letter to his "lord" Balti-lešir (f.)
Nabû-ahu-uṣur	Royal bodyguard	active in Mazamua	SAA V 226	PNA no. 1, cf. no. 2
Nabû-ašared	Priest/official of the Aššur temple	Assur	SAA XIII 34-35	PNA no. 5
Nabû-balassu-iqbi	Priest of the Ninurta temple	Calah	SAA XIII 124-25 (both &Iddinaia/ Nadin-Aia)	PNA no. 11
Nabû-ballissu	–	Assur	BM 103390 (ZA 73 13)	PNA no. 5. Private letter to his mother Kallutu and to Qarruru
Nabû-balliṭanni (a)	– (official)	active in Babylonia, possibly in Lahiru	SAA XV 140-41	PNA no. 1

NAME	PROFESSION	LOCATION	LETTER(S)	OTHER REMARKS
Nabû-balliṭanni (b)	– (official)	Calah	CTN III 1	PNA no. 2. *Private* letter to Ṣilli-Nabû and Adad-aplu-iddin
Nabû-bani-ahhe	– (official)	*Calah*[23]	SAA XIII 127	PNA no. 2
Nabû-bel-šumati	Governor of Sealand	Sealand	ABL 839	PNA no. 10. NB letter, only postscript in NA
Nabû-belšunu	Exorcist and high priest of the Aššur temple	Assur	SAA XIII 39	PNA no. 1. To Aššur-mudammiq
Nabû-belu-ka''in	Governor of Kar-Šarrukin and later *governor of Lubda*	Kar-Šarrukin, *Lubda*	SAA XV 24-47, 83-89, ND 2709 = CTN V 142f	PNA no. 1
Nabû-belu-uṣur	– (official)	*active in the north-east*	SAA I 258 (& Dinanu)	PNA no. 5
Nabû-da''inanni	– (official)	–	SAA XVI 119	PNA no. 3
Nabû-de'iq	– (high official)	active in the west	SAA I 226-32 (229 assignation uncert., see n. ad SAA I 229)	PNA no. 1. 228 to the governor (of Calah), his lord, 232 to [...]-ti-Bel
Nabû-deni-epuš	– (governor of Nineveh and eponym of the year 704?)	– (Nineveh?)	SAA I 151	PNA no. 1, but cf. no. 2
Nabû-dur-makie	– (official)	Hindanu	SAA I 210 (& [Nabû-pašir?])	PNA no. 1
Nabû-duru-uṣur	Deputy governor of Der	Der	SAA XV 129-35	PNA no. 2; 129-31, 133 to the governor of Der, perhaps also 134-35
Nabû-eṭir	– (official)	– (Hubana)	ND 2373 = CTN V 244f	PNA no. 1
Nabû-eṭiranni	– (chief cupbearer?)	–	ND 2392 = CTN V 248f	PNA no. 2, cf. no. 1
Nabû-gamil	Exorcist	Nineveh	SAA X 308	PNA no. 1
Nabû-hamatu'a	Deputy governor of Mazamua	Mazamua	SAA V 210-12	PNA no. 1. Recipient of SAA V 213-14
Nabû-ila'i	–	*Nineveh*	SAA XVI 57	PNA no. 3. Private letter to his "brother" Puṭiširi
Nabû-*IŠ-ibni*	– (official)	– (*middle Euphrates*)	NL 17	–

NAME	PROFESSION	LOCATION	LETTER(S)	OTHER REMARKS
Nabû-kudurri-uṣur	– (member of the personnel of the Nabû temple)	Calah	SAA XIII 130	PNA no. 3
Nabû- [le'i?]	*Governor of Birati*	*Birati*	SAA V 128-31	PNA no. 2
Nabû-mušeṣi (a)	*Scholar* (but cf. LAS II no. 170)	Nineveh	see Adad-šumu-uṣur	PNA no. 1
Nabû-mušeṣi (b)	– (member of the temple personnel)	*Arbela*	SAA XIII 145	PNA no. 4, cf. no. 5 (son of Nabû-reši-iššI)
Nabû-mušeṣi (c)	Goldsmith	Assur	StAT 1 51 (KAV 115)	PNA no. 7. Private letter to his "brother" Nabû-zeru-iddina
Nabû-nadin-šumi	Exorcist	Nineveh	SAA X 273-88 (281 &Adad-šumu-uṣur and Marduk-šakin-šumi, 287 anon.)	PNA no. 2
Nabû-nammir	– (high official, governor or deputy of Šamaš-bunaia?)	active in Babylonia	NL 1, NL 33; ND 2411 = CTN V 76ff, ND 2444 = CTN V 39f, ND 2797 = CTN V 78f, perhaps also ND 2474 = CTN V 271f (NL 1 & Šamaš-bunaia)	PNA no. 2. ND 2444 s.v. Nabû-[...] no. 3. Recipient of ND 2682 = CTN V 289f
Nabû-naṣir	Exorcist	Nineveh	SAA X 296-307 (297 &Urdu-Nanaia; 307 anon.: attribution uncert.)	PNA no. 16. 304 to the "farmer"
Nabû-pašir	Governor(?) of Harran	Harran	SAA I 188-203 (SAA I 187 Nabû-pašir or Inurta-ila'i?) (see also Nabû-dur-makie)	PNA no. 1. 191 to the vizier
Nabû-ra'im-nišešu	– (high military official)	active in Der and its vicinity	SAA XVI 136-47 (136-38, 140, 142, 145 &Salamanu; 146-47 assignation uncert.)	PNA no. 1
Nabû-rehtu-uṣur	– (a servant of the queen mother?)	– (Nineveh?)	SAA XVI 59-61	PNA no. 4, cf. no. 6
Nabû-remanni	*Governor of* Parsua	Parsua	SAA XV 53-58	PNA no. 3

NAME	PROFESSION	LOCATION	LETTER(S)	OTHER REMARKS
Nabû-reši-išši	– (member of the temple personnel, father of Nabû-mušeṣi)	*Arbela*	SAA XIII 144	PNA no. 6
Nabû-riba-ahhe	– (subordinate of the crown prince)	Nineveh	SAA I 153	PNA no. 1. To the crown prince
Nabû-sagib(i)	– (*goldsmith or exorcist*)	Nineveh	SAA XVI 81	PNA no. 1, cf. no. 2
Nabû-šarru-uṣur (a)	– (official)	– (Mount Kirmesi mentioned)	SAA V 83	PNA no. 6
Nabû-šarru-uṣur (b)	– (official concerned with textiles)	Nineveh or Kurbail	SAA XVI 84-85	PNA nos. 14, 16
Nabû-šulmu-ereš	–	Assur	KAV 215	Private letter to his mother Baia
Nabû-šumu-iddina (a)	Fort commander of Lahiru	Lahiru	SAA XV 136-39[24]	PNA no. 7
Nabû-šumu-iddina (b)/Nadinu	Mayor or "inspector" of the Nabû temple	Calah	SAA XIII 78-123, SAA XVI 175-77, K 21982	PNA no. 15. 78 to the crown prince
Nabû-šumu-iddina (c)	Scholar, foreman of the college of ten scribes	Nineveh	SAA X 128-30 (see also Nabû-zeru-lešir)	PNA no. 16. 128 to the "farmer," 130 to the palace scribe
Nabû-šumu-iškun (a)	– (official)	–	ND 2736 = CTN V 202	PNA no. 1
Nabû-šumu-iškun (b)	– (official)	*Nineveh*	SAA XVI 86-87	PNA no. 13
Nabû-šumu-ka''in	Scribe	Assur	SAA XVI 100	PNA no. 2
Nabû-šumu-lešir (a)	– (official)	–	see Nabû-tukulti	PNA no. 8
Nabû-šumu-lešir (b)	*Scribe*	Calah	CTN III 28	PNA no. 14. *Private* letter to Ham-puhi
Nabû-tabni-uṣur	Physician	–	SAA X 334	PNA no. 2
Nabû-taqqinanni	– (involved in overland trade)	Assur	MAss 51 + its envelope (see also Aššur-matu-taqqin [b])	PNA no. 12. Private letter to his lord Duri-Aššur
Nabû-tukulti	– (official)	–	SAA XVI 41 (& Nabû-šumu-lešir, Mutakkil-Adad)	PNA no. 2
Nabû-uṣalla	Governor of Tamnuna	Tamnuna	SAA V 104, ND 2487 = CTN V 120ff	PNA no. 2., cf. no. 3
Nabû-ušabši	– (responsible for building work)	*Dur-Šarrukin*	SAA V 293 (& Iglî)	PNA no. 2

NAME	PROFESSION	LOCATION	LETTER(S)	OTHER REMARKS
Nabû-zer-kitti-lišir (a)	– (official)	working in Dur-Šarrukin	SAA I 152	PNA no. 2
Nabû-zer-kitti-lišir (b)	Overseer of white frit	–	SAA XVI 32-33	PNA no. 4
Nabû-zeru-iddina (a)	Lamentation priest of Sîn and the king	Harran and Nineveh	SAA X 345-46, SAA XVI 174	PNA no. 11
Nabû- [*zeru-iddina*] (b)	Goldsmith	Assur	StAT 2 248/ StAT 1 57 (see also Issar-na'di [b])	PNA no. 21. Private letter to [...]. Recipient of StAT 1 51-52, StAT 2 249)
Nabû-zeru-lešir	Chief scribe/ *exorcist*	Nineveh	SAA X 1-3, SAA XVI 50 (1 & Adad-šumu-uṣur, Nabû-šumu-[iddina], Urdu-Ea and Issar-šumu-ereš, 3 &Adad-šumu-uṣur)	PNA no. 4. SAA X 1-2 to the "farmer," SAA XVI 50 to the palace manager
[Nabû] -zeru-uṣur	Scribe of the palace supervisor	Nineveh	SAA XVI 88	PNA no. 3
Nabû-[...] (a)	– (official)	–	NL 43	–
Nabû-[...] (b)	– (official)	–	NL 97	PNA no. 2
Nabû-[...] (c)	*Priest*	*Nineveh*	SAA XIII 38	–
Nabû-[...] (d)	– (from the archive of exorcists)	Assur	VAT 8688	A broken private letter to Nabû-[...]
Nabû-[…] (e)	–	–	K 22002	–
Na'di-ilu	Chief cupbearer	– (province of the chief cupbearer)	SAA V 62-73, CT 53 74 + 542 (see also Ṭab-ṣill-Ešarra	PNA no. 5
Nadinu see Nabû-šumu-iddina (b)				
Nadin-[...]	– (official)	–	SAA XV 290	PNA no. 1
Nahiš-[...]	– (subordinate of the palace scribe)	active in Babylonia	ND 2786 = CTN V 95ff	to the palace scribe
Nanî	– (official)	*Calah*	SAA XVI 124	PNA no. 17, cf. no. 14. To the crown prince
Nanû	– (official)	*Nineveh*	SAA V 247-48	PNA no. 1
Nashir-Bel/Nashur-Bel (a)	–	Calah	ND 3471 (reign of Adn)	PNA no. 1. To Nabû-le'i
Nashir-Bel/Nashur-Bel (b)	Governor of Amidi and Sinabu (eponym of the year 705)	Amidi	SAA V 1-20	PNA no. 3

NAME	PROFESSION	LOCATION	LETTER(S)	OTHER REMARKS
Naṣiru	Diviner	Nineveh	(SAA X 180 [NB]; see also Marduk-šumu-uṣur)	PNA no. 2. Co-author of several queries
Nergal-a[šared?]	– (military official)	*active in the north*	NL 77	PNA no. 2
Nergal-ballit̩	– (military official)	*Arbela*	SAA I 155	PNA no. 1
Nergal-belu-uṣur	– (official)	–	SAA XV 291	PNA no. 5
Nergal-eṭir (a)	– (subordinate of the governor of Calah)	*Calah* (Rapiqu mentioned)	GPA 194	PNA no. 1. To the governor of Calah
Nergal-eṭir (b)	– (official)	active on the eastern border	SAA XV 65-68	PNA no. 5, cf. nos. 6-7. Recipient of SAA V 81
Nergal-ibni	– (official)	Huzirina	NL 102	PNA no. 1
Nergal-šarrani (a)	– (official: deputy of Aššur-alik-pani)	active on the north-eastern frontier	see Aššur-alik-pani	PNA no. 1
Nergal-šarrani (b)	Priest of Nabû temple	Calah	SAA XIII 70-77	PNA no. 3, cf. no. 5. 75 to the "farmer," 76-77 to the queen mother
Nergal-šumu-iddina	Astrologer	– (Nineveh or Calah?)	SAA X 131-33	PNA no. 6
Nergal-uballiṭ	Governor of Arzuhina (eponym of the year 731)	Arzuhina	NL 41, possibly also SAA XV 292[25]	PNA no. 4
Nurî	– (official?)	*Assur*	StAT 2 63	PNA no. 4. *Private* letter to Kanunaiu
Oilpressers (all names given)	Oilpressers	Assur	KAV 197	Twenty oilpressers write a joint letter to their lord Irmulu
Palace supervisor (a) (ša-pan-ekalli)	Palace supervisor	– (sent by the king to different places)	SAA I 257	–
Palace supervisor (b) (ša-pan-ekalli)	Palace supervisor	Calah	GPA 191	to the governor of Calah
Pan-Aššur-deni	–	Assur	KAV 198	PNA no. 2. Private letter to Mukin-Mina
Pan-Aššur-lamur	– (official, *eunuch*)	–	SAA I 156-57	PNA no. 4

NAME	PROFESSION	LOCATION	LETTER(S)	OTHER REMARKS
Pulu	Lamentation priest of the Nabû temple	Calah	SAA XIII 131-33	PNA no. 8
Qibit-Aššur	Goldsmith	Assur	see Issar-na'di (b)	PNA no. 10
Qurdi-Aššur-lamur (probably also as Qurdi-Aššur)	Governor of Ṣimirra(?)	Ṣimirra(?)	NL 12-14, 21, 69, 98, ND 2662 = CTN V 153f, ND 2716 = CTN V 158ff	–
Rab mugi	Rab mugi	*Calah*	GPA 192	to the governor of Calah
Recruitment officers	Recruitment officers	Calah(?)	SAA I 162	–
Remutu	– (subordinate of Nabû-duru-uṣur involved in pest control)	active in the west	SAA I 221	PNA no. 3. To his lord Nabû-duru-uṣur
Salamanu	– (high military official: *deputy* of Nabû-ra'im-nišešu)	active in Der and its vicinity	see Nabû-ra'im-nišešu	PNA no. 11
Samnuha-belu-uṣur	*City lord*[26] of Šadikanni	Šadikanni	SAA I 222-25	–
Saraia (f.)	– (subordinate of the palace scribe)	Nineveh	SAA XVI 49	to the palace scribe
Sargon II (Šarru-kenu)	King of Assyria (721-705)	Calah, Dur-Šarrukin (at the end of his reign)	SAA I 1-27[27] (1 = NL 39; 26 = NL 32), SAA V 277-80, SAA XV 274-79	SAA I 1 to Aššur-šarru-uṣur, 5-6 to Ašipâ, 10 to Nabû-duru-uṣur, 11 to Mannu-ki-Adad, 25 to 100 b[rick-masons], 26 to the governor (of Calah)?
Scribes of Kilizi	Scribes	Kilizi	SAA X 143-46	–
Sennacherib (Sîn-ahhe-eriba)	Crown prince	Calah, Nineveh, *Dur-Šarrukin*	SAA I 29-40, SAA V 281	–
Shalmaneser V see Ululaiu				
Sîn-ahhe-eriba see Sennacherib				
Sîn-ašared	– (official)	*active in Babylonia*	SAA I 158; ND 2729 = CTN V 36ff	PNA no. 1
Sîn-ila'i	– (official supervising cult centres)	active in Babylonia	SAA XV 241	PNA no. 3
Sîn-na'di (a)	– (official)	active in the upper reaches of the Diyala river	SAA XV 17	PNA no. 7

NAME	PROFESSION	LOCATION	LETTER(S)	OTHER REMARKS
Sîn-na'di (b)	Mayor of the Aššur gate and chief goldsmith of the Aššur temple	Assur	SAA XIII 25-27	PNA no. 16
Ṣallaia	Major domo	–	SAA XVI 42 (& Asalluhi-ereš)	PNA no. 7
Ša-Aššur-dubbu	Governor of Tušhan (eponym of the year 707)	Tušhan	SAA V 31-39	
Šamaš-abu-uṣur	–	active in northern Babylonia	SAA XV 186	to the governor (of Calah?) his lord
Šamaš-ahu-iddina	Governor of Ṣupat(?)	Ṣupat(?) (active in Rablâ)	NL 70	Cf. SAA I 172
Šamaš-belu-uṣur (a) [28]	Governor of Arzuhina (eponym of the year 710)	Arzuhina	SAA V 227-36	
Šamaš-belu-uṣur (b)	Governor of Der	Der	SAA XV 111-28	
Šamaš-bunaia	Assyrian prefect in Babylonia	Babylonia	NL 8, 76, ND 2630 = CTN V 28ff (see also Nabû-nammir)	
Šamaš-ila'i	– (Governor of Halzi-atbar?)	– (Halzi-atbar?)	NL 30, possibly also NL 55	
Šamaš-metu-uballiṭ	Prince	Nineveh	SAA XVI 25-27	
[Šamaš]-re'uwa	– (official)	Calah(?)	SAA XV 293	
Šamaš-šumu-lešir	– (Babylonian scholar or priest?)	letter from the province of the chief cupbearer	SAA XIII 190	–
Šamaš-šumu-ukin	Crown prince of Babylon; King of Babylon	Babylon	SAA XVI 21-24; ABL 426, 809, 1385 and CT 53 140	
Šamaš-taklak	Commander of the *ma'assu* cavalry	Calah, active in Babylonia	SAA XV 294	Cf. CTN III 99 r. ii 12 and 103 r. ii 7
Šamaš-upahhir	governor of Habruri (eponym of the year 708)	Habruri	SAA I 145-46	
Šarru-duri	Governor of Calah	Calah	ND 2626 = CTN V 87f	Recipient of GPA 185-89
Šarru-emuranni (a)	Deputy governor of Isana	Isana	NL 74	
Šarru-emuranni (b)	Governor of Bit-Zamani	Bit-Zamani	SAA V 47	

NAME	PROFESSION	LOCATION	LETTER(S)	OTHER REMARKS
Šarru-emuranni (c)	Governor of Mazamua (eponym of the year 712)	Mazamua	SAA V 199-209	Cf. Šarru-emuranni (d)
Šarru-emuranni (d)	City lord of Qunbuna	Qunbuna (city in Mazamua)	SAA V 243	Cf. Šarru-emuranni (c)[29]
Šarru-emuranni[30] (e)	Governor of Babylon	Babylon	SAA XV 217-39 (220 &Šarru-emuranni!)	Perhaps SAA V 292 is either by him or by (c) or by (b)
Šarru-kenu see Sargon II				
Šarru-lu-dari	– (official)	Laqê	see Išmanni-Aššur	
Šarru-[...]	–	*Calah*	ND 2362 = CTN V 241	to the palace scribe, his son[31]
Šep-šarri	Scribe	Calah	CTN III 4-5	*Private* letters to his "father" the palace manager[32]
Šeru'a-eṭerat	Princess	Nineveh	SAA XVI 28	to Libbali-šarrat (Assurbanipal's wife)
Šulmanu-[...]	– (*moneylende*r investing in the construction of Dur-Šarrukin)	–	SAA I 159	
Šulmu-beli	Deputy of the palace herald	Province of the palace herald	SAA V 133-44, ND 2402 = CTN V 107f	139 anonymous
Šulmu-beli-lašme[33]	– (high official)	–	SAA V 82	
Šulmu-mat-Aššur	Goldsmith	Assur	see Issar-na'di (b)	
Šumaia	*Exorcist and astrologer*	Nineveh	SAA XVI 34-35.	Both to the crown prince. Reports: SAA VIII 175-80
Tabnî	Diviner	Nineveh	SAA X 181-82 (182 assignation uncert.), SAA XVI 48 (by the same man? See also Marduk-šumu-uṣur)	SAA X 182 to the crown prince. SAA XVI 48 to the palace scribe. Co-author of several queries
Taklak-ana-Bel	Governor of Naṣibina (eponym of the year 715)	Naṣibina	SAA I 235-49 (248 attribution uncertain)	244 to the [vizier], his lord
Tammaritu (I or II?)	King of Elam	Susa or Hidalu	ABL 943, 1400	Recipient of ABL 1022, CT 53 908

NAME	PROFESSION	LOCATION	LETTER(S)	OTHER REMARKS
Taqiša	Priest of the Aššur temple	Assur	SAA XIII 40	to (the temple steward) Aššur-šarru-uṣur, his "brother"
Tariba-Issar	– (official collecting barley for palaces)	– (active in Assyrian cities)	SAA I 160-61	
Tartimanni	*Courtier* (later[?] palace manager)	Calah	CTN III 3	to the palace manager
Temple steward ([*a*]*lahhinu*)	Temple steward	Assur	SAA XIII 41-42 (letter and its envelope)	to temple steward, his "brother"
Tiglath-pileser III (Tukulti-apil-Ešarra)	King of Assyria (744-727)	Calah	GPA 183-87, 203; NL 23 (or Sg)	183-84 to Bel-dan, governor of Calah, 185-87 to Šarru-duri,[34] governor of Calah, NL 23 to *Inurta*-belu-uṣur
Tukulti-apil-Ešarra see Tiglath-pileser III				
Ṭab-bet-Aššur	–	Assur	KAV 199	Private letter to his family(?)
Ṭab-ṣill-Ešarra	Governor of Assur (eponym of the year 716)	Assur	SAA I 75-109, (98 &Na'di-ilu), SAA V 291	
Ṭab-šar-Aššur	Treasurer (eponym of the year 717)	Province of the treasurer	SAA I 41-74, SAA V 282-90	
Ṭab-šar-Sîn	– (a high official of the Aššur temple)	Assur	SAA XIII 16 (& Akkullanu, Marduk-šallim-ahhe)	
Ṭudî	– (official)	– (Babylon?)	SAA XVI 152	–
Ubru-ahhe	Priest/official of the Aššur temple	Assur	SAA XIII 36	
Ubru-Libbali	*Recruitment officer of the bodyguard cavalry*	*Arzuhina*	NL 80 + ND 2396 = CTN V 104ff	
Ubru-Nabû (a)[35]	– (subordinate of the governor of Calah)	Calah	GPA 198	to the governor of Calah (8th century)
Ubru-Nabû (b)	Scribe of the new palace	Calah	SAA XVI 105-10	106-107 to the crown prince
Ubru-Nabû (c)	Palace manager[36]	Calah	CTN III 84	to Šamaš-nuri (reign of Asb)
Ululaiu (Shalmaneser V)	Crown Prince	Calah	NL 31, 50-51, 53	

NAME	PROFESSION	LOCATION	LETTER(S)	OTHER REMARKS
Umman-aldaš III	King of Elam	Madaktu	ABL 879	
Unidentified Vassal king	Vassal king	–	SAA V 46	
Upaqa-Šamaš	– (military official: *subordinate of the chief judge*)	active on the Urarṭian border, in Ieri (SAA V 162:10)	SAA V 162-63, K 16498	
Urdî	–[37]	Assur	Rfdn 17 28 (& Mutaqqin-Aššur)	Private letter to their "brother" Aššur-matu-taqqin
Urdu-ahhešu	– (official supervising the restoration of Esaggil and other temples of Babylon)	Babylon	SAA XIII 161-72	166 anonymous memorandum. Cf. "Urdu-ahhešu, *pe*[*rsonal*] 'third man'" SAA VII 9 r. i 10
Urdu-Dagana	*Scholar*	*Nineveh*	SAA X 375	
Urdu-Ea	Lamentation priest	Harran and Nineveh	SAA X 338-44. (see also Adad-šumu-uṣur, Issar-šumu-ereš and Nabû-zeru-lešir)	Reports: SAA VIII 181-83
Urdu-Gula	Exorcist[38]	Nineveh	SAA X 289-94	Recipient of SAA X 295
Urdu-Nabû	Priest	Calah	SAA XIII 56-69	
Urdu-Nanaia	Chief physician	Nineveh	SAA X 314-27, SAA XVI 165 (see also Nabû-naṣir)	325 to the "farmer"
Urdu-Sîn	– (subordinate of the palace herald)	active in the north-east	SAA V 145	to the palace herald
Urzana	King of Muṣaṣir	Muṣaṣir	SAA V 146-47	147 to the palace herald
Zabaiu	Fort commander of Appina	Appina	SAA V 245	Cf. SAA XVII p. xxxiii ad no. 191
Zeru-ibni	Governor of Raṣappa (eponym of the year 718)	Raṣappa	SAA I 204-207	
[...]*aia*	– (official)	–	SAA XV 372	–
[...]*ia*	–	–	SAA XV 371	Private letter to his "brother" Bel-abu-uṣur
[DN]-ila'i	– (official)	–	ND 2740 = CTN V 306	Cf. Aššur-ila'i, Inurta-ila'i (b-d), Sîn-ila'i, and Šamaš-ila'i

NAME	PROFESSION	LOCATION	LETTER(S)	OTHER REMARKS
[...]ipidi and others	–	–	SAA XVI 58	*Private* letter to their lord
[...]su or [...]-SU	–	–	CT 53 174	to the palace supervisor, his lord
[DN]-šarru-uṣur	–	–	ND 2763 = CTN V 311f	
[DN]-šumu-uṣur	–	–	SAA XVI 182	

UNASSIGNED LETTERS

SAA I 154, 163-70, 183 ([...] of Carchemish), 208-209 ([...] of Hindanu), 211-13, 250-51, 253-56, 259-65, 264 (possibly by Mitunu, governor of Isana, eponym of the year 700, see n. ad SAA I 264. Cf. PNA nos. 1-2, 4)
SAA V 41 (Nashir-Bel or Ša-Aššur-dubbu?), 42 (Ša-Aššur-dubbu?), 43, 54 (not Aššur-dur-pani'a), 105, 106-109 (same scribe), 111 (anon.), 112, 148-49, 173-93, 195-98, 249-76, 294-300
SAA VII 15 (uncertain if a letter)
SAA X 147, 148 (anon.), 149, 150-52, 183-84, 310-12 (311 to the "farmer"), 336-37 (anon.), 376-80, 381 (anonymous: Nabû-nadin-šumi?, cf. LAS II p. 350f), 382-89
SAA XIII 28-29 (from Assur, related to Sîn-na'di [b], 29 anon.), 43 (anon.), 44-55, 134 (denouncing Pulu), 135-37, 146 (probably from Arbela), 148 (anon.?), 149 (anon.), 150-51 (*Arbela*), 152, 153 (*Arbela*), 155 (anon.), 156-57, 158 (to the crown prince), 159-60, 184 (hardly Šuma-iddin whose letters were in NB), 188 (from Harran to the queen mother), 189 (Kilizi), 192-211
SAA XV 18-23, 48-52, 73-82, 106-10, 142-54, 189 (anon. denunciation, Il-iada' or Šarru-emuranni?), 190-98, 199 (anon. denunciation), 200-13 (201 + 205?), 214 (not sent to the king), 215-16, 242-73, 280 (Šarru-emuranni?), 281-83 (Dur-Šarrukin), 284 (from Kumme), 285-87 (from Arzuhina), 295-370 (360 [...]ta), 373-91
SAA XVI 36 (not Adad-šumu-uṣur), 37-38 (to the crown prince), 39, 43 (scribe in the service of [...]), 45 (from Naṣibina), 46-47, 51 (not to the king), 52 (anon. to Nabû- [...]), 53 (private letter), 54 (anon. private letter), 55 (anon. private letter), 72-77, 89-93, 94 (to the queen mother), 95 (anon.), 99, 101-104, 122-23, 125, 130, 149-51, 154-64, 166, 168-70, 172-73, 178, 183-246
ABL 1009, 1116, 1142, 1148, 1264, 1364, CT 53 868, 944 and 966 (are all possibly sent to Assurbanipal), ABL 1127,[39] 1352 (all reign of Asb). ABL 1088, 1174, 1254, 1271, 1272, 1281, 1306, 1324, 1357
ADD 91
CT 53 167, 169, 176, 227, 243, 255, 256, 267, 273, 274, 276, 279, 288, 300, 302, 319, 326, 329, 330, 336 (Sg), 361, 366, 373, 375, 378, 379, 383, 385 (Sg), 402 (Sg), 421, 423, 433, 448, 449, 468, 486, 493, 501 (Sg), 512 (Sg), 514, 523, 530, 545, 547, 552, 555, 556, 565, 567, 575, 587, 590, 594, 595, 597, 598, 600, 605, 609, 612, 613, 633, 645, 646, 647, 648, 660, 663, 667, 678, 680, 682, 687, 692, 694, 699, 701, 703, 709, 712, 720, 723, 728, 732, 736, 740, 742, 746, 750, 753, 754, 762, 763, 771, 773, 774, 775, 781, 783, 784, 788, 791, 796, 800, 801, 804, 807, 810, 819, 820, 826 (Sg), 828, 830, 831, 838, 841, 843, 849, 850, 853, 854, 861, 875, 898, 913, 947, 948, 971, 973, 979, 981-82
CTDS 9
GPA 200 (to the governor of Calah), 205-11 (some or even all of them to the governor of Calah)

K 16561 … (cf. n. ad Appendix A)
MAss 17a
ND 2657 (reign of Tgl or Sg, an anonymously written order possibly to Kiribtu-Marduk) , ND 3410, ND 3470 (a shorter duplicate to Kiribtu-Marduk [cf. ND 2657]?)
NL 2-5, 9 (these five: reign of Tgl), NL 21, 22, 27, 40, 45 ([*DN*]-*belu*-[...]), 47, 48, 56, 57, 59, 60, 66, 68, 79, 85, 92, 93, 101, 105; ND 2363 = CTN V 35f, ND 2723 = CTN V 38f, ND 2421 = CTN V 59f, ND 2493 = CTN V 60f, ND 2400 = CTN V 72f, ND 2456 = CTN V 82ff, ND 2384 = CTN V 106f, ND 2427 = CTN V 108f, ND 2445 = CTN V 114f, ND 2488 = CTN V 124f, ND 2755 = CTN V 145f, ND 2772 = CTN V 146f, ND 2064 = CTN V 150f, ND 2417 = CTN V 151f, ND 2767 = CTN V 163f, ND 2737 = CTN V 166f, ND 2668 = CTN V 177f, ND 2676 = CTN V 179f, ND 2733 = CTN V 181f, ND 2610 = CTN V 184ff, ND 2719 = CTN V 200f, ND 2731 = CTN V 201f, ND 2481 = CTN V 214f, ND 2770 = CTN V 221f, ND 2616 = CTN V 224f, ND 2062 = CTN V 236, ND 2067 = CTN V 236, ND 2087 = CTN V 237, ND 2351 = CTN V 237f, ND 2369 = CTN V 243, ND 2376 = CTN V 245, ND 2394 = CTN V 249f, ND 2801 = CTN V 250f, ND 2395 = CTN V 251, ND 2413 = CTN V 254f, ND 2420 = CTN V 255f, ND 2422 = CTN V 256f, ND 2423 = CTN V 257f, ND 2425 = CTN V 258f, ND 2426 = CTN V 259f, ND 2428 = CTN V 260f, ND 2429 = CTN V 261f, ND 2432 = CTN V 262f, ND 2459 = CTN V 264f, ND 2472 = CTN V 265f, ND 2467 = CTN V 268f, ND 2468 = CTN V 269f, ND 2469 = CTN V 270, ND 2747 = CTN V 271 (possibly part of the same tablet as the previous one), ND 2473 = CTN V 271, ND 2627 = CTN V 278ff, ND 2639 = CTN V 280f, ND 2654 = CTN V 284f, ND 2658 = CTN V 285f, ND 2675 = CTN V 287f, ND 2708 = CTN V 296f, ND 2718 = CTN V 300ff, ND 2724 = CTN V 303f, ND 2743 = CTN V 306f, ND 2746 = CTN V 307, ND 2752 = CTN V 308, ND 2756 = CTN V 309, ND 2775 = CTN V 313ff, ND 2793 = CTN V 318, ND 2794 = CTN V 318f, ND 2802 = CTN V 320, ND 2688 = CTN V 320f, ND 2704 = CTN V 321
SÉ 152 (AfO 42/43 96) (anon. private letter)
StAT 1 55 (VAT 15580, private letter)
StAT 2 12 (A 2129; from the Assur archive N4: exorcists), 85, 316-18 (private letters)
TH 2 (confirmation of a delivered message to the governor of Guzana)
TIM 11 29 (A fragmentary private letter)
VAT 8655 (anon. written order), VAT 8699 (anon.)

Notes to Appendix B:

[1] See Fadhil and Radner (1996) 420f. Note that this format was also chosen for some short official letters. Originally, the "longest" of these extant short oval letters was probably SAA XVI 71 (CT 53 44). Presumably the maximum number of lines in this letter type was approximately ten lines per side.

[2] See Nissinen (1998) 78ff.

[3] CTN V 139: "Ahu-illaka (or Babba)". Possibly Ahu-illika, cf. Ambos (2003) 74.

[4] For the concordance between the NL and ND numbers and the CTN V page numbers, see CTN V, pp. 323-325.

[5] See Frame (1992) 172f.

[6] The writer may have introduced himself twice in the letter, cf. LAS II n. ad no. 239 r.4.

[7] Cf. Watanabe (1985) 140, 147.

[8] Parpola and Porter (2001) 3 D3 and 17 (Gazetteer), however, define Tidu as a fortress.

[9] These two letters, however, may originate from two different scribes. According to the copies of CTN V, several signs look slightly different, cf. *bu*, *mu*, *te* (in ND 2711, these signs regularly seem to have five diagonal wedges), and also *ba*, *ša*.

[10] I suggest interpreting Aššur-nirka-da''in as the governor of Assur. In the introductory formula of ND 2795 (CTN V 97ff) Aššur-nirka-da''in invokes the gods Aššur and Mullissu. This implies that Aššur-nirka-da''in is from Assur (cf. especially the introductory formula of the letters of Ṭab-ṣill-Ešarra, governor of Assur, SAA I 75-109, but also SAA XIII 32 by Mutakkil-Aššur). Moreover, as Aššur-nirka-da''in is recorded as the eponym of the year 720, it is more than likely that he was the governor of Assur at that time.

[11] I do not know whether this man is the same as Aššur-reṣuwa (a). However, the fact that the author of SAA XV 288-89 writes the latter part of his name as *re-ṣi-u-a* may arouse suspicions that we are dealing with two different men. Contrary to PNA 1/I p. 212 s.v. Aššur-reṣuwa 2.a., ABL 382 (and its envelope ABL 383 = SAA XV 288-89) is not a letter to the king about the relations with Urarṭu, as the letters by Aššur-reṣuwa (a), but a petition to a deputy (governor) that the writer should be returned to his (former) office. This suggests a lower office than Aššur-reṣuwa's (a royal agent/delegate). Therefore, if we really deal with the same Aššur-reṣuwa, then it is likely that there was a considerable temporal difference between the writing of SAA XV 288-89 and SAA V 83ff.

[12] Cf. SAA V, p. xii. I prefer this interpretation to that of PNA 1/II p. 311 s.v. Bel-iddina no. 5 ("Military official active on the northeastern border of Assyria") because the author's orthography is not very convincing, cf. Parpola (1997A) 319 n.12.

[13] See SAA XVI, p. xliv and ibid. n. ad no. 110:6.

[14] See SAA XVI, p. xliv.

[15] Assurbanipal could also be possible, see LAS II ad discussion of no. 226. On the other hand, Urdu-Gula, the addressee of the royal order, probably fell into disgrace with Assurbanipal soon after his accession. Of course, it is possible that Assurbanipal sent the grumbling Urdu-Gula to Babylonia (SAA X 295 was found in Sippar). For the career of Urdu-Gula, see Parpola (1987B) 268ff.

[16] For the Neo-Assyrian royal letters and their characteristics, see Watanabe (1985) .

[17] Note that Mannî writes his own name before that of the recipient. If Mannî was really a subordinate of Isseme-ili, this is a violation of the usual letter hierarchy, cf. n. 20 below.

[18] Saggs suggests (CTN V 220) to read the sender's name as *Nabû-balliṭ*. To me, Marduk-remanni appears to be a more likely reading, although not as m]⌈d!MES!⌉–*rém*-[*a-ni*] (as in SAA I 110:2 and PNA 2/II p. 721 s.v. Marduk-remanni 5.) but as m⌈d⌉ŠÚ–*rém*-[*a-ni*]. In any case, the contents of the letter clearly favour its assignation to the governor of Calah.

[19] Is he the same man as Marduk-šarru-uṣur (b)? See SAA XV p. xxxviii.

[20] Cf. already Weidner in TH (1940) 18. The usual letter hierarchy seems to confirm that a governor (of Naṣibina) sent a letter to another governor (of Guzana): when a sender's rank is either higher than or equal to that of a recipient then the sender mentions his own name first after which the name of the recipient follows.

[21] This Mušezib-[*ilu*] and the Mušezib-ilu of NL 72 have different handwritings, cf., e.g., the signs for LUGAL, and KÁM; also *annurig* ~ *annurag*, KASKAL ~ KASKAL.2.

[22] In SAA XVI, we did not suggest to identify the writer of SAA X 153 with the one of SAA XVI 181, but see LAS II A p. 38. Although both of these letters are badly broken (esp. SAA X 153), orthographically they seem to match well.

[23] According to PNA 2/II p. 809 s.v. Nabû-bani-ahhe no. 2 "Official in Babylonia," but cf. SAA XIII p. xiii.

[24] SAA XV 137 reads erroneously Nab[û-belu-ka''in].

[25] If correct, this indicates that Nergal-uballiṭ still was the governor of Arzuhina during the reign of Sargon II, possibly until the governorship of Šamaš-belu-uṣur (eponym of the year 710).

[26]The title given here is conjectural, cf. "Ubru-[...], city lord of Šadikanni" SAA VI 286:1-2. Another possibility could be "vice-regent of Šadikanni," see PNA 3/I p. 1085 s.v. Samnuha-šar-ilani. SAA I pp. x, 235 and PNA 3/I, p. 1084 s.v. Samnuha-belu-uṣur, give him the title "governor of Šadikanni". But can this be correct? At least according to Parpola and Porter, (2001) 15 (Gazetteer), Šadikanni is a city, not a province.

[27] Note that SAA I 28 is later republished as part of SAA X 216. It is thus not a fragment by Sargon, but a letter by Esarhaddon.

[28] In my interpretation, Šamaš-belu-uṣur, the governor of Arzuhina, is a different individual than Šamaš-belu-uṣur, the governor of Der, but cf. SAA XV p. liv n. 127.

[29] See Lanfranchi (1998) 109.

[30] See SAA XV pp. xxxviii and liv (n. 130).

[31] Another possibility here is to render DUMU as "lord" (see 7.3), but because the author writes his own name first, his status was probably higher than or equal to that of the palace scribe.

[32] Probably Isseme-ili, see CTN III p. 55.

[33] The same Šulmu-beli-lašme may be mentioned in SAA V 97 s.1.

[34] For the dating of Šarru-duri's governorship, see GPA p. 11.

[35] The same Ubru-Nabû may be attested in SAA VI 19 r.14e (734 BCE), but cf. also SAA VI 11 r.11′ (717 BCE), ND 2498:14′ and SAA XV 284:4′.

[36] See ND 2314 r.5, ND 2328 r.17, ND 2344:1, 4, ND 3425:7, SAA XII 92 r.6, 93 r.13, 94 r.17e. Cf. CTN III pp. 97, 140.

[37] Cf. "Urdî, priest of Ninurta" StAT 2 10:7 and "Nabû-dur-[...], son of Urdî, architect" VAT 21000 r.40.

[38] Note also "Urdu-Gula, deputy of the chief physician" in SAA VI 193 r.8-9 (681 BCE).

[39] For the date of this fragmentary letter, cf. Waters (2000) 60 n. 23.

BIBLIOGRAPHY

Ambos, C.
2003 Review of "H. W. F. Saggs, *The Nimrud Letters, 1952*," *OLZ* 98, 71-75.

Aro, J.
1953 "Abnormal Plene Writings in Akkadian Texts," *StOr* 19:11, 1-19.

Baker, H. D. (ed.) (see also Radner, K. [ed.])
2000- *Prosopography of the Neo-Assyrian Empire*. Helsinki.

Borger, R.
1986[3] *Assyrisch-babylonische Zeichenliste*. AOAT 33/33A. Neukirchen-Vluyn.

Buccellati, G.
1995 *A Structural Grammar of Babylonian*. Wiesbaden.

Bussmann, H.
1996 *Routledge Dictionary of Language and Linguistics*. London.

Cancik-Kirschbaum, E. C.
1996 *Die mittelassyrischen Briefe aus Tall Šēh Hamad / Dūr-Katlimmu*. Berichte der Ausgrabung Tall Šēh Hamad / Dūr-Katlimmu (BATSH) 4. Berlin.

Carr, P.
1993 *Phonology*. Chatham.

Clyne, M.
1999 "Typology and Language Change in Bilingualism and Trilingualism," in C. F. Justus and E. C. Polomé (eds.) *Language Change and Typological Variation: In Honor of W. P. Lehmann on the Occasion of His 83rd Birthday. Volume II: Grammatical Universals and Typology*. Journal of Indo-European Studies. Monograph 31 (Washington D.C.) 444-63.

Cole, S. W. and P. Machinist
1998 *Letters from Priests to the Kings Esarhaddon and Assurbanipal*. SAA XIII. Helsinki.

Comrie, B.
1989[2] *Language Universals and Linguistic Typology*. Oxford.

Crystal, D. and R. Quirk
1964 *Systems of Prosodic and Paralinguistic Features in English*. Janua Linguarum. Series Minor 39. The Hague 1964.

Dalley, S.
1996-1997 "Neo-Assyrian Tablets from Til-Barsib," *Abr-Nahrain* 34, 66-99.

Dalley, S. and J. N. Postgate
1984 *The Tablets from Fort Shalmaneser*. CTN III. London.

Degen, R.
1969 *Altaramäische Grammatik der Inschriften des 10.-8. Jh. v. Chr.* Wiesbaden.

Deller, K.
1957A "Zur sprachlichen Einordnung der Inschriften Aššurnaṣirpals II. (883-59)," *Or.* 26, 144-56.
1957B "Assyrisches Sprachgut bei Tukulti-Ninurta II (888-884)," *Or.* 26, 268-72.
1959 *Lautlehre des Neuassyrischen.* Unpublished PhD Dissertation. Vienna.
1961A "^{LÚ}LUL = ^{LÚ}*parriṣu* und ^{LÚ}*sarru*," *Or.* 30, 249-57.
1961B "Die Verdrängung des Grundstamms von *ezēbu* durch *rammû* im Neuassyrischen," *Or.* 30, 345-54.
1962A "Zweisilbige Lautwerte des Typs KVKV im Neuassyrischen," *Or.* 31, 7-26.
1962B "Studien zur neuassyrischen Orthographie," *Or.* 31, 186-96.
1962C "Zur Syntax des Infinitivs im Neuassyrischen," *Or.* 31, 225-35.
1965A "Comparative Semitics – Some Remarks on a Recent Publication," *Or.* 34, 35-41.
1965B Review of "*From the Workshop of the Chicago Assyrian Dictionary. Studies presented to A. Leo Oppenheim*," *Or.* 34, 73-77.
1965C Review of "A. Ungnad, *Grammatik des Akkadischen*. Edited by L. Matouš," *Or.* 34, 77-79.
1967 "Notes brèves: ABL 2 r. 1-3," *RA* 61, 189.
1969 "Die Briefe des Adad-šumu-uṣur," in W. Röllig and M. Dietrich (eds.), *lišān mithurti: Fs. W. von Soden.* AOAT 1, 45-64.
1971 "Die Rolle des Richters im neuassyrischen Prozessrecht," in *Studi in onore di Edoardo Volterra*, Volume VI, 639-53.
1984 "Drei wiederentdeckte neuassyrische Rechtsurkunden aus Assur," *BaM* 15, 225-51.
1986 "Ein Assyrer tilgt Schulden," *Oriens Antiquus* 25, 21-27.
1985-1986 "Old Assyrian Kanwarta, Middle Assyrian Kalmarte, and Neo-Assyrian Garmarte," *Ex Oriente Lux* 29, 43-49.
1987 Review of "CAD N," *Or.* 56, 177-89 (i.e., pages concerning NA and MA).

Deller, K. and I. L. Finkel
1984 "A Neo-Assyrian Inventory Tablet of Unknown Provenance," *ZA* 74, 76-91.

Deller, K. and S. Parpola
1966A "Die Schreibungen des Wortes *etinnu* 'Baumeister' im Neuassyrischen," *RA* 60, 59-70.
1966B "Neuassyrisch 'unser Herr' = *bēlīni*, nicht **bēlni*," *Or.* 35, 121-22.
1967 "Progressive Vokalassimilation im Neuassyrischen," *Or.* 36, 337-38.

Dietrich, M.
1969 "Untersuchungen zur Grammatik des Neubabylonischen I. Die neubabylonischen Subjunktionen," in W. Röllig and M. Dietrich (eds.) *lišān mithurti: Fs. W. von Soden.* AOAT 1, 65-99.

Donbaz, V.
2002 "A Neo-Assyrian Text of unknown Provenance," *Nouvelles Assyriologiques Brèves et Utilitaires* 2002/90.

Donbaz, V. and S. Parpola
2001 *Neo-Assyrian Legal Texts in Istanbul.* StAT 2. Saarbrücken.

Fabritius, K.
1995 "Vowel Dissimilation as a Marker of Plurality in Neo-Assyrian," *JCS* 47, 51-55.

Fadhil, A. and K. Radner
1996 "Äste, Gras und Esel," *BaM* 27, 419-28.

Fales, F. M.
1983 "Studies on Neo-Assyrian Texts II: 'Deeds and documents' from the British Museum," *ZA* 73, 232-55.
2000 "*bīt bēli*: An Assyrian Institutional Concept," in E. Rova (ed.), *Patavina Orientalia Selecta*. History of the Ancient Near East, Monographs IV (Padova), 231-49.

Fales, F. M. and J. N. Postgate
1992 *Imperial Administrative Records. Part I. Palace and Temple Administration*. SAA VII. Helsinki.
1995 *Imperial Administrative Records. Part II. Provincial and Military Administration*. SAA XI. Helsinki.

Frame, G.
1992 *Babylonia 689-627 B.C. A Political History*. PIHANS 69. Istanbul.

Freydank, H.
1985 "Die 'Söhne' des Šallim-pî-Ea," *AoF* 12, 362-64.

Friedrich, J., G. R. Meyer, A. Ungnad, and E. F. Weidner
1940 *Die Inschriften vom Tell Halaf. Keilschrifttexte und aramäische Urkunden aus einer assyrischen Provinzhauptstadt*. AfO Beiheft 6. Berlin.

Fuchs, A. and S. Parpola
2001 *The Correspondence of Sargon II. Part III. Letters from Babylonia and the Eastern Provinces*. SAA XV. Helsinki.

Garr, W. R.
1986 "On Voicing and Devoicing in Ugaritic," *JNES* 45, 45-52.

Gelb, I. J.
1955 "Notes on von Soden's Grammar of Akkadian," *BiOr* 12, 93-111.
1970A "A Note on Morphographemics," in D. Cohen (ed.) *Mélanges Marcel Cohen*, 73-77.
1970B "Comments on the Akkadian Syllabary," *Or.* 39, 516-46.

Grayson, A. K.
1972 *Assyrian Royal Inscriptions. Volume I. From the Beginning to Ashur-resha-ishi I.* Wiesbaden.
1991 "Three Neo-Assyrian Documents," in D. Charpin and F. Joannès (eds.) *Marchands, diplomates et empereurs. Fs. P. Garelli* (Paris) 357-62.

Groneberg, B.
1980 "Zu den 'gebrochenen Schreibungen'," *JCS* 32, 151-67.

Hecker, K.
1968 *Grammatik der Kültepe-Texte*. AnOr 44. Roma.

Hunger, H.
1992 *Astrological Reports to Assyrian Kings*. SAA VIII. Helsinki.

Hämeen-Anttila, J.
2000 *A Sketch of Neo-Assyrian Grammar*. SAAS XIII. Helsinki.

Ihalainen, O.
1991 "On grammatical Diffusion in Somerset Folk Speech," in P. Trudgill and J. K. Chambers (eds.) *Dialects of English: Studies in Grammatical Variation*. Linguistics Library (Singapore) 104-19.

Itkonen, T.
1970 "Ovatko äänteenmuutokset vähittäisiä vai harppauksellisia?" *Virittäjä* 74, 411-38.

Jas, R.
1990 "A Neo-Assyrian Letter Without Address," *SAAB* 4, 3-5.

Joüon, P. and T. Muraoka
1991 *A Grammar of Biblical Hebrew*. Subsidia Biblica 14/I. Roma.

Jursa, M. and K. Radner
1995/1996 "Keilschrifttexte aus Jerusalem," *AfO* 42/43, 89-108.

Kataja, L.
1987 "A Neo-Assyrian Document on Two Cases of River Ordeal," *SAAB* 1, 65-68.

Kataja, L. and R. Whiting
1995 *Grants, Decrees and Gifts of the Neo-Assyrian Period*. SAA XII. Helsinki.

Kaufman, S.
1974 *The Akkadian Influences on Aramaic*. AS 19. Chicago - London.

Kohler, J. and A. Ungnad
1913 *Assyrische Rechtsurkunden in Umschrift und Übersetzung nebst einem Index der Personen-Namen und Rechtserläuterungen*. Leipzig.

Kraus, F. R.
1987 *Sonderformen akkadischer Parataxe. Die Koppelungen*. Mededelingen der Koninklijke Nederlandse Akademie van Wetenschappen, Afd. Letterkunde, N.R., 50 I. Amsterdam.

Kwasman, T.
2001/2002 Review of "K. Radner, *Ein neuassyrisches Privatarchiv der Tempelgoldschmiede von Assur*," AfO 48/49, 221-23.

Kwasman, T. and S. Parpola
1991 *Legal Transactions of the Royal Court of Nineveh. Part I. Tiglath-Pileser III through Esarhaddon*. SAA VI. Helsinki.

Lambert, W. G.
1959 "The Sultantepe Tablets. A Review Article," *RA* 53, 119-38.

Lanfranchi, G.
1998 "Esarhaddon, Assyria and Media," *SAAB* 12, 99-109.

Lanfranchi, G. and S. Parpola
1990 *The Correspondence of Sargon II. Part II. Letters from the Northern and North-eastern Provinces*. SAA V. Helsinki.

Leichty, E.
1970 *The Omen Series šumma izbu*. TCS 4. Glückstadt.

Lipiński, E.
1994 *Studies in Aramaic Inscriptions and Onomastics II*. OLA 57. Leuven.
1997 *Semitic Languages – Outline of a Comparative Grammar*. OLA 80. Leuven.

Livingstone, A.
1989 *Court Poetry and Literary Miscellanea*. SAA III. Helsinki.

Luukko, M. and G. Van Buylaere
2002 *The Political Correspondence of Esarhaddon*. SAA XVI. Helsinki.

Matouš, L. and K. Petrácek
1956 "Beiträge zur akkadischen Grammatik I. Die Liquiden in ihrem Verhältnis zum Vokal im Assyrischen," *ArOr* 24, 1-14.

Mattila, R.
1987 "The Political Status of Elam after 653 B.C. According to ABL 839," *SAAB* 1, 27-30.
2002 *Legal Transactions of the Royal Court of Nineveh, Part II*. SAA XIV. Helsinki.

Mayer, W.
1971 *Untersuchungen zur Grammatik des Mittelassyrischen*. AOATS 2. Neukirchen-Vluyn.

Mayer, W. R.
1992 "Ein Hymnus auf Ninurta als Helfer in der Not," *Or.* 61, 17-57.

Millard, A. R.
1980 "The Homeland of Zakkur," *Semitica* 39, 47-52.

Neumann, H.
1997 "Gläubiger oder Schuldner? Anmerkungen zu einem neuassyrischen Privatbrief," in Beate Pongratz-Leisten, Hartmut Kühne, Paolo Xella (eds.), *Ana šadî Labnāni lū allik: Beiträge zu altorientalischen und mittelmeerischen Kulturen: Festschrift für Wolfgang Röllig*. AOAT 247, 281-93.

Nissinen, M.
1998 *References to Prophecy in Neo-Assyrian Sources*. SAAS 7. Helsinki.

Paddock, H.
1991 "The Actuation Problem for Gender Change in Wessex versus Newfoundland," in P. Trudgill and J. K. Chambers (eds.) *Dialects of English: Studies in Grammatical Variation*. Linguistics Library (Singapore) 29-46.

Pardee, D. and R. M. Whiting
1987 "Aspects of Epistolary Verbal Usage in Ugaritic and Akkadian," *Bulletin of the School of Oriental and African Studies* 50, 1-31

Parker, B. J.
1997A "Garrisoning the Empire: Aspects of the Construction and Maintenance of Forts on the Assyrian Border," *Iraq* 59, 77-87.
1997B "The Real and the Irreal: The Multiple Meanings of *maṣi* in Neo-Assyrian," *SAAB* 11 (1997), 37-54.

Parpola, S.
1970 *Neo-Assyrian Toponyms*. AOAT 6. Neukirchen-Vluyn.
1971 *Letters from Assyrian Scholars to the Kings Esarhaddon and Assurbanipal. Part II A: Introduction and Appendices*. Kevelaer and Neukirchen-Vluyn.
1972 "A Letter from Samaš-šumu-ukīn to Esarhaddon," *Iraq* 34, 21-34.
1974 "The Alleged Middle/Neo-Assyrian Irregular Verb **naṣṣ* and the Assyrian Sound Change *Š* > *S*," *Assur* 1/1, 1-10.
1975 "Neo-Assyrian Prosodies," Unpublished Paper, XXIIe Rencontre Assyriologique Internationale, Göttingen, 9 June 1975.
1979 Review of "W. von Soden, *Akkadisches Handwörterbuch. Band II und III/1*," *OLZ* 74, 23-36.
1980 "The Murderer of Sennacherib," in B. Alster (ed.) *Death in Mesopotamia*. Mesopotamia 8 (Copenhagen) 171-82.
1981 "Assyrian Royal Inscriptions and Neo-Assyrian Letters," in F.M. Fales (ed.) *Assyrian Royal Inscriptions: New Horizons in Literary, Ideological and Historical Analysis* (Roma) 117-34.
1983 *Letters from Assyrian Scholars to the Kings Esarhaddon and Assurbanipal. Part II: Commentary and Appendices*. AOAT 5/2. Neukirchen-Vluyn.
1984 "*Likalka ittatakku* – Two Notes on the Morphology of the Verb *alāku* in Neo-Assyrian," *StOr* 55, 185-209.
1987A *The Correspondence of Sargon II. Part I. Letters from Assyria and the West*. SAA I. Helsinki.
1987B "The Forlorn Scholar," in F. Rochberg-Halton (ed.), *Language, Literature, and History: Philological and Historical Studies Presented to Erica Reiner*, 257-78.
1988A "The Neo-Assyrian Word for 'Queen'," *SAAB* 2, 73-76.
1988B "The Reading of the Neo-Assyrian Logogram ^LÚ^SIMUG.KUG.GI 'Goldsmith'," *SAAB* 2, 77-80.

1990 "A Letter from Marduk-apla-uṣur of Anah to Rudamu/Urtamis, King of Hamath," in P.J. Riis and M.-L. Buhl, *Hama* II 2, (Nationalmuseets Skrifter. Storre Beretningar XII, København) 257-65 (Appendix 1).
1993 *Letters from Assyrian and Babylonian Scholars*. SAA X. Helsinki.
1997A "The Man Without a Scribe and the Question of Literacy in the Assyrian Empire," in *Ana šadî Labnāni lū allik. Fs. für W. Röllig*, 315-24.
1997B *Assyrian Prophecies*. SAA IX. Helsinki.
1998 "The Esoteric Meaning of the Name of Gilgamesh," in J. Prosecký (ed.) *Intellectual Life of the Ancient Near East. Papers Presented at the 43rd RAI, Prague*, 315-29.

Parpola, S. and M. Porter (eds.)
2001 *The Helsinki Atlas of the Near East in the Neo-Assyrian Period*. Helsinki.

Parpola, S. and K. Watanabe
1988 *Neo-Assyrian Treaties and Loyalty Oaths*. SAA II. Helsinki.

Paunonen, H.
1973 "On Free Variation," *Suomalais-ugrilaisen seuran aikakauskirja* 72, 285-300.

Pečírková, J.
1977 "The Administrative Organization of the Neo-Assyrian Empire," *ArOr* 45, 211-28.

Pedersén, O.
1997 "Use of Writing among the Assyrians," in H. Hauptmann and H. Waetzold (eds.) *Assyrien im Wandel der Zeiten*. CRRAI 39. HSAO 6, 139-52.
1998 *Archives and Libraries in the Ancient Near East 1500-300 B.C.* Bethesda.

Postgate, J. N.
1973 *The Governor's Palace Archive*. CTN II. London.
1974 Review of "W. Mayer, *Untersuchungen zur Grammatik des Mittelassyrischen*," BiOr 31, 273-4.
1980 "The Place of the *šaknu* in Assyrian Government," *AnSt* 30, 67-76.
1995 "Some Latter-Day Merchants of Aššur," in M. Dietrich and O. Loretz (eds.) *Vom Alten Orient zum Alten Testament. Fs. W. von Soden*. AOAT 240, 403-406.
1997 "Middle Assyrian to Neo-Assyrian: the Nature of the Shift," in H. Hauptmann and H. Waetzold (eds.) *Assyrien im Wandel der Zeiten*. CRRAI 39. HSAO 6, 159-68.

Quirk, R.
1995 *Grammatical and Lexical Variance in English*. Singapore.

Radner, K.
1995 "The Relation Between Format and Content of Neo-Assyrian Texts," in R. Mattila (ed.), *Nineveh 612 BC. The Glory and Fall of the Assyrian Empire* (Helsinki), 63-78.
1997 *Die neuassyrischen Privatrechtsurkunden als Quelle für Mensch und Umwelt*. SAAS VI. Helsinki.
1999A *Ein neuassyrisches Privatarchiv der Tempelgoldschmiede von Assur*. StAT 1. Saarbrücken.
1999B "Traders in the Neo-Assyrian Period," in J. G. Dercksen (ed.), *Trade and Finance in Ancient Mesopotamia*, 101-26.

Radner, K. (ed.) (see also Baker, H. D. [ed.])
1998-99 *The Prosopography of the Neo-Assyrian Empire*. Helsinki.

Reiner, E.
1964 "The Phonological Interpretation of a Subsystem in the Akkadian Syllabary," in *Studies Presented to A. Leo Oppenheim*, 167-80.
1966 *A Linguistic Analysis of Akkadian*. Janua Linguarum, Series Practica 21. The Hague.
1973 "How We Read Cuneiform Texts," *JCS* 25, 1-58.
1973B "New Cases of Morphophonemic Spellings," *Or.* 42, 35-38.

Rosenthal, F.
1974[4] *A Grammar of Biblical Aramaic*. Wiesbaden.

Saggs, H. W. F.
2001 *Nimrud Letters, 1952*. CTN V. London.

Salonen, E.
1976 *Die Gruss- und Höflichkeitsformeln in babylonisch-assyrischen Briefen*. StOr 38. Helsinki.

Soden, W. von
1948 "Vokalfärbungen im Akkadischen," *JCS* 2, 291-303.
1950 "Verbalformen mit doppeltem t-infix im Akkadischen," *Or.* 19, 385-96.
1952 "Unregelmässige Verben im Akkadischen," *ZA* 50, 163-81.
1957 "Zur Laut- und Formenlehre des Neuassyrischen," *AfO* 18, 121-22.
1983 "Kritische Notizen," *ZA* 73, 92-95.
1952/69/95 *Grundriss der akkadischen Grammatik*. AnOr 35. Roma.

Soden, W. von and W. Röllig
1967[2] *Das Akkadische Syllabar*. AnOr 42. Roma.

Tropper, J.
1992 "Sam'alisch *mt* 'wahrlich' und das Phänomen der Aphärese im Semitischen," *Or.* 61, 448-53.
1997 "Probleme des akkadischen Verbalparadigmas," *AoF* 24, 189-210.

Trudgill, P. and J. K. Chambers (eds.)
1991 *Dialects of English: Studies in Grammatical Variation*. Linguistics Library. Singapore.

Watanabe, K.
1985 "Die Briefe der neuassyrischen Könige," *Acta Sumerologica* 7, 139-56.

Waters, M. W.
2000 *A Survey of Neo-Elamite History*. SAAS XII. Helsinki.

Wilhelm, G.
1970 "*Ta/erdennu, ta/urtannu, ta/urtānu*," *UF* 2, 277-82.

Wiseman, D. J.
1955 "Assyrian Writing-boards," *Iraq* 17, 3-13.

Woodington, N.
1982 *A Grammar of the Neo-Babylonian Letters of the Kuyunjik Collection*. Unpublished PhD Dissertation. Yale.

Ylvisaker, S.
1912 *Zur babylonischen und assyrischen Grammatik*. Leipziger Semitistische Studien V 6. Leipzig.

INDICES

Grammatical Index

abbreviations: 206
abnormal syllabification: 9, 27
accent (marker): 6
accusative: 84, 93, 157, 166, 168f, 173
adjectives: 38, 41, 80, 87, 90, 110, 137
  nisbe: 37, 183
  verbal adjective: 145, 147
adverbs: 12, 80, 82, 109f, 116, 121, 124, 127, 136, 146, 153, 172
Akkadian: 2f, 6, 27, 31, 37, 39f, 124, 145f, 149, 172, 175f, 179
allographs: 176
allophones: 5, 40, 42f, 74, 76, 82, 85, 87f, 138, 150
allophones of vowels
  of /a/: 82
  of /i/: 85
  of /u/: 87
allophonic: 40, 42, 82, 86
alphabetic writing: 2
anaptyctic or epenthetic vowels: 35, 70, 99, 102, 104-108, 115
aphesis: 118, 120ff, 188
apocopal forms: 151
apocope: 33, 109f, 115
Aramaic/Aramaic influence/Aramaisms: 1f, 11, 29, 38f, 53, 70f, 80, 89, 137, 140, 149, 156f, 178f, 187, 189f
archaisms: 64, 67, 137, 165, 188
articles: 156
aspectual use of present: 164
assimilation: 9, 74, 76ff, 80, 90, 121f, 145f
  consonantal assimilations: 76
  partial assimilations: 77, 79, 81
  progressive assimilation: 78
  progressive vowel assimilations: 87, 90, 137, 166, 168
  reciprocal consonantal assimilations: 80
  regressive assimilation: 76
  vowel assimilations: 89f
  assimilations: 80, 188
attributes: 184
auxiliary vowels: 27, 70, 98f, 108, 140, 142
Babylonian influence: 78, 80, 86, 88, 147, 151, 168, 190
Babylonianisms: 8, 13, 51, 54, 72, 76, 80f, 87, 92f, 138, 168, 176, 181, 183, 190
bilingual: 3, 188
cases: 13, 27, 51, 118, 166, 175, 179
characteristic features: 9, 12, 23
chronological (variation): 15, 25
circumflex: 6, 140
closed syllables: 82-85, 99, 124, 126, 128
collective: 137
collective nouns: 137
colon: 9, 23, 26
comparative: 4, 175, 187
compound logogram: 175
compound prepositions: 156
compound words: 118, 156, 175, 182
conditional clauses: 10, 170, 172
conditional variation: 10
conjugation: 12, 75, 146, 149, 189
consecutive clauses: 89, 109, 170
consonantal gemination (cf. gemination of consonants): 31, 35, 117, 140
coordination: 90, 108, 131
coordinative: 31, 89
copula: 154
cuneiform: 2-5, 8f, 14, 16, 21, 69, 137, 213
CV-signs: 44, 68
CVC-signs: 41, 50f, 68, 79
dative: 93
defective writings: 36
defricativized: 72
deixis: 134f
descriptive principles: 4
determinative(s): 139, 176, 179, 183
diachronic: 15, 19, 72, 144
dialectal variation: 40, 72
dialectology: 7
diphthong: 37
direct object: 169, 174
dissimilations: 94f, 115
disyllabic (words): 6, 37, 39, 69, 93, 142
dividing line/horizontal ruling/end line: 23ff
D-stem: 71, 79, 95, 105, 146f
Dtt-stem: 123, 145f
dual: 39
ellipsis: 165, 178
elliptical: 109, 156, 164ff
emphasis: 6, 35, 38, 108, 125, 163
emphatic: 31, 35, 69f, 80, 85, 100, 109, 113, 134, 155
emphatic stress: 31, 100
enclitic(s): 38, 97, 108, 140
epenthetic vowels: 102
etymology: 82, 85, 137
feminine: 14, 76, 80, 137, 184f
free variation: 9ff, 35, 40, 42, 69, 87, 108, 118, 121, 124, 128, 131, 148, 176, 188
fricativization: 71
geminated (consonant): 11, 32, 35, 122
gemination of consonants: 31f, 98, 123f

voicing: 69, 73
vowel contractions: 6
vowel dissimilation: 94f, 142, 188
vowel harmony: 95, 97, 110f, 115, 140, 144, 148
V-signs: 44
weak verbs: 43, 114, 146f
West Semitic: 92, 157, 187, 190
word order: 153-57, 166, 190
writing system(s): 2, 5, 8, 11, 14, 70

Personal Names

Geographical Names

Divine and Temple Names

Akkadian Words Discussed

Textual References

41 r.30: 10
43:4: 177
43:10: 117, 124
43 r.4-5: 164
43 r.15: 177
43 r.16-17: 26
44:3: 83
44:10: 141
44 r.5: 103
44 r.8: 83
45:9: 79
45: 24, 31, 38, 79, 88, 95, 134
45 r.3: 134
45 r.5: 88
45 r.8: 31, 88
45 r.10: 88, 95
45 r.14: 38
46: 25
47:7: 81
47: 24, 81
48:5: 36
48:7: 36
48:13-14: 108
48:15: 27
48 r.7: 106
50:6: 110
50:11: 71
50 e.17: 147
50 r.14: 95
52:5: 94
52:11: 43
52: 24, 43, 94
53:8: 110
54:3: 80
54:6: 37
54:9: 166
54:13: 147
54 e.18: 59
54 r.2: 106
54 r.12-13: 158
55:6-7: 84
55:11: 106
56:4′-6: 135
56:4: 135
57 r.2: 104
60:7: 123, 146
60 e.12: 38
62: 24
64:10-11: 83
64:11: 107
64:17: 28
64:19: 146
64: 24, 28, 77, 83, 107, 116, 131, 146
64 r.3: 131
64 r.4: 77, 116
64 r.5: 116
65:4-5: 84
65:5: 41
65:6: 37, 74
65:9: 131
65:10: 47, 106
65:11: 47, 80, 106
65:14: 57
67:9: 28
67:11: 137
67: 24, 28, 72, 92, 114, 137
67 r.13: 92
69:6: 84
69:9: 146
69 r.5: 68
70:8: 129
70:10: 140
70 r.2: 129
70 r.4: 129
70 r.16: 150
70 r.18: 150
71:6: 122
71:12: 131
71: 24, 45, 80, 107, 122, 131
71 e.15: 80
71 r.5: 45, 107
72:4: 174
72:5: 79
72:8: 63, 82, 85
74:4-7: 165
74:4: 116, 165
74:5: 76, 116, 119
74:11: 147
74: 24, 39, 76, 88, 100, 116, 119, 147, 151, 165
74 r.13: 39, 88, 100
74 r.16: 151
75:12: 67
75: 24, 67
78: 24, 36, 65, 100
78 r.6: 36, 100
78 r.7: 65
79:4: 85
79:7: 122
79:12: 60
79 r.3: 74
81:5-6: 23
81: 23f, 41, 78, 92
81 r.3: 92
81 r.5: 41
81 r.8: 78
85:9: 103
85:16: 131
85 r.6-7: 160
85 r.6: 124, 160
85 r.10: 90, 151
85 r.14: 103
86:9: 167
86:10: 96, 133
86:11: 59
86:16: 97
86 r.1: 125
87:8: 101
87:10: 101
87 r.7: 138
87 r.10: 104
87 r.11: 104
87 r.12: 107
92:11: 123, 146
93:5: 70, 104
93 r.3: 70, 104
95:4: 177
96:7: 131, 138
96:8: 106
96:9: 127
96:10: 138
96:15: 39
96 r.14: 98
96 r.19: 117
97:11: 49
97: 24, 49, 87
97 r.10: 87
98:8: 92, 137
99:12: 104, 123
99 r.8: 124
99 r.19: 123
99 r.21: 77, 99
100:7: 74, 129, 148
100:9: 73
100:10: 99
101:8: 42, 129
101:10: 42, 129
101 r.5: 110
102:9: 90
102: 24, 76, 90, 113, 119
102 r.11: 76, 119
102 r.13: 113
102 r.13e-14e: 113
103: 24
104: 24
105 r.8: 70, 79, 81

Rfdn 17
28:5: 181
28:7: 46, 92
28:9: 72
28:10: 130
28 r.8: 22
29 r.6: 117
29 r.7: 147
29 r.18e: 151

RIMA 2
A.0.101.40:33: 122

SAA I
1:5: 43
1:13: 103
1:15: 93
1:18: 98
1:19: 43
1:23: 171
1:34: 131
1 r.42: 141
1 r.49: 121f
1 r.50: 141
1 r.62: 156
1 r.66: 106
2:4: 38
2:5: 129
2 r.1: 45
4:10: 84
4:13: 98
7:8: 106
8 r.9: 168
8 r.10: 94
8 r.12: 107
8 r.14: 38, 61
10:3: 176
10:6: 96
10:12: 176
10 r.6: 167
10 r.12-13: 158
11:2: 155
11:6: 92
11:8: 61
11:11: 176
11:13-14: 99
11:19: 103
11 r.1: 129
11 r.8: 66
12:9′-12: 165
12:12: 115
12 r.1: 81, 150
12 r.2: 137
12 s.3: 76
13:15: 52
14:3: 143
14:5: 104
14:12: 119
14 r.11-12: 170
14 s.2: 70
15:11: 120
15:13: 143
15:14: 59
15:15: 127
16 r.5: 61
18:10: 119
18 r.9: 80
18 r.10: 130
18 s.1: 54
20:3: 45, 116, 119
20 r.1: 116, 119
21:2: 147
21:10: 130, 147
21 r.3: 130
22:9: 101
22 r.5: 36
23:2: 106
23:3: 63
23:4: 105
24:6: 64
24:8: 101
25:5: 67
25:9: 96
25:16: 119
26:3: 87
26:5: 181
26 r.10: 156
29:16: 119, 130
29:18: 120
29:19: 32, 91
29:27: 37
29:29: 37
29:31: 98
29 e.34: 28, 91
29 r.1: 43, 116, 122
29 r.2: 37, 80
29 r.3: 146
29 r.4: 37, 140
29 r.6: 67
29 r.7: 40, 106
29 r.9: 101

139 r.1: 120
141:4: 103
141:5: 68
141 r.2: 181
142 r.2: 55
143:2: 49
143:10: 157
143:14′-16: 162
143:14: 116, 162
143 r.10-11: 113
143 r.10: 33, 113
144 e.11: 124
145 r.8e: 91
146:2: 55
147:5: 96
147:15: 74, 129, 148
147 r.11: 27
147 r.12: 94, 144
148:5: 36
148 r.2: 73
148 r.11e: 94
149:8-9: 120
149:10: 151
150 r.8: 59
150 r.15: 37
152:14: 79
152 r.9-12: 156
152 r.12: 127
153 r.4: 124
153 r.5: 39
154 r.4: 124
154 r.7: 22
155:4: 59
155:8-9: 112
155 r.3: 115
156 e.2: 83
158:4: 53
158:5: 68
158:6: 53
158:13: 53
159:7: 94
159 e.20: 94
159 r.6: 94
159 r.11: 94
159 r.14: 28, 129
160:6-9: 165
160:6: 150, 165
160:12: 91
160 r.3: 105
160 r.7: 28
163 e.6′-7: 156
166:7: 180
170:6: 182
170:8: 62
171 r.19: 131
171 r.35: 106
172:6: 99
172:7-8: 169
172:9-10: 112
172:10: 134
172:12: 74, 105, 182
172:13: 182
172 e.19: 116
172 r.31: 78
172 r.32: 133
172 r.36e: 133
175:13: 105
175 r.31: 72
176:14: 49, 79
176 r.38: 134
177:8-9: 109
177:11-12: 157
177:16-19: 160
177:19: 95
177 r.8: 76, 119
177 r.15: 74, 138
179:1: 54, 68, 79, 130
179:8: 182
179:11: 68
179:16: 79
179:18: 130
179:20: 30, 121
179:22: 130
179 e.26: 44
179 e.27-28: 156
179 r.7: 157
179 r.8: 105
179 r.9: 105
179 r.12: 151
180 e.12: 62, 124
181:9: 37, 117
181:12-13: 156
181 r.5: 82
181 r.7: 92
181 r.8: 28, 65, 129, 140
181 r.9: 28, 67, 129, 140
182:8: 105, 119
182:9: 182
182:11: 97
182 r.10: 182
183:5: 156
183:7′-8: 156
183:9: 63
183:10: 74, 77
183:21: 96
183 r.6: 77
183 r.8: 77
183 r.11: 142
183 r.13: 89
184 r.7: 84
188:9: 44
188:12: 167
188 r.1: 182
188 r.7: 131
190:10: 94
190 r.6: 36, 103
190 r.9: 67, 100
191 r.2-3: 166
191 r.2: 166, 174
191 r.6: 63, 82
191 r.7: 28, 73
191 r.14-15: 158
191 r.14: 106, 158
192:8: 84
192:11: 87, 101, 106
192 r.4: 108, 181
193 r.4: 84
194 r.1: 104
194 r.2: 76
194 r.3: 106
194 r.4: 46, 124
194 r.5: 106
195 r.2: 97
195 r.13e-14e: 159
195 r.17: 88
204:4: 60
204:9: 130
204 r.1: 103, 111, 116
204 r.5: 27
204 r.11: 103, 111
205:5: 142
205:14: 98
205:15: 91
205 e.19: 131, 166
205 r.9: 37
205 r.14: 62, 92
205 r.19e-21: 159
208 r.8′-9: 171
208 r.9: 66
210:12: 84
210:15: 30, 61
210 e.17: 81, 141
210 r.1: 98, 101, 124, 180
210 r.11: 180
210 r.14: 98, 101
215:1-3: 179
216:4: 182
219:11: 143
219:13: 64, 103, 122
219:16: 103
220:1-3: 179
220:3: 39
220:5: 107
220 r.5: 117
220 r.8e: 106, 171
221:1: 179
221:4: 103
221:8: 108
221 r.6: 131
221 r.8: 119, 131
223:5: 83
223 r.9: 39
224:10: 176
224:15: 83
225:3: 83
226:4: 87
226:6: 87
226:7: 87
226:11: 107
226 r.1: 53, 81
226 r.2: 57
226 r.9: 87
226 r.10: 81
227:7: 60
227 r.2: 104
227 r.10: 91
229:10: 117
229 r.5: 145
230:5: 177
230:8: 181
230:10: 181
230 r.2: 181
231 r.4: 34
232:8: 40
233:13: 118
233:17: 83
233:18: 124
233:19: 180
233:20: 124
233:21: 76, 116
233:24: 180
233:25: 82, 180
233 r.12: 180
233 r.13: 180
234:12: 103
234:16: 104
234:17: 104
235:11: 106
235:13: 40, 106
235:15: 130, 150
235:17: 120
235:19: 129, 140
235:20: 101, 143
235:21: 101
235 r.2: 117
235 s.1: 130
236:4: 81
236:8: 37, 146
236 e.14: 32
236 r.4: 84
236 r.6: 37
236 r.9: 120
236 r.12: 107
236 s.1: 37
237:5: 77
237 r.15: 77
237 r.16-17: 113
238:6: 153
238:7: 64, 116
239:6: 97
240:4: 29
240:9: 42, 79
240:14: 78
240 r.4: 105, 125
240 r.10: 116
241 e.4′-r.1: 160
241 r.7: 22
241 r.8: 73
241 r.13: 33
243:3: 183
244:11-12: 169
244:18: 181
244 r.7: 79
244 r.8: 78, 140
244 r.12: 149, 183
244 r.16: 128
245:2: 130
245:5′-8: 125
245:5: 101, 125
245:8: 101
245 r.3-5: 159
245 r.3: 154, 159
246:10: 130
246:11: 95
246 r.5: 73
247 e.11: 68
247 r.5: 98, 105
248 r.5: 167
250:2′-3: 159

STATE ARCHIVES OF ASSYRIA

VOLUME I
THE CORRESPONDENCE OF SARGON II, PART I
Letters from Assyria and the West
Edited by Simo Parpola
1987

VOLUME II
NEO-ASSYRIAN TREATIES AND LOYALTY OATHS
Edited by Simo Parpola and Kazuko Watanabe
1988

VOLUME III
COURT POETRY AND LITERARY MISCELLANEA
Edited by Alasdair Livingstone
1989

VOLUME IV
QUERIES TO THE SUNGOD
Divination and Politics in Sargonid Assyria
Edited by Ivan Starr
1990

VOLUME V
THE CORRESPONDENCE OF SARGON II, PART II
Letters from the Northern and Northeastern Provinces
Edited by Giovanni B. Lanfranchi and Simo Parpola
1990

VOLUME VI
LEGAL TRANSACTIONS OF THE ROYAL COURT OF NINEVEH, PART I
Tiglath-Pileser III through Esarhaddon
Edited by Theodore Kwasman and Simo Parpola
1991

VOLUME VII
IMPERIAL ADMINISTRATIVE RECORDS, PART I
Palace and Temple Administration
Edited by F. M. Fales and J. N. Postgate
1992

VOLUME VIII
ASTROLOGICAL REPORTS TO ASSYRIAN KINGS
Edited by Hermann Hunger
1992

VOLUME IX
ASSYRIAN PROPHECIES
Edited by Simo Parpola
1997

VOLUME X

LETTERS FROM ASSYRIAN AND BABYLONIAN SCHOLARS

Edited by Simo Parpola

1993

VOLUME XI

IMPERIAL ADMINISTRATIVE RECORDS, PART II

Provincial and Military Administration

Edited by F. M. Fales and J. N. Postgate

1995

VOLUME XII

GRANTS, DECREES AND GIFTS OF THE NEO-ASSYRIAN PERIOD

Edited by L. Kataja and R. Whiting

1995

VOLUME XIII

LETTERS FROM PRIESTS TO THE KINGS ESARHADDON AND ASSURBANIPAL

Edited by Steven W. Cole and Peter Machinist

1998

VOLUME XIV

LEGAL TRANSACTIONS OF THE ROYAL COURT OF NINEVEH, PART II

Assurbanipal through Sin-šarru-iškun

Raija Mattila

2002

VOLUME XV

THE CORRESPONDENCE OF SARGON II, PART III

Letters from Babylonia and the Eastern Provinces

Andreas Fuchs and Simo Parpola

2002

VOLUME XVI

THE POLITICAL CORRESPONDENCE OF ESARHADDON

Mikko Luukko and Greta Van Buylaere

2002

VOLUME XVII

THE BABYLONIAN CORRESPONDENCE OF SARGON AND SENNACHERIB

Manfried Dietrich

2003

VOLUME XVIII

THE BABYLONIAN CORRESPONDENCE OF ESARHADDON

and Letters to Assurbanipal and Sin-šarru-iškun from Northern and Central Babylonia

Frances Reynolds

2003

State Archives of Assyria Studies

VOLUME I
Neuassyrische Glyptik des 8.-7. Jh. v. Chr.
unter besonderer Berücksichtigung der Siegelungen
auf Tafeln und Tonverschlüsse
by Suzanne Herbordt
1992

VOLUME II
The Eponyms of the Assyrian Empire 910–612 BC
by Alan Millard
1994

VOLUME III
The Use of Numbers and Quantifications
in the Assyrian Royal Inscriptions
by Marco De Odorico
1995

VOLUME IV
Nippur in Late Assyrian Times
c. 755–612 BC
by Steven W. Cole
1996

VOLUME V
Neo-Assyrian Judicial Procedures
by Remko Jas
1996

VOLUME VI
Die neuassyrischen Privatrechtsurkunden
als Quelle für Mensch und Umwelt
by Karen Radner
1997

VOLUME VII
References to Prophecy in Neo-Assyrian Sources
by Martti Nissinen
1998

VOLUME VIII
Die Annalen des Jahres 711 v. Chr.
nach Prismenfragmenten aus Ninive und Assur
by Andreas Fuchs
1998

VOLUME IX
The Role of Naqia/Zakutu in Sargonid Politics
by Sarah C. Melville
1999

VOLUME X
Herrschaftswissen in Mesopotamien:
Formen der Kommunikation zwischen Gott und König
im 2. und 1. Jahrtausend v.Chr.
by Beate Pongratz-Leisten
1999

VOLUME XI
The King's Magnates:
A Study of the Highest Officials of the Neo-Assyrian Empire
by Raija Mattila
2000

VOLUME XII
A Survey of Neo-Elamite History
by Matthew W. Waters
2000

VOLUME XIII
A Sketch of Neo-Assyrian Grammar
by Jaakko Hämeen-Anttila
2000

VOLUME XIV
The God Ninurta in the Mythology and Royal Ideology
of Ancient Mesopotamia
by Amar Annus
2002

VOLUME XV
The Sumerian Sacred Marriage
in the Light of Comparative Evidence
by Pirjo Lapinkivi
2004

VOLUME XVI
Grammatical Variation in Neo-Assyrian
by Mikko Luukko
2004

STATE ARCHIVES OF ASSYRIA CUNEIFORM TEXTS

VOLUME I
The Standard Babylonian Epic of Gilgamesh
by Simo Parpola
1997

VOLUME II
The Standard Babylonian Etana Epic
by Jamie R. Novotny
2001

VOLUME III
The Standard Babylonian Anzu Epic
by Amar Annus
2001

MELAMMU SYMPOSIA

VOLUME I
The Heirs of Assyria
Proceedings of the Opening Symposium of
The Assyrian and Babylonian Intellectual Heritage Project
Held in Tvärminne, Finland, October 8-11, 1998
Edited by Sanna Aro and R. M. Whiting
2000

VOLUME II
Mythology and Mythologies
Methodological Approaches to Intercultural Influences
Proceedings of the Second Annual Symposium of
The Assyrian and Babylonian Intellectual Heritage Project
Held in Paris, France, October 4-7, 1999
Edited by R. M. Whiting
2001

STATE ARCHIVES OF ASSYRIA LITERARY TEXTS

VOLUME I
The Induction of the Cult Image in Ancient Mesopotamia
The Mesopotamian Mīs Pî Ritual
by Christopher Walker and Michael Dick
2001

PROSOPOGRAPHY OF THE NEO-ASSYRIAN EMPIRE

VOLUME 1 A-G
edited by Karen Radner
1998/99

VOLUME 2 Ḫ-N
edited by Heather D. Baker
2000/2001

VOLUME 3, Part I P-Ṣ
edited by Heather D. Baker
2002

OTHER TITLES

ASSYRIA 1995
Proceedings of the 10th Annivesary Symposium of
The Neo-Assyrian Text Corpus Project
Helsinki, September 7-11, 1995
edited by S. Parpola and R. M. Whiting
1997

NINEVEH, 612 BC
The Glory and Fall of the Assyrian Empire
Catalogue of the 10th Anniversary Exhibition of the
Neo-Assyrian Text Corpus Project
edited by Raija Mattila
1995

The Mechanics of Empire
The Northern Frontier of Assyria as a Case Study in Imperial Dynamics
by Bradley J. Parker
2001